SPEER

MARTIN KITCHEN

SPEER

HITLER'S ARCHITECT

YALE UNIVERSITY PRESS
NEW HAVEN AND LONDON

For information about this and other Yale University Press publications, please contact:
U.S. Office: sales.press@yale.edu   www.yalebooks.com
Europe Office: sales@yaleup.co.uk   www.yalebooks.co.uk

Typeset in Minion Pro by IDSUK (DataConnection) Ltd
Printed in the United States of America

Library of Congress Cataloging-in-Publication Data

Kitchen, Martin.
    Speer: Hitler's architect/Martin Kitchen.
      pages cm
    ISBN 978-0-300-19044-1 (cloth: alkaline paper)
1. Speer, Albert, 1905–1981. 2. Speer, Albert, 1905–1981—Political and social views.
3. Cabinet officers—Germany—Biography. 4. Architects—Germany—Biography.
5. Nazis—Biography. 6. War criminals—Germany—Biography. 7. Germany—Politics and government—1933–1945. 8. Germany—Military policy. I. Title.
    DD247.S63K57 2015
    943.086092—dc23
    [B]
                                                                          2015023355

A catalogue record for this book is available from the British Library.

10 9 8 7 6 5 4 3 2 1

ALFRED FRANKE

In memoriam

Ein König, der Unmenschliches verlangt,
Findt Diener gnug, die gegen Gnad und Lohn
Den halben Fluch der Tat begierig fassen.
Goethe, *Iphigenie auf Tauris*, Act 5 Scene 3

A king who enjoins inhuman deeds
Will find enough retainers, who for grace and payment
Avidly accept half the anathema.

CONTENTS

ILLUSTRATIONS

ABBREVIATIONS

DAF   Deutsche Arbeitsfront (German Work Front)

DEST   Deutsche Erd- und Steinwerke GmbH (German Earth and Stone Works Company)

GBI   Generalbauinspektor für die Reichshauptstadt (Inspector General of Buildings in the Reich Capital)

GSW   Gemeinnützigen Siedlungs- und Wohnungsbaugesellschaft (Building Association for Settlements and Housing in the Public Interest)

IMT   International Military Tribunal (Nuremberg)

KfdK   Kampfbund für deutsche Kultur (Action Group for German Culture)

KPD   Kommunistische Partei Deutschlands (German Communist Party)

NSDAP   Nationalsozialistische Deutsche Arbeiterpartei (National Socialist German Workers' Party)

NSDStB   Nationalsozialistischer Deutscher Studentenbund (National Socialist German Students' Association)

NSKK   Nationalsozialistisches Kraftfahrkorps (National Socialist Automobile Corps)

NSV   Nationalsozialistische Volkswohlfahrt (National Socialist People's Welfare)

OKH   Oberkommando des Heeres (Army High Command)

OKW   Oberkommando der Wehrmacht (Supreme Command of the Armed Forces)

OT   Organisation Todt

RSHA   Reichssicherheitshauptamt (Reich Security Main Office)

RVE   Reichsvereinigung Eisen (Reich Iron Association)

RVK   Reichsvereinigung Kohle (Reich Coal Association)

SA   Sturmabteilung

SPD   Sozialdemokratische Partei Deutschlands (Social Democratic Party)

SS   Schutzstaffel

USAAF   United States Army Air Forces

ZRPT   Zweckverband Reichsparteitagsgelände Nürnberg (Reich Party Rally Grounds Association Nuremberg)

ACKNOWLEDGMENTS

Although it is becoming increasingly common to reduce acknowledgments down to thanks for permission to reproduce material from copyright works, archives or picture agencies I feel duty bound to express my gratitude and thanks to those without whose help this book would never have reached its present state.

First there are all the many historians and journalists who have sought to understand the multiple aspects of Albert Speer's life – as architect, Minister of Armaments, Major War criminal condemned to twenty years' imprisonment and 'Good Nazi' who provided an alibi for a nation. Thanks are due to all those whose names appear in my endnotes and bibliography. In addition I am most grateful to Kirsten Brast for his insightful comments on Speer's efforts to come to terms with his past. Then there are those friends and colleagues whose interest, encouragement and support were so important to me. They are too many to mention by name.

None of this would have been possible without the skilful assistance of Vera Yuen and Sonny Wong from the Interlibrary Loans department of the Simon Fraser University Library who tracked down a treasure trove of rare material. I am also most grateful to the staff of the Bundesarchiv, Berlin-Lichterfelde whose assistance was invaluable.

Thanks are also due to Professor John Craig, Dean of Arts and Sciences at Simon Fraser University, who made up for the Social Sciences and Research Council of Canada's parsimony in refusing to fund research by professors emeriti by providing modest but most welcome financial aid.

At Yale University Press Anne Bihan, Jane Birkett, Candida Brazil, Loulou Brown, Tami Halliday and Stephanie Pierre did a superb job sorting out a shameful number of typographical errors and compensating for my total inability to proof-read my own work. Needless to say any errors that remain are entirely my own. Rachael Lonsdale gave expert assistance in tracking down the images and was always ready to help. Meg Davies made the index and spotted a number of errors that had fallen through the net. My greatest debt of gratitude is to Heather McCallum, with whom I have had the good fortune to work on a number occasions. She first suggested that I should take another look at Albert Speer. It proved to be a challenging, fascinating and often daunting task. She unfailingly provided guidance, constructive criticism and encouragement in often frustrating times.

Lastly my thanks are due to Bettina, to whose father the book is dedicated. She put up with an unwanted house-guest for far longer than had been anticipated, but our conversations about him always proved lively, fruitful and challenging. We got to know him very well.

INTRODUCTION

THE OXFORD HISTORIAN Hugh Trevor-Roper, whom British Intelligence had appointed to counter Soviet claims that Hitler was not dead but had sought refuge with the Western Allies, interviewed Speer while he was in custody at Kransberg Castle, where he awaited trial at Nuremberg.[1] He had found him to be polite, sympathetic and informative. He was neither an autocrat nor a courtier, but an unassuming intellectual, who seemed oddly out of place among the 'opprobrious tomfools' who surrounded the Führer. Indeed, Trevor-Roper paid him the highest compliment by saying that he hardly seemed to be a German. The mystery for him was how such a man, who grew in stature when compared with Hitler's other closest associates, should have been so close an admirer of the dictator and how he could have served him so diligently.

Speer was for Trevor-Roper an organisational genius who could have served any other type of politician equally well. He had the courage to stand up to Hitler when it was obvious that all was lost and the honesty to admit his guilt. His admiration for Speer was enhanced by his belief that he had carried out a 'Speer revolution' by converting a peacetime economy into a wartime economy. He had seized the opportunities available in the 'leadership state' (*Führerstaat*) to take control over all aspects of armaments production, but he was wise enough to give industry its head and refused to burden it with unnecessary regulation.

By 1945 Speer saw that his task was becoming impossible. Raw materials were in short supply. The Allied air offensive was causing havoc. The enemy's overwhelming superiority in men and materiel could not possibly be matched. Dreams of 'miracle weapons' that would turn the tide were shattered. Realising that victory was out of the question, Speer now tried to save what could be saved in order to prepare the way for the transition back to a peace-time economy. By the autumn of 1944 Trevor-Roper saw Speer and Hitler on a collision course, to the point that he believed Speer's tale about planning to destroy Hitler's entire court by introducing poison gas into the bunker in the Reich Chancellery's garden. But he also realised that it was precisely Speer and his ilk that had made the implementation of Hitler's abhorrent ideas possible, so that in spite of his many fine qualities future historians would see him as one of Nazi Germany's major criminals.[2]

Trevor-Roper continued to be fascinated by Speer. He even considered writing a biography about him. In 1978, when questioned by Speer's ghost-writer and biographer, Joachim Fest, he said that he had been so favourably inclined towards Speer at Kransberg because he was in such marked contrast to the contemptible and servile 'jackasses' in the Nazi leadership. Now he had found the key to the 'Speer mystery'. He was not wicked, hard-hearted or mean-spirited. He was something much worse. He was morally and emotionally empty.[3] Speer was deeply hurt when Fest maliciously repeated these words. He protested that his conclusions were far-fetched and the line of argument tortuous.[4] But Speer missed the point. Trevor-Roper realised that Speer's deeply flawed character was a key to the understanding of the Third Reich. Whereas studies of political desperados, sadistic adventurers and peddlers of noxious notions revealed little but psycho-portraits of criminally inclined outsiders, for whom it is impossible to feel little other than the deepest revulsion, it was the Speers that made the regime possible. Speer's circumscribed confession of guilt was part of a deliberate attempt to distance himself as far as possible from this unsavoury bunch, in the hope thereby of absolving himself from the regime's worst crimes. In fact it only served to show how closely they worked together.

This was something of which Speer was uncomfortably aware. In a note dated 11 October 1946 he wrote: 'It seems to me that the Himmlers, Bormanns and Streichers do not explain Hitler's success with the German people. On the contrary, Hitler was buttressed by the idealism and devotion of people like me. We, who put everything else first, made it all possible. Crooks and criminal elements are always there. They explain nothing.'[5] Speer was of the new managerial type, untroubled by moral preoccupations, determined to make his way in the world, willing unquestioningly to submit to the exigencies of the times and to enjoy its fruits.

Albert Speer had all the prerequisites for a successful career. He was born into a wealthy family, was exceptionally intelligent, passed effortlessly through his training as an architect and at the age of twenty-three he was appointed assistant to Heinrich Tessenow, one of the Weimar Republic's most distinguished architects and town planners. But the opportunities for a young architect, even one with such impressive credentials, were slim in 1928. With the onset of the Great Depression they disappeared altogether.

He was typical of his class and his generation. Too young to have fought in the First World War, he affected to be in revolt against the bourgeois certainties of his liberal father. Reticent by nature, he was something of a loner, adopting a mildly unconventional attitude, deliberately antagonising his parents by marrying below his station. Although professing only to find fulfilment in a simple outdoor life, camping, canoeing and indulging in semi-mystical contemplation of the wonders of nature that were then much in vogue among German youth, he remained much smitten by material pleasures. Fast cars, fine fare and a patrician lifestyle soon replaced canoes, campfires and tents.

Although he was seen as the exemplary young gentleman among the Nazi elite, Speer did not quite fit the ideal. He lacked the cultural capital that was an essential component of the German concept of the cultured bourgeois. He also had a slight touch of the parvenu, inherited perhaps from his father, whose obsession with displaying his considerable wealth never troubled him, in spite of his frequent assertions of his predilection for simple living. None of this mattered in Hitler's intimate circle. In spite of the efforts of his Munich hostesses, Helene Bechstein, Helene Hanfstaengl and Elsa Bruckmann as well as his close friend Winifred Wagner, Hitler remained somewhat socially inept. He never mastered the delicate art of kissing hands. His bows were both too stiff and too low. The bouquets he presented were invariably grotesquely large. He was not quite a gentleman, as Speer's mother cattily remarked after a visit to the Berghof. He imagined that Joachim von Ribbentrop was a sophisticated man of the world. He was also something of a snob. Two of his closest associates – his naval adjutant Karl-Jesko von Puttkamer and his Luftwaffe adjutant Nicolaus von Below – were of impeccably aristocratic stock. The cruder members of the Nazi elite, such as Julius Streicher, Fritz Sauckel and Robert Ley, were kept outside the pale. Speer met all the necessary criteria. He was socially on a par with the solidly middle class General Wilhelm Keitel and Dr Hans Lammers. At the Berghof only the sinister Martin Bormann stood clearly apart.

Speer owed his exalted position in large part to his exceptionally close relationship with Hitler. Just as Hermann Göring would have been merely an odd-jobbing air force veteran, Joseph Goebbels the author of second-rate novels, pitiable plays and occasional newspaper articles and Heinrich Himmler a chicken farmer or village schoolmaster, Speer would have merely had a modest career as a small-town architect without this essential connection. This was something that he found exceedingly hard to accept. He came to see himself as an artist who would have been capable of great things had he not been led astray by Hitler and forced to realise his fantastic plans for a New Berlin. After the war it was cold comfort that Andy Warhol was virtually alone in professing his admiration for Speer's contributions to this outlandish 'Germania' project. In fact he had limited originality as an architect. His success was not due to his artistic ability, but because he was a devoted follower of Hitler as well as an unscrupulous, value-free power broker, untroubled by any moral considerations. From the outset of his career he had to live with the uncomfortable realisation that without Hitler he would have been of little consequence.

Thanks to a series of fortuitous encounters and odd jobs, in 1933 Speer became Hitler's intimate at the age of twenty-eight. When Hitler's favourite architect, Paul Troost, died suddenly on 21 January 1934 Speer was appointed to succeed him. Once Tessenow's devoted disciple, Speer had already wholeheartedly embraced Troost's architectural style that seemed likely to become the Third Reich's vernacular. Once in this exalted position he quickly showed those qualities that were to ensure him such a staggeringly successful career. His exceptional organisational talents were already apparent. He was now in a position to delegate authority and did so to people of real ability. He did what he was told by Hitler and had a handpicked team to make sure that the job was well done. He was in many ways a modernist. Unlike the Nazi radicals he was an unashamed supporter of big business. Although at heart a traditional nationalist, he was soon to become the architect of atavistic cult monuments. From the outset he had no qualms about employing vast amounts of slave labour from Himmler's concentration camps. He enthusiastically endorsed Hitler's decision to risk war in 1939, even though it might involve putting some of his mammoth building projects on hold until the 'Final Victory'.

In July 1933 the Nuremberg City Council, impressed by the work he had done for the May Day celebration in Berlin, commissioned him to design the setting for the party's 'Victory Rally' to begin at the end of August. Speer then designed a number of permanent structures in Nuremberg. They were built in Troost's spare and restrained style, but they were on a far grander scale. Speer's intent was to build monumental structures as permanent memorials to the Thousand Year Reich.

Soon after Troost's death Hitler ordered Speer to make preliminary drawings for a vast new chancellery in Berlin. This was to be Speer's major completed work, in which he successfully realised Hitler's vision of a representational building that exemplified the power and grandeur of the Third Reich. It was a structure designed to overawe and intimidate by its sheer size. As such it was built on an inhuman scale and was thus totally impractical as a working environment. Built at vast expense, it was seldom used until Hitler spent his final days in a bunker in the Chancellery garden. By then it was a pile of rubble, with only the exterior walls still standing. Its saving grace was the rear façade facing the garden. Speer adopted a conventional neo-classicism, but it is well proportioned and admirably suited for an important representational building.

In January 1937 he was appointed Generalbauinspektor für die Reichshauptstadt or Inspector General of Buildings in the Reich Capital (GBI).

His task was to draw up plans for a new Berlin, to be called 'Germania'. Limitless funds were made available for the construction of a 'World Capital'. To this end the SS founded the Deutsche Erd- und Steinwerke GmbH or German Earth and Stone Works Company (DEST) in April 1938. It was funded by Speer as GBI. In close consultation with Speer new concentration camps were built at Oranienburg, Flossenbürg, Mauthausen, Gusen, Groß-Rosen and Natzweiler-Struthof to quarry the stone and make the bricks that he had selected for the Germania project. Working conditions in these camps beggar description. They were an integral part of Himmler's method of 'extermination by work'. Speer was fortunate that the prosecution overlooked this aspect of his work as an architect when he stood trial as a major war criminal at Nuremberg. Oswald Pohl, whom Himmler put in charge of DEST, was condemned to death.

As GBI Speer ran roughshod over established practice and legal norms. He made vast sums of money by employing his own firm as a consultant for the Germania project, thereby substantially augmenting the generous emolument he received in his official position. He also made handsome profits from real estate speculation. With enthusiastic support from Goebbels he managed to secure the dismissal of Berlin's mayor, Julius Lippert. Although a devout National Socialist and impassioned anti-Semite, Lippert had serious qualms about the astronomic economic and human cost of Hitler and Speer's plans for rebuilding the city.

Speer's worst offence as GBI was the role he played in the persecution and expulsion of Berlin's large Jewish community. There was already an acute housing shortage in the city when he was put in charge of the construction of a new capital. Additional housing had to be found for people forced to move from areas scheduled for redevelopment. During the war there was the additional problem of finding shelter for those rendered homeless by the bombing. With sovereign disregard for landlord and tenant rights Speer cooperated enthusiastically with Goebbels, the Nazi Party and the SS, first to herd the Jews into over-crowded alternative housing, then into camps until they were transported to the death factories in eastern Europe. After the invasion of the Soviet Union in June 1941 Speer worked closely with the SS to employ slave labour, much of which was Jewish, to build a motorway through the Ukraine that was designed to link Berlin to the Crimean Riviera. He also lent his expertise to the Reichsführer-SS, Himmler, by helping to design his model cities in a future eastern empire to house a new race of German settlers.

Speer visited Hitler's headquarters at Rastenburg on 7 February 1942 having made an extensive and arduous visit to his operations in the Soviet Union. The Minister of Armaments, Fritz Todt, was also present. He had come in the hope of convincing Hitler that the entire system of armaments production and allocation had to be drastically altered for a further offensive in the East to have any chance of success. The result was a long and heated debate that went on until midnight. Early the next morning the plane that was to fly Todt back to Berlin exploded shortly after take-off. All on board were killed. Speer had intended to take this flight, but Hitler insisted on discussing his plans for rebuilding Berlin after he had spoken to Todt. Their conversation went on until three o'clock in the morning. Dog-tired and in desperate need of a good night's sleep Speer cancelled the trip.

Without hesitation Hitler appointed Speer to replace Fritz Todt both as Minister of Armaments and as head of the colossal government-controlled construction company Organisation Todt. He did not relinquish any of his tasks as Hitler's principal architect and town planner. For the second time Speer stepped into a dead man's shoes. The appointment of the court favourite to high office caused considerable consternation in some quarters, but it proved to be an excellent choice. Speer was young, energetic and utterly loyal to Hitler. He had proved himself to be an outstanding organiser. Hitler thought the fact that, like Todt, he had no direct experience in the armaments industry was a major asset. He loathed experts, particularly those who had the impertinence to contradict him. Even though Speer's recent visit to Dnepropetrovsk had been far from encouraging he did not share Todt's pessimistic outlook with regard to Germany's long-term prospects. He had no power base. His position within the Nazi hierarchy depended solely on his close relationship with Hitler.

Speer had already made some important contacts and gathered sufficient experience to give him a head start in his new office. He had established excellent relations with General Friedrich Fromm, who as head of the Reserve Army was responsible for the army's armaments. He had worked closely with the military authorities in the Ukraine, building roads and repairing the railway network. He had built a special factory for the Junkers aircraft company. He was responsible for all the Luftwaffe's building requirements. But he had serious shortcomings. He gave the impression of being cold, aloof and arrogant. He had neither Todt's warmth of personality nor his professional expertise. Todt had joined the Nazi Party in 1922, whereas Speer was seen as something of an opportunistic latecomer, who had precious few close contacts within the party. Although he was to accumulate vast powers, he was never a match for the likes of Goebbels, Bormann, Himmler or even Göring until the latter relapsed into a drug-induced torpor. From the outset he was confronted by a number of ambitious underlings who were determined to assert their independence. He selected an outstanding team of experts, many of whom had served under his predecessor, but he soon had to deal with dissent within his own ministry, while being constantly involved in jockeying for power among an envious elite. Everything therefore depended on his relationship with Hitler. When Hitler's support weakened Speer was lost.

The situation that Speer inherited from Fritz Todt was highly confusing. The Ministry of Armaments was only responsible for the army's weaponry, although it provided munitions for all three services. It therefore had to compete with a number of other agencies. The Oberkommando der Wehrmacht or Supreme Command of the Armed Forces (OKW) and General Georg Thomas as head of the Armaments Office had extensive powers, as did Göring as head of the Four-Year Plan. The navy and the Luftwaffe were each responsible for their own armaments. The Minister of Economics and head of the Reichsbank Walther Funk had considerable influence over the allocation of resources. The Nazi Party and the Gauleiters, who tended to stand up for small businesses, fought against the 'plutocrats' who were bent on rationalisation and centralisation. Industry struggled to break free from irksome government control. Yet in spite of all this confusion and duplicated effort, by February 1942 the achievements of the German armaments industry were truly remarkable. Speer did not work a miracle, as he was later to claim. He built on solid foundations and reaped the benefits of past efforts.

Surrounded by a highly talented team of experts, in both Nuremberg and Berlin, Speer set about extending the powers and influence of the Ministry of Armaments. He did so with such ruthless determination, boundless ambition, and total disregard for established practice as to alarm and dismay many of the key figures in Hitler's entourage. Principal among them were the chief of the OKW, Wilhelm Keitel; the head of the Party Chancellery, Martin Bormann; and the head of the Reich Chancellery, Hans Lammers. Certain of Hitler's unconditional support, Speer was undaunted. Fuelled by an unexpected appetite for power, with astonishing speed he accumulated such a wide range of responsibilities as to make him one of the most formidable figures in the Third Reich.

Within two months Speer managed take over all questions concerning armaments from Göring's powerful Four-Year Plan with the establishment of Central Planning, an organisation that gave him control over 90 per cent of the armaments industry. Within a matter of weeks the army lost its control over armaments. The Luftwaffe under the able leadership of Field Marshal Erhard Milch felt that its interests were best served by cooperating closely with Speer, who wrested the allocation of fuel and energy from the Ministry of Economics, undermined the authority of the Gauleiters and the local party authorities and extended his powers over occupied Europe. Industry was freed from tiresome bureaucratic control and burdensome taxation to profit from expedient price fixing. Speer exercised indirect control over the navy by excluding them from Central Planning and by dictating the allocation of steel. He took over formal control over naval armaments in July 1943. In the following month he absorbed much of the Ministry of Economics to become, in Admiral Dönitz's words, 'Europe's economic dictator'. This was reflected in the change of his title from Reich Minister for Weapons and Munitions to Reich Minister for Armaments and War Production.

The industrialists were treated to some tempting carrots, while the work-force got nothing but sticks. In close cooperation with Fritz Sauckel, the Gauleiter of Thuringia, Speer combed occupied Europe for workers whether free, forced or slave. He threatened all those considered as slackers or malin-gerers with such ferocious punishments that a shocked Himmler pleaded for leniency. Speer ignored all such concerns and ordered the arrest of critics of Himmler's seriously mismanaged U-boat building programme. In other respects, however, the two men were in such accord that there was talk of a Speer–Himmler axis. Speer provided Himmler with building materials for his concentration camps, including the wherewithal for 'the implementation of special treatments' at Auschwitz. He did however complain that the accom-modation in certain concentration camps was altogether too luxurious. Himmler kept his side of the bargain by providing ample supplies of slave labour for his architectural projects and the armaments industry.

During a visit to Organisation Todt troops in Lapland during Christmas 1943 Speer damaged his knee. Combined with exhaustion and what would seem to have been a severe depression he fell seriously ill and spent several months in the care of Himmler's somewhat dubious personal physician, Professor Karl Gebhardt. His rivals, both within the Ministry of Armaments and without, seized this opportunity seriously to undermine his authority and to sow doubt in Hitler's mind about his favourite protégé. Speer fought back as best he could, but by the summer of 1944 he had effectively lost control over Organisation Todt to Franz Xaver Dorsch. Karl-Otto Saur was firmly in charge of armaments, while SS-Brigadeführer Hans Kammler, who had overall responsibility for the concen-tration camps, including the gas chambers and crematoria, ran the V2 rocket programme. In March 1945 he was put in charge of aircraft production. Hans Kehrl had full control over those sections of the Ministry of Economics that had been absorbed by Speer's ministry. Albert Ganzenmüller, although only Deputy Director General of the State Railways, acted fully independently, even though he was formally under Speer. Thus, although he had accumulated vast powers, with Hitler's support no longer unconditional, Speer's position was significantly weakened. In the aftermath of the attempt on Hitler's life on 20 July 1944 his rivals launched a series of attacks on a number of his closest associates, while his system of industrial self-determination came under ferocious attack both from National Socialist radicals among the Gauleiters and the Nazi Party, and from Hans Kehrl, a key figure in both the Ministry of Armaments and the

Ministry of Economics, who called for rigid planning in place of the complex series of overlapping rings, committees, business groups and special staff that Speer had inherited from Fritz Todt.

Speer tried to bolster his position with shamelessly doctored production figures, exhortations for an all-out war effort and wild promises that wonderful new weapons would bring Final Victory. Even though the V1 and V2 proved to be militarily worthless, supplies of raw materials were running desperately low and the transportation network had broken down, he refused to draw the obvious conclusion that the war could not possibly be won. He continued to give Hitler the impression that the tide would soon turn. In the final months of the war, Speer was a lonely figure. On paper he had accumulated exceptional powers to become one of the key figures of the Third Reich, but in reality he no longer enjoyed Hitler's unconditional support without which he was virtually powerless. At the same time power over his vastly expanded ministry was slipping out of his hands as influential rivals schemed against him. The Central Planning Office under Hans Kehrl, formed in late 1944, robbed Speer of much of his power, but as communications and transport were disrupted by Allied bombing, central control was no longer possible. Power now rested with local authorities. Central planning gave way to hasty improvisation. By 1943 Hermann Giesler had replaced Speer as Hitler's favourite architect. As the Third Reich fell apart Hitler ignored Speer's models for Germania, the gaudy monument to his future victories. He now found solace in the contemplation of Giesler's plans for rebuilding Linz, where he intended to be buried.

Speer's behaviour in the final stages of the war was confused and ambiguous. He showed considerable courage in defying Hitler's attempt to destroy everything in sight in a grisly act of national self-immolation, while at the same time doing everything he possibly could to supply the armed forces with the means to continue what had become a senseless fight. At times he got carried away into the realm of fantasy. He imagined that Field Marshal Model's Army Group B could save the Ruhr. He suggested a suicidal bombing mission against Soviet power stations in which he would take part. In more sober moments, mindful of his future career, he showed due concern for Germany's post-war needs. He did his utmost to stop the destruction of industrial plant as the Allied armies advanced. He ordered the removal of explosives from key bridges and ensured the mines were not put out of action. Well aware that the country would soon face a chronic shortage of food, he paid particular attention to the needs of agriculture. But he showed total indifference to the number of casualties and disregarded the pressing needs of hundreds of thousands of hapless refugees.

Although he had been effectively stripped of much of his power and influence, Speer still imagined that Hitler might appoint him as his successor. This would seem to be the only plausible explanation for his hazardous flight to Berlin on 23 April 1945. He hoped that the result would justify the considerable risks involved. The day before he set out on this precarious journey he wrote to his wife: 'My Dear Gretel, I am so much looking forward to a new life together . . . much that is unnatural will disappear and things will be so much better . . . My aim is to look after you and the children. I am sure that I shall succeed. Until now I have always achieved what I set out to do.'[6] He had already bidden Hitler farewell during his dreary birthday celebration three days previously. This could hardly have been a final attempt to patch up their tattered relationship. Hitler now had no time for his former favourite, who was not even mentioned in his list of future appointments. Speer, however, was still profoundly attached to a man who had showered him with power and glory and to whom he had extended something resembling friendship. News of Hitler's suicide left him utterly shattered. For the first time in his life he was overcome with profound emotion. But this did not last for long. His attention was now focussed on securing a position in the post-war world. For this he needed to ingratiate himself with the Allies and to reinvent himself as an apolitical penitent, unaware of the crimes committed by the regime he had served in highest office, an innocent victim of a remorseless technocratic age.

Captured by the Allies, Speer was anxious to prove himself fully cooperative and win their trust. He offered the United States Army Air Forces expert advice on the appropriate bombing strategy to adopt against Japan. Thereby he enhanced his reputation as a miracle worker by claiming against all the evidence that, due to faulty targeting, he had managed to increase production during the bomber offensive. He also used the distrust between the Allies and the Soviet Union to his own advantage by warning that it would be unfortunate were he forced to give testimony in court that might be valuable to the Soviets. Speer impressed his interlocutors. Here was a gentlemanly and highly intelligent man who was in such marked contrast to most of the other members of the Nazi elite. He was so successful in this endeavour that he managed to lay the firm foundations for the Speer legend by convincing a number of critical minds that he was an apolitical technocrat who had worked miracles and who had stood in staunch opposition to Hitler's destructive genius.

His performance during the Nuremberg Trials was most impressive. He acknowledged the regime's wrongdoings and admitted to an adroitly ill-defined degree of responsibility for its criminal actions. He deftly distanced himself from Fritz Sauckel and Himmler without losing credibility. He answered questions calmly, cogently and convincingly. He avoided the death sentence not only because a great deal of highly incriminating evidence was not available to the court, but also because of the marked contrast between his demeanour and that of most of the other defendants. Amid a collection of outraged men who claimed only to have done their duty, proudly defiant National Socialists and colourless functionaries, Speer was a man apart, somehow distanced from the horrific world of the Third Reich, an anomaly and an exception. By claiming that he was the victim of an amoral technological age that now threatened to destroy civilisation and by arguing that the Germans were also victims because of a morally unjustifiable bomber offensive, he contributed further to his carefully constructed post-war image as a man who had remained fundamentally decent by playing the part of a critical outsider during these dreadful times. Most of the judges were duly impressed, but a few saw through him. Some even considered him to be the worst of the lot.

Although there are a number of excellent studies of the Ministry of Armaments, Speer has not aroused the interest of many biographers, even though he was one of the key figures in the Third Reich.[7] Two notable exceptions are studies by Joachim Fest and Gitta Sereny.[8] Both knew Speer very well. Fest worked closely with him in writing his memoirs, *Inside the Third Reich,* and then *Spandau: The Secret Diaries,* and he remained in close touch with him until his death. Sereny spent twelve years interviewing him and his close associates. Both writers accepted Speer's insistence that he knew nothing of the true nature of the crimes committed by the regime in which he held high office. Sereny, as in her studies of the child murderer Mary Bell and Franz Stangl, the commandant of Sobibór and Treblinka death camps, shows considerably more sympathy for the perpetrators than for their victims. Indeed she finds all three of her subjects to have been themselves victims of their early environment and upbringing. Thus she came to believe that Speer's cold and unloving parents caused him to seek a father figure in Hitler, that he had a dim awareness of some dark secret and that he accepted his share of an unspecific overall responsibility for what had happened, but of which he was unaware. This is a modest and questionable conclusion for a book of inordinate length, but although there are some interesting snippets, her portrait of a man battling with the truth is unconvincing.

The case of Joachim Fest is even more interesting. Although he had long since come to the realisation that he had been hoodwinked by Speer, he makes no mention of this in his biography that was published in 1999, eighteen years after the subject's death. Fest not only dismissed all the evidence against Speer produced by historians, he also challenged Gitta Sereny's assertion that Speer had exercised a certain economy of truth when claiming that he knew nothing of the Final Solution. The end result was a rehashing of Speer's memoirs, which was their joint effort. In 2005, six years after his biography of Speer, Fest published selections of interviews he had held with him that clearly showed how he had been misled.[9] Fest's admission of guilt was every bit as circumspect as Speer's. In many ways they were kindred souls. Both found it exceptionally hard to admit to any wrongdoing.

Speer's career in the Third Reich is of particular interest in that he was typical of the well-educated, cultivated and well-mannered middle-class and aristocratic people who played key roles in all aspects of the Third Reich. It is a reflection of the fact that the existing German society and the National Socialist dictatorship were in a broadly harmonious relationship. Class distinctions remained virtually unchanged. The aristocracy still played a key role in the armed services, the diplomatic corps and the upper echelons of the civil service and the SS. Germany could never have achieved so much had it been the exclusive domain of the misfits, psychopaths and sadists of the popular imagination. This 'Dual State' was marked by struggles between the old hierarchical administrative structures and the party apparatus. This resulted in a degree of organisational chaos, but it remained dynamic, competitive and was held together by a series of networks. It was a system that enabled skilful players like Speer to become immensely powerful, but it left him vulnerable to attack from ambitious underlings. The realisation that it was these fundamentally decent individuals with doctorates, professional qualifications, culture and civic responsibility who made it all possible was very hard to accept. Since their hands were not dripping with blood and they were mostly not directly connected with the monstrous crimes committed by the National Socialist regime, their consciences were untroubled. They passed smoothly through the de-nazification process after the war to be quickly integrated into post-war Germany in both West and East.

Speer was somewhat different in two respects. He was appointed Minister of Armaments even though he was neither a technician nor a specialist. As an architect he had already shown determined leadership and organisational skill in handling major projects, but he knew nothing of weaponry and left such technical matters to carefully selected experts. Secondly, as one of the Third Reich's most important officials he was held to account at Nuremberg where he skilfully managed to avoid the death sentence. He then set about the task of presenting himself as a man anxious to atone for his sins of omission, but remained resolute in his denial that he was aware of the depravity around him. He was hugely successful in this endeavour, in large part because his self-portrait as a man who played a key role in Nazi Germany but managed to keep his hands clean, provided a comforting alibi for a whole generation.

Speer maintained that he had worked an armaments miracle, in spite of intense Allied bombing and although the Red Army's advance gradually cut off essential supplies of raw materials. Vanity was not the sole motive for this assertion. Impressive production statistics, even when clearly doctored, were a guarantee of Hitler's approval and support. An armaments miracle and later the promise of miracle weapons were grist to Goebbels' propaganda machine that began to run out of plausible materiel after the defeats at Stalingrad and Tunis. The promise of miracle weapons kept hopes alive even when the Wehrmacht was on its last legs. Speer's armaments miracle also provided an explanation for Germany's defeat. According to this scenario the country was insufficiently prepared for a lengthy war and it was only when Speer was appointed Minister of Armaments in February 1942, when Operation Barbarossa had failed that serious attention was paid to the question of armaments in depth and in breadth. Speer stuck to this narrative when he was interviewed by the Allies. By insisting that the bomber offensive had been ineffective he was not only able to shift part of the blame for the horrors of Germany's war on to the Allies. He used this Allied bombing strategy at Nuremberg as an excuse for the appalling conditions in which forced labourers had to live. Later he was to argue that there was no moral distinction between the bombing of Dresden and the massacre of women and children by the Waffen-SS at Oradour–sur-Glane.

Such moral relativism was combined with pride in his achievements and an insistence that he knew nothing beyond an inkling, an inward perception and an imaginative awareness of the crimes committed by those with whom he was in such close contact. By maintaining a detached and courteous demeanour and by making a circumspect confession of limited guilt, he was able to pass as the honourable exception among Hitler's paladins. How far does this ingenious construct correspond to the historical record?

CHAPTER ONE

THE YOUNG ARCHITECT

A CCORDING TO ALBERT Speer's own account, his birth, precisely at midday on 19 March 1905 at Prinz-Wilhelm-Straße 19 in Mannheim, was dramatically orchestrated. Amid crashes of thunder the bells of the nearby Christ Church could distinctly be heard. This entry into the world, reminiscent of Babylonian birth omens or the burning of the temple of Diana at Ephesus that coincided with the birth of Alexander the Great, was not quite so dramatic. There was indeed a thunderstorm in Mannheim that day, but it occurred between three and five that afternoon. The bells of Christ Church could not possibly have been heard. Young Albert was already six years old when the church – an unhappy mixture of neo-baroque and art nouveau – was completed.[1]

Mannheim, situated on the confluence of the rivers Rhine and Neckar, began as a fortress built by the Elector Palatine Friedrich IV in 1606, around which a small town developed. It suffered terribly in the Thirty Years War and was sacked by Louis XIV's army in 1688. In 1720 the Elector Palatine Carl Philipp moved his capital from Heidelberg to Mannheim where he built a fine palace that now houses the university. The town became a distinguished cultural and artistic centre and enjoyed great prosperity until the Elector Palatine Carl Theodor moved to Munich in 1778 as the Prince Elector and Duke of Bavaria.

There followed a period of rapid decline, but in the course of the nineteenth century it became an important industrial centre. By 1905 it was a prosperous, solidly bourgeois, Protestant town with 150,000 inhabitants. The Speers were an established upper-middle-class family typical of Mannheim's elite. Berthold Konrad Hermann Albert Speer was named after his paternal grandfather Berthold Speer, a successful architect in Dortmund who made a small fortune by designing run-of-the-mill neo-classical buildings. He died young, but left enough money for his four sons to be given a proper education and for his stern matriarchal widow to live in appropriate style. Speer's father, Albert

Friedrich Speer, established a highly successful architectural firm in Mannheim. At first he built in the neo-renaissance style that was much in favour at the time, but then he became influenced by Ludwig Hoffmann's neo-classicism.[2] Both these styles come under the umbrella heading of 'historicism', traces of which can be found in young Speer's work during the Third Reich. By 1900 Albert senior was in a position to marry the daughter of a taciturn self-made man from Mainz, the owner of a substantial machine-tool company. Luise Hommel was sixteen years younger than her husband. She was an unemotional young woman with social ambitions. She brought more money into the marriage than did her husband: a bonus that Albert Senior was later to claim was the principal reason why he married her.[3] Speer's maternal grandfather was the only one of his relatives who was capable of showing him any love or affection. His maternal grandmother, by contrast, was so stingy that she even locked away her precious hoard of sugar cubes.[4] This lack of affection, all too common in similar families, was also characterised in Speer's own family, where his mother-in-law was his children's only source of emotional warmth from within the immediate family.

Speer's father candidly admitted that his sole interest in architecture was that it was an excellent way to make a lot of money.[5] He was not ashamed to make a display of his success in this endeavour. The apartment in Mannheim consisted of fourteen rooms comprising one floor of a vast townhouse that Speer's grandfather had built. In 1905 Speer's father bought a plot of land in the Schloss-Wolfsbrunnenweg in Heidelberg. Here he built a large mansion with elaborate wrought-iron gates and a sweeping driveway that ended with a flight of steps leading to an imposing entrance. One of the two Mercedes – an open one for summer use and a saloon for winter – was parked in front of the house. It was attended by a liveried chauffeur. The Speers were the only family in Mannheim that owned two cars.[6] The staff included a nanny named Berta, a cook, three uniformed maids and a manservant in violet livery. The gold-plated buttons bore a phoney family crest. The house was lavishly furnished, with heavy Dutch furniture in the hallway and a stove encased in costly Delft tiles. There was a winter garden with exotic Indian furniture that his father had bought at the Paris exhibition in 1900. The dining room was decorated in a neo-gothic style that was already outmoded. The drawing room was panelled in dark woods and massively furnished. Initially the house was designed as a summer retreat, but in the summer of 1918 the Mannheim house was let and the Speers moved to Heidelberg. The house was then enlarged to include a garage and an additional apartment.

Young Albert's older brother Hermann was their mother's favourite. His younger brother Ernst was that of his father. But all three were taken largely on sufferance.[7] They were forbidden to enter the house by the front door and forced to take the tradesmen's entrance. Similarly they were obliged to use the back stairs when going to their rooms. The children were brought up in a cold and frequently hostile atmosphere made worse by their parents' strained relationship. As Albert was to remark many years later: 'love was not included in the marriage contract'.[8] Speer's misery in this emotionally cold atmosphere was partially relieved by the presence of Mademoiselle Blum, the children's lovable French governess, of whom he was later to say that she was the principal source of affection during his childhood.[9] His childhood was made all the more miserable by his delicate health. He was given to dizzy spells and fainting fits, which a distinguished professor of medicine from Heidelberg imaginatively diagnosed as 'weakness of the vascular nerves', but for which he was unable to prescribe a therapy. This led Albert to withdraw even more, adopting a slyly accommodating attitude that was to serve him well later in life when having to deal with people whom he disliked.[10] Banned from playing in the park with the children of hoi polloi, young Albert found an agreeable friend in Frieda, the caretaker's daughter, whose skimpily furnished basement apartment he found more congenial than the theatrical pomposity of his own home upstairs.

Albert's formal education began in a small private school that catered for the children of Mannheim's elite. In the summer of 1918 the family moved permanently to their summer estate in Heidelberg. He was then sent to the Hermann von Helmholtz Senior Secondary School, which came as something as a shock to him, because he now came in contact with some rough and ready types lower down the social order.[11] He soon made friends with one of them, a boy named Quenzer, who persuaded him to part with some of his pocket money to buy a football. His parents were horrified when they learnt that Albert was showing some enthusiasm for this resolutely plebeian sport. His new friend introduced him to the fun to be had by defying authority: playing pranks and impressing fellow pupils with the number of times their names were entered for misbehaviour in the class register.

All this was mere playfulness. Speer was no teenage rebel. Although Germany underwent considerable and often extremely violent changes in the immediate post-war years, there were no profound changes in the social structure. Traditional values were still widely accepted and customs remained unchallenged. Politically his father moved with the times, leaving little room for outright confrontation. He was a liberal, an enthusiastic reader of the *Frankfurter Zeitung*, a paper that endorsed the Versailles Treaty, supported Stresemann's fulfilment policy and – with prominent left-wing contributors such as Siegfried Kracauer, Walter Benjamin and Bertold Brecht – was anathema to the nationalist right. Albert senior subscribed to the critical weekly *Simplicissimus*, which featured work by Erich Kästner, Käthe Kollwitz, Kurt Tucholsky and Joachim Ringelnatz. He endorsed Count Richard Nikolaus von Coudenhove-Kalergi's idealistic vision of a united Europe and

Friedrich Naumann's programme for social reform, but at home there were no political discussions and the Helmholtz School did not encourage critical thought or political debate.

In one important respect he challenged his parents' authority and values. One day on his way to school the seventeen-year-old Albert met a young woman named Margarete (Gretel) Weber. She was a year younger than him, the daughter of a highly respected cabinet-maker, who was a member of Heidelberg's city council and a successful entrepreneur. He soon became a frequent guest at the Webers' house, where he found something of the warmth and affection that was so sadly lacking at home.[12] Albert's parents were snobbishly horrified by this friendship. At first they tried to comfort themselves by the thought that this was merely a fit of calf love, but gradually they realised that it was indeed to be a lasting relationship. The Webers were also far from thrilled with Gretel's affection for the poor little rich boy. They packed her off to a boarding school in an attempt to keep her out of harm's way. Speer's letters to her make for curious reading. They were stiff, pretentious and affected, without a hint of the spontaneity and rapture characteristic of a love letter, but they had the desired effect. One year after their first meeting she agreed to marry him, once he had finished his studies.

Albert's health improved greatly during his school years. The everyday walk to school took three-quarters of an hour. At fourteen he joined a rowing club, much to his mother's dismay. She considered the sport, like football, to be distinctly proletarian. Eventually he became the stroke of the school fours and eights. He enjoyed being part of a team, but he abhorred the social side of the club. He disapproved of the dancing, smoking and drinking in which his fellow oarsmen indulged. He remained throughout his life something of a loner and an outsider, hiding his awkwardness behind a façade of impersonal superiority and detached indifference.

As a young man Speer was a passionate skier, mountaineer and hiker. He also developed a love of music. In Mannheim he went to concerts conducted by Wilhelm Furtwängler and Erich Kleiber when both great artists were at the beginning of their distinguished careers. He was particularly moved by the dramatic, romantic and sorrowful, such as Bruckner's fourth symphony, Isolde's *Liebestod* and Mahler's fifth symphony. Later in life he was moved to tears when his friend Wilhelm Kempff played Chopin's enigmatic second piano sonata. It would seem that he had an emotional response to music and nature that was lacking in his personal relationships.

Speer excelled at school. He received the highest marks of all in his school-leaving examination, the *Abitur*.[13] His particular strength was in mathematics, so he decided that he would continue to study the subject at university. His father was horrified that he should opt for such an excellent way to starve for a living. After lengthy argument he persuaded his son to follow in the family tradition and study architecture. He began his studies in 1923 amid the horrendous inflation that rendered the German mark worthless. He described a supper at a simple guesthouse for 1.8 million marks as 'cheap' and later 400 million for a theatre ticket as perfectly in order.

Speer's father survived the crisis relatively well by selling his father-in-law's factory for dollars, but nevertheless certain economies had to be made. Albert was sent to the technical university in nearby Karlsruhe. With the princely monthly allowance of 16 dollars he could easily afford the 20,000 million marks needed to pay for an evening meal.[14] In November 1923 Hjalmar Schacht was appointed Currency Commissioner. He waved his magic wand and stopped the inflation by introducing a new currency known as the Rentenmark that knocked twelve noughts off the Papiermark. In December he was appointed head of the Reichsbank. In August 1924 the Reichsmark was introduced at par with the Rentenmark.

With inflation now under control, Speer was able to pursue his studies in Munich in the spring of 1924. Here he could go mountaineering and canoeing, often accompanied by Gretel. He did not join any of the youth clubs that flourished in the Weimar Republic, preferring to savour the wonders of nature in relative isolation, thereby seeking refuge from the frustrating complexity of the everyday world.[15] He thus espoused the then fashionable distrust of civilisation and an inchoate revolt against convention. This rebellion had been powerfully articulated by Ludwig Klages in his opening address at the inaugural meeting of the Free German Youth in 1913, in which he delivered an intoxicatingly confusing denunciation of modern technological society.[16] Speer claimed, like Klages, that nature was the site of the authentic. His daughter Hilde said that her father never really understood the modern world. His was a Manichean vision, infused with a simplistic social Darwinism.[17] He was fascinated with technology, but he was later to claim that he was also its prey. Klages claimed that 'most people do not live – they merely exist. They are enslaved by their jobs, mere machines exploited by large concerns, serfs of mammon, entrapped in a delirium of shares and flotations. They are enthralled by the distractions of urban life, leaving many with a sense of emptiness and increasing wretchedness.'[18] Speer was later to find in such apocalyptic rhapsodies a convenient alibi for his behaviour during the Third Reich, and he who indulged in much of the best that the modern world had to offer was also to claim to have been its victim.

In the autumn of 1925, along with a number of his fellow students, Speer went to Berlin to study at the renowned Technical University Berlin-Charlottenburg. They hoped to study with Hans Poelzig, a distinguished representative of the school of architecture called *Neue Sachlichkeit* or New Objectivity. He had joined the teaching staff in 1923, and was best known for the *Grosses Schauspielhaus* (Grand Theatre) in Berlin, built in 1919, with its remarkable auditorium featuring clusters of plaster stalactites and its elegant foyer. Max Reinhardt's production of Aeschylus's *Oresteia* for the opening ceremony was one of the major theatrical events of the decade.[19] As a teacher Poelzig was resolutely practical. Since he felt that it was impossible to teach art, he concentrated on the practical matter of organising space so as best to meet its purpose. He told his students that 'there are two very difficult assignments . . . a large theatre and a really small house. The small house is the more difficult of the two'.[20] He liked to shock his students by saying that he saw nothing wrong with plagiarism, citing Handel, Mozart, Shakespeare and himself as distinguished copycats.

Poelzig encouraged individuality and inventiveness so that each of his students could develop his or her own style. They were set specific tasks, whether a factory, a church, a detached house or an office block. On Thursdays and Fridays preliminary sketches were submitted for his inspection. If they were approved, the student was ordered to complete the project. If rejected, the student had to enter the next competition. Having completed three such projects, the student was ready for the final examination. Such was Poelzig's fame that competition was fierce among those eager to sit at the feet of 'The Master'.[21] Speer, who lacked imagination and originality and whose drawing technique was inadequate, was refused entry to this select circle.

Speer took this all in his stride. In his second semester Heinrich Tessenow joined the faculty, having previously taught at the Dresden Academy of Art. He was a leading figure in the movement known as Reform Architecture, which laid great emphasis on the simple, the unpretentious and the down-to-earth. He was greatly influenced by Ebenezer Howard and the British Garden City movement, as can been seen in his work for the Hellerau estate in Dresden and the Hopfengarten in Magdeburg. He was almost the polar opposite of Poelzig. He had followed in his father's footsteps as a cabinet-maker before training as an architect. He always stressed the importance of craft over intellect and imagination. Echoing William Morris, he argued that a craftsman was only at home in a small town. The city was for intellectuals and artists.[22] It was a form of anti-modernism that was echoed by the radical Nazis and survives today, often in surprising places.

As a teacher Tessenow insisted that his pupils should be firmly grounded in the basics of the architect's craft. They should concentrate on the essentials and keep their buildings as simple as possible. In a typically gnomic statement he claimed that: 'The simple is not always the best, but the best is always simple'.[23] Whereas Poelzig's students were encouraged to go their own way, Tessenow's classroom was full of aspiring Tessenows. He was a stimulating if eccentric teacher, who either inspired fierce loyalty or met with outright rejection. Speer was passionately among the former. His adulation of his teacher was such that he decorated his apartment in the Nikolassee district of Berlin in his teacher's style. In a letter to Gretel he wrote: 'My new professor is the most important and clear-headed man I have ever met.'[24]

Speer was also greatly impressed by the archaeologist and architectural historian Daniel Krencker, whose work in Baalbek, Palmyra, Aksum, Ankara, Quedlinburg and the Roman baths in Trier was highly regarded. Here Speer found rich material for his historicist eclecticism and inspiration for his ideas about 'ruin value' – discussed in the next chapter – that was to make such an impression on Adolf Hitler.

As a student Speer was sloppily dressed and appeared to take a nonchalant attitude towards his studies. Rudolf Wolters, who first met him in Munich, described him as an 'amiable loafer', who paid less wealthy pupils to do the architectural drawings for which he showed no great talent. He was generous, often helping out fellow students such as Wolters when they ran short of cash. Once he came under Tessenow's sway Speer seems to have had a change of heart. He hid his boundless ambition behind an outward display of smoothly elegant indifference. He breezed through his diploma in 1927. Six months later, when he became Tessenow's assistant, he was the youngest in the entire university. In 1928, underlining his membership of the educated and cultivated middle class, Speer chose Goethe's birthday, 28 August, to marry Gretel. He sent his parents, who had still not met his bride, a telegram that read: 'MARRIED TODAY STOP WITH LOVE STOP ALBERT AND GRETEL STOP.'[25] Speer's mother, an inveterate social climber, was outraged when she heard that her worst fears had thus been confirmed. It took seven years for Speer's parents to overcome their resentment and invite Gretel to their home.[26] Three weeks of honeymoon were spent canoeing and camping in the Mecklenburg Lake District.

Tessenow's pessimistic view of the modern world as an industrialised Moloch, driven by soulless mass production, creating the alienation of big cities and an extravagant display of new wealth, made a great impression on Speer. It was reinforced by the fashionable cultural pessimism of Oswald Spengler, as articulated in *Prussianism and Socialism* (1919), which argued that the evils of both capitalism and Marxism could be overcome by an alliance of workers, soldiers, technocrats and right-wing intellectuals. Together they would smash the 'dictatorship of money' and keep the mob under control. Speer was much taken by Tessenow's remark that 'perhaps, before handicrafts and small towns can once again flourish, we shall first have to go through fire and brimstone. The next heyday will be that of peoples who have gone through hell.'[27] This modishly apocalyptic vision was a component of National Socialism.

Speer made much of his love of the simple life and his acceptance of Tessenow's adage that the best is always simple. Later, during his years of imprisonment he professed to have come to the conclusion that a room not much larger than a prison cell was all that a normal person needed. This sentimental nonsense is belied by his lifestyle when not a guest of the Allies. He always lived the comfortable life of a successful man. Simplicity is hardly the hallmark of his designs for rebuilding Berlin as 'Germania', as he was later to regret. However, it is greatly to his credit that he adapted remarkably well to wartime hardship and imprisonment under exceptionally stringent conditions. He was also capable of considerable courage and fortitude in defending himself against his rivals and in his single-minded pursuit of the main chance. This same strength of mind protected his conscience from any troubling thoughts and enabled him to feel unpolluted by the garishness and iniquity of the regime that he so loyally and effectively served.

The late 1920s were perplexing times for Germany's youth. The appeal of radical solutions, false prophets and counterfeit messiahs were hard to resist. Defeat in war had been followed by outbursts of revolutionary violence. The *Diktat* of the Treaty of Versailles laid a heavy burden on the country, both materially and emotionally, that was hard to accept. It was widely felt that the German army had indeed been 'stabbed in the back' in 1918 by the democratic parties and their dubious hangers-on. This version of events was after all based on the unquestionable authority of the demi-gods Paul von Hindenburg and Erich Ludendorff. There followed a series of attempted coups, both from the left and the right. In an atmosphere of lawlessness and unbridled violence, political assassinations became commonplace. On top of all this came the shattering experience of the Allied occupation of the Rhineland in 1923, followed by hyperinflation. In the universities there were few that accepted the democratic republic as a legitimate state. With the Great Depression capitalism seemed to be on its last legs and offered no hope for a better future. Some agreed with the American journalist Lincoln Steffens that the Soviet Union had found a future that worked, but others saw Communism as a god that had failed. Many felt that American capitalism was no longer a viable alternative. An increasing number of people felt that Adolf Hitler's Nationalsozialistische Deutsche Arbeiterpartei or National Socialist German Workers' Party (NSDAP) offered a viable answer. A great many, even though they had considerable reservations about the Nazis, came to believe that they were the only alternative to the dictatorship of the Kommunistische Partei Deutschlands or German Communist Party (KPD).

The Technical University of Berlin was a bastion of National Socialism. In 1928 Baldur von Schirach's Nationalsozialistischer Deutscher Studentenbund or National Socialist German Students' Association (NSDStB) won 13 per cent of the vote for the Allgemeiner Studenten Ausschuss or student council (AStA). One year later it got 66 per cent. A large number of Tessenow's students were enthusiastic adherents of 'The Movement'. Speer, ever anxious to portray himself as an apolitical professional and technocrat, claims that he was 'unconvinced but still uncertain' until he went along with some fellow students to hear Hitler address university students in Berlin in December 1930. It was a rally to drum up support for the NSDAP in the forthcoming student council elections.[28] There is ample evidence that Speer's attitude towards National Socialism was far from being lukewarm. One of his students, Peter Koller, who later under Speer was to plan the town of Wolfsburg as a base housing for the Volkswagen works, tells of lengthy discussions at Speer's apartment about National Socialism, particularly its proposals for creating a corporate state that would set right an economy that was in ruins.[29] Speer was later on occasion to let slip his identification with Nazi racial prejudice and with other unattractive aspects of this offensive ideology.[30] The NSDStB's policy statement was unambiguous. It denounced the 'War Guilt Lie' and the Young Plan for reparations. It called for professorships in 'racial science' and 'military science'. It demanded a strict limitation of the number of Jewish students and other 'elements alien to the Germanic race'.[31]

Tessenow, although not a party member, was sympathetic to the Hitler movement. He was known on occasion to have read *Die Tat* (The Deed), the only journal on the radical right that was intellectually challenging, with contributors such as Ernst Jünger, Dorothy Thompson and Sefton Delmer which helped to give it an international reputation. A common theme was that modern technology and authoritarian politics were well matched. They believed that Germany could find a sense of community that would avoid both the soulless materialism of the United States and the soulless collectivism of the Soviet Union.

Another theme was that the cultural crisis of modern society was not due to technology itself, as Speer was later to claim, but rather that technology was harnessed to selfish commercial interests. Environmental destruction, the commodification of culture and contempt for spiritual values were all due to enslavement to economic forces rather than to technology. The engineer-artist opposed brutish commercial interests that were blind to the 'metaphysical foundations' of technology. Often technology was confused with what was seen as the curse of Americanism. Technology was falsely identified with production and use-value, whereas it should be seen as creative. Parasitic and selfish finance capital was soullessly concerned with circulation and exchange value.[32] The young conservatives in the *Tat* circle argued that a strong state was needed to protect the masses from the rapacious greed of the few. The radical journalist and pacifist Carl von Ossietzky said that: 'it clearly shows the befuddlement of the liberal bourgeoisie, who in the face of a world-wide economic crisis throw themselves yelling, screaming and ecstatically gesturing into the arms of right-wing radicals'.[33] The *Tat* circle was closely associated with the left-wing Nazis around Otto Strasser, who was a regular contributor to the journal. The British journalist Sefton Delmer, head of the *Daily Express* Berlin bureau, was a friend of Ernst Röhm, the leader of the brown-shirted radicals in the SA. The Nazi left took many of the ideas expressed in *Die Tat* on board.[34] Tessenow would therefore not have been particularly alarmed when his assistant became involved with the Nazis.

Speer combined such modish cultural pessimism and anti-modernism with a fascination with technology that was so typical of conservative intellectuals in the Weimar Republic. This 'reactionary modernism' was to find its radical expression in National Socialism.[35] It was a strange mixture. It combined a rhapsodic love of nature, canoeing and hiking in the Alps with a rejection of the degenerate urban world. But it also involved a fascination with technology, fast cars, cinema and Max Reinhardt's innovative stage productions. As Minister of Armaments Speer cautioned that although technology could solve future problems, there was a danger of mankind becoming its slave.[36] After the war technology became Speer's strongest alibi. An autonomous technology exonerated technocrats from moral responsibility as well as the political consequences of their efforts.

Over 5,000 students crowded into the Neue Welt beer hall in the Berlin district of Neukölln on 4 December 1930 to hear Adolf Hitler speak.[37] News that two members of the brown-shirted SA had become 'the victims of murderous red beasts' further served to electrify the atmosphere. Hitler made an impassioned appeal for moderation and compromise, calling for an end to the self-destructive struggle between left and right. He appealed for a renewal of the traditional values of honour and heroism, insisting that 'a heroic idea attracts heroes' whereas 'a cowardly idea collects cowards'. The present misery was caused, he claimed, by the fact that the war had destroyed all the best while preserving the inferior, resulting in rule by the mediocre, so that politics had been reduced to mere egotism. It was the task of National Socialism to put the elite back in power – by which he clearly meant his present audience – so that national unity might be restored. He closed by telling the students that they must 'find a way to integrate themselves into the nation's life and future'. It was an intoxicating message for the young and ambitious, whose future amidst a shattering depression, rapidly rising unemployment and a political system that was falling apart appeared hopelessly grim.[38] It is testament to the hypnotic power possessed by Hitler that such a highly educated group should be carried away by a speech given in far from faultless German, riddled with contradictions, illogical argument and empty promises. It was delivered in a raucous voice with outbursts of screaming and yelling, punctuated by foot-stamping and wild gesticulation.

While his students discussed Hitler's speech over glasses of beer, Speer drove through the night to a pine forest in the Havelland where he wandered alone deep in thought. Some weeks after this epiphany, he went to hear Goebbels speak. He later claimed to have been revolted by the hectoring, crude and violent tone of his lengthy tirade, but this did not cause him to have any second thoughts about the Nazi Party.[39] It was Goebbels who helped ease Speer's way to the top, and in a speech he gave in the Berlin Sports Palace in 1943 he spoke highly of Berlin's Gauleiter: 'During the Time of Struggle I used to sit among you as an unknown party comrade, experiencing the Führer's unique rallies. The passionate words of our Gauleiter Dr Goebbels renewed my strength to carry on the struggle.'[40] In January 1931 Speer applied for membership. On 1 March he became Party Comrade number 474,481.[41] In the German original of his memoirs Speer states that his decision to join the party was 'not dramatic'. In the English version he reassures the reader that had Hitler announced his intention to go to war, burn down the synagogues and kill Jews and political prisoners before 1933 he would have lost most of his followers.[42] Hitler's speech to the students did not include an anti-Semitic rant, nor did it give any hint that he was contemplating going to war, but party literature was full of such presentiments. Speer could not have avoided being aware of National Socialism's fundamental intents. His political commitment, he assures his English-speaking readers, consisted merely in paying his modest monthly party dues. Speer obviously thought that his German readers would not be quite so gullible. He told them that the Nazi Party offered 'new ideals, new insights and a new mission'.[43] He was more forthright when speaking to the British journalist William Hamsher. He told him that he had joined the party in order to save Germany from Communism.[44] Ever the opportunist, Speer presented himself as a dedicated and devout party comrade during the Third Reich. After the war he claimed to have had no interest in politics and had become a party member almost by chance. The truth lies somewhere in between these two extremes. Like many of the leading figures in the Third Reich, Speer was never an ideologue. Nor was he anything more than an instinctive anti-Semite. He was frequently locked in battle with the Nazi Party. But it was his party connections that made his meteoric rise to power possible. In this too he was typical of the well-educated and skilled middle class that gave the Third Reich its compliant support, despite some reservations and occasional feelings of remorse.

That he was merely an indifferent fellow traveller is pure myth. Soon after becoming a party member Speer joined the ranks of the radical brown-shirted bullyboys in the SA. In 1932 he enlisted in the Nationalsozialistisches Kraftfahrkorps or National Socialist Automobile Corps (NSKK), the SA's motorised section, in which he played an active role. He also promptly joined the

Kampfbund deutscher Architekten und Ingenieure or Action Group of German Architects and Engineers, an organisation founded by Gottfried Feder and Paul Schultze-Naumburg in 1931 as a section of Alfred Rosenberg's Kampfbund für deutsche Kultur or Action Group for German Culture (KfdK). Speer's friend Rudolf Wolters, who had serious reservations about Hitler, asked him why on earth he had joined the party. Speer replied: 'Come on, you'll see. The man is not that stupid. He'll be somebody one day.'[45]

Thanks to Speer's engagement in Nazi politics, the Western District Party Organiser in Berlin, Karl Hanke – a man who was to rise to great heights in the Third Reich – asked him in 1931 to refurbish his office in a villa he had rented in the exclusive Grünewald neighbourhood. The Nazi Party, having achieved a breakthrough in the elections in September 1930, was attempting to appear more respectable so as to strengthen its support among the middle class. Eagerly seizing this opportunity Speer undertook the task free of charge. Hanke, now Ward Leader in Berlin's West End – the most exciting part of the city during the 'Golden Twenties' – was delighted with the results. With scant regard for party orthodoxy, he selected 'communist' wallpaper that came from the ideologically suspect Bauhaus on the grounds that only the best was good enough for the Nazis, regardless of provenance.[46]

In early 1932 the rigorous austerity programme instituted by the Brüning government resulted in the stipends of university assistants being drastically cut, whereupon Speer decided to try his luck as an independent architect. These were exceedingly difficult times for someone unknown in this field. He had no clients and prospects were grim. Unable to find work in Berlin he returned to Mannheim hoping to land a few assignments through his father's many contacts. His luck did not turn, so his father gave him a job managing his various properties. Since this was hardly full-time employment he decided to go on a canoeing holiday in the Masurian Lake District, then in East Prussia. On 28 July 1932, just as he was about to set out on this trip, he received a telephone call from Wilhelm Nagel, the head of the NSKK asking him to return to Berlin. It was a call that was to change his life.[47] Nagel spoke on behalf of Karl Hanke, who had requested that Speer renovate the Nazi Party's recently acquired headquarters at Vossstraße 11 in the heart of the governmental district. Speer claims that his return to Berlin was due to pure chance. Had Nagel called a few hours later he would have already left on holiday and would have been out of touch with the outside world.

There is a good reason to doubt this story. In June 1932 Franz von Papen, a man of whom the French ambassador said that 'he enjoyed the peculiarity of being taken seriously neither by his friends nor by his enemies' and who had virtually no support in parliament, asked President Hindenburg to dissolve the Reichstag three days after his appointment as chancellor.[48] The two months of campaigning that followed were the bloodiest and most violent in the history of the republic. Elections for the Reichstag were held on 31 July. Speer admits in his memoirs that he returned to Berlin 'to savour the exciting election atmosphere and – wherever possible – to help out'. As he was one of the very few Nazis in Berlin who owned a car, he would have been very much in demand during the election campaign. The results marked the decisive breakthrough of the Nazi Party, which was returned as the largest party, increasing the number of seats from 107 in 1930 to 230. With 13,745,680 votes cast in its favour it had almost twice the number as its closest rival, the Sozialdemokratische Partei Deutschlands or Social Democratic Party (SPD). In such a heady atmosphere, when the fate of the republic hung in the balance and when the SA was in urgent need of his services, it is somewhat unlikely that Speer would have contemplated going on a canoeing holiday just three days before the election.

Whatever the case, Speer's work in the *Gauhaus* at Vossstraße 11 was soon completed. All he was asked to do was to undertake a few minor renovations, repaint the interior and select furniture for Goebbels' office and the conference room. His main problem was that he was still completely under the influence of Tessenow's doctrine that the best is always simple. This was hard to realise in an ornate building typical of the Wilhelmine style. He hardly ever saw Goebbels, who was frantically preparing for yet another election. The work was completed on time, but well over budget. In the election of 6 November 1932 the Nazi Party lost a significant number of seats. Party membership dropped. The till was empty. The craftsmen had to accept a deferment of payments for several months, by which time Hitler was in power and cash was no longer a problem.[49]

With no more work to do in Berlin, Speer returned to Mannheim where the situation was as miserable as ever. The only good news was that Speer was told that Hitler was delighted with the work he had done at Vossstraße 11.[50] Hitler was appointed chancellor on 30 January 1933. Elections were held on 5 March. One week later Hanke, who had just been appointed adjutant and personal assistant to the Minister of Propaganda, telephoned Speer and asked him to return to Berlin to advise Goebbels on refurbishing his new ministry in the Prince Friedrich Leopold Palace in the Wilhelmplatz. Goebbels told Speer to get on with the job at once. He was far too impatient to wait for an estimate so that Speer, mindful that the Propaganda Ministry as yet had no official budget and true to his training under Tessenow, opted for relatively modest furnishings. Goebbels, considering these to be unworthy of his high office, ordered furniture directly from the United Workshops in Munich, which specialised in Paul Ludwig Troost's 'ocean liner style' much favoured by Hitler.[51]

For his personal use Goebbels grabbed the official residence of the Minister of Food and Agriculture on the Friedrich-Ebert-Straße, soon to be renamed

Hermann-Göring-Straße. Alfred Hugenberg, who was leader of the German National People's Party and Minister for Economics, Agriculture and Food in Hitler's first cabinet, was outraged. He put up a strong resistance, but was eventually forced to give way. Speer was commissioned to renovate the interior and to add a substantial living area. Goebbels was once again in a mad rush, but Speer rashly promised to have the job completed within two months. Hitler pronounced this to be an impossibility, but Speer handed over the keys on 30 June 1933, well within the time limit. Goebbels pronounced his new home to be 'fabulous', a 'fairy-tale castle' set in a 'magnificent park'. In mid-July Joseph and Magda Goebbels gave a house-warming party in their new home to which Hitler was invited. Hitler spotted some 'degenerate' paintings, including watercolours by Emil Nolde that Speer had managed to borrow from the National Gallery and which the Goebbels's had found delightful. Hitler judged them to be totally unacceptable and Goebbels ordered Speer to return them at once.[52] In spite of this gaffe, Hitler was greatly impressed by Speer's work.[53]

Hitler decided that 1 May should be celebrated as the 'Day of National Labour', thereby wresting May Day out of the hands of Communists, Social Democrats and the trades unions, all of which he denounced as playing critical roles in the 'Jewish-Bolshevik world conspiracy'. He hoped thereby to win over the working class to National Socialism. As part of the celebrations the Propaganda Ministry was ordered to organise a mass demonstration on the evening of 1 May in the Tempelhof Field in Berlin. The file landed on Hanke's desk. When shown some initial sketches for the celebration, Speer remarked that they looked like the arrangements for a village fete, whereupon Hanke said that if he could do something better he was welcome to have a try.

Speer set to work that very evening and made the initial sketches. Realising that there would not be sufficient time to make any elaborate preparations, he came up with a brilliant solution. From Max Reinhardt's detailed stage productions and from his enthusiasm for the cinema he had developed a vivid sense of the theatrical. He proposed to place nine flagpoles behind the speakers' tribune, each of them 33 metres high, from which hung flags as if they were sails. The effect was dramatic, but it would have been disastrous had there been a high wind. Searchlights, borrowed from the UFA film studios at Babelsberg, were placed around the perimeter pointing directly upwards, creating columns of light. Clusters of flags were placed between the searchlights.[54]

According to much exaggerated official sources 1.5 million people attended the rally. Goebbels gave the opening address. Hitler promised to put an end to political strife and divisiveness by creating a genuine 'racial community' (*Volksgemeinschaft*). He then unveiled a make-work programme based on building a network of highways. The rally ended with a lavish fireworks display and the singing of the national anthem. The whole event was broadcast, with a commentary from a Zeppelin that circled overhead.[55]

After the carrot – a holiday with pay on 1 May for which the Social Democrats and Communists had struggled in vain for years – came the stick. On 2 May the SA raided the offices of the trades unions. Their property was seized. On 10 May all workers from the chairman of the board to the unskilled labourers were obliged to join the Deutsche Arbeitsfront or German Work Front (DAF), which thereby became the largest organisation in the world. To add salt to the wound, workers' wages on the Autobahn were below the welfare level.

Speer proudly took Tessenow on a tour of the Tempelhof site. He was appalled, dismissing it as nothing but empty show that was contrary to all his fundamental ideas. 'Do you think that you have created anything?' he asked. 'All you have done is create an impression.' Much the same can be said of the bulk of Speer's subsequent work as an architect. Hanke's message was more positive. He told Speer that Hitler had been delighted.[56] With such praise from on high Speer was given the official position of Director General for the artistic decoration of the Propaganda Ministry's major rallies. Thereby at the age of twenty-eight he had made a significant step forward on his way to becoming the Third Reich's principal architect.

CHAPTER TWO

NUREMBERG AND BERLIN

B Y MAY 1933 Speer had had some success with relatively small projects and had shown considerable improvisatory skill with the May Day Rally, but his future prospects did not look particularly promising. Hitherto his only experience with bricks and mortar was in building a suburban villa for his parents-in-law and a couple of garages in the Wannsee district of Berlin. In the unlikely event of him being assigned a major public project he would have to shake himself free from Tessenow's influence, whose functionalist style was not deemed appropriate for representational buildings in the New Germany. But where was he to turn? In his inaugural speech as Chancellor on 23 March 1933 Hitler had told the Reichstag that artistic vision had henceforth to be based on blood and race; but no one knew quite what that was supposed to mean. Lacking any strikingly original ideas, Speer would have to decide which alternative style he should adopt.

Regional elections in Thuringia in December 1929 had resulted in Wilhelm Frick becoming the first member of the NSDAP to hold ministerial office. One of his first acts as Minister of the Interior and of Education was to close down the Bauhaus, the state-sponsored modernist school of architecture and design in Dessau. He then appointed Paul Schultze-Naumburg head of the State College for Architecture and Crafts in Weimar. Frick promptly fired virtually the entire teaching staff. He also rid the Weimar museum of 'degenerate' works by artists such as Kandinsky, Klee and Nolde. This was a practical application of the principles enumerated in Schultze-Naumburg's book *Art and Race* of 1928, thereby providing a grim foretaste of National Socialist cultural politics.[1]

Schultze-Naumburg had established a considerable reputation as an architect. His best-known work is the Cecilienhof in Potsdam, built for Crown Prince Wilhelm and completed in 1917. Although it is a vast building with 176 rooms, it still manages to be unpretentious and peaceful with its steeply pitched roof and neo-Tudor half-timbering.[2] His buildings were imbued with regionalism and nationalism, based on the traditional farmhouse and the village community. He detested modernism and its deliberate break with tradition, describing the Weissenhof Estate, built for an international architectural exhibition with houses by, among others, Walter Gropius, Mies van der Rohe, Le Corbusier and Hans Poelzig, as 'Casablanca in Stuttgart'. The principles of his 'Blood and Soil' architecture were laid out in Karl Willy Straub's *Architecture in the Third Reich* of 1932, which seemed destined to be the guide book for a distinctly National Socialist architecture.[3]

In the 1920s Schultze-Naumburg entertained Hitler, Himmler and Goebbels at his studio in Saaleck. It was here that Walther Darré, who was to become Minister of Agriculture in Hitler's government, wrote his magnum opus *The New Aristocracy of Blood and Soil* in 1930.[4] Heinrich Tessenow also worked in Schultze-Naumburg's studio. In 1929 Schultze-Naumburg joined Alfred Rosenberg's Action Group for German Culture (KfdK), which specialised in disrupting concerts at which 'degenerate' modern music was played, denouncing 'Jewish and Negro' influence in the arts and in distributing rabble-rousing anti-Semitic pamphlets. The KfdK worked closely with the SA, which used its strong-arm tactics against 'enemies of German culture'. Schultze-Naumburg was intimately associated with two of the most appalling racists in these insalubrious circles: Alfred Ploetz, the co-founder with Wilhelm Schallmayer of 'racial hygiene' and the extremist 'Race Pope' Hans F.K. Günther, a eugenicist who was Professor for Racial Science, Racial Biology and Regional Sociology at Berlin University.[5] Schultze-Naumburg's relationship with Wilhelm Frick was so close that when he went through an extremely ugly divorce in 1934 resulting from Frick's relationship with Schultze-Naumburg's wife Margarete, whom he subsequently married, they still remained on friendly terms. In 1932 he joined the Nazi caucus in the Reichstag and remained a member of this redundant organisation until 1945.

With such a background, impeccable credentials and powerful friends, Schultze-Naumburg seemed destined to become Nazi Germany's leading architect. But he fell foul of the Nazi Party and his career rapidly unravelled. After 1935 he received no more major contracts. In 1938 Speer tried desperately to stop the distribution of a catalogue sponsored by the Ministry of Finance entitled *The Movement's Buildings* on the grounds that there were too many reproductions of Schultze-Naumburg's work.[6] In 1941 Schultze-Naumburg was forced into retirement from his position in Weimar and was threatened with a party disciplinary procedure, but was partly reinstated in 1944 when honours were bestowed upon him more for his ideological orthodoxy than for his buildings.[7] He was included in the list of 'Divinely Blessed Artists', who were so precious that they were to be exempted from military service. His cardinal sin was that he, like Tessenow, was violently opposed to anything

that smacked of ostentation, of excessive ornamentation and of the monumental. He described such buildings, increasingly favoured as the regime
gained in confidence, with devastating accuracy as 'wantonly parvenu'. This
was the style that Speer brought to full fruition in his designs for Germania.
Schultze-Naumburg had a particular aversion to roofs that were partly hidden
or flat, claiming that they gave buildings an additional heaviness. His vision
was in accord with the thinking of the National Socialist left, associated with
the likes of Otto Strasser, Gottfried Feder and Franz Lawaczeck, whose version
of National Socialism was anti-capitalist in that it warned of the dangers of
industrial technology, and called for a return to an essentially artisanal mode of
production.[8] Hitler smashed these radical elements, associated with Ernst
Röhm and the SA, in the 'Night of the Long Knives' in June 1934, which marked
a new phase in the development of Nazi Germany. Speer put an end to Schultze-
Naumburg's lingering influence when in 1939 he ordered Ernst Neufert to
write a new edition of his book *Architects' Data*, first published in 1936. It called
for the normalisation and rationalisation of building methods, thereby
sounding the death knoll of all craft production in the event of a 'Final Victory'.[9]

Hitler made a somewhat surprising choice for his chief architect. Paul
Ludwig Troost was essentially an interior designer who had gained an international reputation for his stunning interiors of luxury liners. He had also
designed furniture for Schultze-Naumburg's Cecilienhof. Hitler began to
collect his costly furniture in 1926. The two men met in 1930, when Hitler
appointed him to renovate the NSDAP's headquarters in Munich, known as
the Brown House. Troost's architecture was eclectic. It ranged from the neo-
classical, flat-roofed Villa Becker in 1904 to his own house built in 1924, much
in the style of Schultze-Naumburg.[10] His first building for the Party was the
Führer's Building, or *Führerbau*, in the Königsplatz in Munich. It was here that
the Munich Agreement was signed in 1938. With its restrained neo-classical
style, flat roof and columned portico it was the antithesis of Schultze-
Naumburg's Germanic 'blood and soil' aesthetic.

Early in 1933 Hitler commissioned Troost to design a replacement for the
Glass Palace, an exhibition hall in the Botanical Garden in Munich, built in
1854 as Bavaria's answer to the Crystal Palace. It burnt down in 1931, five years
before its precursor in London. The result was Troost's best-known work – the
House of German Art. This was the Third Reich's first monumental building
that set the style for the next five years. The design was based on the colon-
naded façade of Schinkel's Old Museum on the Museum Island in Berlin.[11]
Hitler temporarily abandoned his love for Viennese Ringstraße baroque in
favour of a less flamboyant style. With its neo-classical façade, flat roof and
columned arcade it was a typical example of the international style of stripped-
down classicism and modernised antique. The locals were not impressed. It

was popularly known as the 'Weißwurst Temple'. Peter Behrens' Imperial German Embassy in St Petersburg (1913), Albert Kahn's Angell Hall at the University of Michigan (1924), Paul Philippe Cret's Eccles Building for the Federal Reserve in Washington (1935–7), K.S. Alabyan and V.N. Simbirtzev's Red Army Theatre in Moscow (1940), Henri Paul Nénot's League of Nations Palace in Geneva (1929–36) and Léon Azéma, Jacques Carlu and Louis-Hippolyte Boileau's Palais de Chaillot (1935–7), are all built in much the same style. It would be difficult to read Troost's building as specifically National Socialist, just as Cret's building is hardly a hymn of praise to American capitalism or the Palais de Chaillot a monument to republican virtues.

The problem is that Troost's building is so closely associated with the evil regime that sponsored it that it is difficult to view it dispassionately within the context of an international style. Thus Charles Holden's Senate House of the University of London (1932–7), an imposing example of the international modernist style, was seen by the architect of the British welfare state, William Beveridge, as 'an academic island in swirling tides of traffic, a world of learning in a world of affairs'. But it has also been described as 'Hitler's headquarters', 'Stalinist' and 'totalitarian'.[12] This serves to show how the semiotics of architecture is frequently confusing. The problem is that art historians, particularly in Germany, have tended to see all works of art as symbolic. According to this paradigm Nazi architecture is as perverse as the regime under which it was built. By analogy any building built in a similar style is equally tainted. Speer was perfectly correct when he wrote that there was no such thing as a specifically National Socialist architecture, merely an emphasis on the colossal and the overpowering. He perceptively wrote: 'Ideology was apparent in the definition of the commission, but not in the style of its execution.'[13]

The Nazis faced a difficult dilemma. Rosenberg issued a resounding denunciation of modern architecture as 'un-German' in July of 1933, but Schultze-Naumburg's aesthetic, although ideologically defensible, was simply not suitable for representational buildings. But where were they to turn? The classicism of Friedrich David Gilly and Karl Friedrich Schinkel, both of whom Speer greatly admired, was somewhat tainted with French revolutionary overtones and the liberal aspects of the war against Napoleon, even though they were magisterially endorsed by Moeller van den Bruck as embodiments of the *Prussian style*.[14] Otto Wagner's work in Vienna in the 1890s, which greatly impressed Hitler, had to be surpassed, not imitated. Stripped-down neo-classicism would have to suffice during this transitional stage until the regime found its feet. The addition of weighty eagles and swastikas would have to serve as a National Socialist variant of an international style until a new vernacular was found.

Meanwhile the modernistic style, although condemned, was still alive and struggled on. There was nothing to rival Giuseppi Terragni's Casa del Fascio in

Como – a modern masterpiece directly sponsored by the Italian Fascist Party. Nor was any building in the Third Reich ever to match Emil Fahrenkamp's Shell House in Berlin, opened in 1932. Ernst Sagebiel, who had worked briefly as project manager for the great German-Jewish modernist Erich Mendelsohn, designed the Air Ministry of 1935–6, the first major building under National Socialism. It is a solid example of the international style, a descendant of Albert Kahn's General Motors Building in Detroit (1919) and of Hans Poelzig's IG-Farben-Haus in Frankfurt (1931). The building, with over 55,000 square metres and 2,000 rooms, was a clear indication that Nazi Germany was set on defying the Treaty of Versailles, which prohibited the country from building an air force. Its main distinguishing features were its vastness and the speed with which it was completed, both aspects designed as expressions of the regime's unbounded energy and determination.[15] It is now a listed building, which houses the Federal Ministry of Finance. Sagebiel was also responsible for building the new airport at Tempelhof, at the time the world's largest. It was designed largely for its propagandistic effect as a demonstration of the regime's modernity and strength of purpose. Sagebiel's style was soon known as 'Luftwaffe modern'.[16]

The struggle to find an explicitly National Socialist German architecture was symptomatic of a fundamental dichotomy within the regime's confused ideology. It tried to resolve the contradictions that had perplexed German intellectuals for the last half century, from Ferdinand Tönnies and Max Weber to Thomas Mann, Ernst Jünger, Oswald Spengler, Carl Schmitt and Martin Heidegger. How was it possible to reconcile culture and civilisation, tradition and modernity, community and society? Was there an alternative to the selfish individualism and insensitive commercialism of the United States and the faceless collectivism and soulless materialism of the Soviet Union? How could technology be made to serve loftier aims than sordid greed and commercial advantage? How could the contradiction between the pastoral idyll of 'Blood and Soil' and the exigencies of modern technology be resolved? Was it conceivable that a comradely community could survive in an industrial world of Taylorism and rationalisation? How could technology transcend the anarchy of capitalist reproduction? The answers offered by the likes of Goebbels were glib evasions. Filling the utilitarian framework of technology with the fire and energy of National Socialism seemed on reflection to be nothing but empty sloganeering. National Socialism was both modern and atavistic, divided within itself and unable to reconcile its inherent contradictions. Albert Speer is a personification of this ambiguity. As Minister of Armaments he stood for modern technology, mass production, rationalisation, big business and unrestrained capitalism – even though subject to certain wartime controls. As Hitler's Haussmann and Le Nôtre, he planned to build massive atavistic cult monuments that were a defiant rejection of modernity.

As a result of all this confusion a host of different architectural styles were adopted in the Third Reich. Various forms of classicism, later loaded with neo-baroque excrescences as in Speer's designs for the new Berlin, were favoured for state and party buildings and for various propagandistic structures such as the Party Rally Grounds at Nuremberg. Variations of Paul Schultze-Naumburg and Heinrich Tessenow's rustic 'Save the Homeland' style were used for suburban housing developments as well as for the schools for training a National Socialist elite known as Order Castles (*Ordensburgen*). Modified forms of modernism were considered appropriate for apartment blocks and office buildings. A forceful functionalism was favoured for army barracks and head offices, while a more restrained version can be seen in sports facilities and stadiums. Lastly, the Bauhaus' New Objectivity lived on, in spite of being ideologically suspect, in industrial buildings and research centres. Mies van der Rohe was even commissioned to design gas stations for Fritz Todt's highways.[17] Speer was surprised when Hitler expressed great admiration for Herbert Rimpl's modernist Hermann Göring Works outside Linz, which he visited in 1943.[18] The style was also adapted for much of the new housing built after 1933. Such eclecticism enabled many of Nazi Germany's leading architects to adapt quickly to post-war conditions and to pursue highly successful careers in the Federal Republic. Speer showed genuine inventiveness in his ad hoc arrangements for the party rallies, but he was lacking in creativity as an architect. He was successful in using light as a building material, but showed no originality when using more conventional materials. Having abandoned Tessenow, who was clearly a hindrance to his career, he dutifully followed Troost and then Hitler.

His genius lay in providing the dictator with exactly what he wanted: theatrical backdrops to enhance his stature and the realisation of his dreams of building vast monuments to his boundless imperial ambitions, designed to survive for thousands of years – even as ruins – as a permanent reminder of his staggering achievements. Hence the preposterous notion of the 'ruin value' of buildings that were to last for two thousand years – in more euphoric moments for four thousand – as monuments to bygone splendour. In fact many of those buildings that survived bombing and artillery fire were to show serious signs of decay within twenty years.[19] Speer's buildings were made with reinforced concrete faced with stone because Hitler demanded that they be built as quickly as possible. They would have made exceedingly ugly ruins.

The idea of 'ruin value' was far from original. In 1771, Horace Walpole predicted that there would 'be a Thucydides at Boston, a Xenophon at New York, and in time a Virgil at Mexico, and a Newton at Peru. At last some curious traveller from Lima will visit England and give a description of the ruins of St. Paul's, like the editions of Baalbek and Palmyra.' Macaulay prophesied that one day a New Zealander would visit a derelict London, sit among the remains of London Bridge and sketch St Paul's in ruins. Caspar David Friedrich painted St James' church in Greifswald as a ruin. John Soane did the same in his water-colours of the Bank of England, while Gustav Doré in *London: a Pilgrimage* showed the city in an advanced state of decay.[20]

Speer may not have been particularly creative, but he had an exceptional organisational talent. He knew how to pick a team, delegate responsibility and deliver the goods.[21] This was something that Hitler clearly recognised. He was not an artist who was eager to leave his personal mark. He did what he was told and got the job done quickly and efficiently in the spirit intended. It was precisely these qualities that made Hitler decide to appoint him Minister of Armaments and which account for his astonishing success in an area of which he had no previous knowledge or experience. They were also his undoing. His willingness to delegate left him wide open to jealous rivals, eager to push him aside at the first possible opportunity.

Hitler's first major architectural project was to build a 'national place of pilgrimage' at Nuremberg, but he was hesitant as to whom he should entrust this task. The natural choice would have been his chosen architect, Paul Ludwig Troost, but the situation was a trifle delicate. Speer already had a position in the Ministry of Propaganda as the official designer for party rallies. Furthermore, Speer had received a formal invitation from the Nuremberg city council in July 1933, just as he was putting the finishing touches to Goebbels' private residence, to draw up plans for a temporary structure on the Zeppelin Field for the forth-coming party rally. Since all such plans had to be approved by Hitler, Speer went to Munich to present his portfolio. His design was a modified version of the May Day celebrations. Instead of enormous flags behind the tribune he placed a gigantic eagle with outstretched wings, clutching a swastika in its claws. This time the entire complement of the Luftwaffe's anti-aircraft section's 152 searchlights were to be borrowed – much to Göring's displeasure – to create an impression that the British ambassador, Sir Neville Henderson, described as 'both solemn and beautiful . . . like being in a cathedral of ice'.[22] Hitler, who was engrossed in cleaning an automatic pistol that lay in pieces on his desk, gave a nod, grunted 'approved' and began to reassemble the weapon. Such was Speer's brief first encounter with the man who was to change his life.[23] He was later to bemoan the fact that this 'immaterial' lightshow was remembered as his greatest architectural achievement. We do not know his reactions when it was revived in David Bowie's *Station to Station* tour of 1976.[24]

Speer's next commission was to design the Harvest Festival to be held on 1 October 1933 on the northern slope of the Bückeberg. This was a mystical spot for the National Socialists. It was here that Arminius was said to have defeated the Romans and where the Saxon leader Widukin had defeated Charlemagne's Franks. The Nazi hero Horst Wessel came from the region, which was irrigated

by the 'pure German' River Weser. Speer's design, drawn up in close consultation with the Minister of Agriculture, Walther Darré, was a simple oval planted
with thousands of flags. There were two platforms at opposite ends, connected
by 600 metres of raised walkway known as 'The Führer's Way'. It took Hitler an
hour to press his way along it through a throng of adulating peasantry. It was
later replaced by a cobblestone road that is now classified as a historic monument. There was a speakers' podium at the north-western end of the oval and a
stand to the south-east for 3,000 special guests, photographers and journalists.
To stress the simplicity and directness of farming, all structures were made of
wood. The concrete foundations still remain. The Harvest Festival was a gigantic
spectacle, even greater in scale than the annual Nuremberg Party Rally. 500,000
participants attended the initial ceremony. By 1937 the figure had risen to 1.2
million. Over the years more permanent structures were added and the arena
was designated as a 'Thing Site' for use as an outdoor theatre. Here was the
perfect setting for various manifestations of Darré's 'Blood and Soil' ideology.[25]

During his visit to Nuremberg Speer made a number of other important
contacts. Among them was the city planner, Walter Brugmann, who was later
to become one of his closest associates. For this mammoth project in Nuremberg
he coordinated the work of slave labour from all over Europe. Brugmann also
assisted Speer in his efforts to build a new Berlin that was rid of its Jewish
population.[26]

As a result of this visit Speer was entrusted with building permanent stands
on the Zeppelin Field in 1933. His design, with its arcade of unadorned rectan-
gular pillars, was a direct quote from Troost's House of German Art. Anxious
to prove that he was not a mere imitator of Hitler's chief architect, Speer insisted
that he had been inspired by the Pergamon Altar in Berlin's Museum Island.
There were, however, two major differences that gave a strong indication of
what was to come. The first was the sheer size of the structure. It was 390
metres wide and 24 metres high.[27] Secondly, he placed a gigantic swastika,
carved in stone and framed in a laurel wreath, on its flat roof. On 25 April 1945
a film was made of American engineers blowing up this hated emblem of
Nazism. It was to become a powerful symbol of the defeat of Nazi Germany.

Willy Liebel, the mayor of Nuremberg, had also commissioned a local
architect, Ludwig Ruff, to build a massive congress hall along a central axis
connecting a vast arena on the Luitpoldhain, on which the rallies were to
be held, with the Märzfeld – a rectangle of some 60 hectares of sandy heath,
fenced off by 30-metre-high swastika flags that were spanned between 24
massive stone towers. Provision was made for 160,000 spectators to watch
the Wehrmacht's display manoeuvres. The Congress Hall was modelled after
the Roman Colosseum. Ruff had a close relationship with Hitler, thanks to the
intermediary of the Gauleiter of Thuringia, Fritz Sauckel, a man who was to

play a key role as slave driver in Speer's armaments empire. Hitler approved this plan, but Ruff was unable to bring it to fruition. He died in August 1934 as a result of an operation. His son Franz, who was soon to establish a reputation as one of Nazi Germany's leading architects, readily agreed to finish his father's work.[28] Franz's major work was the massive SS barracks in Nuremberg, the designs for which were carefully vetted by Speer and Hitler. Ironically it now houses the Federal Bureau for Migration and Refugees.

Speer's design for the Luitpold Hall, which was originally intended to house exhibitions and events and was now to be rebuilt as a convention centre, bears a close resemblance to the work of one of his teachers. In this case it was Daniel Krencker's assistant Walter Andrae, whose drawings of a reconstruction of the Assyrian temple of Tukulti-Ninurta at Assur had made a great impression on him. Speer replaced the art nouveau façade of the 1907 building with a monumental entrance that had a gigantic swastika above the doorway. He modified the interior, draped it with Nazi flags and provided seating for 16,000 people. It was badly damaged by Allied bombing and was demolished in 1950. It is now a parking lot.[29]

Speer was well pleased with the initial stages of the work in Nuremberg. In an essay published in 1936 he wrote of the 'Führer's buildings': 'His great buildings that are under construction in a number of places are designed to be an expression of the nature of the Movement that will last a thousand years. They are thus part of the Movement itself. The Führer created the Movement, came to power because of its might and even today influences it down to the smallest details . . . He is driven to build like a National Socialist.' It would have been embarrassing for Speer had he been reminded of such an effusion when, after the war, he was assiduously working on his image as an architect and technocrat who was untainted by politics. He went on to write: 'It will be unique in the history of the German people that at a decisive turning point their Führer began not only with the philosophical and political rearrangement of our history, but at the same time, with his unparalleled expertise as a masterbuilder, he also began to create stone buildings that will last for thousands of years as a testament to the political will and the cultural talent of our times.'[30] This turgid prose is a perfect example of what Thomas Mann meant when he wrote: 'the really characteristic and dangerous aspect of National Socialism was the mixture of robust modernity and an affirmative stance towards progress combined with dreams of the past: a high technological romanticism.'[31]

The first phase of building in Nuremberg was rushed through so as to be ready for the party rally in 1936. In the following year Speer began work on the final stage – the design for the enormous German Stadium. The Zweckverband Reichsparteitagsgelände Nürnberg or Reich Party Rally Grounds Association Nuremberg (ZRPT) – a public corporation founded in March 1935, which coordinated the financial contributions of the city, the state of Bavaria, the NSDAP and the Reich government – approved a sum of 95 million Reichsmarks for the initial planning.[32] When Speer pointed out the enormous cost of the project – 211 million Reichsmarks had already been approved by August 1938 and the sum was soon to reach between 700 and 800 million for the entire complex – Hitler brushed this off with the remark that it was no more than that of two battleships of the *Bismarck* class.[33] He laid the foundation stone on 9 September 1937.

The basic plan for this oversize structure was a vast horseshoe of stands, modelled on the Odeon in Athens sponsored by Herodes Atticus.[34] The Odeon was built on a slope, but here the land was flat, so that Speer had to support the tiers of seating with massive barrel vaulting on the Roman model. The end result would thus have been far more Roman than it was Greek. Speer placed an immense propylaea (monumental gateway) across the opening of the oval-shaped horseshoe, as a tribune for dignitaries and representatives of the press. On the roof was to be a colossal female statue 14 metres taller than the Statue of Liberty. The stadium was designed to provide 150 rows of seating for 405,000 spectators at the Aryan Games, a racially purified version of the Olympic Games from which the likes of Jesse Owens, the black athlete who won four gold medals at the Berlin Olympics, would have been rigorously excluded.

Work began on building a scale model on a steep slope at nearby Oberklausen in 1938. The foundations for the stadium were completed in March 1940. By this time Speer and Walter Brugmann had the entire project firmly in their hands, with the ZRPT reduced to providing the funds, raw materials and manpower. The task was greatly simplified when the Ministry of Labour put the project in the special category of being 'of political importance to the state'.[35] It proved to be an awesome task. Speer needed 350,000 cubic metres of special pink granite for the stadium – seventy times more stone than was needed for his Reich Chancellery. This would mean that the granite quarries – most of the suitable ones were near Dresden – would have to be expanded. Building firms would have to hire large numbers of new workers; Himmler's slave labourers would be further exploited. An alliance between Speer and Himmler was formalised with the foundation of the SS-owned German Earth and Stone Works Company (DEST) on 29 April 1938. It was headed by Oswald Pohl, a man of exceptional organisational talent, who ran the SS Wirtschafts-Verwaltungshauptamt or SS Main Office for Administration and Economics. Pohl combined an enthusiasm for the exploitation of slave labour with a firm belief in racial purification. He ran the SS maternity homes and orphanages known as 'Spring of Life' (*Lebensborn*) as well as the German branch of the Red Cross. DEST was a curious organisation, not untypical of Nazi Germany. Legally it was a private company, but its officers were all members of the SS and were answerable to Pohl. It was of dubious legality in that it was a party organisation acting as a private company and thus – as other firms in the building sector were quick to point out – had an unfair advantage. The SS replied that they were not in the business for profit, but that they were solely concerned with 'reforming' concentration camp inmates.[36]

Pohl was perfectly candid in stating during his trial in 1947 that DEST had been specifically founded to produce building materials for Speer's projected 'Buildings for the Führer'. He pointed out that private industry could only provide 18 per cent of the two billion bricks per year that Speer required for rebuilding Berlin. In fact this was his principal justification for a party institution to operate as a private business. His secondary consideration was that it was a useful way to find employment for concentration camp inmates to the benefit of the SS. The new organisation resulted from discussions between Speer, Himmler and Hitler, although there is some debate as to who took the initiative.[37] Whatever the case, there can be no question that DEST was as much a terror organisation as it was a supplier of building materials. The Nuremberg Trials clearly established that it formed an essential part of Himmler's murderous policy of 'annihilation through work'.[38] Speer, with vast sums of money at his disposal, thereby enabled Himmler to establish a business empire.

From the outset Speer worked closely with DEST and the SS. Along with his close associates – Brugmann, Karl Hettlage and Dietrich Clahes – he met frequently with key figures in the SS economics and political departments such as Himmler, Pohl and Karl Mummenthey from DEST, and Himmler's right-hand-man Reinhard Heydrich. Speer was not a mere technocrat, but an active agent who from the outset decisively influenced the policies of the SS and other organisations.[39]

Although Speer knew full well that war would inevitably have a major effect on his building operations in both Berlin and Nuremberg, he was an enthusiastic supporter of a radical solution to 'national questions'. He regarded those like Göring and Goebbels, who had second thoughts about Germany's chances in what was likely to become another world war, as 'feeble people, rendered degenerate by power, who did not wish to risk losing the privileges they had won'.[40]

Regardless of political importance, building work stopped as soon as the war began. Workers were switched to various branches of the armaments industry. Speer, doubtless in close consultation with Brugmann, decided what should continue to be built once the ban was lifted. By now his main interest was to lay the groundwork for rebuilding Berlin. The mayor of Nuremberg, Willy Liebel, was most distressed when ordered to stop construction. He insisted that: 'Further employment of the stone quarries and stone-processing concerns, at least at the current level of productivity ... has been expressly ordered by the Führer, according to information from the General Building Inspector Professor Speer.'

He suggested that 170,000 Reichsmarks per month be provided for the upkeep of various building sites and 15.5 million Reichsmarks to cover stone orders up until August 1940.[41] DEST would thereby keep its order books full and Himmler's 're-education' programme for concentration camp inmates would not be interrupted. Willy Liebel remained a close associate of Speer. Having organised the deportation of Nuremberg's Jews to Riga, Lublin and Theresienstadt, where virtually all were murdered, he joined Speer's Ministry of Armaments in 1942 as head of the Central Office.[42]

Construction ceased, but planning and the stockpiling of stone continued. The Party Rally Grounds were still given top priority so that a couple of weeks before the armistice with France was signed on 22 June 1940 Hitler and Speer considered using prisoners of war to resume construction. By April 1941 there were five hundred POWs working on the site. ZRPT was raring to go, imagining that Britain would be defeated in the next few months so that the party rallies could resume in 1941. To speed up the delivery of stone for Nuremberg, as well as for Speer's buildings in Berlin, a new company called Arge Nuremberg (Arbeitsgemeinschaft Natursteinlieferungen Reichsparteitagsbauten Nürnberg GmbH) was formed, but it was pushed aside when the Four-Year Plan took over responsibility for the distribution of stone.[43] To underline the fact that rebuilding Berlin was his top priority, Speer moved Brugmann to the capital in November 1940 to supervise construction.

As the war dragged on, work at Nuremberg gradually came to a standstill. Prisoners of war working on the site were detailed to work in the armaments industry. The vast expense of building up reserves of stone could no longer be sustained when all available resources had to be concentrated on armaments, which was now Speer's responsibility. In 1943 Brugmann took charge of Organisation Todt's construction teams in eastern Europe. ZRPT had shrunk to insignificance. Stone was still being delivered to the Party Rally Grounds, but the rate was dwindling. Deliveries continued until the spring of 1944, but by then the site had been partially transformed into a military facility. There was now precious little hope that Speer's Greco-Roman fantasy would ever be realised.

Speer's sudden rise to power, wealth and fame really began in 1933, not with the commission in Nuremberg but when he became site manager to Professor Troost at the age of twenty-eight with the task of overseeing the renovation of the chancellery in Berlin. Hitler had proved to himself that he was a political mastermind and was soon to test his skills on the field of battle, but he remained a frustrated artistic genius. Troost was a man with an international reputation and an imposing personality. Hitler was somewhat in awe of him. Speer was a young man whose career had hardly begun. He was the ideal person through whom Hitler could realise his architectural vision.

Almost as soon as he had been appointed chancellor, Hitler was determined to make some drastic changes to the chancellery. Eduard Jobst Siedler had designed a classically modern and functional addition to Bismarck's chancellery in the Schulenberg-Radziwill Palace on the Wilhelmstraße. It was built between 1928 and 1930, but Hitler dismissed the new wing as a 'cigar box' that looked like 'the administrative offices of a soap factory'.[44] Due to the renovation of the presidential palace next door to the old chancellery, Hindenburg had been obliged to move his official residence into the old chancellery, thus leaving Hitler to make do with the new administrative wing. His official lodgings were in an apartment designed for the chancellor's state secretary. It was therefore not until the autumn of 1933, after Hindenburg had moved back to the presidential palace, that Hitler was able to give Paul Ludwig Troost the contract to renovate the entire building.

Troost readily agreed to undertake the renovations, but his office was in Munich and he was unfamiliar with the building companies in Berlin. Hitler wanted the job done in a hurry. Having been greatly impressed by the prompt work that he had done for Goebbels, he felt that Speer was the ideal person to act as site manager on Troost's behalf. Speer was officially appointed to undertake this task and was paid the first instalment of his honorarium on 22 June 1936.

In his speech on the occasion of the inauguration of the new chancellery in January 1939 Hitler claimed that the old building had been in an appalling state, symbolic, he thought, of the decay and rottenness of the Weimar Republic. The roof leaked the floorboards were rotting, and the chancellor's study in the annexe looked 'both in size and shape like the tasteless office of an agent for a medium-sized cigarette and tobacco firm'.[45] In other words the building was fit for demolition. This was a pure fabrication, although there were certain shortcomings. There was only one bath in the entire building. The kitchen was badly equipped and dreadfully dark; but on the whole it was in reasonable condition. The building had been handed over to the new government on 8 December 1918 and was said to have been 'thoroughly satisfactory'. It had been renovated in 1926. Hindenburg had recently been living there for some time and there had been no complaints. Nor is it credible that, even in such difficult times, the head of state should have been given sub-standard housing.

Hitler watched Speer closely. He inspected the site daily at noon. Speer found him 'not unfriendly, but abrupt'.[46] Hitler was very impressed by the young man. He gave precise and direct answers to all his many questions. He never made the slightest attempt to curry favour. He appeared not to be intimidated by his immense power and prestige. Hitler admired his impeccable manners and self-confidence. He was a pleasant contrast to the toadying courtiers, adulating acolytes and heel-clicking automata in his customary entourage.

The atmosphere was informal. There were no 'Heil Hitlers', no raised right arms or exaggerated marks of servility. The workers wished him good day and went on with their tasks. One day, having finished his tour of inspection, Hitler invited Speer to lunch. Speer was well mannered, discreet, handsome and suitably reverential. This suave young product of the educated middle class enchanted the Führer, who deep down suffered from the insecurity of an autodidact of humble origins. Speer was flattered by this invitation, but felt embarrassed. He had some plaster on his suit jacket. Hitler noticed this and told him not to worry. Back in his private quarters Hitler told his valet to bring Speer a dark jacket. At table Goebbels was outraged that young Speer was sitting there wearing Hitler's unique gold party badge. Hitler explained what had happened and spent the entire lunch with Speer as his sole conversational partner, much to the Propaganda Minister's chagrin.[47]

He was soon a frequent guest at Hitler's table, both for lunch and dinner. Among the usual crowd were his chauffeur, the former actor Julius Schreck, who was Party Comrade number 53; the commander of the Leibstandarte SS Adolf Hitler, Sepp Dietrich; Hitler's adjutants Wilhelm Brückner and Julius Schaub; his Press Chief, SS-Obergruppenführer Otto Dietrich; and his personal photographer, Heinrich Hoffmann. Frequent guests included his companions from Munich: the publisher Max Amann; the party's treasurer Franz Xaver Schwarz; the paedophile editor of the party newspaper *Völkischer Beobachter*, Hermann Esser; and the notoriously anti-Semitic Gauleiter of Munich, Adolf Wagner. Jakob Werlin, a car salesman for Mercedes in Munich, who provided Hitler with his cars, was often present.[48] The table only sat ten people, so Speer was suddenly among a very select group of Hitler's closest associates. After the evening meal Hitler liked to watch one or two films. He preferred light comedies, love stories and musicals, especially when there were plenty of well-turned legs on display.

At the table, Speer sat beside Hitler and spoke openly of personal matters, quickly establishing the closest thing to a friendship that Hitler ever managed to enjoy. In some ways they were similar. Speer's raffish and easy-going attitude was a front that covered up an emotionally inhibited personality. He had no intimate friends, was uneasy in society, his behaviour was often awkward and bashful. Most of the time, unable to hide his self-consciousness behind a nonchalant youthfulness and an offhand manner, he affected an icy, laconic aloofness that gradually hardened into arrogance. Speer's fellow architect and bitter rival, Hermann Giesler, found him so aloof that he described him as a 'pillar saint' or stylite.[49] Hitler likewise erected a barrier around himself that was impossible to penetrate. Both men were emotionally impoverished, insatiably hungry for power and consummate showmen. Their most marked difference was that Speer, conscious of his shortcomings and weaknesses, was willing to delegate.

Hitler and Speer were bound together by their passion for architecture. Hitler had long since dreamt of building vast symbols of Germany's might. His taste, as Troost's wife Gerdy remarked, had unfortunately got stuck in the 1890s; but this presented no problem to Speer. He was quick to realise that Hitler's favoured style of architecture was Habsburg rather than Prussian. He liked the domes, curves, eclecticism, ornamentation and opulence of Vienna's Ringstraße, or Charles Garnier's monumental and overly ornate Paris Opera.[50] Indeed he found it difficult to understand quite what it was that Hitler found so appealing in Troost's severe style.[51] For Hitler, Bruno Schmitz's ponderous and top-heavy essay in historicism, the Landesmuseum in Linz, was 'the pinnacle of German architecture'.[52] Speer had readily abandoned Poelzig's New Objectivity to embrace Tessenow's bucolic Reform Architecture. He then quickly adjusted to Troost's pared down neo-classicism, soon to abandon that to reach his apotheosis in the realisation of Hitler's bloated fin-de-siècle imperialist vision. Speer was the means whereby Hitler could realise his wildest artistic dreams. Hitler provided him with the opportunity to design buildings the sheer size of which beggared the imagination. Speer fantasised that he would be remembered as one of the great German architects – a second Balthasar Neumann or Karl Friedrich Schinkel. But for one thing it was an almost perfect relationship. Unlike the great patrons of the past, Hitler constantly supervised, controlled and interfered with Speer's work. Once Speer caustically remarked to Furtwängler that he should count himself lucky that Hitler did not fancy himself as a conductor, otherwise he would have been constantly advising him on tempi, phrasing and dynamics.[53]

Speer also attributed Hitler's 'mad hatred of Jews' to his being emotionally and intellectually stuck in Vienna at the turn of the century. He saw it as a 'vulgar trapping, a relic of his days in Vienna. God knows why he never dropped it'. He asked himself whether Hitler's anti-Semitism was 'a tactical means to whip up mass instincts', or did he really mean what he said when he spoke of the war as a fight to the death between National Socialism and 'world Jewry'? All remained silent as Hitler ranted on about the 'annihilation', 'extermination' or 'eradication' of the Jews. Such phrases were so often repeated that they seemed to be empty of meaning, depositories of an inchoate predisposition, not a matter of life and death.[54] He thus grossly trivialised Hitler's pathological hatred of Jews. It was not merely a rhetorical device or coffee-house twaddle from pre-war Vienna. As part of his elaborate alibi he refused to acknowledge that the solution to Hitler's obsession with the Jews involved mass murder on an unimaginable scale.

Speer, like Hitler, heartily disliked modern art, but whereas Hitler got stuck in the 1890s, Speer's great love was romantic German art from the early nineteenth century to Arnold Böcklin's ironic symbolism that was to inspire the surrealists. He assembled a splendid collection of paintings from this period, including a Böcklin, most of which was said to have been of unknown provenance. He enjoyed the opportunity to mix architectural styles, just as Schinkel had done. His 'Führer's Palace' in Berlin was thus to be a cross between Pompeii and the Palazzo Pitti. Speer later asked himself quite what this was – a forerunner of post-modernism or a late form of historicism?[55]

Speer did not share Hitler's taste in painting. He positively loathed Adolf Ziegler's lifeless nudes in which Hitler delighted, but which earned him the derisive popular title of the 'Master of German Pubic Hair'. He disliked Paul Mathias Padua's 'Blood and Soil' peasant families listening eagerly to Hitler speaking on the radio. He found his heroic battle scenes equally unappealing. But he had a weakness for Werner Peiner's neo-Altdorfers and Breughels. He commissioned him to design some tapestries for the new chancellery.[56]

Speer shared Hitler's enthusiasm for sculpture, feeling that it brought vast public spaces down to a human scale. He was friendly with Arnold Breker and Josef Thorak, who churned out sculptures of muscular Aryans, gigantic horses and monumental nudes on an industrial scale and at staggering expense. He also greatly admired Fritz Klimsch's anodyne nudes.[57] Speer claimed to have helped restore the reputations of Georg Kolbe, whose Heine memorial in Frankfurt and Rathenau memorial in Berlin inevitably offended the Nazis because of the distinguished German Jews they honoured, and of Richard Scheibe, whose memorial to Friedrich Ebert outside St Paul's church in Frankfurt in the form of a naked youth excited outrage among some Nazis for its subject, the prudish for its blatant homoeroticism and the more discerning for its absurdity. Hitler purchased Scheibe's *Philosopher* in 1938 for 10,000 Reichsmarks, even though he had been briefly dismissed from the Städel Art Institute in Frankfurt by Nazi zealots in 1933. Kolbe, although condemned by ardent Nazis as 'humanistic' and 'unheroic', found a number of admirers among those who found the bombast of officially sponsored sculpture distinctly vulgar. Speer thought it grossly unfair that Breker, Klimsch and Peiner were later tarred with the Nazi brush.[58]

In November 1933 Hitler entrusted Speer with reorganising the floor plan of Siedler's extension to the chancellery. Then, on 21 January 1934, Troost suddenly died. Hitler's next move was obvious to all around him. Walther Funk, who was then serving as state secretary in Goebbels' propaganda ministry, with singular lack of delicacy said to Speer: 'Congratulations – you are now number one.'[59] But Speer's position was somewhat unclear. He had his remit from Hitler, but he was left in an ambiguous situation typical of the Third Reich. He might have been Hitler's plenipotentiary, but the Nuremberg project was still the overall responsibility of the municipal authorities. It was unclear who was responsible for funding his growing number of projects. The chain of command was likewise ambiguous. Above all there was Hitler, who considered himself to be 'the real architect of the Third Reich'.[60]

After Troost's death his widow Gerdy, assisted by Leonhard Gall, took over responsibility for refurbishing Bismarck's chancellery. Speer remained as site manager with responsibility for renovating the annexe. They designed an apartment for Hitler, including a bedroom and bathroom for Eva Braun and a suitably imposing study. Hitler's privacy was jealously guarded, so that no photographs were ever taken of these private rooms. The entire building, both the original palace and the extension, was renovated from top to bottom. Hitler moved into his new apartment in May 1934. Hans Lammers, the head of the Reich Chancellery, took possession of Hitler's ten-room apartment in the Siedler annexe. Cost was of no concern. Accounts were no longer submitted to the Ministry of Finance. The 'will of the Führer' was enough to cover all the bills.

Speer's next commission in Berlin was to renovate the Italianate Palais Borsig on the corner of Vossstraße and Wilhelmstraße – next door to the chancellery extension – as a headquarters for the SA. After the 'Röhm Putsch' of July 1934 Hitler decided to move this troublesome organisation from Munich so as to keep it under close observation. Speer's first task was to move Vice-Chancellor von Papen and his staff out of the building. He sent a team of workmen to make as much noise and mess as possible by demolishing the plasterwork in the entrance hall, corridors and antechambers. In one of the rooms he saw a bloodstain marking the spot where Herbert von Bose, Papen's press secretary and a prominent figure in the conservative opposition to Hitler, had been gunned down during the Röhm Putsch. This was Speer's only comment on an event that changed the face of National Socialism and made much of the elite complicit in large-scale murder.[61]

In 1935 Speer, following a sketch by Hitler, added a balcony to Siedler's annexe to the chancellery, upon which Hitler was to make his public appearances before the crowds in the Wilhelmplatz.[62] Hitler previously had only been seen as a shadowy figure framed in a window when he watched the torchlight parade that celebrated his appointment as chancellor. Now, as he put it, he wished to be seen in three dimensions, to be able to lean over the balcony so as to drink in the applause, as he did after the victory over France. Speer, who still faithfully followed Troost's style, simplified Hitler's design and narrowed it by one third; but even though he skilfully placed the balcony to counterbalance the massive entrance, it was still an awkward protrusion that seriously disturbed the symmetry of Siedler's severe façade.

Although a vast amount of money had been spent on the thorough renovation of the Reich Chancellery and all adjacent buildings, this was still not enough for Hitler. He now decided to build an entirely new chancellery that would provide a more adequate expression of the power and prestige of his regime. In his speech at the topping-out ceremony of the new building on 2 August 1938 he said: 'In late December and early January 1937–8 I decided to solve the Austrian question, thereby creating a greater Germany. The old Reich Chancellery was totally unsuitable for the purely official and representative functions that were necessarily involved. Therefore on 11 January 1938 I entrusted the Inspector General of Buildings, Professor Speer, with the building of a new chancellery in the Vossstraße and ordered it to be finished by 10 January 1939.' Hitler claimed that Speer returned six hours after receiving this order with detailed plans of the building.[63]

In his memoirs Speer tells us that at the end of January 1938 Hitler told him that as he would soon have to hold a series of important discussions, he needed a number of large reception rooms designed to impress 'little potentates'. A site was available for the building. The cost was immaterial. He had ordered the new chancellery to be finished by the end of the year so as to be ready for the New Year's reception for the diplomatic corps in January 1939. Speer wrote that he immediately ordered the demolition of the houses on the Vossstraße.[64]

Speer's account of this meeting with Hitler is blatantly untrue. Hitler was anxious to prove that he had planned the Anschluss with Austria as early as December 1937. Speer wanted to show that he had managed to build the vast new chancellery in less than a year. After all, Hitler had publicly announced that this was 'not American, but German alacrity'.[65] The new chancellery was thus seen as further proof of the vitality of National Socialism. This was an impression that Speer did not wish to correct in his memoirs.

Hitler and Speer deliberately hid the truth. Hans Lammers made the official announcement on 22 June 1936: 'The Führer and Reichskanzler has given the architect Albert Speer, Lindenallee 18, Berlin-Charlottenburg 9, the task of preparing plans for the Vossstraße. The Reich treasury has been ordered to pay Albert Speer 30,000 Reichsmarks as an advance of his honorarium, the final amount of which is not yet determined.'[66] This was an immense sum of money for a young architect. Detailed plans on a scale of 1:100 were drawn up in July 1937. They show all the main features of the completed building. But the initial planning began much earlier. Preliminary sketches had been made in 1934. Purchasing the land on the Vossstraße began at the end of 1935. Buildings were demolished as early as March 1936. The shell of the first stage of the new chancellery was complete on 1 January 1938 – ten days before the date on which Hitler claimed to have made his decision to build it.[67]

It is hardly surprising, given the unflattering remarks Hitler made about Bismarck's chancellery and the new wing built under the Weimar Republic, that a conference was held in the chancellery in 1934, attended by representatives from the municipal government, to discuss building a new residence for the Führer. The mayor, Dr Solm, agreed that, 'taking the Führer's remarks into consideration', a new building should be constructed near the present chancellery. On 5 July that year a further meeting was held at which Hitler suggested that the Vossstraße should be widened and the 'ugly', 'old fashioned' and 'confusing' buildings on the north side pulled down. This was the spot where Vossstraße crossed the Wilhelmstraße, the street in which most of the government buildings including the Reich Chancellery were to be found. The significance of these two meetings is that Hitler was thinking of building a new official residence, even though President Hindenburg was still alive. His decision to build a palace for himself was a clear indication that he fully intended to take over the office of President as soon as Hindenburg died. The latter was eighty-seven years old and in poor health. He died less than a month later, on 2 August 1934.

Under existing law the buildings on the Vossstraße could not simply be appropriated. They would have to be bought. This presented a problem. Among the buildings in this narrow side street were the Ministry of Justice and the local offices of the NSDAP, both recently renovated. The Bavarian, Saxon and Württemberg legations as well as some imposing private residences would also have to be demolished. By the end of 1937 all these buildings had been bought by the government for a total of 13.5 million Reichsmarks.[68]

In 1935 Hitler had made some sketches of the floor plan of a new chancellery. They were for a building on the Vossstraße that was half the size of the eventual building. Speer was involved in the process virtually from the beginning. In January 1936 he told Lammers that building would begin that spring. In March 1936 he submitted an estimate for all the plans for the new building, including scale models and the initial preparation of the site, for which he demanded the handsome sum of 80,000 Reichsmarks.[69]

The buildings at Vossstraße 2 and 3 were demolished in March 1936. In May Speer wrote to Lammers to tell him that a year's preliminary work for the 'Vossstraße project' had been completed and that it met with Hitler's approval. On 22 June Speer resubmitted his estimate of 80,000 Reichsmarks, adding a personal honorarium of 30,000 Reichsmarks. Lammers prudently made no reference to the larger sum in his public announcement months later. The purchase of buildings on the Vossstraße continued throughout 1936. In October Speer announced that the building would be completed within three to four years. For this to be possible all the remaining properties on the Vossstraße would have to be purchased by mid-1938. Owners and tenants would graciously be allowed to remain in residence until the houses were to be torn down.

One major problem remained. The Four-Year Plan, instigated in 1936, came into effect on 1 January 1937. Its principal aim was to concentrate on armaments.[70] As a result there was a severe shortage of building materials, particularly of iron and steel. In February 1937 Speer complained to Lammers that Hitler's wish to have a new building on the Vossstraße was being frustrated by various agencies acting by the book. He asked that it be made perfectly clear that the Führer's will should under no circumstances be challenged or frustrated. Lammers replied that since this was Hitler's wish the project was to be given top priority.

It was at this point that Hitler appointed Speer Inspector General for Buildings in the Nation's Capital. Now faced with the onerous task of converting Berlin into the new capital 'Germania', Speer asked that he hand over responsibility for the technical drawings and the job of site manager to another architect. Hitler agreed to Speer's suggestion that Karl Piepenburg was an ideal choice.[71] The estimate for the new building, drawn up to the last pfennig in March 1937, was 4,295,957.43 Reichsmarks.

Speer resubmitted the estimates in September. They had now swollen to a staggering 28,016,310 Reichsmarks. This was a substantial addition to the burden of debt caused by the massive rearmament programme. Partly for this reason the whole project was kept from the public. Hitler had already laid the foundation stone for the Military Technical Institute, the first stage in Speer's plans for rebuilding Berlin; but this was seen as an integral part of the rearmament programme. Even at the architectural exhibition in Munich in January 1938, which Hitler duly attended, no mention was made of the plans for the new chancellery. On 3 February 1938 the official newspaper, *Völkischer Beobachter,* published a major article on Albert Speer – the 'movement's great master-builder' – that concentrated on his plans for rebuilding Berlin. Brief mention was made of a planned extension to the chancellery, but that this was to be an entirely new building on a vast scale was carefully concealed.[72]

Hitler now urged Speer to get the new chancellery built as quickly as possible. He was a man in a hurry. The rearmament programme was placing an intolerable burden on the economy. Foreign currency reserves were drained. The problem of unemployment had been solved, but Germany now faced a chronic shortage of labour. On 5 November 1937 Hitler called together the heads of the armed services and the foreign office to discuss the problems arising from the forced armaments programme, particularly the shortage of steel. In the course of the meeting he argued that Germany suffered from a 'lack of space'. This had to be overcome in order that Germany would no longer be dependent on imports. The country therefore had to be fully prepared to 'solve the space question' by 1943–5, by force if necessary. Should France fall apart due to 'social tensions' or become involved in a war with another power, Germany would seize Czechoslovakia and Austria.[73] Hitler was thinking aloud. He was provoking those who had second thoughts about the forced pace of rearmament, such as the Minister of War and Commander-in-Chief of the Armed Forces Field Marshal Blomberg, the Commander-in-Chief of the Army

General Fritsch and the Foreign Minister Neurath, all of whom were present. Hjalmar Schacht, a critic of the rearmament programme, resigned his posts as Minister of Economics and Plenipotentiary for the War Economy three weeks after the meeting. Blomberg was forced to resign in January 1938, Fritsch in February, and Neurath was sacked in the same month. Hitler appointed himself Commander-in-Chief of the Armed Forces. Hitler's new chancellery and the hectic pace at which it was built, along with Speer's appointment on 30 January 1937 to oversee the rebuilding of Berlin to become the 'world capital' Germania, were all evidence that the Third Reich was entering a new, desperate and aggressive phase.[74]

On the day that Blomberg was obliged to resign, 27 January 1938, Hitler gave Speer plenipotentiary powers to ensure that the new chancellery would be finished by 1 January the following year. He ordained that all obstacles to achieving this goal be overcome and that the project be given absolute priority.[75] All went according to plan, so that the topping-out ceremony was duly held on 2 August. A feast, attended by 4,500 construction workers along with a host of dignitaries, was held in the Deutschlandhalle. In his speech Hitler made reference to the annexation of Austria in March 1938, and gloated over the fact that Vienna, 'a beautiful, imposing, great German city with an outstanding old culture and wonderful buildings', had been incorporated in the German Reich. It was for this reason that he had ordered 'Master-Builder Speer' to have the new 'House of the Greater German Reich' ready for the reception of the diplomatic corps on 10 January 1939. Hitler made the preposterous claim that 'this year' he had ordered Speer to have the building ready in time. He boasted that a country that could absorb a sovereign state within three or four days was capable of finishing a building within one to two years. The history of the new chancellery was thus rewritten to strengthen the impression of National Socialism's vigour, organisational skill and sense of purpose. It is an impression that is echoed in Speer's memoirs and in much of the literature on the topic.[76]

Speer's private office in the Lindenallee was solely responsible for the new chancellery, whereas a special new department was formed for the rebuilding of Berlin. He was assisted by a number of other architects. Among them was Otto Apel, who also worked as Tessenow's assistant. Hans Peter Klinke, who had been one of Speer's fellow students at the Technical University in Berlin, worked on integrating the Palais Borsig at Vossstraße 1 into the new chancellery rather than tearing it down. In 1942, having claimed that Speer had taken all the credit for his work, Klinke resigned and joined the elite Waffen-SS Leibstandarte Adolf Hitler. He died of wounds received in Kiev in 1943. Speer gave the eulogy at his funeral. Speer also offered important assignments to his protégé Cäsar Pinnau. He was responsible for the interior decoration of the offices of the head of the Reich

Chancellery, Lammers, the head of the Presidential Chancellery, Otto Meissner, and the head of the NSDAP leader's Chancellery, Philipp Bouhler.[77]

Mosaics in the new chancellery were the work of Speer's close associate Hermann Kaspar, who was one of the Third Reich's stellar artists. He had risen to fame for his work in the German Museum in Munich and Troost's House of German Art. Kaspar's mosaics in the chancellery made extensive use of swastikas, eagles and depressingly obvious symbolic representations of life, energy and strength. He also designed the intaglio for Speer's monumental furniture. On the wall behind Hitler's desk he placed an inlaid half-sheathed sword. This was an image that particularly pleased Hitler. When diplomats saw that, he chuckled, saying it would 'send fear into their hearts'.[78] His mosaics, made by the renowned Puhl and Wagner Company, were extremely costly. In part this was due to Speer insisting that the mosaic stones should be small – not more than five millimetres across. The huge eagle in the Mosaic Room alone cost 321,750 Reichsmarks. Kaspar was rather slow in giving his designs to Puhl and Wagner, and making the mosaics was a lengthy business. As a result a number of them were not ready for the inauguration ceremony. A carpet had to be laid on the unfinished floor of the Mosaic Room.

For Hitler the costly new Reich Chancellery was only to be a temporary building. He was already thinking of moving into a new, even larger and more flamboyant palace in Germania. His deputy Rudolf Hess was then to move into the building. Hitler's sole interest in architecture was its effect. Speer's chancellery was thus designed as a theatrical set, a backdrop that would serve to enhance his charismatic status as Führer and Chancellor. The building had two aspects. The two wings on the 421-metre-long façade housed three stories of offices. The central tract, almost three metres higher than the two wings and set further back, was a massive stone block with a neo-classical portico over which hovered a giant eagle with outspread wings measuring 7.75 metres, proudly standing atop a swastika surrounded by a wreath. The stone bird seemed to be somewhat squashed by the weight of an overhanging cornice. This forbidding entrance led to an inner court of honour adorned with Arno Breker's two gigantic naked torch-bearing males ostensibly representing the party and the armed forces, the twin pillars of the Third Reich. Another massive eagle, this time in bronze, was fixed to the end wall.

The exterior created the impression that the building was a hive of administrative activity, but in fact there was very little office space available. Virtually the entire interior was devoted to pomp and circumstance. The visitor had to undergo a long march through a series of representational rooms before reaching Hitler's study. After the entrance hall came the 46.2 by 19.2 metre Mosaic Room, a gloomy windowless space reminiscent of an Egyptian tomb. Next came the Round Room, also in marble but more baroque in flavour. The two massive doors on the main axis were surmounted by reliefs, one a male figure in a threatening pose representing 'The Warrior', the other a classically draped woman holding a lictor's fasces symbolising 'Genius'. This space was designed as a setting for a number of sculptures by Arnold Breker. Next came the 146-metre-long 'Gallery of Mirrors' – exactly twice the length of the Hall of Mirrors at Versailles – at the end of which was the imposing entrance to Hitler's study. The walls were decorated with tapestries recounting the life of Alexander the Great. They were eventually to be replaced by a series depicting great German battles to be designed by Werner Peiner. Speer had wanted to lay a carpet on the floor, but Hitler insisted that his visitors should be made to walk on a 'slippery slope' of polished marble so as to render them all the more uneasy before entering his study.[79]

Two soldiers guarded the entrance to Hitler's study. They were dwarfed by the immense door over which were carved the initials 'A.H.' surrounded by oak leaves. The room was 27 metres long, 14.5 metres wide and 9.75 metres high. It was thus more like a throne room than a study. The room was decorated with an equestrian statue of Frederick the Great, a magnificent portrait of Bismarck by Lenbach and a bust of Hindenburg, as heavy-handed reminders that Hitler saw himself as their legitimate successor, both as politician and as soldier. A workman dropped and smashed a bust of Bismarck by the neo-baroque sculptor Reinhild Begas, which Speer took to be an ill omen because Hitler had once told him that at the outbreak of the First World War the imperial eagle on the roof of the central post office in Vienna had fallen down: a portent of the collapse of the German Empire. He therefore asked his friend Arno Breker to make an exact copy. It was aged by soaking it in tea.[80]

Among the art works on the walls were four huge tapestries. To the right of the fireplace was one of a bearded man wearing a cowl, with a globe, a pair of compasses and a book representing learning and wisdom. Next there was a knight with sword and shield, bearing a striking facial resemblance to Hitler, heavy-handedly symbolising valour. Then came a youth in Attic attire, holding scales in one hand and a book in the other, personifying justice. Lastly, there was another knightly Hitler accompanied, as in Dürer's famous engraving, 'Knight Death and the Devil': an exemplification of fearlessness.

The room was littered with symbolic representations. There were bare-breasted women bearing sheaves of wheat. Muscle-bound men stripped to the waist wielded blacksmiths' hammers. Naked youths with conch shells and tridents rode on the backs of dolphins. Mars and Medusa jostled with Dido and Aeneas, Hercules conversed with Omphale, Hector bade farewell to Andromache, Pallas was buried – all this amid a mass of swastikas, cornucopias, eagles and laurel wreaths. At the end of the room Hitler sat enthroned behind a desk measuring 3.5 by 1.4 metres. Although the propaganda claimed that Hitler worked day and night in this overwhelming space, the arrangements belie this tale. The telephone was out of reach. Books, not files, were carefully arranged on the desk. Writing material was obviously there as decoration, not for use. The whole thing was a theatrical setting that was seldom used.

The furniture was arranged in three groups. At the desk Hitler was the statesman. A vast marble map table halfway down the room against the rear wall was where he played the role of commander-in-chief. A cluster of heavy furniture around the fireplace was a place for him to relax with his friends as a normal citizen. The overall impression left by this almost 400 square metre space was of a fantasy staggering under symbolic overkill. It was totally lacking in proportion or coherence. Such hollow ostentation would have made a perfect setting for Charlie Chaplin as the Great Dictator.

The style of furniture that was extolled in the professional journals of the day as 'furniture for the German people' that reflected 'the honesty, solidity and directness of a natural lifestyle' was not to be found in the new chancellery.[81] Aping the styles of bygone ages, particularly if foreign and essentially aristocratic, was roundly condemned. Such gaudy luxury and ostentatious grandeur had no place in the new Germany. Tessenow's conservative functionalism and the straightforward designs of the Werkbund were seen as ideals. But the Werkbund was banned in 1938 for its association with the Bauhaus and New Objectivity. Speer's approach was radically different. His was the exact reverse of the Werkbund's. He had no taste for furniture that was designed somehow to reflect German racial characteristics. His furniture was heavy, extravagant and brazen. The new chancellery reflected in all its aspects the assertiveness and blustering self-confidence of a regime that was securely in power, but in its eclecticism, exaggeration and sensationalism it was a monumental effort to conceal a lack of direction and of legitimacy based on sound historical foundations. Speer's contribution to the new chancellery, both the architecture and the furniture, is based on Troost's work. As mentioned in Chapter 1, he even used the same company to make the furniture.[82] But it is already much heavier, more oppressive and overly decorated. It is lacking in Troost's restrained elegance and luxurious theatricality.

Ideologically sound National Socialist furniture makers, true to the 'Blood and Soil' ideology, insisted that Germans should have furniture made of German woods such as pine, beech or elm. For special occasions walnut, ash or larch might be considered. Hitler and Speer wanted nothing to do with such nonsense. Only mahogany, ebony, rosewood and other tropical woods, for which scarce foreign exchange was needed, were good enough for them. This at a time when the average German had increasingly to make do with plywood, laminates and hardboard as the Four-Year Plan extended its control over civilian production. Speer in his capacity as head of the office 'Beauty of Work' within the German Work Front, a post to which he was appointed in early

1934, was more rigorously orthodox. Furniture produced for works canteens, or housing for workers on the *Autobahnen* or the Westwall (the Siegfried Line) was sternly utilitarian, based on traditional farmhouse designs and using cheap German materials. Even in furniture there was a marked contrast between that of the leadership and the masses that revealed the true nature of National Socialism and exposed the concept of the 'racial community' as an empty sham.[83] For Speer, however, this was 'contemporary German socialism'.[84]

It is noticeable that although a large number of contemporary paintings were exhibited in the new chancellery, precious few of them had any specific political message. In Hitler's study, apart from Lenbach's portrait of Bismarck, all the paintings were from the seventeenth and eighteenth centuries. No one seemed to have noticed the irony of Tintoretto's painting of the discovery of Moses among the bulrushes hanging in the cabinet room. Hitler did eventually order Anselm Feuerbach's huge painting of Plato's symposium to be removed once he was told of Alcibiades's fate.[85]

The garden façade of the new chancellery was Speer's most successful piece of work. It had none of the overblown ornamentation and threatening monumentality of the Germania project, but looked back to Troost in its dignified restraint, while at the same time creating a worthy setting for a head of state. The effect was somewhat diminished by two oversized statues of horses by Josef Thorak.

In spite of many delays due to sub-contractors being given far too short notice, the building was ready for opening on 7 January 1939, even though not all the furniture and decorations were in place. A finishing ceremony had already been held on 3 January attended by 8,000 workers, 2,000 of whom were quarrymen. Hitler, having been handed the key, congratulated all those involved in a building that he described as the 'crowning glory of the greater German political empire'.[86]

Hitler gave a special luncheon in his private apartment for Speer and his closest associates at which Speer was awarded the golden Party badge as well as a pedestrian watercolour of the Minorites Church in Vienna that Hitler had painted in 1909. Speer was harshly critical of this 'pedantic', 'lifeless', 'nondescript' and 'painstaking' work.[87] He confessed to having been impressed by some of Hitler's architectural sketches made in the 1920s, but he could never understand why he still stood by these wretched earlier paintings.

A rally was held in the Sports Palace for 4,500 workers, suppliers and others involved in building the new chancellery. Hitler announced that this was 'the first building of the new Reich' that would last for 'many centuries' and praised Speer as an architect of genius. Tessenow was less enthusiastic. He dismissed the new building as a rushed job. It would, he told Speer, have been better had he spent nine years on the project.[88]

The reception for the diplomatic corps was held on 12 January 1939. The *Völkischer Beobachter* predictably sang the praises of the new building. It was described as a superb expression of the increase of Germany's power and greatness and a symbolic representation of the country's historical ascendancy. Speer had achieved his goal of giving architectural expression to National Socialist Germany's achievements and destiny. In finishing it so rapidly he bore witness to the know-how and creative genius of the New Germany. Hitler was enthralled, but was still not entirely satisfied. On 31 January he held a lavish reception for senior officers in the armed forces and their wives. He proudly gave the ladies a guided tour of the building, but having thought things over he decided that the reception hall was altogether too small. He ordered Speer to double its size from 404 to 870 square metres.[89] Work soon began, but made slow progress. It was halted in 1943.

Hitler found the chancellery to be an admirable setting for the intimidation and browbeating of lesser mortals. It was in his study on 13 March 1939 that the Slovak leader Monsignor Tiso was bullied into breaking away from Czechoslovakia. The following day the 66-year-old Czech President Emil Hácha was obliged to march from the entrance courtyard along the 'diplomat's route' to Hitler's office, where he was treated to a ferocious harangue. The strain was too much for him and he fainted. Having been revived by an injection from Hitler's unsavoury personal physician Dr Morell, he signed away his country.

Further propagandistic displays were held at the new chancellery. A lavish reception was held there on 20 April 1939 to celebrate the Führer's fiftieth birthday. Then on 7 June an audience was given for the Condor Legion, the bombers of Guernica. Speer had done an excellent job in providing the theatrical backdrop for such bombastic scenes, but in practical terms the building was a gigantic white elephant. The staterooms on the *bel étage* were vast spaces that Hitler hardly ever used. Lammers, who ran the government while Hitler sat on his Bavarian mountaintop, had his office here; but it was neither congenial nor efficient as a workplace. The cabinet never met in the cabinet room – or anywhere else for that matter – but Lammers occasionally used it for conferences with various ministers. There were 130 small windowless rooms in the cellar, originally designed as storage space, where most of the staff had to work and some had to live. Many of the offices in the administrative wing were left empty. There were a total of 315 offices in the entire building, most of them tiny cramped spaces, due to Speer's obsession with corridors that were 6.5 metres wide, thereby wasting valuable space. With his fascination for technology Speer had installed an air-conditioning system that seldom worked and two escalators that needed constant attention. Two men to service the machinery had to be on permanent duty, artfully using their essential skills to extort wages that were well above the norm. Along with forty-eight cleaning women and fourteen flunkies this resulted in exorbitant maintenance costs.

The building was represented as a masterpiece of German craftsmanship, the work of German artisans who were feted as heroic figures by National Socialist ideologues. They were championed by radicals within the party, whose brand of socialism was little more than a rejection of industrial capitalism, an ingrained hatred of 'plutocrats' and a deep suspicion of technology. The radical leadership of this left-wing Nazism had been eliminated in the Röhm Putsch in 1934, but the sentiment lived on within the party and the SA, to be revived in the later stages of the war. It was an attitude with which Speer initially had some sympathy.[90] The Nazis still had an ambivalent attitude towards technology, so that although it was not rejected it had to be hidden away behind handcrafted objects. Light switches were disguised in marble casings. Light bulbs were designed to look like candles.[91] It was not until he became Minister of Armaments that Speer was able openly to display his fascination with technology.

That the new chancellery was built so quickly was due in large part to the remorseless exploitation of labour. Speer had hoped to have three eight-hour shifts per day, but shortages of manpower meant that the men had to work in two ten- to twelve-hour shifts. As a special privilege they were given a hot meal in mid-shift. The *Völkischer Beobachter* shamelessly claimed that the new buildings were designed in part to overcome the problem of unemployment and could thus be seen as a major part of National Socialist welfare policy.[92] From early 1937 there was a shortage of labour that was rapidly becoming a serious problem due to the ambitious projects of the Four-Year Plan that included a staggering rearmament programme and building of the fortifications along the Westwall. As soon as the new chancellery was finished the workers were made to work on the Westwall or for Speer in Berlin. Weekly newsreels made much of the fact that the chancellery was built in only nine months – evidence of the regime's energy, expertise and resolve – and thereby conveniently overlooking the years of planning and the time it took to demolish an entire city block. Nothing was said about the sacrifices the workers were called upon to make. Construction workers on the chancellery site and elsewhere were prone to serious injury as a result of being required to work excessively long hours with inadequate nutrition and rudimentary safety precautions. In order to meet the growing demand for emergency medical services a special hospital was built where workers were hastily patched up and sent back to work as quickly as possible.[93]

This 'stone monument to the Greater German Reich' was extravagantly praised in the press and the cinema, but there was very little positive response. Although the building was touted as a representation of the 'racial community', none of the photographs of the building showed any human beings. Not even Hitler was photographed in his new surroundings. The reason for this is simple. This overwhelming architecture was designed to intimidate and humiliate, a Sarastro's castle where those who entered would be submitted to an ordeal before coming into the presence of the dictator. Had Hitler been photographed sitting behind his Brobdingnagian desk he would also have been dwarfed and the absurdity of the entire setting would have been exposed. The new chancellery was a vast, cold, bombastic and empty space, in which nothing was on a human scale. In these hard times there was much comment about the vast amount of money that had been frittered away on it.[94] Few could have imagined that the building would only last for six years. All but the exterior walls were destroyed by Allied bombing, while Hitler lived in the Führer Bunker in a corner of the chancellery garden under four metres of reinforced concrete.

After the war there were various rumours about where valuable material from the remains had ended up. Theories ranged from the Humboldt University, the Mohrenstraße metro station or the Soviet war memorials in the Treptower Park, the Tiergarten and the Schönholzer Heide in Pankow. None are true. The Soviets graciously gave Kurt Schmid-Ehmen's bronze eagle that decorated the court of honour to the British military authorities. It now rests in the Imperial War Museum. Hitler's desk and globe are in the Historical Museum in Berlin. Some of the paintings from the chancellery hang in the Pentagon. Arno Breker's naked man representing the party is in the Arno Breker Museum in Nörvenich in the Cologne region. Josef Thorak's enormous equestrian statues ended up in Soviet Army barracks in the German Democratic Republic. For years the site of Speer's chancellery was an empty space in the no man's land along the Berlin Wall. There is now a nondescript apartment building on the site.

CHAPTER THREE

GERMANIA

On 30 January 1937 Hitlar appointed Albert Speer as Berlin's Inspector General of Buildings. In doing so he decreed that Speer's personal staff were neither a government agency nor a branch of municipal government: they were answerable to Speer alone. Berlin's town planning was no longer a municipal affair, but was solely in the hands of Professor Speer. His was the task of rebuilding Berlin as 'Germania', home of National Socialism, an expression of the conquest and subjugation of lesser peoples and a potential world power. Speer was now as much a propagandist as an architect. He was certainly not a conventional city planner. Although Berlin faced a severe housing crisis, in the end the realisation of Speer's plans would make the situation worse. Third Reich housing would never be a match for that of the Weimar Republic. Nevertheless, to Speer Berlin should become the showpiece of the regime's architectural self-expression, just as Nuremberg was for its cultic rituals.

Hitler had long been obsessed with the idea of completely rebuilding Berlin, as he implies in *Mein Kampf.* In the summer of 1926 Goebbels spoke of Hitler's determination to shape 'the country's future architectural image'. On 3 February 1932 Goebbels wrote that for a long time Hitler had been planning how to rebuild the city. 'In his leisure hours the Führer occupies himself with plans for a new party headquarters and the grandiose rebuilding of the Reich's capital. He has the whole thing all set. One is amazed at the expert way in which he deals with so many problems.'[1]

Speer, too, had been involved in planning Germania since March 1936 when Hitler showed him drawings of a triumphal arch and a great hall that he had drawn ten years previously.[2] Some ten co-workers worked in the Lindenstraße in Berlin's Mitte in Kreuzberg. This was at a time when his Nuremberg project was going full steam ahead in a blaze of publicity. His appointment as GBI in January the following year therefore came as no surprise. He already had a carefully considered plan of action and got to work at once. The importance of his new post was underlined when the Prussian Academy of Arts, which was founded in 1694, was unceremoniously turfed out of its fine building, the former Palais Arnim, at Pariser Platz 4, by the Brandenburg Gate, to make way for Speer's headquarters.³ This move enabled Hitler to walk unnoticed from his office in the chancellery and through the garden to Speer's office. Speer was well aware of his privileged position and exploited it to the full. He had a princely sum of money at his disposal. For planning alone he was guaranteed 60 million Reichsmarks per year until 1960. The municipality of Berlin was required to allocate 70 million Reichsmarks per year to buy and demolish property to make way for Speer's new buildings. Not only was he given the right to ignore the city's building regulations, but also any future building in Berlin that was outside the area he intended to rebuild that exceeded a volume of 50,000 cubic metres had to meet with his approval. Similarly, any building within the area scheduled to be rebuilt that cost more than a paltry 5,000 Reichsmarks had to be authorised by him.⁴

Speer was initially uncertain what style to adopt for Germania. Very few monumental building projects had been realised since 1933. Exceptions were Paul Ludwig Troost's House of German Art in Munich, Werner March's stadium for the 1936 Olympics and some buildings for the party in Munich. Speer had already cut his teeth with the Zeppelin Field in Nuremberg. Of all Hitler's architects, Troost had come closest to overcoming the fundamental contradiction at the heart of a concept of architecture that was supposed to be both conservative and modern. In his designs for the décor of transatlantic liners he had successfully managed to overcome opposites. He combined the modern with the traditional, simplicity with opulence, and the dynamic of the ocean-going with land-bound elegance. The stripped-down classicism of his architecture was likewise both contemporary and time-honoured.

Very little had been done to tackle Berlin's housing problems beyond shamelessly blaming them on the incompetence of the Weimar Republic. When in 1871 Berlin suddenly changed from being the capital of Prussia to that of the most powerful country in Europe, the population had been 826,341. By 1933 it was 4,242,501 and rising. There were some new settlements in the suburbs that were expressions of the romantically rural and the anti-urban that accorded well with certain aspects of National Socialist ideology. Housing for Siemens workers in Berlin and a massive administrative building were designed by the firm's house architect, Hans Hertlein. As a prominent representative of New Objectivity, a movement spurned by the Nazis for official buildings, Hertlein was given no government contracts. He now concentrated on office buildings Hertlein Siemens, Carl Zeiss and Telefunken. It took time for the Nazis, many of whom were imbued with strong anti-urban prejudice, to realise that cities were important not only as cultural centres, but also for their economic and industrial potential.[5]

In *Mein Kampf* Hitler expressed his contempt for modern cities. He argued that whereas Athens and Rome had left behind magnificent public buildings such as the Acropolis and the Pantheon, were Berlin to go the way of Rome all that future generations would be left with would be 'a few Jewish department stores and hotels built by limited companies'. Berlin needed some 'outstanding emblems of the racial community', rather than monuments to 'small-minded expediency' and materialism. It was hardly surprising, he argued, that those who worshipped mammon had no concept of heroism.[6] Rebuilding Berlin, as well as a number of other cities, remained an obsession with Hitler. After the death of Paul Ludwig Troost in January 1934 he felt that he had found the ideal man to do the job: the young, handsome, energetic, fiercely ambitious and utterly devoted 31-year-old Albert Speer.

Speer was eager and willing slavishly to realise his master's gargantuan vision, as he had already shown in Nuremberg. Troost's widow Gerdy, herself an architect, who ran her husband's office after his death, was once asked by Goebbels, in the presence of Hitler, what she thought of Speer. She replied that had Hitler asked her husband to design a building 100 metres wide, he would have thought about it and the next day would let him know that out of consideration for statics and aesthetics, it would have to be 96 metres wide. Turning to Hitler, she said: 'But if you said to Speer, "I need a building of 100 metres," he would immediately reply, "Mein Führer, 200 metres!" and you would say, "You are my man!"' Hitler laughed heartily at this, without a hint of the sarcasm that Speer insisted was an essential ingredient of his sense of humour.[7]

Speer's task was to render the political in aesthetic terms, to find an adequate architectural expression of the spirit of National Socialism, to provide a setting that would give the 'racial comrades' a feeling of self-confidence, strength and superiority, while at the same time disciplining and manipulating them into becoming the regime's willing instruments.[8] This was no easy task. National Socialism had yet to find a unique architectural style that would meet Hitler's lofty criteria as Hitler awkwardly stated to Gerdy Troost: 'When a people inwardly experience great times, they find outward expression of them. Their word is more convincing than the spoken: it is the word in stone.'[9] Speer was a promising talent, willing to undertake the task of expressing the Führer's word in stone. As Tessenow had disdainfully remarked, making an impression was the be-all and end-all of Nazi architecture. It was both its strength and its weakness. It was designed to make the maximum impact and as such it certainly succeeded.[10] Its artistic merit is more open to dispute. Speer's colossal German

Pavilion at the Paris Exhibition of 1937 was awarded the gold medal. But so too was Boris Iofan's stylistically similar Soviet Pavilion, which stood in its over-powering shadow. It is questionable how far political rather than aesthetic considerations lay behind this Solomonic decision. There can be little doubt that the Soviet Pavilion was the superior design. Frank Lloyd Wright described Iofan's building as 'the most dramatic and successful exhibition building at the Paris fair . . . Here, on the whole, is a master architect's conception that walks away with the Paris fair.'[11] His admiration for Vera Mukhina's 24-metre-high stainless steel structure with a statue of a sturdy factory worker, hammer in hand, and an energetic sickle-wielding kolkhoz woman atop this dynamic structure, is more open to question. This iconic image is, however, an arche-typical piece of socialist realism.

Speer's design for the German Pavilion was skilfully adapted to the neo-classicism of the exhibition site. It was deliberately planned to eclipse the Soviet Pavilion, designed by Stalin's favourite architect. He was, however, at the insist-ence of the exhibition's chief architect, Jacques Gréber, obliged to reduce the building's height by one-fifth so as not to disrupt the harmony of the ensemble.[12] Speer clad the pavilion's innovative steel structure, developed by Siemens and Krupp, with Bavarian granite. At night the spaces between the pillars, which were decorated with gold and red mosaics interspersed with swastikas, were illuminated by concealed lighting specially designed by Zeiss-Ikon. This created an effect similar to the Nuremberg 'cathedral of light'. The 54-metre-tall building was topped by Kurt Schmidt-Ehmen's 9-metre-tall gilded eagle, for which he was awarded the grand prize of the French Republic.[13]

The pavilion's windowless interior, a gloomy tomb-like space illuminated by forty hideous chandeliers, was dominated by a Zeppelin engine mounted on a sturdy pedestal. It was cluttered with an assortment of German products ranging from a Mercedes racing car, scientific instruments and chemical products to beer, children's toys and overstuffed furniture in a superfluity of overdetermined repre-sentations and symbols.[14] Vast naturalistic paintings, mostly of industrial plant such as the Krupp works in Essen, covered the walls. But whereas Stalin was omnipresent in the Soviet Pavilion, there were no portraits of Hitler in the German pavilion. At the entrance stood Josef Thorak's gargantuan sculpture of two muscle-bound male nudes holding hands. They have since been resurrected as gay icons.

There was nothing new in the grammar and syntax of the new architectural language chosen to convert the Nazi word into German granite. Its basics – columns, pillars, arches, loggias, balconies, massive symbols such as swastikas and eagles, sharp outlines, weighty proportions, hierarchical symmetry, all in indigenous stone – were characteristic of the monumental architecture of the Wilhelmine Empire and the heavy-handed functionalism of the Weimar Republic.[15] The problem was to combine all these elements convincingly into a new language. The word was unambiguous. 'You are nothing. The Führer and the *Volk* are everything.'

Hitler was obsessed with size. He was determined to build the world's largest stadium in Nuremberg, the tallest skyscraper in Hamburg, the largest seaside resort in Rügen and the most powerful radio transmitter in the Niederlausitz.[16] It was an appetite that Speer was determined to satisfy. Size was also the dominant feature of Werner March's stadium for the 1936 Olympic Games, with seating for 100,000 and a vast parade ground with room for 250,000 spectators, with stands for a further 60,000. Among the other buildings were a 78-metre-tall Olympic Tower – also known as the Führer's Tower – the German Hall (Deutschlandhalle) opened by Hitler in 1935, an open-air theatre and a host of smaller buildings for various sports.[17]

According to Speer's account, March's original design for the stadium made extensive use of steel and glass, but Hitler was horrified. This did not meet his criteria for home-grown Germanic simplicity, durability and stability that alone could express National Socialist power and importance. He promptly handed over the plans to young Speer, who 'overnight' wrapped March's structure in freestone, which met with Hitler's enthusiastic approval.[18] In fact Hitler had visited the site in October 1934 and suggested that the buildings should be clad in stone. March promptly consulted Speer. They soon reached agreement. There is no evidence whatsoever that Hitler was outraged at March's modernistic design and had turned to Speer for help. Hitler honoured March by awarding him the rank of professor and by suggesting that he help design the new headquarters for the navy. Had he disapproved too strongly of the original designs for the Olympic stadium March's career would have come to an abrupt end.[19]

A number of head offices of major companies were also built at this time. Although most of these buildings had distinct propagandistic and political overtones, they were built according to principles laid down by major architects of the Weimar Republic such as Peter Behrens, Wilhelm Kreis, Ernst Sagebiel and Paul Bonatz, or by promising young talents such as Speer's associate Cäsar Pinnau. Their designs were functional and rational. Although often monumental and conservative, they were well proportioned, without menace and were built on a human scale. Bonatz' design for the Stuttgart main railway station gained wide acceptance as a modern masterpiece and today is fiercely defended against any radical modification by such modernists as David Chipperfield and Richard Meier.[20] By contrast, such clearly National Socialist buildings as the Führer Building and the House of German Art in Munich, although they share certain stylistic similarities, placed a greater emphasis on monumentality, order and effect.[21]

Speer's task was to transcend these earlier examples of an as-yet fledgling party architecture, in order to build a National Socialist capital, a massive symbolic representation of power and might, an overwhelming space where human beings would be dwarfed and homogenised into a slavishly obedient and unthinkingly dutiful community. This marked a decisive change in direction. Until 1938 there had been a number of successful combinations of the traditional and the modern, such as Cäsar Pinnau and Ludwig Moshammer's design for the Japanese embassy. Speer's Reich Chancellery marks the beginning of a new phase. The regime had consolidated its power and demanded that it be adequately expressed in buildings on a colossal scale. Speer's team of architects seem to have entered a trance-like state, dreaming up grossly inflated versions of Roman forts, Babylonian palaces, sacrificial altars and castles fit for the Nibelungs. It was a dictatorial architecture, an expression of unbridled power, inhuman in scale. A number of individual buildings were announced in a bombastic propaganda campaign, but the sheer vastness of the overall plan was carefully concealed. Times were hard for the average German. Consumer goods were in short supply as the armaments programme was stepped up. Working conditions were hard, employees were left virtually without rights and real wages were dropping. It was felt prudent to disguise the enormous cost that all this would entail.[22] The city fathers of Berlin, appalled at the colossal expense entailed, felt that this was a case of 'beware of Greeks bearing gifts'. Hitler threatened to build a new capital like Canberra or Washington on the banks of Lake Müritz in Mecklenburg if the municipal authorities did not bow to his wishes. This shocked them into compliance. Had they known that Hitler regarded artificial capitals as lifeless they might perhaps have tried to bargain with him.[23] The blatantly militaristic and Caesaristic elements of this vast project were downplayed. The announcement of the Four-Year Plan with its clearly aggressive intent had already alarmed many of the more cautious. In such circumstances it was deemed prudent not to publicise such an unimaginably costly project.

From the outset Speer as GBI showed a sovereign disregard for the law and established institutional practice. He seized whatever land he wished and issued decrees without consideration for their long-term consequences. Lammers and his staff at the chancellery despaired at the resulting chaos, while the Auditor General was aghast at the projected costs and the shoddy bookkeeping. The naivety and recklessness of Speer's approach, which in his memoirs he tries to present as that of an apolitical technocrat, was typical of National Socialism. Pseudo-legality, pseudo-constitutionality and even pseudo-democratic practices were dressed up as politically neutral efficiency while openly avoiding bureaucratic inertia and practice. This mixture of the radically political and the pragmatically efficient, of reactionary romanticism and the worship of technological progress, was at the heart of National Socialism. This startling discrepancy between theory and practice resulted in a dynamic synthesis of the conservative and the radical, the emotional and the rational. The end effect was a startling contradiction between the regime's aims and its means.[24]

Hitler believed that the young and pliable Albert Speer was admirably suited to overcome such polarities and do his bidding, but he was obviously quite unsuited to developing a plan for post-war housing. For this, Hitler established a commission that included Rudolf Hess as the Führer's deputy, the Minister of Finance, Fritz Todt in his capacity as Plenipotentiary for Building, the head of the German Work Front Robert Ley, and the Lord Mayor of Munich, Karl Fiehler. Speer as GBI was included, but in a subordinate role. As a result of their deliberations Hitler appointed Robert Ley as the Reich Commissioner for Housing. This was a clearly ideological decision. Ley's remit was to provide accommodation for racially pure 'stallions at stud and broodmares' plus their impeccably Aryan offspring.[25] Speer makes no mention of this setback in his memoirs, even though he later made every effort to gain control over housing by arguing that Ley did not have direct access to the Führer without which no plan could come to fruition. Hitler, who wanted Speer to concentrate on the Germania project, countered this presumptuous argument by saying that Speer already had more than enough on his plate.[26]

Speer had overall responsibility for this vast project, but he commissioned a number of prominent architects to design individual buildings. Despite the vigorous protests of the party's hierophant Alfred Rosenberg, these included the industrial designer, typographer and architect Peter Behrens, a man for whom the likes of Walter Gropius, Mies van der Rohe and Le Corbusier had worked and who enjoyed an enviable international reputation.[27] Herbert Rimpl, the chief architect for the Hermann Göring Works, was a much younger man of limited talent but was ideologically sounder. Wilhelm Kreis was a far more creative architect, but he was treated with deep suspicion for having had a considerable number of Jewish clients during the Weimar Republic. His wife was related to the 'degenerate' poetess Ricarda Huch. Kreis's Hygiene Museum in Dresden, built in 1930, is a fine example of Weimar modernism, but his Dresden District Air Command III/IV of 1937 fully embraced the Nazi 'word in stone' style. A monolithic stone block is adorned with a relief of soldiers fighting and dying to form a sacrificial altar to the Führer cult. By this remarkable metamorphosis Kreis managed to overcome all obstacles and ingratiate himself with the Nazis to the point that Hitler included him on a short list of 12 'irreplaceable' visual artists among the 1,051 'divinely blessed' artists whose lives were so precious that they had to be protected from all danger.[28] Paul Bonatz, who specialised in building ideologically neutral bridges during the Nazi period, was also given commissions, even though he was under investigation by the Gestapo for harbouring Jews and for criticising Hitler. Both Kreis and Rimpl had successful careers in post-war Germany. Hitler violently objected to Bonatz' plans for a new railway station in Munich. He wanted it to be replaced by a monstrosity that was to be even larger than the Great Hall in Berlin. Speer was furious that his masterpiece was thus to be overshadowed and Bonatz, thinking that the Führer had lost his mind, prudently moved to Ankara where he built a number of important buildings. He did not return to Germany until 1954.[29] Hitler then gave Speer's rival, Hermann Giesler, the task of rebuilding Munich according to his designs. Much of Speer's success both as an architect and as Minister of Armaments was due to his willingness to delegate to men of real talent. In Berlin these included Wilhelm Kreis, Peter Behrens, German Bestelmeyer and Gropius' Bauhaus associates Hanns Dustmann, Ernst Neufert and Herbert Rimpl.[30]

Speer won a certain amount of approval within Germany's architectural establishment for sponsoring the likes of Kreis and Behrens, both of whom were respected members of their guild, but his sponsorship had a disastrous effect on many of them. As Germany's situation became increasingly precarious they entertained fantasies of a mythical past, imperial splendour and racial purity. Kreis' designs in 1942 for rebuilding the Museum Island in Berlin were particularly grotesque. The Egyptian Museum was an alarming piece of neo-Babylonian kitsch. The designs for both the Germanic and the East Asian Museums were so badly proportioned that they appeared to be sinking into the ground under their ponderous weight. Speer awarded the design for a new Anthropological Museum – also known as the Museum of Racial Theory – on the south bank of the Spree to Gropius' former assistant Hanns Dustmann, the Reich Architect of the Hitler Youth. In Speer's words, this was to be 'a kind of racial museum' based on 'the fundamental ideals of the new world-view'. This was in accord with the ideas of Dustmann's superior, Alfred Rosenberg, who demanded a 'new revolutionary museum' that would oppose all forms of cultural relativism by being 'based on racial philosophy and taking account of Germany's future mission'.[31] The resulting design of 1941 was unique in its overblown proportions and bombastic unsightliness.

Peter Behrens' design for AEG's main office on Germania's north-south axis was for a hypertrophic castle in Hollywood-Roman style. Speer particularly favoured Herbert Rimpl, who, having specialised in industrial architecture, found it relatively easy to adapt to the new Pharaonic style. His headquarters for the Oberkommando des Heeres or Army High Command (OKH), fronted by a vast Soldier's Hall, and based on a rough sketch by Hitler, was an unpleasant National Socialist appropriation of the Hatshepsut temple at Deir el-Bahari. Here Hitler wished to move the remains of Erich and Mathilde Ludendorff. He was undecided as to whether this was also an appropriate final resting place for Frederick the Great.[32] Kreis' model for a World War Museum had all the appearance of a gigantic bunker. It would seem that Speer and his colleagues shared in the *Götterdämmerung* atmosphere of the final war years, allowing their imaginations to run riot, designing their individual Valhallas, which they must have known would never be built.

Speer's basic plan was to build along two axes running from north to south and east to west, crossing at the Brandenburg Gate. Work on the 50-kilometre-long east–west axis, pretentiously named the 'Via Triumphalis', had begun in 1935. According to 'the will of the Führer and Reich Chancellor Adolf Hitler and on the instructions of the General Building Inspector Albert Speer', the Victory Column of 1873 was moved from its position in front of the Reichstag in the Königsplatz (now known as the Platz der Republik) to the Großer Stern, which was to form the centrepiece of the east–west axis. This important crossroads was to be widened from 80 to 200 metres to relieve traffic congestion and to provide room for monuments to Bismarck, Moltke and Roon. Hitler formally inaugurated the remodelled square on 20 April 1939, as part of the celebrations for his fiftieth birthday. Speer's designs for the lighting along the street from the Großer Stern to the Brandenburg Gate, and an indestructible 12,000-metric-ton concrete block in Schöneberg, built to test whether the sandy soil would bear the weight of a colossal triumphal arch, is all that remains today of his work in Berlin.[33]

At the western end of the east–west axis the vast Military Technical Institute was to be built. Hans Malwitz's plan looked more like a barracks than an institution of higher learning. Hitler laid the foundation stone in November 1937, but the building was never finished. It now lies buried under 75 million cubic metres of rubble cleared from the ruins of Berlin, known as the Devil's Mountain (*Teufelsberg*). Further plans for the Grünewald district included a University City. According to Speer's instructions for the competition it was to be enhanced by towers, triumphal arches and plazas that would not 'be of direct practical use . . . but would for future generations . . . be testament to a glorious past'.[34] The monstrous assembly hall of the university with the word 'Langemark' over the entrance, in memory of the students who lost their lives in a suicide attack in Flanders in November 1914, was the work of Hanns Dustmann, who had formerly worked for Gropius. He rejected all the master's principles in his plans for one of the less fortunate of Speer's projects for the New Berlin.[35] It would have glowered menacingly at the end of the boulevard leading to what is now the Platz der Republik, standing as a grim necropolis and a shrine to the death wish.

The new north–south axis would go from the airport at Tempelhof and the Southern Railway Station at Tempelhof-Schöneberg through central Berlin to a through station in Moabit, on the site of which now stands Berlin's main station. The whole north–south axis was 38.5 kilometres long. Both axes would be linked to an Autobahn ring around the city that was already under construction and which was to form the new city limits. All Berlin's terminus stations were to be dismantled, to be replaced by a suburban railway network. The central section of the north–south axis was a 5-kilometre-long 'Boulevard of Splendours', closed to traffic, with a standardised cornice line, as in Haussmann's boulevards in Paris, the height of which was to be set by Peter Behrens' new headquarters for AEG.[36] The new city was to be completed by 1950 when a world exhibition was to be held and the city formally renamed.

The boulevard began at the Southern Railway Station. Unlike all the other buildings along the north–south axis, it made extensive use of steel and glass. It was also a colossal building, far larger in scale than New York's Grand Central Station. The first design by Emil Kleinschmidt, an architect attached to the Reich Railway offices in Mainz, must have seemed far too modernistic for Speer, because it was drastically modified by Herbert Rimpl and by Speer himself. As visitors left the station they would face a vast space, 1,000 metres long and 330 metres wide, at the end of which would stand a triumphal arch. The Great Hall would loom 5 kilometres away. The area would be littered with captured weapons – testament to Germany's invincible might. On 20 August 1941 Speer, on Hitler's orders, told a somewhat astonished Admiral Hermann Lorey, the director of the Army Museum, that thirty pieces of heavy artillery captured from the enemy were to be placed between the Southern Railway Station and a triumphal arch in a manner similar to the rows of rams at Karnak. Captured tanks were to be placed outside other important public buildings.[37]

As mentioned above, Hitler himself designed the monstrous triumphal arch that was intended to greet and overwhelm visitors as they emerged from the Southern Railway Station. It was a monstrously overpowering hulk which, at 117 metres high and 170 metres wide, would have overshadowed all the surrounding buildings. The names of the 1.8 million servicemen who had been killed in the Great War were to be inscribed on it, in the style of the Tyne Cot Memorial to the Missing or the Menin Gate at Ypres. Speer claimed to have tried to persuade Hitler to agree to a more modest memorial to the dead, but to no avail. It was somewhat questionable whether the earth with its layers of marl would bear such a colossal weight.

To the north of the triumphal arch a Runde Platz (Round Plaza) was to be built where Mies van der Rohe's New National Gallery now stands. Speer was responsible for the overall design. It was to be enhanced with a fountain designed by Arno Breker, Nazi Germany's most highly regarded sculptor. The architecture here was noticeably more restrained than most of the other buildings in Germania. The curved façades rested on a well-proportioned colonnade, clearly influenced by Italian Fascist architecture. The whole was a somewhat heavy-handed Teutonic version of the sort of architecture reflected in de Chirico's paintings.[38] On the eastern side of the plaza was the head office of the Allianz insurance company, an enterprise that profited shamefully from its close association with the Nazi Party.[39] A House of German Tourism was planned on the opposite side of the plaza. The shell of the house was completed, but building was halted during the war. Other buildings on the Runde Platz were to include a cinema with six thousand seats, an officers' mess, the House of German Artists and Hermann Giesler's Thuringia House. It was assumed that these buildings would jointly carry the cost of the entire project.[40]

Speer's plan for Berlin underlined the fact that the headquarters of the Armed Forces and of Germany's leading companies did not merely share the same address, but lived together in harmony. That the tourist office and the headquarters of the secret police were in close proximity suggested that they had more in common than a postal code. Ernst Petersen's project for the washing powder manufacturer Henkel was next door to Herbert Rimpl's building for the Hermann Göring Works. IG Farben was placed opposite Hitler's palace. AEG was across the street from the Ministry of Propaganda. This sense of togetherness and of monumentality was strengthened by bunching these huge buildings together along the north–south axis. Thus these representative buildings were not dwarfed by vast open spaces as they are in Washington, New Delhi, Chandigarh or Brasilia.

Further north was the Kemperplatz – then known as the Skagerrakplatz – where the Berlin Philharmonic is now housed.[41] It was to be dominated by a colossal Soldier's Hall, a grotesque parody of Schinkel's Doric Neue Wache that Tessenow had converted into a memorial to the fallen in the Great War. Speer asked Wilhelm Kreis to design this temple to militarism. It was somewhat unclear what purpose this was supposed to serve, except that it was intended to form a fitting setting for the restaurant car in which the armistice had been signed in Compiègne in November 1918 and where the roles were reversed in June 1940. Kreis decided that it should be a shrine to the heroes who were yet to fall on the field of honour. As such, it was to be a 'truly German cathedral'. A vast crypt under the entire building was to provide a Valhalla for those 'who had sacrificed that which they held to be most precious so that future generations might live.'[42] The building's repugnant message was that the living should prepare to die in order to preserve and strengthen the 'racial community'.[43]

Adjacent to the Soldier's Hall a new headquarters for the Army High Command was to be built. When the drawings were shown to Göring he decided that his new Air Ministry building in the Wilhelmstraße did not reflect his importance. He therefore ordered a palace to be built opposite the Soldier's Hall. Göring asked Speer to design a building that was to underline heavily his exalted status. Speer, who was allowed by Hitler to continue with his private practice in addition to acting as GBI, readily accepted this lucrative contract. As GBI he was the head of a public-private partnership, but it was one in which he bore no financial, technical or operational risk and was not subject to outside control. It was a corrupt system, typical of Nazi Germany, in which Speer could help himself as he saw fit. Hitler complained that the proposed building was far too big for Göring. He also deeply resented that Reichsmarschall Göring had hired 'his' architect to build it. But such remarks were without consequence. Hitler, anxious to avoid a confrontation with Göring, amused himself by making caustic comments behind his back, mocking his ludicrous hedonism and love of splendour.[44]

Speer's design for what was to be called the Office of the Reichsmarschall was a palace intended more for pleasure than for business. In it, Speer's architectural vision reached its hysterical apogee. It was a stone colossus of unparalleled ostentatiousness, a parvenu's palace in bloated baroque. An elaborate staircase dominated the entrance hall, but Speer prudently provided for an elevator to save Göring from hauling his vast bulk up this imposing obstacle. When the Italian architect Luigi Nervi was shown a photograph of a scale model he exclaimed: 'Unbelievable! They must have gone mad!'[45] The roof was to be protected from air raids by earth four metres deep, to be planted with trees and a shrubbery to provide a pleasing setting for garden parties. The three acres of park to the rear of the building were to accommodate a swimming pool, tennis courts, pavilions, pergolas, bowers and fountains. It was also to include a sizeable outdoor theatre, where his wife's theatrical friends could entertain his guests.[46]

Göring allotted all the Luftwaffe's buildings to private architects so as to make sure that they were at least equal to, and wherever possible outshone, those built for his Führer. Thus in the palace that Speer planned for Göring, Nazi architecture reached its zenith. Had it ever been built, Göring would have trumped Hitler once again, as he did when he installed a panoramic window in his country estate, Carinhall, that was even larger than that at Hitler's mountaintop residence in Berchtesgaden.

Speer would have liked to have demolished Paul Wallot's Reichstag building, but Hitler insisted that it should remain, possibly because it stood as a monument to a defeated enemy.[47] Facing it to the west, a huge 'Führer's Palace' with a windowless façade was to be built in roughly the place where the comparatively modest German Chancellery (*Bundeskanzleramt*) now stands. It was a pompously ornate design, an overblown gingerbread version of the Palazzo Pitti that, with its 500-metre-long gallery and Hitler's 900-square-metre study, dwarfed Speer's new chancellery.[48] Hitler, terrified that there might eventually be an uprising against him, wanted the palace built as an impenetrable fortress. To provide extra security OKW agreed that the Großdeutschland Regiment should guard his residence. A new barracks was to be built for them 800 metres away. They were to be instructed to act immediately were there any protest demonstrations.

The Führer's Palace was to provide secure and adequate accommodation for the ruler of the world. 15,000 square metres of space was provided just to entertain his visitors. The dining hall seated more than 1,000 guests. There was to be a theatre seating up to 950 people, with a special box for the Führer. Hitler's bedroom was to be in marked contrast to his study, providing modest space for his simple white lacquered bed.[49] In order to maintain the myth that Hitler led a modest and Spartan life, plans for this immense building were kept secret.

Hitler ordered that a new parliament was to be built adjacent to the old Reichstag. It was to be adequate for the representation of a 'racial community' of 140 million Germanic peoples. The population of Germany in 1940, including Austria, the Sudetenland and Memel, was about 80 million, which gives some indication of Hitler's territorial ambitions. For some strange reason he wanted to keep the Weimar Republic's electoral system, which allotted one member of parliament for every 60,000 voters. Space would therefore have to be adequate for the needs of 2,333 members. To underline the pointlessness of the new Reichstag it was to be totally dwarfed by the Great Hall of the People, with fifty times the volume of the powerless parliament.

The Great Hall was the crowning horror of Speer's plan. This was a National Socialist variation of a prevalent utopian vision of an assembly hall for the community, such as Karl Friedrich Schinkel's Cathedral of Liberty in the early nineteenth century, Bruno Taut's elitist Nietzschean vision of the City Crown of 1917, or Walter Gropius' futuristic vision in the 1920s of a Socialist Cathedral.[50] Speer's architects were much taken by Taut's ideas and frequently spoke of the Great Hall as the Crown or even the City Crown. In the summer of 1936 Hitler had shown Speer a sketch of a huge domed building that he had made in the 1920s. Speer worked on this design and presented Hitler with detailed drawings and a scale model for his forty-eighth birthday on 20 April the following year. Speer chose, much to the celebrant's delight, to sign his work as 'based on the Führer's ideas'. On his fiftieth birthday Speer presented Hitler with a detailed 3-metre-high wooden model of the Great Hall, as well as a scale model of the interior. It was set up in Speer's offices in the former Prussian Academy of the Arts – now purified of its degenerate and Jewish membership – where Hitler made frequent visits to contemplate his masterpiece. Remembering that his ideas had once been dismissed as idle fantasies, he was given to muttering 'Who was prepared to believe me that it ever would be built?'[51] It never was.

The building was designed to provide standing room for 180,000 people. By contrast, the vast Soviet Congress Hall in Moscow seated a mere 15,000 delegates and Beijing's more modest Great Hall of the People has room for the 10,000 attending the National Congress of the world's largest political party. It would have been sixteen times the size of St Peter's in Rome. The dome was to have been just over three hundred metres high. It was to be covered with copper, so would loom mountainously over the surrounding resplendence. It was to be topped by a glass lantern 40 metres high with an enormous swastika upon which perched a massive eagle from Schmid-Ehman's studio. After the fall of France, Hitler felt it more appropriate to replace the swastika with a globe. Germania was, after all, to be a 'World Capital'.[52] The entrance was to be flanked by two 15-metre-high figures, one representing Atlas holding the heavens and the other Tellus holding the world. Ninety-four parcels of land would have to be cleared, twenty-seven of which were already government property, to provide space to build the Great Hall. The value of these properties was 40,212,800 Reichsmarks, a sum that included 11,105,900 Reichsmarks for the property already owned by the government. Preparations had been made for these purchases as soon as the Führer gave the order.[53]

On 8 May 1941 Goebbels wrote in his diary: 'The Führer expresses his adamant certainty that some day the Reich will dominate all of Europe. For this to be so we shall have to fight many battles, but without a doubt they will be brilliant successes. Then the way will be open to world domination. Whoever possesses Europe will be able to seize leadership over the world.'[54] Germania was thus to be not only a World Capital, it would be Capital of the World. When Speer pointed out to Hitler that the dome would rise above the clouds and provide an ideal marker for enemy aircraft, he was told that Göring had guaranteed that not a single bomber would ever reach Germany.[55] It would certainly have fulfilled its intention to overwhelm, although one post-war admirer of Speer's architecture saw it as a symbolic representation of 'mother Europe's bosom and womb'.[56]

Speer, who professed to be an enthusiast for water sports, designed a vast pool between the Northern Railway Station and the Great Hall that could be used for bathing and boating. In would be bordered by cabins for changing clothes. This version of Paris-Plages *avant la lettre* was designed to be in sharp contrast to the industrial filth in the Spree. It would also have been a very curious sight in the context of the surrounding architecture. At the northern end was a massive railway station; to the south the overpowering Great Hall, whose reflection would make it seem all the more imposing. Along the eastern side the navy was to have its headquarters in appropriately watery surroundings. On the other side of the pool was to be an enormous new City Hall designed by German Bestelmeyer, who was another of Hitler's favourite architects. Along with Paul Bonatz, Wilhelm Kreis and Paul Schultze-Naumburg, he had formed 'The Block', in staunch opposition to Bestelmeyer modernists such as Walter Gropius, Mies van der Rohe and Erich Mendelsohn. He was also a leading member of Alfred Rosenberg's viciously anti-Semitic Action League for German Culture (KfdK). Among its other distinguished members were Hitler's favourite, Winifred Wagner, and Othmar Spann. It was from such circles that Speer chose the men to realise his dreams.

These plans did make some modest provision for housing the tens of thousands that were to be displaced. New housing estates were planned to the south and east of the city. The 'Southern Town' was to provide housing for 210,000 people, half of whom were expected to be employed by industrial enterprises scheduled to open in what was to be essentially a working-class district. Much of the overall planning, which had begun under the aegis of the municipality, was entrusted to Hermann Jansen, one of Speer's instructors in city planning, who in 1929 had won an international competition for rebuilding Ankara. His design showed a concern to provide sufficient green spaces and sports facilities, while avoiding traffic congestion. Speer as GBI modified these plans by abandoning Jansen's grid system, which he found monotonous, dividing up the area into sub-districts, building tower blocks along the ring road to form a new city wall and extending the north–south axis to join the new district at a point where a number of official buildings would be constructed. A sports stadium to be designed by Werner March, as well as a parade ground, were intended to give the area an appropriately National Socialist flavour. This plan was then modified, returning to a more rigid street plan, but providing for a number of single dwellings and additional green spaces. Among the monumental new buildings planned along the extension of the north–south axis were a Customs School, a Police Technical College, the Army War Academy, offices for the Air Ministry, the High Command of the Waffen-SS, the Reich Archives, the Reich Insurance Office (whose offices on the Skagerrakplatz were to be demolished to make way for the Army High Command's new building) and the Department of Public Works. All these designs were pedestrian variations on the fustian norms of National Socialist architecture. In them the pretentious hovers on the brink of the preposterous.[57]

Had it been realised, the whole scheme would have been a nightmare of deadly conformity, reducing a vital city into lifeless homogeneity. It was an architectural expression of boundless ambition that bore no relation whatsoever to Berlin's immediate needs or future requirements. But in one sense Hitler and Speer's plans were a perfect marriage of form and function. This would have been a capital worthy of the 'Germanic Reich' of which Hitler dreamed. It would have been an overwhelming representation, in reinforced concrete faced with granite, of a horrific dystopia.

Germania was designed to be the backdrop for a permanent display of the regime's awesome might. Its architecture was intended as a power-political instrument at the service of National Socialism. The North–South Axis as the 'Victory Avenue of the Third Reich' was intended to trump the Wilhelmine Siegesallee or 'Victory Avenue' of the Second Reich, popularly known as 'Doll's

Avenue' because of the thirty-two statues of the rulers of Brandenburg and Prussia that lined the route.[58] There was no room in this concept for any consideration of the acute housing shortage, estimated to be in the region of 600,000 to 700,000 units.

The Germania undertaking would have been incredibly expensive, would have called for about 200,000 workers and would have consumed vast amounts of raw materials. Almost from the outset of his work in Nuremberg Speer had worked closely with the SS. Himmler, a man whom Speer described as 'friendly with a somewhat formal properness', was more than happy to provide him with the granite and bricks that he required, provided that Speer's organisation picked up the tab. On 1 July 1938 an agreement was signed to this effect. Almost immediately 10,000 concentration camp inmates were selected in a programme waggishly entitled 'Slothful', whereby Himmler made a handsome profit out of his campaign of 'racial prevention' in which he rounded up 'anti-social elements' and then hired them out.[59]

The decision to open concentration camps at Mauthausen and Flossenbürg, both built in 1938, was made in consultation with Speer after an examination of the quality and quantity of the stone available in local quarries. Inmates of the concentration camps slaved away in unimaginable conditions on behalf of the GBI. When Himmler decided to expand his system of concentration camps in 1940 he went with Oswald Pohl to seek Speer's advice. Speer told them that he needed the bluish-grey granite from Groß-Rosen (Rogoźnica) in Silesia and the reddish granite from Natzweiler-Struthof in Alsace, the latter for his gigantic German Stadium in Nuremberg. Special concentration camps were built at Speer's behest at both sites. In September 1941 the Reich Party Rally Grounds Association in Nuremberg signed a contract with DEST for the Natzweiler-Struthof quarry to meet Speer's requirements.[60] Speer ordered Oswald Pohl to give Natzweiler-Struthof top priority. Steel was made readily available and he sent his deputy, SS-Hauptsturmführer Franz Liebermann, to liaise with DEST's representative at Natzweiler-Struthof. The geologist SS-Standartenführer Karl Blumberg ensured that all ran smoothly.[61] The brick factory at Oranienburg, built at Speer's request in 1938, was made of stones quarried by inmates from the concentration camp at Sachsenhausen. The workers were DEST's slaves. When someone remarked on the wretched conditions at Oranienburg, Speer replied that 'The Yids got used to making bricks while in Egyptian captivity.'[62] In 1941 a special 'Speer Commando' was created to work in the recently built concentration camp Oranienburg II.[63] Even when the Germania project had to be shelved, Oranienburg still remained part of Speer's empire, no longer as Inspector General of Buildings, but as Minister of Armaments. It was now used as a branch plant for the Heinkel aircraft company. Speer also travelled throughout German-occupied Europe in search of stone for his projects in Nuremberg and Berlin. The concentration camps were thus an essential part of his plans to rebuild Berlin. National Socialist monumental architecture, of which Speer was the outstanding proponent, was inextricably linked to the oppression, terror and murderous intent of Himmler's SS.

Like so much else in Nazi Germany, the alliance between Speer and Himmler was fraught with contradictions. The concentration camp commandants and their staff regarded the camps primarily as instruments of political oppression, designed to punish enemies of the state and to eliminate the undesirable. They looked down upon the pen-pushing bureaucrats in DEST with their obsession with output and efficiency. The situation was further complicated when Speer became Minister of Armaments. Forced labour in the concentration camps was now increasingly used in the armaments industries as weapons took precedence over monumental buildings.

By May 1943 all the quarries had been closed down, with the exception of Flossenbürg and Mauthausen, where there were frequent complaints about the poor quality of a labour force that had been brutalised, half-starved and literally worked to death. Such was the cruel absurdity of trying to combine efficiency with merciless coercion.

Speer and Himmler's interests remained distinct, but they were still convergent. Speer believed in the self-determination of industry and close cooperation between the state and private enterprise, whereas Himmler's economic empire was essentially an instrument of terror. But Speer needed workers, which Himmler had in ample supply.

Speer's lawyer at the Nuremberg trials, Hans Flächsner, was successful in insisting that there was a manifest caesura in Speer's life in February 1942. Before that date he was an architect; afterwards he was a technocrat. Speer's *mea culpa* on the witness stand only referred to his activities as Minister of Armaments. But the political dimension of his activities both as architect and minister is clearly apparent. In each capacity he was closely involved with the murderous intent of the SS.

As noted above, Berlin already suffered from an acute housing shortage. It would have reached crisis proportions with the extensive demolition needed for building a world capital. Speer had made a vague promise to build 650,000 new dwellings, to compensate for the deliberately underestimated loss of 100,000 to 150,000 housing units pulled down to make way for his vision for a new capital. His immediate plans called for the demolition of a number of dwellings that equalled the total amount of all new building in Berlin during the previous ten years. The municipal authorities were naturally aghast at the consequences of destruction on such a scale and were deeply concerned that evictions should be strictly within the limits of existing law. Speer haughtily brushed such concerns aside by claiming that a measure that had been discussed with and approved by the Führer should not be questioned. Quasi-legal sanction for this despotic approach had already been given in the Law for Rebuilding of German Towns of 4 October 1937, which was drafted by Speer in conjunction with the Ministry of Labour, the body hitherto responsible for urban planning and housing. It soon became known as the 'Expropriation Law'. This gave Speer absolute authority to seize whatever property he wished and to award compensation according to the minimal requirements of the law.[64]

Speer's new organisation was an example of the public-private partnerships that resulted from an increasing trend towards privatisation in Nazi Germany. It was eventually freed from most bureaucratic and legal restraints, checks and balances. On the public side it was funded directly by the Reich Chancellery, while offering private business ample opportunities for bribery, corruption and influence peddling without being subject to controls from the municipal authorities.

Berlin already had a Gemeinnützigen Siedlungs- und Wohnungsbau-gesellschaft, or Building Association for Settlements and Housing in the Public Interest (GSW), with responsibility for building new housing. It worked closely with Speer, with two of his closest associates on its board of directors. Speer's deputy, Karl Maria Hettlage, was given responsibility for finances and the acquisition of property, without reference to the municipal authorities. He was typical of a number of people who had been employed by the city of Berlin and now worked for the GBI.[65] Speer's closest young colleagues were Rudolf Wolters, Willi Schelkes and Hans Stephan, all of whom had been fellow students. They were soon known as the 'Three Planners'.[66]

Speer had a total of twenty-eight architects working under him, but the 'Three Planners' formed an inner circle. Wolters was sent on a tour of America to look at road traffic. Speer and Schelkes lived in the German embassy in London to study the city's architecture. Schelkes also travelled to Italy with Speer and his wife Gretel. In 1937, Schelkes and Stephan accompanied Speer to the International Exhibition dedicated to Art and Technology in Modern Life in Paris, where Speer received the gold medal for the German Pavilion.

Speer was now fully in command. Not only had power shifted radically from the municipal authorities, the financial inducement to work for the GBI was considerable. Salaries were topped up beyond the normal levels, an extra month's pay was awarded as a Christmas bonus, and the staff's privileged status as civil servants was maintained. But this was not enough for Speer. When the Ministry of Finance turned down his application for a salary increase that was well in excess of the established scale, he appealed directly to Hitler, who ordered the minister to make an exception in this case. Speer as GBI had a vast budget of 60 million Reichsmarks at his disposal, thereby enabling him to distribute considerable largesse to architects, artists, model builders and draughtsmen. As GBI he received 1,500 Reichsmarks per month, which was the ceiling salary for a secretary of state. It was an amount that he described as 'insignificant' when compared with his honorarium as an architect.[67] He awarded his own architectural firm 60,000 Reichsmarks per month for services rendered to himself as GBI, a chunk of which landed up in his own pocket.[68] But he did not always have it his own way. Hans Lammers as head of the Reich Chancellery firmly turned down his request to be included in the state pension scheme 'for the sake of (his) family's security'.[69]

An important part of Speer's carefully constructed self-image was his assertion that, in contrast to the vulgar parvenus among the Third Reich's elite, he led an extremely modest life. In Spandau gaol he claimed to have learnt the value of Spartan simplicity and to scorn material values. In his memoirs he described the sybaritic excesses of his colleagues, who even in the later stages of the war used their vast mansions, hunting lodges, landed estates and castles for spurious 'official functions' in which a host of servants served elegant meals washed down with the finest wines.[70] Speer drew a clear distinction between his lifestyle and that of the corrupt and degenerate leadership.

Initially there was a grain of truth in this assertion. The house in Berlin-Schlachtensee, which he built in 1935, was a charming and relatively modest villa of 125 square metres that cost 70,000 Reichsmarks, 30,000 Reichsmarks of which was borrowed from his father.[71] Speer was not yet a member of the elite and was still under the restraining influence of Tessenow. One note of luxury was a swimming pool – a rarity in those days. The house was totally destroyed by Allied bombing after the Speer family had moved out. In 1932 he had declared an income of 1,660 Reichsmarks. By 1943 it had risen to 211,933 Reichsmarks. Very little of this substantial sum came from his income as Minister of Armaments. He continued to earn handsomely from his architectural firm, the proceeds of which were tax-free, thanks to a special dispensation from the Ministry of Finance. By 1940 he had already accumulated a personal fortune of 1,423,000 Reichsmarks. Apart from Ribbentrop, who was a partner in his father-in-law's sparkling wine company and who also ran a successful export-import business, Speer was already the richest of the Nazi grandees.[72] His future income would have been truly spectacular if the war had not intervened. He was to have been given a 2 per cent honorarium for his buildings for Germania. The triumphal arch was estimated to cost 130 million Reichsmarks, which would have earned him 2.6 million Reichsmarks. In February 1943 he was paid 650,000 Reichsmarks for his preliminary drawings of this monstrosity. The Great Hall was to cost 2,150,000,000 Reichsmarks, earning him 43 million Reichsmarks. The sum of 1,935,000 Reichsmarks was to be paid as an advance on this project in February 1943. Lammers wrote in May 1943 that Speer had claim to 7 million

Reichsmarks in honorarium for his work in Berlin. This did not include all the work he had done in Nuremberg, for which similar sums were due.[73]

Admittedly most of this was purely theoretical, because Germania was never built, but Speer did receive substantial advances for a number of projects. By the end of the financial year 1942 he had been paid a total of 3,893,000 Reichsmarks for the Headquarters of the High Command of the Armed Forces, the Führer's Palace and the Triumphal Arch. In 1943 he received an additional 200,000 Reichsmarks. It would seem that he was also paid 710,000 Reichsmarks for the Headquarters of the Luftwaffe and his design for the Adolf-Hitler–Platz. This adds up to the breathtaking sum of 4.8 million Reichsmarks. When held prisoner at Kransberg, the Allies requested him to list his assets. He claimed to possess a total of 1,112,750 Reichsmarks.[74] The missing millions are a mystery about which Speer remained silent. In his memoirs he wrote: 'At the end of my career as an architect my assets had grown to about 1.5 million Reichsmarks. The Reich owed me another million, which I was never paid.'[75]

Work on building Germania virtually ceased with the outbreak of the war, but with the swift victory over France Speer was anxious to get back to work. According to his memoirs Hitler was in such a euphoric state after his visit to Paris that he signed a 'Führer's Decree', drafted by Speer and backdated to 25 June 1940, the date of the armistice, demanding that Berlin be rebuilt as 'the capital of a powerful new Reich and as an expression of the greatness of our victory'. The work was to be completed by 1950.[76] When warned that sufficient funds would not be available because of wartime economies, he told the Reich Chancellery that Hitler had said that he wished planning to go ahead so that construction work could begin as soon as the war ended. For this to be possible he demanded an increase in the budget. Speer left it to Karl Maria Hettlage, who was now on the board of the Commerzbank, to find the necessary funds. This he managed with remarkable cunning, enabling Speer to increase the GBI's staff from 52 in 1938 to 1,400 by 1942. The cost of rebuilding as well as the purchase of property was the responsibility of the relevant authority, whether the Reich Railways, the Reich Post, the NSDAP or a particular ministry. Hettlage also managed to get these various bodies to bear a proportion of the administrative cost of the GBI's office, thereby substantially increasing an already grossly inflated budget. His continued link with the Commerzbank throughout the war was also greatly to the bank's advantage.[77]

Speer was exceedingly heavy-handed with the municipal government, claiming plenipotentiary rights to interfere at all levels based on the powers vested in the GBI by Hitler. In June 1940 he drafted a decree that reduced the municipal government to an organisation that was to fund his operations, provide information as requested and lend him every assistance. On 9 July

Berlin's mayor, Dr Julius Lippert, wrote to Speer complaining that he was trying to humiliate him by showing no respect whatsoever for the rights of the municipal government. Speer immediately took the matter to Hitler, who in Bormann's presence ordered that Lippert, a man whom Hitler had previously described as 'incompetent, an idiot, a failure and a nonentity', should be instantly dismissed.[78] Bormann thereupon instructed Lammers to take the necessary steps to remove him from office. He was summarily fired on 19 July. Lippert, although a fervent National Socialist and one of Goebbels' protégés, had never been enthusiastic about Hitler's grandiose plans for rebuilding Berlin and was thus already out of favour. His subsequent career was undistinguished, in part perhaps because Speer unscrupulously handed over his entire correspondence with Lippert to Himmler.[79] The whole incident is an example of Speer's utter ruthlessness and makes a mockery of his claim to have been simply an 'apolitical' architect.

The outcome of a protracted and bitter struggle between Speer and Mayor Lippert infuriated Goebbels. As early as 1 January 1939 he wrote in his diary: 'Hanke . . . told me about an infamous press attack planned by Speer against Lippert. I make no secret of my opinion. So much is certain: he is too cowardly to attack openly, so he insidiously attacks from behind. We really appreciate that. Such things cut no ice with me.'[80] But Goebbels was powerless to intervene as long as Speer had Hitler's support.

From the outset of the war Speer was concerned to protect stoneworkers from being drafted into the armed forces. He was determined that they should continue to stockpile material for the new Berlin, particularly the 180,000 cubic metres of stone that Wilhelm Kreis estimated he needed for his OKH headquarters and the Soldier's Hall. Speer received Hitler's approval for his request that over 180 quarries in the private sector should continue production in wartime, their workers exempted from military service. These efforts were intensified with the rapid defeat of France, much of the work being coordinated by Walter Brugmann from the company Arge Nuremberg, Speer's site manager in Berlin. On 29 November 1941, in a brief moment of euphoria, even though his campaign in the Soviet Union was rapidly unravelling, Hitler told Speer and Kreis over dinner that he did not want the war to interfere with his plans for Berlin and that he hoped that work could soon begin on the Soldier's Hall.[81] Within a few days the Red Army dashed all such hopes. Speer now had limitless supplies of stone available from quarries all over Europe, but it was impossible to see how it could be put to use until the war ended in victory. For Speer, stone procurement was the only way that he could keep his operations in Berlin and Nuremberg going. He had natural allies in Himmler, the SS and DEST. The alliance was further strengthened in 1941 when DEST's manager, Karl Mummenthey, was appointed to the board of Arge Nuremberg.

Speer grabbed labour wherever he found it, making little distinction between volunteer workers from Italy, French prisoners of war or Czechs drafted to do wartime service in the Reich. His major problem was that Göring had a monopoly over the use of Soviet prisoners of war.[82] Speer solved this difficulty in the usual manner by going directly to Hitler, who gave him permission to use 30,000 Soviet POWs to work in Berlin. By the end of 1941 Speer had 130,000 workers from all over Europe under his command. He made a similar deal with Heydrich, who, in his capacity of Deputy Reich Protector of Bohemia and Moravia, was ruthlessly exploiting Czech labour. In return for 15,000 Czech workers, Speer promised to help Heydrich with his plans to rebuild Prague.[83] Heydrich's assassination and the exigencies of war denied Speer this opportunity.

The use of large numbers of prisoners of war presented a major security problem. Speer, who was already working in close cooperation with the SS on a number of projects, including the eviction of Jewish tenants – a procedure now known as 'de-renting' (Entmietung) – turned to the Waffen-SS for help. His friend Sepp Dietrich, who commanded the Leibstandarte SS Adolf Hitler in Berlin along with some other Waffen-SS units, was ready to oblige.[84]

With massive building operations in Berlin on hold for the duration of hostilities, Speer's office took over part of the task of Organisation Todt: a civil and military engineering group organised along military lines and named after its leader, Fritz Todt. It is characteristic of Nazi Germany that one organisation should duplicate the task of another and that areas of competence should overlap. That in this case it worked relatively well was due to the fact that Speer respected Todt as an exceptionally talented man. He was also the most affable of the Third Reich's leading figures – an admittedly narrow field. The GBI was responsible for building air-raid shelters, clearing bomb damage and demolishing buildings, for which purpose large numbers of Jews were forced to work. Speer also made use of regular German workers from Organisation Todt. In November 1939 he was given responsibility for meeting the Luftwaffe's construction needs. In 1941 he built industrial plant for Göring's Four-Year Plan. He also handled contracts from the army and the navy. On 27 December 1941 Hitler charged him with 'duties in the East'.[85] In mid-January 1942 he established the Baustab Speer–Ostbau or Speer Construction Staff East with 30,000 workers. It cooperated closely with Organisation Todt in construction projects in the Ukraine and the southern sector of the Eastern Front. Speer's rival, the architect Hermann Giesler, headed a similar organisation that operated in the northern sector of Army Groups Centre and North. Giesler also assisted Organisation Todt in Bavaria and along the Danube.[86]

This Baustab Speer–Ostbau was in fact a moving concentration camp in which inmates, mostly Jews, were forced to work on an Autobahn through the Ukraine known as Thoroughfare IV. Speer's right-hand man Rudolf Wolters inspected the project in 1942. With reference to this part of Himmler's plan for 'Annihilation Through Work' in which thousands died, he told Speer that some worked two shifts in a row, apparently voluntarily, adding 'you know what this is all about'.[87] This road, also known as SS Road, was a joint venture of Speer, Himmler and the Wehrmacht. The SS provided movable concentration camps for Jewish workers. The Wehrmacht made 50,000 prisoners of war available. Press-gangs rounded up thousands of Ukrainians. Those who were no longer capable of working were 'selected' and then killed. This resulted in some 25,000 Jews being murdered in eighty-four mass executions.[88] Speer's men were thus from the very beginning dutifully carrying out one of the Wannsee Conference's appalling recommendations: 'Under proper leadership, the Jews must now in the course of the Final Solution be given suitable assignments for work in the East. Such Jews that are capable of working are to be separated by sex and sent in large work gangs to these areas to build roads, whereby a majority is bound to fall by the wayside through a process of natural diminution. Those who remain will undoubtedly be among the toughest. They must be treated appropriately, since by the process of natural selection they would form the kernel of a new Jewish resistance should they be released.'[89]

As GBI, Speer made extensive use of Soviet prisoners of war both for preparatory work to build the new Berlin and to clear away bomb damage. Hettlage's Main Office II (Organisation and Economics) built two camps in Berlin at Kaulsdorf and Falkensee where it was proudly announced that no soup was served on Saturdays and Sundays. The prisoners were hired by private construction companies, with the result that from October 1941 to March 1942 Hettlage's office made a profit of 110,000 Reichsmarks.[90]

On 11 October 1943 Hitler entrusted Speer, in addition to his duties as Minister of Armaments, with the awesome task of rebuilding Germany's bombed towns. He thereby assumed responsibilities that hitherto had been the province of the Minister of Labour and of local municipal authorities. In the last months of the war Speer as GBI began to sell government property and equipment to private investors. They saw excellent opportunities for the building industry in the post-war world. In 1944 Speer and Goebbels set up a competition for the reconstruction of Berlin. Speer's central core was to be built as planned, but the rest of the city, with an estimated population of 10 million and thus the largest in Europe, was to be converted into a garden city. All roads and railways were to be underground and the Spree widened.[91] Gleams of realism were apparent when, in March 1945, Speer's planning staff prudently awarded themselves three months advance pay and packed their bags.[92]

From the very outset it seemed somewhat dubious whether, as Mayor Lippert had argued, the grandiose twenty- to thirty-year plan for building Germania could ever be realised. Even under normal circumstances the cost was likely to be prohibitive. With the colossal investment in armaments even before the war it was virtually impossible. Then there were the legal problems involved in gaining government control over a vast area of central Berlin, given that existing real estate law remained in force, in spite of Speer's exceptional powers. Even Jewish tenants were still protected. It was not until 25 July 1938 that landlords were permitted to terminate leases of office space to Jewish doctors.[93] It was highly questionable whether the building industry had the capacity to undertake such an enormous task within the allotted time. Above all, there was the exceptional difficulty of drawing up a plan that would coordinate all these aspects into a coherent effort. Attention was now concentrated on tearing down existing buildings and clearing the way for future construction.

Speer published some details of his plans for Hitler's 'world capital' in the newspapers, beginning in January 1938, but he was careful to keep secret the areas he intended to demolish. A series of confidential meetings with local authorities and party officials was held to coordinate efforts and prepare alternative housing for those affected. They were given short notice before demolition was to begin, thereby creating the serious problem of quickly finding new housing for those left homeless. In 1938, 17,000 apartments were designated for destruction, thus significantly adding to an existing shortage of 190,000 apartments. Such was the result of ignoring Berlin's mounting housing requirements during the first five years of the Third Reich, during which time the housing shortage had doubled. Difficulties were further compounded by the fact that a large number of dwellings were in an exceptionally poor state of repair, with many scheduled for demolition. In most instances where alternative housing was available the rents were considerably higher, often well beyond the means of those affected. The Ministry of Economics protested vigorously against the ridiculously short notice that was to be given before owners and tenants were evicted. Offices and institutes were to be allowed six weeks, individuals sometimes merely one week. Speer replied that such cases always implied hardship and that it was absurd that the Architectural Institute of the German Reich claimed to be unable to move its sizeable library and archive within six weeks.[94]

The lack of alternative housing, made all the more acute by the slowdown in new building because of lack of funds, meant that demolition plans had to be shelved. In May 1938 one of Speer's associates pointed out that 30,000 new dwellings had been planned to replace 17,000 that were to be demolished and to provide 13,000 new ones to relieve the housing shortage. In fact only 8,000 new homes had been built by the combined efforts of the city's construction company GSW and private investors. There was no relief in sight due to a lack of resources.[95]

The greatest number of housing units built in Berlin was the yearly average of 33,000 during the depression years between 1929 and 1931. Between 1932 and 1935 the average fell to 8,700. The figure then steadily rose, reaching 18,750 in 1937. Given these figures, it is truly astonishing that in October 1937 during a discussion between Speer, the municipality and the GSW, it was agreed that 30-40,000 new housing units were to be built in the following year. After a fierce struggle between Speer and the municipal authorities over who should build what and when, the end result was that only 14,935 new units were built in 1938.[96]

Speer and his department, having failed to work out a viable plan and having made inexcusable miscalculations about the resources available, were locked in a fruitless battle with the city. Speer obtained a 'Führer's Decision' that enabled him to order the GBI's Implementation Agency to ensure that 30,000 new units would be built in Berlin in 1939. The requirements for men and material for the Westwall alone were enough to render this impossible. If the new dwellings could not be built, houses could not be demolished and building could not begin. Where demolition was possible there were loud complaints from tenants who were suddenly faced with the problem of finding alternative accommodation in a saturated market. In the case of the Air Ministry's intention to build a new headquarters in Tempelhof, there was such a public outcry that Göring was obliged to postpone the demolition of the housing needed to clear the site. Similarly the building plans of AEG, Maggi and the armaments concern Fritz Werner AG could not go ahead because of the lack of alternative accommodation.

Speer was outraged that his building plans were being frustrated by the inability to provide adequate housing for those forced to move. He told the municipal authorities that they should put tenants on notice that they would have to move not later than February 1940. A further problem was that those who were able to find alternative accommodation served to reduce the number of units available for the Nationalsozialistische Volkswohlfahrt or National Socialist People's Welfare (NSV) that was responsible for providing housing for the poor and homeless. The Security Service of the SS reported that there were also complaints about the lack of Kindergarten space due to widespread demolition.[97] Speer's plans for Germania, even at this early stage, placed an intolerable strain on the National Socialist welfare state, which was a core element in the ideological construct of the 'racial community'.

It was then that Speer suffered his first setbacks. Hitler, spurred on by Bormann, appointed Hermann Giesler to supervise the rebuilding of Munich as the 'Movement's Capital'. In March 1939 Roderich Fick, a traditionalist architect who had designed a number of buildings on the Obersalzberg, was appointed to convert Linz from a provincial backwater into a 'world city' to which Hitler intended to retire and where he was to be buried in a suitably imposing mausoleum. Speer reacted to Fick's appointment by petulantly resigning from several of his positions, including 'Beauty of Work', which had once meant so much to him.[98]

Little was achieved by designating new housing for those whose dwellings had been demolished. The lifting of the Ministry of Economics' restrictions on mortgages and loans in August 1938 for tenants whose homes were to be destroyed and who wished to become owner-occupiers did not bring much relief. The GSW only managed to build 4,500 units in 1939, instead of the 30,000 planned. The main reasons for this were the chronic scarcity of building materials, labour and capital. Speer was well aware of this, but he was unable to accept that his vision for Germania was unrealisable and that he had failed in the task that Hitler had set him. He issued orders and decrees that were impossible to carry out. He even threatened to tear down buildings regardless of whether alternative housing was available for tenants who had been evicted. He intended to place the blame on the city of Berlin for having failed to meet their needs. This was clearly unacceptable, but Speer did not give up. He could not afford to admit that his loudly trumpeted plans could not be realised, thus putting his co-workers, planners, architects and artists out of work. Nor could this fiasco be made public. Then, at last, a partial solution was found. One section of the population could be evicted without compensation, thereby providing accommodation for those who had to make way for Speer's new buildings – Berlin's Jews. In other German cities the local authorities were accountable for measures against Jewish tenants. In Berlin, Speer as GBI played a key role.[99]

On 10 September 1938 the Ministry of Finance turned down Speer's request for additional funding for new housing units. Four days later Speer invited representatives of Berlin's administration to a meeting at which 'Professor Speer made the suggestion that, as far as the building of mid-sized and large apartments was concerned, the large apartments that are needed could be made available by the forcible eviction of Jews. Then, instead of 2,500 large apartments, approximately 2,700 small ones would have to be built.' Speer insisted that this matter should be treated in the utmost confidence because he first had to ask the Führer for his permission and then obtain the necessary legal authority.[100]

Thus even before the pogrom on 9 November 1938 Speer was calling for measures against Jews that went well beyond anything hitherto in Nazi Germany. The Ministry of Justice took up the issue of Jewish tenants' rights on the same day and worked closely with Speer to provide him with the legal sanctions. The resulting plan, known as the 'Jewish Settlement', called for the eviction of Jews living in the centre of the city in apartments with four or more rooms. It was an operation that Speer calculated would save 40 million Reichsmarks. By building only 2,500 small apartments a further 5 million Reichsmarks could be saved. Adalbert Pfeil, the municipal official responsible for construction, was highly sceptical of the plan. He pointed out that it would probably exceed the need for spacious apartments, while doing nothing to solve the shortage of smaller ones. Nor did it address the problem of finding accommodation for the Jews who had been evicted from their homes.

It was now very unlikely that Speer's intentions would remain strictly confidential and he had not yet obtained Hitler's approval. Nevertheless he ordered that the eviction of Berlin's Jews should go ahead, without even waiting for a final decision from the Ministry of Justice. On 7 November 1938 he wrote a letter to a senior official in the Ministry of Justice marked 'personal and confidential' in which he bluntly stated: 'Although obviously the total removal of tenants' rights from Jews, particularly in the cities, gives rise to some difficulties because of the present impossibility of finding alternative accommodation, nevertheless I suggest that in Berlin we start tackling this problem by eviction from large apartments.' These 'could then provide accommodation for German racial comrades in so far as the emigration of the Jews continues to increase.'[101] On the following day Speer ordered Gerhard Petrik from the Municipal Department of Works to start building a settlement in the north-eastern suburb of Buch that would be sufficiently large to accommodate tenants evicted from 1,500 apartments. It was to be finished by the following October.[102]

A number of problems had to be solved before the Jewish Settlement could go ahead. There were no details available that indicated which apartments were owned by Jews or were rented by them. Tenants, even though Jewish, were still legally protected. It was unclear what was to happen with property that was owned by Jews but was let to non-Jews, or when Jews were tenants of non-Jews. Local party officials in the Berlin Party District, of which Goebbels was the Gauleiter, set to work in September to compile a census of large apartments in which Jews were living, but they soon found that this task was beyond their means. On 27 September 1938 Speer convened a meeting attended by representatives of the city planning and statistical offices, the police, the Nazi Party and the German Work Front (DAF), but little came of it. The names and addresses of Jews who had been deprived of their voting rights were available, but it was not possible to deduce from this list who rented which apartment or from whom. Both the police and the party said they had better things to do. The DAF smugly announced that they had already collected all the information that Speer needed and that it would be relatively easy to draw up a list of the large apartments that he required.[103]

Speer had a useful ally in his friend Rudolf Schmeer, a man who had joined the Nazi Party in 1922 and had been an active right-wing terrorist during the occupation of the Ruhr in 1923. Having held high office in the Nazi Party and in the DAF, he was now a senior official in the Ministry of Economics, where he was responsible for the 'Jewish Question'. He was an enthusiastic supporter of Speer's plans to evict Jews. Göring said of him that if he wanted anyone to deal with anti-Jewish measures Schmeer was the man to consult: 'it will be dealt with in five minutes'.[104] Speer's next move was to persuade the Ministry of Justice to remove all legal restraints on such evictions.

The pogrom of 9 November 1938, a horror that has been trivialised as Kristallnacht or the 'Night of Broken Glass', presented Speer with certain problems. There were now others with greedy eyes on Jewish property and Speer's activities, which had exacerbated the already desperate housing situation in Berlin, were likely to come to light. For this reason he was exceedingly reluctant to make any mention of the pogrom in his memoirs. At Joachim Fest's insistence he added one trite and disingenuous paragraph.[105] A young architect on Speer's team, Hans Simon, showed exemplary courage and moral fortitude. He resigned after these events, saying 'For people like that, I don't work', thereby ruining a promising career.[106] Speer, who directly profited, had no such qualms of conscience. He made the meaningless distinction between the 'repulsive bourgeois revolutionaries' who were responsible for such violence and brutality and those like himself who supported Hitler for reasons of 'idealism and devotion'.[107] He was unable to show where the line could be drawn.

The question was now raised whether it was desirable to create a ghetto in Berlin. On 12 November 1938 a high-level meeting was held to discuss this issue. It was attended by Göring as head of the Four-Year Plan, Heydrich from the SS Reich Security Main Office and Goebbels as Gauleiter of Berlin and Minister of Propaganda. On the agenda were Jewish property rights and the 'Aryanisation' of the German economy.[108] Heydrich objected strongly to Speer's proposal to concentrate evicted Jews in settlements. He argued that such ghettos would become hideouts for criminals and breeding grounds for disease. It would be far better to have them living among German racial comrades, who would keep an eye on them. The meeting concluded that although Jewish property rights were on the whole to be respected, they were to be honoured more in the breach than the observance.

On 21 November Speer, Goebbels and Lippert met to discuss how best to divide the loot from the pogrom. The following day Goebbels gave a rousing account of the outcome of this meeting in a speech at the former Kroll Opera House. He blandly announced that there was no conflict of interest between building the New Berlin, the construction of new apartments and the renovation of old housing stock to relieve the housing shortage. This was to be tackled with 'National Socialist diligence'. For maximum political effect Goebbels, Lippert and Speer's disreputable deputy, Dr Ernst Zörner, who had recently been dismissed as mayor of Dresden for what were tactfully called 'irregularities', drove together in a magnificent open motorcar through the working-class districts of Berlin.[109] Speer prudently did not take part in this unseemly farce, but behind the scenes he concentrated on taking over as many spacious apartments as could be found in the most desirable districts that had Jewish tenants. His task was made much easier when Göring, as head of the Four-Year Plan, gave him pre-emptive rights over all property with Jewish tenants.[110]

The intensification of anti-Jewish measures after 9 November relieved Speer of the problem of finding alternative housing for those Jewish tenants who had been evicted. On 25 January 1939 Speer ensured that his office would be informed when property that had been rented by Jews became free. Landlords would then have to gain permission from the GBI before accepting new tenants. If repairs were required, half the cost was to be borne by the Berlin Jewish Association.[111] Speer was gradually gaining a virtual monopoly over the disposal of all the property in Berlin that had been rented or owned by Jews.

After the pogrom on 9 November 1938 an average of 3,000 Jews left Berlin every month, thereby freeing some 1,000 apartments. But even this did little to relieve the housing crisis. The percentage of free apartments rose, but it was only from 0.2 to 0.3 per cent. In January 1939 the Danzig senator Paul Batzer, who had been hauled up in front of a party court for skulduggery and removed from office, was made head of Department II/4 within Speer's organisation, charged with 'the acquisition and letting of Jewish apartments, businesses and industrial plant'. This new agency worked in close cooperation with the city authorities concerned with the 'Aryanisation' of Jewish property and with the agencies charged with finding alternative accommodation for those affected by the demolition programme. In July the GBI reviewed the past six months and concluded: 'Clearing areas on time depends entirely on getting alternative accommodation ready . . . Taking apartments in older buildings from which Jews have been removed has made things much easier and is the reason why some areas have already been emptied.'[112]

The problem of moving large offices, workshops and small businesses was even more complex than finding new apartments for those forced to move. In most instances offices moved into residential housing in the fashionable districts in the west of Berlin, with larger companies building office blocks in the same area. This further reduced the amount of available housing for those who were being forcibly moved. Thousands of valuable housing units were taken over by ministries, the armed forces, the NSDAP and the administrative offices of the armaments industry. All these moves were under the control of the GBI, which showed scant regard for legal norms and current practice. This caused the Ministry of Finance to begin asking some probing questions. The armed forces deeply resented being told by Speer what they could and could not do. They asked which was more important – the needs of the military or rebuilding Berlin, and threatened to take the matter to Hitler for adjudication. However, the outbreak of war presented them with more pressing concerns.

Speer's office decided who got what. Thus when Volkswagen set its sights on three houses in Charlottenburg that were in 'non-Aryan hands' and where most of the fifty-nine tenants were Jews, permission to move in was refused. The German Work Front was also interested in this valuable property but they were turned down as well. It was finally given as an olive branch to the Ministry of Finance, with which Speer needed to remain on good terms.[113]

A housing boom followed the pogrom of 9 November 1938 as Jews were evicted, forced into exile, terrorised or rounded up in concentration camps. Speer's main concern during these frantic months was to make sure that enough residential property remained available for government offices, while major firms hastily gobbled up some of Berlin's most desirable properties at bargain basement prices. The man responsible within the municipal authority for implementing the plans for rebuilding Berlin, Dr Werner Dickmann, wrote to Speer in June 1939: 'It seems to me to be absolutely essential that when we consider these questions, we must ensure that certain residential areas are preserved as such. It is our experience that generally speaking these areas are the same as those from which you decided to expel the Jews.'[114] Certain districts were henceforth designated as residential, to provide homes for non-Jewish tenants evicted to make way for the building of Germania. These areas were known as *Judenrein* (cleansed of Jews). This led to some strange situations. In some instances Speer insisted that Jewish tenants should be left untouched until their apartments were needed for those racial comrades who were to be displaced.

A further complication was that there were no legal means of forcing an 'Aryan' landlord to evict a Jewish tenant. The Berlin NSDAP therefore set about encouraging landlords to do so. The party's local propaganda chief met with some of Speer's principal associates to work out a 'campaign for the forcible evacuation of Jewish apartments that are owned by Aryans'. Paul Batzer pointed out that this would be most unpopular. Since Jews were under such enormous pressure they made ideal tenants. They were anxious not to cause any trouble. They were quiet, paid the rent regularly and made no demands on their landlords for repairs or redecoration. Landlords were anxious to keep them for as long as possible.[115] Batzer also had to deal with the problem that local Nazi officials had their eyes on these desirable apartments, so he had to fight hard with the local party authorities to ensure that they went to evicted tenants from areas designated for reconstruction and not to party notables.

The law concerning 'Rental Conditions for Jews' of 30 April 1939 made Speer's task much easier. Instead of building new apartments for Jews who had been evicted from their homes, they could now be forced to live in houses owned or rented by other Jews – a method known as 'packaging'. Speer circumvented the existing law on tenants' rights by calling upon the Nazi Party to exert pressure on those who were reluctant to move. On 17 May 1939 Speer's senior staff held a meeting at which it was decided that he was to designate areas that were to be 'cleansed of Jews'. Local party officials (*Ortsgruppenleiter*) were to 'apply pressure' to achieve the necessary decontamination. In return for this signal service party officials were to be given any apartments that were in excess of the needs of 'racial comrades' who had been forced out of their homes to make way for the building of Germania.[116]

In order to have a clear indication of the resources available through the 'Aryanisation' of the property market, Speer's organisation created a card index catalogue of all apartments in non-Jewish hands that were rented by Jews, their size and the amount of rent paid. The GBI worked in close conjunction with the local housing authorities to find accommodation for Jews who had been forced out of their apartments to make way for 'Aryans' displaced by the rebuilding project.[117] In May 1939 Mayor Lippert issued a decree 'recommending' that Jews living in buildings not owned by Jews should 'voluntarily' vacate their apartments to make way for those affected by Speer's building plans.[118]

This decree was an admission that there was no legal basis either for evicting Jews or obliging landlords to evict tenants with whom they were perfectly satisfied. The only way to evict Jews legally was for the GBI to use the powers given to him in the Reconstruction Order of 8 February 1939. This made it possible to evict Jewish tenants whose landlords were non-Jewish, to provide accommodation for those who were to be evicted so that Speer's plans for Germania could be realised. Batzer's Section II/4 had already drawn maps of areas that were to be rendered 'cleansed of Jews' by such means. It soon became clear that these measures did not make enough accommodation available to meet the demand. The GBI then called upon the municipal authorities to provide a detailed list of all Jewish tenants in Jewish-owned buildings, not simply in those areas designated to be 'de-Jewed' (*entjüdet*), but throughout Berlin.[119]

On 31 August 1939, on the eve of the invasion of Poland, Speer ordered all building for the new Berlin to stop. His organisation was rendered smaller and leaner. Concentration was now on building for the military so as to keep at least a skeleton operation ready to begin rebuilding Berlin once the war was over. Speer's workforce of 60,000 was rapidly diminished, as men were obliged to work in the armaments industry. Administrators were drafted into the armed services, but planning still went ahead. A considerable amount of stone was still being imported from abroad in readiness for building Germania. It gradually had to be reduced for want of foreign currency, the shortage of manpower and transportation difficulties.[120] It was not until 14 February 1943 that Speer, as part of the total war effort, announced the end of all planning for the rebuilding of Berlin. All those involved in the project were now free to join the Wehrmacht or Organisation Todt, or to work in the armaments industry.[121]

Speer as GBI profited from the persecution of the Jews by the SS, the SA, the Nazi Party and the Berlin Gestapo, and also from the wretched housing conditions imposed upon the Jewish community. He seized the apartments of Jewish tenants, but he was not directly involved in any plans to expel the Jews from Berlin along the lines of the expulsion of Austrian and Czechoslovakian Jews in October or Polish Jews in December 1939. Plans were, however, drawn up in mid-1940 by his Implementation Office to deport Berlin's Jews as soon as the war was over.[122]

Although there could be no question of beginning to build a new capital in wartime, it was still possible to continue moving people out of designated areas. Speer and Hettlage decided that Jews who lived in areas designated for reconstruction should be evicted and effectively left to fend for themselves. The GBI was but one of the rival organisations anxious to extend its real estate holdings. The Reich Railway needed land for its north and south through-stations. The municipal housing authorities were desperately short of accommodation. The National Socialist People's Welfare needed more and more housing as 'catastrophe housing' for those whose homes had been bombed out. Homes also had to be found for the influx of foreign workers needed by the armaments factories. Speer, secure in the knowledge that he had Hitler's full support, soon showed his mastery as an in-fighter. Although he was clearly set on achieving his goals, he knew when to concede a point, when to stand firm and when to keep a low profile. He was ruthless in the pursuit of his objectives and blatantly disregarded both the letter and the spirit of the law. Thus his new rental agreements of mid-January 1940, known as 'Speer Contracts', greatly diminished tenants' rights, leaving them without any legal protection.[123] He knew that in Nazi Germany there was no need to show any deference to due practice or the exigencies of the law. All that mattered was whether or not, in the last resort, Hitler's support was forthcoming. Legal approval of the 'Speer Contracts' was not given until September 1940 with the 'Statutory Order to Change and Supplement Rental Relationships with Jews'.

In early April 1940 Himmler demanded the right to buy a Jewish property in Berlin for his SS, but he met with Speer's blank refusal. Fearful that Himmler was trying to undermine his position in the city, he told the Reichsführer-SS that he had nothing available that was large enough and within his price range. Speer's relationship with the municipal authorities in Berlin was more cordial. They were in full agreement that all Jews should be forced out of property in the centre of the city and that their right of residence should be strictly temporary. It was now no longer a question of removing Jews from areas designated for rebuilding, but also from any desirable part of the city. Goebbels was bent on ensuring that all Berlin's Jews should be expelled. Speer now had a stock of apartments to give to those he wished to favour: the diplomatic corps, Heydrich's colleagues or Goebbels' actors and directors. The majority of Jewish apartments went to such people and were not in areas designated for rebuilding.[124] A confrontation with Himmler was thereby avoided.

On 28 June 1940 Hitler made a four-hour visit to Paris accompanied by Speer, his rival architect Hermann Giesler and his friend the sculptor Arno Breker. Landing at Le Bourget at five in the morning, they drove through the empty streets to visit Garnier's opera house of which Hitler had a remarkably detailed knowledge. Then they drove past the Madeleine to the Place de la Concorde and up the Champs-Elysées. Hitler was singularly unimpressed by the Arc de Triomphe, which was to be dwarfed by his triulmphal arch in Berlin. The party then went to the Trocadero and on to the Palais de Chaillot. Hitler spent some time pondering Napoleon's tomb. He then told Giesler that he had decided that he should design his sarcophagus. Speer's reaction to this deliberate snub was not recorded, but can be imagined. The party then drove past the Louvre and Notre Dame to the Place des Vosges. Another visit was made to the Palais Garnier, this time in daylight. The visit ended in Montmartre where the group stood on the terrace of the Sacré Coeur. They were ignored by the worshippers leaving the basilica.

On their return to Berlin Hitler ordered Speer to begin the rebuilding programme even in wartime. 'Wasn't Paris lovely?' he said. 'But Berlin must be even more beautiful.'[125] Building was also to go ahead in Munich, Linz, Hamburg and the Party Rally grounds in Nuremberg. Speer's men now imagined that the war would be over by September and that they could then set to work in earnest. This soon proved to be an illusion. The GBI was now hard at work building shelters and clearing bomb damage. Speer was thereby able to rebuild and expand his organisation so as to be ready to set to work again once the war was over. A further excuse was now found for evicting Jews: their apartments were needed to house 'racial comrades' left homeless by air raids.

In the summer of 1940 the GBI estimated that there were still between five and seven thousand apartments with Jewish tenants. It was decided that the creation of 'areas cleansed of Jews' should continue by 'de-Jewing' these apartments. The municipal housing authorities were told that any apartments in excess of those needed to house people moved from districts scheduled for demolition could be added to the city's housing pool. The GBI, the city and the NSDAP were in full agreement that once the war was over Berlin would be *Judenrein*. In July 1940 the GBI insisted that all apartments rented by Jews should be under its control. Goebbels' state secretary, Hans Hinkel, discussed with the police the transportation of five hundred Jews per month to

Poland.[126] This figure coincided with Speer's plans for clearing Jews out of certain areas.

Speer met with determined opposition to his plans to rebuild Berlin from the traditional bureaucracy within the Reich Chancellery, the Ministry of Finance and the Ministry of Labour. As a result, in the summer of 1940 there was very little movement, apart from within those areas already designated for reconstruction. But in September Speer embarked on a new campaign, arguing that housing had to be made available for the victims of bomb damage, so that the rehousing programme was now styled as essential to the war effort. At the end of the month he announced a 'campaign for a thousand Jewish apartments' that had Hitler's support. The Jews were to be thrown out and their apartments made available for those who had been rendered homeless by bombing. Speer showed no interest whatsoever in the fate of those affected. His sole concern was to get his clearance programme going again, particularly with regard to the double lot on Lichtensteinallee 3 and 3a, where he planned to build his residence and studio. No wonder then that he sent an urgent note from the Obersalzberg to Dietrich Clahes, the head of his Resettlement Office, asking how the one thousand Jewish apartments programme was going, 'especially clearing Lichtensteinallee'. Clahes promptly ordered that twelve households in the Lichtensteinallee be cleared of their Jewish tenants.[127]

The process of moving people from the Spreebogen – the point near the Reichstag where the river takes a sharp bend – to make room for Speer's monumental Great Hall began in November 1940. In January 1941 Speer sent Clahes an urgent note from the Obersalzberg saying that: 'The Führer is strongly in favour of the plan that I have presented to him suggesting that one thousand Jewish apartments should be made temporarily available for those made homeless by the air raids.'[128] This caused some concern to those living in the designated area. Fritz Wintermantel, a director of the Deutsche Bank, had to be reassured that a commensurate apartment would be made available from the stock of Jewish apartments. The Foreign Office told the Finnish military attaché that: 'It is intended to give tenants in this house Jewish apartments as soon as they are made available.'[129]

Speer had succeeded in giving top priority to preparing the ground for his luxurious residence and studio in the Lichtensteinallee, by disguising it as a wartime measure designed to provide housing for victims of the RAF. As further measures to 'maintain the German people's will to work and withstand' he concentrated on bomb damage removal and the building of air-raid shelters. This enabled him to recruit a workforce of 120,000 men by January 1941, who would be able to set about building Germania as soon as the war was over. As an empire builder of considerable resourcefulness, Speer had thereby managed to maintain a huge organisation in singularly unfavourable circumstances. The rebuilding of Berlin was put on hold, but the GBI still had command over a large workforce that paralleled, but never challenged, Organisation Todt.

Large numbers of prisoners of war were at the ready to clear bomb damage, with specialist craftsmen housed in temporary camps. This workforce was enhanced by the forced labour of four hundred Jews. Until the Battle of Berlin, which began in November 1943, bomb damage was relatively minor, so the municipal authorities enlisted the Jews for garbage removal, promising that were the bomb damage to become severe they would be given back to Speer's organisation. Speer now had tens of thousands of workers, the vehicle fleet *Transportstandarte Speer* and a yearly budget of one billion Reichsmarks. This would have been fully sufficient to meet the requirements for rebuilding the city once the war was over.

On 20 March 1941 representatives of the GBI met with members of the Reichssicherheitshauptamt or Reich Security Main Office (RSHA) and Goebbels' state secretary to discuss the expulsion of the Jews. Goebbels, who had an absolute obsession with rendering the city *Judenrein*, had mentioned the question of Berlin's 60,000 to 70,000 Jews over lunch with Hitler, but true to form the Führer gave him no clear instructions. He concluded that 'a suitable suggestion for evacuation would meet with the Führer's approval'. Adolf Eichmann, who attended the meeting on behalf of the RSHA, said that Hitler had given him written permission to expel 60,000 Jews from Vienna, but that he had only managed to get his hands on 45,000. He therefore made the outrageous suggestion that at least 15,000 of Berlin's Jews could be added to make up the shortfall. Speer had instructed his spokesman to make it clear that there were still 20,000 apartments left with Jewish tenants. He wanted them all to house people rendered homeless by bombing raids as well as those he would eventually have to move to make way for his building programme. Speer and Goebbels' representatives suggested that since there was a shortage of 160,000 to 180,000 apartments in Berlin, Eichmann should draw up a plan for the expulsion of the Jews from the city.[130]

Preparations for the deportation of Jews from Berlin began in August 1941. The GBI gave the police lists of Jewish apartments. The Gestapo ordered the Jewish Cultural Association to hand over information from its housing section. Deportation to Poland, the Baltic States and Belarus began in October. By 2 November 4,200 Berlin Jews had been deported to Łódź.[131] Speer soon had 10,000 more apartments at his disposal. One thousand of these were kept as an 'Emergency Inventory' – later known as 'Blocked Apartments' – as suitable for tenants from areas due for rebuilding, or to be disposed of as Speer saw fit.[132]

Initially Jews who had been evicted from their apartments had to fend for themselves, somehow finding a new apartment in a glutted market or staying with friends. Those who found no alternative were forced into 'Jewish Houses'. On 28 January 1941 Speer's financial expert, Karl Maria Hettlage, chaired a meeting to discuss evicting people from various parts of Berlin to provide housing for those who had lost their homes in air raids. Those attending included representatives from the Main Real Property Office, the Association of Property Owners in Berlin, the local Party District and Heydrich's Reich Security Main Office.[133] Hettlage's GBI Main Office II (Organisation and Economics), whose task it was to coordinate the eviction of Jews, was concerned that the SS would not be able to clear 100 residences within two weeks and a further 250 Jewish residences by the end of February.[134] He was immediately assured otherwise. Dietrich Clahes, GBI's resettlement specialist, insisted that evicted Jews must be placed in housing owned by Jews. The SS was to be provided with lists of such housing. Exceptions were to be made in cases where a spouse was non-Jewish or when there were children in the household.

In April another top-level meeting was convened with representatives of the Ministries of Justice, the Interior and Labour, the Deputy Führer's Office and the GBI to extend the eviction law.[135] Hitherto Jews could only be evicted from property owned by non-Jews. Now it included Jewish-owned property, so that Speer at last had power over the fate of all Berlin's Jews.

Thus by the summer of 1941 all tiresome constraints had been removed. Evicted Jews were simply deported to the death camps in the East. The press, inspired by Goebbels, wrote of this horror: 'In recent days a number of Jews have fled from Germany, leaving their debts behind them.'[136] Internally the expulsion of the Jews was dressed up as an essential war measure. Clahes made this quite clear in a letter to the Minister of the Interior on 20 June 1941: 'The decree to clear 1,000 Jewish apartments in order eventually to provide housing for racial comrades who have been made homeless by air raids has been given orally by the Führer and Reich Chancellor to Professor Speer.' Apartments from which Jews had been evicted were then renovated for tenants whose homes were due to be torn down. The expense was borne by the evicted tenants and the landlords, with the Jewish Cultural Association acting as joint and several debtors. 'Aryan' tenants who were forced to move were found suitable apartments from those seized from Jews, but the empty dwellings on the Lichtensteinallee were not to be included in those to be made available for racial comrades made homeless by the RAF. These were for Speer's exclusive use.[137]

It soon transpired that all the talk about keeping apartments empty, ready to house the homeless, was pure propaganda. In 1941 more than 10,000 people were left homeless after bombing raids, but there were only 16 apartments available in buildings due to be torn down. Temporary shelters were provided in schools and churches; people stayed with relatives and friends or left the city. The situation improved greatly in 1942 because in that year there were very few raids on Berlin. By now there were 1,000 empty apartments ready to house the homeless. But raids in January 1943 left over 11,000 people temporarily homeless. Of these, only 113 moved into 'catastrophe housing'. The raid on 1 March 1943 left 35,000 people without a home, with 6,000 dwellings totally destroyed.

This presented Speer with yet another problem. If bombed-out Berliners were to move into houses that were destined for demolition, how was he to get rid of them once the war was over? A solution to this problem was found by using these buildings as temporary housing for government offices, as hotels and hostels and makeshift accommodation for workers and soldiers. Speer was delighted with this arrangement, which he saw as 'a great relief in that the eviction of individual tenants with all the practical and legal difficulties involved is no longer a problem'.[138]

This was all part of Speer's determined effort to win favour with the military, bureaucracy and industry. He was tireless in providing offices for them, where possible in buildings seized from Jews. He soon enjoyed an excellent reputation in influential circles and was able to forge alliances that were to stand him in good stead when he was appointed Minister of Armaments. Having reconsidered his attitude towards Himmler, he supplied the SS with fifty new apartments per month as Himmler's empire rapidly expanded. Adolf Eichmann was provided with special housing for his expanding Section IVB4 (Matters Concerning Jews and Evacuation) in the SS Reich Security Main Office. Speer obliged Goebbels with ten apartments per month to house artists for his film studios. He kept on good terms with the National Socialist People's Welfare organisation (NSV), and made every effort to meet the requirements of the NSDAP. Office space from sequestered Jewish apartments was provided for the Reich Colonial Office, a vast bureaucratic organisation that ruled over Germany's imaginary colonies.[139] This particular deal was made between the GBI and the Prussian Government through the intermediary of Hans Mohr, an ingenious real estate broker who made handsome profits out of the GBI's rehousing programme.[140] Himmler's new Reich Commission for Strengthening the German Race had to be provided with headquarters adequate for the seriousness of its purpose. Much of this housing came from the five thousand apartments from which Jews had been evicted. The Reich Post took over the offices of the Reich Jewish Association.

Few could resist such rich pickings. Karl Blessing, who along with his minister, Hjalmar Schacht, had resigned from the Ministry of Economics in November 1937, having warned of the dire consequences of the forced armaments programme, also cast a greedy eye on Jewish property.[141] On 28 November 1941 he asked Hettlage not to house Jewish families in Kaiserdamm 82, but to make the property available for Kontinentale Öl AG (Konti Öl), on whose board he served. The GBI obliged by evicting six Jews. Blessing had a brilliant career in the Federal Republic of Germany, becoming president of the Bundesbank or Federal Bank.[142] The fate of the Jews whose eviction he secured is unknown, but can be imagined.

A number of other companies followed the example set by Kontinentale Öl. Senior management went directly to Speer in search of large apartments or villas to rent, lease or buy. Speer, who insisted that such deals should be in strictest confidence, was soon so flooded with requests that by mid-1941 he had to warn that very little was left available. The GBI began to operate like a shady real estate operator. Speer had pre-emption rights on a large number of properties designated for public housing, many of which had been taken from Jews. Much of this property was sold to private parties, using dubious accounting methods to disguise any hint of corruption. Many influential figures profited from these attractive deals and often expressed their gratitude to Speer, the consummate networker. He undertook a number of special favours for Gerhard Engel, Hitler's adjutant at OKW. On one such occasion the power-conscious Speer wrote to the heavily indebted Engel: 'if your three protégés can't shut their traps, I'll order their houses to be demolished, so as to leave them once again with nowhere to live'.[143]

There were some who had qualms about moving into apartments from which the owner or tenant had been forcibly ejected. Rommel asked Speer to provide housing for his newly-wed adjutant, Baron Melchior von Schlippenbach, who was taken to see an apartment by a city official. He turned down the offer when he realised that it was occupied by a Jewish family designated for eviction. When an outraged von Schlippenbach reported this to Rommel he was told that his friend Speer could not possibly have known of this.[144]

The demand for housing soon became so great that Speer felt obliged to call a halt. By late 1941 he had turned down numerous applications, insisting that he only had housing available for people being moved from houses due to be demolished, and that on Hitler's orders he had to keep a large number of apartments free for the victims of air raids. He found it necessary to warn Bormann to keep his hands off Jewish property in Berlin, reminding him that Hitler had placed Jewish property at his disposal and that it was intended that it be kept ready for those left homeless as a result of bomb damage.[145] On 26 January 1942 Speer wrote to Rosenberg, who had put in a request for fifteen apartments, saying that this would not be possible because the expulsion of Jews from Berlin had been held up 'until about April due to technical problems with the railways'.[146]

One thing was certain: from now on if one was not in the GBI's good books and if one had no quid pro quo to offer, the chances of getting housing in Berlin were extremely slim. The situation was rendered more difficult when Speer became Minister of Armaments in February 1942. Much of the available office space was swallowed up as his ministry rapidly expanded. Most of the

Jewish apartments were now unavailable – even to the most illustrious. Thus Dr Joachim Pfaffenberger, a metallurgist with close links to the armaments industry and who was on the board of AEG, was unable to get his hands on a large house at Witzlebenplatz 6, which had been divided up into three Jewish apartments. When he first made this request it was pointed out that only two of the Jewish tenants had been evicted, but that he could renew the application when the third party was removed. When this happened Clahes told him that his request was denied, because the GBI needed large apartments for special purposes. The married couple Benno and Guste Pakscher, aged eighty-three and seventy-three, the tenants of this third apartment, were rendered homeless to make way for one Paul Hoffmann, who had been forced to move from his lodgings at Lichtensteinallee 3 and 3a to make way for Speer's studio and residence.[147]

Methods of eviction varied. Some Jews were thrown out on the street without warning. In other cases the Jewish Cultural Association was involved. In one such instance Speer told the Association to evict Jewish tenants from a thousand apartments owned by 'Aryans', ostensibly to make room for the victims of bombing raids. Those evicted were to become subtenants in Jewish apartments.[148] Not a single one of these apartments was reserved for 'catastrophe relief'. Almost all were used to accommodate people evicted from houses Speer intended to demolish. In general, evictions were carried out in close cooperation with the GBI, the municipal housing authorities, the NSDAP's District Office, the SS, the Berlin Police and the Ministry of the Interior.

The GBI's list of the number of Jews evicted from these apartments was greater than the number that the SS Reich Security Main Office (RSHA) had foreseen for transportation to Łódź in September 1941. The second wave of transportation in January 1942, to Lublin, Warsaw and Chełmno, was also oversubscribed. The GBI handed over some 10,000 Jews to the Gestapo. There is no evidence that Speer and his colleagues showed the slightest sign of concern or even interest as to their fate. They cooperated fully with the Gestapo, handing over all their meticulously gathered information so as to speed up the process of eviction and deportation, the latter cynically called 'emigration'. The dubious legal basis for the Gestapo's seizure of the assets of Jewish Berliners was the law on the seizure of Communist assets of 26 May 1933, the law on the seizure of the assets of enemies of the state of 14 July 1933 and the Führer's decree on the appropriation of the assets of enemies of the state of 29 May 1941. Jews were thus stripped of all their possessions and murdered because they were defined as 'enemies of the state', thereby piling falsehood on perversity. Their fate was sealed as a result of eviction orders, given without any warning, by the GBI. Speer was thereby a key player in the murder of thousands of Jewish Berliners.

Jews were deported to relieve an already severe housing shortage in Berlin. Relief was quickly found as 10,000 were sent to ghettos in eastern Europe, 35,000

to the death camps in Poland and 15,000 of those considered 'privileged' to the
transfer camp at Theresienstadt. Hundreds committed suicide. Others ended
up in forced labour camps, where more often than not they were worked to
death. When the deportations began in 1941 there were 64,720 Jews in Berlin
'listed by religion' and 73,842 'listed by race'.[149] Precious few survived. Most of
those that did were Jews living in mixed marriages or 'half-breeds'. They were
isolated, humiliated and used as forced labour. An order from the RSHA that
all those in mixed marriages should be sent to Theresienstadt could not
be carried out due to chaotic transport conditions and popular protest.[150] In a
final irony, Speer's enthusiasm for deporting Jews as GBI was later to run
counter to his interests as Minister of Armaments. Officials of his ministry
voiced frequent complaints that Jews, who were doing useful work in the armaments industry, were being deported, even though adequate replacements were
not yet available.[151]

Although there can be no doubt that Goebbels, ably supported by Berlin's
duplicitous police chief, Count von Helldorf, was the driving force behind the
persecution of the Jews in Berlin, their deportation was in part a result of the
need to find alternative accommodation for tenants evicted to make way for
Speer's grandiose plans for rebuilding Berlin as Germania, or to find desirable
accommodation for those he wished to favour. Speer's organisation coordinated the seizure, exploitation and allocation of Jewish assets after the pogrom
of 9 November 1938. All the apartments of those Jews who had been forcibly
evicted were left in the hands of the GBI's organisation, which thereby effectively controlled a critical section of the housing market.

By the time Speer was appointed Minister of Armaments on 8 February
1942 his plans to rebuild Berlin had created a nightmare. In close collaboration
with the SS, he ruthlessly exploited the labour of concentration camp inmates
in quarries, brickyards and factories producing building materials. They
worked under appalling conditions and the mortality rate was shockingly high.
Speer made thousands of Jewish families homeless, most of whom were handed
over to the Gestapo to be shipped to what was delicately described as 'the East'.
He continued this grim work while Minister of Armaments until October
1942, by which time there were precious few Jews left to deport, apart from
those slaving away in his armaments factories. They too were soon deported.

At the end of October 1942 Clahes proudly listed the achievements of the
Inspector General of Buildings with regard to 'resettlement matters'. By then
23,765 Jewish apartments had been seized and by 15 November 1942 75,000
people would have been 'resettled'. Many of their apartments had been given to
seriously wounded soldiers and men who had been awarded either the Knight's
Cross or the Iron Cross First Class.[152] There were no longer any apartments available for the Nazi elite or for industrial and banking magnates because, as Speer

wrote to Rosenberg on 12 November 1942: 'I have achieved the aims that I set.'[153] On Hitler's orders, Adolf Eichmann dealt with the remaining Jewish Berliners. In the raid of 26 February 1943, later known as the 'Factory Action', some 8,000 Jews working in armaments factories in Berlin were rounded up and deported to the death camps. Half of these managed to escape, much to Goebbels' disappointment and disgust. His diary entry for 2 March 1943 reads: 'Unfortunately once again in the best circles, particularly among intellectuals, our Jewish policy is not understood and some even support the Jews. As a result our move was betrayed ahead of time, so that a lot of Jews slipped through our fingers.'[154]

Soon a man of power and considerable wealth, Speer felt that the elegant but relatively small house in the Schopenhauerstraße in Berlin-Schlachtensee that he had built in 1935 was no longer up to his standards. Although he had bought a hunting lodge in Ostertal in the Allgäu, Hitler insisted that his court favourite now move into a house on the Obersalzberg that had formerly belonged to the Bechstein family. He subsequently built a large new house with a studio nearby, where the family lived close to Hitler's Berghof, which was completed in May 1937. Speer, Göring and Bormann were the only members of a select group of Obersalzbergers living within the 1,730-acre security zone around Hitler's mountain retreat.[155] It was here that his family lived, but Speer was seldom at home. He was either in Berlin or at the Berghof, where he was part of Hitler's inner circle. He had no time for family life.

Speer now let his house in Berlin and rented a magnificent 'Aryanised' villa owned by the movie star Gustav Fröhlich in Schwanenwerder, a luxurious island in the Havel that was the most expensive property in the German version of Monopoly.[156] It had been the playground of Jewish high society, their properties bought at bargain prices by the likes of Goebbels, Hitler's physician Theodor Morell and the Reich's Women's Leader Gertrud Scholtz-Klink. Speer also profited from the 'Aryanisation' of Jewish property in Berlin. In 1938, just prior to the pogrom of 9 November, he joined this illustrious group of property owners by acquiring a highly desirable plot of land at Inselstraße 50. It belonged to Marie-Anne von Goldschmidt-Rothschild, a remarkable woman best known for her correspondence with the poet Rainer Maria Rilke between 1914 and 1918. She needed to sell in order to pay the tax levied on those who wished to emigrate. Although the price of 150,000 Reichsmarks was ludicrously low for such a fine property, it was a substantial sum for a young man at the outset of his career and is an indication of the enormous wealth Speer had already accumulated. A plot was even reserved for him to build a house for Hitler, but nothing came of this and it may be for this reason that Speer decided to sell the Goldschmidt-Rothschild property. He kept a boathouse on the island and also built an air-raid shelter there.

Shortly after his appointment as Minister of Armaments Speer bought a substantial property at Altranft near Bad Freienwalde in the Oderbruch, near his friend Arno Breker's studio, for which he paid 250,000 Reichsmarks. He designed a grotesque pseudo-mediaeval castle for this property that was to be built after the 'Final Victory' at an estimated cost of 2.5 million Reichsmarks.[157] His son Albert was horrified when he saw the drawings in the archives in Munich.[158] In March 1943 Göring presented Speer with 250 acres of forest that belonged to the Prussian government to complete the estate. The Ministry of Finance gave special permission to free this transaction from all the usual taxes. Its value is unknown, because Speer refused to answer the Ministry of Finance's request for a tax return on 1 January 1944.[159]

On 1 September 1943 Speer moved into a large house in the Lichtensteinallee, which had been cleared of its mostly Jewish tenants. The property, which also contained his studio, was renovated at government expense for the staggering sum of 1,673,631 Reichsmarks.[160] He did not live there for long. On 22 November it was totally destroyed in a bombing raid.[161]

In 1943 he sold the Schwanenwerder lot to the German Reich for 389,000 Reichsmarks, thereby pocketing a substantial profit. The property was returned to the rightful owner in 1952. It was sold ten years later to the Steglitz district authority for use as a public park. As part of the post-war compensation process Speer was ordered to pay the difference between the purchase price of 150,000 Reichsmarks and the sale to the Reich for 389,506 Reichsmarks – 239,506 Reichsmarks – to be paid on the basis of 10 Reichsmarks to 1 Deutschmark. Speer thus owed a mere 23,950.60 Deutschmarks on what had been a windfall profit. His friend Rudolf Wolters somehow managed to reduce this to 10,000 Deutschmarks, which was paid without a murmur to avoid any adverse publicity.[162]

In October 1966 several former members of the Gestapo in Berlin were charged with having been accessories to the murder of Berlin's Jews. This was an alarm signal to Speer, who had recently been released from jail. Fear of 'witch-hunts' against so-called 'desktop murderers' had already prompted Speer's amanuensis, Rudolf Wolters, to delete certain compromising passages concerning his activities as GBI from the diary known as the 'Speer Chronicle'. The trial went ahead without any mention being made of the organisation whose instructions these Gestapo officers were following. The offences came under a statute of limitations for Nazi crimes and resulted in the two officers being cleared of all charges. Another Gestapo officer was charged with being an accessory to murder in April 1971, but it was argued that deportation was not 'a concrete act of encouragement' to commit murder.[163] Whether the numerous suicides resulting from Speer's eviction orders would have been similarly considered was never considered.

Speer made a clumsy attempt to disguise his role in the expulsion and murder of Berlin's Jews in his book *Der Sklavenstaat* (Infiltration) by claiming that as he drove to work along the AVUS – a stretch of Autobahn that was often used for motor races – every day he saw large numbers of Jews boarding a train heading east from the Nicolassee station.[164] This sight gave him 'an uncomfortable feeling. Perhaps I was conscious of grim procedures.'[165] In fact the transport for Jews to Łódź, Kowno, Minsk, Riga, Lublin, Chełmno and Warsaw between mid-October 1941 and April 1942 was from the Grünewald station. This did not occur on a daily basis, but on thirteen separate occasions. It is impossible to see the Nicolassee station from the AVUS. Speer admitted that 75,000 Jews were deported from Berlin, but had the gall to point out that this began 'under my predecessor Todt'. He made no mention of the fact that it was he, as Inspector General of Buildings, who decided their fate. On the contrary he attributes this to Goebbels' determination to render Berlin 'cleansed of Jews' or *Judenrein*.[166]

Fully confident that the Wehrmacht would soon bring the Soviet Union to its knees, Speer devoted himself enthusiastically to dreaming up and planning the remodelling and expansion of towns in Russia and the Baltic States and the foundation of German towns to be built in the conquered eastern territories. Three days after his appointment as Minister of Armaments, in his capacity as Inspector General of Buildings, he wrote to Alfred Rosenberg, the Reich Minister for the Occupied Eastern Territories, outlining his views.[167] The plan, all part of General Plan East, is so divorced from reality that it is extremely hard to take it seriously. By contrast Himmler's crazed vision of German colonisation in the East seems positively modest.[168]

The new towns, to be known as 'The Führer's Foundations', were to avoid uniformity and to be designed with future expansion in mind. Since German cities are so diverse, Speer thought it best to model these on those that already existed. Thus the likes of a new Stuttgart, Augsburg, Nuremberg, Hamburg, Cologne, Bremen, Königsberg, Danzig, Leipzig, Dresden or Vienna could be built in the East, creating a series of twinned towns and cities closely linked to the originals and reflecting their 'significant aspects'. According to Speer's own calculations this would provide accommodation for 7,852,000 people at a cost of 785 billion Reichsmarks. No thought was given to where these people were to come from or how this could ever have been financed. General Plan East estimated a modest 14.5 billion Reichsmarks for its extensive building projects in the East.[169] Hitler endorsed this plan and in September 1942 he gave his approval to Speer's 'Proposals for the Foundation of New German Towns and the Expansion of German Towns in the East'.[170]

Hitler and Speer had quite different ideas about what a German town should look like. Hitler's ideal was the picture-postcard medieval idyll of a Dinkelsbühl or Rothenburg ob der Tauber, with their narrow, winding streets and half-timbered buildings. Speer was more of a modernist, preferring a carefully planned geometrical layout, broad streets and adequate provision for motor vehicles. The first example of a new German town was built at Usedom for those working at the rocket research station at Peenemünde. Speer made some preliminary sketches and laid down a set of principles for the new town, but handed the task over to a young architect, Heinrich Eggerstedt, assisted by another architect, Walter Schlempp, the head of Baugruppe or Construction Group Schlempp that was under Speer's aegis as GBI.[171]

Another model town was 'Town X for 20,000 inhabitants', the details of which were published in the magazine *Baukunst* (Architecture) in November 1941.[172] This was designed by Speer and Eggerstedt as an architectural expression of the National Socialist racial community. A 'People's Hall' on the lakeside stood at the end of the central axis that led to a circular forum, thence to a settlement of single family homes on the edge of a forest. Further details of future towns in the East are contained in the *Building Handbook for Construction in the East*, published in 1943 under the auspices of Heinrich Himmler and Albert Speer.[173] Future cities in eastern Europe were to be exclusively inhabited by Germans. There was no place here for the 'racially foreign'. In other words, such people were either to be evicted or killed.[174] Himmler and Speer were living in a world of fantasy and murderous intent, but after Stalingrad there was mercifully little chance that these plans could ever be realised.

Speer's men were also involved in planning for the future of Litzmannstadt (Łódź). The city, the third largest in Poland, is about 135 kilometres south-west of Warsaw. In September 1939 a mere 10 per cent of the population was of German origin. The town was extremely crowded, with an average of 5.8 persons per room. There was a wholly inadequate sewage system and rudimentary water mains. The plan was first to move industry out of the city centre, then to build a settlement for 25,000 Germans to the west of the main railway station. Eventually the centre would be rebuilt, the Polish population having been 'removed'.[175] The city had a population of 665,000, of whom 223,000 were Jewish. How they were to be 'removed' was a matter to be decided by Himmler's Rasse- und Siedlungshauptamt-SS or Main Office for Race and Settlement. On 10 December 1939 Friedrich Uebelhoer, the District Governor, ordered the 164,000 Jews who had the misfortune to have remained in the city, with the exception of those that were considered strong enough to work, to be crammed together into a ghetto. This was to be only a temporary measure. 'The goal must be to cauterise this pestilential tumour.'[176] Thus from the outset Speer, his team of planners and architects were intimately involved in the 'Final Solution'.

CHAPTER FOUR

THE STATE OF GERMAN ARMAMENTS
IN 1942

D RAWING ON INFORMATION gleaned from his work on the US Strategic
Bombing Survey, John Kenneth Galbraith published an article in 1945
attempting to explain why Germany had lost the war.[1] His answer was very
simple. Germany had been slow to mobilise industry for wartime production.
Before the war the books had been cooked to create the impression that the
country was armed to the teeth. In 1940 Britain outstripped Germany in the
production of both tanks and aircraft, and did so again in 1941. Civilian
consumption in Germany dropped a mere 10 per cent in 1940 and again in
1941. With the fall of France the leadership, imagining that the war was already
won, apart from some mopping-up operations in Britain and the Soviet Union,
cut back on armaments production. Confident that Operation Barbarossa would
be over within four months, no preparations were made for a lengthy campaign.
Even though the Wehrmacht was meeting with ferocious opposition in freezing
conditions, armaments production was further reduced. By December 1941,
30 per cent fewer weapons were produced than in July the previous year. With
their army halted before Moscow and Operation Barbarossa in ruins, the
Germans, under the forceful leadership of Albert Speer, at last began the serious
business of war production. Output increased in spite of Allied bombing, but
even so civilian consumption continued to provide for a comfortable standard
of living, with a mere 20 per cent reduction from the pre-war level.

   This plausible account was to be reinforced in Speer's skilfully trimmed
memoirs, as well as by the testimony of a number of his closest associates.[2] In
their version Hitler, mindful of the disastrous collapse of morale on the home
front in 1918, which resulted in the army being 'stabbed in the back', opted for
a 'civilian economy in wartime' and a strategy of *Blitzkrieg* – limited campaigns
with limited resources. As a result Germany was inadequately prepared for the
invasion of the Soviet Union, and Speer could claim that had he been in charge
of armaments from the outset of the war he would have provided the Wehrmacht

with the tools to do the job.[3] Speer's chief statistician, Rolf Wagenführ, produced a mass of figures to reinforce the Speer legend. They seemed to confirm the assessment of the United States Strategic Bombing Survey.[4]

In order to test Speer's claim to have orchestrated an 'armaments miracle' it is essential to examine the situation that he inherited on being appointed Minister of Armaments in February 1942. The German economy had made rapid progress after Hitler's appointment as chancellor in January 1933. The situation was in some ways analogous to the 'economic miracle' (*Wirtschaftswunder*) after the currency reform in 1948. A booming economy resulted in full employment within three years, but the question remained as to what caused this rapid rate of growth. Was it due to deliberate measures to stimulate the economy and to create jobs, or was it the result of massive expenditure on armaments?[5] Was it a case of 'guns before butter' or the result of Keynesian pump priming, which had been initiated before the Nazis came to power?[6]

The programme for work creation, initiated by the state secretary in the Ministry of Finance, Fritz Reinhardt, only came into effect on 1 June 1933. Thus the sharp increase in employment in the first three-quarters of 1933 was due to pump priming by the Papen and Schleicher governments.[7] A further stimulus to growth was that on account of the depression prices for raw materials and semi-finished products were falling.[8]

From the very outset the regime decided to spend staggering sums on a massive rearmament programme. This contributed decisively to the reduction of unemployment, but it also caused a dramatic increase in the national debt. It is not quite clear when the decision was taken to commit 35 billion Reichsmarks to armaments over an eight-year period, because the Wehrmacht documented the rearmament process retrospectively in 1938. It was probably at a cabinet meeting held on 8 June 1933.[9]

By 1935 the stimulus measures of the Brüning and Schleicher governments were no longer applied. Full employment was now largely due to a marked increase in armaments production. The Nazis' 'economic miracle' was thus conceived on an unsound basis. It threatened international stability, resulted in a chronic lack of foreign exchange, led to deficit spending on an alarming scale, made industry reluctant to make further investments, and cut Germany off from the world market.[10]

Nevertheless the ill effects of large-scale military Keynesianism on consumers have often been exaggerated.[11] Per capita real consumption expressed as an index number was 88 in 1933, rose to 100 in 1936 and to 108 in 1939. It did not fall back to the 1936 level until 1942.[12] The industrial production of consumer goods followed the same trend. Taking 1936 as 100, it rose to 110 in 1939 and dropped back to 100 in 1942. The Nazis were thus able to produce 'as much butter as necessary, as many guns as possible'.[13]

Spending on rearmament rapidly got out of control. The initial plan envisaged spending at the rate of slightly over 4.3 billion Reichsmarks per year over an eight-year period in order to build a military force strong enough to launch a credible offensive. By 1935 expenditure had reached almost 6 billion Reichsmarks and was bound to rise even higher as France, Britain and the Soviet Union began to rearm in response. The military, certain of Hitler's enthusiastic support, started clamouring for modern weaponry. The War Minister Werner Blomberg went on a wild spending spree, deliberately ignoring all budgetary restraints.[14]

As soon as what the Nazis called the 'Liberation of the Rhineland' was successfully completed in 1936, with German troops occupying the demilitarised Rhineland in defiance of the Treaty of Versailles, Hitler appointed Hermann Göring, Schacht's most powerful opponent, to take charge of foreign exchange and the import of raw materials. Hitler outlined the new approach in a memorandum announcing a Four-Year Plan.[15] He argued that Germany's economic problems could only be solved by war and the conquest of 'living space' (*Lebensraum*) to secure adequate supplies of food and raw materials. War was in any case essential because Bolshevism, behind which stood world Jewry, had to be destroyed or the Judeo-Bolshevik front would cause 'the final destruction, in other words the annihilation of the German people'. The armed forces and the economy had therefore to be ready for war within four years. This was a clear signal to the military to abandon all restraint and they acted accordingly. The army, restricted to a hundred thousand men by the Treaty of Versailles, was to expand to over four million within four years, but it was still an old-fashioned force. It was to march on foot, its materiel moved by hundreds of thousands of horses. Expenditure on tanks was still relatively small, but the projected total cost was nevertheless astronomical.

The Four-Year Plan created more problems than it solved. The autarchy programme required colossal investments in what were unlikely ever to be economically viable projects. Shortages of steel were such that it had to be strictly rationed. The chronic dearth of foreign exchange had to be addressed, were the rearmament programme ever to reach its goals. Even the most extreme proponents of autarchy and National Socialist economics had to admit that bitter reality simply had to be faced. Exports had to be boosted by the Schachtian method of generous subsidies combined with the allocation of more steel to export industries than to armaments and the Four-Year Plan combined.[16] This was effective, due largely to an upswing in world trade, but only because the military were forced to accept drastic cuts. The army warned that it would not be able to meet its target of reaching full fighting strength for the foreseeable future. The Luftwaffe talked of cutting aircraft production by 25 per cent.

It soon became apparent that the shortage of steel meant that the rearmament goals set in 1936 could not possibly be met. Since it would be years before the Hermann Göring Works began large-scale production, the only solution was to lift the restriction on steel production, but this in turn would involve increasing imports, thereby placing an intolerable strain on the meagre foreign currency reserves. Faced with this intractable situation Hitler, who once said that his only call was to go for broke, decided in 1938 to intensify tensions both at home and abroad.

The annexation of Austria in March 1938, known as the *Anschluss*, was the first dramatic act of the new course. Shortly thereafter Hitler began to put pressure on Czechoslovakia by heightening tensions in the Sudetenland. Hitler fanned the crisis throughout the summer until Chamberlain and Daladier sold out their ally at Munich in September. On 21 October 1938 Hitler, having been given the Sudetenland at Munich, issued orders for the 'destruction of the remainder of Czechoslovakia'.

Hitler's speech to the Reichstag on 30 January 1939 is best known for his promise that: 'if the Jews that control finance in Europe and elsewhere are once again successful in plunging the nations into a world war, the result will not be the bolshevisation of the earth and thus the victory of Jewry, but the annihilation of the Jewish race in Europe.' Amid this vile tirade he made it quite clear that the only solution to the problems facing the German economy, especially the dependence on imports, was the extension of Germany's *Lebensraum*. To this end the Four-Year Plan had to be intensified and the reserves of labour fully exploited.[17] War was thus designed as a pre-emptive strike against Jewish financiers as well as to ensure that Germany's import and foreign exchange problems, caused in large part by armaments, were finally solved.

On 23 May 1939 Hitler told the heads of the armed services of his intention to attack Poland, warning that this could very well lead to a war that would last for ten to fifteen years. The strategy was now to transform the economy to meet the requirements of a lengthy war. The army argued that they were far from being prepared for a new world war, to which Hitler retorted that a swift campaign against Poland would provide the additional resources required to fight a full-scale war. General Thomas at the Armed Forces High Command (OKW) had already used the argument that the defeat of Poland would relieve the problem of the shortage of raw materials. This was also the view of a number of leading industrialists.[18]

The German-Soviet Commercial Agreement of 19 August 1939 and the Molotov-Ribbentrop Pact four days later encouraged Walther Funk to make the extravagant claim to Hitler that the economy was fully prepared for any eventuality in the next two years, by which time the Four-Year Plan would have reached its armaments goal. General Thomas rightly considered Funk's attitude to be utterly irresponsible. He felt that Germany was not sufficiently armed in depth and that the economy was nowhere near to being on a war footing. He now argued that war should be avoided until the country was prepared for every eventuality.[19] The navy and the Luftwaffe were equally pessimistic, but Keitel at OKW was not one to stand in Hitler's way. Hitler was well aware of the risks involved. He knew all too well that the time factor was not on Germany's side, announcing at the onset of the war that Germany could only hang on for a few years, adding that Göring agreed with him.[20] He used this argument to throw caution to the winds, opting to launch a series of offensives in rapid succession before his enemies brought their massive economic advantage to bear. It was a desperate gamble that very nearly paid off.

In spite of the distortion of the peacetime economy by an emphasis on armaments, historians are reluctant to speak of a 'wartime economy' until Speer took command. Various alternatives have been mooted such as a 'peace-time economy in wartime' or '*blitzkrieg* economy'. It was argued that Hitler was determined to ease the burden on the home front by rapid campaigns with limited resources and that this *blitzkrieg* strategy was a means to escape from the bottlenecks caused by a 'wartime economy in peacetime' and relieve the pressure on the population by giving them the fruits of a swift predatory war.[21] These ideas soon came under attack when it was argued that since the Nazis thought in terms of a long war, from the outset they strove for the total mobi-lisation of the economy.[22] Indeed it soon became questionable whether the term *blitzkrieg* had any meaning whatsoever.[23]

In the euphoric atmosphere after the swift defeat of Poland the ideologues' arguments were strengthened, as the need for rigorous controls no longer seemed such a pressing concern. Further confusion arose from Hitler's uncer-tainty as to whether an attack on France would get bogged down in a lengthy campaign or result in another swift victory. The end result was a proliferation of power centres and decision-making bodies. Old structures collapsed amid a confusing search for political direction, resulting in disorganisation and waste-fulness characteristic of the mounting polycentric tendencies typical of the Third Reich.[24]

Hitler persistently demanded all-out rearmament, regardless of the consumer sector, immediate needs or long-term projections. He arbitrarily picked 1 October 1941 as the date when armaments production was to peak. General Thomas argued that for this to be possible a militarised command economy that paid no heed to the exigencies of a post-war economy was absolutely imperative. For this to be possible a powerful person had to be put in command. He would have to be assisted by a committee comprising leading figures in the military and the relevant civilian ministries. Thomas considered Göring to be the ideal man for the job. Industry would then be placed under strict military control. Hitler rejected this suggestion out of hand, realising that it was an attempt to create an all-powerful armaments minister. Instead he abolished Funk's office of Chief Plenipotentiary for Economics and gave Göring additional authority over the war economy. The General Council of the Four-Year Plan was thereby expanded to include representatives of the military and relevant ministries. It was a stop-gap measure that solved nothing.[25]

It was soon obvious that these new arrangements would not deliver the goods. Göring therefore sought to be appointed Minister of Armaments, but Hitler turned down the suggestion, repeating his conviction that industry should be the province of industrialists and those sympathetic to them. Ruhr barons might shower the Field Marshal with lavish gifts, but they resented his despotic meddling and self-important posturing. The ineffectual Funk, Minister of Economics and president of the Reichsbank, was much less of a threat. He stood for private enterprise, whereas Göring with his Four-Year Plan was the personification of a command economy combined with the nebulous Nazi concept of an 'economic racial community'.[26] Hitler was opposed to further centralisation and bureaucratisation, whether in the hands of the Four-Year Plan or the Ministry of Economics.[27] This to him smacked of Bolshevism. Nazi ideology also favoured a decentralised economy that strengthened small businesses. The wellbeing of the butcher, the baker and the candlestick-maker was an integral part of 'German socialism', as against the selfish interests of the 'plutocrats' on the Rhine and Ruhr. A National Socialist war economy should thus be based on small enterprises, not encourage big business to make windfall profits and drive their rivals to the wall. But smaller companies saw no reason to switch over to armaments production – a lengthy and expensive undertaking with uncertain prospects – unless they were forced to do so. They knew that a war economy meant that they would either be forced to close down or would become fully dependent on the big industrial combines. They had significant support within the Nazi Party.

Neither the Ministry of Economics nor the military wanted to be held responsible for creating a command economy, thereby opening themselves to the charge of 'Bolshevism'. It was not until 3 February 1940 that Göring, having discussed the matter with Hitler, wrote to Funk suggesting that non-essential sectors of the economy should be diverted to war work. The emphasis was to be on converting existing capacity rather than building new facilities.[28] The Ministry of Economics promptly sent instructions to its regional offices calling for 'drastic' action in this regard; but this was empty rhetoric. Fearing fierce resistance, Funk was reluctant to take further action. He knew that businesses would appeal to local party officials, who would sympathise with their plight. On 21 February he ordered that a comprehensive review of non-essential production be completed by 26 March 1940. This was an impossible undertaking, not least because no clear criteria had been established as to what constituted 'non-essential'.

A number of firms were forced to close or were in serious difficulties because of a harsh winter, inadequate transport facilities and coal shortages, but this did not help the military. Often the local Nazi Party officials came to the rescue, or things were kept going by shortening the working week. By this time there was general agreement that something drastic had to be done to radically improve the output of materiel, but there was widespread reluctance to act. Most important of all, during the 'Phoney War' there was no sense of urgency, as there had been for the Germans by 1917, when they had established a mechanism for closing down or amalgamating inessential firms. Even the prospect of a lengthy and bloody campaign in the West was insufficient incentive for them to take decisive action.

There was one man who completely transformed the situation by establishing a viable structure that made possible a significant increase in armaments production. Fritz Todt, an engineer specialising in road building, had been appointed Generalinspektor für das deutsche Straßenwesen or Inspector General of German Roads immediately on Hitler's appointment as chancellor. In 1938 he founded Organisation Todt (OT), made up of government firms, private companies and the Reichsarbeitsdienst or German Labour Service. The latter was a military auxiliary organisation in which all young men were required to do six months of compulsory service. OT's main task was to build the Westwall or Siegfried Line that ran from the Dutch border at Kleve to the Swiss frontier at Weil am Rhein. Todt completed this gigantic project with exceptional speed and efficiency. From his experience in building the Autobahns he firmly believed in the principle of 'industrial self-determination' (Selbstverantwortung der Industrie), in other words letting private industry make decisions independently within an overall plan. It was a system that had proved its worth under Walther Rathenau during the First World War. The free exchange of technical information, the division of labour between different factories, rationalisation and standardisation led to a doubling of production using the same amount of industrial plant and without any increase in labour costs. Industry was assured that the system was to be strictly limited to the duration of the war.[29] Todt thereby won many friends and supporters in the private sector. Having joined the Nazi Party in January 1922, he was one of the oldest of the 'Old Warriors' and was particularly close to Hitler. This gave him considerable power and influence within the party.[30] He also enjoyed the respect of his professional colleagues.

In the early stages of the war Todt used his closeness to Hitler to free himself from the control of the military, thereby ensuring that he had adequate supplies of manpower and raw materials for his various projects. He sided with the entrepreneurs, managers and technicians who were critical of the military procurement offices, whose officers mostly lacked technical know-how and whose military training left them unable to fathom the foreign culture of the business world. Todt fed Hitler with complaints about the military procurement offices. Hitler, who was locked in battle with the army over a number of issues, lent him a willing ear. Todt soon got the upper hand over Robert Ley, a chronic alcoholic and murderous anti-Semite, who was leader of the German Work Front and Organisational Head of the NSDAP. He tried to strengthen the party's influence over industry, but he was no match for Todt in the ensuing struggle for power and influence.[31] Hitler gave Ley the task of formulating a comprehensive programme of social insurance that was to relieve much of the hardship among 'racial comrades' caused by wartime sacrifices. Ley's ambitious schemes alarmed the business sector, which regarded his ideas as suspiciously socialist.

In February 1940 Göring appointed Todt General Inspector for Special Duties in the Four-Year Plan or Generalinspektor für Sonderaufgaben im Vierjahresplan, with the task of finding ways to save metals.[32] This gave him considerable influence over the military's armaments programme, but for him to consolidate his position he needed Hitler's full support. The situation was advantageous. The military saw Todt as a villain who was hoarding raw materials for his construction projects that were needed for armaments. They demanded that his allocations should be halved. Todt told Hitler that the section of the Westwall he was building near Saarbrücken could not be completed because the military refused to cooperate. Hitler, who at that time was obsessed with defences and heavy artillery, was outraged. Alarming reports that the French armaments industry was roaring ahead caused him to fear that his forthcoming offensive might get stuck, resulting in a static war in which Todt's defensive emplacements would play a critical role. Hitler blamed the complex bureaucratic apparatus of the Army Armaments Office for the sluggish performance in the armaments sector. He now began to think in terms of appointing a civilian as Minister of Armaments and blamed himself for rejecting the idea the previous autumn.[33] When Keitel heard from Göring that Hitler was thinking in these terms he suggested that the future ministry should be within OKW and that General Thomas was the obvious man for the job, but Hitler had already made up his mind.

Keitel and Thomas soon recovered from the initial shock at the suggestion that Todt be appointed Minister of Armaments. They fondly imagined that Todt would concentrate of the technical problems of production, while they could continue making demands on industry as they saw fit. They hoped that Todt would fully respect their needs and would work closely with the military procurement offices. They were therefore highly alarmed when, at a meeting in the chancellery to discuss the functions of a new ministry, it was established that Todt was not only to have overall responsibility for munitions production but was also to be responsible for weapons development. The military's hopes that Todt would be obliged to cooperate closely with them were dashed when Hitler ordered that the new minister was to be fully independent.[34] The military were appalled, the industrialists delighted. Todt was sympathetic to the industrialists' demands to have a greater say in how contracts were awarded. He endorsed their due concern for economies of scale. He agreed to reconsider how profits were to be calculated. He promised to end the price freeze and even offered some fiscal relief.

Todt was officially appointed Reichsminister für Bewaffnung und Munition or Reich Minister for Armaments and Munitions on 17 May 1940, one week after the campaign in the West began. It was an impressive title, but although he was responsible for munitions in all three services, he was only responsible for the army's weapons requirements, and then only to a certain extent. He was head of a pseudo-ministry that was typical of the Third Reich. It was in effect a commissariat rather than a traditional ministry. It was a managerial organisation, led by a charismatic figure, whose executive power was not restrained by bureaucratic practice or legal norms, but depended on his ability to enforce his decisions by decrees from Hitler and his skill in outwitting his rivals within the hierarchy. Like the Four-Year Plan of Himmler as Reich Commissar for the Strengthening of the German Race, it was an example of the National Socialist 'Leadership Principle' in action.[35] After due consultation, industry presented Todt with a list of its main concerns: relaxation of price controls, greater freedom in the system of awarding contracts and the channelling of more resources to the larger firms. Thus from the outset the Ministry of Armaments established a very close relationship with heavy industry and was prepared to make major concessions to its demands.[36]

Todt had no time for the military's notion that industry should do its soldierly duty for Führer and Fatherland. He agreed with the industrialists that it was profit that motivates business ventures and that a sense of patriotic obligation was not a viable alternative; but he did not want to abolish all forms of price control. He adopted the system that had proved effective when building the Westwall. Where possible, fixed prices at a reasonable level gave enterprises room to rationalise and increase profits. The industrialists had to wait until Speer took office for the profit motive to take priority.[37]

The industrialists used their considerable influence to make sure how contracts were awarded. The system had become hopelessly inefficient because OKW and the Army Armaments Office were frequently at loggerheads. Todt supported the Reich Industrial Group's proposal that the procedure be decentralised, with working groups from different manufacturing sectors deciding how best to allocate the military's requirements. He also supported industry's request to have a greater say in research and development. The Professional Association of the Iron and Metal Industry (Fachgemeinschaft Eisen und Metallindustrie) established a Munitions Advisory Board (Munitionsbeirat) in Berlin that coordinated the efforts of the regional munitions committees. General Karl Becker as head of the Army Weapons Office made a desperate effort to counter these measures and reassert the primacy of the military. Hitler was sympathetic to Becker's proposals, but when Erich 'Cannon' Müller, head of artillery development at Friedrich Krupp AG, heard of this he told Hitler bluntly that industry did not want to have the military interfering in its affairs and indignantly spoke of certain problems in the Becker household. Becker was informed by telephone not only that Hitler had changed his mind, but also that his character had been defamed. This was the last straw for a man who suffered from long bouts of depression and was blamed for all the bottlenecks in the production of munitions. His suicide at his home in Berlin on 8 April 1940 was symbolic of the victory of the industrialists over the officers, but although they had won a battle they had yet to win the war.[38] Becker was given a state funeral that was attended by Hitler.

Becker's death did not solve Todt's problems with the Army Armaments Office. His successor, General Emil Leeb, was determined to resist Todt's attempts to assert the primacy of industry. He begged General Thomas to do all he could to get rid of the Ministry of Armaments and to ensure that decision-making and allocation should be according to the wishes of the military and not those of industry.[39] For his part Thomas began to imagine that he and Todt were not so very far apart. They agreed that OKW stood in the way of effective planning and that each arm of the services should be treated independently. It was decided that a committee should be formed to coordinate the demands of the army, navy and Luftwaffe and then discuss them with representatives of industry. General Thomas was to be in the chair.[40]

Todt, realising that he would thereby give Thomas and the military too much power, promptly suggested an alternative arrangement whereby a new planning committee should be formed. It was strikingly similar to the one to which he had just agreed. The only significant difference was that Todt rather than Thomas was to be the chairman. None of this solved the fundamental problem that the committee had no executive power. It could merely forward its desiderata to Hitler or Göring. Keitel, who objected to Thomas's willingness to place military experts at the minister's disposal, fiercely contested Todt's initiative. He urged Thomas to work together with Göring, who also saw Todt as a dangerous rival. Thomas's main concern was now to preserve the power and influence of his office. Todt, unlike his successor Speer, saw Thomas as a potential ally rather than as a rival. Thomas in turn, bent on further weakening the influence of the Ministry of Economics, saw Göring as a useful confederate.

In the early stages Todt's ministry consisted merely of three of his closest associates: Karl-Otto Saur, an engineer who was his right-hand-man at OT and an exceptionally forceful character, the architect Eduard Schönleben and Günther Schulze-Fielitz, a civil engineer. Inevitably the ministry expanded, but by the end of 1940 it comprised only fifty people – minuscule in comparison with the Army Armaments Office of five thousand or General Thomas's staff of five hundred. Were the ministry to be effective it had to break free from this bureaucratic tangle, the indistinct command structures and the struggles between the military, the Four-Year Plan, the party and the industrialists. It then had to have executive power. Todt wanted to ensure that the industrialists were fully integrated into the decision-making process. He was determined to resist any attempt to militarise the economy or to establish a bureaucratised command economy. He was thus bound to meet with considerable opposition from both the military and the party.

The swift victory over France threw the whole system into turmoil. Planning had been based on the presumption that this would be a lengthy campaign that might well get bogged down in positional warfare. Now, in his euphoria over his lightning victory, Hitler turned his attention once again to his monumental building projects in Berlin. Resources were diverted from armaments to these pharaonic monuments; but this did not mean that there was a return to a peace-time economy. The war was to continue, even though it was imagined that Britain would soon throw in the towel. Assuming that his campaign against the Soviet Union would result in yet another swift victory, Hitler told Keitel that it would be 'child's play'.[41] As far as armaments were concerned the emphasis was to be on tanks and mobilised infantry for the campaign in the East, while the Luftwaffe and the navy were to be prepared for operations against Britain.

Todt's ministry was totally in the dark as to Hitler's plans for the future. It was generally assumed that the war would soon be over. Hitler briefly ordered a degree of industrial demobilisation in order to increase the manufacture of consumer goods. The directive was soon rescinded, but the armaments industry was thereby seriously disrupted. Funk tried to reduce the wartime tax burden on both capital and labour. Robert Ley promised that his German Work Front would introduce extensive welfare reforms for the working population as a step towards the creation of a genuine 'racial community' (Volksgemeinschaft) – an initiative that was viewed by management with considerable alarm. Industry, fearing a confrontation with the party, thought it wise to treat the workforce with circum-spection. The agreement between the military and industry that workers should be harshly disciplined and further exploited was thus no longer binding.[42]

In this period of confusion the various arms of the services vied with one another with renewed vigour. The navy demanded the concentration of resources to build U-boats. Göring insisted that the Luftwaffe should be the absolute priority. The army called for an emphasis on tanks and troop carriers. There was at least general agreement that weapons should now take precedence over munitions, an indication that the next campaign was intended to be short and swift. Hitler then decided that Britain, having stubbornly refused to admit defeat, was to be the next objective. Thereupon OKW ordered that the demands of all three services be met. Each was to list their priorities.

Todt was left sidelined, awaiting the outcome of these struggles. Realising that the military was intent on undermining his position, he strengthened his links with industry. He created a Tank Committee under the capable chairmanship of Walther Rohland from United Steel (*Vereinigte Stahlwerke*), who as 'Panzer' Rohland was soon to play a key role in the Ministry of Armaments by wresting control over tank production from the army. Todt seized the opportunity offered by the change of emphasis from munitions to weapons to strengthen his position against OKW. His intention was that his local Armaments Committees (*Rüstungsausschüssen*) should work together with the Army Armaments Office's local bodies, thereby bypassing OKW's Armaments Inspectors (*Rüstungsinspektoren*). 'Panzer' Rohland gave Todt his energetic support with his apodictic pronouncement that: 'Industrial self-determination is more effective than quotas. Quotas spell the death of industry.'[43] For the time being, however, these hopes could not be fulfilled. The armaments industry remained under military control, but the divisions and rivalries within the armed services still left them vulnerable to a determined attack on their primacy. The basic problem was that the Treaty of Versailles had forbidden Germany to produce a wide range of armaments. These had therefore been produced clandestinely during the Weimar Republic. Since they could not be developed by private industry, an overblown military bureaucracy had evolved to oversee weapons production. This made it all the harder to hand over responsibility to the private sector.[44]

Yet for all the shortcomings, rivalries, uncertainties and lack of coherent planning, the achievements of the German armaments industry in the first seven months of 1940 were truly amazing. Between the beginning of January and the end of July, production doubled. Nothing during Speer's time in office was to match these figures. In a concerted effort by all concerned, the seemingly impossible had been achieved. The figures suggest that perhaps the harshly criticised officials in the army procurement offices and the regional armaments inspectorates did not do quite such a bad job.[45] Particularly impressive were the figures for ammunition and front-line aircraft, foremost of which was the Junkers Ju 88 twin-engine bomber intended to knock Britain out of the war.[46] The basic reason for this success was the huge increase in the allotment of metals to the armaments industries once the war began. After all, it takes about six months for raw materials to be transformed into an aircraft.

In August 1940 General Fromm, the Army Armaments Chief, issued instructions for the forthcoming invasion of the Soviet Union. Armaments Plan B called for an army of 180 divisions to be supplied with minimum equipment within nine months. It was to be fully equipped within three years.[47] This is a truly astonishing document. Germany intended to attack numerically stronger forces with far greater resources and the advantage of vast space with a minimally equipped army and inadequate logistical support. The Germans were not only going to launch a major campaign without the armaments industry going flat out, they were going to do so with a system which by general consent was hopelessly inefficient, even though the numbers looked impressive. On the military side, the weapons inspectors complained about the duplication of work in an overblown bureaucracy. Speaking both for the Ministry of Economics and the Four-Year Plan, Hans Kehrl complained that the various civilian and military bodies involved were 'opposed, juxtaposed, interposed and superimposed'.[48] He considered the military bureaucracy to be 'laggardly, accommodative and indolent'.[49]

The hopeless confusion and lack of clear direction in the armaments sector was compounded by the fact that Nazi Germany had no effective central government. Hitler gave ambiguous guidelines, OKW seemed incapable of providing clear plans and setting priorities, the civilians were unable to assert themselves and the industrialists were frustrated by the frequent chops and changes in the orders they received. On behalf of the Army Armaments Office, General Leeb pronounced the whole system to be a 'dog's breakfast' (*Planungswirrwarr*) and complained that Todt's planning staff had been lulled to sleep (*sanft einge-schlafen*). Funk, having no real understanding of the economy, but with a modest competence in monetary policy, concentrated on his duties as head of the Reichsbank. He left economic policy to his State Secretary Friedrich Landfried, a man whom Kehrl considered to be an unimaginative plodder.[50]

The demands of the army – even for the minimum requirements specified in Armaments Plan B – were such that the navy was unable to build the number of U-boats it needed for the campaign in the Atlantic. Aircraft production stagnated. Raw materials, thanks to the ruthless exploitation of the resources of occupied Europe, were hardly a problem. Hopeless bureaucratic confusion and sclerosis were the major hindrances to an effective armaments programme. Todt gradually strengthened his position, first by lending full support to 'Panzer' Rohland and giving his Tank Committee greater responsibilities. He then created an analogous Special Committee 'X' under 'Cannon' Müller – another of Hitler's intimates – to deal with weapons. Todt's initiatives were highly alarming to the Army Armaments Office and to OKW. General Thomas now turned to Göring for support against Todt's attempts to gain control over his Defence Economy and the Armaments Office.

In November 1940 Hitler ordered the army to report on its preparations for the offensive in the East. The results were alarming. The goals set by the minimum programme had not been met. There was little improvement in the following months, but Hitler still did not want to hear about the serious problems in the war economy. In his view, if resources were not available to build enough hydrogenation plants to produce synthetic fuel, then Germany must seize the oil wells in the Caucasus. For this to be possible the army had to be given priority. This strengthened Todt's position because he and 'Panzer' Rohland had by now gained almost complete control over tank production, the most important weapon in the forthcoming campaign. Germany was thus in the difficult position of planning a campaign with inadequate means in order to overcome the shortcomings within its armament programme. Small wonder then that a number of prominent figures were uncomfortably aware of this contradiction, but none would dare confront the dictator.

The armaments industry was still working well below capacity, even when figures based on the daily production of only one shift were used. Even so there were already serious shortages in the consumer sector. Food rations were reduced on 1 May 1941. This led to the widespread impression that the country had reached an economic impasse. Civilian morale was rapidly sinking and Goebbels' boasting that Germany was sufficiently armed to meet all eventualities found few takers.[51]

At times Hitler seems to have realised that the economy was fundamentally unsound. In June 1941 he told Goebbels that he needed Ukrainian grain to feed the population as well as labour from the Soviet Union to build the weapons he was going to need against the United States. With the Red Army concentrated near the frontier and with Germany's superior weapons he was confident that the campaign would be over within four months. Goebbels believed that it would be even shorter.[52] Hitler told Todt that it was 'better and cheaper' to get hold of raw materials by conquest than to build the plant that Carl Krauch was demanding for the production of synthetic fuel and rubber. He had forgotten that six weeks previously he had ordered priority to be given to basic materials at the expense of the armaments industry.[53] The great gambler imagined that he could destroy the Soviet Union in a swift campaign, thereby solving all Germany's immediate difficulties, and then prepare for the next round. The question remained whether the armed forces were up to the job. Many senior officers doubted that they were.

By late June 1941, even though the German army was rapidly advancing in the East, General Thomas came to the alarming realisation that Germany was in serious difficulties. Grave mistakes had been made. It had been assumed that Britain and France would remain neutral in 1939. In 1940 Britain was expected to negotiate an end to the war. Now the British, with increasing support from the United States, were playing a waiting game, preparing to wear down a Germany that was already affected by the naval blockade and would soon be disrupted by a large-scale bomber offensive. A decision had therefore been taken to think in terms of a lengthy war of attrition.[54]

A report in July from Generals Thomas and Udet warned that by the following spring Britain and America would have an ever-increasing superiority over the Axis. Friedrich Siebel, the engineer in charge of the Air Ministry's own factory in Halle, wrote a report on the American aircraft industry, which Udet presented to Hitler. It showed that the Americans were producing two or three times more aircraft than the Germans and that their technology was far more advanced. Hitler was not at all impressed. He said to Udet: 'What you've written here is all very well. Maybe the gentlemen are correct, but I've already got victory in my pocket.'[55] Hitler agreed with Udet and Göring that air power would be all-important in future campaigns, but the priority given to the Luftwaffe was compromised by Hitler's other pet schemes, such as the heavy 'Tiger' tank, which was classified as 'urgent'. The demands made on the armaments industry were out of all proportion to its capacity, while productivity was steadily declining due to a workforce weakened by poor nutrition and lengthy working hours. Increasing productivity by technical innovation was hardly possible because of the shortage of machine tools owing to the armed forces hogging all the resources. Rationalisation and centralisation were hampered by strong political objections to closing down small businesses. Where such action was taken it was often counter-productive.

Hitler continued to insist that victory in the Soviet Union was imminent and that all the shortcomings in the economy would thereby be overcome. General Thomas was not so confident. He argued that any gains made from the occupation of the western part of the Soviet Union would be offset by the export of American weaponry.[56] Hitler was not impressed. He considered American weapons to be of poor quality. In his view German weapons were of such superior quality that they compensated for the enemy's numerical advantage. Speer was soon to convince himself that this was true and it was to become a leitmotiv of his public pronouncements.

In December 1941 the Army Armaments Office published its estimates for the army in the following year.[57] It made alarming reading. In the first quarter, 60 per cent fewer motor vehicles would be manufactured. There would be a severe shortage of optical devices. The output of ammunition, with the exception of that for tanks and anti-tank guns, would dry up. Thirty per cent fewer tanks would be produced, even though they had been given top priority. A number of important research projects, such as the rocket programme in Peenemünde, would have to be curtailed owing to a chronic shortage of non-ferrous metals. A similar report from Erich Raeder showed that the navy would be hamstrung without a sizeable increase in the amount of raw materials allocated. The situation was rendered even worse when Hitler promised the Romanians that he would equip ten to fifteen armoured divisions in return for a guaranteed supply of oil. This prompted the Hungarians to ask Hitler for the gift of one division as recompense for their support of Germany in the Soviet Union. Hitler ignored these warnings. He told Goebbels that he had conquered enough territory in the East. The important thing now was to organise the German sphere of influence so effectively that victory would not be compromised.[58]

When Hitler appointed himself commander-in-chief of the army in December 1941, General Fromm, who had recently been talking of an urgent need to end the war, felt that he could now break free from General Thomas and OKW and appeal directly to the Führer so that the army, like the navy and the Luftwaffe, could act independently with regard to armaments. This did not worry Thomas. He concentrated on shoring up his position by arguing that the question of the allocation of resources to each of the services had to be settled and that the military had to stand up to Todt, whose influence was steadily increasing.[59] There was general agreement that with Operation Barbarossa in ruins the army had to be given top priority, so that additional divisions could be created to enable the offensive to continue in 1942. Even though the United States was now in the war the navy would have to economise. Only the U-boat programme was to continue; other projects had to be abandoned. The Luftwaffe also had to make sacrifices. Thomas assumed that these measures would have to continue well into 1943.[60]

Hitler did not agree. Having recovered from a brief bout of depression and gloom he confidently predicted that the campaign in the Soviet Union would be victoriously concluded in 1942. Every effort would then be concentrated on fighting the British and the Americans. That would mean that the navy and the Luftwaffe would be privileged at the expense of the army. Once again planners had to face the difficulty of squaring the need for a long-term agenda with short-term changes of priorities. For the moment the services simply had to make the best of what they had. For Erhard Milch and the Luftwaffe this meant rationalisation in order to make more with less. His experts estimated that by such means output could be increased by up to 50 per cent. The danger for Thomas remained that General Fromm's insatiable appetite would result in both the navy and the Luftwaffe being starved of resources. The Ministry of Armaments and the Army Armaments Office would thereby be greatly strengthened at the expense of Thomas's Defence Economy and Armaments Office.

Hitler had ordered that the army on the eastern front should be refreshed and strengthened by 1 May 1942, but General Fromm had to admit that this was not possible. He reported to Hitler that a choice had to be made between freshening up the existing army – even though it would be impossible to bring it up to the strength it had enjoyed at the beginning of Barbarossa – or to arm brand new units, leaving the existing formations seriously under strength.[61] OKH, like Hitler, preferred the second alternative, which was the only way to make further operations possible even though, for the time being at least, the eastern army would be starved of materiel. Fromm cautioned that this would mean that the army would resume operations in 1942 without any reserves; furthermore it would be impossible to build up any reserves, even by 1943. Blaming OKW for mishandling the allocation of raw materials, Fromm called for a major change in armaments policy. Thomas had proposed to cut the army's allocation by 40 per cent in the third quarter of 1942 in order to meet the Luftwaffe and the navy's requirements. This would make it impossible for the army to be adequately supplied. General Fromm also blamed Thomas for resisting the army's request that workers in the armaments industry be enlisted and replaced by prisoners of war. General Franz Halder, the army's chief of staff, gave Fromm his full support, saying that it was time to 'get some life into the joint', but Hitler ignored Fromm's appeal. He still had faith in Keitel, who was not given to making such pessimistic assessments. He boldly claimed that Todt would make sure that the production side worked effectively.[62]

Todt skilfully tutored Hitler on the major problems concerning the war economy. German industry was based on coal, therefore output had to be significantly increased. Industry was working at nowhere near full capacity, therefore attention must be paid to the rational apportioning of labour and raw materials. Wherever possible factories should employ two or three shifts. Industry had to be centralised to increase efficiency and reduce the pressure on an overworked transport system. Mass production had to replace traditional German workmanship, which was time-consuming and wasteful. On 13 January 1941 Todt told the General Council of the Reich Industrial Group that the setback at Moscow meant that armaments production had to be greatly increased. Wilhelm Zangen, the group's chairman, responded by quoting Frederick the Great: 'Battles are won with bayonets; wars can only be won by the economy.'[63]

On 7 February 1942 Todt went to Hitler's headquarters in the Masurian woods near Rastenburg (Kętrzyn) in East Prussia, determined to enlist the Führer's support for the reorganisation of the war economy. Hitler approved of his plans for fixed prices, the expansion of his committees and a diminution of the influence of the military, particularly that of the Army Armaments Office. There was heated discussion of Goebbels and Ley's contrary ideas, Hitler having agreed with the Propaganda Minister's views only a few hours before Todt arrived. The other thorny question was whether Todt could be made independent of Göring, from whom he had become ever more estranged. Göring had given Werner Mansfeld, an undersecretary in the Ministry of

Labour and deputy director of labour in the Four-Year Plan, plenipotentiary powers over the allocation of labour. This was a direct challenge to Todt, whom Hitler had already given control over the employment of Soviet prisoners of war and who wanted to extend this power to include all sources of labour. OKW in turn was determined to frustrate Todt's bid for power over the work-force. Hitler was as usual unwilling to make a decision on this key matter and the interview ended on a disagreeably frustrating note.

Hitler then demanded to see Speer, who was at headquarters to report on his recent inspection of building operations in the Ukraine, to discuss the rebuilding of Berlin. It was now one o'clock in the morning. Hitler was tired and ill-tempered, but soon perked up as Speer briefed him on progress in Berlin. The interview ended at three. In view of the late hour Speer cancelled his early morning flight with Todt.

After a brief sleep Todt boarded a plane to fly back to Berlin. A few seconds after take-off it veered sharply to the left as if attempting an emergency landing. The plane then exploded and all on board were killed. 'Panzer' Rohland was convinced that the SS, probably at Hitler's urging, had murdered Todt. There is no evidence to support this view, but the very fact that such rumours should circulate was indicative of the tensions and strains within the leadership after the disastrous failure of Barbarossa and with the recent declaration of war on the United States.[64]

Speer gives a number of different accounts of Todt's death.[65] In the 1953 draft of his memoirs he wrote: 'Immediately after Todt's accident Hitler ordered Milch to investigate the causes. He had a suspicion that there was something odd about it.' In the 1967 draft this was changed to: 'Upon Hitler's orders – as he suspected something odd about the accident – the Air Ministry undertook an investigation as to whether my predecessor's crash could have been due to sabotage . . . they came to the conclusion that sabotage could be excluded.' This passage is followed by the closing remarks of the Air Ministry's inquiry: 'Judging from the examination of the wreck it certainly seems reasonable to suppose that the plane (which according to the inquiry had a self-destruction mechanism) exploded at low altitude. But how, by whom and due to what was the mechanism activated? It is a question which allows latitude to all specula-tion, however fantastic.'

In the fourth and final draft of his memoirs in 1968 this is again changed to read: 'Hitler seemed to treat Todt's death with the stoic calm of a man who must reckon with such incidents as part of the general picture . . . [Hitler] thought it was a successful act by the secret service of our enemies. But then, it is doubtful that he would have expressed to me any mere conjecture.' In the German version this was changed to: 'He thought it was a successful stroke by the secret services.' Whether he meant the British, the American, the Soviet or his own is left unclear. The English version is quite different: 'he was going to have the secret services look into the matter'.

The machine, a Heinkel 111 converted to passenger use, had been placed at Todt's disposal by Field Marshal Hugo Sperrle, because his own plane was undergoing repairs. It was said, like all courier planes, to have been fitted with a self-destruction device, operated by a lever beside the pilot's seat. Shortly after the accident, Todt's eighteen-year-old fighter-pilot son was able to prove that the plane was not equipped with such a device. Nicolaus von Below, Hitler's Luftwaffe adjutant, makes no mention of such a device in his account of the accident. He does however record that he had an argument with Todt because Hitler had issued an order that his top people were not to fly in twin-engine planes. Todt was furious and told him to mind his own business.

We may never know the true cause of the crash, just as we shall never know what Hitler said to Speer that night after Todt had gone to bed. Had he persuaded him not to board the same plane as Todt? Had he already decided to replace the pessimistic Todt with his faithful vassal Speer?

CHAPTER FIVE

MINISTER OF ARMAMENTS

TODT'S VIOLENT DEATH under somewhat suspicious circumstances gave rise to a host of rumours. An official investigation ruled out sabotage and suggested that the pilot had mistakenly triggered the self-destruction mechanism, but this was not enough to silence the conspiracy theorists, who were quick to point out that Hitler banned any discussion of the circumstances of Todt's death. This was the third violent death in the upper echelon of the armaments industry, following the suicides of General Karl Becker in 1940 and Udet in 1941.[1] After the war 'Panzer' Rohland claimed that Todt had come to the conclusion that the war was lost and had urged Hitler to bring it to an end. There is no supporting evidence for this attempt to depict Todt, and by implication his successor, as being at one with the 'resisters'.[2] Both Todt and Rohland knew that the situation was precarious and Hans Kehrl was in full agreement, but they attributed this in large part to organisational chaos within the armaments industry and to Hitler's reluctance to take decisive action. Even though he had fundamental differences with party functionaries, Todt was a passionate National Socialist, who was doggedly loyal to his Führer. Hitler had full confidence in him and was in agreement with his plan to grant his ministry and the industrialists joint authority over the armaments industry, but the problem was that this would involve clipping the wings of a number of his principal satraps: Göring, Keitel, Goebbels, Funk and Ley among them.[3]

Todt's dramatic death provided the impetus for Hitler to overcome his reluctance to act. Göring flew to the Wolf's Lair – as Hitler's headquarters near Rastenburg were known – as soon as he heard of Todt's death, in the hope that Hitler would agree to the Four-Year Plan taking over the Armaments Ministry. Much to his consternation he found that Hitler had already appointed the court favourite Albert Speer as Todt's successor. It was not such a surprising choice. Hitler had a very close relationship with his architect and could count on his undivided loyalty. Speer already had enough experience to qualify him for the job. He was responsible for all the buildings in the aircraft industry. He had organised the repair of the railway network and built roads in the Soviet Union. He had worked closely with General Friedrich Fromm, the head of the Reserve Army and the officer responsible for armaments. He had built a special plant in Dessau for the Junkers medium-range dive-bomber, the Ju 87 Stuka. He was known to be a diligent organiser and a forceful leader. Unlike Todt, Speer would be neither an uncomfortable bearer of bad news nor treat Hitler to lectures on what needed to be done. He was young and energetic, not yet worn down by bureaucratic infighting and wrangles over areas of competence. Unlike the other Nazi grandees he had no power base. Even at the height of his power and influence he was punching above his weight when confronted with Goebbels, Himmler or Bormann. Hitler liked the fact that, just like Todt, Speer had no expertise in the armaments field. He detested experts, whom he regarded as argumentative know-alls who sometimes even dared to contradict him. Above all he considered Speer to be a loyal vassal, who would never dare step out of line.

In his first address as Armaments Minister Speer claimed that 'until recently I lived in a world of ideals.' He was constantly to harp on this theme as he made himself out to have been nothing more than an architect, who was suddenly thrust into the armaments industry, an artist who overnight had to transform himself into a technocrat. He used this line of defence at Nuremberg so as to disguise the more sordid aspects of his career. While the *Baustab Speer* was busy building motorways and work camps in the Soviet Union, the *Transportstandarte Speer* supplied the frontline units of the Luftwaffe. In preparation for Barbarossa the unit was expanded to three regiments to form the NSKK Transport Brigade Speer. It provided logistical support for the offensive. The organisation was soon expanded to ten regiments.[4] On 20 October 1941 a special unit of the Transport Regiment Speer was formed in Stettin to be sent to North Africa. Another unit was made responsible for supplying the Luftwaffe in North Africa and Crete. There were 54,000 workers in the Building Corps in December 1939. This increased to 92,000 by September 1940 and 98,000 in October 1941.[5] One of the Building Corps Speer's principal tasks was building prisoner of war camps in Poland and the Soviet Union. These were also built at Kaulsdorf and Falkensee to provide workers in Berlin. A handsome profit was made by hiring out the prisoners. Corners were cut to increase profits.[6] Small wonder, then, that Speer was anxious to run his own prisoner of war camps, telling the military authorities that he would thereby save them trouble and expense. Such was the 'world of ideals' in which the mere architect Albert Speer had lived before he was suddenly cast into the real world as Minister of Armaments. The brutal treatment of Berlin's Jews and the construction of a number of concentration camps for the slave labour he required for his mammoth building projects were a significant part of this ideal world.

That Hitler appointed Speer both Minister of Armaments and head of Organisation Todt was a clear indication that he was determined to follow the course set by Speer's predecessor. On the other hand he characteristically did not give Speer any clear instructions or guidelines. He left it to him to carve out his own empire, for which he had the necessary ambition, self-assertiveness and ruthlessness. Speer had had a close relationship with Todt, whom he greatly admired. He fully endorsed Todt's notion of industrial self-determination, although he was later to claim that he revived the system adopted in the First World War, rather than inheriting it directly from his predecessor.[7] He shared Todt's passion for technology and modern management techniques, but he differed from Todt in one important respect. Todt was a pleasant man for whom to work. He was mindful of the sensitivity of others, had no time for internal power struggles and acknowledged the merits of his colleagues.[8] Speer, however, remained aloof and unapproachable. He shunned convivial meetings with his colleagues, offering them instead an occasional Bruckner symphony or piano recital as an appropriate 'synthesis of art and war'.[9]

Speer knew that with virtually unlimited access to Hitler he held the key to power in the Third Reich. Hitler had worked closely with Speer for almost a decade. His closeness to Hitler enabled him to show scant concern for established rules of procedure or legal constraints. He set himself the daunting task of winning the war by providing high-quality weapons in sufficient numbers to overcome the combined industrial might of the United States, the Soviet Union and Britain and its Commonwealth. He imagined that this would only be possible if the entire economy were placed under his direction. Goebbels was initially enormously impressed by Speer, whom he felt was 'outdoing the great Todt'. He waxed lyrical about his idealism, his expert knowledge, his efforts to streamline and rationalise the entire system of arms procurement. He wrote: 'we work splendidly together – at last a kindred mind'.[10] Few shared the Propaganda Minister's enthusiasm.

Göring, who was furious that he had not been chosen to replace Todt, was the first to go on the attack. He told Speer that Todt had given him a written promise not to interfere in the affairs of the Four-Year Plan and that he would forward this paper for his perusal. Speer ignored this threat and awaited the outcome of a major conference on armaments to be held on 13 February 1942.[11] Field Marshal Erhard Milch dominated the discussion at this meeting, but by concentrating on complaints that the Luftwaffe had been seriously disadvantaged and that there had been a sinister alliance between Todt and the commander of the Reserve Army, General Friedrich Fromm, he missed the opportunity to create a common front of all the services against the new Armaments Minister. Vice-Admiral Kurt von dem Borne for the navy countered with complaints about the Luftwaffe, accusing Milch of being an unscrupulous empire builder. He hoped that Speer might be able to cut him down to size. General Thomas talked in terms of vertical rearmament, which should be the province of the armed forces, with horizontal rearmament the responsibility of the Reich Industrial Group. The German Work Front was to provide another unspecified dimension. Thomas was all in favour of rationalisation, but insisted that Speer did not have sufficient experience or insight into the complexity of the situation to make the necessary decisions.

Speaking on behalf of the industrialists, Albert Vögler from United Steel announced that he was sick and tired of the chops and changes in the procurement orders given to industry resulting from the infighting between various competing organisations. He concluded that 'one person must decide everything. Industry is not interested in whom that should be'.[12] Funk followed up this suggestion by proposing that Milch was the man for the job, whereupon Speer played his trump card. He calmly stated that the mission was his and that Hitler wished to speak to the assembled group in order to clarify the matter. Hitler promptly appeared and treated the meeting to a one-hour address.

After a preamble stressing the vital importance of increasing the performance of the armaments industry, Hitler glibly announced that Göring and the Four-Year Plan were incapable of mastering the situation and that those present should behave as 'gentlemen' towards Speer. Once again Hitler had failed to take any decisive action, but he had pushed Speer's main rivals aside, leaving Speer 'in an empty space without any obstacles, so that I could do more or less what I wanted'.[13]

Seeing that Speer enjoyed Hitler's full support, Funk prudently decided to fall into line. In a private discussion with Bormann and Speer, Hitler advised his new minister to work closely with industry. Bormann had to swallow this pill so that for the time being the Nazi Party remained silent. Speer's position was further strengthened when the Nazi Party's Main Office for Technology, which since 1934 had been headed by Fritz Todt, was formally handed over to him. Similarly, the German Work Front's Technology Office also became part of Speer's ministry.[14] Speer took pains not to crow too loudly, having, at least for the moment, outwitted Bormann and Ley. While treating them both with distant courtesy, he artfully fuelled the conflict between them. Ley wanted to gain Hitler's support for his suggestion that all residential construction should be under the aegis of the German Work Front. Bormann opposed this, fearing that it would enable Ley to frustrate his ambitious building plans for Hitler's estate in Berchtesgaden and thwart the Gauleiters' ambitions to leave their architectural marks. Hitler initially agreed with Bormann, but Speer artfully supported Ley, even though buildings were part of his responsibilities both as Inspector General of Buildings in the Reich Capital (GBI) and now as head of Organisation Todt. In a remarkable demonstration of Speer's influence over Hitler a 'Führer Order' was signed giving Ley the authority he had requested.[15]

Speer, having little to fear from Ley, thereby won the first round against Bormann, his most dangerous rival.

Speer was determined to retain the initiative. On 18 February 1942 he presented the outline of a plan for the reorganisation of the armaments industry at a meeting attended by Funk and General Hermann von Hanneken from the Ministry of Economics, Colonel Adolf von Schell, Plenipotentiary for Motor Vehicles within the Four-Year Plan and Wilhelm Zangen and Karl Lange from the Reich Industrial Group, along with a number of armaments experts from the military. His basic intention was to reaffirm Todt's determination to direct armaments from the production end and to make sure that the Ministry of Armaments was solely responsible for the apportionment of armaments orders and production management. The military gave its exceptionally reluctant approval to this concept. General Thomas and the head of the navy's weapons office, Admiral Karl Witzell, expressed their 'serious reservations'. General Friedrich Olbricht, representing the reserve army, argued that with his new powers over the allocation of labour, Speer would be able to influence army recruitment. Speer and Milch assured him that would not be the case. General agreement was reached and Hitler's approval secured.[16]

On 24 February 1942 Speer addressed a meeting of the Gauleiters in Munich. He told them to halt all non-essential building operations and to concentrate on the war effort. No thought should be given to peacetime planning. Industry must concentrate solely on armaments, with the private sector totally subordinate to the requirements of the state. With youthful arrogance Speer complained that too many leading figures in industry were too old to do an effective job. He promised a rejuvenation programme to bring in a large number of forty-year-olds to replace them. He called for a concentrated effort from all concerned, combined with a continuation and extension of Todt's rationalisation programme. Anyone who was found to have given false information in order to procure materials or workers would be condemned to death or serve a severe prison sentence. Speer demanded sacrifices from all concerned, and ended by saying that he had been obliged to abandon his vocation as an architect in order to devote himself selflessly to the war effort.[17] Aware of the propaganda value of this speech, Bormann had it printed and circulated to all the Reichsleiters, Gauleiters and other senior officials. Not all of them were pleased with what they read. They did not like the threats against their extravagant building plans and references to their hunting lodges, domestic staff, luxurious automobiles and flamboyant lifestyles. Bormann immediately obtained an order from Hitler so that he could continue building on the Obersalzberg. The Gauleiters similarly disregarded the economy measures.

Speer then drafted a decree for Hitler's signature threatening anyone who gave a false account of the raw materials, labour or machinery at their disposal with the death penalty. On the same day he announced to the press that he had sent two managers to a concentration camp for employing labour for their own purposes at the expense of the armaments industry.[18]

The reaction was prompt and predictable. At the Reich Chancellery Lammers objected on the grounds that the decree had not passed through the normal channels. Göring protested that Speer was stepping out of line by trying to assert his authority over the Four-Year Plan. The Wehrmacht tried to protect its own by arguing that any member of the military charged under these provisions should be tried in a civilian court rather than the People's Court. Otto Thierack as Minister of Justice insisted that the definition of new crimes was the province of his ministry. The Minister of the Interior, Wilhelm Frick, argued that Speer was not only bound by existing laws and regulations but also had to consult with other ministers when their interests were directly involved. Speer brusquely countered these objections by stating that he was acting on Hitler's initiative. After heated discussion agreement was finally reached when, on 21 March 1942, Hitler signed a decree, countersigned by Lammers and Keitel, making it a crime to falsify information about labour, raw materials, products or machinery in the armaments industry. Punishments ranged from fines to the death sentence. Cases were to be brought before the People's Court, a judicial body not known for clemency or respect for due procedure. Speer won a significant victory in that he was given responsibility for laying the charges. One month later he also managed to get these sanctions applied to the building industry. Funk was given analogous powers with respect to raw materials.[19]

Himmler considered Speer's initiative to be unduly harsh. He pronounced that: 'The most severe forms of punishment become blunt instruments and therefore worthless if they are used as threats at every possible opportunity ... Being sent to a concentration camp involves separation from one's family, isolation from the outside world and hard work ... it is a severe punishment.' There was no need for such threats because 'on the whole the German people are extraordinarily respectable.'[20] In his memoirs Speer claimed that such threats were merely designed as propaganda but they were never put into practice. His sole motive was to protect those who worked for him from the Gestapo, hence Himmler's objection. He argued that the decree was to prove invaluable during the wave of arrests after the attempt on Hitler's life on 20 July 1944.[21] If that was indeed the reason, it did not prove very effective.

Speer soon realised that even with Hitler's support there were strict limits to his power. His initial attempts to recruit Soviet labour into the armaments industry were frustrated by the Reich Security Main Office and also by the Gauleiters. Dr Werner Mansfeld from the Ministry of Labour informed him that his request 'for a few hundred thousand' Soviet construction workers had to be turned down because the Gauleiters refused permission for them to move from one Gau to another.[22] Speer remained locked in battle with most of the Gauleiters until the bitter end. Since the Gauleiters were also Reich Commissioners for Defence, conflict with the Ministry of Armaments was inevitable. They fought over the allocation of labour, the closing down of firms considered to be non-essential, the protection of small businesses and pet building projects in their respective fiefdoms. They saw themselves as guardians of National Socialist orthodoxy against Speer and his 'plutocratic' cronies. As long as Speer had Hitler's support he was able to defend himself against the Gauleiters and the party machine, but Bormann worked tirelessly to cut his rival down to size.[23]

As Minister of Armaments, Speer tried to create a position analogous to that of the GBI. In Berlin he had acted directly under Hitler. His office was completely autonomous and beyond outside control. Armaments were too complex an issue for this ever to be possible. Thousands of decisions made by Hitler during his conferences with Speer were converted into 'Führer's Decrees', so that he could thereby continue to ignore conventional channels.[24] But Bormann for the party and Lammers at the chancellery did what they could to rein in this over-confident maverick, while within his own ministry he faced challenges from power-hungry subordinates such as the weapons expert Karl-Otto Saur and Franz Xaver Dorsch at Organisation Todt.

Hitler made all the decisions at the frequent armaments conferences. He never sought advice, very seldom asked for an opinion and was furious when Speer lobbied delegates before a meeting in an attempt to influence its outcome. For Hitler, Speer was merely an executant of his will, which in turn gave Speer exceptional power in a state where the Führer's will was the ultimate authority. Hitler had an astonishing memory, coupled with a detailed knowledge of armaments that Speer could not possibly match. Within the Ministry of Armaments only Saur had such a comprehensive overview of technical factors, which he unscrupulously used to undermine his minister's unique place in Hitler's favour.[25]

Armaments conferences with Hitler were convened at roughly two-week intervals. Speer also met Hitler frequently on a one–to-one basis, regularly going to his headquarters and spending lengthy visits in Berchtesgaden. Speer's success depended on his ability to feed Hitler's 'hallucinatory optimism' with carefully doctored statistics.[26] As Hitler's health began its rapid decline his attention span shortened and he had fits of absent-mindedness. He began to avoid large conferences and disliked unfamiliar faces. With Hitler no longer able to remember all the details, Speer had to rely on the expertise of Saur and Dorsch, both of whom were intent on replacing him.

Speer's immediate concern was to ward off his many rivals. Funk had his eye on energy, thus threatening Speer's position as Inspector General for Water and Energy.[27] Ley argued that his German Work Front should be entrusted with technology. Both OKW and Göring were determined to extend their powers. General Thomas sought to reassert his independence, while Field Marshal Milch saw Todt's death as an opportunity to score against his rival, Thomas, and to ward off the meddlesome Ministry of Armaments. The weapons agencies of all three services were determined to assert their autonomy. Party officials were deeply concerned about the social consequences of an armaments policy, which they felt threatened to undermine the 'racial community'.

But in spite of such powerful rivals Speer was in a strong position. Heavy industry and its various interest groups, enthusiastically supported by Fritz Todt, had prepared the ground for reform. Speer was the beneficiary. He had the drive and determination to seize the opportunity to make a successful bid for power. Heavy industry triumphed over the burdensome civil and military bureaucracies and trampled on the smaller enterprises and their zealous supporters within the NSDAP.[28] Industrialists needed centralised planning, along with decisive and unambiguous orders and the appropriate allocation of resources. They had favoured Todt over Milch or Thomas, because he was sympathetic to industry's needs and was a champion of self-determination. They were therefore much relieved to find that Speer followed closely in his predecessor's footsteps.[29] Heavy industry thus had a congenial man in the key position, but Speer was certainly not its marionette. He also had to maintain his position against determined opposition from all sides. As General Thomas remarked to a British interrogating officer in August 1945, 'as far as the economy was concerned the so-called Leadership State (*Führerstaat*) was marked by a total lack of leadership along with unimaginable confusion and conflict, because Hitler did not see the necessity for clear and far-sighted planning, Göring had no understanding of business and the relevant specialists had no authority.'[30] These problems were never solved; indeed, they were compounded by a growing awareness in certain quarters that the war could not be won.

As Minister of Armaments, Speer, like Todt, was only responsible for providing the army with weapons. As Minister of Munitions he was responsible for ammunition across the three services. Wisely he turned to Milch for advice and guidance. Milch in turn knew that since there was no point in challenging Speer it was best to cooperate with him. Speer's success as Minister of Armaments was due in very large part to his close cooperation with the Field Marshal. After all, 40 per cent of the 'Speer Miracle' between February 1942 and the summer of 1943 was achieved by Milch and the Luftwaffe. Ten per cent came from the navy and Carl Krauch's chemicals from the Four-Year Plan. Thus Speer only deserves half the credit.[31] This, in turn, was largely due to Todt's groundwork.

Speer's relationship with General Thomas was more difficult. Deciding for the moment to avoid an outright confrontation, he pointed out that he had the means to get things done because he had Hitler's backing, whereas Thomas had the experience and the expertise. He cruelly added that all Göring had was a name. Thomas was surprised and delighted at Speer's offer of a collegial relationship, but he was soon to learn that he had other things in mind.[32]

Todt's ministry was a most unusual institution. Rather than working within a traditional bureaucratic structure he had preferred to rely on a handful of experts, who were given extensive leeway. Lacking experience of the inner workings of the armaments industry, Speer was reliant upon Todt's handpicked team, who regarded the new minister with varying degrees of suspicion and hostility. The decision to retain most of Todt's closest associates was to cause Speer considerable problems in the future, but he had no choice. He tried to strengthen his position by bringing a number of his most trusted associates into the ministry, but as architects and structural engineers they lacked specialised expertise.

Todt's right-hand man, Karl-Otto Saur, remained as head of the Technical Office, which had been established to supervise the various committees that dealt with specific issues such as ammunition, tanks, weapons and electrical equipment. Saur was an engineer who had been a director at Thyssen. He joined the Nazi Party in 1931. He had been Todt's deputy in Organisation Todt before being made responsible for weapons development in the Ministry of Armaments, working closely with the Army Weapons Office. He had become popularly known as 'Todt's raucous weekly newsreel' for his obstreperous self-promotion.[33] He was an utterly ruthless and unscrupulous man, whose bullyboy tactics earned him the nickname 'Speer's Rottweiler'.[34] He was soon to challenge his minister and seek to unseat him.

Dr Walther Schieber had also joined the NSDAP in 1931 and the SS in 1933, becoming a member of Himmler's Circle of Friends that provided a mutually beneficial link between business and the regime. He coupled a doctorate in chemical engineering with exceptional business acumen. He was also a highly decorated veteran and a devout National Socialist. He worked for IG Farben before becoming head of the Armaments Consignment Office. His task was to supply the raw materials, labour and components for Saur's end products. It was a thankless task. Saur got all the glory, while Schieber's efforts were ignored. From the outset he was very impressed by Speer. Here was a highly intelligent young man, full of energy and in excellent health. He was obviously someone who would demand every effort from those around him and who would be equally unsparing of himself. This from Schieber, who had a reputation for being an incredibly hard worker, was indeed impressive testimony. In the crisis situation that faced the Reich, Speer seemed to be the ideal man. His main fault was that, quite unlike Todt, he was devoid of any sign of human warmth. He appeared to be ice-cold and only concerned with the matter at hand.[35]

Karl Maria Hettlage was head of the Business and Finance Department, having held an equivalent position in Speer's Berlin Building Inspectorate. His main responsibility was the procurement of goods and raw materials that were in short supply, most of which came from the occupied areas. Although a man of exceptional ability, Hettlage prudently kept a low profile and possibly for this reason rose to high office in post-war Germany.[36]

Speer left Organisation Todt in the hands of Todt's deputy, Franz Xaver Dorsch. He was a civil engineer who had worked closely with Todt on the motorways and the Westwall since 1933. From the outset Dorsch was antagonistic towards Speer. On his appointment as Minister of Armaments Speer had asked his senior officials to put their trust in him. Dorsch haughtily replied: 'We trusted Dr Todt unreservedly. Trust is not automatic. It has to be earned.' Speer never forgave him for this remark.[37] Organisation Todt was a Europe-wide concern that was divided into several sections: West Europe, South-eastern Europe, Southern Russia, Central Russia, Northern Russia, 'Viking' (Norway and Denmark) and Finland.[38]

Speer appointed the mayor of Nuremberg, Willy Liebel, head of the Central Office, with Karl Maria Hettlage as his deputy. Originally designed to deal with personnel, it eventually had five main sections:

1. Organisation and administration;
2. Economics and finance directly under Hettlage;
3. Law and industrial self-determination;
4. Personnel;
5. Culture and propaganda.[39]

Liebel and Speer had worked closely together while building the arena for the party rallies in Nuremberg. He was entrusted with keeping control over Dorsch's often wilful personnel management in OT. Speer relied on Liebel's advice to such an extent that he left his duties as mayor of Nuremberg to a deputy, to become one of Speer's closest colleagues.

The administrative structure of Speer's ministry was in a constant state of flux. New committees were established to meet immediate contingencies. Existing structures were frequently modified. Thus by October 1943 the Central Office was still run by Liebel, but its subsections were now:

1. Raw Materials under Kehrl, with responsibility for coal, metals, wood, textiles, oil and rubber;
2. Armaments Procurement under Schieber, dealing with iron, steel, glass, electrical goods, optics and spare parts; it also oversaw seventeen subordinate 'rings' dealing with specific commodities;

3. Consumer Goods under Georg Seebauer, which controlled ten groups and associations for consumer goods;
4. The Technical Office for Armaments Production under Saur, with subordinate committees for weapons, ammunition, tanks and shipping;
5. The Building Office under Carl Stobbe-Dethleffsen; which also included Speer's office as Inspector General of Buildings in the Reich Capital;
6. The Energy Office under Günther Schulze-Fielitz, with overall responsibility for electricity, gas and water.[40]

To these were added a series of independent offices dealing with specific issues.

Speer always prided himself on not being hidebound by bureaucracy, but in fact he presided over a vast administrative structure that was continually changed and modified. This gave the ministry a certain dynamism, but it fostered interdepartmental rivalry and the duplication of effort, together with the back-biting and power struggles that bedevilled less flexible structures. Nor could Speer, even when he enjoyed Hitler's unconditional support, overlook the rival claims of the armed forces, the Nazi Party, the SS and the civilian administration.

The Armaments Ministry was housed in Speer's offices as GBI on the Pariser Platz near the Brandenburg Gate. It was a remarkably small organisation. Even as late as June 1944 there were only 218 people working there. Speer preferred to work through a vast network of subordinate committees, task forces and teams. Embracing Todt's belief in the self-determination of industry, he gave the industrialists a significant say in the decision-making process. He relied heavily on the expertise of a number of leading figures in industry. Edmund Geilenberg, who came from the weapons manufacturer Rheinmetall-Borsig, was put in overall charge of munitions. Arthur Tix from the coal and steel conglomerates United Steel and Bochumer Verein with its subsidiary Hanomag, which specialised in building tanks and trucks, was given overall responsibility for weapons. 'Panzer' Rohland from United Steel was put in charge of tank production.

From the outset, with single-minded determination, Speer set out to gain control over the armaments of all three services. Considering the military to be singularly ill-equipped to understand the complexities of modern industrial production, he was determined to supervise the Luftwaffe and the navy's weapons requirements. With the United States now in the war the navy would have to play a greater role. The prospects were not good. By January 1942 Dönitz's stock of U-boats had been reduced to 91, of which only 12 were suitable for operation in the Atlantic. On 20 March Speer managed to convince Hitler that the system of industrial self-determination should also be applied to the navy. Rudolf Blohm from the shipbuilding firm Blohm & Voss, a company that ran its own concentration camp, whose inmates came mostly from Poland and the Soviet Union, was made responsible for warships. Gottlieb Paulus from Mercedes-Benz was put in charge of torpedoes and special instruments for the navy.[41] This arrangement soon proved to be unworkable.

The Luftwaffe turned out to be much more cooperative. Speer got Milch's consent to three new committees, with Karl Frydag from the Heinkel aircraft company responsible for airframes, William Werner, from Auto Union/Junkers, responsible for engines, and Hans Heyne from the electrical equipment combine AEG responsible for technical equipment.[42]

There were further committees within the Ministry of Armaments for general supplies under Wilhelm Zangen from the industrial conglomerate Mannesmann. He was a merciless careerist, who profited greatly from 'Aryanised' property and the exploitation of slave labour. Machine tools were handled by Karl Lange from the Four-Year Plan, a man who had for many years called for greater freedom for industry from excessive government control. Railway rolling stock was the responsibility of Gerhard Degenkolb from the engineering firm Demag. Motor vehicles were placed under Colonel Fritz Holzhäuer from the Weapons Testing Office at OKH. Speer added two further committees: for locomotives to meet an immediate crisis and for shipping so as to gain more control over the navy. Carl Krauch's immense chemical empire within the Four-Year Plan became in effect a committee of the Ministry of Armaments. All these committees were concerned with end products and were thus the responsibility of Karl-Otto Saur, who soon became dangerously powerful.[43]

Whereas these committees were responsible for end products, supplied products were controlled by a number of rings. Albert Vögler had long argued in favour of such rings, in part because he thought that they would wrest armaments production from the tiresome interference of the Ministry of Economics. Initially there were four main rings: iron and steel under Albert Nöll from United Steel; other metals under Otto Fitzner from the Silesian mining company Georg von Giesches Erben; mechanical components under Hans Kluy from the Hermann Göring Works; and electrical products under Friedrich Lüschen from Siemens. In July 1942 further rings were added: for explosives under Otto Sarrazin from Wasag and IG Farben, and for iron ore under the Saarland industrialist Hermann Röchling, who sat on the boards of numerous firms in the coal and steel industry.[44] Albert Nöll, having lost overall control of the iron and steel ring to Röchling, was made responsible for iron processing. The system of committees and sub-committees, rings and sub-rings rapidly multiplied. The telephone book of the Ministry of Armaments listed 249 such bodies by the end of 1942.[45] The personnel of Speer's ministry soon made up a virtual Who's Who of German industry. The rings were for the most part staffed by people with an engineering background, whose task it was to select the most efficient companies and to ensure that production was rationalised and standardised. They also gave advice to the less efficient companies on how to increase output and reduce costs.[46]

Armaments production was thereby organised vertically in committees and horizontally in rings. This structure worked well because individuals often served both in the committees and in the rings. Thus, for example, someone responsible for crankshafts in 'Panzer' Rohland's committee also looked after the production of crankshafts for tanks in Hans Kluy's ring.[47] Within a few weeks Speer had energetically and ruthlessly tightened the organisational structure he inherited from Todt. With Hitler's full support he achieved some major changes in personnel, even in other ministries. Such success whetted his appetite. He was not satisfied with simply producing armaments, he wanted to have a major say in the development of new weapons, thereby eclipsing the Army Armaments Office.[48] The main argument in support of this move was that weapons had to be designed that were suitable for mass production by unskilled labour. They had to be simple and have relatively few standardised components.

Speer inherited the system of committees and rings from Todt, but he extended them almost beyond recognition. He also took up Todt's suggestion for reforming the pricing system. On 15 January 1942 Hans Fischböck, an Austrian lawyer with a banking background, known as 'Austria's Göring', had been appointed Reich Commissioner for Pricing. He was an acknowledged expert in plundering Jews, ransacking the Dutch economy and rounding up forced labour.[49] He was a callous brute, but he was more favourably disposed towards industry than his predecessor, the somewhat ridiculous 'old warrior' Josef Wagner, who had been stripped of all his offices in November. Fischböck found great favour among the industrialists by agreeing to a standardised system of set prices. All questions of excess profits were left to the Ministry of Finance, whose attitude was equally accommodating. Only profits that were 50 per cent higher than those in 1938 were subject to tax. This was a huge advantage to major firms that had made vast profits in the early stages of rearmament. Furthermore, firms had generous legal means by which they could avoid the full effect of such a tax.[50]

In March 1942, Speer entered into negotiations with General Emil Leeb, head of the Army Armaments Office, to relinquish responsibility for weapons development. Henceforth this would be the concern of the development committees and technical offices of the Ministry of Armaments.

A series of Development Commissions were created in the next few months to deal with research and development: in April, for tanks under the automobile manufacturer Ferdinand Porsche; in July, for weapons under Erich 'Cannon'

Müller from Krupp; for munitions, under Albert Wolff from the Deutsche-Waffen und Munitionsfabriken AG, a firm best known as the manufacturer of the Luger Parabellum gun, and for explosives under Paul Müller from Dynamit Nobel and IG Farben. In August, Karl Küpfmüller from Siemens and Halske chaired a commission dealing with signals and communication systems.[51] All these men gave their services on an honorary basis, although the firms they represented made handsome profits from their efforts. Speer announced that his self-determination system was completed in the summer of 1942, but it continued to expand well into 1944, by which time it had become a gigantic complex of groups, commissions, rings and committees that was barely comprehensible and virtually unmanageable.

Speer was anxious to ensure that these various groups did not become fossilised and deteriorate into rigid bureaucratic departments. He believed that improvisation rather than planning was the most effective way to ensure that idle plants got back to work while inefficient firms closed. Hitler gave his full endorsement to Speer's determination to leave it to the industrialists to get on with the job. In March 1942 he announced that 'German managers must, without constant supervision, consider the wartime economic interests of the Reich as their own', but he cautioned that 'whoever abuses this confidence and violates the integrity of the manager will be severely punished'. Hitler thereby once again upheld the notion of the 'leadership principle' (*Führerprinzip*) and applied it to the business world. This idea did not go down well with the Nazi Party, many of whose functionaries still clung to the pseudo-socialism of the early radical 'storm and stress' period. They saw this approach simply as a means whereby the barons of the Rhine and the Ruhr lined their pockets. Why, they asked, should a group of tycoons run the economy of the nation at war? The primacy of National Socialist politics should once again be asserted. The military was equally disgruntled. They had been largely excluded from the armaments industry, their role reduced to that of a suppliant, dependent on industry's largesse.

By the late summer of 1942 these critical voices had been largely silenced, at least for the time being, because the system seemed to be working well. Bottlenecks were removed, production ran smoothly and output figures improved impressively. The system was Todt's, but Speer gained most of the credit. It had needed the shock of the dramatic setback outside Moscow and Fritz Todt's sudden death to shake Hitler into action. He realised that something drastic had to be done. He mistrusted bureaucracy, which he was convinced led to inertia, preferring a free-for-all where the strongest and ablest would come out on top. He had lost confidence in the muddle-headed National Socialist gurus, whose outlandish economic conceits had once impressed him. He shared Speer's belief that technology held most of the answers. Within a few weeks Speer had made himself into one of the most powerful figures in the Third Reich. He had managed to absorb most of the effective parts of Göring's Four-Year Plan into his ministry by recruiting its leading figures into his committees and rings. He had gained control over the army by placing his men in the Industrial Council of the Commander-in-Chief of the Army. He had already made moves to bring the navy and the Luftwaffe under his sway.

There remained the problem of General Thomas and his Defence Economy and Armaments Office. Thomas controlled the regional armaments inspections and the local armaments authorities. Speer had his own men at the top and at the local level, but Thomas's organisations were placed in between.[52] On 2 March 1942 Speer artfully admitted to Thomas that his armaments programme was unworkable without his cooperation. Thomas, who was in Hitler and Göring's bad books because of his pessimistic reports, felt it prudent to give way to this glamorous young star who basked in the Führer's favour, but Speer was not in the least bit interested in cooperating with Thomas. On 7 May he obtained an order from Hitler whereby those sections within Thomas' office that dealt with the production of armaments should come under his control. Thomas was furious but powerless. He was an introspective man who, without access to Hitler and with insufficient backing from Keitel, was loathe to get involved in power struggles. He attributed his demise to the favouritism showered by Hitler upon the industrialists and to the ruthless ambition of Speer who, with the able support of his immediate colleagues, seemed intent on taking command over the entire economy.[53] Speer's closest associates, Karl-Otto Saur and Walther Schieber, were also determined to push Thomas aside. For the time being he remained in office as head of the Armaments Office, the key part of his organisation, but it was now an empty shell within Speer's ministry.[54] Worn down, exhausted and in poor health, Thomas was forced out in November to be replaced by a colourless nonentity, General Kurt Waeger. Thomas's earlier association with oppositional figures such as General Ludwig Beck and Karl Friedrich Goerdeler, as well as his pessimistic assessment of Germany's chances in a lengthy war, were uncovered after the attempt on Hitler's life on 20 July 1944. He was arrested on 11 October and spent the rest of the war in various concentration camps.

General Fromm also shared Thomas's pessimism. At the end of September 1942 he boldly submitted a memorandum to Hitler in which he argued that Germany was heading for disaster and that a negotiated end to the war was the only option.[55] Speer was informed of Fromm's alarmingly prescient analysis, but remained silent. At the same time Speer and Milch both knew that if Germany failed to gain its objectives in 1942, the chances of ultimate success would be very slim. Fromm was gradually pushed aside. He was executed in March 1945, having been implicated in the 20 July plot to assassinate Hitler.

A powerless rump organisation – the War Economics Directorate (*Wehrwirtschaftsamt*) of OKW – remained. Henceforth the services were to send their requests to this organisation to test their value and feasibility. When approved, Keitel was to forward these requests to Hitler. When Hitler agreed, they were passed to Speer's ministry for action. First they were examined by technical experts, then production facilities were sought, allocations made, raw materials and labour allocated. The result of these changes was that the military was excluded from the armaments industry, which was now the virtually exclusive preserve of the industrialists through their influence in Speer's committees and rings.

Thomas's authority had extended to enterprises in the occupied countries. General Erich Stud, who had headed the Armaments Inspection in France since August 1940 under OKW, was placed under Speer's ministry in February 1943. Speer made him responsible for procuring weapons in France in May. Similar organisations in Belgium and Holland were swallowed up in the following months. In September he appointed General Hans Leyers – an exceptionally energetic officer, a glamorous society figure and a patron of Herbert von Karajan – as his man in Italy.[56] Captain Walter Forstmann, whose U-boat U39 sank 146 ships in the First World War, for which he was awarded the Pour le Mérite, played a similar role in Denmark. A liaison officer to the Reich Commissioner was appointed in Norway and 'German Industrial Commissions' were established in Slovakia and Hungary. In all these countries Speer's men set about the ruthless exploitation of all available resources, resulting in the ruination of their domestic economies.[57] Speer was never held to account for these actions and saw no reason to mention them in his memoirs.

Speer's Armaments Inspection in the Reich Commission Ostland (Baltic States and Belarus) ran up against similar bodies from the Ministry of Economics, the Four-Year Plan and the Supreme Command of the Armed Forces. But his main rival here was Alfred Rosenberg, the Reich Minister for the Occupied Eastern Territories. His Eastern Economics Office under Werner Schlotterer jealously guarded its authority.[58] Speer sought to extend his powers as Inspector General for Roads and hoped to win Hitler's support against Rosenberg. Hitler was initially reluctant, but once again Speer got his way. As an expression of his 'limitless confidence' at the beginning of June 1942 Hitler gave Speer responsibility for technology in the occupied territories, but it was not quite clear what this involved. At the end of the month he was put in charge of all building operations. In September these powers were extended to the General Government of Poland. Göring welcomed these moves, but made sure that Speer kept his hands off the Protectorate of Bohemia and Moravia where the Hermann Göring Works had important interests that included the Škoda factory.[59]

On 17 September 1942 Göring ordered the immediate creation of Armaments Commissions to be charged with directing all matters concerning armaments within the areas of competence of the Armaments Inspectors and Reich Defence Commissioners. This gave Speer additional powers, because Göring's order stressed that the commissions were to remove all obstacles to industrial self-determination. The commissions were also given plenipotentiary powers over the allocation of labour, so that they were able to resist the demands of the military's recruitment officers.[60] Speer's executive order of 10 October created twenty-six Armaments Commissions. Each consisted of a District Armaments Agent, a delegate from Speer's ministry, the head of the local Agricultural Office and the District Economic Adviser. To these was to be added a member of the District Chamber of Commerce.

These new Armaments Commissions were chaired by commissioners handpicked by Walther Schieber from the Armaments Consignment Office in the Ministry of Armaments and by Wilhelm Zangen from the Reich Industrial Group. Working closely with the Gauleiters they selected a number of highly qualified representatives of the armaments industry. These middlemen could overrule all military and civil officials, including those of the Ministry of Economics and the German Work Front, even their own ministry's committees and rings. The Commissions took precedence over the Armaments Inspectors, the Military Districts and even the Gauleiters. Speer was anxious to avoid conflict with the Gauleiters, who also functioned as Reich Defence Commissioners, and sought to cooperate with the local military officials. The local party officials, such as the Party District Technical Officers, were subordinate to Speer as head of the Nazi Party's Main Office for Technology. This confusing combination of state and party offices provided Speer with a useful conduit to Bormann, with whom at this early stage he was on reasonably good terms.[61] This was not to last for long. As Speer rapidly accumulated power the ever-watchful Bormann came to see him as a dangerous rival, while the Gauleiters and the Nazi Party were in fundamental opposition both to his policies and his methods.

With characteristic resolve Speer seized the opportunity offered by the transport crisis in the spring of 1942 further to expand his domain. At the end of May, Hitler formed a committee under Milch to tackle the transport problem. Once its work was done it was dissolved. Having served on the committee, Speer resolved to maintain and strengthen his influence over a sector that was of critical importance to the armaments industry. To this end he appointed a special section at the Pariser Platz to deal with transportation. Speer worked closely with Albert Ganzenmüller, a fervent National Socialist who had taken part in the Hitler Putsch in 1923 while still a schoolboy. He had attracted Speer's attention for his excellent work sorting out the railway problems behind the Eastern Front during the Soviet counter-offensive in December 1941. In May 1942 Speer secured Hitler's approval for Ganzenmüller's appointment as deputy to Julius Dorpmüller, Director General of the Reich Railways, and as state secretary under Dorpmüller in his capacity as Minister of Transport. Dorpmüller was an elderly gentleman who lacked the energy to tackle the many difficulties that faced the railways.[62] Such backstairs intrigue came as a shock to him, because he had no reason to be dissatisfied with his state secretary, Wilhelm Kleinmann, a solid National Socialist and experienced technician with whom he had worked for many years. Ganzenmüller, in addition to his new duties, continued his work in the East. He organised the transportation of Jews to the death camps in *Aktion Reinhardt* in the summer of 1942. In early 1943 Himmler called upon Ganzenmüller's expertise to supervise the transportation of Jews to Auschwitz-Birkenau. He also superintended the shipment of German Jews to Theresienstadt.[63] Speer would have us believe that he knew nothing of this aspect of his protégé's work.

It was hardly surprising that the railway system was sorely taxed. The network now ran from Bordeaux to the Black Sea, from Flensburg to Athens. It had to supply the armed forces, move tens of thousands of tons of coal and deliver components and finished goods in addition to playing a key role as an instrument of judeocide. Shortage of manpower meant that too much equipment was awaiting repair, while loading and unloading of goods trains was painfully slow.

Dorpmüller soon became dependent on Ganzenmüller's expertise, Speer thereby gaining absolute control over the railways. He delegated Hans Kehrl to act on his behalf.[64] In July Speer appointed Transport Agents who were attached to each of the committees and rings. They ensured that absolute priority was given to the requirements of the armaments industry, according to its own set of priorities. As a result of these efforts the number of wagons per day on the Reichsbahn increased from 120,000 to 150,000.[65]

Speer developed a master plan for road transport in an attempt to reduce fuel consumption. Funk protested vigorously when he removed the allocation of fuel from the local economics offices of his ministry, but to no avail. Although Speer had no authority to do so, he handed over responsibility for civilian transport to the Ministry of Transport, knowing full well that Dorpmüller would give Ganzenmüller a free hand.[66] Military vehicles were placed under the supervision of General Richard Koll, head of the Armed Services Transportation Office.[67]

Speer was clever enough to avoid a head-on collision with Göring, who was still one of the most powerful figures in the Third Reich. Having first suggested to Thomas that a central planning committee for all aspects of the war economy be established under Göring, he went to the Reich Marshal's opulent country estate Carinhall on 3 March 1942, accompanied by Field Marshal Milch, Walther Schieber and Carl Krauch. Here, Speer bluntly announced that Hitler had charged him with establishing a central planning committee. Göring, when presented with what appeared to be an order from the all-highest, felt that he had no choice but to agree. In order not to be totally excluded, Göring suggested that his state secretary, Paul 'Pilli' Körner, should be a member of the new committee.[68] Speer was initially opposed to the idea, fearing that he would have too powerful a voice, but Milch persuaded him that it would be useful to have a line open to Göring and that Körner was little more than a 'harmless plant'.[69] Hitler gave his approval to the idea, appointing Speer, Milch and Körner as supra-ministerial officials, not as representatives of their respective organisations. This subtle distinction did not escape the notice of the navy, who realised that a deal had been made behind their backs. Speer was in such a powerful position that he could advise Hitler to turn down the navy's request to have a representative on the new committee.[70]

Within a few months Speer had gained full control over the army's armaments. He had managed to infiltrate and undermine the jealously guarded fiefs of the Gauleiters. He had effective control over transportation. He was steadily increasing his power over all of occupied Europe. He had proved himself to be a consummate infighter. Göring had huffed and puffed, Rosenberg had whined, Funk was resentful, Bormann and the NSDAP swore revenge, the Wehrmacht grumbled, and even within his own ministry there was considerable discontent; but they had all been forced to give way to Speer, who always had a 'Führer Order' at hand. His next move was an attempt to snatch the entire raw materials sector from Hermann Göring's mighty Four-Year Plan.

Business was conducted in a hectic and unconventional manner. When in Berlin, Speer held a continuous series of meetings to deal with the succession of orders and directives that he received from Hitler. These meetings, at which a series of important questions were raised, were usually convened at very short notice. Thus in the course of one day Hans Kehrl was called to three separate meetings at which the following issues were discussed: increasing coal production, improvements in nutrition for foreign workers, accommodation for prisoners of war working in the coal mines, economic planning in Norway and relations with the Reich Industrial Group.[71]

Such meetings were devoted almost exclusively to details. Fundamental issues were seldom discussed. Speer's approach was informal, breezy and optimistic. He preferred to avoid uncomfortable decisions and awkward facts by adopting a flippant and ironic tone that some found particularly irritating, especially in moments of crisis. When other departments faced particular difficulties Speer's staff argued that the department concerned should simply be absorbed by the Ministry of Armaments, as if that were a magic formula that could solve all problems. As a result Speer was slow to achieve a funda-mental shift in the economy towards a concentration on armaments produc-tion. When he took office 43.5 per cent of iron production was devoted to armaments. It rose to between 48 and 50 per cent during the next few quarters, but it did not reach 60 per cent until after the Stalingrad crisis.[72]

In April 1942 Speer drew up a schematic outline of the armaments industry. He divided it into four sections: transport, raw materials, labour and weapons production. He now had weapons production, at least for the army, firmly under his control. After securing major changes in personnel in the Ministry of Transport he did not foresee any serious problems in that area. He had managed to outwit Göring, whom he regarded with ill-concealed contempt, dismissing him as a ludicrously vain, drug-addled and pompous has-been, to gain virtual control over raw materials.

On 4 April 1942 Göring gave his formal approval to a decree written by Speer that established Central Planning. Among its allotted tasks were the exploitation and allocation of existing resources of raw materials and energy. It had overall control over all forms of transport as well as the allocation of labour. Its responsibilities were so complex that it is hardly surprising that it took almost two months of intense negotiations to get it into working order.[73]

Although a somewhat amorphous body, Central Planning was the key to Speer's success. It is a prime example of his ability to improvise, delegate authority and to achieve the cooperation of people with real power, ability and influence. In the short run it paid off, but in the cut-throat atmosphere of Nazi Germany, where ambitious subordinates were eager to claw their way to the top, it was fraught with tension. Central Planning was plagued by a hectic schedule and a host of duties. It was an organisation that, in spite of its impressive title, was an inchoate body without offices or a clear organisational structure. Over time a routine was established that ensured a relatively smooth operation. It was not until the third quarter of 1944 when the Allied bomber offensive had caused such disruption that effective planning gave way to frantic improvisation.[74]

Speer included a number of key figures in Central Planning in addition to 'Pilli' Körner and Milch. These included his friend Herbert Backe who had taken over control of the Ministry of Agriculture from the nominal minister, the incompetent ideologue Walther Darré. The Ministry of Transport, which was now under Albert Ganzenmüller's effective control, was also represented. Hans Kehrl from the Ministry of Economics frequently attended meetings, as did the coal tsar Paul Pleiger. The Third Reich's slave driver, Fritz Sauckel, played a significant role in its deliberations. The coal and iron associations were formally under the Minister of Economics, but due to their critical role in Central Planning in practice they were subordinate to the Ministry of Armaments.[75] Through Central Planning Speer and Milch controlled 90 per cent of Germany's armaments. Milch had the expertise combined with organisational genius, but Speer had unlimited access to Hitler, without which no decisive action could be taken.[76]

On 22 April 1942 Speer and Milch, along with Krauch, Pleiger and Schieber, gained Göring's approval for enhanced powers for what was now called the Central Planning Office of the Four-Year Plan. Although the troika of Speer, Milch and Körner formally headed Central Planning, there was no question that this was Speer's organisation. Within a few weeks he had accumulated astonishing powers by outwitting Göring, pushing Funk aside, effectively excluding OKW and the navy from the decision-making process, and by winning the industrialists' enthusiastic support. As Milch had predicted, Göring's man Körner played little part in Central Planning. Apart from making repeated pleas for the allocation of raw materials for agriculture, he remained silently passive. Milch realised that it was in his best interests to follow Speer's lead. Göring did not attend a single meeting, possibly because Speer condescendingly told him that he was not needed.[77]

As head of Organisation Todt, as well as with his duties in Berlin and Nuremberg, Speer was Germany's master builder. Göring had long since ordered Fritz Todt to concentrate on projects that were essential for the war effort, but in practice this had been largely ignored. Projects such as plants for the production of synthetic oil and nitrogen were shelved in the vain belief that victory in the Soviet Union would solve all Germany's problems. By February 1942 it was obvious that such complacency was totally inappropriate. In early March Speer obtained Hitler's approval for his scheme to make building for the armaments sector the top priority. Hitler even agreed that all civilian building should cease, sanctimoniously including his estate on the Obersalzberg.[78] This was an order that Bormann, with his ability to read Hitler's inner thoughts, simply ignored. 500,000 construction workers were now moved from the building trades to provide second and third shifts in the armaments industry. Hitler's architects – most of whom were Speer's rivals – were disinclined to follow these orders, knowing how precious their plans were to Hitler and the Gauleiters, but Speer brought them into line by cutting off supplies of raw materials. He also put an end to all post-war planning and research. From now on, all efforts had to be directed towards the Final Victory. Whatever the short-term benefits of this approach might have been, the concentration on immediate needs at the expense of future-oriented research proved disastrous in 1944 when work on weapons such as jet-propelled aircraft and the new generation of U-boats was insufficiently advanced for them to play a decisive role.

A substantial increase in the output of weapons could not be achieved without an effective system for the allocation of iron and steel. At Speer's urging, Walther Funk ordered Hans Kehrl, his representative on Central

Planning, to rethink the entire process of the management and allotment of raw materials.[79] Kehrl concluded that the existing system had to be fundamentally revised. All existing allocations were to be cancelled and re-examined by Central Planning. At a meeting on 15 May Kehrl managed to get all three branches of the Wehrmacht – represented by Fromm, Milch and Dönitz – to agree to his streamlined allocation scheme.[80] Dönitz worked in close cooperation with Speer, thereby easing the way for the Ministry of Armaments to take over responsibility for shipbuilding and naval armaments.[81] In 1942 Dönitz commanded the U-boats. In January 1943 he was to succeed Erich Raeder as Supreme Commander of the Navy.

Coal, iron and steel were formally in the hands of the Ministry of Economics, but the coal barons, with their Reichsvereinigung Kohle or Reich Coal Association, were virtually autonomous. They were fully prepared to cooperate with Central Planning, provided that their interests were respected. Iron and steel proved to be a much more difficult problem. Speer's object was to cut through the maze of separate organisations dealing with the iron and steel industry and above all to bring the wilful Paul Pleiger and the Hermann Göring Works into line. It was a challenging task because the industry was divided into different sectors and cartels, often with conflicting interests. The most powerful were the regional groups that in effect were run directly by the major firms: Oberhütten-Ballestrem in Upper Silesia, Flick in central Germany, Hermann Röchling in the south-west and Ernst Poensgen from United Steel in the north-west.[82]

Ernst Poensgen, who was one of the few industrialists to have kept an almost clean record during the Nazi years, was strongly opposed to the proposal to create a Reichsvereinigung Eisen or Reich Iron Association (RVE) because it threatened to undermine his leading role in the Ruhr. Speer suggested that Albert Vögler, the managing director of United Steel, should head this new organisation, but Hitler preferred his crony Hermann Röchling. As a leading crusader against the world Jewish conspiracy Röchling had protested vigorously that the Saarland was in danger of becoming a 'Jewish nature reserve' when anti-Semitism was temporarily downplayed in the region in preparation for the plebiscite in January 1935. Poensgen on the other hand was a conservative nationalist who was appalled at National Socialist anti-Semitism, racism and intolerance.[83]

On 29 May 1942 Speer duly appointed Hermann Röchling to head the RVE. It controlled all aspects of the iron industry from raw materials to sales. At the same time Walter 'Panzer' Rohland replaced Poensgen as head of the north-western group.[84] Poensgen resigned from all his official positions, including his position as Chairman of the board of United Steel, and retired to Kitzbühel. Funk appointed Alfried Krupp von Bohlen und Halbach and 'Panzer' Rohland as Röchling's RVE deputies to lend additional weight to the new organisation. Rohland, as Alfred Vögler's right-hand man at United Steel and Speer's intimate, effectively controlled the iron production ring, in addition to having a powerful voice in the RVE. Röchling, along with Alfried Krupp and 'Panzer' Rohland, now had virtually dictatorial powers. They were known in the RVE either as the 'Three Wise Men' or the 'Three Kings'.[85]

For Röchling, by the spring of 1942 Germany's campaign in the Soviet Union had turned into an apocalyptic struggle between Capitalism and Communism in which the performance of the steel industry played a pivotal role. This was not merely a war between states; it was the acid test for private enterprise. Röchling was staggered by the performance of the Soviet economy. The Red Air Force had lost 20,000 aircraft, but they were rapidly replaced. Tanks were being produced even in besieged and starving Leningrad. Entire factories had been moved eastwards. In certain respects, especially in tanks, the Soviets were technologically superior. Röchling feared that if the capitalist system failed to deliver the goods it might well be replaced by an alternative model; either a command economy along Soviet lines, or one based on radical National Socialist ideology. Although he endorsed National Socialism's racial and anti-Semitic policies as well as its predatory foreign political aims, he was appalled by the radical Nazis' confused notions of 'German Socialism', its attacks on 'plutocrats' and its concern for the welfare of small businesses. Speer was in full agreement with this assessment. Röchling was determined to show that private enterprise, spurred on by the profit motive and left as far as possible to its own devices, was the most efficient way of providing the armed forces with the means to win the war. Capitalism had to take up the daunting Communist challenge. Woe if it failed.[86]

It took some time for Röchling and the Reich Iron Association to get organised. The presidium first met in August 1942. All the major industrialists in the iron and steel industries were present. Along with Röchling, Krupp and Rohland were Friedrich Flick, Wilhelm Zangen from Mannesmann, Paul Pleiger from the Hermann Göring Works and Alfred Pott from Oberhütten-Ballestrem, who with Alfred Vögler in 1926 had founded Ruhrgas AG, Germany's largest gas company. In addition there were representatives from Saxony and Austria – now the Ostmark – as well as from the German Work Front. The association was further strengthened because Flick and Krupp also played key roles in the Reich Coal Association (RVK). The board of directors included all these powerful industrialists. Hans-Günther Sohl from United Steel and Eugen Langen from the Röchling works were the chief executive officers.[87] It is noticeable that the Hermann Göring Works had relatively little influence in this new organisation. The RVE was thus a perfect example of Speer's industrial self-determination in action. The Ministry of Economics had no influence over it, even though it was formally under its control, and Göring was eclipsed. Speer, at least for the moment, was the hands-off man in charge and gratefully acknowledged as such. There was no input from labour, no political control and no irksome outside interference, as long as he delivered the goods.

The fundamental problem now was how to get RVE and RVK to work together so that the steel industry's demands for coal could be met. This task was rendered all the more difficult by Hitler's unrealistic demands for increased output. On 28 October 1942 a meeting was held at the Ministry of Armaments in an attempt to settle the problem of iron and coal allocations. Hitler was present. 'Panzer' Rohland, who had been chosen to speak on behalf of the iron and steel industries because of his outspokenness, bitterly complained that the agreement made with Hitler on 13 August to produce 2.65 million metric tons of steel per month was totally unrealistic. Pleiger, the chairman of the Reich Coal Association, clearly listed the difficulties facing the coal industry. Coal production in Belgium and northern France had dropped significantly, because of the shortage of manpower, undernourishment and inadequate transport facilities. Norway and Sweden were running desperately short of supplies and were demanding relief. In Germany there was widespread discontent over the shortage of household coal. Krauch's insatiable demand for coal for his chemical industries further exacerbated the situation.[88] At this point Hitler lost his temper and warned the hapless Pleiger that if he could not meet the requirements of the steel industry the war would be lost. A stunned Pleiger could only mutter that he would do his best. Again Hitler had shown, in a moment of depression and desperation, that deep down he knew that the chances of winning the war were very slim.[89] The results of the summer offensive were disappointing. The situation at Stalingrad was beginning to cause concern and the Wehrmacht had not met its objectives in the Caucasus. The Panzer Army in Africa was in a desperate situation at El Alamein.

Rohland estimated that it might just be possible for the monthly rate of steel production to reach 2.4 million metric tons, but by January this would drop to 2.2 million metric tons at most. Even these disappointing figures could only be met if coal supplies were sufficient. He blamed Pleiger for this situation, pointing out that coal supplies had fallen drastically. Rohland then made the absurd claim that he could produce the 2.65 million metric tons monthly as demanded by Hitler, but only in the forlorn hope that Pleiger could increase coal production as Hitler had ordered. Speer tried to calm things down by ordering Rohland, Pleiger and Schieber to get together and sort out their differences, but Rohland remained adamant. He called for a substantial increase in coal deliveries, for which he demanded an allocation of 68,000 additional workers.[90]

In November 1942 Speer announced at a meeting of Central Planning that the failure of the coal and steel industries to meet their targets put the entire private enterprise system in question. If the policy of industrial self-determination, coupled with systematic rationalisation to save raw materials and manpower, failed to work, then Central Planning would have to hand over the reins to Göring and Hitler.[91]

Speer now reduced the figure promised to Hitler to 2.5 million metric tons of steel per month. Rohland now insisted that 2.4 million was the absolute limit of the possible, whereupon Speer made a scantily disguised threat. His entire system of industrial self-determination was now put in question. The theory that if industry were left alone it would do the job had been put to the test and had been found wanting. When Speer presented the plans for the first quarter of 1943 to Hitler in early December, he had to admit that the navy and munitions would have their iron and steel allocations cut. The prospects for the future were bleak. It was estimated that there would be severe shortages of iron and steel in the second quarter of 1943, which meant that a number of important programmes would have to be shelved. The situation worsened when the demands for air-raid precautions rose dramatically as the Allied air offensive gathered momentum. Increasing demands from the Waffen-SS placed further strain on the system. Speer tried to put an optimistic gloss on this parlous state of affairs, but he had to admit that his efforts significantly to increase iron and steel production had failed due to shortages of coal, ore, labour and industrial capacity. Knowing that the situation was intractable, he was not prepared to apportion blame. He loyally defended Pleiger against Rohland's unwarranted attacks. The question remains open as to whether, even had these production figures for coal and iron been met, it would have been possible to significantly increase armaments production. Speer knew that industrial capacity was already stretched to the limit, so that much of this steel would never have entered the production process.[92]

Due to exceptional efforts by all concerned, including a significant cut in the already minimal allocation of household coal, the results were nevertheless impressive. At the beginning of December 1942 Hitler congratulated Pleiger for raising annual coal production from 317.9 million metric tons to 340.4 million metric tons.[93] In spite of Speer's dire predictions, steel production reached a record high of 2.7 million metric tons per month in the first quarter of 1943.

Speer had achieved impressive results, but Milch had done even better by taking a quite different approach. From May 1941 procurement was conducted by an Industrial Council in the Air Ministry that severely limited the influence of major firms.[94] Milch had no truck with industrial self-determination, preferring to intervene directly to achieve his ends. In 1934 Hugo Junkers had been forced to sell 51 per cent of his aircraft company along with all his patents. Friedrich Flick's close associate, Heinrich Koppenberg, was put in charge of the company. He was a brutal bully with no knowledge of the aircraft industry who set illusory production targets. Milch summarily dismissed him later that year.

When BMW faced problems with its radial engines Milch put the deputy chairman of the Industrial Council, William Werner, in charge of production. He was an American-born engineer from Junkers/Auto Union who had studied mass production techniques in Detroit.[95] In April 1942 Milch used the serious design flaws in the Messerschmitt Me 210 ground-attack aircraft as an excuse to wrest control of the company from Willy Messerschmitt. Financial difficulties at Heinkel led to Ernst Heinkel's dismissal in 1943. Thus the Air Ministry now had direct control over all three major aircraft companies.

In spite of bureaucratic control and a total lack of entrepreneurial freedom, the aircraft industry achieved some astonishing results. Aircraft production doubled between 1942 and 1943. Mass-production techniques using smaller numbers of unskilled and semi-skilled labour and the adoption of processes that greatly reduced the wastage of metals made it possible to increase production without significant increases in labour and raw materials. Milch's decision to concentrate on the mass production of tried and tested models boosted output, but it was at the cost of developing new models that were already on the drawing board. The Luftwaffe's trusted workhorses – such as the Me 109 fighter and the He 111 bomber – were rapidly becoming obsolete. Opting for quantity rather than quality, Milch was forcing aircrews into machines that were rapidly reducing their chances of survival.

From the outset Speer realised that it would be impossible to increase the production of each and every imaginable product needed by the military. Priority had to be given to things that in his view would decide the outcome of the war. These included munitions, tanks, trucks and locomotives. In July 1942, in addition to the categories S (special category) and SS (extra special category), he added the category DE for projects that needed to be rapidly developed and produced on a relatively small scale. Priorities were set by a select group within the committees and sanctioned by Speer in consultation with Hitler. The problem was that Hitler was constantly changing his mind. A minimal change in priorities could put entire programmes out of kilter. Hitler also had the tiresome habit of demanding the impossible. In 1942 the exceptionally high cost of ammunition on the Eastern Front led him to demand a dramatic increase in production. Since the basic raw materials, especially chemicals, were not available in sufficient quantities, Speer had to use all his powers of persuasion to get Hitler to accept less ambitious target figures.[96] Shortage of ammunition was to plague the Wehrmacht throughout the war and was to become chronic as it drew to an end.

Speer was in full agreement with Hitler that the tank would be the decisive weapon. Hitler, insisting that weight was more important than speed, commissioned Ferdinand Porsche and the Krupp concern in March 1942 to build a 100-metric-ton tank, making it three times heavier than the Soviet T-34. Giving this project top priority and calling for a prototype to be ready by early 1943, he stopped all further development of motor vehicles. Henceforth only existing models would be built.[97] Production of the Panzer II was significantly reduced and self-propelled guns were henceforth to be equipped with the powerful 7.5 cm Pak 40 anti-tank gun. Production of the Panzer IIIs was stepped up in 1942. Although it proved worthless against Soviet armour, when equipped with a 7.5 cm L24 gun it proved relatively effective as infantry support. The Panzer IV was now equipped with a high-velocity 75mm gun that was effective against Soviet armour. Hitler's monster tank, however, never went into production. The Wehrmacht's heaviest tank, the Tiger II, weighed a more modest 69.8 metric tons.[98]

Speer wanted to concentrate on the manufacture of assault guns at the expense of tanks, because with their fixed turrets they were easier to manufacture, but Hitler insisted that work on the Panzer V Panther should go ahead. He took a lively interest in the Panther, thereby causing Speer many headaches. His constant calls for changes in the design made an effective programme virtually impossible. Suddenly, in May 1942, he insisted that all tanks should be equipped with the 75mm KwK 40 gun, even before adequate tests had been carried out. He dismissed Speer's objections, claiming that even if the gun did not prove suitable, the tanks could still be used when rearmed. In June Hitler ordered front armour to be increased to 80 mm. Two weeks later he countermanded this order, thereby causing considerable material waste.[99]

Work went ahead on the 56.9-metric-ton Tiger I for which both Hitler and Speer had high hopes. In March 1942 Speer made the extravagant claim that Ferdinand Porsche would be able to produce 60 Tigers by October and Henschel 25, before even deciding which model should go into large-scale production. It soon turned out that the Porsche Tiger was a disaster. Its chassis was used to build a 65-ton tank destroyer, first known as the Elephant and then as Ferdinand. Once again Hitler constantly called for changes and modifications while demanding that the Tiger I be tested at the front as soon as possible. It was first used in combat at Leningrad in the summer of 1942. Early reports suggested that the tank was too heavy, but Hitler ignored these criticisms. He ordered Speer to increase its weight to 120 metric tons and arm it with a very powerful gun. Tests showed that this was impossible. The main armament was to be increased to 88mm and its range increased from 50 to 150 kilometres. In spite of all these difficulties 78 Tigers reached the front by the end of 1942, whereas not a single Panther was ready for combat.[100]

Hitler wanted Daimler-Benz to build the Panther, but Speer managed to persuade him that MAN was better suited to the task. He promised that 250 would be built by May 1943. It was a rash pledge. Production was hampered by there being six different types of tank under construction at the same time and by Hitler's persistent demands for modifications. Speer's tank specialists – Rohland,

Porsche, Erich Müller from Krupp and Gerhard Stieler von Heydekamp from Opel's Brandenburg Works – were sorely tried by Hitler's meddling and his insistence that in every instance armour was more important than speed. This was something that Speer had reluctantly to accept. 'The Führer's decision,' he remarked wearily, 'must be regarded as final.'[101] In spite of all these wrangles the number of tanks produced increased, but Speer was unable to achieve the mass production of standard models for which he had hoped.

Hitler's fixation on armour prompted Porsche to propose a 188-metric-ton monster, the Panzer VIII 'Mouse', armed with two guns of 128 and 150mm that would require a turret weighing 50 metric tons. Two of these behemoths went into action in the final stages of the war. They did nothing to stop the Red Army's advance. Even more grotesque was Hitler's request for two engineers from Krupp to draw up plans for the Land Cruiser 1000 'Rat', a 1,500-ton tank armed with a 800mm gun and powered by eight Daimler-Benz marine diesel engines. Unsurprisingly this monstrosity never saw the light of day.[102]

Throughout the summer and autumn of 1942 Hitler modified, chopped and changed Speer's tank programme. In November Speer drew up a new set of priorities in the 'Adolf Hitler Panzer Programme', which was discussed at length in late November and finalised at a three-day conference at Hitler's headquarters, ending on 1 December.[103] Rohland gave a measured presentation, carefully pointing out all the many problems that had to be overcome, principal among them the lack of metals and machine tools. Hitler brushed these aside, blandly remarking that the tanks had to be delivered regardless of any obstacles. On 22 January 1943 the programme was made public in a massive publicity campaign. It promised a fourfold increase in tank production within two years, even though Speer had warned Hitler that he could only manage to guarantee an increase in the production of Panzer IVs and assault guns.[104] He would have to wait until the Panther programme got up to full stream before making any promises. Tanks were nevertheless given top priority for raw materials and transport, skilled workers working on tanks were not to be enlisted and those already serving in the armed services were to be released. Speer was given exceptional powers to make sure that these measures were enforced. Any who failed to do their bit were to be brought before the People's Court.[105] Workers in tank factories were required to put in a 72-hour week, with firms adopting a two-shift daily routine. It was reported that some workers volunteered to work 24-hour shifts. A few modest perks were offered: extra rations, vitamin pills, an extra clothing allowance and holidays in a 'Strength Through Joy' resort in the Tyrol.[106]

In industrial circles the Adolf Hitler Panzer Programme was renamed the 'Saur Action', Speer having handed over the reins to his deputy. It was a decision he was to live to regret. Hitler, encouraged by Saur, continued to demand the impossible. In July 1943 Germany did not have enough tanks to trap the Red Army in the Kursk salient. According to Field Marshal Manstein, Hitler promised him a large quantity of Tigers, Panthers, Ferdinands and assault guns for 'Operation Citadel'. It was all in vain.[107] The Soviets had twice the number of tanks. The Panzer III was already obsolete. The Panthers had severe teething problems, frequently breaking down and easily catching fire. The Tigers with their heavy armour proved difficult to kill, but there were not enough of them to play a decisive role. The lumbering Ferdinand was virtually immune to anti-tank fire. Armed with an 88mm gun it proved devastating in a tank-to-tank engagement, but since it did not have a machine gun it was very vulnerable to infantry attack. The Soviets were quick to counter the Tiger by equipping their updated T-34/85 with an 85mm gun that could pierce the Tiger's armour from a distance of 500 metres.

Yet in spite of all the emphasis placed on the tank, only 7 per cent of the armaments budget was devoted to its production. The Adolf Hitler Panzer Programme did not have a significant effect on the increase in the total amount of armaments, the lion's share of which was attributable to Milch and his aircraft. Even though tanks were given absolute priority, they often disrupted other weapons programmes, Milch was able to produce 2,200 aircraft in a single month, thereby overshadowing the Panzer Programme's heavily publicised 1,270 vehicles in the same period, most of which were obsolete.[108]

During his first year in office Speer had achieved a great deal. Building on the solid foundations laid by Todt, with no substantial increase in raw materials and in spite of an acute shortage of skilled labour, he had managed significantly to increase output by concentration, standardisation and rationalisation as well as by increasing the transport available to the armaments industry. Hitler had given Speer authority to shut down all branches of industry that were not directly or indirectly connected to armaments and supported him in almost all instances. Speer's success gave him immense authority over the military and industry, but there were already some cracks in the system. The Gauleiters and the party were far from enthusiastic about him, and his more ambitious underlings were already beginning to threaten his position.

It took some time for those involved to realise that Speer's calls for 'rationalisation', which seemed to be self-evident, were in fact little more than an expression of his determination to extend his power and influence over every aspect of the armaments industry. This necessarily resulted in economic and military considerations giving way to instrumental rationality. Armaments production was now marked by inflexibility and a concentration on mega-projects of questionable value. 'Rationalisation' was thus little more than the National Socialist 'Leadership Principle' in another guise. It was a call for heedless leadership and blind obedience. For all the talk of the self-determination of industry, initiative was stifled, innovation discouraged and compromise difficult to reach.[109] Even though, like Todt, he never had anything that might be described as a system, Speer was widely regarded as a miracle worker who would be able to provide Germany with the means to overcome its enemies. All now depended on the army's ability to secure Nazi Germany's sphere of influence, so that raw materials and labour were available in sufficient quantities, and on the Luftwaffe guaranteeing that the roof over Fortress Germany remained intact.

CHAPTER SIX

LABOUR: FREE, FORCED AND SLAVE

THE IDEA OF appointing a 'manpower dictator' – the expression came from Todt – had been discussed soon after the setback at Moscow in December 1941 in a series of discussions between the Ministry of Armaments, OKW, the Four-Year Plan, the Ministry of Labour and industry in the guise of the Reich Industrial Group, the Reich Coal Association and Carl Krauch as Plenipotentiary for Chemicals. In January 1942 Göring gave Dr Werner Mansfeld, an efficiency expert from the Ministry of Labour – a man who specialised in the ruthless exploitation of Soviet prisoners of war – 'unrestrained and exceptional power to control the allocation of all available labour once the recruitment require- ments of the armed services had been met'.[1] He thereby replaced Friedrich Syrup, the man responsible for labour within the Four-Year Plan, who had suffered a nervous breakdown.[2]

Todt objected strongly to appointing a bureaucrat from the Ministry of Labour, seconded to the Four-Year Plan, in order to deal with the allocation of labour. He felt that this should be the sole responsibility of his ministry. But Mansfeld soon proved to be something of a damp squib. His powers were never clearly defined. Speer felt that he lacked sufficient drive. The Gauleiters, who had control over labour in their districts, put up stiff resistance to any form of centralisation. Hitler was unsure about appointing a manpower dictator, who was bound to step on a number of sensitive toes and who would likely have a deleterious influence on social policy.

Speer and the coterie of powerful industrialists who surrounded him were determined to rationalise and centralise the allocation of manpower. Six million workers had been drafted into the armed forces and were only partially replaced by shifting manpower from trades and crafts, or by setting prisoners of war to work. Speer realised that manpower was a major problem that needed to be addressed immediately. There is some indication that he hoped to gain personal control over the allocation of labour, but he doubted that he would be able to overcome the fierce objections of the Gauleiters. He therefore suggested that his old friend Karl Hanke, the ruthless Gauleiter of Lower Silesia, would be the ideal man for the job. Both Hitler and Göring thought that this was an acceptable choice, but Hanke was a controversial figure. In 1938 the Propaganda Minister had fallen for a young Czech starlet, Lída Baarová, prompting his sorely tried wife Magda to seek solace in Hanke's arms, who at that time was secretary of state in Goebbels' ministry. Bormann played on this episode in order to persuade Hitler to appoint someone in his stead who would be easier to control.[3] He suggested that his friend Fritz Sauckel, the Gauleiter of Thuringia, was more suitable for the task. Speer concurred with Bormann's choice, because he was preferable to Robert Ley, who was desperately trying to secure the job. Speer argued that it would be a bad idea to give the task of commandeering labour to an organisation that in theory represented workers' interests.[4] Hitler agreed that it would be politically unwise to give the job to Ley – an itinerant preacher for 'German Socialism' – whose German Work Front was designed as the cornerstone of the Nazi welfare state. This would be hard to reconcile with the task of allocating forced labour to the armaments industry or obliging German women to become factory workers. The myth of the 'racial community' had to be preserved.

On 21 March 1942 Hitler duly appointed Fritz Sauckel General-bevollmächtigter für den Arbeitseinsatz or Plenipotentiary for the Employment of Labour. He seemed to be an ideal choice. As a Gauleiter he was in an advantageous position to deal with others of his ilk. As a bullnecked demagogue with impeccable Jew-baiting credentials and dogged devotion to his Führer, he was politically beyond reproof. He also had some knowledge of the armaments industry, having in 1936 founded the armaments firm the Wilhelm Gustloff Foundation in Suhl. It was based on a company established by Löb and Moses Simson that had been 'Aryanised'. Through this firm Sauckel had close ties to Carl Goetz, the head of the Dresdner Bank, and to Walther Schieber in the Ministry of Armaments.[5] As was soon apparent during the Nuremberg trials, Speer and Sauckel were totally different personalities in social background, education, comportment and temperament. As a result there was potential friction between the two men. Sauckel made it quite clear that he was willing to meet Speer's labour requirements, but refused to accept them as orders.[6] Bormann was delighted at thus having at least partially frustrated Speer's plan to have direct control over the allocation of labour.

Hitler initially thought of placing Sauckel under Speer's command. Hans Lammers, his tirelessly vigilant head of chancellery, vigorously objected to this suggestion, ostensibly on administrative grounds, but almost certainly because he felt that Speer was rapidly accumulating too much power. This was Speer's first setback in his campaign to take over control of the entire economy. He had to make do with Sauckel's 'collegial cooperation'.[7]

Hitler initially agreed to Göring's suggestion that Sauckel should be his subordinate in the Four-Year Plan. Speer was outraged. In Hitler's presence he brusquely told Sauckel that he had to work for him. Speer pointed out that he was also Plenipotentiary for Armaments within the Four-Year Plan and as such Sauckel was his subordinate.[8] This nicety was overlooked in practice, thereby providing a blessing in disguise, because it enabled Speer to claim at Nuremberg that his relationship with Sauckel was at arm's length. Speer's contention, not only that Sauckel acted independently from him, but that he was also his adversary, helped save his neck. A number of historians have swallowed this tale, making Sauckel alone responsible for all the gruesome inhumanity associated with the recruitment and employment of forced labour.[9]

One thing was certain. Output could not be boosted without a significant increase in a labour force that had been drastically depleted owing to the recruitment requirements of the military after the failure of Operation Barbarossa. Hitler and the Nazi Party were loath to exploit the already sorely pressed domestic labour market fully for fear of political repercussions. Hitler's charismatic power rested on the faith the people invested in him. To demand excessive sacrifices, principally from women, at this stage of the war would tarnish his image. A remarkably high percentage of German women were already in the workforce: 52 per cent of German women between the ages of 15 and 60 were gainfully employed in 1939. In Britain the figure was 45 per cent, in the USA only 36 per cent. German women worked mainly on small-scale peasant farms, in domestic service, in the retail trade and as clerical workers.[10] Even in the final stages of the war German women were not called upon to enter the armaments factories. The National Socialist ideology of the 'subhuman' provided a simple answer. The vast resources of labour in the East could be ruthlessly exploited to fill the gaps in the domestic market.

On 3 May 1942 Keitel circulated a memorandum to Speer, Göring and Sauckel in which he stated that he intended to recruit 115,000 workers classified as 'indispensable' ('unabkömmlich gestellt', shortened to 'uk-gestellt'). Speer set about ensuring that wherever possible skilled workers in the armaments industry were safe from OKW's predatory hands. By June, with the military having suffered unexpectedly heavy losses and about to launch the summer offensive, the need for manpower was pressing. Speer promptly visited Hitler and managed to get the numbers reduced, but he had to promise that the criteria for 'indispensability' would be made more stringent. This left a relatively small number of absolutely indispensable workers, whom Hitler guaranteed would not be required to do military service.[11] He was prepared to make this concession because he was in an optimistic mood, claiming that casualties in Army Group South were relatively light.

Sauckel provided a vast number of workers to replace those recruited by the military, but they were mostly in such poor health that they did not solve Speer's problems. Speer agreed with Sauckel that industrial workers needed to be reasonably well fed in order to function effectively. Almost as soon as he was appointed Armaments Minister he told Hitler that Soviet workers had to be properly fed if they were to be of any use. Somewhat surprisingly, Hitler was in full agreement with this. Herbert Backe at the Ministry of Food and Agriculture was ordered to provide the food. This was a curious commission for a man who cold-bloodedly planned to starve thirty million Soviet citizens to death.[12] In a fit of righteous indignation Hitler, temporarily casting his racist theories aside, said that it was outrageous that Soviet civilians should be treated like prisoners of war. Eastern workers were to be given the same rations as other foreign workers, their wages were increased and they were allowed greater freedom of movement. In a remarkable ideological U-turn it was announced that 'Russian labour is the most valuable booty that the German economy has won from the Russian campaign.'[13] This new approach did not last for long, however. As rations for ordinary Germans were reduced there were widespread complaints that the *Ostarbeiter* were better fed than the average 'racial comrade'. On 17 April 1942, less than a month after Hitler had increased the rations for Soviet workers, they were once again reduced.

The Krupp concern was quick to complain. It reported that 30 per cent of their Soviet prisoners of war were unable to work due to undernourishment. Twelve had already died. Civilian Soviet workers, who appeared to be in excellent health when they arrived, were also showing signs of severe malnutrition. The ELFI Works in Hildesheim reported that Ukrainians who were perfectly willing to work were collapsing on the shop floor due to hunger.[14] Defending themselves against any possible charge of 'sentimentality' they insisted that these workers be given adequate rations in order that they might work at maximum efficiency. The Reich Industrial Group submitted a memorandum stating that although the minimal rations given to Soviet workers might be politically desirable, from a practical point of view they were indefensible. OKW agreed, arguing that the categories of 'labour', 'heavy labour' and 'heaviest labour', used to determine the number of calories per day required, should not take 'racial provenance' into consideration.[15] Speer was equally unsentimental. He disagreed with Himmler, not on moral but on practical grounds. Starving workers to death was not an effective way to run a business. For the same reason Speer was determined to frustrate Himmler's efforts to build an armaments industry within the concentration camps. This was not merely a threat to the industrialists' profits, which Speer saw as the motivating force behind an efficient economy, it was also grossly inefficient.

Himmler and the SS indeed took a very different approach. They saw industrial labour as an alternative method for the elimination of inferior races. 'Extermination by Work' was a practical alternative to the gas chamber. On 31 January 1942 Himmler told Oswald Pohl, the head of his Main Economics and Organisational Office, that henceforth 80 per cent of the armaments of the SS were to be made by the SS itself. Extensive use was to be made of concentration camp inmates. The camps were no longer to be seen as mainly 'political' institutions, but as sources of labour.[16] Pohl aimed to produce armaments within the concentration camp system, thereby avoiding any contact with the industrialists. From the outset Speer was determined to meet this challenge. He aimed to exploit the labour harboured by Himmler in his concentration camps in the armaments industry, just as he had done for his projects in Nuremberg and Berlin. He was thereby following the example set by Erhard Milch, who had used workers from the concentration camps in the aviation industry six months before Speer signed an agreement with Oswald Pohl.[17] Every week clerks from Speer and Sauckel's offices would present Pohl with detailed requests for labour from the concentration camps. Pohl would send these lists to the Inspector General of the Concentration Camps, SS-Gruppenführer Richard Gluecks in Oranienburg, for immediate action. Pohl frequently met Speer to discuss questions of housing, food and medical attention for workers taken from the concentration camps. Pohl had to admit that their minimum requirements were seldom met.[18]

In July Himmler told Walther Schieber, head of the Armaments Consignment Office, that he intended to build a factory in Kattowitz (Katowice) that would make heavy mortars, machine guns and the coachwork for trucks. Speer was deeply suspicious of this initiative. He was determined to resist Himmler's attempt to build armaments factories in the concentration camps. This would not only threaten Speer's hold over armaments production but would also reduce the amount of slave labour available to him. He ordered Schieber, who held high office within the SS, to conduct further negotiations with Himmler and Pohl.[19]

Karl-Otto Saur was also utterly opposed to the idea of building an armaments factory in Auschwitz. Pohl advised Himmler not to push this point. He agreed to Saur's suggestion that labour from concentration camps should be made available for the armaments industry and that special concentration camps were to be built close to certain armaments factories. Speer requested that 50,000 Jewish prisoners should be made available to work in existing factories. 'Appropriate accommodation' would be made available for them. Speer also secured Pohl's agreement for the concentration camps to produce building materials, such as standardised window frames and doors, to be used to repair bomb-damaged houses. Building Brigades, each of one thousand men, were to be formed in Sachsenhausen, Neuengamme and Buchenwald.

Armed with picks and shovels they were to act under Speer's orders, clearing debris after air raids. After the Final Victory these would be converted into Peace Brigades with the task of building the new Germany. Speer and the SS worked closely together clearing bomb damage and repairing damaged housing. For this, Himmler's organisation earned the thanks of the public, which was thus diverted from the less attractive activities of the SS.[20]

Although Speer wanted Himmler to provide him with slave labour, he still saw the Reichsführer-SS as a potential rival. He vetoed Pohl's request for the SS to build a foundry at the Volkswagen works in Fallersleben, whereupon Pohl, anxious to avoid any direct confrontation with Speer, discreetly went ahead with his own plans. He started to manufacture carbines in Buchenwald, pistols in Neuengamme and 37mm anti-aircraft guns in Auschwitz. Women in Ravensbrück were employed to make radios for the Waffen-SS. None of these schemes was worthwhile.[21]

Pohl had to admit that the few factories run by the SS were hopelessly inefficient and that Himmler had admitted that they produced nothing but 'dribs and drabs'. Both Speer and Himmler were frustrated. The concentration camps were incapable of providing a suitable labour force and the SS had neither the technical expertise nor sufficient management skills to run armaments factories effectively.[22] In conferences with Hitler on 20 and 22 September 1942 Speer managed to convince him that neither moving factories into the concentration camps, nor having the SS running factories outside them, was practical. A proposed alternative was that there should be a second shift in certain key factories made up of concentration camp inmates. Hitler agreed to this suggestion, adding that between 3 and 5 per cent of the weapons thereby produced should go to the SS.[23]

Speer suggested to Hitler that private industry should be allowed to hire concentration camp inmates directly, rather than having to go through the Ministry of Armaments and Sauckel. Hitler endorsed this plan so that henceforth industrialists made their needs known to Oswald Pohl's SS Economics and Armaments Office.[24] Firms such as Heinkel, Messerschmitt, Volkswagen and IG Farben, promptly asked for workers from Himmler's concentration camps.[25] Soon most of Germany's leading firms, from Krupp to the Hermann Göring Works, Daimler Benz and BMW, and the construction companies Hochtief and Philipp Holzmann, were employing workers from the camps. They got them on the cheap. Initially they cost 1 Reichsmark per day, but this soon rose to 6 Reichsmarks for skilled and 4 Reichsmarks for unskilled labour and women. 110,000 such workers were employed by the end of September 1942. The figure rose steadily to reach 700,000 by early 1945.[26] Among the most energetic of the recruiters of workers from the camps were Speer's deputy head of Organisation Todt, Franz Xaver Dorsch, as well as his intimates Paul Pleiger and Ferdinand Porsche.

As head of Organisation Todt, Speer was also directly involved in the concentration camps. In September 1942 he chaired a meeting with Pohl and SS-Oberführer Hans Kammler, the man responsible for building the camps, the gas chambers and the crematoria. Saur and Schieber from his ministry were also in attendance.[27] Speer agreed to Kammler's request to expand Auschwitz and other camps, allocating 13.7 million Reichsmarks for this purpose. This would enable 300 more huts to be built, providing housing for 132,000 in Auschwitz. Included in the requirements for 'Prisoner of War Camp Auschwitz (Implementation of Special Treatments)' was material to build crematoria, morgues and 'disinfestation facilities'. Henceforth the building programme at Auschwitz was known in the SS as 'Professor Speer's Special Programme'.[28] Oswald Pohl told Himmler on 19 April 1943 that Speer had been fully informed of the details of these grim structures.

On 21 May 1943 Speer sent two of his men, Friedrich Desch and Armin Sander, to Auschwitz to examine the work that had been done to extend the camp and build new crematoria.[29] Speer's inspection team, together with two representatives from his OT construction team in Silesia, met Kammler and the camp commandant, SS-Obersturmbannführer Rudolf Höss, to discuss his requirements for steel and the use of inmates as forced labour. In the course of the discussions Höss pointed out that the main purpose of the camp was 'the solution of the Jewish question'. Desch and Sander gave Speer an 'in-depth' report of this meeting, whereupon Speer told Himmler that he agreed to all of Höss's demands.[30] On 30 May Speer agreed to give Himmler the materials he had requested to extend the concentration camps, including Auschwitz, but he disingenuously regretted that he would not be able to provide an additional allowance for the Waffen-SS. In a handwritten note below his signature he added: 'I am delighted that the visit to other concentration camps made a very positive impression.'[31]

Speer was also closely involved in providing building materials for the expansion of the concentration camps. In a letter to Himmler in April 1943 he said that he had allocated 7 million Reichsmarks and 1,000 metric tons of steel to expand the camps during 1943. A smaller amount would be available the following year. The largest sum was designated for Auschwitz. Speer admonished the SS for being spendthrift with building materials for concentration camps and suggested they could use cheaper construction methods. He was clearly dissatisfied with the number of slave labourers he was getting following the agreement made with Himmler in September. Faced with a crisis situation after the Stalingrad debacle, Speer was determined to act.[32]

Oswald Pohl affected to be outraged by Speer's remarks. He rejected the charge of wastefulness out of hand, insisting that they had enough of a problem with poor sanitary conditions, disease and high death rates for it to be possible to provide even more primitive accommodation for inmates. Pohl was particularly upset by Speer's complaint that the buildings at Mauthausen were so substantial: 'It is utterly absurd to start using primitive construction methods in concentration camps. Reich Minister Speer does not seem to realise that at the moment we have 160,000 prisoners. Returning to primitive building methods would probably cause a hitherto unimaginable death rate in the camps.' He pointed out that all projected buildings in the concentration camps had to be approved by Speer's ministry, the printed forms required having been provided by him as Inspector General of Buildings. Mauthausen had, after all, been built at a time when there was no great shortage of building materials.[33]

Further evidence that Speer was well informed about the details of the Final Solution is contained in a letter he wrote to Himmler on 1 February 1943.[34] Himmler intended to 'evacuate' 40,000 Jews from the ghetto in Bialystok to make way for 40,000 White Russian peasants evacuated from an area that was teeming with partisans. He felt that for them to have adequate accommodation he would need building materials for 20,000 housing units. Speer wrote to Himmler regretting that he was unable to help. He explained that he needed all available building material for housing workers in the armaments industry and for 'racial comrades' who had been bombed out. When confronted with this document after the war Speer claimed that although it had been sent under his signature, he had never seen it.[35]

Although Speer and Pohl were often at loggerheads, Pohl agreed to select able-bodied Jews from eastern Europe so that they 'could interrupt their journey and work in the armaments industry'. In other words, they would be given temporary remission from the gas chambers.[36] Since Hitler and Himmler were determined to make Germany 'free from Jews', or *Judenfrei*, and Sauckel provided a sufficient quantity of foreign labour, however, nothing much came of this scheme. Those Jews capable of working were now sent to Auschwitz-Monowitz.

Speer was later to argue that he had done what he could to save Jews from the concentration camps by employing them in the armaments industry, although he had to admit that the death rate among workers was exceedingly high. Some might argue that the distinction between being an undernourished, overworked slave living in appalling conditions and being a concentration camp inmate was often only one of degree. Speer's humanitarian efforts to persuade Hitler to permit him to keep his skilled Jewish workers were frustrated as early as 28 May 1942 when Hitler assured Goebbels that he would order Speer 'as soon as possible to ensure that all the Jews employed in the German armaments industry were replaced by foreign workers'.[37] Sauckel said to Hitler that this could easily be done. A shortage of transport saved a few Jewish armaments workers from being deported immediately, but Speer did very little to protect those who remained under his aegis. The Wehrmacht and

Hans Frank in the General Government had a far better record, however suspect their motives.[38] Goebbels found Speer's efforts to spare Jewish workers 'laughable'. He confided in his diary that: 'Now we believe that we cannot do without skilled Jewish workers, when not so long ago we repeatedly claimed that Jews never work and don't even know the meaning of the word.'[39] He did not seem to notice that therein lay yet another absurd contradiction within National Socialist anti-Semitism.

By the autumn of 1942, with the Red Army fighting desperately amid the ruins of Stalingrad, Speer found it increasingly difficult to resist the pressure from the armed forces to recruit workers from his armaments factories. He used this threat to discipline his workforce. In October 1942 he wrote: 'The problem of scrimshanking has reached the point when we really must do something. Ley has found out that whenever a doctor is present the number of sick people is reduced by between one-quarter and one-fifth. The SS and police should get tough. Known scrimshankers should be sent to concentration camps. There is no other solution.'[40] Speer added that special attention should be paid to Soviet workers. They were known to be particularly skilful at feigning sickness.

On 22 November 1942 – the day that the Red Army entrapped Paulus' 6th Army in Stalingrad – Hitler appointed General Walter von Unruh to head a special commission that would comb the rear echelons of the armed forces, the civil service and industry to find more men for active service. Unruh was the scion of an ancient aristocratic family, a zealous National Socialist and outspoken anti-Semite. Speer was determined to keep this man, who was soon nicknamed the 'Hero Snatcher', at arm's length. He managed to get Hitler's agreement to his proposal that none of those workers designated as essential should be called up before the end of the year. In December Hitler ordered the release of 50,000 workers from the consumer goods industries in three instalments. These workers were to be replaced by older members of the armed forces. This was to be followed by the recruitment of 100,000 armaments workers hitherto classified as indispensable.[41] Speer managed to ensure that certain programmes, such as 'Panzer' Rohland's tanks and special operations within Organisation Todt, were left untouched. He interpreted this agreement in the widest possible sense. Thus when party authorities in Brandenburg began to investigate whether there was some excess fat in the Organisation for Trade and Industry, the Reich Industrial Group immediately objected. Their appeal was upheld.[42] 'Industrial self-determination' was thus exempted from scrutiny, at least for the moment.

There followed a series of clashes between the Unruh Commission and Speer's ministry that was typical of the wrangling over areas of competence in the polycratic Nazi state.[43] A three-man commission of Keitel, Lammers and Bormann that Göring also facetiously called the 'Three Kings' proved singularly ineffective in solving the Wehrmacht's manpower problems. All three were totally submissive to Hitler's fractious moods and high-handed behaviour, so that they were incapable of independent action. Speer did what he could to sabotage their efforts. Goebbels, who was angered by the failure of the 'Three Kings' to give the country effective leadership, gave Speer his full support. In the late summer of 1943 the Unruh Commission was finally disbanded. Its failure showed that it was exceedingly difficult in the 'Führer state' to achieve any measure of rational governance.

As the battle for Stalingrad headed towards a catastrophic conclusion, Keitel made fresh demands on Speer. He responded by calling upon Sauckel to provide him with at least one million foreign workers, to be recruited on a voluntary basis. Sauckel justifiably replied that he could not meet this figure, adding testily that Speer was unable to absorb the mass of foreign workers he had already provided. Even when applying a very generous definition to the term 'volunteer', there were only 200,000 foreign workers who came more or less of their own accord. Of these, a considerable number came from France, lured by Speer's false promises to skilled labourers.[44]

Since the French, Belgian and Dutch authorities were understandably somewhat reluctant to help the Germans overcome their labour shortage, Sauckel felt obliged to take the Erlking's approach: 'if thou'rt unwilling, then force I'll employ'. In order to meet Speer's insatiable appetite for labour – free, forced or slave – he rounded up whole villages in France, Belgium and Holland and shipped them off to work in Speer's factories. Speer was delighted when Hitler gave Sauckel permission to use whatever means of compulsion he deemed necessary to meet his needs. Sauckel heartily agreed with Hans Frank, the Governor General of occupied Poland – popularly known as Frank-Reich – that defeated Poles were 'slaves of the German Reich'. Two million Poles were rounded up in the autumn of 1942 and sent to Germany, for which achievement Sauckel received the Führer's hearty congratulations.[45]

Speer's demands were so excessive that even the Reich Minister for the Occupied Eastern Territories, Alfred Rosenberg, felt that the figures requested and the methods employed were disproportionate. The Nazi Party's leading ideologue was an obsessive anti-Semite, but he held the heterodox view that Slavs, although inferior, were Aryans and should be treated as such. Neither Sauckel nor Speer had any such qualms. They ignored his protests, and 700,000 workers were sent to Germany from Rosenberg's fiefdom in August 1942. By the end of the year the number had risen to between two and three million.

In early 1943, Keitel announced that he needed 700,000 recruits, 200,000 of whom would be skilled workers in the armaments industry. Sauckel knew that suitable replacements were only available in France, and that he would have to use force to get them. On 4 January 1943 Speer telephoned Sauckel from

Hitler's headquarters telling him that 'when enlisting skilled and unskilled workers in France it is no longer necessary to take the French into considera- tion. Ruthless measures may be used when recruiting'.[46] Sauckel had no compunction about using force as the prime method of recruitment. At a meeting of Gauleiters in Posen in March he stated: 'The unheard-of severity of the war forces me, in the name of the Führer, to mobilize many millions of foreigners to work for the German war economy.'[47]

The military was not at all pleased with Speer and Sauckel's activities because they also had a pressing need for labour. Officials from the Ministry of Economics, the Four-Year Plan and Hans Frank's General Government, all of whom were trying to develop local industry, seconded their objections. But there were exceptions. When Sauckel visited the southern sector of the Eastern Front, Field Marshal Fedor von Bock promised him his 'unqualified support'. He assured Sauckel that he had already ordered his subordinates to back his efforts, but he added that there was concern in some quarters that these measures would encourage the partisans and be helpful to Soviet propaganda efforts.[48] Sauckel, backed by Hitler and urged on by Speer, ignored such reserv- ations. In April 1943, when recruitment in France had dwindled to a mere trickle, he ordered the French authorities to provide 500,000 workers for tran- sportation to Germany. In the East he called for one million men and women to work on the land in Germany, thereby turning the Nazi 'Blood and Soil' ideology on its head. Slav blood now tilled German soil.

By April 1943, Sauckel had added 3,638,056 men and women to the 2.1 million foreign workers already working in Germany. Sixty per cent of them were Soviet citizens. 1,568,801 were employed in Speer's armaments industry. Sauckel had hoped to improve on these figures by extending his grasp to Soviet prisoners of war, but this was energetically resisted by Keitel. These unfortunates would require extra rations if they were to be fit enough to work in the armaments industry. It was considered more economical to starve these 'useless eaters' to death.[49]

On 13 January 1943, with the Germans in Stalingrad about to surrender, Hitler issued a decree calling for an all-out effort to achieve a 'victorious peace'. This was largely due to Speer's influence. For some time he had been lobbying with Lammers to force more women into the armaments industry and get the armed forces to comb the rear echelons for men to be sent into active service. Sauckel continued to insist that there was no need for such drastic measures, but he reluctantly agreed that a large number of shop assistants could be enlisted to work in armaments factories.[50] Hitler's decree did not go as far as Speer had hoped. It called for the maximum possible number of men to be enlisted. The files of those registered as 'indispensable' had to be once again carefully combed. Similarly, all regional and local administrative bodies had to be drastically pruned. Men between the ages of sixteen and sixty-five and women between seventeen and fifty had to register. Speer saw this as a golden opportunity to bring the entire economy under his control. Central Planning energetically set to work to increase output, but soon found itself in difficulties. The maximum age for women workers was then reduced to forty-five. There were far too many loopholes in the system of reporting for duty. Hitler refused to force German women to work in the armaments industry. When pressed by Speer on 13 March, he replied: 'sacrificing my most valued principles is too high a price to pay'. Hitler had obviously taken to heart Bormann's paper on the dire demographic consequences of women being forced to work in armaments factories. He argued that it would cause a fall in the birth rate, leading to 'racially undesirable conditions'.[51] On 29 January 1943 the party newspaper *Völkischer Beobachter* had tried to calm people's nerves by announcing that labour service would only be made mandatory in exceptional circumstances. Speer's ambition to find one million additional German workers for the armaments industry was overly ambitious. It would, as he admitted, lead to a 'proletarianisation' of the German upper classes for the duration of the war. His determination to close down unessential enterprises was bound to meet with determined resistance from the Ministry of Economics, the Gauleiters and the Nazi Party.

On 29 January 1943 Speer gave an address to leading figures in the armaments industry in which he called for an all-out effort, adding that this meant that reserves of German labour would have to be ruthlessly exploited. Industrialists had to become the 'smiths of victory'. The entire 'racial community' had to devote all its efforts to the pursuit of victory. Industrial production that was not linked to armaments had to cease. All workers had to adjust their lifestyles to meet wartime obligations.[52] This was clearly a challenge to the party, which did all that it could to resist any move towards a full wartime economy.

Speer's appeal met with a lukewarm response. It was argued that there was no apparent degree of urgency about forcing German men and women to work in industry due to the simple fact that foreign labour was considered to be more productive and considerably cheaper. The system was also bedevilled by what Speer called '*Gau* particularism'. Sauckel's authority over labour stopped at the boundaries of the Party District. The implementation of measures dealing with compulsory labour was left to the local party authorities, which meant that there was no nationwide programme and no central control. Local party officials looked after the immediate needs of firms within their own districts and were not concerned with overall requirements.

Sauckel told Hitler that the reserves of German labour were totally exhausted. Speer refused to accept this, but Hitler was anxious not to upset his people unduly. They were already disheartened by the news from North Africa and the Eastern Front. The result was a series of feeble compromises. On 25 April 1943 Hitler told Speer that he thought that stopping the production of cosmetics and hair dyes was preferable to an outright ban on the use of cosmetics, and that banning the repair of devices used for permanent waves was better than banning permanent waves. These remarks were in response to the Ministry of Economics' attempt to stop the production of the chemicals and devices used for permanent waves, which had provoked a chorus of 'ill-tempered consternation' amongst the female population.[53]

Sauckel assured Speer that he would solve the labour problem. He promised 1 to 1.5 million foreign workers, but with the local German authorities in the East wanting to retain all available labour, combined with mounting resistance from the partisans, he said that most of this additional labour would have to come from western Europe. Speer pointed out that a large number of workers in France were already working in factories controlled by Germany and that they should not be touched. Since Hitler was impressed by statistics, Sauckel wanted to collect workers, whereas Speer was concerned that companies working for German interests abroad should not be affected.[54]

Hitler had grown increasingly dissatisfied with Sauckel and the military authorities over the allocation of labour from France. Speer cautioned that the entire approach was mistaken. He felt that consumer goods should henceforth be manufactured in France, thereby freeing skilled German labour to work in the armaments industry. He also undermined Sauckel's authority by taking charge of the labour required to build the Atlantic Wall, the coastal defences designed to ward off an Allied invasion. Goaded by Hitler and in the knowl-edge that all sources of voluntary labour had dried up, Sauckel told his men to 'shake off all traces of wishy-washy humanitarian sentimentality' in rounding up foreign labour.[55]

Laval returned to power in Vichy France in April 1942, almost at the same time as Sauckel arrived in search of French workers, thereby earning the title 'Europe's slave-trader'. By then some 100,000 Frenchmen had volunteered to work in Germany. Laval somewhat reluctantly agreed to the idea of conscripting workers, but demanded the release of one French prisoner of war for every three workers sent to Germany. He assured Ribbentrop that he desired a German victory and saw this agreement as part of an effort to assist the German struggle against Bolshevism.[56] Laval managed to procrastinate until 4 September when the Vichy government passed the requisite law, despite the opposition of four ministers. All males from eighteen to fifty and all single women from twenty-one to thirty-five were to be conscripted so as to 'be subject to do any work that the government deems necessary'. By the end of the year, at Sauckel's insistence, 250,000 workers had been shipped off to Germany under police escort.[57] They proved to be something of a mixed blessing. Because French workers showed an increasing tendency not to return to Germany at the end of their holidays, Sauckel then suggested that no more leave should be granted.[58] Speer continued to insist that the answer to this problem was to establish protected factories in France that would work for the Germans. This would also solve the additional problem that French workers were failing to report to work for fear that they would be sent to Germany.[59]

In September 1943, Laval's minister of Labour, Jean Bichelonne, a young, brilliant and amoral technocrat, who was also an enthusiastic collaborator, came to Berlin for discussions with Speer. The two men were remarkably similar in background and temperament. They agreed to work closely together.[60] Bichelonne, who was renowned for his arrogance and condescension, said of Speer: 'I met a man in Berlin who carries on his shoulders a head that is twice as big as mine.'[61] He readily agreed to Speer's request that French factories should work for German industry, but asked that Sauckel should not be involved in the recruitment of labour in France and that he should keep his hands off these protected firms. Speer managed to get Sauckel's reluctant consent to this arrangement.

The initiative for this new approach came not from Speer, as he claimed at Nuremberg, but from the Reich Commissar for the Netherlands, Arthur Seyß-Inquart, and the military commanders in France and Belgium, all of whom objected to Sauckel's disruptive press-gang tactics. They approached the Minister of Economics with a request to address this matter, but Funk was too feeble a character to confront the likes of Sauckel. They therefore turned to Speer,[62] who seized this opportunity to vet all contracts in western Europe, whether military or civil. The Wehrmacht and private firms were not to act independently, but were to submit to the decisions of Speer's committees and rings.[63]

The system of 'protected firms' was extended to Belgium, Holland and Italy, thereby seriously limiting Sauckel's disruptive actions. Speer's plan to give Bichelonne full control over the iron and steel industries in France came to nothing, due to opposition from the Foreign Office, which insisted that this was a foreign policy issue. The system was thus incomplete, but at least Sauckel was now held in check.

It was not long before Sauckel began to realise that Speer had outwitted him. In mid-December 1943 Hitler was apprised of the fundamental differences between Speer, who wanted the French to work for Germany in France and Sauckel, who was anxious to present the Führer with impressive lists of foreign workers forced to work in Germany.[64] Hitler, as usual, wished to combine both approaches. Sauckel was left in a difficult position. He was called upon to provide Speer with the labour he needed, but political decisions were made by the foreign section of the RSHA, while Central Planning laid down the guidelines for the allocation of labour in consultation with Section V of the

Ministry of Labour, whose Section IV determined wages. The situation was further complicated by intervention from Ribbentrop and the Foreign Office. Sauckel was Gauleiter of Thuringia and one of the Nazi Party's 'old warriors', but he lacked decision-making authority. He could only work effectively at the level of the Gauleiters and local party officials, but he still had direct access to Hitler.[65]

On 21 December 1943 Central Planning discussed the question of Sauckel's deportations, which were placing an impossible strain on the transportation network. It was pointed out that his activities in the West had led directly to an increase in acts of sabotage and resistance from workers threatened with being 'Sauckeled'. With one million workers in protected factories, Sauckel had been trumped. Clearly a decision was needed from Hitler to put an end to this rivalry. On 4 January 1944 Hitler called a meeting that was attended by Speer, Sauckel, Keitel, Milch, Himmler, Backe and Lammers.[66] He posed two fundamental questions: how many additional workers were needed to maintain the present level of production and how many were needed to achieve a significant increase.

Sauckel's reply was that 2.5 to 3 million additional workers were required to maintain present production. Speer said that for production to increase, an additional 1.3 million workers would be needed, but he cautioned that all depended on adequate additional supplies of iron ore. Speer got Hitler's agreement that those already working for German firms should be protected from Sauckel's agents. Hitler then called for 250,000 workers for air-raid protection and up to 2,500 to remove the bomb damage in Vienna. Sauckel announced that he would provide four million additional workers, 500,000 coming from within Germany, without touching Speer's protected factories. In true National Socialist spirit he promised to set about this Herculean task 'with fanatical willpower', but he soon began to doubt whether he could meet this target. Himmler promised that the SS would help him out. This was all totally unrealistic. There was no need for such a number of workers, no work places for them, no food to feed them and no housing available. Speer was profoundly depressed by the outcome of this meeting. He had managed to save his protected firms, but Sauckel had won this round, even though it was a Pyrrhic victory. To safeguard them from Sauckel's rapacity, Speer ordered that as many firms as possible should be declared to be protected. There were soon 14,000 such firms in France alone.[67] Sauckel was furious, calling the protected firms *le Maquis légal*, but there was little he could do about this.

Speer and Sauckel's attitudes towards the use of foreign labour were irreconcilable. Sauckel argued that armaments production in Germany could not be increased without recruiting workers from western Europe, and that it was not possible to release German workers for service in the Wehrmacht without them. Furthermore, were French workers to remain in France they would not be subjected to the same discipline as they would be in Germany. Productivity would suffer as a result. He believed that the ruthless exploitation of foreign labour was essential for National Socialist Germany to achieve 'Final Victory'. Speer argued that a degree of cooperation within a Europe-wide plan was preferable to Sauckel's more aggressive approach.

Speer's concept was nevertheless firmly rooted in National Socialist ideology. Western Europe was to survive as an industrialised region under German leadership and control, while eastern, south-eastern and, after 1943, southern Europe were to be ruthlessly exploited both for raw materials and labour. The division within this concept of an 'expansive economy' (*Großraumwirtschaft*) was on strictly racial lines. As far as eastern Europe was concerned, Speer and Sauckel began to sing from the same hymn sheet. Speer also benefited from the labour of 600,000 to 650,000 French workers sent to Germany under Compulsory Work Service between June 1942 and July 1944, as well as some 250,000 French prisoners of war. It was the French government rather than Sauckel that did the dirty work.

Speer did not think that German workers should be given special treatment. All workers in the armaments industry, whether foreign or German, were pushed to the absolute limit. A report by the Reich Chamber of Commerce in 1943 said that workers had been exploited 'to the limits of human ability', due to the introduction of piecework and premiums. In June, Speer proudly announced to Hitler and a group of leading industrialists that 'the workforce's output had been exploited to the full'. The Chamber of Commerce in Kattowitz (Katowice) announced at the end of 1943 that average output per worker had increased by 100 per cent since 1941. An overall analysis of the armaments industry indicated that productivity had risen by 57 per cent between 1941/42 and 1942/43. By the end of 1943 it had risen by 89 per cent and by the middle of 1944 by 134 per cent.[68] Although much of the increase in productivity was due to rationalisation and centralisation, as Speer underlined in his speech in the Sports Palace on 5 June 1943, the increased exploitation of labour still played a significant role. In the course of this speech to 10,000 munitions workers he once again harped on a familiar theme: 'In present-day war, in which technology is so intimately involved, quantity can not only be matched by quality, it can be surmounted by it.'[69] This was empty propaganda. Speer of necessity was obliged to opt for the mass production of shoddy weapons while frittering away vast amounts on prestige projects such as rockets, exotic models of jet aircraft and state-of-the-art submarines.

In July 1943 Speer took part in discussions with Himmler in which it was decided that all males in areas in the Soviet Union in which there was partisan activity were to be considered as prisoners of war and forced to work in mines.

Himmler added that all healthy females should also be considered as prisoners of war and sent to work in Germany. It was noted that rounding up workers should take precedence over 'measures taken by the Security Police' – in other words, mass executions. Hitler then decreed that these methods were to be extended to all recently occupied territories in the East.[70]

Speer was by no means alone in his struggle to frustrate Sauckel's efforts. Himmler was determined to ensure that he kept his hands off his SS empire. The Wehrmacht insisted that there was no excess fat in its rear echelons. The Nazi Party considered itself to be untouchable. Sauckel complained bitterly when Hitler insisted that 'long-legged and thin German women' were unsuited for work in factories, unlike 'squat, primitive and healthy' Russians. In a series of conferences Sauckel tried to get his hands on Speer's protected factories, but he met with determined opposition from Speer, Milch, Kehrl and the military. The Allied invasion in June put an end to his ambitions to act 'à la Staline' in France, with absolute powers to force every able-bodied man and woman to work for Germany.

CHAPTER SEVEN

THE CONSOLIDATION OF POWER

FROM THE OUTSET Speer was determined to gain control over armaments in all three services. He had rapidly consolidated his authority over the army. Milch and the Luftwaffe were willing to cooperate. Only the navy remained intransigent in its determination to run its own affairs. The shipbuilder Rudolf Blohm, to whom in March 1942 he had entrusted the task of introducing industrial self-determination into the construction of warships, had been unable to stand up to the naval establishment. In July Speer replaced him with Otto Merker, a brilliant young engineer specialising in tracked vehicles, who was general manager of Klöckner-Humboldt-Deutz and a member of the NSDAP since 1927. For Speer he was the perfect example of the innovative, forceful and imaginative technicians he added to his team. He saw it as a positive advantage that Merker had no knowledge whatsoever of the shipbuilding industry. That his appointment was a deliberate slap in the face for an old-fashioned reactionary like Blohm was an added attraction.[1] Responsibility for merchant shipping was handed over to Hamburg's populist Gauleiter, Karl Kaufmann, a man whose nebulous vision of 'socialism in action' had won him a degree of popularity. He was one of the few Gauleiters who worked closely with Speer. Without education, profession or trade, he owed his first gainful employment to the NSDAP. He was staggeringly corrupt, even by Nazi standards, was ruthless in the pursuit of Jews and other undesirables, suffered bouts of severe depression, and, following the Hamburg raid, was almost solely concerned with saving his skin after Nazi Germany's defeat, which he now thought inevitable. In this respect he was remarkably successful.[2]

The main problem for the navy was that the development of the new model U-boats – types XXI and the much smaller XXIII – was a painfully lengthy process. Admiral Werner Fuchs, the navy's head of the Warship Building Office, viewed the entire project with distinct scepticism. He thought that if they were given top priority it might be possible to have two XXI U-boats ready

for preliminary tests by the end of 1944. If successful they could go into production in 1945 and be ready for action in 1946. Dönitz, refusing to accept this
gloomy assessment, turned to Merker, who argued that there was no need for
extensive tests and suggested that the U-boats be built in sections, in much the
same manner as Henry J. Kaiser's 'Liberty Ships'. Only the final assembly would
take place in the slipways, where the boats were vulnerable to Allied bombers.
The navy's technical staff was highly sceptical of the idea of building U-boats
in sections, given the enormous pressure they had to resist when submerged,
and their vulnerability to depth charges. Dönitz then sought the opinion of the
navy's leading civilian expert on U-boat construction. He agreed with Merker
that building U-boats in sections to avoid Allied bombers was a viable option,
but Merker's ingenious proposal soon proved to be disastrous.[3]

For Speer, Merker's U-boat programme promised to be a repeat performance of the triumph of the Adolf Hitler Panzer Programme. The first of these
wonder weapons was scheduled to be ready for Hitler's fifty-fifth birthday on
20 April 1944. The navy was promised delivery of thirty Mark XXIs by the end
of the summer of 1944, followed by a steady flow of thirty new submarines per
month. But this proved to be wildly over-optimistic. Building U-boats in
sections soon proved exceedingly difficult. Firms that had no previous experience in shipbuilding were required to build the eight separate sections. This
resulted in lengthy post-production work to fix a number of serious deficiencies. In order to protect the final assembly facilities from air attack ten thousand concentration camp inmates were forced to build a hugely expensive
concrete pen, 'Valentin', near Bremen. After two years of construction work it
was seriously damaged in March 1945 by the RAF's 617 'Dambuster' squadron.
It remained unfinished at the end of the war.

Dönitz and Speer boldly assured Hitler that the new U-boats were faster,
could dive deeper and could remain under water longer than conventional
submarines. They would be ready for action by November 1944. This was far
too late for Hitler. He wanted to have these innovative U-boats in action as
soon as possible. Whereas previous submarines spent most of the time above
water, the Mark XXI, fitted with the revolutionary snorkel, could operate under
water for days at a time. Its sleek design and powerful electric motors enabled
it to move underwater at up to 16.5 knots, making it hard to chase and destroy.
It was in fact the first true submarine.[4]

Admiral Raeder, the navy's commander-in-chief (*Oberbehlshaber der
Kriegsmarine*), was in a difficult position. Unlike Speer or Milch, he did not have
ready access to Hitler. Speer had deliberately excluded the navy from Central
Planning. It controlled the allocation of steel, which was the key component of
the naval building programme. When Dönitz took over command of the navy
in January 1943 he was determined to rectify this situation. He managed to get

an increase in the amount of steel allotted to the navy, but this advantage was cancelled out by heavy losses in action as well as by Allied bombing raids on the shipyards. He now felt that the only hope was to hand over the naval building programme to the ambitious young Minister of Armaments.

This was a most unpopular suggestion. Naval technicians knew from the fate of the Army Armaments Office that they would be pushed aside.[5] They also doubted that this change would bring much relief. Speer warned that there would be no increase in the allocation of steel unless Hitler agreed to a significant reduction in the manufacture of consumer goods.[6] This was questionable, given that the Nazi Party was opposed to any such move for fear of losing what was left of its dwindling popularity.

In spite of these caveats, on 3 July 1943 Merker's shipbuilding commission reported that a 30 per cent increase in shipbuilding was feasible. On the basis of this wildly optimistic assessment Speer readily agreed to take over responsibility for shipbuilding. On 22 July 1943 he signed an agreement with Dönitz stipulating that future shipbuilding plans presented by the Naval High Command were to be vetted by experts from Speer's ministry. Once the deal was done Speer announced: 'Now we begin a new life!'[7] By taking over responsibility for naval armaments it seemed that he was, in Dönitz's ambiguous words, 'Europe's economic dictator' and the most powerful of all Hitler's paladins. But it was difficult to see how he could possibly make good on his promise.

A Shipbuilding Commission was created, chaired by Rear Admiral Erich Topp, a U-boat hero who had been awarded the Knight's Cross with oak leaves and swords for sinking thirty-five merchant ships. Its task was to ensure the implementation of Dönitz's ambitious plans for U-boat and motor-torpedo boat construction that he had presented to Hitler in April 1943.[8] This plan faced Speer and Röchling with the impossible task of increasing steel production by 30,000 tons per month, at a time when steel production was steadily declining. One month later Dönitz announced that the thirty U-boats per month that he had ordered would not be enough. He now demanded a minimum of forty. Hitler agreed, having first consulted Speer.

The first Mark XXI U-boat was duly launched at Schichau the day before Hitler's birthday. It was a dubious birthday present. It was a hastily assembled prototype that leaked like a sieve and had to be towed back to the dock once the crowd of admiring dignitaries had dispersed. Thereafter progress was painfully slow. Regardless of all the difficulties, Speer, once he had recovered from a long illness, launched a massive and totally irresponsible propaganda campaign. In May 1944 he addressed a mass meeting of Hamburg dock-workers, in which he announced that they were building a weapon that was a key to 'Final Victory'. He repeated this empty boast at the annual meeting of Gauleiters in Posen in August.[9]

Speer was caught in an impossible situation. The U-boat programme that included the older types, the XXI and XXIII, as well as Dönitz's new-found enthusiasm for one-man submarines, consumed a vast amount of raw materials, skilled labour and building materials. Even worse was the incontrovertible fact that it was a strategically pointless weapon. The naval war had been irrevocably lost. All of the eighty Mark XXIs that were built in 1944 were so defective that they were unfit for action. By the end of the war, four of the magnificent XXIs were at last ready to go on patrol, but only two of them ventured out. Whether or not U-2511 got within sight of the enemy is open to doubt. Whatever the case, it never fired a shot. Six of the XXIIIs saw active service and managed to sink five ships. All the other fifty-five boats of this type that were built had such serious deficiencies that they could not be deployed before the war's end. Speer could have used the steel that was wasted in the U-boat programme to build the five thousand tanks that were desperately needed as the enemy advanced on all fronts. Hitler of course wanted both U-boats and tanks. It was impossible to convince him that he had to make a choice.[10]

In the end the scepticism of conservative shipbuilders like Rudolf and Walther Blohm, naval engineers like Friedrich Schürer and experienced naval officers such as Admiral Werner Fuchs was proven completely justified. Speer and Merker, with their arrogant belief that the root of the problem in the ship-building industry was one of attitude and *Weltanschauung*, refused to take the blame for this fiasco. They continued to insist, against overwhelming evidence to the contrary, that their approach was correct and that the critical attitude of the Blohm brothers amounted to sabotage. Walther Blohm in return charged Merker with incompetence. The struggle between the two sides reached the point whereby Walther Blohm was court-martialled on a trumped-up charge of failing to take adequate air-raid precautions and sentenced to six months imprisonment.[11]

The Blohm family, with their powerful contacts in Hamburg and Berlin, managed to get the sentence overturned. Frank Stapelfeldt, the head of Krupp's Deschimag shipyard in Bremen, was less fortunate. As an outspoken critic of Merker's approach he insisted that his target figures were impossible to achieve. Such criticism of the Minister of Armaments was swiftly silenced. Stapelfeldt was arrested by the Gestapo on 3 October 1944 and detained until the end of the war. Krupp was obliged to replace him with someone acceptably subser-vient to Speer.[12] These unpleasant episodes show that there were some limita-tions to Speer's system of industrial self-determination. He showed no compunction in using brute force to silence his critics.

In less than eighteen months in office, Speer had reorganised his ministry, accumulated considerable power and achieved impressive results. That he had been able to do so relatively easily had served to spur his ambition. It also provoked a fierce reaction from those who were determined to put him in his place. Bormann, Keitel and Lammers formed an alliance against him. Bormann deeply resented Speer's intimacy with Hitler, his lack of ideological fervour and his cosy relationship with big business – the 'plutocrats' who played a central role in National Socialist demonology. Keitel resented Speer's control over armaments. His demands for manpower also compromised the military's target figures for recruitment. Keitel presented Hitler with an impressive list of technical objections to Speer's policies. Discontent with Speer's heavy-handed approach was widespread in the navy. Lammers complained about administrative and legal irregularities. Speer flaunted established executive procedures and obtained decrees from Hitler without due consultation.

With such powerful opposition Speer could no longer rely on Hitler's unconditional support, upon which his power depended.[13] He therefore needed a powerful ally and felt that he had found one in Joseph Goebbels. The Propaganda Minister was also frustrated. As the campaign in the East got into difficulties his propaganda began to ring hollow. His radio addresses were now popularly dismissed as 'Clubfoot's fairy tales'. He had proved unable to accrue as much power as the newcomer Speer. His control over propaganda was far from complete. Alfred Rosenberg, who was responsible for ideological schooling in the Nazi Party, remained a powerful rival. Max Amann as Reich Press Chief and Otto Dietrich as Party Press Chief limited Goebbels' control over the press. Frick, as Minister of the Interior, supported the Gauleiters and local government authorities against Goebbels' encroachments. Robert Ley was solely responsible for the extensive cultural offerings of the German Work Front. Philipp Bouhler, the head of Hitler's private chancellery, was responsible for the censorship of party literature. Most important of all, Goebbels also met the determined opposition of Keitel, Lammers and Bormann. With common enemies, Goebbels and Speer seemed to be ideal allies.

On 4 February 1943, two days after the surrender of the 6th Army at Stalingrad, Goebbels invited Speer and his wife to dinner to test the waters. Describing Speer as 'an organisational genius' and agreeing with Hitler's assessment that he was 'a very advantageous swap for Todt', he got him to agree to help unseat the 'evil trio' of Keitel, Lammers and Bormann. They hoped to enlist Göring, Funk and Ley in this endeavour. Goebbels' idea was to set up a Council of Ministers to advise Hitler, run the country's domestic affairs and restructure defence policy.[14] Goebbels then invited Speer, Funk and Ley to tea and cognac in his vast palace in Berlin. He told his guests that the problem was not so much that Germany faced a 'leadership crisis'. The real problem was that they were faced with a 'leader crisis'.[15] Speer was in full agreement, but there was precious little that could be done.[16] There was no suggestion that Hitler should be toppled. Would the removal of the triumvirate of Keitel, Lammers and Bormann, who controlled access to Hitler, really make any difference? Could Göring be roused from his sybaritic lethargy to act as an effective counterweight to the Führer by resuscitating the Ministerial Council for the Defence of the Reich? This was unlikely. Göring and Goebbels were on very bad terms partly because the Propaganda Minister wanted to close Horcher, the Reichsmarschall's – and also Speer's – favourite restaurant in Berlin.

Nothing came of a scheme that was little more than wishful thinking. This is hardly surprising. The Diadochi were an unimpressive lot. Bormann, backed by Himmler, led a vigorous counter-attack. With the Luftwaffe's failure to deal with the Allied bomber offensive Göring was in no position to challenge the status quo. Speer was out of his depth and Goebbels, who had better ideas how to enhance his position, feigned sickness.[17]

The differences between the two sides were not apparent at a meeting in Posen on 5 and 6 February 1943, attended by Speer, Bormann, Goebbels, Funk, Ley, Sauckel, State Secretary Backe from the Ministry of Agriculture, the Minister of Transport Julius Dorpmüller and OKW's manpower specialist, General Walter von Unruh. A large number of senior military and party officials were also in attendance. All of them called for a total commitment to the war effort, while studiously avoiding any concrete proposals.[18] The particularly sensitive issues of the employment of women in industry and the closure of non-essential plant were not addressed. No one wished to speak openly in such a forum. It was all to be done backstairs as they jockeyed for Hitler's favour. Goebbels' speech on the need for a total war effort was sufficiently vague for it to meet with general approval. Sauckel's address on the manpower situation was not only unbelievably boring but, in contrast to Goebbels' contribution, exceptionally smug. He claimed that he could find all the labour that was needed abroad and insisted that there was no need to recruit German women.

After the meeting the dignitaries repaired to Hitler's headquarters where, on 7 February, they were treated to a two-hour harangue on the current situation. Hitler placed the blame for the defeat at Stalingrad on the Romanians, Hungarians and Italians. The Bolsheviks had mobilised the people far more effectively than the Germans, but the main reason for the enemy's success was that they had the 'driving force of Jewry' behind them. From this it followed that 'we must exterminate Jewry not only in the territory of the German Reich but throughout Europe'. Goebbels was entranced by these words. Hitler had endorsed his inchoate plans for Total War and he had also been given authority to remove the few remaining Jews from Berlin.[19] Speer prudently made no mention of this meeting in his memoirs or elsewhere.

Goebbels saw Hitler's speech as an excellent chance to regain some of his tarnished glory in an all-out propaganda campaign for a maximum war effort. Speer was delighted that the Propaganda Minister was thus putting himself in

the limelight. He would thereby take most of the blame for the harsh consequences of such a programme.[20] But Goebbels had set himself a daunting task.
It was proving increasingly difficult to work up much enthusiasm for a war that
was going badly after El Alamein, the Torch landings and Stalingrad. On 18
February 1943 Goebbels gave a carefully orchestrated speech before a vast
crowd at the Sports Palace in Berlin in which he asked the rhetorical question:
'Do You Want Total War?' An enthusiastic crowd, selected from the party
faithful, eagerly welcomed the suggestion that others should work for fourteen
hours per day and that women should be fully engaged in war work so that
men could go to the front to face the menace of an 'invasion from the Steppes'
and the accompanying 'Jewish liquidation commandos'. Goebbels concluded
this rousing harangue with a reference to the romantic nationalist poet Theodor
Körner, who fell fighting in the Free Corps during the Napoleonic wars, by
demanding: 'People, arise and let a storm break loose!'[21]

Speer sat in the front row during Goebbels' lengthy tirade. The man who
later claimed that he knew nothing of the fate of the European Jews listened to
a harangue that echoed Hitler's recent words at Rastenburg:

> The Jews are an infectious disease. We shall not be hindered from doing the
> necessary, just because foreign countries hypocritically protest about our
> anti-Jewish policies and weep crocodile tears over the measures we have
> taken against the Jews. Germany does not intend to give way to this menace
> but will confront it in a timely manner and when necessary will take the
> most radical measures.

The speech was here interrupted by a chorus of approval that lasted several
minutes.

> We shall not be deterred by the clamouring of international Jewry
> throughout the world from leading the titanic struggle against this universal
> pestilence in a courageous and earnest manner. It can and must end in
> victory.

Cries of 'German men to arms, German women to work!' were heard.

Goebbels' dramatic speech was an admission by the party leadership that all
was not well, but no immediate consequences were drawn. In large part this
was due to the vigorous reaction of Bormann and the Gauleiters to his attack.
Göring was certainly not in favour of austerity, especially if it meant closing his
favourite restaurant. Ribbentrop was justifiably suspicious that Goebbels
intended to take his place as Foreign Minister. Lammers saw it as a direct attack
on his position. His opponents were soon able to win Hitler over to their side.

After his speech Goebbels invited a number of prominent figures to his house. Among them were Speer, Milch, Ley, Wilhelm Stuckart from the Ministry of the Interior, Göring's right-hand man Paul Körner and the Minister of Justice, Otto Thierack. He told this somewhat bemused group that he had pulled off a silent *coup d'état*. Although Hitler described the speech as 'a first rate psychological and propagandistic masterpiece', it was soon obvious that this was a gross exaggeration.[22] The Propaganda Minister was once again forced to realise that his power was strictly limited. His speech had made an impression, but it was by no means always positive. Goebbels' silent coup resulted in little more than a fruitless bid to gain control over the allocation of labour. 3.5 million men and women were duly registered under his scheme, but only 20 per cent of them actually joined the labour force: 400,000 women and 300,000 men.[23] The German bourgeoisie was thus saved from descending into the ranks of the proletariat as he had threatened.

Goebbels decided to give another major speech at the Sports Palace on 5 June 1943.[24] It was preceded by an address by Speer. This was the first time that he had addressed such a large crowd and it was a role to which he was ill suited. He boasted of his achievements during his first year in office. He tried to create the impression that Germany had such an arsenal at its disposal, thanks to his efforts, that the war could not possibly be lost. He repeated the extravagant claim that any apparent shortage in the number of German weapons was cancelled out by their superior quality. The men at the front knew this to be untrue. Speer's ministry was increasingly putting quantity before quality, mainly to boost production figures. Speer then played his trump card by mentioning 'vengeance weapons' that would soon turn the tide. He told the crowd that his success was due to his policy of giving industry a free rein, reeling off a list of prominent industrialists who counted as his closest collaborators.[25] Although Speer was a poor speaker, totally lacking Goebbels' power, passion and biting irony, these extravagant claims were widely disseminated and initially found to be encouraging.

Speer's audience in the Sports Palace was no doubt somewhat bored by his sober and low-key delivery, but the immediate effect of the speech was considerable. The statistics he presented appeared to be most impressive. But on consideration it did not go unnoticed that the chosen baseline was at a time when production figures were particularly low. He also pointed out that he had the convenient excuse that he was unable to give any total figures for reasons of security.[26] Speer also prudently avoided making any mention of the extremely heavy losses sustained since he took office in February 1942. That would have put the measure of his achievements in some sort of perspective. Statistical juggling of this sort did not go unnoticed by the general public. The Security Service reported that there was widespread scepticism about Speer's statistics and an uneasy feeling that Germany could never match the enemy's industrial might. All depended on the courage and skill of their soldiers and the strength of the home front.[27]

Goebbels' speech was full of praise for the 'long suffering population' in western Germany that was bearing the brunt of the Allied bomber offensive. His vision was of 'a new epoch of German socialism'. Together with Speer he was determined to fight a 'Total War' that in turn called for the whole-hearted commitment of the entire 'racial community'. Speer was once again witness to a murderous anti-Semitic harangue. Goebbels promised that the Jews would be 'radically removed' so that 'Lucifer would once again fall':

> The complete exclusion of the Jews from Europe is not a moral issue. It is a question of state security ... Just as the Colorado beetle destroys the potato field – indeed it is compelled to do so by its very nature – so the Jew destroys states and peoples. There is only one antidote. The menace must be utterly annihilated.[28]

Once again Speer makes only brief mention of this speech, and makes no mention at all of Goebbels' contribution in his memoirs.

Speer's overly confident and self-congratulatory speech backfired. Bormann and the Gauleiters took his impressive statistics to mean that there was no need for the German people to make further sacrifices. Why cut back on the butter when so many guns were being produced? The party could thereby be saved from further criticism. By contrast, soldiers at the front, who were fully aware of the shortage of weapons and munitions, took a very sceptical view of Speer's facts and figures.[29]

Smaller enterprises were highly alarmed by Speer's efforts to concentrate and centralise production.[30] Cartels and similar expedient arrangements had to be dissolved for rationalisation and centralisation to be achieved. Of the 2,500 existing cartels, 2,000 were promptly eliminated. Speer left the task of reorganisation of industrial production in large part to Hans Kehrl and the Reich Industrial Group. Small fry either had to switch over to armaments production, which often meant being swallowed up by one of the larger concerns, or they were forced to close down. In June 1943 Hitler signed a decree drafted by Speer that closed the majority of smaller armaments factories. Lammers was furious because Speer, going directly to Hitler, had once again ignored customary procedure.

Speer's relative optimism was due to the Eastern Front having stabilised after the Stalingrad debacle. Provided that Manstein could hold on to the iron-mining region of Kryvyi Rih, the manganese deposits at Bol'shoy Tokmak and coal from the Donbas, it was still possible to envisage a significant increase in steel production in 1943. But in spite of the Panzer Programme's impressive results, German tanks at the Battle of Kursk in July 1943 were outnumbered two to one.[31] Bol'shoy Tokmak and the Donbas were soon lost. Kryvyi Rih came under heavy attack in November, but a German counter-attack was successful. A renewed offensive by the 3rd Ukrainian Front against Kleist's Army Group A was successfully completed in February 1944, thereby cutting off vital supplies of manganese.

By the summer of 1943 it seemed that Speer's position was weakening. He no longer enjoyed Hitler's unconditional confidence. His propaganda offensive had backfired. The Red Army had gained the strategic initiative. Essential sources of raw materials were under threat. Keitel, Lammers and Bormann were determined to thwart him at every turn. But Speer was undaunted. Having gained control over naval armaments he was emboldened to approach Hitler and ask that his powers be extended to include all aspects of civilian production. He argued that the Allied bomber offensive had begun to have an alarming effect and he therefore needed additional powers to meet the crisis. He requested that Hans Kehrl, who was the key figure in Walther Funk's Ministry of Economics, should become his subordinate. Kehrl was outraged at this suggestion. He violently disapproved of Speer's approach to management, which he contemptuously described as 'organised improvisation'. He felt that Speer had no strategic concept for a comprehensive war effort. His objections were short-lived, however. Speer convinced Kehrl that his powers would be greatly enhanced as head of a Planning Office within Central Planning. He assured him that he would be given a free hand. Thereupon Kehrl asked for permission to resign from the Ministry of Economics. He was warned that resignation would amount to desertion and that he would be treated accordingly.[32] Henceforth Kehrl worked for Speer in the Planning Office, but remained within the Ministry of Economics. It took a long time before relations between Speer and Kehrl – the Ministry of Armaments and the Ministry of Economics – were at least partially restored. But such conflicts of interest were endemic in the Third Reich.[33] For all the talk of a 'leadership state', struggles over areas of competence were seldom settled by firm decision-making at the highest level.

On the evening of 27 July 1943 Speer convened a meeting at his apartment in the Rauchstrasse in Berlin. It was attended by Karl-Otto Saur, the director of consignments Walther Schieber, General Thomas' successor in the Armaments Office Kurt Waeger, the head of the Central Office Willy Liebel and Hans Kehrl. Speer had just returned from Hitler's headquarters with the announcement that there was to be a Battle for Armaments (*Rüstungsschlacht*). The Ministry of Armaments would have to be reorganised to meet the challenge. Kehrl asked Speer to comment on the political situation, which looked grim after the fall of Mussolini and the disaster at Kursk. Speer angrily replied that his colleagues should not expect him to reveal what the Führer had told him in the course of a confidential conversation. Kehrl was incensed. As head of an important new organisation, while still playing a key role in the Ministry of Economics, he felt that he had the right to be kept informed about the overall political situation. Restraining himself with some difficulty, he decided to confront Speer in private rather than in front of his closest collaborators.

Kehrl returned home in an angry mood. He received an agitated call from Gauleiter Kaufmann of Hamburg, who gave him the horrific details of Operation Gomorrah that was still raging. The Allied raid resulted in a firestorm that left 42,000 people dead and 37,000 wounded. One million people were forced to leave the city. Thereupon Kehrl told his wife that the war was lost.[34] He soon recovered his composure when he was assured that the bomber offensive had not yet had much of an impact on the production of armaments. But Kehrl was convinced that the only solution to Germany's predicament was to get rid of Ribbentrop and negotiate a separate peace with the Soviet Union.[35] Speer dismissed Kehrl's claim that there was no alternative to a separate peace as an example of 'defeatism' that would simply land him in jail. He pointed out that with the massive attacks on the hydrogenation plants seriously disrupting fuel supplies, and the Allied landings in Sicily, the Soviets were most unlikely to consider a separate peace.

Speer's 'economic dictatorship' was further strengthened when a somewhat mollified Hans Kehrl and his close friend Walther Schieber drafted a memorandum proposing that Speer's ministry absorb Kehrl's key Section II of the Ministry of Economics. The state secretary in the Ministry of Economics, Friedrich Landfried, strongly objected to this suggestion, but Walther Funk felt that the centralisation of production made eminent sense. Since he was only really interested in his position as president of the Reichsbank, he even offered to hand over his entire ministry to Speer.[36] On 9 August 1943 Funk and Speer presented this extraordinary proposal to Lammers for approval. Bormann put up a stiff resistance to a measure that would give Speer additional authority. Speer was furious at having to wait for a decision. On 18 August he wrote to Bormann: 'The demand for the most rapid possible expansion of armaments is dictated by the enemy.'

The matter was finally settled on 2 September in the Führer's Decree for the Concentration of the Wartime Economy. It marked the greatest change in the organisation of the German economy since the Four-Year Plan in 1936. This was reflected in the name change of Speer's ministry from the Reich Ministry for Weapons and Munitions to the Reich Ministry for Armaments and War Production. Speer now had virtually dictatorial powers over the economy at home and in the occupied territories. Only agriculture and aircraft production remained beyond his grasp, but he had close ties to the de facto minister, Herbert Backe and Milch, who was dependent on Speer for supplies and repairs as Allied bombers wreaked havoc on aircraft production, was fully cooperative.

His powers extended from the Soviet Union, Poland and the Protectorate of Bohemia and Moravia to Luxemburg, Alsace Lorraine, Carinthia, Carniola and Lower Styria.

Funk was left with authority over 'fundamental economic policies', but it was difficult to see quite what this involved. He was still responsible for the provision of consumer goods and for deciding how they should be apportioned. He was in charge of all credit institutions, most of whose cupboards were already bare. Speer was unwilling to take over responsibility for such matters, knowing that it would only lead to further fights with the Gauleiters over consumer goods. Since he determined the allocation of raw materials to the civilian economy he had decisive influence, while Funk took the blame from dissatisfied consumers. Speer admitted that he knew absolutely nothing about finance. He therefore preferred to keep Funk in office in the shell of his ministry.[37]

Kehrl was determined to play a key role in Speer's ministry. To relieve Walther Schieber from his excessive workload, he made Willy Schlieker, an energetic and resourceful self-made man, responsible for the procurement of coal, iron and chemicals. Speer requested Sauckel to provide him with 500,000 more workers, to be culled from the consumer goods sector. Göring was singularly displeased with these developments, his discontent fuelled by Bormann and Lammers, who seized every opportunity to frustrate Speer's ambitions. But he had already become so lethargic that he was unwilling to take any action.[38]

Although Speer was now in a position that had no parallel in any of the belligerent countries, the prospects were far from encouraging.[39] His ministry had been expanded and renamed. He had been given the assurance that non-essential production would be drastically reduced, but this meant that he would inevitably meet with the determined opposition of the Gauleiters and the Nazi Party. Labour and raw materials were in such short supply that even the minimal demands of the three services could not possibly be met. Speer would have to overcome the appalling problems that confronted the German economy in order to be certain of Hitler's support. He also had to ward off attacks from his powerful rivals, both within his ministry and among the power-hungry members of Hitler's inner circle. Seemingly at the height of his powers, it gradually became apparent that Speer had taken on far too many responsibilities for one man to manage.

On 29 October 1943 he signed a decree drafted by Hans Kehrl on the reorganisation of the ministry so as to include the civilian sector. It was presented as the Magna Carta of the wartime economy. It resulted from discussions in the Reichsbank between Funk, Speer, Kehrl and Schieber that continued late into the night. Its more familiar name was the 'Tapeworm Decree' because of its exceptional length.[40] Three new departments were created: for raw materials, planning and consumer goods. Hans Kehrl was put in charge of the first two departments. He had fought hard to gain this position. Initially Speer had wanted to separate raw materials from planning, but Kehrl had argued that this would lead to organisational chaos. He refused point blank to work under Speer unless these two departments were combined. Speer was furious, telling Kehrl that the men in his ministry were soldiers who should obey orders. Kehrl stood firm. Speer, appreciative of Kehrl's outstanding ability and experience, eventually backed down.[41] Speer secured Göring's approval of Kehrl as head of the new Planning Office. He was thereby accorded plenipotentiary powers within the Four-Year Plan. The Consumer Goods Department was soon to be renamed the Exploitation Department, because its main task was to divert workers into the armaments sector.

The 'Tapeworm Decree' was an uneasy compromise that pleased no one. Kehrl felt that there were 'too many cooks' for it to work effectively. Speer regarded it as excessively bureaucratic. But Kehrl wisely pointed out that no such organisational structure could ever be perfect. In his view it contained enough checks and balances to avoid structural confusion and serious conflicts over areas of competence. It thus marked a real step forward.[42]

As part of this major restructuring of the ministry Kehrl established a Central Office for Statistics (*Hauptabteilung Statistik*) under Dr Rolf Wagenführ, an acknowledged expert in the field. The statistical information he gathered was vital for the Planning Office, but the data was exceedingly misleading. Wagenführ took the figures for February 1942, the month that Speer took office, as the baseline for his calculations. Taking February 1942 as 100, the production of weapons rose to 180 by the end of the year, to 222 at the end of 1943 and to 322 in July 1944. Then, largely due to the bomber offensive, it dropped to 273 by September and 227 by January 1945.[43] It was on the basis of these figures that the 'Speer miracle' was constructed. They failed to take into account the fact that February 1942 was a low point in armaments output, in large part because weapons that were in production or in the planning stage were not yet end products. Furthermore, these overall figures did not take account of particular weapons. Thus the early rise was largely due to a concentration on munitions and tanks.[44] The fact that overall figures did not fall further after the summer of 1944 was due to aircraft production, which was still largely Milch's concern. Speer's achievements were considerable, but they only become miraculous by statistical juggling. Any comparison with Allied production figures was carefully avoided. During the war the United States, the Soviet Union and Britain produced a total of 599,444 military aircraft, Germany 119,307.[45] With figures such as these Speer would indeed have to produce a miracle for him to fulfil his dream of a 'victorious peace'.

None of these new measures solved the fundamental question of how to deal with the consumer industries. Self-regulation worked well for armaments, but it was ineffective in the consumer sector. Many firms that were registered as being involved in war production only devoted a fraction of their productive capacity to the war effort. Small firms in poor areas were often protected by the local Gauleiter so as to provide adequate employment and a sufficient supply of consumer goods to provide for the immediate needs of a hard-pressed population. Speer felt that the only solution was to impose rigorous state control over the production of consumer goods, but this met with fierce resistance from the Gauleiters, the Nazi Party and powerful figures in the SS such as Otto Ohlendorf, who denounced such an approach as 'Bolshevistic'. Speer's main opponents in this regard were Bormann, Sauckel and Kaltenbrunner, all of whom were violently opposed to strict restrictions on consumer goods.[46]

Speer addressed these questions at a high-level meeting of Reichsleiters and Gauleiters in Posen on 6 October 1943.[47] It was also attended by a number of leading industrialists and armaments experts. Himmler was to give the keynote address in the afternoon. The proceedings began with presentations by 'Panzer' Rohland on armaments for the army, Karl Frydag on the Luftwaffe, Otto Merker on shipbuilding and Willy Schlieker on iron and steel. All stressed that skilled labour had to be in sufficient supply and exempted from military service. All non-essential companies should be closed down, with workers transferred to the armaments industry. Rohland warned the Gauleiters that their 'special requirements' would henceforth be ignored. The morning's proceedings ended with Speer's speech. He confronted the opposition by announcing that he intended to take over a number of factories producing goods for the civilian sector, thereby freeing up enough workers for twenty new divisions. This was music to Goebbels' ears.[48] Speer pulled no punches when describing the parlous state of the armaments industry. In his Sports Palace address he had promised a 15 to 20 per cent increase in armaments per month, but the RAF's Battle of the Ruhr had rendered this impossible. He claimed that the quality of German weapons was still very high, but the quantity was still insufficient. This could be overcome, but only if all pulled together. An all-out war against 'skivers and malingerers' was imperative.[49] Speer warned the Gauleiters not to stand in the way. He cautioned that he now had the backing of Himmler and the SS, who would ensure that all consumer goods such as radio sets, refrigerators and electric heating pads – items that made excellent bribes – were no longer produced. Should a Gauleiter fail to comply with orders from the Sicherheitsdienst or Security Service to close down specific enterprises within two weeks they would be confronted with the 'full authority of the Reich'.

Speer's speech ended with a three-point definition of his notion of 'Total War':

1. Reduction of living standards at home to the level of that at the front;
2. Maximum effort from all workers;
3. Extreme frugality with regard to consumer goods.

He was fully confident that with Himmler's support and the Gauleiters' compliance the war would be won. He also made mention of a secret weapon – presumably the V2 rocket – that was not yet quite ready.[50]

Speer later claimed that after lunch he left the meeting to go with 'Panzer' Rohland to Hitler's headquarters in order to pre-empt the Gauleiters' predictable complaints.[51] Most of the afternoon session was devoted to a three-hour address by Heinrich Himmler, in which he gave a remarkably candid account of Germany's overall situation and which included a section on the mass murder of the European Jews. This ended with the words:

> And with this I want to finish by talking about the matter of the Jews. You are now informed, and you will keep the knowledge to yourselves. Later, perhaps, we can consider whether the German people should be told about this. But I think it is better that we – we together – carry for our people the burden of responsibility for an achievement, not just an idea . . . and then take the secret with us to our graves.

In the course of this speech Himmler addressed Speer in person, an embarrassing fact that Speer later attempted to brush aside. Himmler's speech was a full endorsement of Speer's 'Total War' approach to armaments. He assured the Gauleiters that he would be as ruthless in the pursuit of industrial efficiency as he was in his determination to exterminate the Jews. But he also cautioned that murdering Jews took priority over war production:

> You must understand that economic factors presented us with considerable difficulties, particularly with regard to clearing the ghettos. In Warsaw we fought street battles for four weeks . . . Because that ghetto produced coats and textiles, we were prevented from taking it over when it would have been easy. We were told that we were interfering with essential production. 'Halt!' they called, 'this is war production!'

At this point Himmler addressed Speer directly:

> Of course this has nothing to do with Party Comrade Speer. It was not something you did. In the next few weeks Party Comrade Speer and I will put an end to precisely this sort of self-styled 'war production'. We will take a tough approach as is appropriate in this fifth year of the war.[52]

The whole purpose of the Posen meeting was to celebrate an agreement between the Security Service, the Security Police and the Ministry of Armaments, known as the Iron Pact, that had been reached the day before. It was designed to impress upon the Gauleiters that they were now subordinate to the 'Speer-Himmler Axis'.[53] Speer's close association with Himmler was something that he was understandably determined to conceal after the war.

The Gauleiters were quick to respond. They complained to Hitler and Bormann that these drastic measures would have a disastrous effect on civilian morale. Himmler, both in his capacity as Minister of the Interior and as the guarantor of domestic stability, began to have second thoughts. Bormann and the Gauleiters – in particular Fritz Sauckel in Thuringia, Josef Bürckel in the Westmark and Karl Kaufmann in Hamburg – were determined to thwart Speer's plans. They managed to convince Hitler to distance himself from his favourite, so that at the high point of his meteoric career Speer's power and influence began to wane.[54] Hitler, in a deliberate snub, now asked Saur rather than Speer to present the monthly production figures.[55] Speer managed to recover some of the lost ground by including a few architectural drawings among the documents he showed Hitler. These diverted his attention, acting, as Speer said, as amulets against the malignant influence of the Gauleiters.[56] But irrevocable damage had been done to his relationship with Hitler.

Political exigencies were thus in conflict with the requirements of a war economy. Speer's power-political ambitions ran up against the entrenched interests of the Nazi Party. Hitler, as usual, wavered between these two positions. This did not result from a fundamental opposition between the rational approach of Speer and the industrialists and the ideologically blinkered Bormann and his Gauleiter cronies. Rather, it was a reflection of the hopeless position into which Nazi Germany had manoeuvred itself. There was a fundamental contradiction between the need to maximise armaments production and the necessity of maintaining a high level of civilian morale. It was a contradiction that was impossible to overcome. Goebbels could run the gamut of emotions and play on deep-rooted fears. He had command of an inexhaustible supply of abstract nouns, but his exhortations began to lack conviction.

Prospects were so grim that in October 1943 Speer first raised the question with Hans Kehrl as to who was likely to succeed Hitler. Himmler was dismissed as a schoolmasterly crank and a petty-minded vacillator, who was not at all to Hitler's taste. The club-footed Goebbels was out of the question due to his outward appearance, wildly extravagant promises and his unpopularity in the party. Rommel was a possibility, but Hitler was unlikely to select a military personality as his successor. The same applied to Dönitz. Speer unashamedly asked Kehrl whether Hitler might consider him as his successor. Kehrl replied in the affirmative. Hitler and Speer both had artistic temperaments, they were emotionally compatible, no one was closer to Hitler than Speer and he was undoubtedly impressed with Speer's outstanding abilities and leadership qualities. Speer nodded his head in complacent affirmation.[57]

Another major problem was that the bomber offensive was at last beginning to have a significant impact on war production. In March 1943 Air Marshal Arthur Harris launched a campaign against the Ruhr, Germany's industrial heartland. The initial raids were relatively ineffective, with H2S radar unable to penetrate the smog that lay over the area. On the night of 2/3 March the Krupp factory in Essen was hit in the first of a series of attacks in the spring and summer that caused damage estimated at 485 million marks. 'Bomber' Harris now set a list of armaments targets in order of importance: U-boat construction, the aircraft industry, oil production and transportation.[58]

The Eighth Air Force of the United States Army Air Forces (USAAF) took a very different approach. Attacking by day, initially with unescorted bombers, they sought out specific targets. Their aim was first of all to destroy the Luftwaffe, then to concentrate on the armaments industry. The first major success for the Americans was the daytime attack on Schweinfurt on 17 August 1943, which resulted in ball-bearing production being reduced by 35 per cent, prompting Speer once again to ask Hitler for better protection of the armaments industry from Allied bombers. This resulted in the Germans being prepared for the second attack on Schweinfurt on 14 October. The USAAF suffered its worst defeat in the war on 'Black Thursday'. Of the 291 B17 'Flying Fortresses', 77 were lost and 121 damaged. Aircrew killed in action numbered 590, while 65 were taken prisoner. The Allies had temporarily lost air superiority over Germany.[59]

There was one particularly vulnerable area in the Ruhr: the Möhne, Eder and Sorpe dams. The Armaments Inspector in the area, General Kurt Erdmann, had persistently warned that the dams had to be protected.[60] They provided five million people with drinking water and 70 per cent of the water used in the Ruhr's factories. They were also used to control flooding by the Eder, Fulda and Weser rivers as well as regulating the flow of water to hydroelectric stations. On 17 May 1943 Bomber Command's 'Dambusters' under Wing Commander Guy Gibson launched 'Operation Chastise' against the three dams. The Möhne and Eder dams were breached, but the Sorpe dam received only minor damage.[61]

The raid was technically brilliant, but the results for Bomber Command were very disappointing. Speer rushed to inspect the dams and was reassured that the Sorpe dam still provided drinking water, so there was no health hazard. He ordered Organisation Todt to set to work immediately to repair the dams. By 23 September they had been repaired and provided with greatly improved anti-aircraft protection. Although considerable damage was done to roads and bridges, and for months generating plants and water works operated at 35 per cent below full capacity while sewage treatment plants were seriously affected, nevertheless the major effect was on morale.

Speer was later to claim that the Allied bomber offensive caused him few problems and that armaments production continued to rise in spite of it. Both assertions are untrue. As early as June 1943 Speer, no doubt alarmed by the Dambusters raid, pointed out that Allied bombers were skilled at selecting vulnerable targets. Arguing that Germany should respond in kind, he formed a committee that included Rohland, Pleiger and Saur to select armaments factories in England for attack by the Luftwaffe.[62] Göring's men were in no position to make much use of this valuable information.

The Battle of the Ruhr between 5 March and 31 July 1943 was a decisive turning point in the war, a fact that is often overlooked because of an underestimation of its effect by both the United States Strategic Bombing Survey and the British Bombing Survey Unit. Speer's boastful reports on the speed with which the damage was repaired, and the minimal effect on armaments production that it caused, served further to lessen its impact. Serious moral qualms about aerial warfare made it uncomfortable for the Reich to accept that the Allied bomber offensive drastically weakened Germany's fighting strength.[63]

At the time Speer had no such illusions. He declared the Ruhr to be a war zone. An emergency meeting was held in July at what Rudolf Wolters' Chronicle sarcastically described as Krupp's 'little villa' outside Essen, which had been offered to Speer as temporary accommodation. As a result of this conference a Ruhr Staff Speer was formed.[64] It was housed in Friedrich Flick's immense Charlottenhof in Kettwig, popularly known as 'Schloss Flick'. General Kurt Erdmann was put in charge. His staff included 'Panzer' Rohland, Albert Vögler, a construction manager from Organisation Todt and representatives from the Flick Corporation, the Rheinland-Westphalian Coal Syndicate and the German Work Front. Speer gave the organisation exceptional powers to override existing organisations and the right to decide what action was appropriate when a factory was damaged in an air raid.[65] This new organisation was typical of Speer's ad hoc approach and his belief in the self-determination of industry. It became increasingly powerful in the later stages of the war, often ignoring the directions from the 'bureaucrats' in the Pariser Platz as well as the local Nazi Party officials. It ensured that cool heads prevailed during the chaotic final stages of the war.

The effects of the bomber offensive by the summer of 1943 were already considerable, especially in certain areas of the Ruhr where there was a drop of 25 per cent in coal production and 24 per cent in iron production.[66] Damage to the transportation network caused incalculable complications. The effects on the civilian population were calamitous. Constant air-raid warnings deprived the workforce of sleep. In the Ruhr there were often up to three warnings per night, so that a good night's sleep was nigh on impossible. Widespread destruction in residential areas had a shattering effect on morale.

The Hamburg raid at the end of July and early August seemed to be a shocking foretaste of things to come.[67] Widespread destruction resulted in an increased demand for scarce building materials and for everyday items such as cooking utensils, cutlery, tableware and clothing. The task of removing bomb damage and providing temporary shelter soon proved too much for local authorities to handle. Organisation Todt was forced to divert manpower to this task, thereby seriously compromising the building of new armaments factories, the protection of existing facilities and the construction of defences such as the Atlantic Wall.[68]

There was a widespread feeling that if the Allies continued with raids like 'Gomorrah' on Hamburg, they were bound to prevail. Combined with the Red Army's victory at Kursk it was obvious to some that the writing was on the wall. Field Marshal Milch panicked. He told a shocked meeting of Gauleiters, ministers and senior civil servants that the war was definitely lost. The indefatigable Hans Kehrl suffered a mental breakdown.[69] Speer was highly alarmed. At a meeting of Central Planning on 29 July 1943 he announced that: 'If air raids on this scale continue, within twelve weeks we will no longer have to bother about the questions with which we are now concerned. There will then be a straight-forward and fairly rapid slide downhill . . . We can then convene the final session of Central Planning.' He concluded that the only solution was to concentrate on building fighter aircraft. Speer went directly to Hitler and told him that if there were attacks on six more German cities on the same scale as that on Hamburg the armaments industry would grind to a halt. Hitler did not seem to be much concerned. He simply remarked: 'You will get things under control again.'[70]

The Battle of Berlin, which began in November 1943, marked the next phase in the air war. Far better results would have been achieved by continuing to concentrate on the Ruhr, the centre of Germany's coal and steel industries. Thanks to the concentration on Berlin, Speer and the Ruhr Staff were able to avoid the catastrophe that they had feared. Berlin was a difficult mission for the RAF, being at the extreme limit of the Lancaster's range. The results were disappointing. The raids resulted in Speer's ministry being partially destroyed which, given his dislike for bureaucracy and paperwork, did not cause him much anguish. On 23 November 1943 he published a memorandum in which he said that: 'I believe that thanks to this [raid] the question of the bureaucratic treatment of problems that should best be dealt with in a manner free from administrative restraints, is automatically resolved.' He repeated this sentiment in a speech in Essen:

> During one of the first heavy raids on Berlin we had the good fortune that a large part of the current files was burnt, so that for a time we were rid of unnecessary ballast; but we cannot expect in future that such events will bring this much-needed freshness to our work.[71]

These flippant remarks made the highly organised and meticulous Hans Kehrl furious. Speer might dismiss paperwork as irrelevant, but he should remember that he was always painstakingly briefed by his hard-working and conscientious staff. Knowing that the executive branch of the ministry relied on detailed administrative spadework, Kehrl came to the conclusion that Speer had no real idea how his office functioned. For Kehrl these remarks were as thoughtless as Goebbels' comment on the bombing of Berlin: 'It's easier to march without kit.'[72]

Hans Kehrl admired Speer's energy, determination and ability to find imaginative solutions to seemingly intractable problems, but he also knew that it was not enough simply to lay plans and issue orders. Without an effective administrative structure none of these ideas, however ingenious, could be put into practice. That was a fundamental structural failure of the Third Reich. The glorification of leadership in the 'leadership principle' led to an underestimation of the importance of subordinates. Speer was an excellent example of the National Socialist leader in this respect.[73] He once told Kehrl that he felt that mistrust was a positive quality. Kehrl violently disagreed, arguing that reciprocal loyalty was essential to the smooth running of the ministry. He took this opportunity to take Speer to task for often playing off his subordinates one against another. Speer complacently replied with the well-worn adage '*divide et impera* – divide and rule'. Kehrl pointed out that this stratagem was used by the Romans against their enemies and rivals, not their colleagues and friends.[74]

A crash programme to produce anti-aircraft guns was hastily improvised to counteract the bomber offensive. This resulted in a noteworthy reduction in the number of anti-tank guns sent to the Eastern Front.[75] Speer endorsed the Luftwaffe's demands for a significant increase in fighters, thereby reducing the resources available to the army and the navy. By the autumn the Luftwaffe began planning for a major bomber offensive aimed at Soviet industry. They now called for a 30 per cent reduction of fighter production in favour of bombers, thereby further weakening Germany's air defences. The Allied bomber offensive thus confronted Speer and Milch with a set of intractable choices. How could they meet the threat from the air without compromising the strength of the ground forces?

CHAPTER EIGHT

THE CHALLENGE TO POWER

FRITZ SAUCKEL, WHO ran his own armaments factories in his Thuringian demesne in which he made extensive use of labour from the concentration camp at Buchenwald, acted as a spokesman for his fellow Gauleiters when, on 4 December 1943, he gave a speech in Weimar in which he made a frontal attack on Speer's system of industrial self-determination. He proclaimed the Soviet system of 'force as a matter of course' as being obviously a far more efficient alternative. On the following day at a press conference he stepped on Speer's toes by calling for an all-out effort in the armaments industry. Speer complained bitterly to Hitler that 'after all it is I who must decide the time and the form for an appeal for an all-out effort.'[1]

Sauckel's attack rankled, but Speer faced even stronger opposition within his own organisation. He had taken over command of Organisation Todt on his appointment as Todt's successor, but had left it in the hands of his deputy, Franz Xaver Dorsch. He was a civil engineer and fervent National Socialist, who was determined to go his own way. From the outset Speer was at loggerheads with Dorsch and the 'inflexible bureaucrats' in Organisation Todt.[2] Determined to make Dorsch aware that he was his subordinate, Speer went on the attack accusing him of megalomania, complaisance and bureaucratic inertia. He began by moving some of Dorsch's key associates to the armaments section of his ministry, but was far too busy with armaments and munitions to pay much attention to OT. Dorsch, furious at what he considered to be Speer's overblown sense of self-importance, refused to toe the line and set about creating an independent fiefdom. When Speer visited OT troops in Lapland at Christmas 1943 he invited Dorsch to a conciliatory meeting but Dorsch refused to come.[3]

This trip provided a welcome escape, but on his return to Germany Speer was subjected to a tongue-lashing from Hitler when he suggested that it would be better to recruit domestic labour rather than depend on Sauckel's efforts to get hold of four million foreign workers.[4] Undaunted, he returned to his habitual routine. On 5 January 1944 he chaired a ministerial conference that addressed a series of pressing problems: the need for more anti-aircraft guns, the supply of energy and gas in bomb-damaged towns, the granting of armaments contracts to French firms, the redeployment of workers from factories deemed inessential, the employment of the SS in Estonia, the reorganisation of fire brigades, the simplification of payment procedures, problems within the postal service, trade relations with Sweden, locomotive repairs, building projects in Norway, the agenda for a major armaments conference, the export of weapons, control over transport in Italy and the use of caves as bomb-proof factories.[5] This staggering list of topics gives some indication of the vast range of activities covered by Speer's ministry.

On 10 January Speer hosted a conference of local officials of the Ministry of Propaganda in Berlin at which he outlined his plans for rebuilding Germany's bomb-damaged towns after the war. He began with the absurd boast that 'terror bombing' had had no effect whatsoever on armaments production. In fact, he claimed, output had steadily increased. No mention was made of the urgent calls for more anti-aircraft guns and fighters or the need to move factories underground that had been voiced just a few days earlier. In a similarly wildly optimistic tone Speer announced that: 'In the course of this year a series of technological innovations will give the enemy fresh surprises.' His insistence that, inflamed with true National Socialist spirit and enjoying the trust of the working class, Germany would overcome all difficulties, sounded somewhat bland when followed by a warning that complacency had to be avoided. The country had to prepare for the massive task of rebuilding after the 'Final Victory'. The many mistakes that had been made after the defeat of France in 1871 had at all costs to be prevented.[6]

Shortly after delivering this abstruse speech Speer fell seriously ill. He had injured his knee during his visit to Lapland and was suffering from 'exhaustion'.[7] He was admitted to SS-Gruppenführer Professor Dr Karl Gebhardt's clinic at Hohenlychen, a fashionable establishment north of Berlin much favoured by the Nazi elite. Gebhardt, an orthopaedic surgeon specialising in knee injuries, was Himmler's personal physician. Among his many distinguished patients were the King of the Belgians and a number of leading personalities from the world of sports. To many Gebhardt was seen as the Reichsführer-SS's evil genius. Walter Schellenberg, the head of Himmler's secret service, described him as 'detestable'. The head of the domestic section of the Security Service, SS-Gruppenführer Otto Ohlendorf, contemptuously dismissed him as a corrupt, self-seeking schemer with a keen eye for the main chance.[8]

Hohenlychen was a somewhat dubious establishment in that a number of prominent patients mysteriously failed to survive. Gebhardt's treatment of what would seem to have included acute depression very nearly killed Speer. He was officially diagnosed as suffering from 'a purulent rheumatoid infection of the left knee-joint combined with damaged ligaments.'[9] On 8 February – having spent three weeks without leaving his bed while receiving a daily flood of visitors, who regularly kept him busy until after midnight – he suffered a near-fatal lung embolism. His life was saved by the intervention of Professor Friedrich Koch from the Hufeland Hospital in Berlin, who went to Hohenlychen at the prompting of Speer's friend SS-Gruppenführer Professor Dr Karl Brandt. In September 1943 Hitler, delighted with the work he had done murdering more than 70,000 physically and mentally handicapped patients in 'Action T4', had made Brandt responsible for the 'medical research' conducted in the concentration camps.[10] When Gebhardt claimed that Speer's heart was so weak that he was unable to work, Brandt dismissed this as total rubbish. There was nothing whatsoever wrong with Speer's heart.[11] Throughout Speer's illness there was considerable doubt as to the exact nature of his complaint. This served to fan the suspicion that something devious was afoot. Speer, all too aware of his rivals within the ministry, decided not to appoint a deputy while he was indisposed. He remained hard at work, in spite of Gebhardt's agitated protests.[12]

American bombers were his major concern. 'Big Week', from 20 to 25 February 1944, dealt a devastating blow to the Luftwaffe's aircraft factories. The Flying Fortresses and Liberators were now accompanied by P-51 Mustangs fitted with disposable fuel tanks, enabling them to give the bombers constant fighter protection. Milch convened an emergency bedside meeting at Hohenlychen at which it was unanimously agreed that the aircraft industry had where possible to be moved to safe locations. Milch made an extensive tour of the damaged aircraft factories in what was codenamed 'Operation Hamburg'. The results were sobering. He had to confess that the Luftwaffe's aircraft construction programme was bankrupt. Two thousand aircraft per month had been promised; now it would seem that they would be lucky to build six hundred.

On 1 March Saur went to Hohenlychen. He reported that the bomb damage was so extensive that it would be impossible to meet the target figures for fighter aircraft. To meet this crisis Speer ordered the formation of a Fighter Staff with Milch as his deputy and Saur as chief of staff.[13] Speer made it clear that this would mean that his ministry would take charge of the Luftwaffe's armaments programme. With the Allied bomber offensive strangling the Luftwaffe's supplies, Milch felt that he had no alternative but to comply.[14] That same day Hitler signed a decree, drafted by Speer, formally creating the Fighter Staff. The Fighter Staff's offices were in the Air Ministry, with both Speer and Milch having equal authority, but with Speer indisposed real executive power over the Fighter Staff rested in the hands of Karl-Otto Saur. He was ably assisted by another ambitious rival, SS-Obergruppenführer and Waffen-SS General Hans Kammler.

Himmler's role during Speer's illness is difficult to read. He was resentful of Speer's staggering accumulation of power that now totally overshadowed Oswald Pohl's SS Economics and Armaments Office. He had clashed with Speer over a number of issues but Speer was to be no threat to the SS. He may well have wanted to keep Speer on the sidelines as long as possible but it is difficult to imagine that he seriously considered permanently removing a man who was still a key player in Hitler's inner circle. Professor Koch, on the contrary, was absolutely convinced that Himmler did everything he could to hinder Speer's recovery.[15] Speer was later to claim that he had narrowly escaped being murdered at Hohenlychen.[16]

None of this squares with a letter that Gebhardt wrote to Himmler on 21 February 1944 in which he said that since Speer intended to leave Hohenlychen in a week or two, he had requested the Gauleiter of South Tyrol to find him a property with sixteen to twenty rooms at an altitude of 1,500 to 1,800 metres. Speer had requested that Gebhardt and his family accompany him. Gebhardt wanted to know how he could contact Himmler's chief of staff, SS-Gruppenführer Karl Wolff, so as to make the necessary security arrangements. Himmler promptly telexed 'Wölffchen' ordering him to make sure that Speer's temporary residence should be made absolutely secure and protected from air raids.[17]

That Speer was on excellent terms with Gebhardt is also clear from by a letter thanking him for 'everything you did for my family [and] for your understanding and comradeship'. Six weeks later Speer wrote to Gebhardt warmly congratulating him on a high honour that Hitler had bestowed upon him. To cap it all he was later to recommend Gebhardt's medical skills to his friend the French Minister of Labour, Transport and Communications, Jean Bichelonne, who unfortunately took his advice and died at Hohenlychen.[18]

The only possible explanation for this discrepancy can be that as Speer set about the reconstruction of his past he had to distance himself as far as possible from both Gebhardt and Himmler. In spite of some disagreements, Speer maintained an excellent working relationship with 'Dear Party Comrade Himmler'. While at Hohenlychen he told Himmler that he needed concentration camp inmates to help build the Atlantic Wall. He said that he had a camp ready, with an adequate number of guards to oversee 6,500 prisoners. He would soon be able to accommodate 1,000 more. In addition he asked for 10,000 prisoners from Auschwitz to work in the chemical industry in Upper Silesia. The camps and guards were ready for immediate use. Himmler was most accommodating.[19]

Determined to hang on to the reins of power, Speer had a steady stream of bedside visitors, including frequent discussions with Milch. He had good reason to be concerned. Göring took advantage of his indisposition to make an attempt to regain some of his lost powers, but Hitler quickly put a stop to that.

Dorsch presented a far greater challenge. As an 'old warrior' who had taken part in Hitler's putsch attempt in 1923 and as a friend of Himmler since his youth, he had easy access to the top. Shortly after he was admitted to the clinic, Speer received alarming news from his chief of personnel, Erwin Bohr, that at Dorsch's instigation the Berlin Party District Office had ordered that a safe containing the political evaluations of all those who worked at the Ministry of Armaments was to be sent to Organisation Todt's head office. Speer, knowing full well that this was part of Dorsch's plan to undermine his position, ordered that the safe remain in Bohr's office. Party officials then sealed the safe's door. On Speer's orders, the back of the safe was removed, a number of sensitive documents with some less than flattering reports on some of Speer's principal associates were removed, and the back replaced. Willy Liebel, as head of the ministry's Central Office, ordered Dorsch to give a written explanation why a demand had been made for confidential documents to leave the ministry. Speer asked Bormann to find out who had initiated this action.[20]

Dorsch was ordered to go to Hitler's headquarters where he was asked to list his complaints. He blandly stated that he had none, but Bormann pressed the point in the hope of undermining Hitler's confidence in Speer. Nothing resulted from this meeting with Hitler, beyond providing further evidence of the discord between Speer and Dorsch. Speer laid down a set of conditions for Dorsch, warning him that if he did not fall into line he would be dismissed.

From his bed in Hohenlychen, Speer issued a decree threatening to send anyone in the ministry who spread rumours and disaffection to a concentration camp. He also decided to tell Hitler that he intended to fire Dorsch, but wanted to wait until he was well enough to go to Hitler's headquarters to argue his case in person. On 26 January 1944 he wrote to Goebbels saying that Dorsch had allowed politics to cloud his judgment and therefore he had to be removed. Although Dorsch gave Speer an empty expression of his loyalty, he continued to intrigue behind his back. He told General Kurt Zeitzler, the army's chief of staff, that he would soon take over responsibility for all construction projects because Speer was incurably ill.[21] Dorsch assiduously spread this rumour around Hitler's headquarters, thereby giving considerable encouragement to Speer's rivals.

Speer had long been locked in battle with Dorsch over the promotion of one of Speer's associates, Dr Carl Birkenholz, who was an expert in labour law.[22] As a result of his report on working conditions, men were to work for seventy-two hours and women for sixty-six hours per week. In return they were to receive special rations, consumer goods, tobacco, alcohol and medical assistance. Extra clothing was to be provided, especially for those working outdoors. The system was monstrously unfair in that these privileges were only awarded to those who worked hard – in other words, those who were physically capable of working such long hours. Ferocious punishment was meted out to 'skivers'. The end result was that the healthy benefited from the incentives; the weak fell by the wayside.[23]

Dorsch, who was opposed to such generosity, objected to Birkenholz's promotion on the grounds that he had received several bad references. Bormann's office let it be known that he was not considered to be a sufficiently ardent National Socialist to be promoted to the rank of Permanent Secretary. He was considered to be 'uncomradely', 'arrogant' and a 'weak character'. Speer was furious. He wrote back claiming that Birkenholz's papers had been destroyed in a 'terror attack' by the RAF on Berlin so he was unable to produce concrete evidence to support his case. He attributed this underhand attack on a trusted colleague to Frau Stürtz, the meddlesome wife of the Gauleiter of Brandenburg, who worked in Birkenholz's department on a part-time basis. In mid-January Birkenholz's immediate superior, Dietrich Clahes, renewed the attempt to secure Birkenholz's promotion, but Bormann again refused, citing his lack of a truly National Socialist spirit.[24]

Speer did not give in. He was now convinced that Dorsch and Konrad Haasemann, the chief of the personnel department, were intriguing against him. Karl-Otto Saur leapt to Birkenholz's defence, insisting that the charges against him were false. He had done excellent work under Fritz Todt and had overcome many difficulties to improve rations for munitions workers. Dorsch replied that he considered Birkenholz to be 'uncreative' and argued that he had every right to mention his reservations about him to Haasemann. Speer wrote again to Bormann in early March complaining bitterly that Dorsch and Haasemann were indulging in 'sinister backstairs politics' at his expense and repeated that they were using political criteria to influence their judgment. He warned Bormann that he intended to hold both men to account. Speer ordered Haasemann to be arrested by Transport Brigade Speer and called for a thorough investigation of the case. Haasemann, admitting that he had been caught in a conflict of loyalty between Dorsch and Speer, expressed his regret that he had backed the wrong side. Having narrowly escaped being sent to a concentration camp, he was dismissed from Speer's ministry and sent off to build roads in Saxony. Saur kept up the pressure on Bormann, but it was not until early May that he finally gave way and Birkenholz was promoted. Speer was unforgiving. Haasemann was cast into the wilderness. In November he came grovelling to Speer, pleading to be given a decent job. Speer turned a deaf ear to his entreaties, so that Haasemann's career was now in ruins.[25]

Having failed to use the Haasemann affair to dislodge Dorsch, Speer revived plans to restructure Organisation Todt. He wrote to Hitler suggesting that Willi Henne, one of Todt's closest assistants, should be put in charge of construction in the Reich. Dorsch would then only be responsible for construction in the occupied countries. Walter Brugmann, who had been his right-hand man in

Berlin and was now in charge of Organisation Todt in the south of the Soviet Union, would be given overall responsibility for it. An angry Hitler rejected this proposal out of hand. He told his senior secretary, Johanna Wolf, that: 'Speer must realise that even for him reason of state applies.' Five weeks later Brugmann was killed in a plane crash that at first appeared to be similar to that which had killed Speer's predecessor.[26] But this time there was no question of sabotage. The accident happened when flying through a mountain pass at low altitude in thick fog. The plane hit a treetop and exploded on impact.[27] Brugmann was a man of integrity who was widely respected. He was given a ceremonial funeral and buried in a heroes' graveyard in the Ukraine.[28]

Speer responded to these attempts to undermine his position with a series of 'submissions for the Führer' dictated from his sickbed. In the first he pointed out that his sole concern was to do everything possible to increase all sectors of the armaments industry during 1944. For this to be possible the Gauleiters and the NSDAP had to be fully committed to following his 'specialised competence' in all matters pertaining to the armaments industry. Sauckel had to follow instructions, not set the priorities of the armaments industry. That was Speer's sole responsibility. He asked Hitler to tell the Gauleiters, and Sauckel as Generalbevollmächtigter für den Arbeitseinsatz, or Plenipotentiary for the Employment of Labour, to cooperate with his ministry. To this end he requested that a meeting be held at which he could address the Gauleiters.[29]

In a second memorandum Speer asked Hitler to counter the rumours emanating from the upper echelons of the army, to the effect that the armaments industry was failing to produce the weapons, tanks and munitions needed for victory. Hitler should endorse Speer's 'Success Report'. The third submission had little of substance, but the fourth contained a blistering attack on the Gau Economics Advisors, whom he claimed had no idea of the problems facing the armaments industry. They were meddlesome and totally superfluous. There was also a testy complaint about Sauckel's remarks regarding the superiority of Soviet industry and his call for an all-out effort. Lastly, he complained that Otto Dietrich, the Reich Press Chief, was permitting articles to be published about armaments that had not been vetted by his ministry. Speer insisted that he alone should decide what information should be released and when it should appear.[30]

The crotchety tone of these submissions is clear evidence that Speer was deeply concerned. All now depended on Hitler's reaction. Speer later claimed to have emerged the winner, but it is difficult to see how he could have reached this conclusion.[31] He was saved not by an energetic counter-attack, but by the critical problems facing Germany in the months to come, combined with Hitler's reluctance to settle arguments amongst his subordinates.

Speer finally left Hohenlychen on 17 March 1944. The night before he left, his friend Wilhelm Kempff gave a piano recital for the staff. The next day,

travelling with a physician, Frau Hofmann, and a physiotherapist, Fräulein
Dültgen, he stopped at Hitler's official guesthouse at Klessheim, near Salzburg.
Hitler was in residence at the castle where he met Hungary's Admiral Horthy,
who was promptly placed under what amounted to house arrest. He was ordered
to dismiss Miklós Kállay's government, which had been trying to negotiate a
separate peace with the Allies. Henceforth he was to take orders from a Reich
Plenipotentiary, SS-Brigadeführer Edmund Veesenmayer, a man who had
specialised in deporting Serbian Jews. SS-Gruppenführer Otto Winckelmann
was entrusted with performing 'the tasks of the SS and police concerning
Hungary and especially police duties in connection with the Jewish question'.[32]
In this he was to be assisted by Ernst Kaltenbrunner and Adolf Eichmann. Two
days later German troops marched into Hungary. While these dramatic events
were taking place in the castle, Speer was temporarily housed in a baroque
pavilion in the park that was designed by the great Austrian architect Fischer von
Erlach. In his memoirs Speer made no mention of the circumstances that led to
the deportation of 437,402 Hungarian Jews, 90 per cent of whom were murdered.

Hitler paid Speer a personal visit to his pavilion. They had not seen one
another for ten weeks. Speer later claimed that for the first time he was struck by
Hitler's unsightliness: his sallow complexion, ugly nose and constant twitching.[33]
Speer was to tell his biographer, Gitta Sereny, that he first began to have doubts
about Hitler when, during a formal dinner at the Hotel Vierjahreszeiten in
Munich, he saw him hand Eva Braun an envelope full of banknotes without
saying a word. She blushed deeply. Speer was also shocked when Hitler remarked
at the Berghof that intelligent men should always choose primitive and stupid
women.[34] It is typical that Speer should be offended not by Hitler's brutality,
arbitrariness and lack of moral scruples, but by the shape of his nose or such
things as his ungallant attitude to women, his lack of decorum and his poor taste.

Hitler visited Speer again to wish him a happy birthday on 19 March and
presented him with an enormous bouquet of flowers. Hitler's Luftwaffe adjutant
Nicolaus von Below and his physician Dr Morell also congratulated him personally.[35] Hitler came once again to bid him farewell. He thereby gave his vassal
ample evidence of his support and appreciation. After five days of court intrigue
Speer was relieved to move to Burg Goyen near Meran, a magnificent castle
built in the twelfth century and extended in the sixteenth. The reception was
inauspicious. In spite of elaborate preparations the water supply broke down.
The Speer children were delighted as it meant they could go to bed without
washing. Speer recuperated gradually, taking it easy and sunning himself on the
veranda while his wife enjoyed the company of Heydrich's young widow, Lina.
Before long there was a steady stream of visitors as his strength recovered.

While in Burg Goyen, Speer wrote an irritable letter to Hitler complaining
that he had been ignored when major new building contracts were discussed.

He peevishly protested that while he allowed the architects who worked under him to get on with the job, they frequently broke faith and intrigued against him. He countered Hitler's charge that building within the boundaries of the Reich had been neglected by producing a mound of statistics. He pointed out that he had appointed a Main Building Committee under the energetic young Carl Stobbe-Dethleffsen that had done splendid work, in spite of Sauckel's inability to provide him with a sufficient supply of foreign workers. Speer's concluding argument was that at this critical stage of the war, industry and construction had to go hand in hand.[36]

Dorsch's intrigues during Speer's illness had considerable effect. Hitler made a series of disparaging remarks about Speer in the presence of Milch, Saur and Dorsch during his fifty-fifth birthday celebrations at the Obersalzberg on 20 April 1944. In a private conversation with Hitler, Milch pointed out that were he to lose confidence in Speer, the entire armaments industry would be plunged into chaos. Hitler then asked Milch what he should say to Speer. Milch gave the somewhat strange reply that he should tell Speer that he was fond of him. Hitler agreed and told Milch to pass on a message to this effect.[37] Speer's response to Milch was brief and to the point: 'The Führer can lick my arse!' Milch, although frequently given to choleric outbursts, was appalled. He told Speer that he was far too insignificant to speak of the Führer in such terms.[38]

Hans Kehrl thought that Speer had made a good recovery, but was weighed down by the Dorsch affair. He had moments of absent-mindedness, seemed to lack his former vitality and showed little interest in the production figures.[39] 'Panzer' Rohland was highly alarmed at Hitler's changed attitude towards Speer and was horrified when he heard rumours that Speer had threatened to resign. He told him that he had to stay in office both for the good of the country and for industry. Were he to go, industry would fall into the hands of sundry radical cranks within the Nazi Party. The resulting chaos would be unimaginable. He caustically added that since the war was obviously lost it was vital to consider how to keep the economy going and the people fed once the fighting stopped.[40]

While Speer was recuperating in Meran, Dorsch went straight to Hitler and Göring to win their approval for building 'Fighter Bunkers'. These included reinforced concrete hangars and bombproof factories for aircraft production. He made the extravagant promise to have these structures completed by November.[41] He obviously hoped that this underhand move would strengthen Speer's rumoured resolve to resign. Dorsch might well then become his successor. The proposal also appealed to Himmler, who had an ample supply of slave labour ready to be worked to death. With Göring's support he managed to persuade Hitler to give Dorsch absolute priority for his ambitious building projects.[42] Bormann was also delighted to see Speer's position thus significantly undermined.

This was altogether too much for Speer. He had always strongly objected to the idea of building massive bomb-proof factories on the grounds that it would mean putting all other building projects – including the Atlantic Wall – on hold. His immediate reaction was to send a close associate to Hitler with a letter of resignation, in an attempt to force Hitler to decide between him and Dorsch. Hitler refused to accept it, and gave Speer a warm welcome when he went to the Obersalzberg on 23 April. Convinced that Dorsch's schemes were bound to fail, Speer asked to be relieved of all responsibility for the building industry. Hitler again refused. Speer then suggested that Dorsch be made fully responsible for all building matters. Hitler turned this request down and confirmed Speer in all his powers, but did not cancel the orders he had given to Dorsch.[43] Speer decided to put Dorsch on the spot by appointing him head of the Building Office in place of Carl Stobbe-Dethleffsen. He also made him his deputy as General Plenipotentiary for Building within the Four-Year Plan. He also officially appointed him his deputy in Organisation Todt.[44] Speer hoped that he had thereby given Dorsch enough rope to hang himself.

Dorsch went ahead with planning these gigantic bunkers, although not on quite the scale that he had first envisioned. They were to be built by covering a colossal pile of earth with reinforced concrete. The earth would then be removed. The bunker was to be extended by digging down to provide space for several stories. The method was hideously expensive, labour-intensive and used enormous quantities of concrete. Speer preferred the less costly method of hollowing out caves, but this was even more dangerous for the workers involved.

At least 3,000 workers from the local concentration camp died building the bunker Weingut I (Vineyard I) at Mühldorf am Inn. Vineyard II, Diana II and Walnut (Walnuss) II were to be built in a pine forest near Landsberg. Vineyard II would have involved shifting 1 million cubic metres of earth and pouring on more than 3 million cubic metres of concrete. In February 1945 Speer paid an official visit to Weingut I and the adjacent concentration camp where thousands of prisoners from Auschwitz and Dachau were housed in appalling conditions and brutally mistreated.[45] None of these projects were finished by the war's end.

Speer did not return to work work in what remained of his office on the Pariser Platz until the beginning of May 1944. He celebrated his return by giving three hundred of his associates medals and bottles of cognac. All the children who remained in Berlin were given packets of sweets.[46] On 10 May he held his first meeting as minister after a five-months absence. It was attended by Goebbels, Kehrl, Fromm, Milch, Schieber and Saur along with a host of other important officials. With biting irony he praised his colleagues for the loyalty they had shown him during his long absence. Grudgingly admitting that production figures had peaked while he was away, he pointed out that even though he was on the sicklist he had still held the reins. He generously thanked Saur and Liebel for their sterling efforts during this hiatus, but warned that he was again in charge and determined to take all major decisions. He had no intention of allowing Fromm, Dönitz, Himmler or Göring to go their own ways as they had attempted to do in his absence.[47]

Speer used the farewell ceremony for Stobbe-Dethleffsen as an opportunity to make some remarks about the recent crisis in his ministry. He told the large gathering of his closest associates that Hitler had said that he wished that he had both a Todt and a Speer, the one as minister of works, the other as minister of armaments. During Speer's illness Hitler had again felt that these two functions should be separated and Speer had called his bluff by offering to hand over responsibility for building to someone else 'without being upset or aggrieved'. Hitler had refused, saying that there was no other person to whom he could entrust the job.[48] Dorsch was now in effective control of Organisation Todt, but was still subordinate to Speer. This formal reorganisation had no opportunity to be put to the test. The USAAF's attacks on the hydrogenation plants presented the construction industry with a new set of challenges for which a totally new organisation was required.[49]

Since returning to work Speer had managed to repair much of the damage and reassert control. As an outward sign of his revitalised status Bormann even suggested that they should use the familiar 'Du'. He was now back in Hitler's inner circle at the Berghof, where he was submitted to tirades about the evils of smoking, artificial honey and the churches, all spiced with what passed for jokes in such company. The threat from Dorsch had been neutralised, but tensions between the two men were barely concealed in their outwardly courteous correspondence. Dorsch, backed by Göring and Bormann, had chosen to attack Speer openly and emerged from the struggle with greatly enhanced powers. His other great rival, Karl-Otto Saur, preferred to intrigue behind his back. As the man in charge of end production he was able to soothe Hitler on the evening of the first day of each month with a recitation of production figures. Saur was a man very much to Hitler's taste. He was intelligent, wily, unscrupulous and totally unprincipled. During Speer's illness he had spent as much time as possible at Hitler's headquarters where he blew his own trumpet to deafening effect. He aroused all manner of unfounded hopes that solutions to Germany's mounting difficulties would soon be found. Milch frequently warned Speer that Saur was out to harm him, but the former continued to take Saur's egregious professions of loyalty at face value.

Speer had been seriously weakened during his illness and his relationship with Hitler was never again so close. Dorsch now had virtually full control over construction. Saur had taken charge of armaments. SS-Obergruppenführer Hans Kammler, whom Göring had put in charge of the underground factories on 4 March 1944, was steadily undermining his position.[50] Nevertheless, the production figures were most encouraging, but no one knew that this was the last good news that Speer's ministry was ever to get.[51] On 13 May he asked Hitler to award Saur the Knight's Cross with swords and in gold in recognition of his 'loyal and untiring work during my illness'.[52] This must have given Saur some wry amusement. He knew that the devil was in the detail and that it was precisely these details – in the form of production figures, tonnage, calibres and ranges – that fascinated Hitler, whereas Speer was content to concentrate on fundamental issues. Dorsch and Saur had powerful allies in Bormann and the Gauleiters with their District Economic Advisers, most of whom detested Speer's cosy arrangement with industry. For two years Speer had enjoyed Hitler's full support and had thus been invulnerable. Now Dorsch had got a Führer's Decree to build his bunkers, while Saur had won Hitler's confidence.

The Gauleiters stepped up their attack on Speer's lieutenants in the building sector, accusing them of not being 'wholeheartedly behind the state and the movement' and of lacking sufficient 'politico-economic understanding'. It was even suggested that there might be some opposition elements lurking in the Pariser Platz.[53]

Friction between Speer and the Gauleiters increased as the Allied bomber offensive began to have disastrous effects. Although armaments production peaked in July 1944, the Allied bomber offensive also intensified. Sixty per cent of the bombs dropped on Germany during the entire war fell after that date. The Gauleiters played an active role in clearing bomb damage, building temporary dwellings and improving air-raid protection. Speer welcomed a helping hand with this increasingly daunting task, but serious problems arose when the Gauleiters began to divert raw materials required for armaments production to provide for the welfare of the civilian population. Speer was solely concerned with maintaining and increasing the output of armaments. The Gauleiters as politicians had, even in a dictatorship, to take public opinion into consideration in the interests of maintaining at least the fiction of a 'racial community'.

In June Speer went to Berchtesgaden to be close to Hitler. He stayed there for several weeks and did not visit Berlin, much to the annoyance of many of his close associates, who accused him of being curiously inactive at a critical time.[54] The Allies had landed in Normandy. Raw steel production was 500,000 metric tons less than in the previous month. Reserves were rapidly dwindling. The manufacture of railway engines and rolling stock was seriously affected. Building had almost stopped because of Dorsch's requirements for his massive bunkers. Repairs to the hydrogenation plants that were being ravaged by the USAAF put a further strain on the construction industry. Raw materials were becoming increasingly scarce. The Swiss were proving to be difficult trading partners. With the Allies in France, exports of coal from Spain and Normandy ceased.[55] Soon there was no more manganese from Nikopol, chromium from Turkey, tungsten from Spain and Portugal, oil from Romania, ores from the Balkans, bauxite from southern France, nickel from Finland or minette ore from Lorraine.[56]

Speer energetically set about reasserting his position at court that had been seriously compromised by his months of absence. His first move was a request for permission to address a meeting of Gauleiters and senior party officials in order to give an account of the successes his ministry had achieved. He was determined to get back into the limelight and reassert his power. This was going be difficult. Bormann and his supporters had no desire to be given a repeat performance of the Posen meeting in October. A number of Gauleiters had complained to Hitler that they had found Speer's remarks at Posen highly offensive. Sauckel was determined to get his hands on the workers in Speer's protected factories in France.[57] Hitler also demanded to vet the text of a major speech that Speer was to give in Friedrich Flick's villa, so as to make sure that it contained nothing that might be offensive to the Gauleiters.[58]

The meeting was held in Essen on 9 June 1944. The mood was astonishingly optimistic, given that it was only three days after the Allies had landed in Normandy. Saur opened the proceedings by examining the relative potential of Germany and its enemies with respect to the production of iron and steel. He put the figure somewhat optimistically at 1:2.5 – a great improvement on World War I when it was 1:3.5. He pointed to the success of the U-boat programme as an example of what could be achieved by rationalisation. He forgot to add that there were serious production problems and that none of the new models were operational. Nor did he mention that the older models were hopelessly obsolete, or that most of them were at the bottom of the Atlantic.

Kehrl then addressed the issue of control over the European economy. He had become disillusioned with the increasingly chaotic system of rings, committees, business groups and special staffs. He concluded that since a free economy had proved unworkable and a Bolshevik command economy was out of the question, industrial production would have to be carefully planned and controlled, now and after the war. Goals would be set by selected 'personalities' from government and put into effect by the self-determination of entrepreneurs. It was highly doubtful whether 'self-determination' under such terms would amount to much, as the examples of Messerschmitt and Heinkel had already shown.

Friedrich Scheid was the man responsible for 'industrial self-determination' in Speer's ministry. His presentation was a direct response to Kehrl's approach. He described in pragmatic terms how some firms found it difficult to function in a system that operated without free enterprise and competitive bidding, that called for the open exchange of experience and research results, rationalisation, the abolition of patent protection and the closing down of non-essential plant. There was need for improvement, but drastic changes at this stage of the war would only lead to disaster.

Speer's keynote address, which had been carefully prepared in consultation with Saur, Kehrl and Rohland and approved by Hitler, was full of rousing expressions of confidence in victory.[59] It listed his ministry's astonishing successes and underlined the key role he had played to make this possible. He rejoiced in having achieved an 'armaments miracle', smugly announcing that: 'The steady increase up until May this year and the fact that terror bombing caused us no losses, is in my opinion the most amazing and wonderful achievement of our armaments and war production.' In an unambiguous warning to the Gauleiters he said that he would defend the principle of industrial self-determination against any attack, because it was 'the unconditional requirement of the Reich's leadership'. The Gauleiters there present – Friedrich Karl Florian of Düsseldorf, Albert Hoffmann of Southern Westphalia and Alfred Meyer of Northern Westphalia – did not feel threatened. They all had cosy relationships with the industrialists.

At a press conference after the speech Speer admitted that there had been some attacks on this central idea during his illness and that some industrialists did not like being obliged to switch to armaments production. He admitted that there was a trend towards bureaucratisation, which threatened to stifle initiative. There were brief moments when he sounded a more cautious note. Leaving aside his euphoric promises of 'miracle weapons' for a moment, he said that the armed forces would have to 'tough it out' with the weapons at hand.

When asked whether the system of industrial self-determination would remain in place after the war Speer was unable to give a clear answer. He did however concede that the present organisational form was dictated by the exigencies of war. By the summer of 1944 an increasing number of industrialists were beginning to think about post-war planning. Their spokesman in the Ministry of Armaments was 'Panzer' Rohland, who had long since given up any hope of a 'Final Victory'.[60]

Speer ended the session by expressing his absolute confidence that the Allies would be pushed back into the sea, after which it would be necessary to find various means of 'vexing' the enemy, thereby grinding them down. One such measure was the new model of U-boat, but he cautioned that this would not be ready for service for at least a year. His main objective was to stress the importance of understanding that Germany was in for the long haul. 'I cannot accept the idea that the war will be over the day after tomorrow. It could last for another five years.'[61]

This was a truly astonishing performance. Having recovered from his depression, Speer appears to have entered a manic phase. The Allies had established a bridgehead in Normandy. Only a few weeks previously the 'terror bombers' had delivered a very nasty shock by dealing a crippling blow to the fuel industry. Shortly after this speech Speer admitted that Allied bombers had become exceptionally skilled at selecting critical sectors of industry and attacking in force. In desperation he argued that morale should be boosted by making extravagant promises of 'miracle weapons'.[62]

A 'Victory Plan' for armaments had been drafted in March 1944. It made the extravagant prediction that output could be increased by 58.5 per cent by the end of the year. Speer imagined that he would be able to repeat the performance of his first year in office. But the situation in 1942 had been very different. There had been considerable room for rationalisation and concentration. Labour was readily available, whether forced or freely recruited. A vast area was open for ruthless exploitation. Allied bombing had not yet begun to take its toll and, most important of all, a number of projects that had been put in train by Fritz Todt had just begun to go into production. The subsequent drop in the rate of growth indicated that the limit would soon be reached. Speer, like Hitler, was beginning to believe that willpower could overcome all obstacles and that high target figures, even if totally unrealistic, would act as an incentive to maximum effort.

Speer was by no means alone in thinking that it would be possible to achieve a significant increase in the output of armaments in 1944. The indefatigably ambitious Karl-Otto Saur was firmly convinced that there were sufficient reserves available for him to be able to produce a staggering number of Me 262 jet fighters by the end of the year. Even the normally cautiously realistic Hans Kehrl had managed to convince himself that with maximum effort it would be possible to achieve the 'Final Victory'.[63]

Speer considered the Essen event to have been a rousing success. He therefore planned a repeat performance to be held in Linz on 24 June 1944,[64] when 350 of the leading figures in the armaments sector were brought in special trains to the Audorf barracks. Most of Speer's senior staff attended the meeting. Fritz Sauckel, with whom Speer had recently buried the hatchet, was also present. The Ministry of Agriculture was represented by Backe's deputy, Hans-Joachim Riecke, a man directly responsible for starving millions of Soviet citizens to death. The meeting was hosted by the local Gauleiter, August Eigruber, who presided over the Mauthausen concentration camp and who was also on the board of Steyr-Daimler-Puch AG.[65] Albert Vögler, Speer's grey eminence, hovered in the background.

Speer's speech lasted for three hours and was marked by a tone of irrational elation.[66] He confused his audience with an overload of statistics. He spoke in vague terms of the reserves of 'effectiveness' and 'potential manpower'. He warned against 'resignation' and ended on a somewhat sombre note by assuring those present that 'we do our duty . . . so that our fellow Germans may be preserved'.[67]

On the third day of the meeting, 26 June, a select group was invited to meet Hitler at the Platterhof, a guesthouse near his mountaintop residence at Obersalzberg, which had been turned into a military hospital and rehabilitation centre. In contrast to the Nazi grandees in their magnificent limousines, Hitler appeared on the scene in a Volkswagen.[68] This was to prove to be Hitler's last speech to a sizeable audience. It was carefully drafted by Speer, but was punctuated by rhetorical outbursts in Hitler's characteristic style.[69] It stressed that the system of industrial self-determination had to be strengthened. Although these were 'difficult times of crisis' there was 'no cause for resignation'. Then Hitler, in shrewd anticipation of the Morgenthau Plan, warned that, were the war to be lost, the result would be the 'destruction of German industry'.[70] Hitler, who had obviously heard that the industrialists were already thinking seriously about post-war planning, decided to put an end to such defeatism. 'Gentlemen,' he disdainfully announced, 'if the war is lost you will not have to worry about changing over to a peacetime economy. Each one of you will have to make his own decision how to get from the here-and-now into the hereafter. Either you do it yourself, or you will be hanged. The choice is whether you want a shot in the back of the neck, to starve to death or go to work in Siberia. These are the only things that an individual will have to consider.'

He then turned his attention to post-war industrial organisation after the 'Final Victory'. Industry had been complaining that Speer's words about the dangers of bureaucratisation were empty rhetoric designed to disguise the interference and meddling of his officials. Hitler promised that there would be no question of the 'nationalisation of industry' after a German victory, or of the state socialism favoured by many radicals in the party. On the contrary, there would be 'an incredible boom' in all areas that would greatly benefit industry. In a final flourish, he promised that 'impending revolutionary innovations', such as jet-propelled bombers, were 'a guarantee of Final Victory'.[71]

There was something frighteningly unreal about this speech. Hitler appeared to Hans Kehrl to be 'a man in a state of acute exhaustion, given at times to absence of mind'. He could hardly walk. His arms hung awkwardly. His speech was hesitant with sentences frequently left unfinished. The man was clearly no longer in a condition to rule.[72] Four days previously, on 22 June 1944 – the anniversary of the German invasion in 1941 – the Red Army had launched 'Operation Bagration', a massive offensive in Belarus that destroyed Model's Army Group Centre in what was Germany's most disastrous defeat in the entire war. In the West the Allies had established a secure foothold in Normandy. Rome had been captured on 4 June. In such circumstances the speech only served to increase the feelings of dismay shared by many of the industrialists present. Few can have been encouraged by Hitler's prescient statement that: 'After this war the German economy will possibly witness its biggest boom ever.' There was also little relief to this ghostly and unreal atmosphere offered by the evening concerts in the collegiate church devoted to Bruckner's 4th symphony and a suitably sombre recital by Wilhelm Kempff and Georg Kulenkampff.

His position having been seriously undermined during his illness, Speer sought mass support by addressing workers in a series of demagogic speeches. He bombarded them with production figures designed to boost their morale and flatter their pride. He told a group of shipyard labourers in Hamburg: 'We can honestly say that we have witnessed a true miracle. None of us thought this possible. When the air raids first began, particularly after the heavy raid here in Hamburg, we said to ourselves: if this goes on for a few months we'll go bust. But although it did go on, as far as armaments are concerned things were not so bad. That should be cause for encouragement.'[73] Speer the miracle worker was beginning to believe his own propaganda. At a speech in the Wartburg on 16 July he had made the extravagant claim that Germany's production of fighters was equal to that of the United States and England combined. In fact the United States produced three times more front-line aircraft than Germany in 1944 and almost twice as many fighters.[74]

On 18 July General Fromm, the commander of the Home Army, sent General Werner Kennes – his director of armaments, his liaison officer with OKH and his representative on Edmund Geilenberg's bomb damage repair group in Speer's ministry – to invite Speer to a luncheon meeting at his headquarters in the Bendlerstraße on 20 July.[75] There was nothing unusual about this invitation. The two men were close colleagues and on friendly terms. But since he was due to give a major speech at the Propaganda Ministry that morning, Speer felt obliged to refuse.

Thus when Stauffenberg's bomb was detonated at Rastenburg, Speer was giving another of his highly emotional speeches to a selection of ministers, their senior officials and a group of journalists in the banqueting hall at the Propaganda Ministry. Having shown some slides of the V1 rocket he announced some staggering increases in the target figures for the 'Victory Programme'.[76]

Much of this was simply juggling with figures. Even though the armaments industry had suffered severe losses in early 1944 as a result of the bomber offensive, some major increases in production in certain areas could be expected. But any such increases were likely to be offset by ever mounting losses, so that the armed forces' weapons stock would be steadily depleted. Even the most encouraging production statistics were becoming increasingly meaningless. Weapons might be produced, but there was a desperate shortage of transportation to bring them up to the front. Aircraft lacked the fuel needed to fly and new pilots could not be given adequate training. Increases in aircraft production were offset by even heavier losses. The Luftwaffe was rapidly shrinking.[77]

Speer maintained that, having delivered this pep talk at the Propaganda Ministry, he was invited by Goebbels for a drink. It was then that the Reich Press Chief, Otto Dietrich, informed Goebbels that a bomb had gone off in Hitler's headquarters. Speer then returned to his ministry, where he had a late lunch with Colonel Gerhard Engel, Hitler's former army adjutant who was now on active service. They discussed the likely effect on the troops of the appointment of a 'deputy dictator' charged with ensuring a total war effort. Noticing that soldiers had surrounded the building, Speer phoned General Fromm to find out what all this meant. When told that Fromm was unavailable, he demanded to speak to General Friedrich Olbricht, who held important positions at both OKH and OKW. Olbricht apologised profusely when an outraged Speer told him that he was virtually a prisoner in his own ministry. He said that it was an unfortunate mistake.[78]

Shortly after Speer had spoken to Olbricht, Goebbels phoned, asking him to come to his residence immediately. He was then given details of the coup attempt. Goebbels told him that Hitler had charged him with re-establishing legitimate authority in Berlin and asked Speer to give him a helping hand. Goebbels ordered a relatively junior officer, Major Otto Ernst Remer, to crush the insurgency. Remer, who commanded the Infantry Regiment *Großdeutschland* that was responsible for security in Berlin, replied that he had heard that Hitler was dead and that he was acting on the authority of General Paul von Hase, the City Commandant of Berlin. Goebbels immediately put a call through to Rastenburg so that Hitler could speak directly to Remer and convince him otherwise.

Later that evening Goebbels and Speer heard from General Ernst Bolbringer, the head of the tank department at OKH, that Fromm had arrested General Ludwig Beck, Olbricht and Stauffenberg, and was about to hold a summary court martial in the Bendlerstraße. Speer then drove to Fromm's headquarters, together with Bolbringer and Remer. The group was stopped by an SS patrol, but they were released when SS-Obergruppenführer Ernst Kaltenbrunner, the head of the Reich Security Main Office, identified Speer. When Speer said that they were going to the Bendlerstraße to stop the court martial Kaltenbrunner brusquely replied that it was the army's affair and that the matter had already been settled.

Speer was in no way implicated in the 20 July plot. Far from arguing that, since the war could not be won, a compromise peace had to be negotiated, he had spent the weeks before Stauffenberg planted the bomb calling for a coordinated effort by Himmler, Lammers, Keitel, Sauckel and Goebbels, in conjunction with the Ministry of Armaments, to achieve the Victory Programme. This was not the attitude of a man who had lost faith in Hitler and the National Socialist state, nor of one who believed that the war was lost.[79] Speer's speech on the morning of 20 July had loudly proclaimed the opposite.

In papers seized in the Bendlerstraße, Speer's name was mentioned as a possible minister should the plot succeed, but it was noted that he should only be approached when Hitler was dead. Speer was in fact totally opposed to the putsch attempt. He was convinced that victory was still possible and that it could only be achieved under Hitler. In the Spandau draft of his memoirs he had been quite frank about his role in crushing the coup. Later, when the men of 20 July were seen as national heroes, he was anxious to present himself as having been in sympathy with them, and attributed Hitler's subsequent coolness towards him to the fact that he had been chosen by them as a suitable minister. Both were key components in Speer's ingeniously constructed self-image. In his memoirs Speer claims that Kaltenbrunner visited him the following morning while he was lying in bed. With a look of 'jovial menace' he announced that the conspirators had chosen him as the future Armaments Minister. Someone had added 'if possible' and a question mark. Here he tries to heighten the drama by claiming that this was the first time he had heard that he had been considered for high office in the unlikely event that 'Operation Walküre' had been successful.[80] In fact the list of potential ministers was disclosed late in the evening of 20 July. Speer and Goebbels had a hearty laugh when they saw that he was included.[81]

The 'Chronicle' of Speer's ministry shows that he was at the centre of events on 20 July, but his day was somewhat less eventful than he subsequently claimed. Having given his speech at the Ministry of Propaganda he returned to his office. That afternoon he received a visit from Karl Claudius, the foreign office's special envoy to Romania, to discuss the oil crisis caused by the lack of transport and the mining of the Danube.[82] It was decided that it was imperative to build a pipeline in order to overcome these difficulties. During this discussion an adjutant had burst into the room with the news that there had been an attempt on Hitler's life, but that he was unharmed. Speer had already been informed of this by headquarters in Rastenburg, but had not been given any details. Goebbels had telephoned while he was still talking to Claudius. Speer immediately left for Goebbels' house, where he remained until late that night, by which time Goebbels had established full control over the capital. Troops appeared at the Brandenburg Gate and surrounded all government buildings, including the Ministry of Armaments on the Pariser Platz, but not until Speer had left his office.[83]

All the top ministers were summoned to Rastenburg the day after the assassination attempt, but only Speer was required to bring along his two top aides, Dorsch and Saur. Hitler paid noticeably more attention to them and was particularly cool towards Speer. People fell silent when Speer entered the room.

Hitler was somewhat friendlier the following day when Speer was invited to his teahouse along with Bormann, Himmler, Keitel and Goebbels. It was in these informal surroundings that Hitler decided to appoint Goebbels Reich Plenipotentiary for Total War.[84] Speer was later to claim that henceforth he seldom went to meetings with Hitler, because he was determined to maintain his independence and not be browbeaten by the Führer or play second fiddle to Saur.[85] The real reason, however, was that Saur and Dorsch had managed to gain the upper hand during his long illness.

While at Hitler's headquarters Speer drafted a memorandum that vividly conveys the reckless atmosphere that prevailed. He wrote:

> In his decree on the concentration of armaments and war production, dated 19 July 1944, the Führer issued a series of orders for a concerted effort to focus on the development of those weapons and devices which, because of their revolutionary new qualities, will give us a significant advantage over our enemies' innovations. At the same time we must put an end to the excessive amount of modifications made to those models whose development may be considered as completed.

Speer ordered that all research and development on new weapons must cease, unless it was officially sanctioned by Saur's Technical Office.[86]

On 22 July Speer told Hans Lammers that, having consulted with his top advisers, Hermann Röchling, Paul Pleiger, Carl Krauch and Albert Vögler, he had decided that an all-out effort to increase armaments production was essential. Exceptional powers were needed so that leading personalities could act as they saw fit, without being tied up in red tape or blocked by bureaucratic inertia.[87] Speer saw the botched coup attempt as an excellent opportunity finally to get things done. Now he could dispense with bus conductors, save fuel by stopping the use of traffic lights and drastically reduce the number of domestic servants.[88] The appointment of Himmler as commander of the reserve army on 21 July and Goebbels as Reich Plenipotentiary for Total War on 25 July was very much in the same spirit. Speer had supported both these appointments; whether by prudence or conviction is open to question. On his return to Berlin on 24 July he addressed his staff at the Pariser Platz.[89] He claimed with hollow rhetoric that the attempt on Hitler's life marked a 'watershed moment in destiny's struggle' and a 'decisive change that will lead to victory'. He ended this tirade with a rousing 'Heil Hitler!'[90]

Speer had taken two memoranda with him to Rastenburg. The first was concerned with labour. He pointed out that whereas only 6.22 million workers were employed in industry and mining there were 7.63 million in administration, trade and banking. In the armed forces the situation was even worse. Of the 10.5 million in uniform only 2.3 million were at the sharp end. A strong personality was needed to sort this out. Speer considered Keitel to be too weak and suggested that Himmler should be made responsible for personnel in the armed forces. On 2 August 1944 Hitler acted upon this suggestion by making Himmler responsible for investigating the armed forces, Waffen-SS, the police and Organisation Todt.

In the second memorandum Speer complained that his colleagues were denounced in party circles as reactionaries who were only interested in the economy and kept the party at arm's length. Bormann and Goebbels described his system of 'industrial self-determination' as a 'catchment basin for reactionary bosses' and 'enemies of the party'. Speer, however, insisted that his task was 'apolitical' and that his efforts should not be judged in party political terms. He argued that all party organisations that dealt with matters concerning armaments had to be subordinate to the Ministry of Armaments and that Hitler should make his support for the industrialists clear and defend them against party zealots. He asked that his performance be judged on purely objective grounds. He insisted that his system of industrial self-determination had worked wonders and that it would be seriously compromised were the NSDAP to interfere.[91] Hitler, visibly shaken after the attempt on his life the previous day, took the memoranda without saying a word, pressed a bell, and handed it over to an adjutant, who was told to pass it on to Bormann. Speer knew at once that he had lost this round. Hitler, as usual, was unwilling to get involved in a struggle between his ministers. He had simply passed the material on to Speer's most formidable rival.[92]

Things did not go quite as Speer had hoped. Himmler placed army armaments in the hands of SS-Obergruppenführer Hans Jüttner, the head of the SS Main Leadership Office and deputy to Himmler in his new capacity as Head of Army Armaments and Commander of the Reserve Army.[93] As a passionate opponent of the idea of self-determination of industry – like Himmler, Ohlendorf and Berger – Jüttner was determined to break free from Speer's control. Speer got Saur to persuade Hitler to remove Jüttner and replace him with the more amenable General Walter Buhle, a man who had been injured in the bomb blast on 20 July.[94] On 15 February 1945 Buhle was placed in charge of a new Armed Forces' Weapons Office that amalgamated the Weapons Offices of all three branches of the armed services. It was responsible for weapons, munitions, motor transport, tanks and electrical equipment.[95] This move greatly simplified the development of new weapons, but it backfired on Speer. Saur's influence on Hitler was thereby greatly strengthened and Himmler was left – in Speer's words – 'not in a friendly mood'.[96]

Speer had hoped that his alliance with Goebbels would hold, but after the attempt on Hitler's life and the subsequent intensified repression there was little chance that this would happen. He unwisely agreed to release one-third of his workforce to meet the Propaganda Minister's demand for more men in the armed forces – a request that was enthusiastically endorsed by both Bormann and Keitel. Speer loyally refused to find a job for one of Goebbels' senior staff, whom the Propaganda Minister had dismissed for defeatism after a visit to Rommel's headquarters in France.[97] But this did nothing to strengthen his position because he could not possibly meet Goebbels' inflated demands for manpower for the military. The relationship between the armed forces and the Ministry of Armaments was also radically changed. The recruitment of personnel for the armed forces from the industrial workforce was no longer the province of Keitel and OKW, but was handled by Goebbels in his capacity as Reich Plenipotentiary for Total War. He used Speer's bitter rivals among the Gauleiters as his local representatives. This left the Ministry of Armaments having to deal, in the caustic words of one official, with 'a much stronger partner'.[98] Bormann, who was determined to assert the primacy of National Socialist politics over the technocrats, saw this as a welcome opportunity to infringe upon Speer's demesne. At Goebbels' insistence, on 16 August Hitler gave the Gauleiters additional powers to seek information and issue directives.[99] Sorcerer Speer had imagined that Goebbels was an ally who would do his bidding. Now he discovered in Goebbels a most troublesome apprentice.

Speer was well aware that his rivals would use every available opportunity offered by the attempted coup to sow doubt and suspicion. Bormann felt that the conspirators' trust in Speer was further evidence that he was at best a luke-warm National Socialist. A number of leading industrialists in Speer's entourage came under investigation in the ensuing witch-hunt. They included Albert Vögler, Hermann Bücher from AEG, Alfred Meyer from MAN, Paul Reusch and Curt-Berthold Haniel from the Gutehoffnungshütte, Hans Reuter from Demag, and Hugo Stinnes junior. That Speer did all that he could to protect such people only served to fuel the suspicions of his rivals. He spoke up for General Fromm and for his colleague Eberhard Barth, who had been arrested as a family member of a conspirator.[100] He also defended Count Ulrich-Wilhelm von Schwerin von Schwanenfeld, General Speidel – General von Kluge's chief of staff – and the publisher Peter Suhrkamp. His efforts were largely unsuccessful, but he did manage to secure Barth's release. Schwerin was executed in September. On 8 December 1944 General Kennes was arrested along with Fromm and sent to Ravensbrück concentration camp. He was released at the end of the month, but Fromm was executed in March 1945. Speidel had the good fortune not to be hauled up in front of the People's Court, but remained in prison until he managed to escape in April 1945. Suhrkamp remained in Sachsenhausen until the leader of the Hitler Youth and Gauleiter of Vienna, Baldur von Schirach, secured his release in February 1945.

Speer's attempt to defend Fromm was an act of considerable courage. Otto Thierack, the Reich Minister of Justice, went to Hitler for advice on how to handle the case. Hitler issued an unambiguous warning to Speer that he was not to appear as a witness for Fromm.[101] Had Speer been capable of genuine companionship, Fromm would certainly have been one of his friends. They had worked closely together and Fromm had always been a loyal supporter. Speer also had a sincere admiration for Stauffenberg's many fine qualities, but he was utterly opposed to the attempt to kill the dictator.

The failure of the 20 July plot gave the regime a new lease of life. The charismatic leader's life had been saved as if by providence. Schemes to circumscribe his power or implement a regime change were doomed.[102] Speer now had to contend with the additional powers given to Himmler as commander-in-chief of the Reserve Army. His former ally, Goebbels, soon became a bitter rival. He joined forces with Bormann and the party in a concerted effort to push Speer aside.[103] He no longer enjoyed Hitler's automatic support. His efforts to strengthen his position after his return to full duties were to no avail. He was never to regain the unique position he had enjoyed before his illness. The crisis caused his damaged leg to swell to twice its size – an outward and visible sign of inner turmoil. Dr Brandt gave him anti-inflammatory pills, but believing the disorder to be largely psychosomatic he also prescribed a homeopathic preparation of valerian.

Although Speer was in no way involved in the plot against Hitler, his name had appeared as a man with whom the conspirators felt they could do business. The Gauleiters were in no mood to be impressed either by a long list of production figures or by professions of gratitude for the splendid work done by the NSDAP that had made all this possible. Speer had lost all credibility in their eyes, so that they believed neither his data nor his words of appreciation. What they did not know was that the production figures Speer had given them were as much as 50 per cent higher than those circulated in internal memoranda in his ministry. What he pretentiously called 'German Industry's Manifestation of Fidelity' was yet another piece of propagandistic ego-boosting based on statistical juggling.[104] Speer boasted that July 1944 should not be looked upon as a record month. Production figures would continue to rise. He claimed that a series of weapons 'of exceptional significance' would soon be available and which the enemy would be unable to match. Thanks to them, 'Final Victory' was a certainty. He ended by promising 'to produce more weapons and new weapons while at the same time providing more soldiers'. No one seems to have realised that this was an impossibility, or that it was yet another glaring example of the hopeless quandary with which the Nazis were confronted.

There was some grumbling about the glaring discrepancies in Speer's figures, but blame for this was placed on his co-workers. Hitler continued to believe implicitly in the data Speer provided. He got away with it because the 'Armaments Miracle' was a powerful propaganda weapon that helped boost morale. The military was well aware that Speer was cooking the books, but as long as Hitler still believed him they were loath to unmask the miracle worker. Speer forged ahead regardless of mounting scepticism. He exhorted his co-workers to accentuate the positive, to be optimistic and to remember that it would be most unfortunate were the 'racial comrades' to underestimate the achievements of the armaments industry. Regardless of whether the figures were right or wrong, as Hitler put it in his address at the Platterhof, 'correct is that which is useful'.[105]

Speer did not get a better reception when he presented the production figures at a meeting of leading figures in the Propaganda Ministry at the end of August. By this time his ministry was beginning to fall apart, rent by internal rivalries and mounting discontent. Speer's efforts to overcome this crisis only served to make matters worse. On 19 September 1944 he addressed a meeting of heads of the Armaments Commissions at which he said: 'The enthusiasm with which the Gauleiters are ready unquestioningly to support our efforts is exceptional. The measures that we want to put into effect are only possible to achieve if we work together with the Party'.[106] Unable to defeat the Gauleiters, Speer offered them an olive branch. Henceforth when an individual Gauleiter began to interfere with the armaments industry he dealt with him directly without first seeking Hitler's support.

No one person could possibly hold such a vast organisation together once the centrifugal forces gathered strength. By mid-1944 Speer's organisation had become so complex that a conspectus was virtually impossible. There were twenty-one main committees with hundreds of sub-committees and working groups. Then there were the rings and commissions in forty-two Reich Defence Districts that were not compatible with the Armaments Inspectorates in the Army Districts. Further confusion resulted from the reorganisation of industry for armaments production. A chocolate factory that was converted to make hand grenades remained within the Confectionary Business Group. Speer's Reich Associations for various branches of industry caused further problems. These were only partly overcome by the fact that their leading figures were also prominent in other committees and organisations. Speer proudly announced that his system was not bureaucratic, but this was often another way of saying that it was unsystematic and not infrequently chaotic. In such a system Karl-Otto Saur, with his exceptional knowledge of the minute details, was in a much stronger position than Speer, who lacked the detailed information necessary for him to maintain full control.

Speer now transformed himself into an itinerant preacher for industrial self-determination. He rushed around the country giving a series of virtually identical speeches, claiming that he had discovered the magical answer to Germany's economic problems. But he had to admit that there was considerable resistance to his approach. The building industry, encouraged by Dorsch, refused to cooperate fully. The shipbuilding sector proved similarly intransigent. Speer refused to accept that this was a reflection of certain difficulties within the system itself. He attributed it solely to the failure of the building and shipbuilding industries to adapt to meet the challenges of total war. The aeronautical industry was much more flexible, but he felt that it was still kept on too tight a rein by the Luftwaffe. Only in armaments for the army, where Speer had fought and won a long battle, had his system reached its full potential. Even where there were serious problems, he claimed to be able to force all those involved to sit down and talk things over, so that their fundamental differences did not become public.[107] Speer would not hear of any criticism of industrial self-determination, which he described as 'the most important instrument in the German people's struggle for existence'.[108] He thus continued to support the 'Three Kings' – Röchling, Rohland and Krupp – in the Reich Industrial Group against Paul Pleiger and the state-owned Hermann Göring Works.[109] But it gradually became apparent that the rapid growth of the system of industrial self-determination since the spring of 1942 had led to further organisational confusion and overlapping areas of competence. Speer came to realise the mistakes of the past, but lacked the technical understanding and administrative discernment to bring some order into this disorderly system.

He was generous in his praise of the workers in the armaments industry and repeatedly promised them adequate housing and improved social services once the war was over, but these were empty words. It is doubtful whether such assurances brought much comfort to Germany's hard-pressed industrial working class that was worn down by sleepless nights due to air-raid warnings, inhuman working hours and poor nutrition. By 1944 the number of Germans working in industry had declined sharply. Most of them were now over the age of fifty. An increasing number of childless and older women were employed as unskilled workers. The 7 million foreign workers, including prisoners of war, formed a sub-proletariat.[110]

In spite of this influx of foreign workers the actual number of workers in industry had declined drastically, but thanks to rationalisation and a reduction in the number of different types of weaponry, production increased. But the major cause of this increase was the intensified exploitation of labour. Concentration camp inmates and forced labourers were treated inhumanely, with tens of thousands worked to death. Regular workers were obliged to work for up to seventy-two hours per week. In such conditions it is hardly surprising that the number of those reporting sick rose alarmingly. The principal causes of sickness were colds caused by inadequate clothing and heating, problems related to a poor diet with a chronic lack of fresh fruit and vegetables, and exhaustion due to overwork.

German workers remained remarkably docile in the face of such deprivations. The Gestapo wielded a heavy stick, threatening the recalcitrant with internment in a concentration camp. Workers feared that if they did not pull their weight they would cease to be categorised as 'indispensable' and would be sent to the front. But there were substantial carrots in the form of goods plundered from the occupied countries and the social services provided for the 'racial comrades'. Most German workers supported the regime and found that the majority of their enslaved fellow workers confirmed the propaganda about the inferiority of Slav 'sub-humans' and the perfidy of Bolsheviks and Jews. It was very tempting for German workers to behave on the shop floor as if they were indeed members of a master race.

Speer was indifferent to the millions who slaved away in his factories. He was content to give them a few pats on the back and make some vacuous promises about the good life awaiting German workers after the war. He was now solely concerned with defending his system of industrial self-determination against attacks from Bormann and Goebbels. As usual, Hitler refused to take sides in this struggle, preferring to let his followers fight it out among themselves. Bormann took advantage of Hitler's withdrawal into virtual isolation by the autumn of 1944 to seize control over domestic policy, but his hold weakened as Germany began to fall apart in the final months of the war.[111]

CHAPTER NINE

MIRACLE WEAPONS

THE LUFTWAFFE WAS locked in a lengthy debate over whether to concentrate on bombers or fighters. Germany, unlike the United States and Britain, could not afford both. After the Hamburg raid in the summer of 1943, the Luftwaffe argued that the only solution to the bomber threat was to concentrate on building fighters so as to fight a defensive air war. When Göring put this to Hitler, he was brusquely admonished. The Luftwaffe had failed him, a defensive war was out of the question, and planning should go ahead for a major bomber offensive against England. Göring, by now a broken man, meekly agreed. The result was Operation Capricorn (*Steinbock*) between January and May 1944. The British contemptuously nicknamed it the 'Baby Blitz'. It was a miserable failure. Crews were poorly trained and left helpless against the greater numbers and technological superiority of Air Defence Great Britain. The operation seriously weakened the Luftwaffe, leaving it, as Field Marshal Hugo Sperrle had predicted, worthless against the Allied invasion fleet.[1]

Milch, regardless of *Steinbock*, tried desperately to convince Saur that the only hope for survival was a crash programme to produce jet-propelled fighters. He argued that without this weapon, within four to eight months Allied bombers would make it impossible for Germany to produce either U-boats or tanks.[2] After a heated exchange Saur agreed to consider the idea, but he wanted to continue building the old Me 109 and FW 190 as well as the jet-propelled Me 262 fighter. He would do so only if the Luftwaffe was placed under the command of the Ministry of Armaments, thereby putting Saur in charge. This was something that Milch was not yet prepared to accept. Saur was only interested in production figures. He did not care about what type of aircraft was built, or whether sufficient aviation fuel or landing strips were available. He had no patience with Speer's self-determination of industry. 'Speer's Rottweiler' believed in the ruthless exploitation of labour, regimentation, severe punishments and constant harangues. The German engineer, not the industrialist, was the man of the hour. He must devote all his energy to increasing production, thereby providing Saur with the figures with which to impress Hitler. The issue was settled at Speer's bedside at Hohenlychen with the formation of the Fighter Staff.

Speer did not attend a meeting of the Fighter Staff until 26 May 1944, so that Milch managed to retain much of his power and influence over aircraft production. The Fighter Staff was a flexible and largely improvised body that acted as a mini-ministry.[3] Backed by the authority of both the Ministry of Armaments and the Air Ministry, it could override other programmes within the armaments sector. This frequently caused severe disruptions. The challenge with which it was faced was daunting. In March half of the Luftwaffe's fighters were destroyed. In April a third of the remainder was lost.

On 4 June 1944 Speer asked Hitler to place the aircraft industry formally under his ministry, thereby abolishing Milch's position as State Secretary and Head of Aircraft Production. He already had nominal control over the Fighter Staff and the bomber programme, so it made little sense to leave the rest of Luftwaffe's concerns under a separate organisation. Speer asked Hitler to persuade Göring that this step was necessary. He suggested that he couch this as a suggestion so as to avoid any unpleasantness. He complained that Göring had claimed that the Ministry of Armaments had deliberately ignored the needs of the Luftwaffe. He pointed out that the Fighter Staff under his aegis had already doubled the production of aircraft in spite of the air raids and without making any cuts in the army's allocations. This argument was somewhat disingenuous. The Fighter Staff had managed to increase the number of fighters built, but at the expense of bombers and using facilities and workers that hitherto had produced weapons for the army.[4] Hitler, who had long since lost faith in Göring, wholeheartedly agreed with Speer's proposal. On 19 June Göring duly informed Milch that his post had been abolished. On the following day he signed over responsibility for aircraft production to Speer, whereupon Milch resigned from all his offices.[5]

Speer had outwitted Göring. His power and influence were lost for ever. All he could do now was to grumble, intrigue and retreat into a fantasy world. Speer appointed Milch as his deputy, but he wisely took the back seat and did not attempt to challenge the all-powerful minister. On paper Speer was now at the height of his powers, with formal control over armaments in all three branches of the Wehrmacht, but in reality his authority had been seriously undermined by rivalry and intrigue both within and without his ministry. Future prospects were grim. Impressive results could only be achieved by giving fighters absolute priority over all other weapons. Technicians and engineers were brought in from other sectors of the armaments industry to offer their expertise. Members of the Fighter Staff had free access to all factories and were empowered to make changes in personnel.[6] Great savings were made by reducing the number of different types of aircraft produced from forty-five to eleven. In order to boost production figures, concentration was on outdated models: the Me 109 and FW 190 fighters and the Ju 88 bomber. Milch's urgent request that the revolutionary Me 262 be given top priority was ignored. The Luftwaffe was to pay a heavy price for ignoring his advice.

Hitler's obsession with 'vengeance' weapons and hare-brained plans for a bomber offensive were the greatest obstacles facing the Fighter Staff. He and most of the Luftwaffe generals felt it dishonourable and self-destructive to fight a defensive campaign. For the armaments industry, the fact that the roof over Fortress Germany was leaking badly and in serious danger of collapsing made it absolutely imperative radically to improve air defences. With USAAF bombers now often flying out of the range of most anti-aircraft guns, fighters were the only viable solution. Saur single mindedly ignored all objections, overrode the Luftwaffe's leadership, freed himself from Speer's tutelage and wherever possible ensured that new priorities set by Hitler did not seriously affect his output figures. He insisted that the situation was so serious that there was no time for long-term planning or research and development. Rushing around in a special train, codenamed 'Hubertus', he hastily improvised, made snap decisions and urged everyone involved to exert maximum effort. Hitler, immensely impressed by such energy and decisiveness, began to lose confidence in Speer who, since his illness, noticeably lacked Saur's drive, self-assurance and resolve. Blinded by his remarkable success, Saur was soon claiming that he would be able to produce four thousand aircraft per month.[7] Optimism had now given way to fantasy.

The achievements of the Fighter Staff were at a staggering human cost. Seventy-two-hour weeks with no holidays and Sunday shifts more often than not caused considerable unrest among the workers. It seemed at times as if ordinary German workers were to be 'scrapped' in much the same manner as the unfortunate slaves from the concentration camps. The concentration camps played a key role in Speer's system, both for the provision of labour and as punishment for the recalcitrant. In a memorandum of December 1943 he wrote: 'A successful experiment has been made to discipline and punish prisoners of war who work badly by means of a double standard for meals. The vast majority of prisoners have tried to gain the benefit of better food by working harder.'[8] Denying food and sending idlers to concentration camps did not prevent foreign workers and prisoners of war from sabotaging the German war effort by working slowly, feigning sickness, creating disruption or attempting to escape. This reached epidemic proportions in 1944 when, according to Speer's figures, 500,000 arrests were made during the year for such misdemeanours.[9]

For all the talk of industrial self-determination, the Fighter Staff exercised a ferocious dictatorship over the aircraft industry. Milch and Saur travelled around in 'Hubertus', submitting works managers and contractors to summary justice when they failed to meet their targets or showed undue concern for the welfare of their workers. As a result of their efforts 1,670 new fighters were built in March – a significant increase over the average of 1,100 over the previous seven months.[10] A total of 3,538 fighters were produced in September.[11] The Allies were now concentrating on bombing fuel plants, which left the factories unscathed; but meant that the new aircraft had no fuel with which fly. As many as 12,807 Me 109s and 7,488 FW 190s are estimated to have been built in 1944, but only 564 Me 262s.[12] Quality gave way to quantity, with outmoded models preferred to state-of-the-art aircraft.

The outstanding technological achievement of Speer's ministry was the fledgling rocket programme, but this was a project for the future that did nothing to help the German war effort. It proved to be a serious drain on resources, manpower and technical expertise. Top-secret work on rockets had begun as early as 1932 under Walter Dornberger from the Army Weapons Office and the twenty-year-old engineer Wernher von Braun. In 1936 their factory moved from Kumersdorf on the outskirts of Berlin to Peenemünde on the Baltic coast. Hitler initially showed little interest in this capital-intensive project and his generals were understandably sceptical as to its military effectiveness. At the beginning of the war Hitler stopped delivery of steel to Peenemünde and it was not until Speer took over the armaments ministry that Dornberger's project was given the go-ahead. On 16 March 1942 Speer ordered him to produce an estimate for the construction of 3,000 'Aggregate 4s' (A4s), the precursor of the V2 rocket.[13]

Speer, with his fascination for technology, enthusiastically supported the rocket programme, but there was also a more practical side to encouraging research and development for this advanced weapons system. The Luftwaffe was never able to build a satisfactory long-distance bomber. The Heinkel He 177 was beset with all manner of technical faults, in part as a result of trying to make a large bomber serve a dual role as a dive-bomber. The ingenious double engines used in combination – so that the machine was four-engined but with only two propellers – frequently overheated and the plane caught fire. Crews were understandably reluctant to fly in what they called the 'Flaming Coffin' (*Brennender Sarg*), the 'Reich's Flare' (*Reichsfackel*) or the 'Reich's Cigarette Lighter' (*Reichsfeuerzeug*). Distrust of the aircraft was greatly increased by putting it into service before it had been properly tested.[14] Even if the Luftwaffe had been able to produce an effective long-range bomber it would have been impossible to build a vast bomber fleet on the scale of the RAF's Bomber Command or the USAAF's Eighth Air Force. Rockets provided a relatively economical alternative.

The first experiments with this weapon were not promising. Two days after Speer issued the go-ahead, a combustion chamber exploded on ignition. The Luftwaffe, which was developing its own rocket, called for a thorough investigation of the army's rival A4 in an attempt to quash the project. Dornberger also had serious reservations about the A4 because the enormous amount of fuel it required was unavailable. Further tests at Peenemünde were not encouraging, so that even Speer began to have serious doubts as to the weapon's feasibility. But on hearing of some successful tests, Speer suggested to Hitler that two types of rocket should go into production with ranges of between 160 and 700 kilometres. Hitler insisted that anything less than 5,000 such rockets would be ineffective. A final decision was deferred.[15]

Speer's faith in Germany's technological superiority and his belief that it was the key to winning the war remained firm, but were sorely tested. There were further setbacks at Peenemünde, but by the end of the year they seem to have been overcome. Speer went to Hitler suggesting that the A4 should go into production. Hitler finally agreed, but he was still not entirely convinced that rockets were the answer. Dornberger was given dictatorial powers to convert the experimental station at Peenemünde into a gigantic factory, with a subsidiary plant at the Zeppelin works at Friedrichshafen on Lake Constance. Speer looked for suitable places to build bomb-proof firing ramps. Rather predictably, he chose Cap Gris Nez, the spot closest to England.[16]

Milch and the Luftwaffe still looked askance at the army's A4. Raw materials desperately needed to build aircraft were being diverted for the construction of a weapon that was deemed to be of questionable value. In June 1942 Milch insisted that the smaller 'Cherrystone' rocket – later known as the V1 – was a more economical alternative and carried one-third more explosives.[17] This was the beginning of a fierce competition between the army's A4 and the Luftwaffe's 'Cherrystone', now officially known as the Fieseler Fi 103.[18] The Volkswagen works was given an order for 3,500 Fi 103s. Other firms were to produce a further 1,500. Dr Detmar Stahlknecht, Speer's production manager at Peenemünde, staunchly backed by Karl-Otto Saur, promised that he could match the Luftwaffe's Fi 103s by building 5,150 A4s by December 1944.[19]

In March 1943 Speer put the entire A4 rocket programme under Dr Waldemar Petersen, director-general of the electrical engineering giant AEG. Having given an enthusiastic report to Speer after a visit to Peenemünde, he was sent off to the Obersalzberg to brief Hitler. Speer, feeling that Stahlknecht's production figures were far too low, replaced him with the engineer and industrialist Gerhard Degenkolb, a director of the heavy equipment manufacturing company Demag, who had proved most effective organising a crash programme for manufacturing locomotives. As head of a Special Committee A4, charged with organising its mass production, he made the totally unrealistic promise to build almost double the number of A4s.[20]

Wernher von Braun was becoming increasingly impatient with the bickering between the army's A4 at Peenemünde East and the Luftwaffe's Fi-103 at

Peenemünde West. In April 1943 he called for a truce. He was, of course, keen to support Degenkolb, but was unable to get much backing from Speer, who was incapable of giving the A4 programme top priority because of the chronic shortage of labour. In May, Sauckel was invited to Peenemünde to witness a rocket launch and was then ordered to round up sufficient labour to meet the ambitious goals set by both Dornberger and Degenkolb. Then, on 20 June, the RAF hit the Zeppelin Works at Friedrichshafen. The aim of Operation Bellicose – the first of the RAF's 'shuttle raids' – had been to bomb a steel works, but it inadvertently interrupted the production of parts for the A4 in Friedrichshafen for months.[21]

Sauckel got to work rounding up foreign workers destined for Peenemünde. Himmler lent his energetic assistance by sending thousands of concentration camp inmates from Buchenwald, Dachau and Sachsenhausen, many of whom were worked to death. Having received a number of complaints about the treatment of these prisoners, Speer asked Kehrl to investigate. Kehrl did not bother to visit the factory until late 1944 and then only saw the part where the rockets were being assembled. He was duly impressed.[22] Workers' welfare was always very low on Speer's list of priorities. Concentration camp inmates hardly counted. Wernher von Braun selected a number of scientists from Buchenwald to be sent to Peenemünde. They were somewhat better treated.

Although A4 was plagued with a series of technical problems, Speer got Hitler's approval to give the programme a top-priority rating. This prompted Goebbels to proclaim in his speech at the Berlin Sports Palace on 5 June 1943 that the hour of vengeance had come. The announcement was premature. It was obvious that the A4 could not possibly go into mass production until all its problems had been ironed out. Speer had yet to be convinced that it was a viable weapon. Milch tried to bypass Speer by appealing directly to Göring and managed to get Hitler's permission to build a series of launching ramps for the Fi 103, now increasingly known as the V1, but a number of further failures at Peenemünde West weakened his hand. Meanwhile, the A4 went through a series of successful tests. At the end of June Speer sent Carl Krauch to make an assessment of the A4, the Me 163 rocket-propelled aircraft, and the surface-to-air missile 'Waterfall'.[23] Horrified at the burden that the A4 and Waterfall would place on the chemical industry, Krauch supported the Me 163 project.[24] Arguing that defensive weapons were more important at this stage in the war than the offensive 'vengeance' weapons, he claimed that Waterfall was preferable both economically and tactically to the A4.

After the war Speer had to admit that his decision to stop work on Waterfall and go ahead with the 'vengeance' weapons was his worst mistake. An effective surface-to-air missile, combined with a sufficient number of Me 262 jet fighters – the Me 163 Komet was not effective in combat – might have provided adequate protection against Allied bombers. The 'V' weapons were the weapons of the future, but they consumed a vast amount of scarce resources and proved to be militarily worthless. A further problem was that development was held up on the Me 262 by lengthy arguments over whether it should be used as a high-speed bomber or as a fighter. Whether or not Waterfall could have been perfected and brought into mass production in time to make a difference is also open to serious question.[25]

Speer, brushing all Krauch's concerns aside, went with Dornberger and von Braun to Hitler's headquarters on 7 July 1943. Hitler was thrilled when shown a colour film of an A4 launch. Egged on by Speer, he got so carried away that he believed that this was the ideal 'vengeance' weapon that perfectly met his requirements for a technological breakthrough that would decide the outcome of the war. In gratitude he gave von Braun the title of professor, personally signing the document.[26] On 25 July Hitler gave Speer plenipotentiary powers over the A4 programme in the 'A4 Decree', whereupon Speer appointed Dr Albin Sawitzki from the Henschel Works – the engineer who supervised the building of the Tiger tank – to organise mass production in a scheme analogous to the Adolf Hitler Panzer Programme. Sawitzki set about this task with such brutality that on 13 April 1945 he was severely beaten by prisoners working at Peenemünde. He died on 1 May.[27] Although the A4 was the army's weapon, Speer told Milch that the Luftwaffe would have to lend its support to what was to become the largest weapons programme in Germany during the entire war. This would necessarily involve restricting aircraft production. The aircraft industry was already desperately short of skilled labour. Now the situation threatened to worsen. Wernher von Braun had already lured a number of engineers away from the aircraft industry. Although Speer had failed to keep his promise to find skilled labour, Milch decided to put the V1 into mass production. On 1 August 1943 Speer met Milch and a group of senior Luftwaffe officers. He was treated to a barrage of complaints, which he blandly dismissed with the remark that the Luftwaffe was strong enough to stand up to any encroachments from the army and their A4 programme.

Speer failed to realise that it was Saur who was raiding the aircraft industry and putting maximum effort into building the A4. He did however begin to worry that the aircraft-building programme was becoming increasingly compromised. He placed aircraft on a higher priority than the A4, but the intermediate bodies within the armaments industry ignored this decision. Milch was furious. On 13 August 1943 he told a staff meeting: 'It seems to me that everything to do with A4 is completely crazy. Either we should lock these people away in a lunatic asylum or we should hit them on the head. Let's first try the latter.'[28] But for the moment both Milch and Speer had more pressing concerns. On 17 August the USAAF delivered a devastating blow to Schweinfurt that destroyed the ball-bearing factories that were pivotal to the entire armaments industry. On the same day the RAF launched Operation Hydra, a raid on Peenemünde, which disrupted work there for six to eight weeks. It was not until 6 October 1943 that another rocket was launched. The raid did not affect the Luftwaffe's research station at Peenemünde West.

Fearing another raid, work began at once on putting A4 production underground. Himmler, anxious to increase his influence over the armaments industry, generously offered thousands of concentration camp inmates to do the job. In August 1943 the Reichsführer-SS appointed his confidant Hans Kammler to supervise this operation. Speer welcomed the labour on offer, but was justifiably fearful that there might be too many strings attached. On 26 August Speer's rocket team met with Kammler and his SS delegation to work out a common plan. Speer was immediately impressed by Kammler's energy and creativity.[29] They had remarkably similar backgrounds. Both were professionals from prosperous middle-class families. They were almost the same age. Both found themselves in positions for which they had not been trained. Their relationship became somewhat strained, however, when Speer heard rumours that Himmler was grooming Kammler as his replacement.[30]

It was agreed that the main works should be underground at the Mittelwerk in the Harz Mountains, where Degenkolb had already established his A4 Special Commission. An underground research station was blasted out of the mountains above Lake Traun in Upper Austria. A special concentration camp – a branch of Mauthausen – was built at nearby Ebensee to provide the necessary labour. A launching ramp was built at the SS troop-training area at Hohenlager, near Blizna in the Sub-Carpathians. Speer had hoped that Kammler as a civil engineer would concentrate on the construction side of the project, but it soon became clear that he had greater ambitions. On 1 September 1943 Himmler appointed him as his Special Representative in the A4 Programme. He was nominally under Oswald Pohl, but was soon acting fully independently.

Although von Braun was full of confidence, announcing on 9 September that the A4's development stage was completed, there were still a host of problems to solve. A number of tests had failed, with the rocket falling apart as it re-entered the earth's atmosphere. The technical problem of how to mass-produce the weapon had yet to be solved. On 10 September Hitler brushed all these objections aside, announcing that England would be bombarded with the new weapon by the end of January 1944. Production began mainly in the Mittelwerk in the Harz mountains, but also in the Zeppelin Works on Lake Constance and in Wiener Neustadt, all of which provided ample employment opportunities for the inmates of local concentration camps. The number of rockets produced was still disappointingly low.

The Mittelwerk was rapidly extended under the energetic management of Georg Rickhey, who had been seconded from the engineering company Demag.[31] On 1 September 1943 Karl Maria Hettlage, Speer's financial expert on secondment from the Commerzbank, created the Mittelwerk GmbH. Hans Kammler, Walter Dornberger, Gerhard Degenkolb and Hettlage formed the board of directors. On 1 October the new company confidently announced that it would produce 1,800 A4 rockets per month in its vast underground factory. An ample supply of labour was provided by the Mittelbau-Dora concentration camp, built in August as a subsidiary of Buchenwald.[32] Of the 60,000 people who had the misfortune to end up in this camp, 20,000 died in the inhuman living and working conditions.

Speer later claimed that the SS ran the underground factories, not his ministry. In fact the SS only ran 22 of the 170 underground works. All the others came under the aegis of Organisation Todt, of which Speer was the head. All produced weapons for the Minister of Armaments.[33] By 1944, 500,000 concentration camp inmates were working for Speer: 230,000 in the armaments industry, 140,000 in the underground factories and 130,000 for Organisation Todt. Speer was later to claim that working for him gave prisoners 'a chance to survive'.[34] This is a shameless perversion of the truth. Underground factories like Dora were death-traps. Workers who were too weak to continue working were sent back to their original concentration camps, where they had a minimal chance of survival. There is no evidence that Speer took even the slightest interest in their fate. He admitted as much in his memoirs where he wrote: 'the sight of people suffering affected my feelings, but not my actions'.[35]

Conditions at Dora beggared description. The air was cold, damp and stank of excrement. Although workers were covered in dust, no washing facilities were provided. There were no latrines, simply an inadequate supply of buckets. The only bedding provided was a thin layer of straw on a cold stone floor, with water constantly dripping from the roof. Many of the inmates went barefoot. Conditions scarcely improved when they were moved from the tunnels to barracks. Discipline was brutal, with frequent executions. The mounting piles of dead bodies were taken to Buchenwald for cremation, but there were soon so many corpses that the crematoria were unable to cope. They had to be burnt in the open.[36]

Speer and his staff visited Dora on 10 December 1943. He was most impressed with what he saw and wrote to Kammler on 17 December congratulating him on having built an underground factory in only two months. It was a feat unequalled in Europe and matched anything built in the US. The more sensitive members of his staff were impressed in a distinctly negative manner. They asked for extra leave to recover from the shock of this visit to hell.[37] Speer wrote to Himmler on 22 December saying that he was so impressed with

Kammler's work at Mittelbau-Dora that he had given him other building projects to supervise.[38] In an unguarded moment in his memoirs Speer does mention the appalling conditions at Dora, where he describes the inmates as 'dahinsiechend' – 'wasting away'.[39]

Dr Poschmann, the man responsible for medical services in the Ministry of Armaments, did not share Speer's enthusiasm for Kammler's achievements. On 13 January 1944 he wrote a detailed report that painted a bleak picture of the situation, describing the scene as 'Dante's Inferno'.[40] Slave labourers worked for a minimum of 72 hours per week. They were provided with a mere 1,100 calories per day. Dampness and intense air pressure made lung and heart disease endemic. An average of 160 men died each day in accordance with Himmler's guiding principle of 'extermination through work'. When a delegation of workers complained to Kammler about these appalling conditions he ordered the summary execution of 80 prisoners.[41]

Carl Stobbe-Dethleffson, the man responsible for buildings in the Ministry of Armaments, was sent to Mittelbau with his associate, Eduard Schönleben, and the structural engineer, Karl Berlitz, to discuss the situation with Kammler.[42] There is no record of any action having been taken to improve conditions on the site as a result of this visit. Speer later claimed that he built accommodation to house 10,000 prisoners, thereby greatly improving living conditions.[43] He failed to mention the obvious fact that he had done so not for humanitarian reasons or in response to Poschmann's report, but because the tunnels in which these troglodytes had been forced to live and work were now being used as factories. In fact conditions worsened. When American troops arrived at Mittelbau they witnessed a ghastly scene. Thousands had been massacred, their corpses piled high. The survivors were gaunt semi-skeletons in striped pyjamas. Film footage of the camp provides one of the most horrific images of the true face of the murderous regime that Speer was never able to look in the eyes.

By March 1944 it seemed that the Luftwaffe's V1 was the favoured weapon. Hitler clutched at this straw, lavished praise on Milch and ordered that Mittelwerk should take over part of the production. Himmler's reaction to this move was to order the arrest of the A4 engineers Karl Wernher and Magnus von Braun, Klaus Riedel and Helmut Göttrub. They were charged – probably correctly – with doubting that the war could be won, and consequently faced the death penalty for defeatism. Dornberger immediately appealed to Speer, pointing out that the entire project was now in danger. Speer managed to secure their release.[44]

Himmler was never to forget that Speer had frustrated his initial attempt to absorb the A4 into his SS empire. Speer and Saur had discussed the rocket programme with him shortly after he had been appointed Minister of the Interior on 24 August 1943. He had then written to Speer claiming that it had been agreed that he should take over A4. Speer already had a guarantee from Hitler that although Himmler was to give him every assistance that he needed – in other words slave labour from the concentration camps – Speer was not to hand over responsibility for A4 to the Reichsführer-SS.[45] Himmler fought back by giving Kammler his full support as he gradually extended his influence over the A4 programme and then over the aircraft industry.

Speer now began to feel that August Coenders from the iron and steel giant Röchling-Buderus had found the answer in the V3, variously known as the High Pressure Pump, 'Busy Lizzy', 'Millipede' or the 'England Cannon'. This massive gun with its 130-metre-long barrel was designed to hit London from emplacements in the Pas de Calais, firing 600 shells per hour. Hitler gave his approval for 5,000 slave labourers that were working as miners in the Ruhr to build a massive bunker at Mimoyecques, a few kilometres southwest of Calais. Speer ordered United Steel, the Gutehoffnungshütte and Krupp to also lend a hand. Saur prudently remained highly sceptical about the V3 and urged Hitler to limit the number of these monster cannons to three, pointing out that the barrels would have to be frequently replaced. Professor Werner Osenberg, head of planning in the Reich Research Office, also poured cold water on the project. He asked Bormann to tell Hitler that the tests had revealed a number of serious problems. He was soon proven correct: 20,000 shells had to be scrapped because of construction problems. The weapon proved utterly worthless. The emplacements at Mimoyecques were attacked in November 1943 by the USAAF in Operation Crossbow and put out of action on 6 July 1944 by the RAF with Barnes Wallis' 'Tallboy' earthquake bombs before a single shot was fired against London.[46]

It was not until after the D-Day landings, on 13 June 1944, that the first of the V1 rockets was fired at London. The results were disappointing. Of the ten V1s fired, one landed in Grove Road, Mile End, killing eight people. The others were way off target, landing at Gravesend, Sevenoaks, Swanscombe and Cuckfield. Five crashed near the launch site. There was a total of 7,488 successful 'doodlebug' launches; 2,419 reached London and the Home Counties, while 2,448 landed in Belgium. By October all the launching sites within range of England were overrun. The V1 did no damage to Britain's armaments industry. Although exceedingly unpleasant for those at the receiving end, it did not significantly undermine civilian morale. Its greatest effect was to raise false hopes among the Germans that another 'miracle weapon' might turn the tide.[47]

With his appointment as Commander of the Reserve Army on 21 July 1944, Himmler finally had command of the V2 programme. He immediately gave plenipotentiary powers to Kammler, even though he was nominally under the command of SS-Obergruppenführer Hans Jüttner, Himmler's deputy as head of the reserve army and of army armaments, who was also subordinate to Speer as Minister of Armaments.

Goebbels' extravagant propaganda had raised hopes to such an extent that the V2 was widely seen as a universal panacea that would solve all problems. On 30 July Goebbels announced in the weekly *Das Reich* – the nearest thing that Nazi Germany had to a quality newspaper – that Germany would soon 'overcome the enemy's advantage' by the deployment of 'terrible weapons' so would bring the war to a victorious end.[48] By this time many soldiers had come to believe that the military situation was so utterly hopeless that 'Adolf' would have ended the war had he not got some sensational new weapon up his sleeve.[49] In August Speer, in a typically convoluted phrase, told the commander of an army training camp that 'shortly' the armaments industry would be able to stem the enemy's 'destructive will'.[50] At the same time he repeatedly reassured Hitler that the present crisis would be over in three or four months.

There was a faint hope that this might be the case. By August 1944 Dornberger had managed to solve the V2s re-entry problems, but then two attempts to fire the rocket on London failed. On 8 September a V2 was launched from The Hague aimed at London. It landed in Chiswick. Another was fired at Paris and landed near the Porte d'Italie. Dornberger was disappointed with the result, describing the V2 as 'an unsatisfactory weapon'. Hitler, however, was not discouraged. He ordered Saur to come to his headquarters. Saur promptly made the wild promise to build nine hundred V2s per month. Speer was appalled. He knew that such a figure could only be achieved by drastically reducing the output of essential weapons. Furthermore, the shortage of raw materials was becoming acute. By cutting back on the production of the V1 to 3,419 units, it was possible to build 629 V2s in September, 628 in October and 662 in November. Himmler got quite carried away by this success. On his initiative Speer was persuaded to get Hitler's approval to award a series of Knight's Crosses to prominent figures in the V1 and V2 programmes.

It began to dawn on Speer that his promises could not be met and that his boasting might very well backfire. He therefore began frantically to back-pedal. In a series of speeches of unaccustomed modesty in late 1944 he warned that he could offer no miracles. Visiting the Western Front in September he was horrified to find that so many, both soldiers and civilians, still had a blind faith in 'miracle weapons', thereby giving rise to undue optimism. 'It is essential', he wrote, 'that every soldier and every racial comrade should be told the truth about the present difficulties with brutal openness.'[51] On 2 November he wrote to Goebbels asking him to desist from all talk of 'miracle weapons'.[52] The problem was that so many people had faith in Speer as a miracle worker, an image that he had hitherto assiduously cultivated; it was rather that they were reluctant to believe such modesty. But he sometimes slipped back into his former boastful mode. On 1 December he told a group of ministers that a surface-to-air missile would soon be ready for service. Although this was far from the truth, he repeated this to officers who were visiting the testing grounds in Rechlin.[53] Kammler was now encouraged to make a bid to add the V1 to his portfolio, but Speer managed to persuade Hitler that since things were running smoothly a change was not required. Kammler did not give up. On 31 January 1945 Hitler ordered the V1 and V2 to be placed under Kammler's command, but by this time the shortage of explosives had become so acute that the rocket programme was already being forced to wind down.[54]

The net result of the V1 and V2 rocket attacks was disappointing for the Germans. In spite of initial anxieties, fuelled by rumour and the unknown, the British soon became used to these weapons, and the V1 'doodlebug', although loaded with a thousand kilograms of explosives, was treated with a certain amused contempt. Travelling beyond the speed of sound and also loaded with a thousand kilograms of explosives, the V2 landed without warning. This was distinctly unnerving, giving rise to a mixture of apprehension and resignation. Neither weapon caused mass panic however. Morale remained remarkably high.[55] The V2 was also a unique weapon in that its manufacture caused more deaths than its deployment.

Speer's support for the V2 was one of his greatest mistakes. The programme was hideously expensive and the weapon was rushed into production long before it had been adequately developed and tested. In this Speer repeated the mistakes he made with the XXI and XXIII U-boats. Goebbels's propaganda raised totally unrealistic hopes. As early as the autumn of 1943 Speer knew that there would not be sufficient quantities of explosive available for these weapons to be effective. Manpower, raw materials and expertise that could have been far better used elsewhere were consumed by a project that was later to have a revolutionary impact, but which brought Germany no relief. Indeed it could well be argued that the V2 had a negative effect on the country's war effort. Speer, blinded by his belief in technology, was clutching at straws.

One miracle weapon for which Speer had little enthusiasm was the atomic bomb.[56] On 4 June 1942 he invited Werner Heisenberg and a group of other physicists to his ministry and asked them whether it would be possible to build such a device. Heisenberg replied that it was theoretically possible to build an atomic bomb within two years, but that the expense would be unimaginable. It was obvious that Germany lacked sufficient sources of energy, workers, raw materials and the financial means to build such a bomb. Heisenberg therefore suggested that a more practical investment would be to build an atomic pile, which at least would be useful after the war. Speer's success depended on reassuring Hitler with impressive production figures. The idea of investing vast sums of money in a long-term project, the outcome of which was uncertain, was clearly an unattractive prospect. He accepted Heisenberg's argument and gave top priority to the building of an atomic reactor in the grounds of the Kaiser-Wilhelm-Institut in Berlin.[57]

The scientists wanted to concentrate on fundamental research. They did not want to be under the military's thumb like their colleagues in Peenemünde. Werner Heisenberg, having been denounced by the SS as a 'White Jew', preferred to keep a low profile. His views deviated radically from the proponents of the dominant 'German Physics', who denounced him and his colleagues for their respect for the work of Jewish physicists. Heisenberg's requests for funding were very unassuming. When the army offered to release hundreds of scientists to help build a German atomic bomb he modestly replied that he had no idea how to run an organisation on such a scale.

Göring, in his capacity as head of the Reich Research Council, had appointed Abraham Esau to chair an atomic research group known as the Uranium Society. He did not have any faith in the atomic bomb as a war-winning weapon and his ideas on how to build an atomic reactor differed radically from Heisenberg's. Speer, who was determined to push Göring aside, frustrated Esau's efforts. On New Year's Day 1944 he finally succeeded in getting him replaced by Walther Gerlach, a remarkable man who believed in the primacy of fundamental research and whose main concern was the peaceful use of atomic energy after the war. Another scientist, Paul Harteck, offered a third solution to the problem by proposing to use enriched uranium with less heavy water in the reactor. Speer was unable to adjudicate. A bunker was built for the reactor, but work soon stalled. There were other demands on the scientists for such things as isotopes for medical use, or luminous material for aircraft instruments. The atomic energy programme limped along, hindered by fundamental disagreements as to which approach was the most promising and by raids by the Resistance on the heavy water plants in Norway. By the summer of 1943, bombing raids forced the scientists to move away from their laboratories in the university towns. In December 1944 Heisenberg and his colleagues were drafted into the *Volkssturm* – ample proof of the low priority afforded to the atomic programme. Gerlach had to use his full authority as the Reich Marshal's Plenipotentiary for Atomic Physics to persuade Bormann of the value of their work and to secure their release from military duty.

CHAPTER TEN

THE END IN SIGHT

THE ALLIES' PLAN for the Completion of Combined Bomber Offensive in March 1944 had made hydrogenation plants and oil refineries their priority targets. This was to present Speer with his major problem in 1944. Hans Kehrl later claimed that he had never ceased to wonder why they had waited until May 1944 to mount such an attack. Along with artificial rubber (*Buna*) and nitrogen, they were the most vulnerable parts of the war economy. He came to the conclusion that the Allies had been deliberately slowing down the Soviet advance until they landed in France. Had they launched these attacks the previous year the war would probably have been over, with the Red Army occupying all of Germany.[1] The simple answer to this ingenious conspiracy theory was that the USAAF took some time to solve the problem of how to attack these plants to maximum effect. Once they had done so the results, although extremely costly, were devastating.

On 12 May 1944 Speer called Kehrl at midnight, asking if he knew about the raids on the hydrogenation plants at Leuna and Brüx (Most). Kehrl replied that he had been fully informed. When Speer asked him for his assessment of the situation he said that if these raids were to continue the war would soon be lost.[2] Speer was in full agreement, saying that they must see Hitler at the earliest opportunity. Four days later the two men went to Leuna where they met Dr Heinrich Bütefisch, the head of IG Farben's Leuna Works and of their branch plant at Auschwitz-Monowitz.[3] IG Farben's Carl Krauch, the man in charge of chemicals in the Four-Year Plan, was also present. They were relieved to find that in spite of considerable damage it would not be long before the plant was back in operation.[4] Although somewhat reassured, the visit convinced Speer that the defence of the hydrogenation plants had to be given absolute priority.

This was to prove an intractable problem. Most anti-aircraft guns were no longer effective against aircraft flying at higher altitudes. The Luftwaffe was spread too thinly. Heavily engaged on the Eastern Front, deployed against the

Allied forces in France and Italy, protecting assets in the Balkans and Norway and giving support to the navy, this meant that there were never enough aircraft to shield Germany's most vulnerable assets. The Luftwaffe did not have enough fighters to be effective against bomber fleets that now had fighter escorts. For fighters to be effective they had to attack en masse. This meant that aircraft would have to be withdrawn from other fronts.

Speer made frantic preparations for his meeting with Hitler. The experts – Krauch, Bütefisch, Pleiger and the Ministry of Economics' oil expert, Ernst Rudolf Fischer – were to give detailed reports on the damage done and to suggest ways to protect these essential assets. On 19 May 1944 Speer flew to the Obersalzberg for preliminary talks with Hitler. The meeting was held on 22 and 23 May. Some thirty people were present, including Göring, Keitel and Milch. Göring insisted that the answer lay in turning the plants into 'anti-aircraft fortresses', but could only bluster when it was pointed out to him that flak was not very effective against bombers flying at such high altitudes. Hitler argued that hydrogenation plants should be protected by artificial fog. He ordered Göring to improve the air defences at these vulnerable plants. Workers, taken mainly from the building sector of Carl Krauch's domain, were to be allocated for rebuilding damaged works. Speer suggested that five hundred electricians and two thousand mechanics should be taken from the armed forces to form a special repair squad. Transportation from Ploetsi had to be better protected. Drastic measures had to be taken to ensure fuel economy. Hitler, who was worried that this latter measure would be most unpopular in party circles, was very reluctant to agree. He specifically ordered that domestic fuel allocations should not be cut back.[5] Speer brought the discussion round to examining the possibility of attacking Moscow's power stations and to sending reconnaissance flights beyond the Urals to seek out suitable targets. The meeting was hopelessly unfocused. Lacking a clear agenda, time was wasted in mutual recrimination. It was a startling example of the leadership's inability to face the country's increasingly desperate predicament.[6]

A further raid on Leuna on 28 May put the plant out of production for ten days. It was still only operating at 75 per cent of capacity by early July, and was attacked again on 7 July. It was back to 53 per cent capacity by 19 July. A raid the following day reduced capacity to 35 per cent. Further attacks in July, August and September put Leuna out of business until 14 October, and it reached 28 per cent of capacity by 20 November. Subsequent attacks reduced output to 15 per cent, at which level the plant staggered on until the final stages of the war. By October attacks on the hydrogenation plants had become a nightmare.[7] Speer was later to confess that in May 1944 the war was lost 'from a technical point of view because without fuel the new tanks and jet aircraft were no good to me'. He was also to claim that all the military leaders he knew argued that if

1. A portrait of the young architect taken in 1933, the year in which he had his first big successes with his designs for the May Day Rally in Berlin and the Nuremberg 'Victory Rally' in August.

2. Albert Speer tutoring his younger brother. Ernst went missing at Stalingrad in 1942. The interior is solidly bourgeois, the mood depressingly serious.

3. Albert and Margarete on their wedding day in Berlin on 28 August 1928. Over the years the distance between them grew ever wider.

4. Paul Ludwig Troost with a model of the House of German Art in Munich. When Troost died in January 1934, Speer stepped into his shoes as Hitler's favourite architect.

5. The conservative architect Wilhelm Kreis gained access to Hitler's inner circle, thanks to his friendship with Troost. He admired the much younger Speer, who commissioned him to build the headquarters for the Army High Command (OKH), the Soldiers' Hall and the Ministry of Transport in Germania. Other projects included the Egyptian Museum, the Museum of the Nineteenth Century and a World War Museum. None of these was built.

6. Hitler and Speer discuss architectural plans at the Obersalzberg. Hitler's obsession with monumental architecture was the key to Speer's power and influence.

7. The Cathedral of Light at the Nuremberg Party Rally in 1934. This was Speer's masterpiece, although Leni Riefenstahl's cameraman Walter Frentz later claimed that the idea was his. Speer was never as successful with bricks and mortar.

8. Speer shows Hitler a scale model of his design for the German Pavilion for the Paris Exhibition of 1937. He shared a gold medal with Boris Iofan for the Soviet Pavilion. Kurt Schmid-Ehman was awarded the Grand Prize of the French Republic for his 9-metre-tall gilded eagle that perched on the roof.

9. Speer and Hitler on an inspection tour of a model for the Nuremberg stadium. This was on a steep slope which meant that the tiered seating would have to be supported by massive barrel vaulting.

10. The garden front of the New Chancellery. Speer's neo-classical façade is somewhat marred by Josef Thorak's massive bronze horses.

11. The Marble Gallery in the New Reich Chancellery. It was exactly twice the length of the Hall of Mirrors in Versailles. The imposing doors to Hitler's vast study were at the end of the gallery. The highly polished marble floor was designed to make visitors feel even more uncertain while walking towards the presence, as if on thin ice.

12. Hitler's study in the New Reich Chancellery was designed as a throne room rather than a workplace. Measuring 4,214 square feet it is testimony to Speer's obsession with effect at the expense of practicality and proportion.

13. A model of the north–south axis of Germania. Beginning at the Tempelhof Airport and Southern Railway Station, the boulevard led to the Triumphal Arch, the Great Hall of the People and ended at the Northern Railway Station.

14. Speer stands between Hitler and his arch-rival, the architect Hermann Giesler, during a brief early-morning visit to Paris on 28 June 1940. Giesler was eventually to replace Speer in Hitler's favour.

15. Arno Breker in 1940 models a portrait bust of Speer in his Berlin studio. Although he enjoyed a highly successful post-war career, since he was National Socialist Germany's star sculptor Breker became a highly controversial figure.

16. Hitler and Speer take a stroll at Hitler's Bavarian mountain retreat on the Obersalzburg. None of Nazi Germany's prominent figures had as close a relationship with Hitler as did Speer.

17. Hitler with three of Speer's children and Margarete at the Berghof. Albert is at the forefront, Hilde next to Hitler. The Speer family lived nearby and were frequent guests.

18. Speer with five of his six children at the wheel of his BMW cabriolet. The children had mixed feelings about driving at high speed through precipitous mountain roads. Adolf (later known as Arnold) – here seen trying to escape the ordeal – was severely traumatised by the experience.

19. Robert Ley, leader of the German Work Front and Speer's friend, the de-facto Minister of Agriculture Herbert Backe, in consultation with the Minister of Armaments. Both Ley and Backe committed suicide at Nuremberg while awaiting trial.

20. Hitler awards Speer the Fritz Todt Prize for technical achievement on 6 February 1943. This was the first and only time that the prize was awarded.

21. Speer stands between his rival Franz Xaver Dorsch and Admiral Karl Dönitz as they watch the launching of a submarine.

22. Speer inspects a Soviet T-34 tank in June 1943. The Adolf Hitler Panzer Programme, launched in December 1942, was a remarkable achievement, but did not provide enough tanks to beat the Red Army at Kursk the following July.

23. Speer treats an entranced Goebbels to a display of his 'miracle weapons' at the rocket research station at Peenemünde in August 1943.

24. Speer and Field Marshal Erhard Milch watching a V1 launch at Peenemünde in October 1943. V1 was the Luftwaffe's weapon, V2 the army's.

25. Albert Speer (second from left) calmly receives instructions from Himmler. The relationship between the two men was far closer than Speer was later prepared to admit.

26. Prisoners at Mittelbau-Dora, a concentration camp built to house workers for the underground factory for V2 rockets. Speer visited the project and pronounced himself to be fully satisfied with working conditions.

27. Prisoners on the 'Staircase of Death' at Mauthausen concentration camp. They were ruthlessly exploited to provide Speer with stone for his mammoth projects in Nuremberg and Berlin.

28. Speer addresses armaments workers in May 1944. Edmund Geilenberg stands behind him, sporting the Knights Cross of the War Merit Cross that Speer awarded him during this ceremony.

29. By means of a skilfully manipulated graph Speer gives a dramatic display of the increase of weapons production since he took over the Ministry of Armaments. Soldiers at the front wondered where all these weapons had gone.

30. An exhausted and depressed Speer during one of his frequent visits to the western front in the winter of 1944.

31. British troops arrest Speer on 23 May 1945. General Jodl walks beside Speer while Admiral Dönitz leads the pack.

32. Speer prepares his defence in his prison cell in Nuremberg. Living conditions for the twenty-four accused were particularly harsh.

33. Speer takes the witness stand at Nuremberg. His impressive performance helped save his life. His baggy suit shows a significant weight loss.

34. Speer begins to clear the undergrowth at Spandau in 1966. Over the years he created an impressive garden in what had been wasteland.

35. Speer and Margarete at the Schlosshotel Gerhus in Grunewald immediately upon his release from Spandau. Theirs had never been a happy marriage and was now beyond repair.

36. Speer, now a best-selling author, presenting the English edition of *Spandauer Tagebücher (1966)*, in 1976.

the war was not won by October or November it would be lost.[8] These reservations were never clearly stated. Pessimistic reports were couched in the conditional. Germany's leadership followed their Führer with almost total credulity, feeding him from time to time with groundless optimism and blind faith. Speer was among those guilty in this respect, for all his later claims that he was one of the first to realise that the other shoe was bound to drop before too long.

On 30 May 1944 Speer obtained Hitler's signature to a 'Führer's Decree' for a 'Commissar General for Immediate Action under the Reich Minister for Armaments and War Production'.[9] He was to be given plenipotentiary powers, including the right to take workers from the armaments industries to ensure the rapid repair of damaged hydrogenation plants. All workers in this task force were to be treated 'ruthlessly'. It was not until 30 June that Speer got Hitler's formal approval for the appointment of Edmund Geilenberg to this new office. At first Hitler argued that Geilenberg's efforts would lead to fewer tanks being built. He changed his mind when Speer and Saur, on the basis of some very dubious figures, assured him that this would not be the case.[10] They could have added that tanks without fuel were of little use. Geilenberg was Paul Pleiger's close friend and the man in charge of munitions in Speer's ministry. He worked in close cooperation with Gerhard Ritter's Special Staff under Carl Krauch in his capacity as plenipotentiary for chemicals in the Four-Year Plan and with the Reconstruction Staff attached to the Leuna Works.[11] As a practical and clear-headed man with enormous energy, he was ideally suited to the job.

Geilenberg's staff expanded exponentially. By the end of July 1944 he had 150,000 workers under his command. Of these, 70,000 were men already employed in the hydrogenation plants, many of whom were prisoners of war, concentration camp inmates or the victims of Sauckel's press-gangs. A further 75,000 came as a result of what Carl Krauch euphemistically called 'special measures'. By November the number had risen to 350,000, all of whom were treated with appropriate 'ruthlessness'.[12] The workforce now included men from the armed forces, the customs service, air-raid wardens, the emergency services and the Reich Labour Service. About 100,000 men were taken from the concentration camps, working in appalling conditions, without winter clothing, wretchedly housed and inadequately fed.[13] There were mounting complaints among industrialists that Geilenberg was starving them of workers and raw materials. They began to mutter treasonably that those who had made pessimistic prognostications were being proved correct.[14]

Geilenberg soon had his hands full. The average daily production of aviation fuel fell from 5,839 tons in March 1944 to 1,733 tons in June. In July, Speer ordered Geilenberg to exploit the oil shale in the Swabian Alps in an attempt to offset this loss. The result was Operation Desert which involved building ten new fuel plants. The workers were to be drawn exclusively from the concentration camps, initially from the camp at Natzweiler-Struthof in Alsace. Geilenberg worked in close cooperation with the SS who built seven small concentration camps to accommodate 10,000 workers. Among them were Jews from the remains of the Warsaw ghetto, Lithuania and Estonia, as well as Gypsies and 'saboteurs' from the occupied countries. The SS charged between four and six Reichsmarks per day in 'rent' for each worker. Conditions in the camps were so appalling that they amounted to death camps. This was in full accordance with Himmler's policy of deliberately working prisoners to death. One camp commander put in a bill for 127.05 Reichsmarks to cover the cost of executing and incinerating twenty intractable prisoners. Prisoners were provided with a striped suit and a cap, which they wore both summer and winter. Unable to wash their clothes, they were riddled with lice and prone to typhus. SS-Scharführer Josef Seuss, the commandant of the Schömberg concentration camp, who had learnt his trade at Dachau, was known affectionately as 'Zack-Zack'. He was particularly proud of his 'Barefoot Commandos', who were forced to work in the quarries with no protection against the sharp rocks.[15] Some privileged prisoners were provided with wooden clogs.

A host of different organisations was involved in planning and research for Operation Desert. They included IG Farben Leuna, the German Oil Shale Research Association, the Early Jurassic Research Association, the Coal–Oil Union, the SS company German Shale Oil, the Hermann Göring Works and Organisation Todt. The results were very disappointing. Only four of the plants went into production before the end of the war. They produced a mere trickle of fuel. The shale was originally broken up with hammers or picks and put by hand into buckets, then carried to the plant. Later, primitive narrow-gauge railways or cableways were built. Since the bitumen content of the shale was only about 5 per cent, the output was very modest and the oil was of such poor quality that it could only be used in specially adapted motors. Altogether these plants produced a mere 1,500 metric tons of mineral oil, for which 52,500 metric tons of shale had to be dug by the prisoners.[16]

On 20 June 1944 Speer told Hitler and Keitel that the effects of the raids were catastrophic. Ten days later he sent a detailed report to Hitler's headquarters on the consequences of the attacks on the fuel plants.[17] Attacks on 22 June had resulted in a 90 per cent drop in the production of aviation fuel. Speedy repairs by Geilenberg's crews had rectified the situation but there was still a chronic shortage. Only 156,000 metric tons of aviation fuel were available, whereas the minimum requirement was 180,000 metric tons. The average daily production was 5,000 metric tons in May. By June it was down to 1,218 metric tons. The July figures were almost certain to be lower. This would mean that by September it would no longer be possible to meet the armed forces' minimum requirements for fuel. 'This', Speeer wrote, 'would have tragic consequences'.

Speer then listed the measures he had already taken. Repairs had been made as quickly as possible. Geilenberg and Dorsch had worked closely together to ensure that vital parts of these plants were protected. Military trucks had been switched to use wood as a fuel when attempts to use coal for motor vehicles were not successful.[18] The Planning Office had made stringent economies in the allocation of fuel. The use of fog machines as protection had proved relatively effective. He ended with a number of urgent requests for future action. The Luftwaffe would have to reduce the amount of fuel used for test flights and training. The armed forces would have to find ways to reduce their fuel requirements. The Luftwaffe had to realise that disaster would be unavoidable if fighter protection of the plants were not significantly improved. Enemy reconnaissance flights over the hydrogenation plants had to be intercepted. More anti-aircraft guns had to be placed around these plants, even if that meant rendering the towns and cities more vulnerable.

At the beginning of July 1944 Speer ordered a crash programme for heavy 12.8cm Flak 40 anti-aircraft guns. This was a formidable weapon. Firing a 27.9-kilogram shell with an effective ceiling of 35,000 feet (10,000 metres), it proved very effective against Allied bombers flying in formation, but there were not enough of these costly guns to bring much relief. At the end of the month Speer sent another detailed report to Hitler on the effects of the Allied bombing raids on fuel production.[19] The figures were alarming. The amount of aviation fuel produced had fallen from 150,000 metric tons in May to 29,500 metric tons in July. Gasoline production had fallen from 125,000 metric tons in April to 56,000 metric tons in July. Diesel fuel had been less affected. An output of 88,000 metric tons in May fell to 62,000 metric tons in July. Nevertheless Speer's predictions for the future remained astonishingly optimistic. He hoped to produce an average of 150,00 to 160,000 metric tons of aviation fuel in the coming months and 142,000 metric tons of gasoline. These figures were based on the vain hope that Allied raids would cease. If they continued to wreak this much damage the Luftwaffe would not be able to fulfil its mission by September or October. It would probably receive an allocation of a mere 10,000 to 20,000 metric tons of aviation fuel, because the deployment of many more anti-aircraft guns had made little impression on the bombers, while the number of fighters protecting the hydrogenation plants had actually decreased. Speer continued to urge that fighters be withdrawn from the front to protect the fuel supplies at home, but this was not a practicable option.

Speer was putting on a brave front, but behind the scenes the atmosphere was close to panic. On 9 July he held an emergency meeting, attended by Krauch, Fischer, Geilenberg and Kehrl, to discuss what immediate steps should be taken to stop the complete breakdown of the oil industry. No solution was found. Geilenberg's taskforce could only do its utmost and hope for the best.[20]

The situation steadily worsened. Speer's statement on 2 August, that although the military situation was desperate he remained optimistic, was hardly encouraging. On 5 August he gave another talk outlining his generous post-war housing plans, this time to workers building U-boats at the Schichau-Werke in Elbing (Elblag). With the Red Army about to spring the trap on Army Group North in the Baltic offensive it is doubtful that this speech was given much credence.[21]

The situation was made even worse when in mid-August Hitler gave orders for 'Action 88', calling for a concentration on anti-aircraft guns at the expense of fighters.[22] Hans Kehrl understandably considered this to be a seriously misguided policy. Arguing that flak was not a viable alternative to fighters, Kehrl issued a memorandum attacking 'Action 88' as a dangerously ill-advised plan. Speer was outraged. In effect, his subordinate was saying that the Führer did not know what he was talking about. This was an outrageous heresy. He ordered Kehrl to telephone all those who had received his memorandum and ask for its return. Kehrl insisted that Saur get a copy, because he had advised Hitler to adopt this disastrous policy simply because it offered him an excellent opportunity to boost his production figures. Speer said he would speak to Saur personally. Milch confided to Kehrl that he was in full agreement with his memorandum. Kehrl asked Keitel's adjutant to make sure that the memorandum was kept from Hitler; he concluded from this episode that Hitler was no longer capable of making rational decisions and that Speer's ministry was leaderless and falling apart.[23] Speer's version of this story is quite different. He claims that both he and Saur agreed that Hitler's emphasis on anti-aircraft guns rather than fighters was gravely mistaken and that for the first time they deliberately ignored the Führer's orders. Speer also claims that he instructed the Armaments Staff to make fighter production its top priority.[24] This is barely credible. Speer could still not risk tolerating any criticism of his omniscient Führer.

Romanian oil was no longer available after 30 August 1944. The industrial region of Silesia with its hydrogenation plants was now within range of the USAAF. Production of aviation fuel continued to fall alarmingly. As Speer had predicted in his clearer moments it was down to 17,000 metric tons in August and 10,000 metric tons in September.[25] On 30 August Speer gave Keitel a memorandum which he asked to be forwarded to Hitler, in which he reported that the Leuna, Brüx (Most), and Pölitz (Police) works had been put out of action for several weeks. Their combined fuel oil production had fallen from 37,000 metric tons in April to 2,500 metric tons in August. There was such a critical shortage of all types of fuel that the armed forces would have to abandon any thought of offensive operations, because the fuel was not available to bring up supplies. Once again Speer pleaded for fighters to be brought back from the front to defend German airspace, his earlier requests having fallen on deaf ears.

A special programme to build at least 1,200 jet fighters had to begin immediately. The future of the Luftwaffe depended on the success of this endeavour. The letter ended with the words: 'If the Allied air forces continue to be successful we shall soon be without the material essential for the continuation of a modern war.' It was signed 'Always your Speer'.[26]

On 19 September Speer appointed yet another team to deal with the fuel crisis. Krauch was to provide the technical know-how, Kehrl the planning skills, Geilenberg the drive and energy. The committee's effectiveness was compromised by serious differences between Geilenberg and Krauch over whether it would be possible to move plant underground. Speer seemed reluctant to intervene in what was largely a technical matter over which he was unable to judge.[27]

Germany was now in a hopeless predicament. In June and July 1944 the production of almost every kind of weapon peaked, but what use were tanks and aircraft without fuel? The Wehrmacht's answer was that if workers were producing weapons that could not be used, they would be of more use to the war effort if they put on a uniform and went to the front. The question of how they were to be armed and equipped was left unanswered. For the fight to continue the home front had to be given adequate protection against Allied bombers. Speer, Milch and the head of the Luftwaffe's Fighter Command, General Galland, tried desperately to assemble an adequate fighter fleet to do the job, but to no avail. All they managed to acquire was a handful of old fighter models and a few jet-propelled Me 262s with precious little fuel to keep them aloft.

It was clear after Hitler's alarming performance at the Platterhof on 26 June 1944 that he was no longer capable of ruling Germany. The Third Reich was now without effective leadership. Himmler, having failed miserably to get wind of the amateurish attempt on Hitler's life on 20 July 1944, was heaped with new responsibilities that were well beyond his limited abilities. Göring had retreated into the dreamland of an oriental potentate. In his more lucid moments Speer knew that the war could not be won. But he still refused to draw any conclusions from this nagging apprehension. For him there appeared to be no alternative but to slog on and hope for the best. With Germany increasingly denied its sources of vital raw materials as the enemy advanced, and with the Allies in full command of German airspace, it was no longer possible to lay any long-term plans. The hopelessness of the situation is reflected in Speer's remarks to his senior staff on 2 August. He repeated the threadbare catchphrase that it was essential to remain optimistic in spite of the difficult military situation. Everyone should avoid defeatism at all costs. He gave a repeat performance of these injunctions a week later, telling members of the Main Weapons Committee that they must create a 'wave of optimism'. Saur went even further. He argued that: 'Even when we think that we have done something really excellent and commendable, it is still our arduous duty not only to do all that the Führer demands of us, but to do even more, better and quicker in order to ensure the German people's final victory'. Hans Kehrl commented that simply doing one's duty, however onerous, was not nearly enough. Such neurotic euphoria and naive optimism was clearly inappropriate when it was revealed that estimates for steel production in the final quarter of 1944 were so miserably low that it was decided not to release them.[28]

Even so, there were still flickers of hope. A record number of fighters were built in September. The bombers had not seriously damaged the oil refineries, most of which were relatively small. As the Wehrmacht retreated and lines of communication shortened, so the demand for fuel fell. This prompted Speer to write an absurdly optimistic letter to Bormann on 16 September loaded with extravagant claims. Possibly this was designed to assuage the Gauleiters. They were becoming increasingly critical of Geilenberg who had first call on labour and raw materials, thereby threatening all their pet projects. Even the indefatigable Geilenberg was beginning to lose heart. Allied reconnaissance flights carefully observed his repair work on the hydrogenation plants. As soon as it was completed a fresh attack was launched. The destruction of the hydrogenation plants was an intractable problem for Speer.[29] Without air cover and with an insufficient number of anti-aircraft guns, all he could do was to hope for bad weather and sufficient cloud cover. Outwardly Speer continued to make light of the situation, announcing that the fuel situation was 'not hopeless'. Geilenberg had managed to get the hydrogenation plants back to 75 per cent capacity. Reserves were still adequate. But Speer warned that if the bombing attacks were to continue, the situation could well become critical.[30] There was no reason to hope that the situation would improve.

On 5 October 1944 Speer sent yet another memorandum to Hitler. It was much the same old story. The Allied attacks were so continuous that Geilenberg's crews could only do hasty repairs on a day-to-day basis. Once again he appealed for more fighter protection, while making a gloomy prognostication of future production figures to drive home the point. Geilenberg had a huge workforce at his command and was given able assistance by Himmler with his vast supply of slave labour, but he was faced with a Sisyphusian task. By the end of November only Leuna and Pölitz were in operation.[31] Hasty repairs brought some of the other plants briefly back into production, but a series of massive raids between 13 and 17 January 1945 put nine hydrogenation plants, including Leuna, permanently out of business. Two days later Speer handed Nicolaus von Below – Hitler's Luftwaffe adjutant and Speer's liaison officer with Hitler – his final memorandum on the hydrogenation plants.[32] It was no longer possible to meet the Luftwaffe's minimum requirements for aviation fuel, and reserves were exhausted. Gasoline came exclusively from Hungarian crude, which would soon be denied. Allied bombing had become much more accurate, the bombs heavier and more destructive. None of this seemed to impress OKW. They continued to make demands for petrol, oil and grease that were far in excess of anything the Speer could possibly provide.[33]

Speer spent very little time in the ministry. He rushed around Germany dealing with immediate problems and visited the front with increasing frequency. As a result, the main committees became increasingly independent. This was particularly true of Hans Kehrl and Central Planning. There was no time for ministerial approval to be given to the immensely complicated technical questions with which this body was confronted. Speer began to see Kehrl as yet another rival bent on undermining his authority. In the final months of the war difficulties with transportation and communications were such that quick decisions had to be made at local level, so that planning had to give way to rapid improvisation. Speer's ambitious associates – Saur, Dorsch, Schieber and Kehrl – were forced to make decisions without due consultation. The Ministry of Armaments no longer had a clearly defined administrative structure. To an increasing degree the ministry was now plagued by rivalry between Kehrl, Saur and Schieber, with Saur clearly gaining the upper hand. Goebbels was enormously impressed by Saur. He said of him: 'The Führer considers Saur to be a stronger personality [than Speer]. Saur is a tough and upright man, who when allotted a task sees it through, if necessary using force. In a sense he is the opposite of Speer.'[34]

The last meeting of all the divisional heads and leading figures in Speer's ministry was held on 15 November 1944. They stood in a vast, almost empty room at Pariser Platz 4, a building that was left virtually a ruin after several bombing raids. For Kehrl, this setting was appropriate for the situation in which the ministry found itself. Speer, having put an unconvincingly optimistic gloss on the October figures, asked his subordinates to look to the future with optimism. Some of the leading personalities were awarded the Knight's Cross with swords for war service, which gave the whole event an air of unreality. Everyone present knew that only a miracle could save Germany from a crushing defeat. These were practical men who had no faith in miracles. All they could do was to carry on and do the best they could until the bitter end.[35]

The shortage of fuel was acute. There was no roof left over Fortress Germany. The army was immobile, the Ardennes offensive having left it exhausted and without reserves of transportation, men and materiel. But Speer kept things going against all the odds. Geilenberg worked frantically patching up the hydrogenation plants. The factories kept working as best they could until Allied and Soviet troops marched through their gates.

Given that Germany was no longer able to deal with the Allied bombers, the factories had to be broken up into smaller units and spread out around the country, either moved underground or buried under massive reinforced concrete bunkers. Saur and Milch had first suggested that mines, caves and tunnels could be converted into bomb-proof factories in January 1944 while Speer was in hospital. Hitler got wind of the idea and was so carried away by it that he began to entertain the utopian vision of burying all of Germany's industry underground, where workers would toil away like Alberich's Nibelungs. It was clear to all concerned that this was pure fantasy, but at least some key industries could be protected in this manner. Speer sought Hitler's approval to place ball-bearings above fighter aircraft on the list of priorities. A special department under Walther Schieber was created to supervise the construction of underground factories, but Dorsch was quick to ask permission to report to Hitler on a monthly basis to say how much underground space had been made available. In January 1945 Speer announced that four million square metres of underground factories were in operation.[36] This was transparently false. He was later to state that the initial programme in early 1944 was for 3 million square metres, but that by February 1945 only 1.2 million square metres were ready for use.[37]

It proved relatively simple to produce ball-bearings and fighters underground, especially as no consideration whatsoever was paid to working conditions and safety measures. The inevitable result was a high mortality rate for the concentration camp inmates who slaved away on a meagre diet and without seeing daylight for days on end. It was much more difficult to move oil refineries underground. The appalling heat caused pressure to rise, resulting in frequent explosions.[38] At the end of July Krauch announced that his department would build twenty small underground refineries that would be able to produce 750,000 metric tons of fuel per year. Further examination of this proposal revealed that the quality of the fuel would be so poor as to be virtually worthless. Krauch then proposed building one large plant underground, code-named 'Badger', that would be capable of producing 1 to 1.5 million metric tons annually. This plan also came to nothing. The machinery was not available and no qualified technicians could be found. A project to produce high-grade jet fuel never left the drawing board. By the time the war came to an end virtually no fuel had been produced underground.[39]

Speer was thus forced to accept the idea of building underground factories, which he had so vehemently opposed while convalescing in Meran. This was a triumph for Dorsch, who had wormed his way into Hitler's inner circle and had won Bormann's support against Speer by championing the proposal to go underground. During his absence Dorsch had been made responsible for all the Luftwaffe's building requirements. Speer was somewhat comforted when it became apparent that Dorsch was well out of his depth. Hitler was irate when he learnt that the two vast factories under reinforced concrete roofs, which Dorsch had recklessly promised would be finished by November 1944, would not be ready until the following spring. Dorsch tried to assuage Hitler's anger by desperately trying to get the job done on time, but this was not possible due to a lack of qualified labour, and with Bormann commandeering part of his workforce to build redoubts in a frenzied attempt to hold off the rapidly advancing armies. By the end of 1944 there were seven hundred small factories working underground.[40] This was far short of fulfilling Hitler's vision of moving all of Germany's industry out of harm's way and it was certainly not enough to make any significant impact on armaments production.

Amid this mounting chaos, in the autumn of 1944 an absurd debate began among the leadership over whether benefits and pensions should be increased. Those in favour argued that this would have 'a psychological effect on hard-working German racial comrades'. It would act as a foretaste of a post-war National Socialist Germany that would offer 'a generous reform of social insurance that would be in the interest of the population at large'. The Minister of Finance, the Minister of Economics and the Head of the Chancellery insisted that this was totally unrealistic. Even Sauckel agreed with them. The 'apolitical technocrat' Albert Speer, along with the ideologues Himmler, Bormann and Bracke, voted in favour of this madcap suggestion.[41] No thought was given as to how this programme was to be financed.

By the autumn of 1944, Allied bombers were concentrating on destroying Germany's transportation network. This gave the hydrogenation plants a degree of respite. Workers from Organisation Todt were sent to the Ruhr to rebuild the railway stations, marshalling yards and bridges. There were also a large number of Organisation Todt workers who had been withdrawn from France after the invasion, where they had been building the Atlantic Wall. Geilenberg therefore had an army of workers at his command, but he still had to contend with the determined opposition of the Gauleiters who considered it pointless to be constantly repairing railway stations when in their view the workforce could be better employed building tank traps. Bormann had the support of OKW, which insisted that the Westwall was holding up the Allied advance, thereby saving the German Army from destruction.[42]

Speer did not have to be reminded that the Ruhr was absolutely essential to the armaments industry. He made an extensive tour of western Germany between 10 and 14 September 1944.[43] From this he concluded that production should continue immediately behind the front. It was a decision dictated by necessity. Moving industry away from the Ruhr was utterly impossible. He made two further trips to the region at the end of September, and on 1 October he discussed the situation with Field Marshal Model, the commander of Army Group B. He stressed the vital importance of hanging on to the area to the west of the Rhine.

On 18 October 1944 Speer addressed an assembly of party functionaries in an attempt to get the Gauleiters to see reason. He pointed out that putting the railways back into operation as quickly as possible was absolutely essential, both for the armaments industry and for supplying the armed forces. He insisted – whether truthfully or not – that the Führer had ordered that repairs to railways and waterways should take priority over the building of tank traps and other defences.[44] Even Bormann saw that this was a reasonable argument. In November he told the Gauleiters that Speer had agreed that top priority should be given to repairing the roads and railways that were being severely disrupted by Allied bombing.[45] Yet in spite of exceptional efforts the situation steadily deteriorated. The transportation system was further overstretched as a rapidly rising number of refugees fled from the Red Army. Given the importance Speer attached to this area, he acted remarkably slowly. It was not until 8 November that he told a group of his leading associates of his concerns. Three days later, having called a special meeting of Central Planning, he handed Hitler a detailed report on the situation in the Ruhr.[46]

Transport was the major problem. It was one that could not be solved from Berlin. A man on the spot was required. Speer therefore appointed Dr Maximilian Lamertz, president of the Reich Railways Directorate in Essen, as a plenipotentiary for transport in Rhineland-Westphalia. To help him out, 4,000 Lanz Bulldog two-stroke hot-bulb tractors were to be sent to the region. They were to be requisitioned from farmers who did not need them during the winter months. They could burn low-grade fuel, even waste oil, and were capable of hauling loads of up to 15 metric tons. In spite of the previously expressed reservations about using coal as an alternative fuel, 8,300 anthracite burners were to be sent to convert trucks from petroleum to run on gas. Bormann had agreed that 50,000 foreign workers, previously used to build defences, should be sent to the Ruhr to repair the transportation network. A further 30,000 workers were also detailed to repair bomb damage to essential armaments factories. In response to Allied target priorities, anti-aircraft guns were to be moved away from factories to protect the transportation network.

Germany now faced the worst coal crisis since the beginning of the war. Reserves were down from 1.84 million metric tons – sufficient for 19 days – on 10 September 1944 to 1.03 million metric tons – sufficient for 10.9 days – on 5 November. The railways faced a daily shortfall of 40,000 metric tons. Locomotives required high-grade coal and used up 80 per cent of this type of fuel. As a result of the shortage of coal a number of electricity works, such as those at Hanau and Oldenburg, were no longer able to function. Several armaments factories in Hamburg, Lübeck, Marburg and Braunschweig had been forced to close because of lack of fuel. An important sugar factory in Hanover and a margarine factory in Hamburg had also been put out of business. Shortages of electricity were causing major problems for hospitals, dairies and bakeries. Allied targeting of the Dortmund–Ems canal had drastically reduced the amount of coal reaching smelters in Salzgitter, Peine and Osnabrück. The production of ammunition was estimated to fall by 25 to 30 per cent by the end of November. In early January 1945 Speer, with astonishing sang-froid, warned that although the situation in the West was 'satisfactory' for the moment, a severe shortage of ammunition could be expected in the near future.[47] Speer's appeal to remain optimistic rang hollow. The implication of his report was that the future was bleak. Only if bad weather hampered the bombers was there any chance of an improvement. The Ruhr, Germany's industrial heartland, was now effectively isolated from the rest of the country. He concluded on a familiar note: 'under no circumstances should we flag in our efforts. We must do everything possible to win the decisive struggle for the Ruhr upon which our people's destiny depends.'

Frost and snow caused further chaos by the end of January. On 23 January 1945 Speer ordered Lamertz to concentrate on providing the population with food and clothing rather than give top priority to the armaments industry. Food was becoming a major concern. The amount of nitrogen produced had dropped by 50 per cent compared with the year before. In 1938/39, 21.5 kilograms per hectare were available. This dropped to 11.5 kilograms by 1943/44. In December 1944 it was a mere 5 kilograms.[48] Germany faced the prospect of a chronic food shortage while the armaments industry was falling apart, with no possible hope of recovery.

At this stage Hitler handed Speer a poisoned chalice. On 18 February 1945 he was made head of a special transportation staff.[49] Two days later he was given total responsibility for transport, thereby eclipsing the Ministry of Transport. It was an impossible task. He had already admitted that unless the volume of transport increased – an exceedingly unlikely eventuality – it would no longer be possible to exploit Germany's industrial capacity or to feed the population. Speer barely had time to address his new responsibilities when, on 22 February, five thousand Allied aircraft based in England, France, Belgium, Holland and Italy launched Operation Clarion. Aimed at railways, roads, ports and bridges, 650,000 square kilometres came under attack from Emden to Lake Constance, from Berlin to Mulhouse.[50] Hitler, secure in the Berlin bunker that he was never now to leave, had no conception of the damage done or of the impossible task he had delegated to Speer. All he could do was to deploy two million underemployed armaments workers to clear the rubble. On 18 March he handed over this responsibility to Eckhard Bürger from Organisation Todt, together with the impressive title of General Commissar for the Repair of the Reich Railways. It was a hopeless assignment. Allied aircraft had finally destroyed Speer's empire, leaving the land forces to finish it off.

For Speer, all that really mattered were armaments, food and transportation: these were for him the 'three pillars' upon which the front depended. He did not wait for Goebbels' instructions before setting about combing his ministry to see how economies could be made. He ordered a 30 per cent reduction of office staff from top to bottom, both in the ministry and in individual companies. Excess personnel were to be trained as skilled workers or to serve in the armed forces. The working week was to be at least sixty hours. All holidays were to be cancelled. Schoolchildren, students and artists were forced to work in armaments factories. It was only when Speer turned his attention to the bloated party bureaucracy, in which the magnificently uniformed 'golden pheasants' or 'old fighters' avoided the unpleasantness of military duty and industrial labour, that he met with any serious resistance. Fritz Schmelter, the man responsible for personnel in the ministry, reported that 1.8 million men were fit for military service, but added the alarming rider that they would almost all have to be withdrawn from essential war work. Goebbels's calculations were very different. He estimated that an additional 7.1 million men could be enlisted. Speer was horrified at what amounted to a threat to the entire armaments industry.[51] Nor, it would seem, was the question asked how these men were to be adequately equipped. Fritz Sauckel played no part in these discussions. As Gauleiter of Thuringia he now concentrated on ruling his Party District from his villa in Weimar.[52]

These two sets of figures were the result of a fundamental difference between Goebbels, Bormann and the majority of the Gauleiters on the one hand and Speer, the Ministry of Armaments and the industrialists on the other. The first group believed that manpower won wars, the second that technology was the key. Speer had failed to see that Goebbels, like all the leading figures in the Third Reich, was solely interested in power. Since Speer's star was waning, Goebbels no longer considered him to be a valuable ally. Hitler's Cerberus, Martin Bormann, was a far more useful partner. During the month of August 1944 the struggle between Speer and Goebbels had intensified, while the Gauleiters were confronted with conflicting orders from Speer, Goebbels and Bormann. In areas near the front, the Gauleiters and SA officers in Operation Mole raided armaments factories and ordered workers to build defences. Speer protested that there was no point in building defences if the men had no weapons, but this argument failed to convince. Within a few weeks Goebbels had removed 200,000 workers from the armaments industry without finding the replacements he had promised.[53] In this situation Speer was left virtually defenceless. His only remaining argument was that the military had far too many men in cushy jobs, far out of harm's way. They, rather than skilled armaments workers, should be armed and sent to the front. He had frequently pointed out the endemic wastefulness of the armed forces, but to remarkably little effect.[54]

Goebbels' prestige had been greatly enhanced by having acted swiftly and decisively in Berlin on 20 July 1944. He now had conditional support from his former rivals Bormann and Keitel. He had the powerful backing of Paul Wegener, the Gauleiter of Weser-Ems, who was also Commissar for Defence of the Reich in northern Germany. But his position was far from secure. His state secretary, Werner Naumann, was a sinister power behind the throne. He was a fanatic bent on replacing Goebbels, whom he considered to be a defeatist. To this end, Naumann intrigued with Himmler and Bormann. He was also bitterly opposed to Speer, and undermined Goebbels on the domestic front by writing soppy love poems to his susceptible wife Magda.[55] Goebbels and the Gauleiters wanted the maximum number of men possible in the armed forces. Speer continued to insist that without weapons they were worthless. In October and November 1944 he made repeated appeals to Hitler, warning him that if these raids on his workforce continued, the armaments industry was likely to fall apart. In desperation Speer suggested that the Gauleiters be made responsible for armaments within their administrative districts and should bear full responsibility for any shortcomings.[56] Hitler was faced with deciding between Speer's requirements for the armaments industry and Goebbels' demands for more soldiers. True to form, he was reluctant to make any decision. He eventually announced that it was not a question of either soldiers or weapons. He demanded both.

Speer's efforts to pare down the administration had begun with the creation of an Armaments Staff on 1 August 1944. It was designed to absorb the Fighter Staff, which had enabled him to reach his goal of creating a unified Armaments Ministry with responsibility for all three services. The new organisation was intended to further strengthen the system of industrial self-determination, relying on improvisation rather than bureaucratic decision-making. All twelve members of the Fighter Staff were included in the new organisation, as was Otto Merker's naval building team and 'Panzer' Rohland's tank experts, along with specialists in weapons, munitions, transport and the V weapons. Thirteen new members included industrialists from such firms as AEG, Messerschmitt, Flick and Auto-Union-Junkers. Representatives of all three branches of the Wehrmacht were also included. Speer was formally the chairman, but he left the bulk of the work to Karl-Otto Saur.[57] Speer made it quite clear that the role of the Armaments Staff was not merely to supply the Wehrmacht with the weapons with which to win the war, but also to act as propagandists, spreading a feeling of optimism and calm. This soon came to mean that it was not only acceptable, but also a patriotic duty, to fiddle the accounts. A Commissioner for the Recognition of Achievement was appointed to provide incentives for greater productivity.

Meetings were held on a daily basis to discuss specific topics: aircraft on Mondays, tanks and tracked vehicles on Tuesdays, the navy, V weapons and trains on alternate Wednesdays, weapons on Thursdays and munitions on Fridays. Speer made a speech at the inaugural meeting that was later widely circulated. The secretary taking the minutes made a short summary that made for curious reading, given the events of 20 July. He wrote that the Armaments Staff had been created to overcome 'the many faults that are inherent in an authoritarian system'. The new organisation was to be 'a band of fanatics, an active block of resistance fighters who, together with other groups of resisters under the leadership of energetic men such as Reichsführer-SS Himmler and Reich Minister Dr Goebbels, will overcome all dangers, so that Germany's destiny shall change for the better'. Saur ironically congratulated the secretary for his political tact. Speer merely laughed at him.[58]

Speer always prided himself on never allowing his ministry to become enmeshed in bureaucracy and red tape. But the Armaments Staff is an example to the contrary. Its Weapons Committee was divided up into sixty sub-committees, one for each calibre of weapon. These sub-committees were then placed in ten groups, the heads of which met individually with Saur every Thursday. A general meeting was held with Speer on a quarterly basis at which luncheon was served.[59]

Thus in his confidently entitled 'Victory Programme', which he unveiled before a meeting of the Gauleiters on 3 August 1944 in Posen, Speer announced that Saur had promised to produce 4,800 jet Me 262s by December.[60] This figure was absurdly optimistic. It concealed the fact that Speer was not nearly so enthusiastic about the plane as he later professed to have been. In the course of the entire war, only 1,294 were built. Of these, 564 were produced in 1944, the remaining 730 in 1945. The highest monthly production of 286 was achieved in March 1945.[61] Speer made equally extravagant claims for other key weapons. Hitler gave him his full support during a meeting with the Gauleiters the following day. He heaped praise upon the Armaments Ministry for its outstanding achievements and professed full confidence in the minister. But none of this could disguise the fact that the armaments industry was in sharp decline. In 1945 it rapidly collapsed.

Another of Speer's schemes involved the production of a 'People's Fighter'. The Heinkel He 162 was a sleek modern design with a BMW turbojet mounted atop the fuselage. Since metals were in short supply it had a wooden airframe. This turned out to be a major problem. At its maximum speed of 750kph the glue became highly corrosive so that the machine threatened to fall apart. The chief test pilot, Captain Gotthard Peter, survived when the nose gear began to come unstuck, but was later killed when an aileron fell off. The plane was initially intended to be flown by members of the Hitler Youth after a brief training course, but it proved to be exceptionally difficult to fly. The controls were light and it was fundamentally unstable, so that only a very experienced pilot was able to master it.

The fighter ace General Adolf Galland, the officer in charge of the fighter programme, was violently opposed to the He 162. He argued that the Allied bombers could only be stopped by technically superior aircraft. He wanted to concentrate on developing and perfecting the superior A-1a fighter model of the Messerschmitt Me 262. Speer, with his obsession with production figures, and with Göring's support, overruled Galland, who was then made the convenient scapegoat for the failure to beat off the bombers.[62] He was relieved of his command in January 1945, placed under house arrest, and returned to active service in March to command the 'Galland Circus' – the elite Fighter Group 44 consisting of carefully selected pilots flying Me 262s.[63] Galland's reservations about the He 162 were borne out in practice. It did not go into combat until mid-April 1945. A number were lost due to engine failure or structural weakness. Since the plane's fuel capacity was exhausted within half an hour, several pilots were killed making emergency landings.

The story of the He 162 is a typical example of Speer's approach to armaments. Although he paid lip service to the idea that quality should always be preferred to quantity, he and Saur were fixated on output figures and percentage increases with which to impress Hitler. The plane was rushed into production before its teething problems had been solved. But, in any case, by April 1945 even the finest of fighter aircraft would not have sufficed to save Nazi Germany.

By the late summer of 1944, Speer knew full well that the situation was desperate, but he was still determined to disguise this unpleasant truth. He liked to point out that when he took office in 1942 the situation had seemed hopeless. The Red Army's counter-attack before Moscow had left Barbarossa in ruins. A number of respected soldiers had felt even then that the war could not be won. But thanks to his efforts things had greatly improved and the output of weapons and munitions had increased substantially. Such talk avoided the real issue. As Himmler complained to Saur, units were being sent to the front only half-equipped. Soldiers often had the guns but lacked ammunition. Speer felt constrained to issue the following appeal to his associates: 'Therefore I beg you not to let the figures to which you are privy be known. You must show by your outward demeanour that we can have every confidence in our armaments and war production.'[64] This was little more than an injunction to whistle in the wind.

Karl-Otto Saur was enormously energetic, travelling around the country inspecting armaments firms, urging them on to maximum effort and meting out harsh justice on those that fell behind. He was a man of action, but certainly not an inspired leader. It is largely due to Saur and the Armaments Staff that the production of U-boats, aircraft, tanks and weapons was more or less maintained up until the end of 1944. Given the steadily worsening situation, this was an astonishing achievement, but one that is subject to substantial qualification. Much of this material was obsolete. The new model U-boats were not yet seaworthy. Midget submarines were worthless weapons, although faulty intelligence made them appear to be an alarming threat to the Royal Navy.[65]

Saur was a highly controversial figure. Many found his dictatorial manner, crude language and lack of consideration for others insufferable. Others admired him as a man who got things done. Speer, whose post-war reputation rested in no small part on Saur's achievements, claimed that Saur had denounced a number of officers in the Army Armaments Office during the witch-hunt after the assassination attempt of 20 July. Due to his influence with Hitler, Speer claimed to have managed to save such figures as General Sebastian Fichtner and General Erich Schneider.[66] Once again Speer's memory is at fault. Far from saving General Fichtner, Speer had set the Gestapo on his track for his 'pro-Soviet sympathies'. He was saved, having been tortured, not by Speer but by his friend Guderian. There is no record of General Schneider, from the Army Weapons Office, ever having been arrested. On 28 December 1944 he was put in command of the 14th Infantry Division in East Prussia.

As early as March 1944 Speer's deputy, Walther Schieber, came under massive attack from Gauleiters Albert Hoffmann of southern Westphalia, Karl Hanke of Lower Silesia and Fritz Sauckel of Thuringia, along with Fritz Kranefuß, Himmler's special representative in the occupied countries, in which capacity he played a key role in the mass murder of the European Jews. Martin Bormann joined in this campaign against one of Speer's key associates. They accused Schieber of having found lucrative positions in industry for his two 'criminal' brothers and for being a spineless traitor. They kept up the pressure on him for months on end until, as an SS-Brigadeführer, he was investigated by a special commission established by Himmler and Kaltenbrunner. Although Schieber was found to be innocent of all charges, Speer felt unable to save him. Pressure from the Gauleiters on Bormann was so great that his deputy would have to go. At Speer's repeated insistence, Himmler told Hitler that 'none of the charges levelled against Dr Schieber have proven to be correct or demonstrable'. Speer asked Hitler to give him a special donation as severance pay and to award him the highest civilian honour: the knight's cross with swords. On 9 November 1944 Schieber ceased to be head of allocations in the ministry, but Speer kept him on as a special envoy, working mostly in Italy.[67] As a wealthy industrialist, he agreed to work pro bono.

Speer used the Schieber affair as an opportunity once again to reorganise his ministry, in part to disguise the fact that he had cravenly given way to pressure from the party, but ostensibly because he wanted to streamline the administration, which had become top-heavy. He took Schieber's departure as an opportunity to abolish the Procurement Office. He then amalgamated General Kurt Waeger's Armaments Office and Willy Liebel's Central Office, creating a new organisation under Theo Hupfauer, the commandant of the SS elite school Ordensburg Sonthofen. As head of a revamped Central Office Hupfauer was now, alongside Saur, one of the most powerful figures in Speer's ministry. Like most of his colleagues, he found Speer far too lofty to be either 'endearing or lovable', but he was swept along by his energy and optimism that created an upbeat atmosphere amid undeniable signs of an inevitable defeat.[68] Himmler regarded Hupfauer as his man within Speer's ministry, while Speer used Hupfauer's connections with Bormann to his own advantage. Hitler also held Hupfauer in high regard, appointing him Minister of Labour in his political testament. At Sonthofen Hupfauer had heard three speeches by Himmler, in May and June 1944, in which he spoke openly and at length about the mass murder of the Jews.[69] Perhaps he followed Himmler's injunction and kept this information to himself.

On leaving the Ministry of Armaments, General Waeger resumed his duties at OKH. Willy Liebel – Hitler's favourite mayor – having collapsed due to overwork, returned to what little remained of Nuremberg, where he died in April 1945 – possibly murdered.[70] Bormann's intrigues against Hitler's doctor, Dr Karl Brandt, resulted in his fall from grace. Speer thereby lost a powerful ally at court.[71] But there were also better moments. In November 1944 the troublesome Franz Xaver Dorsch had fallen seriously ill. Speer replaced him temporarily with one of his more amenable associates.

In February 1945 Saur moved the Planning Office and the Information Service to the delightful spa town of Blankenburg in the Harz Mountains. The statistical office was transferred to nearby Wernigerode.[72] Saur thereby was able to act independently and concentrated on working his way into Hitler's favour by promising that the V weapons would eventually bring victory. As the Allies advanced, Speer's armaments empire dissolved into a series of isolated pockets in which local industrialists and ministerial officials muddled through as best they could, often without contact either with Berlin or Blankenburg.

For several months Speer's efforts had been concentrated on stopping Bormann, Goebbels and Keitel from raiding the armaments factories to make up for the rapidly mounting casualties in the armed forces. The best he could do was to make sure that certain projects were protected from Goebbels and Bormann's predatory grasp. Dönitz managed to get his dockyard workers exempted on 1 November 1944. Two days later, those involved in the production of anti-aircraft guns and munitions were shielded.[73] Soon afterwards 130,000 workers in the Fighter Programme were deemed to be indispensable.[74] This resistance merely whetted Goebbels' appetite. In November Speer insisted that he could not spare more than 10,000 workers. Goebbels called for 100,000. Hitler, as usual, flatly refused to adjudicate. Himmler then demanded that Speer hand over all 'Jewish half-breeds', whereupon Speer protested that he could not spare these highly skilled workers.

On 6 December 1944 Speer gave Hitler a summary of the number of workers he had lost due to Special Conscription Actions.[75] Of the 1,044,000 workers classified as essential since February 1942, only 36 per cent were still at work. Speer begged Hitler at least to spare the mining industry, the workers repairing the railways, the hydrogenation plants and workers preparing underground facilities. But due to constant badgering he agreed to release a further 90,000 armaments workers by March 1945.

Speer's position was rendered even more precarious with the formation of the *Deutsche Volkssturm* on 18 October 1944, the anniversary of the Battle of the Nations in 1813. This was Bormann's pet project in which all males between the ages of sixteen and sixty capable of bearing arms were to be sent into action with minimal training and rudimentary equipment.[76] Its motto 'Victory or Downfall' merely echoed the hopelessness of the situation. Hitler was very sceptical about Bormann's proposal, understandably insisting that the *Volkssturm* would only be effective if it were properly equipped and trained. He made SS-Obergruppenführer Gottlob Berger, chief of staff in the Waffen-SS and head of the SS Main Office, responsible for providing the weapons. He was to work in close conjunction with Speer.[77] Hardly surprisingly, Berger was unable to procure enough weapons. They were mostly of French, Czech and Italian provenance, so there was a serious shortage of suitable ammunition. Speer had virtually nothing to spare.

The *Volkssturm* was an unmitigated disaster. It was militarily worthless and stripped Speer's factories of invaluable workers, managers and engineers. Organisation Todt was also robbed of essential workers. Goebbels and Bormann entertained the fantastic notion that the 'fanatical' defence of the homeland would cause so many enemy casualties that public opinion would force the enemy to call for a compromise peace. Speer now had to contend with an increasing number of men who were living in a madhouse.

Speer's position was being steadily undermined. Kammler had been put in charge of the V2 programme and had his eye on the aircraft industry. A number of Gauleiters, encouraged by Bormann, Goebbels and Himmler, began to follow Sauckel's example and dabble in armaments production. Gradually a group comprising Goebbels, Bormann, Ley, Kaltenbrunner and Sauckel began to think in terms of a dramatic mass suicidal *Götterdämmerung*, while an isolated Speer turned towards such ineffectual figures as Dorpmüller, Schwerin von Krosigk and Backe until Bormann put an end to their 'defeatist evenings at the club'.[78]

Contrary to his later attempts to paint himself as someone who had long since come to the conclusion that the war was irrevocably lost, Speer also fell prey to similar delusions. On 3 December 1944 he addressed a select group of military men at the testing grounds in Rechlin. He told them that, in spite of all the difficulties caused by the loss of sources of raw materials in both East and West, armaments production for all three services was 'satisfactory'. Output was such that thirty entire divisions could be replenished each month. Having made this

highly dubious claim, based on figures that no one present could check, he
went on to make the equally questionable assertion that the Allies would soon
be faced with severe logistical problems that would give Germany a certain
advantage. The clinching argument was the moth-eaten adage that it would be
possible to make up for their opponents' superiority in quantity of armaments
by the quality of future weapons.[79]

This ill-founded and irresponsible optimism was reflected in Speer's 1945
New Year's speech to the Armaments Ministry's personnel. He emphasised the
astonishing achievements of the armaments industry, in spite of the bombing
raids. Once again he stressed the superiority of German weapons, 'which the
enemy is beginning to feel with ever increasing intensity'. He ended with the
rousing appeal: 'The task that we have been set is victory. All our efforts are for
Germany.'[80]

Speer's position was further weakened when the Soviet advance robbed
Germany of its remaining resources in the East and the Allied bomber offensive caused havoc to the railways and put power plants out of action. Industrial
production wound down to the point that there was now an excess of labour.
Attacks on the hydrogenation plants resumed, resulting in a chronic shortage
of aviation fuel.[81] By March 1945 Speer's main concern was to make sure that
there was a sufficient number of agricultural labourers to save the country
from starvation. He gradually realised that the notion he had entertained as
late as July 1944, that it would be possible to produce more weapons as well as
recruit more soldiers, was totally unrealistic.

Hans Kehrl had long been painfully aware of a fundamental weakness in
Speer's system. Speer seems to have been totally oblivious to the financial consequences of his armaments drive. From the outset he had been strongly opposed
to price controls and heavy taxes on profits. As a result inflation became rampant,
threatening to trigger a collapse of the Reichsmark, analogous to that after
World War I. Much of the initial inflationary pressure had been exported to the
occupied countries by manipulating exchange rates, but there was a strict limit
to what could be done by such means.[82] In July 1944 Kehrl produced an alarming
memorandum entitled 'Purchasing Power, Prices and War Finance' that argued
that the German economy was rapidly falling into anarchy.[83] A capitalist system
in which firms responded freely to government requirements had been replaced
by a command economy that was driven either by force or idealism, but unlike
the Soviet planned economy, it failed to maintain a stable monetary system
without which accurate accounting was impossible.

As early as the summer of 1943, Speer's armaments programme had placed
such demands on the economy that it began to fall apart. Ordinary Germans
increasingly resorted to the black market, in spite of ferocious wartime regulations and frequent prosecutions. By the following summer Germany was

having chronic financial difficulties. The situation was exacerbated by the disruption of production due to severe transportation problems. Deliveries were slowed down, resulting in payments being deferred, thereby necessitating bridging loans that in turn placed a severe strain on the banking system. The state provided banks with Reich Security Bonds that guaranteed 30 per cent of loans made by banks to cover armaments orders – *Reichsausfallbürgschaften* – but this was clearly not enough. Funds now flowed into the alternative economy. With a shortage of consumer goods it was no longer possible to use higher wages as an incentive to workers, because there was nothing to buy. Savings were pointless as it was obvious that when the war ended they would be wiped out by hyperinflation. Repression and violence were the only effective motivating forces. Kehrl's remedy was to increase taxation in an effort to stem inflation, but this could only have a limited effect. The fundamental question now was which would be the first to collapse: the Wehrmacht or the economy.[84]

As early as June 1944 discussions had begun to bring sections of the Ministry of Economics under Speer's ministry.[85] Then, in early November 1944, SS-Gruppenführer Otto Ohlendorf suggested to Speer that the Ministry of Armaments, the Ministry of Economics and the Ministry of Food should be amalgamated. Ohlendorf was one of the earlier party members, a talented economist who had been seconded to the Reich Security Main Office where, in his capacity as head of the domestic Security Service, he prepared top-secret reports on German public opinion and morale. In 1941 Himmler appointed him commander of *Einsatzgruppe D* in the Soviet Union, a group of murderers responsible for the deaths of some 90,000 people, mainly Jews. In late 1943, at the initiative of Bormann and Himmler, Ohlendorff was made a state secretary in the Ministry of Economics with responsibility for post-war planning. Here he worked in close association with Ludwig Ehrhardt, the architect of West Germany's 'economic miracle', and with the Deputy Minister, the unimpeach-able Nazi Franz Hayler. Ohlendorf was an advocate of a specifically National Socialist economy based on 'social, that is to say racial, considerations' that encouraged small enterprises and 'active and bold entrepreneurship', as against big business, cartels and monopolies. He was sharply critical of Speer's approach, which he felt was rigidly bureaucratic and 'totally Bolshevistic' with its dislike of small businesses and disregard for the consumer sector.[86] Ohlendorf denounced the system of self-determination of industry because it pandered to big business. This regime of 'hyenas and monopolists' seriously weakened the state.[87] He proposed that he should become state secretary under Funk in a new super-ministry. While Speer was at Hohenlychen he had discussed this 'wartime economic marriage' with Funk, who felt that relations between his ministry and the Ministry of Armaments were on the whole harmonious, but that there was a certain degree of inter-departmental protectiveness. Hayler, Kehrl and Ohlendorf had joined Funk and Speer in a convivial breakfast of beer and veal sausages in the clinic.[88] But Speer soon had good reason to suspect that Ohlendorf's overriding ambition was to assume control. The plan was then put on hold.[89]

Ohlendorf and Hayler, as SS men, worked in close cooperation with Himmler in his capacity as Minister of the Interior to reassert the authority of Funk's Ministry of Economics in opposition to Speer's ministry. But Franz Hayler, an old warrior who had taken part in the Beer Hall Putsch in 1923, got on very well with Speer, who admired his irrepressible optimism. At the end of October 1944 the Ohlendorf group managed to push Speer's Armaments Inspectorates aside, replacing them with officials from the Ministry of Economics.[90] But this was largely cosmetic. Speer was effectively in control of much of the Ministry of Economics through Hans Kehrl.

Bormann and the Gauleiters also stepped up their attacks on Speer and his ministry. They managed to get one of his key associates, Gerhard Degenkolb, suspended from duty pending an investigation for conducting a morning inspection of a locomotive works while intoxicated.[91] Bormann immediately accused Speer's representative in Milan, General Hans Leyers, of being exceedingly lax in plundering Italy's resources. When Speer wished to give Wilhelm Haspel, the chairman of the board of Daimler-Benz, a special honour, the local Gau office and Bormann objected on the grounds that Haspel was not a party member, showed no interest in the 'Movement' and was married to a 'Grade 1 Jewish half-breed'. Speer had to appeal directly to Hitler and Göring before he could award Haspel the title of Armaments Industry Leader.[92]

Communications were beginning to break down. The destruction of the road and railway networks by Allied bombing meant that the postal services functioned only intermittently, causing an administrative nightmare. Central control of the armaments industries was no longer possible.[93] The Speer Telephone Network was established within the Postal Ministry through the intermediary of Heinrich Zerbel, the Postal Ministry's representative on Geilenberg's working group. He was also responsible for communications on the Armaments Staff. A special corps of dispatch riders was formed, but this proved to be totally inadequate. By mid-November the situation was so grave that within the Ruhr communications were becoming sporadic. The railway system had by now completely broken down due to intense bombing, the shortage of coal and the impossibility of replacing rolling stock.[94] Speer therefore decided to revitalise the Ruhr Staff and give it authority to act independently. On 6 December Hitler agreed to Speer's suggestion that Albert Vögler should head this organisation. He thereby became an armaments dictator in the Rhineland and Ruhr.[95]

By the end of February 1945 the transportation network had broken down irrevocably. Speer then divided Germany into eight independent districts, each under an official with plenipotentiary powers. Speer himself was responsible for Berlin and Brandenburg. His control over the other districts rapidly evaporated. Apart from Speer, the plenipotentiaries were all leading industrialists. The self-determination of industry had now reached its final form.[96]

CHAPTER ELEVEN

DEFEAT

SPEER INSPECTED THE Western Front from 26 September to 1 October 1944.[1] He travelled with his adjutant, Manfred von Poser, Willy Liebel and his assistant, SS-Standartenführer Karl Cliever. Milch and Rohland joined the party later. He drove so fast in his convertible BMW that von Poser and Cliever soon lost sight of him. They eventually met up at the delightful Hotel Simonis at Kobern on the Mosel. The following day they moved to the Hotel Porta Negra in Trier for a conference with the local Organisation Todt brigade. During a visit to the front Speer won high praise for his handling of a captured Willys Jeep. The local Gauleiters – Friedrich Florian and through their deputies Albert Hoffmann and Fritz Schlessmann – proved to be surprisingly cooperative. A meeting was arranged with Field Marshal Walter Model at a former rehabilitation centre for alcoholics in Krefeld. 'In a fractious manner' Speer demanded more tanks and weapons. The party then moved on to Arnhem to view the battlefield. Speer lost his temper when he was warned to move back when under artillery fire and had to be calmed down by von Poser. He concluded the trip with a visit to his friend, the sculptor Arno Breker.

Speer returned to the Ruhr on 15 November where he spent a week in close consultation with Model. On 26 November he handed Hitler a list of requests for immediate action. Anti-aircraft defences needed to be strengthened. All available Me 163s – a rocket-propelled fighter that proved to be virtually useless – should be sent to the Ruhr.[2] Long take-off and landing strips had to be built for the Me 262 jet fighter. Between 100,000 and 150,000 additional workers were needed to clear bomb damage. The demand for steel in the Ruhr was such that U-boat construction had to be given a lower priority. Hitler agreed to all these suggestions.[3]

Speer now concentrated on supplying the needs of Model's Army Group B in a desperate attempt to hang on to the Ruhr. On 1 December he gave another of his pep talks to the heads of the Armaments Commissions.[4] They must have been somewhat bemused when he told them there was no need to worry too much about the future. He returned to the Ruhr on 15 December to discuss the final details for supplying Model. He had come to the conclusion that it would indeed be possible to defend the Ruhr. Model's manic self-confidence matched Speer's. They agreed that an all-out effort could meet most of his needs. Bormann managed to convince himself that Speer and Model might succeed. He ordered the Gauleiters in the Ruhr to stop building defences behind the front and put the men to work repairing roads and communications that were coming under heavy attack from the air, the weather having greatly improved. By March Speer had two million workers, most of them foreigners, working on railway repairs.[5] He told Himmler that the operation by Model's Army Group B was the 'decisive battle for Germany' that would enable the Ruhr to continue producing armaments. He added that if necessary he would get decrees from Hitler in support of Model's efforts.[6]

It was not only the Ruhr that was under dire threat. Speer was also deeply concerned about the situation in the East. He stressed the catastrophic consequences were the army to retire to the Nibelungen Line along the Oder from Bratislava to Stettin (Szczecin). This had been established by OKH on 28 November 1944 as part of Guderian's defensive plan for the Eastern Front. It would mean that 60 per cent of Germany's coal supplies would be lost. Since German industry already had to make do with 50 per cent of its needs, the results would be catastrophic. Furthermore, since one third of Germany's steel production was produced to the east of the Nibelungen Line,[7] armaments production would fall by about two thirds. The troops would then be unable to continue fighting. On 16 January Speer alerted Hitler to the importance of the Magistrale – the railway line from Oppeln (Opole) to Litzmannstadt (Łódź) and Gotenhafen (Gdynia) – along which most of Upper Silesia's coal was transported. Five days later he again warned Hitler that General Schörner's Army Group A would have to hold the line. Schörner's basic principle was that his troops should be more afraid of those behind them than those in front. Model would have heartily agreed. For this reason both were among Hitler's favourite generals. Speer promised that he would do everything possible to supply Schörner's needs, but his demand for approximately half of Germany's total armaments output for his rag-tag armies was impossible to meet. Speer suggested, as an alternative, a bomber offensive against the Soviet lines of communication, sourly pointing out that he knew from bitter experience what harm this could cause. Hitler dismissed the suggestion with a 'sarcastic laugh'. The Luftwaffe did not have the aircraft for such a mission.[8]

With the situation unravelling on all fronts it was all too easy to come up with answers. Hitler ordered Speer to concentrate on weapons with 'revolutionary new qualities' that were technologically superior to anything the enemy could produce, but at the same time he supported Bormann's efforts to move hundreds of thousands of workers into the armed forces. The end result was the worst of all worlds. New weapons took far too long to develop before they could be put into mass production. Masses of ill-trained and badly equipped soldiers provided little more than cannon fodder.

The worse the situation became, the greater the emphasis on 'miracle weapons' that would soon become operational and turn the tables on the enemy. Speer did all he could to raise expectations, even appointing a special propaganda section within his ministry to trumpet future wonders. 'Miracle weapons' were as much a propaganda weapon to boost morale and to strengthen the people's faith in their Führer as they were weapons of war. Speer responded to Hitler's orders by stopping work on all projects that were not likely to have a 'revolutionary' effect, thereby rendering the situation even more serious.

Reports from the Security Service and the Propaganda Ministry indicate that by the summer of 1944 the pressure on Speer was mounting. The public appeared to be unimpressed by his upbeat production figures. They were quick to realise that there was no corresponding improvement in the overall situation. Many imagined that Hitler was a reasonable man who would not have continued the war after the D-Day landings unless he had something in the works that might soon change Germany's fortunes. Others, like the U-boat crews, knew that the superiority of Allied technology was such that the war was irredeemably lost. Even with workers slaving away in impossible conditions for 72 hours per week, Germany could not possibly match their opponents' output of conventional weapons. The vast majority of Germans knew that without 'miracle weapons' the war could not be won, and were beginning to fear that they might not arrive in time. The V2 might be a technical marvel, but it did nothing to halt the advancing armies. The Me 262 was a magnificent machine, but there were too few of them to have a decisive effect.

In January 1945 the Armaments Staff decided to stop production of the Messerschmitt Bf 109 fighter that was by now a hopelessly outdated death-trap.[9] Bomber production had virtually ceased by the summer of 1944. An increasingly large number of aircraft could not be used because of the chronic lack of aviation fuel. These were scrapped and the metal used for other weapons. The net result was that a number of factories were unable to continue production. Loath to lose engineers and skilled labour, Speer encouraged companies to develop new models. The result was a frenzy of planning for advanced types of aircraft that were never to go into service. Mercedes-Benz dreamt up the monstrous Projects A to F: huge carrier aircraft with jet bombers and missiles slung under their bellies, grotesque weapons that would never leave the drawing board. Designers in other firms amused themselves with similar futuristic projects that they knew would never fly.[10] That quality was more important than quantity became

Hitler and Speer's weary psittacism.[11] They ended up with neither. Quality weapons that were still on the drawing board were worthless and the production figures for tested weapons were rapidly falling. In January 1945 the production of tanks was only 64 per cent of the projected figure, aircraft 62 per cent, shipping 44 per cent and ammunition 64 per cent.[12]

On 23 January 1945 Speer launched an 'Emergency Programme', due to start in March, to build what were optimistically called 'decisive weapons.' Quite what this meant was unclear. At a meeting with a group of generals at the Krampnitz Barracks in Potsdam on 13 January he had disavowed the propaganda about 'miracle weapons', but he assured his audience that the adversary's material superiority would soon be overcome. He made no mention as to how this could be achieved. The distinction between 'decisive' and 'miracle' weapons was left deliberately vague. The new programme was touted as a stopgap measure until the resources of the Ruhr and Silesia were secured.[13] This was admittedly somewhat less vainglorious than the previous 'Victory Programme', but it was equally unrealistic and inevitably ground to a halt.[14]

It was beginning to become obvious that in spite of his many outstanding achievements Speer had failed to deliver the goods. He now began to look for others to blame. In his report on the overall situation on 27 January he argued that the fundamental mistake was that Germany had not been fully armed by 1940 or at the latest 1941, thereby hinting that there was nothing he could have done to offset this deficiency.[15] Germany's present woes were thus attributed to faulty planning and to Fritz Todt's shortcomings. This was the version of events that Speer was to relate to his captors and repeat in his memoirs. Many found it convincing.

Nevertheless, Speer continued to fan false hopes. At the end of February he told his staff in the Armaments Office that careful planning would lead to an amazing increase in armaments production that would 'astonish the world and bring about a decisive change on the battlefield'.[16] With the 2nd Army encircled in the East Prussian pocket and the 4th Army entrapped at Königsberg, refugees fleeing Breslau, Fritz Todt's Westwall breached, and the Americans about to cross the Rhine at Remagen, it was difficult to imagine that anyone could have taken this latest claim seriously. On 7 March Pleiger told Speer that coal supplies had virtually dried up. The Red Army had overrun Upper Silesia and had encircled Lower Silesia. This resulted in the total collapse of armaments and war production.[17] The Ruhr was starved of coal because the transportation network had been destroyed. The Reich Coal Association was bankrupt. The powerful Rhineland-Westphalian Coal Syndicate had its last meeting on 28 March, paid off its staff and hoped that the war would soon be over.[18]

In a memorandum to Hitler, Speer pointed out that were Rhineland-Westphalia to be lost the economy would be in ruins and it would be impossible to continue the war. The Ruhr was isolated, with all transportation links cut. Armaments production could only be sent to Model's Army Group B. Speer tried to put an optimistic gloss on the situation by making the wild claim that it was roughly analogous to the crisis in the spring of 1943 when the dams were breached. Then it had proved possible to master the situation in spite of great difficulties. Now it was imperative to do likewise in far more difficult circumstances. He ended with this rousing appeal: 'We must not grow weary, however difficult the situation and however unattainable its solution may seem. We must do everything possible to win the battle for the Ruhr upon which the destiny of our Reich depends! *Heil mein Führer*! Signed Speer.' Copies of this effusion were sent to Göring, Himmler, Keitel, Bormann and Dönitz.[19]

Beginning in the spring of 1944, an increasing amount of time and effort was devoted to the problem of closing down, removing or disabling factories in the face of advancing armies. In May, Speer ordered that the Reich Commissars – such as Erich Koch in the East, Seyß-Inquart in the Netherlands and Josef Terboven in Norway – should be made responsible for transferring factories or changing them over to armaments production.[20] These men proved unequal to the task, so that Speer, who was far better at identifying problems than at solving them, handed the whole matter over to the Ministry of Armaments' organisational genius, Karl Maria Hettlage. He drew up an ingenious and detailed memorandum on ways to speed up the process of moving and converting factories, but putting these ideas into practice proved to be a nightmare. Finding adequate accommodation for workers when they were transferred proved to be virtually impossible. The shortage of available transport presented an insurmountable difficulty. Himmler once again promised to give Speer all the assistance he needed, but starved workers from the concentration camps were of little use. Above all, there was the continued resistance from most Gauleiters to any attempt to cut back on consumer goods or to move factories away from their satrapies. Speer constantly complained that things were moving too slowly and urged everyone to make a greater effort, but little changed apart from mounting frustration, resignation and despair.

After Patton's breakthrough at Avranches at the end of July 1944, Hitler had ordered all areas that were not likely to be regained to be devastated. Similar orders were issued as the army withdrew in the East. Speer reacted to these orders by drawing up a 'Deactivation Handbook', the gist of which was that essential equipment should be removed from factories so that they would be of no use to the enemy. Were the factories to be retaken, they could then be quickly put back into working order.[21] Hitler initially found this argument convincing. It suggested that all was not yet lost. A scorched earth policy was never a viable option. The Germans lacked the time, the manpower and the explosives to carry out demolition on this scale. Such a policy would have met with stiff resistance among a population that knew that defeat was imminent. Besides, continual bombing, artillery barrages and urban warfare were likely to be far more devastating than any such policy could ever have been.

As the fronts moved ever closer to the frontiers of Germany, Speer appointed special officers to supervise the deactivation of industrial plant. At a conference at Hitler's headquarters between 18 and 20 August 1944 he managed to get Hitler to agree to deactivation rather than destruction. The appalling devastation caused by the scorched earth policy of the German army as it retreated to the Hindenburg Line in 1917 was thereby avoided.[22]

There was a strong element of wishful thinking in Speer's line of argument. On 5 September he told Gauleiter Gustav Simon – a man popularly known as the 'Poisonous Toadstool of Hermeskeil' who ruled over the civil administration in Luxemburg – that the iron ore deposits in the area had to be saved from destruction. Speer wrote: 'We must count on getting back this ore, because the continuation of the war in the long run is impossible without it.'[23]

The Gauleiters put up a stiff resistance to Speer's deactivation policy and were soon to get their way. In mid-September Gauleiters in the East were given the right to decide whether or not industrial plant and mines should be destroyed. Otto Dietrich, the Reich Press Chief, boldly announced a scorched earth policy in banner headlines in the party newspaper *Völkischer Beobachter*. Speer reacted by presenting the western Gauleiters with detailed plans for deactivation in Rhineland-Westphalia. He ordered an expert in the removal of industrial plant, General Max Schindler, to draft a detailed plan with Field Marshal von Rundstedt, the Supreme Commander West. The matter had added urgency because Nazi Party activists had set about the dismantling of industrial plant with such enthusiasm that the transportation network rapidly became chronically overburdened.[24]

In a desperate attempt to avoid chaos, Speer appealed to Bormann to instruct those Gauleiters who were close to the Western Front to follow his guidelines. Speer told him that Hitler had said that he would soon be able to recapture the ground lost in the West. Therefore industrial plant had to be left in such a condition that it could soon be put back into operation. He also insisted that industry should be kept working up until the very last moment. He stressed the importance of keeping electrical generating plant going as long as possible, otherwise the supply of drinking water would stop, the mines would be flooded and there would be no heavy-duty cranes available to remove essential machinery. Hitler endorsed Speer's initiative, whereupon Speer delegated responsibility for deactivation to his state secretary and deputy, Günther Schulze-Fielitz.

Speer's ministry had already gained considerable experience in deactivating, destroying and dismantling industrial plant. Beginning in late 1943, staggering quantities of industrial equipment, semi-finished products and raw materials were shipped back from Italy. Of the 1,007,000 Italian military internees captured by the Germans 40 per cent were deported to slave away in Speer's armaments industry. Many died in transit. Overworked, undernourished, ill clothed and brutalised, tens of thousands died in the camps.[25] In Holland, Reich Commissar Seyß-Inquart and Speer's special envoy Richard Fiebig set about plundering the country with such vigour that they sent back to Germany far more than could be handled, whereupon Speer ordered them to call a halt.[26] General Schindler was made responsible for 'removals' in the East, where he had served as Armaments Inspector in Kracau. He set to work with such energy that he stripped the area under his command virtually bare.

The failure of these 'removal' actions was testament to the gradual collapse of Speer's ministry. Priorities were set, but were largely ignored. Blind rapacity overrode a careful consideration of real needs. Germany became flooded with material of which no constructive use could be made. The Armaments Ministry, the military and the Gauleiters all went their own ways. Hitler concentrated on planning the Ardennes offensive, preparation for which made Speer's task even more difficult. Saving what could be salvaged was now left to local authorities and agencies in a desperate, uncoordinated effort to delay the inevitable.

A struggle now began over the demolition of key assets in Germany. Speer sent two senior officials from Organisation Todt to remove the explosives that Hitler had ordered to be placed under bridges over the Rhine. These were stored nearby for immediate use when required. Field Marshal Rundstedt sanctioned these orders. In January two regiments from Organisation Todt, under the Supreme Commander West, were detailed to guard the Rhine bridges to make sure that overly zealous local commanders did not destroy them.[27]

Hitherto the military had supported Speer's efforts to stop over-hasty actions, but on 6 December Keitel informed him that Hitler agreed with his view that the mines in the Saar should be destroyed. Speer reacted to this bombshell by ordering Heinrich Kelchner, his Armaments Plenipotentiary in Saarbrücken, to ensure that none of the mines were destroyed, citing Hitler's previous order to this effect.[28] He then issued instructions that the Hungarian oilfields should be left intact. At his request Army Group A left the hydrogenation plants in Blechhammer (Blachownia) and Heydebreck (Kędzierzyn) in southern Poland untouched.

Speer arrived at Hitler's headquarters at Langenhain-Ziegenberg in northern Hesse at two o'clock in the morning on 1 January 1945. Hitler was in remarkably good spirits and full of an infectious optimism that soon had a group of officers, senior party officials and secretaries, all of whom were well lubricated with champagne, in his thrall. He announced that the new year would bring a series of victories. The group gradually began to share this carefree optimism. Perhaps after all the new year would bring new hope, and the Ardennes offensive be brought to a victorious conclusion, in spite of the failure to take Bastogne.[29]

By contrast the atmosphere at the conference on 3 January was sober and extremely tense. Speer received a nasty shock when Goebbels announced that he was calling for a *levée en masse* that would involve Speer losing several hundred thousand workers to form a military force that would be every bit as worthless as the *Volkssturm*. A horrified Speer said that such a move would lead to the collapse of the armaments industry. Goebbels turned to Hitler, saying 'Herr Speer, you bear the historic responsibility for having lost the war because we lacked a few hundred thousand soldiers!' As Speer subsequently sourly remarked, Hitler and Goebbels thereby opted for victory. Hitler now turned a deaf ear to Speer and addressed all his questions to Saur. In front of Speer, Hitler said 'we are lucky to have in Saur an armaments genius. He will overcome all difficulties.'[30] Goebbels later cruelly remarked to Speer that he found it odd that he had allowed Saur to push him aside. Speer was so outraged that henceforth he seldom attended the armaments conferences with Hitler. Saur now took his place. Speer came bitterly to realise that he too had become a victim of Hitler's habit of addressing his senior colleagues' subordinates directly, thereby undermining their authority.[31] For this reason senior officials were reluctant to bring their advisers with them to meetings with Hitler. From now on, whenever possible, Speer spoke to Hitler on a one-on-one basis. Saur was by now so powerful that he was able to get Hitler to agree to the replacement of General Emil Leeb by General Walter Buhle as head of the Army Armaments Office on 1 February 1945 without any objection from Himmler.[32] On 31 March 1945 Hitler announced: 'Saur is superior to Speer in energy and in the art of improvisation.'[33] Speer now faced the united front of Keitel, Bormann and Goebbels, who convinced Hitler that forty thousand men working in the armaments industry who were born in 1906 or later should be enlisted. A further forty thousand men should be taken from those born between 1901 and 1905. Speer objected vigorously, but was ignored.[34]

Speer later claimed that this confrontation with Goebbels had a profound effect on him. Realising that his relationship with Hitler had become undermined, he attempted to distance himself from this charismatic figure, patron, mentor and companion. He now began to restyle himself as a man who, amid the madness of a regime heading for certain destruction, accepted responsibility for the wellbeing of the German people. He, the young apolitical technocrat, was now fighting a lone battle against those who were determined to bring down an entire people with them and destroy their future livelihoods. The following weeks and months, however, show that this was far from the truth.

Germany's situation was rapidly approaching the catastrophic. On 14 January, Speer informed Hitler that only 31 per cent of the army's requirements for anti-tank and tank ammunition could be met. Only 47 per cent of light artillery and 37 per cent of rocket launchers were available. There was also such an acute shortage of ammunition that a catastrophe was almost inevitable.[35] The supremacy of the Soviet Union along the 2,400 kilometres of the Eastern Front was overwhelming. They had eleven times more infantry, seven times more tanks, twenty times more guns and a twenty-fold superiority in the air.

This note was written two days after the Red Army launched the Vistula-Oder offensive. Marshal Konev's 1st Ukrainian front burst into Upper Silesia. The death marches from the concentration camps began. Auschwitz was liberated on 27 January 1945. By the end of the month, the Red Army had crossed the Nibelungen Line and were within 70 kilometres of Berlin.[36] Shortly after he had given absurdly optimistic addresses to munitions workers and senior military officials, Speer told Goebbels that with the loss of the industrial region of Upper Silesia armaments production would fall by 30 per cent and the war was lost. A diplomatic solution had to be found.[37] He repeated this dire message to Hitler on 30 January 1945 – the anniversary of the 'seizure of power' – stressing the devastating consequences of losing Upper Silesia. The loss of the high-quality coal from the region meant that steel production would henceforth be a mere fraction of the anticipated January 1945 output. The German economy would no longer be able to meet the military's minimum requirements. In January 1944, 23.4 million metric tons of coal were produced in Germany and the General Government and 5.8 million metric tons were imported from the occupied countries. With the loss of Lorraine, the Saar and Upper Silesia, coal supplies were down to 12.1 million metric tons, a drop of nearly 60 per cent.[38]

But that was only the beginning of the problem. Owing to a chronic lack of transport, it would only be possible to use 5.5 to 6 million metric tons of coal for armaments production. Even these figures were probably unduly optimistic. The number of railcars in the Ruhr was down from 22,000 daily to 5,000 or 6,000 daily, and was rapidly dwindling. The amount of coal available for the production of electricity and gas was less than half that of the previous year. Steel production was a mere 10 per cent of that of the previous spring. Further complications arose because often where there was electricity there was no gas. Where there was coal there was no transport. Armaments production was now little more than the assembly of previously manufactured parts. It was now no longer possible to replace losses and to arm fresh units. Ammunition was in alarmingly short supply. The sombre conclusion was that the German economy would collapse within a few months. Speer wrote: 'The bravery of our soldiers can no longer compensate for the material superiority of our opponents.' This letter was signed without the usual 'Heil Hitler!'[39] Speer's widely circulated memorandum at the end of January on prospects for the first quarter of 1945 was mostly a repetition of this depressing litany.[40]

The pressing issue now was what to do with factories near the front that were threatened with being overrun by the Soviet advance. On 19 January Speer issued instructions to the Armaments Commissions in Königsberg, Danzig, Posen, Vienna, Oppeln and Breslau to the effect that there was no need to send machine tools back since there were enough at home. In an outward show of bravado, but with a shrewd eye for post-war reconstruction, he ordered that factories were not to be destroyed, but merely disabled so that they could get back to work as soon as they were recaptured.[41] It is difficult to believe that Speer, who knew exactly how critical the situation had become, imagined that a successful counter-attack against the Red Army could be launched. The Ardennes offensive, Germany's last offensive, had failed.

Keitel and OKW agreed that factories producing armaments should continue working until they came under fire. Bridges over the Oder and the Vistula should only be destroyed on orders from army commanders. Gauleiters were responsible for clearing civilians out of the area 30 kilometres behind the front. This latter proved impossible due to lack of transportation and the rapidity of the Soviet advance.[42] Power supplies were to be kept going as long as possible. Mines were not to be flooded. Under no circumstances were factories to be destroyed. Given the lack of transportation there could be no question of moving entire factories back from the front.[43]

By the end of January Speer devoted most of his efforts to meeting the immediate needs of the population and saving what could be saved. Hitler was prepared to listen to Speer's overall assessment of the armaments situation, but he much preferred Saur's optimistic gloss on the production figures. Speer left armaments to Saur, Hans Kehrl and the armaments officials in the Ruhr, while he rushed around Germany meeting his senior officials and captains of industry in an attempt to persuade them to make Saur see reason. This was an odd approach, quite different to that which he had taken against Dorsch. It was evidence that Speer knew that he was treading on very thin ice. Saur was an awkward opponent. Speer described him as being 'as slippery as an eel'.[44] Saur avoided putting anything in writing and carefully shielded Hitler from uncomfortable truths. Yet Speer still remained in close contact with Hitler, frequently warning him of the seriousness of the situation. His cautioning received a testy reception.[45]

On 5 February 1945 Hitler ordered Speer and Saur to come to his Berlin bunker. Speer was much relieved when Hitler gave them a friendly welcome. Saur fuelled his optimism with some carefully doctored statistics, while Speer remained silent. Hitler concluded the meeting by telling Speer that his only duty was to give him facts and figures. He was strictly forbidden to interpret them in any way. Hitler's coolness as he hissed this order was positively frightening.[46] Speer came away from this uncomfortable encounter with an affirmation of Hitler's order that industry near the front should be disabled, but not destroyed. He made sure that this order was widely circulated to which he added the ambiguous rider that the war could only be won if the Wehrmacht were able to recapture Upper Silesia and the Ruhr. Was this an admission that all was lost, or an appeal for a final desperate effort to save Nazi Germany? Lack of transportation was still the major problem. No relief was in sight. Eight hundred thousand workers were needed solely for the repair and maintenance of the roads and railways. It would therefore be sheer madness to demolish the bridges over the Rhine or disrupt inland shipping.[47]

At the armaments conferences on 14 and 26 February Hitler called for a crash programme to produce Tiger tanks, assault guns and various types of jet aircraft. Special attention was to be paid to making the Arado Ar 234, the world's first operational jet-propelled bomber. Special landing strips would have to be built for this technical marvel, because it landed on skids rather than wheels.[48] Speer remained silent while Saur went along with these fantasies, but he managed to get Hitler to put him in charge of the railways during Dorpmüller's absence on sick leave. This was an important step in Speer's move away from armaments and 'Total War' to prepare for post-war reconstruction.

In line with this new approach, on 14 February Speer had written to the Minister of Finance expressing his concerns about stabilising the Reichsmark. Lutz Graf Schwerin von Krosigk was a lofty aristocrat and Rhodes Scholar, who had been appointed Minister of Finance by von Papen in 1932 and remained in office throughout the Third Reich. He owed this longevity to his singular ineffectiveness, lack of political ambition and willingness to delegate to those more able than himself. Speer suggested the radical measure of confiscating all capital gains made since 1933 and even offered to contribute his own personal fortune to a fund for post-war reconstruction.[49]

Schwerin von Krosigk's counter-suggestion was equally divorced from reality. He had become convinced that the main purpose of the Allied bomber offensive was to raze Germany to the ground so that the country's industrial might would be denied to the Soviet Union. From this dubious premise he concluded that it was essential to do everything humanly possible to preserve German industry so as to be an attractive partner for the Western powers in the post-war world.[50] It is impossible to say how far Speer was influenced by this idea. To have expressed it openly would have been to risk either being arrested for defeatism or simply laughed out of court.

Speer, in his new role as de facto Minister of Transport, drafted a decree to be signed by Hitler ordering priorities for transport as follows: 1. Wehrmacht operations. 2. Coal. 3. Food. 4. The Armaments Ministry's emergency programmes. 5. Refugees.[51] This overlooked the fact that there was no transport available for hundreds of thousands of refugees. Hitler repeated his decision that factories near the front should be disabled but not destroyed.[52] Speer now concentrated on repairing the railway network. On 18 March 1945 he appointed Eckhard Bürger from the Transport Division of Organisation Todt Commissar for the Repair of the Reich Railways. His needs were given top priority, even over Geilenberg's repair crews for the hydrogenation plants. Speer appealed directly to Himmler to provide Bürger with as much labour from the concentration camps as he required.[53]

On 27 February Speer met with a small group of his principal associates at Landsberg Castle, the seat of his Ruhr Staff. The main themes of the meeting were 'the preservation of our industrial base' and 'feeding the people'. Two weeks later he addressed a larger meeting in Bernau bei Berlin at which he stated that he would do everything possible to save industrial plant from destruction by friend or foe.[54] These two meetings form the background to Speer's lengthy memorandum on 15 March entitled 'Implications of the Economic Situation from March to April 1945'.[55]

Speer concluded that with the extensive loss of territory in East and West, with the Ruhr under artillery fire, with the transportation network ruined, and with bomber activity day and night, the economy would probably fall apart within four to eight weeks. The duty of the leadership must now be to do what it could to help the German people. It was therefore essential that industrial plant, mines, electrical generating plant and facilities should not be destroyed. Up until now, essential machinery had been removed in order to put industrial plant that might fall into enemy hands out of action for a couple of months, so that when it was regained it could quickly be put into operation again. This principle should still apply. Industry was every bit as important for the country's survival as was agriculture. Just as it would be unthinkable to poison the land to spite the enemy, so industry had to be saved from destruction. Obviously major bridges had to be destroyed, but it would be ridiculous to blow up every single one. That would do more harm than years of bombing, would make feeding the people impossible and would render the restoration of the transportation network after the war almost impossible. Suddenly reverting to appalling National Socialist rhetoric, Speer argued that the inevitable shortages and sufferings of the German people would lead to a process of 'rigorous selection' that would result in the preservation of a 'healthy core'. The memorandum ended with the rousing words: 'We have the duty to give the people every possible opportunity to be able to rebuild in the distant future.'

There were a number of attachments to this document, including Paul Pleiger's gloomy assessment of the coal situation and the drafts of two decrees for Hitler's signature. The first was to forbid the destruction of roads, railways and bridges as well as the sinking of merchant ships. The second was to stop the destruction of industrial plant and to leave all decisions about the deactivation of industry to Speer's ministry.

Speer wrote another lengthy memorandum, dated 18 March 1945. In this he outlined a defensive strategy along the Rhine and the Oder. Arguing that the territory east of the Oder and west of the Rhine could no longer be held, he suggested that a determined defence of these two rivers for a few weeks 'could win our opponents' respect and perhaps have a favourable influence on the outcome of the war'.[56] At no time did he call for an end to the fighting. To have done so would have been singularly foolhardy. In late January Guderian had told Ribbentrop that the war had to be brought to an end. Ribbentrop replied that he did not have the heart to pass this information on to Hitler, whereupon Guderian asked what he would do if the Russians arrived in Berlin within a month. Hitler seems to have got wind of this exchange. During discussions in which Germany's parlous military situation became all too evident, he announced that it would amount to high treason if the Foreign Minister were to be informed of the true state of affairs. He warned Speer to the same effect.

Speer knew from the stark economic facts that the war could not be won. For him, a favourable outcome of the war would have been something other than the unconditional surrender that Roosevelt had proclaimed at the Casablanca Conference in January 1943, which gave Hitler support for his determination to fight to the bitter end. Speer's fatal mistake was his failure to understand that nothing but a bullet in the head would make Hitler change his mind. Stalin and Churchill, who initially had been strongly opposed to the Casablanca Declaration, were now doggedly determined to enforce the policy, in part for fear that one or the other might make a separate deal with the Germans. Speer now called for a last-ditch stand on the Oder and the Rhine, supported by cannon fodder from the ramshackle *Volkssturm*, the Reserve Army and troops withdrawn from Italy and Norway. He suggested that the Nazi Party should hand over control of the *Volkssturm* to the Army High Command and Speer's ally Guderian. Himmler should do the same with the Reserve Army. The memorandum made it plain that were the 'present front' breached the war could not possibly continue. It seems probable that Speer shared the forlorn hope that the uneasy partnership between the Western Allies and the Soviet Union would fall apart. It was held together by a determination to smash Nazi Germany. Now that the country was on its knees, their task virtually completed, tensions were bound to arise. This was Germany's only hope. The analysis was correct, but only after the war was over.[57]

Speer managed to persuade Guderian that destroying all the bridges would lead to total chaos. Keitel, ever meekly subservient to Hitler, refused to support Speer without the Führer's express permission. Predictably, Hitler refused to change his mind.[58] Guderian then tried another tactic. He suggested to Jodl that an army order could be issued to stop the destruction of bridges. But Jodl also refused to act without Hitler's permission. The capture intact of the Ludendorff Bridge at Remagen on 7 March seriously undermined Speer's argument for saving the country's bridges.

On his return from a visit to western Germany on 14 March 1945 Speer told Goebbels that 'from the economic point of view the war is lost'. Goebbels agreed with Speer that a scorched earth policy in such circumstances was utterly pointless. In his view, it was not theirs but the enemies' task to destroy Germany's economy and food supply.[59] Encouraged by Goebbels' support, Speer prepared another memorandum for Hitler.

Carefully avoiding any hint of provocation, Speer offered a choice between slowly winding down the armaments programme and concentrating on meeting the minimal requirements of the civilian population, or continuing to produce a sizeable amount of material – equivalent to a Panzer Army and twenty squadrons of jet fighters – by the end of March.[60] This was hardly a 'declaration of bankruptcy', as he described it in his memoirs.[61] It was also far more reassuring than the report he had given to Goebbels.

Speer had taken a bold stand against the fanatics in the party and those infected by the *Götterdämmerung* atmosphere in Hitler's bunker. He had not ruled out the possibility that at least some factories could be won back after the war, although it is difficult to believe that he ever thought this to be remotely likely. He had also spiced the memorandum with some social Darwinist codswallop, but the overall tone was in clear defiance of the party line. Thinking over Speer's remarks, Goebbels had to admit that his talk of preserving the basis for the German people's continued existence made perfect sense, but then he managed to persuade himself that Speer was under the immediate influence of what he had seen in the Ruhr. He lacked a truly National Socialist worldview. He was far too much concerned with economics and technology to have the detachment and statesmanlike outlook that would enable him to withstand the highs and lows of warfare. Goebbels told himself that it was exactly during such hard times that one had to hold one's nerve.[62]

On 8 March 1945 Goebbels gave another rousing speech to an entranced audience in Görlitz in which he promised massive offensives on the Eastern Front that would reap merciless revenge on the Soviets for the starving children and raped women they left in their wake. Three days later Speer visited the Eastern Front at Freienwalde Castle on the Oder that had once been Walther Rathenau's home.[63] He travelled with one of his favourite generals, Dr Rudolf Hübner, a dentist in civilian life and a dyed-in-the-wool National Socialist, who was in charge of ideological indoctrination at OKW. On his return to Berlin, Hübner told Hitler that there was not enough ammunition to eliminate the Soviet bridgehead over the Oder. Hitler, who gave the impression of being a very sick man, replied that he needed all the ammunition available for General Schörner, who was preparing an offensive against the Red Army's left flank. He promised miracle weapons would soon be available that would enable the Wehrmacht to drive the Red Army out of Germany within the next four weeks. The officers who witnessed this meeting were so appalled at the ineptness of Hitler's performance that they almost felt sorry for him. Hübner went that same day with his notorious 'Flying Drumhead Court-Martial West' (Fliegendes Standgericht West) to Model's headquarters, where he ordered the execution of four officers whom he held responsible for failing to defend the Ludendorff bridge at Remagen.

Speer tells us that Hitler did not bother even to read the documents that he presented to him in the early hours of 19 March. But he had already given them to Nicolaus von Below, Hitler's adjutant and Speer's friend, who may well have informed Hitler of the contents. He dismissed the Armaments Minister with the words: 'If the war is lost, the people will also be lost. It is not necessary to pay any attention to even the most primitive means of keeping the German people alive. On the contrary, it would be better to destroy them. The people have shown themselves to be the weaker. The future belongs to the stronger Eastern Peoples. Only the inferior will remain after this war. The superior are already dead.'[64] This was a startling declaration of the bankruptcy of National Socialist ideology and testament to its utter inhumanity. As Speer was about to leave, Hitler gave him the portrait that he had requested as a present for his fortieth birthday on 19 March. It had a barely readable dedication as a token of his appreciation.

Hitler had already made up his mind. That same day he issued his 'Nero Order', in which he called for the total destruction of all facilities as the army withdrew, thereby 'weakening our enemies' fighting strength'. He argued that it was an absurd illusion to imagine that the enemy would leave disabled plant intact were they forced to retreat. Communications and power supplies were to be destroyed. He made the military, the Gauleiters and the Reich Defence Commissars responsible for the execution of this order, which was to be passed on to all units of the armed forces.[65] Bormann followed this up a couple of days later with an order that all areas threatened by the enemy were to be evacuated. He realised that this would be a difficult task – he might just as well have said that it was an impossible one – but it had to be carried out.[66] The proclamation of a scorched earth policy amounted to a disavowal of Speer and the armaments industry, but Speer still held some trump cards. He had the full support of the industrialists, bankers and business elite, along with all those in the military and the civil administration who refused to accept the preposterous notion that there was no alternative to national suicide. He also had the support of the

vast majority of the German people, who wanted nothing more than an end
to all the misery and suffering. He also had the distinct advantage that the
communications network had broken down. Orders from Hitler's bunker
seldom reached the front line. Even the most enthusiastic of Gauleiters lacked
the explosives and manpower to carry out the Nero Order. Hitler was eyeless in
Gaza, his strength long gone, never to be recovered.

Speer, who had not been informed of the Nero Order, went to visit Field
Marshal Kesselring at his headquarters in Bad Nauheim. Kesselring had only
been in his new command for a week, having taken over from von Rundstedt as
Supreme Commander West on 11 March. Although he was in a hopeless situa-
tion, without weapons and ammunition, with the Allies pouring over the Rhine,
he was deaf to Speer's appeals to reason and moderation. Known as 'Smiling
Albert' – the result of a nervous tic, not because of his jovial disposition –
Kesselring had unleashed a reign of terror in Italy and was in no mood to show
any mercy. His staff, however, was more level-headed and sympathetic to
Speer's approach. Speer and Hermann Röchling then went to visit Heinrich
Kelchner, the Plenipotentiary for Armaments in the south-west, whose headquarters had moved from Saarbrücken to Heidelberg. The next stop was the
headquarters of Army Group G in the Palatinate under Waffen-SS General Paul
'Papa' Hausser. Although formerly one of Hitler's favourite generals, he was
beginning to question the Führer's strategy.

On the following day, 20 March, Speer managed to get Gauleiter Willi Stöhr
of the Saar-Palatinate on board. He then went to visit Field Marshal Model. It
was here that Speer was first informed of the Nero Order. He was shattered. It
was the exact reverse of the memorandum he had just given to Hitler.[67] He then
returned to Berlin. Hans Maltzacher, the Armaments Plenipotentiary Southeast,
was ordered to report to the ministry to be given his instructions. That afternoon Speer went to the chancellery where he tried to hand General Guderian a
copy of his memorandum to Hitler, but Keitel intervened to stop him. Hitler
brushed Speer off with a few curt words.

Undeterred, Speer, accompanied by leading representatives of the coal
industry, conferred with Guderian the following day. Guderian was accompanied by his trusted chief of staff, General Wolfgang Thomale, along with
General Herbert Gundelach, chief of staff in OKH's pioneer division and
General Ivo-Thilo von Trotha, head of operations at OKH. Dönitz was also
present. The meeting was inconclusive, although there was general sympathy
for Speer's opposition to the Nero Order.

On 24 March 1945 Speer held a conference in the ministry for his senior
staff. Goebbels, with whom Speer had had a fierce argument over the Nero
Order, was also present.[68] That evening, urged on by Rohland, Speer went to the
Ruhr, where negotiations between the armaments authorities and the Gauleiters

had reached a deadlock. Operation Plunder, the Allied offensive over the Rhine and the Weser, had begun the day before. At a meeting of the Ruhr Staff it was decided to carry out Hitler's Nero Order only pro forma by concentrating on deactivation rather than destruction. Reliable miners were to be given automatic pistols so that they could fend off any of the Gauleiters' demolition squads. Later in the day Speer met with the Gauleiters from the Ruhr district: Friedrich Florian from Düsseldorf, Albert Hoffmann from Dortmund, Fritz Schlessmann from Essen and Alfred Meyer from Münster. All but Florian agreed that it was impossible to carry out Hitler's orders, that production should continue as long as possible and that power stations and important industrial plant should be deactivated but not destroyed. That evening Speer and Albert Vögler conferred with Model, who agreed that the Nero Order could not be carried out because it would require at least four thousand tons of explosives. The Field Marshal agreed to remain in close contact with 'Panzer' Rohland and his staff.

Speer then went back to Heidelberg, where he discussed plans with Kelchner on how best to stop the fanatical Robert Wagner, Reich Defence Commissar, Gauleiter of Baden and head of the civil administration in Alsace, from carrying out the Nero Order. Having failed to convince Wagner, Speer met again with General Hausser, who promised to do would he could to restrain the Gauleiter, but Hitler relieved him of his command in early April after a serious disagreement. Wagner did what he could to enforce Hitler's orders with twenty-two rag-tag battalions of *Volkssturm* troops, but when the Americans reached Karlsruhe on 4 April they captured his wife and twelve-year-old daughter. Wagner took to his heels.[69]

On 25 March Field Marshal Kesselring ordered the destruction of all supply facilities, communications, telephone lines and radio transmitters, but agreed that industrial plant should be spared. On the following day the navy ordered the destruction of all ports that were threatened by the enemy. Kesselring repeated his order on 29 March, making both Speer's ministry and the Ministry of Transport responsible for seeing that it was carried out. The Ministry of Transport dutifully forwarded this order to all relevant authorities. Jodl then announced that the Allies were in the area of Frankfurt, Marburg and Siegen. No consideration whatsoever was to be given to the needs of the civilian population. A 'fanatical will to fight' was the order of the day.[70] These orders were either ignored or proved impossible to implement.

Speer had greater success with the Gauleiter of Main-Franconia, Otto Hellmuth. On 27 March he was treated to a lavish breakfast in Würzburg, which had been bombed eleven days previously, causing five thousand deaths and leaving ninety thousand homeless. Hellmuth told Speer that he intended to destroy the ball-bearing factories in Schweinfurt. He then said that Goebbels and Bormann had both told him that the 'miracle weapons' would soon be operational. Speer brusquely announced that such weapons did not exist. He then managed to persuade him that Hitler would not be able to lead his troops to victory without ball-bearings.[71] One week later Hellmuth fled the ruined city.

Speer returned to Berlin that day, where he learnt to his horror that Guderian had been dismissed and replaced by General Hans Krebs, an impeccable National Socialist. He also discovered that SS-Obergruppenführer Hans Kammler, who had wormed his way into Hitler's inner circle, had been given full responsibility for aircraft production and development.[72] Speer cannot have been surprised when he heard that Hitler had been fully informed of his activities in the past few days. According to Goebbels, he was very 'indignant', considering Speer to be a defeatist who was manipulated by the industrialists. He was already considering replacing Speer with Saur. On the other hand, Goebbels had to admit that Hitler had suffered a 'severe loss of authority' through the widespread reluctance to enforce the Nero Order and opposition to the evacuation of the civilian population as the Allied armies advanced.[73]

In his 15 March memorandum Speer had used the argument that it would be better to leave the destruction of Germany to the enemy rather than for it to be self-inflicted. In this way the Grand Alliance would bear the 'historical responsibility' for death and destruction. Speer repeated this dubious argument in a handwritten letter to Hitler on 29 March in which he argued that the enemy should 'take the historical blame upon itself'.[74] He hinted that he was thinking of resigning, but hastily added that this would amount to desertion in the face of the enemy. He confessed that he was torn between a realisation that the war could not be won and the hope that things might turn out for the better. Plunging into the bathetic, he wrote:

> Until 18 March I believed that the situation would improve. I am an artist, but I have done great things for Germany. Without me the war would have been lost in 1942/43. I believe in the future of Germany, in a destiny that is just and inexorable, therefore I believe in God. In the face of great victories we went soft in 1940 and failed to arm sufficiently. The weather has been against us: frost in Moscow, fog in Stalingrad and blue skies in the winter of 1944. I still believed that we could secure our destiny.

Speer claimed to have been shattered when Hitler told him that if the war were to be lost Germany deserved to be destroyed. He then abruptly changed his tune, wildly claiming that new weapons and planes would win the day and that heroic sacrifice would prove decisive. He was prepared to do his bit by taking a glider on a suicide mission to bomb a Soviet power plant, 'thereby, thanks to my own effort, helping to change destiny and to set an example'.

Having worked himself into this sacrificial frenzy, Speer argued that it was impossible to believe in eventual success while destroying everything in sight. It was wrong to destroy all that previous generations had achieved. In a desperate appeal he wrote: 'I can only believe in the future if you, my Führer, agree to the preservation of our racial strength.' The Nero Order had a shattering effect on morale, for it was a confession that all was lost. 'Only a better destiny can change our future. Only a positive attitude and an unwavering faith in the eternal future of our race can help us. God protect Germany. Albert Speer.'

Written as General Patton marched into Frankfurt, it is perhaps understandable that all Speer could offer was empty posturing and appeals to such vague notions as 'destiny', National Socialist ideals, self-sacrifice and faith in some lower-case deity. With shameless disregard for the facts, he once again placed the blame for the present hopeless situation on the failure of his predecessor to put the armaments programme into high gear, while attributing Germany's military setbacks to meteorological misfortune. There is no evidence that Speer actually handed this letter to Hitler. He never claimed that he had done so. Hitler backed off from the Nero Order by agreeing to Speer's proposal to put industrial plant temporarily out of action.

The scene at Hitler's bunker was eerie. With the failure of the offensive in Hungary designed to save the oil wells and with the Americans approaching Würzburg, there was a gloomy sense of an impending downfall. Hitler still considered Speer's reputation as a miracle worker to be such that he could not possibly afford to dismiss him. He therefore decided that he should be sent on sick leave. According to Speer's account of this remarkable incident he refused to give up at such a critical stage, whereupon Hitler asked him to admit that the war was not lost. A lengthy argument followed, ending with Hitler giving Speer twenty-four hours to make up his mind.[75] That Hitler acted so leniently with a man whom he had accused of being a traitor is hard to believe. But these were times in which belief was often seriously challenged.

Speer described Hitler as having been 'almost frightened' when he returned to the bunker the following evening. Having sworn his absolute allegiance, Speer claims that he managed to persuade him to change the Nero Order into an injunction to deactivate industrial plant that was likely to be abandoned. He signed a decree to this effect, drafted by Speer, during their night-time meeting on 28/29 March 1945.[76] In doing so, Hitler was caught by his own faulty argument. If the war was not lost, the struggle must continue. It followed that all available industrial capacity was required. Therefore industry had to continue as long as possible and no resources should be destroyed. Hitler reluctantly backed away from the Nero Order by making Speer responsible for carrying out a deactivation programme. Speer had been so confident that he could convince Hitler to change his mind that he had already issued the Gauleiters orders to this effect. The fact of the matter was that there was such opposition to the Nero Order that there was little possibility of it being carried out in full. Industrialists and workers had no desire to destroy the means of their future livelihoods. Generals Heinrici, Thomale, Hausser and Model were in full agreement with Speer. It had been relatively easy to persuade most of the Gauleiters, with the exception of a fanatic like Friedrich Karl Florian in Düsseldorf, that the Nero Order was pointless. Keitel and Jodl at OKW were almost alone in their slavish obedience to Hitler's whims. That the Nero Order proved to be a damp squib was testament to the fact that Hitler was no longer the all-powerful Führer and was rapidly losing control. Speer was quick to realise this. As he later wrote, Hitler ruled in the bunker, but above ground a different system applied.[77]

The new decree, countersigned by Speer – his signature miniaturised so as not to dwarf the tiny stylised 'AH' – ordered factories near the front to continue working for as long as possible, even if there were a possibility that a factory might be captured by the enemy undamaged. Furthermore it was Speer, not the military or the Gauleiters, who was to decide whether a factory should be destroyed.[78] The Nero Order was thereby formally repealed.

In the following days Speer heavily emphasised Hitler's change of heart. On 30 March he sent a widely circulated message stating that Hitler had insisted that a scorched earth policy might be appropriate for a vast country such as Russia, but that in a relatively small space like Germany it was utterly pointless. In a further order he repeated that it was he alone who had the authority to decide which factories were to be destroyed. Since they were to continue working 'until the very last moment, even in the most difficult circumstances', it was unlikely that Speer would ever issue a destruction order.[79] On 31 March Speer attended a meeting of OKW at which he triumphantly presented Hitler's order that factories near the front should be disabled but not destroyed. He also told the generals that the bridge over the Alte Oder at Oderberg was to be left intact.[80]

The more zealous of the Gauleiters elected to ignore Hitler's change of heart. Speer had to remind Gauleiter Siegfried Uiberreither of Styria – the man responsible for a murderous Germanisation programme in Slovenia – that the Nero Order had been rescinded. He felt constrained to repeat that weirs, locks and dams were not to be destroyed until he issued orders to that effect. In another note he pointed out that the 'last moment' order also applied to building sites. Again he repeated that railways, roads and inland waterways were to be left intact, pending his decision. On 5 April 1945 he pointed out that Field Marshal Walther Model desperately needed the railways, roads, shipping and communications in his rear echelons. He issued a series of orders protecting specific factories from the destructive zeal of fanatical Gauleiters and party officials. These included the ball-bearing factories around Schweinfurt,

Daimler-Benz and Bosch in Stuttgart and the Zeiss works in Jena. He was outraged when he learnt that the Henschel works in Kassel that produced Tiger tanks had been put out of action prematurely. The same had happened with light howitzer production in Markstädt (Jelcz-Laskowice). Speer repeatedly insisted that it was his ministry that had to decide when to take action, not the military.[81]

There was some confusion, however, because the nebulous concept of 'military necessity' in certain circumstances gave commanders on-the-spot authority to act without orders from above. Speer reissued an earlier decree from Hitler, which he countersigned, stating that operationally significant bridges could only be demolished on orders from OKW, but other bridges should be kept open as long as possible, as should roads and railways. Communications should only be disrupted, but not disabled. The key point was still that production should continue as long as possible.[82] Model reached an agreement with Speer that 'military objects' were the province of the military, whereas Speer had full responsibility for 'economic objects'. It was further agreed that feeding foreign workers was the responsibility of National Socialist Welfare, the German Work Front and the District Agricultural Offices. Prisoners of war were to be fed by the military.[83] It was a system that guaranteed that precious little would be made available for these poor wretches.

The situation in Germany was rapidly heading towards chaos. Communications had broken down, orders did not reach their destination and when they did there was often no means of carrying them out. Speer rushed around in his open BMW issuing directives that contained little but vacuous appeals to providence, destiny and accountability. It is difficult to imagine how people were expected to respond to a message such as the following, issued in mid-April: 'Everyone who fails in their duty towards the people's continued existence will be marked, even in the distant future, by an historical disgrace that will reap a bitter revenge ... The destiny of this our German people is crucial. Destiny will protect it for ever and ever.'[84] Amid all this turmoil at least Speer earned the heartfelt thanks of the Ruhr barons, such as Albert Vögler and 'Panzer' Rohland, for saving industry from the destructive instincts of Nazi fanatics and suicidal soldiers.[85]

Speer was later to give a graphic account of his desperate struggle with Hitler to countermand the Nero Order. It was a major reason why he did not receive a death sentence at Nuremberg. Did he not deserve a degree of clemency for risking his life to save his country from total destruction by a crazed dictator? None of this is reflected in the archival evidence. Hitler issued the Nero Order, but it was only implemented in a few isolated cases. A few days later it was rescinded, with Hitler returning to his previous position. The Nero Order was an admission that all was lost. This was something Hitler still refused to admit. The logic of Speer's approach was that Germany should continue fighting, buoyed up by the belief that it might be possible to regain at least some of what had been lost. He still refused openly to concede the obvious truth that the end was very near.

Speer's authority had been seriously undermined, but as long as Hitler was reluctant to dismiss him he was relatively secure. The military prepared to topple Hitler's crown prince and drew up plans for a new armaments organisation under OKW, but there was no time left for these fundamental changes to be implemented.[86] After the war Speer claimed to be Germany and Europe's saviour. Had he not saved Germany from Hitler's Nero Order, while at the same time continuing the struggle as long as possible so as to save western Europe from the Bolshevik hordes?[87]

Precisely what happened in these chaotic last few weeks of the Third Reich is very difficult to reconstruct. Speer was successful at Nuremberg in styling himself as Hitler's staunch opponent, who through his tireless efforts spared the country from the consequences of his destructive genius. He was given self-serving support in the testimony of his closest advisers, such as his adjutant Manfred von Poser and 'Panzer' Rohland. It was reinforced by his own carefully edited account.[88] It has to be said, however, that it is to Speer's credit that he put a significant amount of effort, and ran considerable risks, in doing what he could to countermand Hitler's orgy of destruction.

By now Speer was acting more or less in limbo, intent on securing a strong position in the post-war world. On 4 April 1945 he prepared for his new life in civilian clothes by buying a hat from Elizabeth Kraft's millinery shop on the Fasanenstrasse 26, a street where once the liberal synagogue had stood.[89] Speer remained remarkably calm amid all the turmoil and looked forward to a successful career in the post-war world. He organised a highly successful concert in Berlin with Brahms' first symphony and the Schumann Piano Concerto, with Wilhelm Kempff as soloist. He then hosted a musical evening at a villa on the Wannsee. Speer chose Kempff, the young virtuoso violinist Gerhard Taschner and his pianist wife Gerda Netta Taschner to perform for a carefully selected audience. Admiral Dönitz, who was also a music lover, was the guest of honour. Kempff began with some Handel, then at Speer's request he played the Kreutzer Sonata with Taschner. This was followed by the Taschners playing the César Frank Violin Sonata. Then Kempff played pieces by Schumann, Chopin and Liszt. Champagne having been served during the interval, Taschner and Kempff entertained Speer's guests with a display of virtuoso pieces.[90] This lavish soirée does not quite square with Speer's expressions of indignation in his memoirs at the comfortable lifestyle enjoyed by the Nazi elite at a time when ordinary Germans were suffering such deprivation.[91]

The main concern of Speer and the Ruhr Staff in late March and early April 1945 was to stop the unnecessary demolition of bridges during the battle of the Ruhr pocket in which the 430,000 German soldiers in Army Group B were trapped. On 8 April Vögler and Rohland persuaded Model not to destroy bridges that carried water, electricity and gas lines. On 11 April the Americans arrived at the Villa Hügel in Essen, where Alfried Krupp awaited them. By 12 April General von Lüttwitz told the Ruhr Staff that the situation in the Ruhr pocket was hopeless, but on the following day Hitler ordered Army Group B to fight to the last man. A failed attempt was made to persuade General Wagener, Model's chief of staff, that the situation was hopeless and that he should surrender to avoid needless casualties. On 15 April General Fritz Bayerlein, who had served as Rommel's chief of staff in North Africa and now commanded LIII Army Corps, defied Hitler's orders and surrendered at Menden. He was the first German general to lay down his arms. The Americans captured General von Lüttwitz on the following day. Field Marshal Model, who had given his solemn oath to Hitler that he would not surrender, blew his brains out in a wood near Duisburg on 21 April. He left a note behind that read: 'The stress of wartime experience has revealed that a considerable portion of the German people, even among the troops, are poisoned by a Jewish, democratic and materialist way of thinking.' In these circumstances the Field Marshal's boast that 'the victory of the National Socialist idea is indubitable' carried little conviction.[92]

On 15 April Speer met General Heinrici, the commander of Army Group Vistula, General Kinzel, his chief of staff, and General Reymann, the commander of the Berlin Defence Area, in an attempt to get them to persuade Hitler not to defend Berlin to the last and to stop the destruction of essential services in the city. Henrici agreed that a scorched earth policy was misguided. Reymann was not convinced by Speer's arguments, but promised to consult Henrici before undertaking any demolitions. This did not save his skin. Hitler charged him with defeatism and he was dismissed on 22 April. Henrici was relieved of his command one week later.

On 9 April Speer drafted a radio talk that was edited, possibly by Hitler.[93] Again he sang a hymn of praise to the outstanding efforts of the armaments industry, which he claimed was still at the 1943 level. He singled out the primitive anti-tank weapon the *Panzerfaust* as a particular achievement. But he cautioned that 'it is mistaken to believe that miracle weapons will soon appear'. He made the dubious claim that the bombing raids had not affected production, but he failed to mention that the transportation network had been so badly disrupted that such weapons as were produced could not be brought up to the front. In a particularly rich passage he claimed that when the foreigners and prisoners of war who had worked in the armaments industry went home after the war they would be full of praise for the 'social comradeship that had been shown them'. Speer claimed that all 'racial comrades' were convinced that they would overcome every obstacle and challenge, thereby achieving a 'Final Victory'. Fortunately this piece of wishful thinking was never broadcast.

Three days later, on 12 April, at Speer's instigation, the Berlin Philharmonic Orchestra under Wilhelm Furtwängler gave a final concert in the Philharmonic Hall in Berlin. The audience was treated to Beethoven's Violin Concerto, Bruckner's 'Romantic' symphony – Speer's favourite – and, appropriately enough, the end of *Götterdämmerung*. Speer had told the orchestra, as well as a number of friends and colleagues, that when Bruckner's fourth appeared in the programme the end was near. It would then be prudent to go into hiding. It is reported that the significance of the Wagner was underlined when uniformed members of the Hitler Youth held baskets full of cyanide tablets that were offered to the audience as they left. Speer professed to have been horrified at this macabre spectacle, which he attributed to some unknown party functionary.[94] Hitler was in a more buoyant mood that day. He had just heard of Roosevelt's death, which he saw as an omen of victory. This was surely equivalent to the providential death of the Empress Elizabeth of Russia that had saved Frederick the Great from defeat in January 1762. Goebbels, however, was less sanguine.

On 14 April Speer wrote to his old friend and patron, the Gauleiter of Lower Silesia, Karl Hanke, who had been leading a fanatical defence of Breslau since mid-February which was to result in 29,000 civilian and military casualties. He said that Germany would not suffer defeat because of the likes of Hanke, who was one of the country's greatest heroes. He had set an example of inestimable value. Speer wished him a 'wonderful and distinguished death' at the head of his troops.[95] Hanke fled the city in a Fieseler 'Stork', but was captured by Czech troops. He was wounded and then clubbed to death while trying to escape from a column of German prisoners of war. His demise was thus neither wonderful nor distinguished. He died without knowing that in his will Hitler had appointed him to replace Himmler as head of the SS in recognition of his stalwart character.

Speer's motives for writing this curious letter are not clear. Hanke had some time since distanced himself from his former friend, whom he felt was accumulating far too much power and influence. Speer had been very hurt when Hanke had appointed Hermann Giesler as the architect charged with planning the rebuilding of Breslau. Giesler agreed with Hanke that Speer was stepping out of line by aspiring to be Hitler's successor. When Speer complained, Hanke replied that he had felt that he was far too busy to be troubled with such an onerous commission.[96] This gibe was particularly galling because Giesler, strongly supported by Bormann, had by now replaced Speer as Hitler's favourite architect. Hanke was clearly aligned with Himmler, Kammler and Ohlendorf against Speer. The letter was at best a last-minute attempt to mend bridges, but much more likely a cynical expression of the hope that Hanke would indeed meet a gloriously heroic death, thereby ridding Speer of a powerful rival.

On 20 April 1945 Speer attended Hitler's fifty-sixth birthday celebration in the Berlin bunker. The celebrant was treated to a display of new weapons in the courtyard of the Reich Chancellery.[97] It is not recorded whether this offered him any encouragement. Anxious to make financial plans for the uncertain future while in Berlin, Speer obtained a grant of 30,000 Reichsmarks for 'travelling expenses' from the financial section of his Berlin building department (GBI).[98] On the following day he drove to Hamburg, where he recorded a speech at the radio station that was to be broadcast as soon as Berlin fell. Gauleiter Kaufmann was in full agreement with Speer that Hamburg should be surrendered rather than be defended in a pointless last-ditch stand. A request to Hitler to this effect met with a glacial refusal. Kaufmann ignored his orders and surrendered the city on 3 May.

With Berlin encircled, Admiral Dönitz was appointed commander of 'Fortress North', with responsibility for the government's safety. Contrary to his self-constructed post-war image, Dönitz was a zealous Nazi who was utterly devoted to Hitler and determined to fight on until the bitter end. He was widely known as 'Hitlerjunge Quex', after the dauntless young hero of a propaganda film, for his slavish commitment to the Führer.[99] On 21 April 1945 Dönitz moved his cabinet to Eutin in Schleswig-Holstein where Count Lutz Schwerin von Krosigk chaired the daily cabinet meetings. Speer was the only minister who visited Dönitz regularly. Himmler stayed in Lübeck and Ribbentrop in Plön, some 10 kilometres distant. Goebbels and Bormann remained behind in the bunker. Rust and Rosenberg soon moved to Schleswig-Holstein, near Flensburg.

The principal problem facing the 'Cabinet North' was what to do with Himmler. Most wanted to distance themselves from a man who was so clearly identified with the less savoury aspects of the regime. Speer, the Minister of Labour Franz Seldte, Herbert Backe, who had recently been made Minister without Portfolio, and the Minister of Transport, Julius Dorpmüller, argued that Lutz von Schwerin von Krosigk should replace Ribbentrop as Foreign Minister and should be seriously considered as a suitably anodyne successor to Adolf Hitler as Chancellor.[100]

Having left Hamburg, Speer visited Field Marshal Ernst Busch at the headquarters of Army Group Northwest. He faced the hopeless task of stopping Montgomery's advance with utterly demoralised troops and a handful of fanatical officers who showed him no respect. Speer, who was now effectively unemployed because the armaments industry no longer functioned, flew back to Berlin on 23 April 1945 in a single-engined Fieseler 'Stork'. Ostensibly it was to pay a farewell visit to Hitler, but clearly there was another reason. He had already bid adieu to the Führer at the gloomy birthday party three days earlier. He claims to have already reached the conclusion that Hitler was a 'criminal' and that he had nothing but the utmost contempt for all those in his inner circle who remained with him in the bunker. Why was it, then, that he undertook such a hazardous journey? Neither his biographer, Fest, nor his publisher, Siedler, was able to get a satisfactory answer from Speer to this question.[101] One possible explanation is that he wanted to persuade Hitler to appoint him as his successor. He certainly saw himself as a suitable candidate. 'I was for him [Hitler] a gifted artist, who within a short space of time had won a powerful position within the political hierarchy and after all had shown outstanding ability in the military field by my efforts in armaments. It was only in the field of foreign affairs, Hitler's other area of expertise, that I had not shown any particular skills. In his eyes I was probably an artistic genius who was politically artful and thus was indirectly a confirmation of his own career.'[102] His close associates such as Hettlage, Brugmann and Kehrl used to make fun of his political ambitions, pointing out that Göring, Bormann and Goebbels – not to mention Himmler – were far more experienced and effective in-fighters. Speer's position depended entirely on his close relationship with Hitler. Were Hitler to die, he would be left powerless.[103]

Speer persistently regarded himself as number two in the Third Reich, even though Giesler had clearly taken his place as Hitler's favourite architect. Saur was in charge of armaments. Kammler had taken over V2 and aircraft production. Dorsch was effectively in control of Organisation Todt. Without any supporting evidence, Speer imagined that he was a popular figure, who, with his proven ability as an administrator, was the ideal person to head a transitional government after Hitler's death.[104]

Much to his surprise, Speer was given a friendly welcome by his old enemy Bormann, who tried to charm him into persuading Hitler to move to Berchtesgaden in order to establish an alpine redoubt. Ignoring this request, Speer went straight to Hitler. He found him exhausted and lifeless, having been overcome by paroxysms of rage the day before, when he had been told that the Red Army had broken through the Oder front and that General Steiner had been unable to launch a counter-attack. He asked Speer for his opinion of Dönitz, who, as commander of the forces in the north, had offered to send troops to Berlin to defend the bunker. Speer had no choice but to give a positive reply, although he must have been disappointed at this hint that Hitler was thinking of the Grand Admiral as a possible successor.[105] Hitler surprisingly agreed to Speer's extraordinary suggestion that the Czech directors of the Škoda works in Prague, who had excellent relations with the Americans and with whom Speer worked closely, should appeal to the Western Allies to save Czechoslovakia from Soviet communism. Hans Frank, the former 'King of

Poland' who had fled to Bavaria, had come up with the idea of establishing a nationalist anti-communist government in Prague and then moving all German troops, officials and nationals back to Germany.[106] This was but one of many instances of minds becoming unhinged as the Third Reich fell apart.

Hitler could not resist the temptation to deliver a parting blow to his guest. He remarked that he had recently discussed the plans for rebuilding Linz with 'good old Giesler' and that he had given Eva Braun authority over the city's business district, promenades and parks. She had, he stressed, very distinct ideas on the subject.[107] Speer was then dismissed without a handshake. No mention was made of a successor. Speer then went to say farewell to his friends Magda Goebbels and Eva Braun. He spent the hours between midnight and three in the morning with Eva Braun, who unlike all the others in the bunker appeared to be her normal balanced self. They drank champagne and nibbled cakes in her small bedroom. Speer had always made every effort to remain on close terms with Eva Braun, in part because she afforded valuable access to Hitler, but also because he genuinely enjoyed her company.[108] Then he went to say a final goodbye to Hitler, who murmured: 'So you are off. *Auf Wiedersehen*.' Thus ended twelve years of close collaboration and the nearest thing to a friendship that Hitler ever achieved.[109]

Having no desire to take part in the orgy of self-immolation that was being prepared, shortly before dawn Speer and von Poser left Berlin and flew to Rechlin in Mecklenburg. Himmler was at the nearby Hohenlychen clinic where Speer had been treated in 1944. That he chose this spot is further evidence of his closeness to Himmler and Professor Gebhardt, which was soon to prove most embarrassing.[110] Himmler, who was attempting to negotiate with the Allies via contacts in Sweden, told Speer that he hoped to form a new government with Göring as Minister President. Himmler offered Speer a post in the new government, which would immediately begin negotiations with the Allies. Speer, well aware that the Allies were not particularly well disposed towards the Reichsführer-SS, declined the offer. Himmler announced that the Allies would need his expertise in law enforcement in post-war Europe. Half an hour with Eisenhower would suffice to convince him to this effect.[111] Leaving Himmler to ponder his future, Speer hastened on to Hamburg, where he made a new recording of the speech he had given Gauleiter Kaufmann. He asked him to wait for a day or two before it was broadcast. On 30 April 1945 he was with Dönitz in Eutin when he heard that Hitler had committed suicide. He was bitterly disappointed, not only that Dönitz had been appointed Hitler's successor as president, but also that he was not even included in the government. As a final insult Hitler had appointed his old rival Saur in his place. Unpacking his suitcase he discovered Hitler's portrait in its leather case. The shakily written inscription spoke of Hitler's 'everlasting friendship'. Speer found this so moving that he burst into floods of tears.

Disappointment and sorrow soon gave way to relief. The fact that Hitler had rejected him could be used to reinforce Speer's argument that he had resisted him in the final months of the Third Reich. This was to be the basis of his defence at Nuremberg and his subsequent transformation into the exaggeratedly contrite 'Good Nazi'. The way now seemed open for him to transform himself into an apolitical minister of industrial reconstruction.

On 2 May the Dönitz government moved from Eutin to Flensburg on the Danish border, but Speer went with Himmler to Bad Bramstedt. This was a curious move, because Dönitz had already made it plain that he did not want anything to do with Himmler. A possible explanation is that Keitel had assured Himmler of his support and Speer needed to find a way to convince OKW to stop the needless destruction of bridges and communications. Perhaps he was simply waiting upon events. When Himmler heard of the Führer's suicide the champagne was uncorked and toasts were made along the lines of 'The king is dead, long live the king!' He once again announced that as an experienced upholder of law and order, the Allies would welcome his services in the struggle against Bolshevism.[112] Both men then joined Dönitz in Flensburg, but Dönitz refused Himmler's offer of help.

The speech that Speer had recorded in Hamburg was broadcast on 3 May. In the original recorded version Speer was full of praise for the 'hardiness, toughness and faith' of the German people. He warned that faith should not turn into despair, and that exhaustion and indifference should not take the place of hardiness and resilience. He appealed to the Allies to stop the bombing campaign in order to save the German people from hunger and disease. Above all else the German people must be saved from the Red Army. The first priorities were now to repair the railway system and to ensure that agricultural production went into top gear. Explosive charges on bridges must be defused, and further destruction of property stopped. All prisoners of war were to remain in their camps. In the concentration camps political prisoners and Jews were to be separated from the 'anti-social and criminal elements', who were to be sent to correctional institutions. Himmler's 'Werwolf', designed to operate behind enemy lines, was to be disbanded. Speer ended by calling upon the people to be 'inwardly more modest and self-critical'.[113] He had thus already thought of how best to prepare himself against the charges that the victors were likely to lay against him. The reworked version of the speech as broadcast was very different. There was no mention of the Werwolf, the concentration camps, defusing explosives, or of stopping all further destruction. The main emphasis now was on the threat posed by the Red Army.[114]

On 5 May 1945 Speer was appointed Minister of Economics and Production in a newly formed government. But this was an empty appointment. Dönitz's government had no real authority. Keitel and OKW made all major decisions.

Unconditional surrender was a matter to be settled by the military alone. The Allies and the Soviets had no intention of negotiating with civilians and certainly not with Speer. It is therefore hardly surprising that he announced that he saw his appointment as purely temporary. There was little he could do. Six men in the ministry ran the economy with eight assistants, all under the command of Otto Ohlendorf, who was also still head of the domestic section of the Reich Security Main Office.

There were two sides to the Dönitz government. Among the conservative nationalists, most of whom had a certain affinity with National Socialism, were Schwerin von Krosigk, Franz Seldte and Julius Dorpmüller. Then there were the National Socialists: Speer, Herbert Backe, Ohlendorf and the Minister of the Interior Wilhelm Stuckart. The difference between them can clearly be seen in the draft telegrams written in reply to Hitler's appointment of Dönitz as his successor. The first, drafted by Captain von Davidson, head of the navy's intelligence services, read: 'My Führer! I have received your orders. I shall justify your confidence by doing everything possible to ensure that the German people are treated in the best possible manner, just as you would wish.' The second, written by Speer, has quite a different tone: 'My Führer! My loyalty to you is undying and unconditional. I shall therefore do everything possible to help you in Berlin. When destiny demands that I should be your successor to lead the German Reich, as you have determined, I shall bring this war to an end as this unparalleled heroic struggle of the German people demands.' Dönitz accepted Speer's tortuous version.[115]

Both sides knew that the war was lost, that fundamental changes had to be made and that the status quo could not possibly be maintained. The ship was rapidly sinking, but Speer was not yet prepared to swim away from it. In the draft of a speech to be given by Dönitz on 1 May he wrote that Hitler's personal qualities and his visionary understanding of the dire threat posed to Western civilisation by Soviet communism would eventually be appreciated. The struggle had to be continued as long as possible in the East, while in the West it should merely be a holding operation. The destruction of property and infrastructure should be minimal. The speech ended with familiar appeals to comradeship, discipline and hopes for a better future. It concluded on a rousing note: 'Germany shall remain for ever and ever. God protect Germany!'[116] Speer was still totally in thrall to Hitler, his thinking shackled by National Socialist clichés. Dönitz's broadcast version was along much the same lines. He wrote of Hitler's 'heroic death', which he 'mourned in awe', and warned of the 'Bolshevik storm tide'. In marked difference to Speer's more nuanced effort, he blamed the Western Allies for continuing a war that was leading to 'the spread of Bolshevism throughout Europe'.

Speer was wise enough to know that the war had to be ended as soon as possible. He had the full support in this regard from Schwerin von Krosigk.

The alternative was a continuation of the bomber offensive and the destruction of industrial plant, bridges, roads and port facilities, along with the deaths of a countless number of refugees. The modality of the surrender was a matter for the military, but its urgency was a political imperative. In the discussions over whether the fighting should continue in Denmark and Norway, the Wehrmacht and the Reich Commissar in Norway Terboven argued in favour, with the commander of the German troops in Denmark, General Georg Lindemann, promising 'one last decent battle'. Speer and Schwerin von Krosigk, however, called for the immediate cessation of hostilities.[117]

After the surrender of German troops in north-west Germany on 4 May two men who were closely associated with Speer – Herbert Backe as Minister of Agriculture and Julius Dorpmüller as the head of the Reichsbahn – were taken to the Parisian suburb of Le Chesnay to discuss post-war reconstruction.[118] This came as a bitter blow to Speer who had heard through secret service reports from Switzerland that the Allies regarded him and Field Marshal von Brauchitsch as the only two men with whom they could do business. It is strange that Speer could have believed this rumour. Brauchitsch had retired to a hunting lodge in Bohemia on 19 December 1941. Speer's belief that his services might be needed by the victorious powers was as delusional as Himmler's.

On 6 May Dönitz stripped Himmler of all his many offices. Alfred Rosenberg and the Gauleiter and Premier of Schleswig-Holstein, Hinrich Lohse, both of them key players in the murder of the European Jews, were also dismissed. Next day Schwerin von Krosigk, who was effectively head of Dönitz's government, announced Germany's unconditional surrender to the Allies. At one minute past midnight the following day – 8 May 1945 – the war officially ended. The Dönitz government still formally existed, although it was utterly powerless. Speer was entrusted with the affairs of the Minister for Food, Agriculture and Forests but there was nothing for him to do.[119] On 15 May he told Schwerin von Krosigk that he felt that he was not a suitable person to conduct negotiations with the victors because of his political past, thereby overlooking the fact that the Allies had not the slightest intention of negotiating with him. He also felt that he was unsuited to the tasks that lay ahead. With a side-swipe at Ribbentrop he said: 'I am an architect. It is every bit as thankless a task to give an artist responsibility for debt redemption as it was to hand over the foreign ministry to a sparkling wine salesman.'[120] Here he seems to have forgotten that he had not raised this objection to Hitler when he pushed Funk aside in the autumn of 1943. He went on to say that: 'The former leadership of the German people has joint responsibility [Gesamtschuld] for the German people's future. Everyone who took part in this government must carry his share of the burden so that the blame which otherwise would rest on the shoulders of the German people should be borne by individuals.' It was a deliberately ambiguous statement. The German word *Schuld* can also mean guilt, debt, liability, or blame. Was Speer aware that propitiation was to prove even harder than economic recovery, or was he already thinking how best to prepare his defence?

Speer made repeated offers to resign until, on 23 May, he was arrested, along with Jodl and Dönitz, by a unit of the British Army. He was given a preliminary interrogation by three men who were to play leading roles in post-war America: George Ball, John Kenneth Galbraith and Paul Nitze, all from the United States Strategic Bombing Survey. It took place in Speer's headquarters at Glücksburg Castle, the magnificent seat of the Dukes of Schleswig-Holstein, where he had previously been lodged at the duke's invitation. He gave what appeared to be precise and practical information on the effects of Allied bombing. Galbraith found him quite unlike the other Nazis. 'It was evident by his behaviour that he had every intention of putting the greatest distance between himself and the primitives, as he regarded them.'[121] Nitze was struck by the pride Speer showed in his achievements as Minister of Armaments and by his willingness to assist the Allies in bringing the Pacific War to a swift conclusion.[122]

Speer was soon moved to 'Camp Ashcan', the luxurious Palace Hotel at Mondorf-les-Bains, Luxemburg, where the major war criminals were held in temporary custody. A couple of weeks later he was driven in a comfortable limousine to the Trianon Palace Hotel at Versailles. Curiously enough this was a favourite hotel of Speer's. He had stayed there while attending the World Exhibition in 1937. It now served as Eisenhower's headquarters. He was then taken to the elegant chateau at nearby Le Chesnay. There, among a number of prominent experts, engineers and scientists, Speer found some of his close associates. Since he had no idea about the technical side of his former ministry, he told the interrogating officers to address all such questions to his deputy and rival, Karl-Otto Saur. The camp commandant, a charming British paratrooper major, kindly offered to take him for drives to relieve the boredom. They went first to Saint-Germain, then drove past Le Coq Hardi at Bougival where Speer had dined with Cortot, Vlaminck and other famous artists in 1937. They then drove to Paris, where they took a stroll along the Seine, before returning to Le Chesnay via Saint-Cloud. Speer's frequent letters to his wife and family show that he was in good spirits, untroubled by any pangs of conscience and convinced that he would emerge from the interrogation process unscathed. He took comfort in the fact that in Schiller's three-part play, *Wallenstein*, the protagonist, cuts quite a good figure. 'So I have a good chance of being decently treated in subsequent dramas.'[123]

When Eisenhower moved his headquarters to Frankfurt, Speer and the other internees were moved in the back of a truck, sitting on wooden benches,

to Langenhain-Ziegenberg in northern Hesse, where the Allies had set up
'Camp Dustbin' at Kransberg Castle, which Speer and Todt had converted into
the luxurious 'Eagle's Nest' or *Adlerhorst* headquarters for Hitler in September
1939 in preparation for the invasion of France. It was then assigned to Göring
during the Battle of Britain and served as Hitler's headquarters during the
Ardennes offensive. Speer remained there until he was moved to Nuremberg
on 10 August 1945 to await his trial.[124]

CHAPTER TWELVE

NUREMBERG

T HE INMATES OF Camp Dustbin were mostly engineers, industrialists, bankers and civil servants. Among them were Hjalmar Schacht, most of the board of directors of IG Farben, Ferdinand Porsche and Wernher von Braun. A number of Speer's closest associates – Karl-Otto Saur, Karl Maria Hettlage, Walther Dornberger and Theodor Hupfauer – were also among the prisoners.

These men deeply resented being kept in custody, which they considered to be in breach of international law and a further example of the Allies' insufferable habit of vaunting their moral superiority.[1] They imagined that at most they would be called upon as witnesses in the trials of the prominent National Socialists held at Camp Ashcan, the luxurious Palace Hotel in Mondorf-les-Bains, Luxemburg. Speer had no feeling of ever having done anything wrong. His self-righteousness was reinforced when it appeared as if the Allies regarded him as being in a quite different category from the likes of Göring, Sauckel, Streicher or Ribbentrop. The inmates of Camp Dustbin were free to wander around the castle grounds. The wrought-iron gates remained open. They were adequately fed on U.S. Army rations. They passed the time by giving talks, listening to Schacht's poetry and by staging a weekly cabaret mounted by the inmates that made light of their fate.

Speer cooperated fully with the American authorities. He had long conversations with a pleasant interrogation officer, Captain Oleg Hoeffding, during which he gave a detailed account of the politics and politicians of the Third Reich.[2] His assessments of Hitler and the leading figures in the Third Reich were more direct, nuanced and revealing than in the expertly edited and polished version in his memoirs. The same is true of his descriptions of Hitler's loyal followers: Bormann, Göring, Goebbels and Himmler. Speer's account of the shortcomings of the military command structure and the disastrous role played by Keitel is particularly revealing. He had not yet begun the elaborate reconstruction of his past. He admitted that as Minister of Armaments he was 'directly involved in many political decisions'.[3] He spoke well of the vast majority of his associates, but had harsh words for his rivals Dorsch and Saur.[4] The question of anti-Semitism was hardly raised, although Speer did make brief mention of the pogrom of 9 November 1938 unfortunately known as 'The Night of Broken Glass', although he professed not to have remembered the date.[5]

While at Camp Dustbin he wrote a memorandum that he entitled 'The Future Development of the German Problem in Europe'.[6] It makes for curious reading. His admiration for Hitler, the man whose manic destructive urges he had apparently tried to curb, was unreserved: 'Adolf Hitler was rooted in the people [Volk]. His irreproachable lifestyle and unflagging diligence are well known. He is a figure that cannot be ignored.' National Socialism was an ideology that was basically sound. The problem was that Hitler's underlings were second-rate individuals who sent others to a certain death while keeping themselves well out of harm's way.

Speer's plan for a future Germany was based on a modified form of National Socialism. The 'racial community' was to be transformed into a centrally administered 'comradely commonwealth'. For the time being there would be no elections and technocrats rather than professional politicians would be in command. This new Germany closely resembled a vast Ministry of Armaments. Speer, who styled himself as 'a person with a wide range of interests, clear vision and excellent organisational ability', was obviously destined to play a key role. The country was to be firmly allied with the Western powers. His fellow-prisoner Hans Kehrl claims that Speer initially imagined that the Allies would make use of the distinguished experts at Camp Dustbin to help rebuild Germany. He was asked to draw up a list of people with a clean record who would be suitable for such a task.[7] Speer was confident that he would have a splendid career in a future Germany that retained all that was good about Nazism. He was therefore profoundly shocked when at six o'clock one morning he was awoken with the shattering news that he and Hjalmar Schacht were on the list of the major criminals that were to be tried at Nuremberg.[8]

That same day the British camp commandant took Speer for an unguarded drive through the delightful Taunus hillside country. Speer was regaled with stories of bear hunting in Kashmir as they strolled through the forest. Sergeant Williams gave him extra rations so that he could build up his strength for the forthcoming trial. The Americans assured him that he would be acquitted and that his ordeal would soon be over.[9] With such encouragement he quickly recovered his composure and skilfully prepared his defensive strategy. He still believed that the Allies would call upon his services to help rebuild Germany. He tried to assemble staff among those in his ministry who had kept their reputations relatively clean, but wiser folk knew that the game was up.[10] Having decided that a lawyer from among the Western Allies would provide him with the best defence, he approached George Ball, who had cross-examined him on his arrest. He pointed out that he was unlikely ever to find such a prominent client. Ball, however, turned down the brief.[11]

Speer remained aloof throughout his stay at Dustbin. He refused to take part in the gym course that had been arranged for the inmates. He never attended the musical evenings or lectures. When Theo Hupfauer, the former liaison officer between the German Work Front and the Armaments Ministry, asked him why he was so cold and remote, he replied in a moment of depression that he was preparing himself for a twenty-year prison sentence.[12] Hupfauer thought this was nonsense. He told Speer that he would either be shot or acquitted. He later marvelled at Speer's foresight.

Speer's attitude was part carefully considered tactics, part the natural consequence of his personality. He was determined to show his accusers that he was quite a different person from the majority of those who were accused of major crimes. He was surrounded by enemies, even within his own ministry. Dorsch he described as a 'ruthless' and 'reprehensible' character. Saur was 'too ambitious', but had a phenomenal memory for facts and figures.[13] Bormann and the Nazi Party had always been at daggers drawn with him. At the same time he was by nature detached and standoffish, awkward in society, haughty and arrogant, without any real friends and anxious to avoid the company of others. While at Kransberg the only person with whom he had any real contact was his faithful secretary, Annemarie Kempf. The more he considered his own past, the more he came to realise how profoundly he was involved and how impossible it was to separate himself from a regime in which he had played an all-important role. He convinced himself that he was not guilty, but he could not deny that he was deeply implicated. In an early interview at Dustbin Speer said of his many criticisms of Hitler: 'I should not like to be counted among those who malign him in order to exonerate themselves.'[14] This suggested profound inconsistencies within his personality. Richard W. Sonnenfeldt, the chief interpreter for the US prosecution, said of Speer that he made a clear distinction between responsibility and guilt. Speer claimed that he was not an anti-Semite, but he never said that killing people because they were Jewish was wrong. As he pondered the contradictions of his past he began to speak of himself as a stranger in what Sonnenfeldt described as 'an out-of-body experience'.[15]

He appeared to be cool and detached, his feet firmly on the ground, his attitude calmly rational. But he could be swept away by the utopian vision of 'Germania', abandon himself to the missionary zeal of National Socialism or the pursuit of technological perfection. He was torn between the cultural pessimism of Spengler and an optimistic belief that a refined and technically efficient form of National Socialism could offer a solution to post-war Germany's pressing problems. He was never able to overcome the contradictions between reaction and modernity that lay at the heart of National Socialism and which still bedevil much of contemporary thinking.

Conditions in Nuremberg were in sharp contrast to the relaxed atmosphere and relative comfort of Kransberg. Speer was now clearly a prisoner, locked in a cell with a straw mattress, a few dirty blankets, without books, newspapers or a mirror and submitted to a harsh prison routine. Once again his leg began to trouble him, a sure sign that he was living under great stress.[16] Then came the severe shock when he learnt that he was to be charged, along with all the other twenty-one prisoners, on four counts: taking part in a criminal conspiracy, crimes against peace, war crimes and crimes against humanity. He had imagined that each of the accused would receive a separate charge sheet. Lumped together with the others as a perpetrator of monstrous crimes, he realised that he now had to fight for his life. A prominent Berlin lawyer, Dr Hans Flächsner, ably assisted him in this daunting task.[17]

Speer quickly realised that he would have to accept full responsibility for his actions. Flächsner was horrified when he said that he also intended to accept 'overall responsibility' for the crimes of the Nazi regime. The confession that Flächsner felt was almost certain to cost him his life, was in fact a brilliant move that saved him from the hangman's noose. His preferred line of defence was to present Speer as an apolitical architect and technocrat – an approach that Speer was eagerly to adopt as he set about the reconstruction of his past.[18]

Speer was determined to distance himself from Göring and the unrepentant Nazis around him by the admission that he had served an evil regime. But what exactly did he mean by 'overall responsibility'? When the United States prosecutor Robert H. Jackson put this question to him, Speer replied that in his view there were two forms of responsibility in politics. One is fully responsible for everything that happens within one's specific area of competence, but the notion of overall responsibility was limited to fundamental issues. No one could be held accountable for specific actions taken within other ministries or authorities.[19] So defined, the concept of overall responsibility was empty of meaning. By this definition it was up to the prosecution to show that crimes had been committed within Speer's own realm of which he was aware.

Speer's defence at Nuremberg was masterly. As one of the leading figures of the Third Reich he acknowledged overall responsibility, but at the same time he distanced himself from Hitler and the regime. He presented himself as a diligent minister who stuck to the immediate tasks at hand, leaving politics to others. He professed to have had no knowledge whatsoever of the appalling mistreatment of the hundreds of thousands of unfortunates who worked for him. He presented himself as sympathetic to the resistance against Hitler. He claimed to have been totally ignorant of the fate of the European Jews. He remained calm and collected throughout the trial, convincing all who witnessed his performance that he stood apart from his more unsavoury colleagues.

Much of Speer's testimony was designed to win the sympathy of the three Western powers. He detailed the many shortcomings of an authoritarian regime that was bound by its very nature to lead to criminal excesses. Due to its determination to silence all critical voices it was inevitably unimaginative and inefficient. He deliberately played on the Allies' fears and anxieties with regard to the future course of the Soviet Union in his final statement. It contained a rousing call for the defence of Western culture faced with the threat of atomic warfare.

Throughout his life Speer was a consummate role player: as Tessenow's dutiful assistant, Troost's epigone, Hitler's slavishly obedient personal architect, as well as a highly efficient minister of armaments, the virtuoso performer at the Nuremberg trials and as a soul-searching prisoner, and finally as the best-selling penitent who provided an alibi for an entire nation. This was only possible because he closed his eyes to all those uncomfortable things that might have stood in the way of attaining his goals. There was no room here for moral scruples, painful self-questioning or a serious analysis of the consequences of his actions. His limited confession of guilt helped to conceal a much greater culpability that he had neither the courage nor the moral diligence to confront.

Speer's performance at Nuremberg was made all the more dramatic because of his confrontation with Hermann Göring. The grossly overweight, lethargic and drug-befuddled Reichsmarschall had undergone a striking transformation since he had been taken prisoner with forty-seven suitcases, a hoard of precious stones and most of the world's supply of dihydrocodeine. In captivity he had overcome years of drug addiction. He had slimmed drastically. His mind had regained much of its former sharpness. He knew that he was doomed, but was determined to go down fighting. He told the 32-year-old Major Douglas M. Kelley, chief psychiatrist in the U.S. Army's European Theatre of Operations, that he intended to put on such a performance during his trial that in fifty years' time there would be statues in his honour all over Germany.[20]

Göring's intention was for all the accused to stand together in defence of their actions so that future generations would be inspired by their vision of National Socialism. Speer's tactic was the reverse. He knew that his only hope of saving his skin was to condemn the regime he had served so well, while accepting a degree of responsibility for his sins of omission and commission. His transgression was not to have asked any awkward questions and to have looked the other way. His eyes were so riveted to his desk that he never looked out of the window. The contrite Speer, fearful that this might not be enough – certainly not for the Soviets – attempted to strengthen his position by making a deal with the Western Allies.[21]

At the suggestion of an American Intelligence officer, Major John J. Monigan, on 17 November 1945 Speer wrote a statement that he asked to be forwarded to Colonel Lawrence of the British Office of Economic Warfare, or to another appropriate authority.[22] It landed on the desk of the chief American prosecutor, Robert H. Jackson. Speer's expressed concern was that certain 'technical military knowledge' should not be revealed to a 'third party' – in other words, the Soviet Union. He warned that the American Field Intelligence Agency Technical (FIAT) had gained a great deal of information about German science and industry. He had urged all those who had been interviewed at Dustbin, or by the British Combined Intelligence Objectives Sub-Committee in Wimbledon, to cooperate fully. He had also been absolutely open with officers from the United States Strategic Bombing Survey when he had been interviewed at Flensburg between 10 and 23 March 1945. He had pointed out many of the mistakes made by the Allied strategic bombing campaign and offered advice as to how the Americans should proceed against Japan. He insisted that he had done this out of personal conviction and without thought of any possible advantage that it might bring. He ended with the barely veiled warning that he would consider it 'deplorable' were he obliged to reveal this information again in court.

Speer's warning that he had information that might be useful to the Soviets were it to be revealed in court was remarkably successful. On the advice of his assistant, Thomas J. Dodd, Jackson personally led the cross-examination. Dodd had interviewed Speer on several occasions and considered him to be honest, self-effacing and cultured. But he was also struck by the man's exceptional conceitedness and his intense dislike for Göring, who was obviously set on stealing the show. Dodd therefore persuaded Jackson that Speer would be so insulted were he to be cross-examined by Jackson's second-in-command that he would probably refuse to cooperate.[23] Jackson was known to be a somewhat ineffective prosecutor. Even so, there was general surprise at his mild manner when questioning Speer. He greeted him with smiles, treated him with respect and avoided any embarrassing probing. Rumours were rife that a deal had been made between Speer and Jackson.[24] If there had been a deal it was not honoured. When the judges debated the sentences the American Attorney General Francis Biddle initially argued for the death penalty before the French and British judges persuaded him to change his mind.

It was obvious that neither the American nor the British teams would do anything that might lead to the Soviets becoming privy to information that they wished to keep secret. But in Speer's message to Jackson there was an implied threat that he might have something up his sleeve. Speer later made the preposterous claim that he had written to Jackson because the accused had been told that if they were to attempt to sabotage the proceedings they would simply be handed over to the Soviets for summary treatment.[25] Speer's main motive was to soothe his vanity. He wished to be seen as a man of great importance, who was closer to Hitler than anyone else, but who was in a quite different category to the unrepentant Nazis around Göring. For the Americans there was, as Adrian S. Fisher argued, no question at all that Speer was guilty. The only difficulty was to decide whether there was a case to be made for a more lenient sentence than that of death.[26]

The tribunal admitted that under the terms of a decree of 21 March 1942, Sauckel was directly answerable to Göring and the Four-Year Plan. But Speer had ordered Sauckel to provide him with the labour he needed in the armaments industry.[27] Speer knew full well that the workers that Sauckel provided for him were mostly foreigners who had been forced to work. Evidence presented in court showed that he had taken part in a number of meetings that had called for an extension of the forced labour programme. Between 10 and 12 August 1942 Speer and Sauckel had met with Hitler to discuss the use of force to provide the labour that was required. Speer was also present at a meeting at Hitler's headquarters where it was agreed that at least four million workers should be rounded up in the occupied countries to meet Speer's requirements. Sauckel had admitted that this would not be possible without assistance from Himmler and the SS. On 1 March 1944, Speer had complained to Sauckel through an intermediary that he had not met the target figures.

The court considered that Speer's plan to set up factories in the occupied countries, thereby enabling German industry to concentrate on armaments, was 'less inhuman' in that it enabled workers to avoid deportation, but this was only a very small part of Speer's industrial empire. He was the greatest beneficiary of forced labour in the Third Reich, not only as Minister of Armaments, but also as head of Organisation Todt. In addition to the forced labour provided by Sauckel, Speer also made extensive use of labour from the concentration camps. He made the astonishing claim that he was mindful not to press Himmler too hard by making excessive demands upon him. Speer had also made use of prisoners of war in the armaments industry, although he insisted that he had only employed them in branches of industry sanctioned by the Geneva Convention. He was very fortunate that it was not brought to the court's attention that Mittelbau-Dora, the notorious underground factory where the V2 rockets were built and where thousands died due to the appalling conditions, was part of Speer's armaments empire. Nor was any mention made of his complicity with Himmler's policy of deliberately working prisoners to death.

It was admitted that Speer was not directly involved with the mistreatment involved in the forced labour programme, but it was also stated that he was well aware of it. He knew that force was required to meet his needs. At a meeting of Central Planning on 30 October 1942 he asserted that many of the forced workers who claimed to be ill were merely slackers and that anyone who did not pull their weight should be sent to a concentration camp. The tribunal accepted as mitigating circumstances that Speer had shown courage in insisting that the war was lost and had tried to stop the senseless destruction both at home and in the occupied areas, but overlooked the fact that he had also done everything possible to prolong the war.

Speer's claim to have been unaware of the horrendous crimes of the Third Reich and his profession of contrition were at odds with his overbearing vanity. He was determined to present himself as one of the most important figures in what he admitted was a criminal regime. At the same time he claimed ignorance of the appalling things that had happened, even within his own area of competence. Almost as soon as he took the witness stand on the afternoon of 19 June 1946 his arrogance prompted him to say: 'If Hitler had had any friends at all, then I would have certainly been one of his close friends.'[28]

In answer to Flächsner's question whether he had taken part in planning and preparing for a war of aggression, he replied that none of his buildings were military and that all the workers, materials and money involved in them were thereby denied to the armed forces. He claimed that Hitler's buildings were a hindrance to the rearmament programme. Flächsner's questioning was designed to show that Speer was a pragmatist who found the best-qualified people, most of them coming from industry, to work in the armaments ministry. He had tried wherever possible to keep his ministry free from the Nazi Party's interference. From the outset Flächsner was determined to present his client as an apolitical technocrat and manager who was totally absorbed in running a vast enterprise that by 1944 had fourteen million employees in Germany alone and a monthly budget of between three and four billion Reichsmarks. The entire enterprise was administered by a staff of six thousand, many of whom were volunteers. He took pains to show that his ministry was not run by professional civil servants but was an ad hoc arrangement that was viewed with deep suspicion by the Nazi Party. Bormann and Goebbels felt that Speer was 'alien to the party' and 'hostile to the party'.[29] Speer denied that he had ever received a lump-sum payment from Hitler as many others had done, but he kept discreetly silent about the vast sums of money he had earned as Hitler's architect and from a number of shady property deals, including a substantial gift of land from Göring. Nor did he mention the lavish sums of money handed out to his key associates, or the profits made by the industries they represented.

On the key question of the mistreatment of workers in the armaments industry Speer firmly asserted that this was neither his responsibility nor that of his ministry. He was solely concerned with technical matters. The welfare of workers was the responsibility of the Ministry of Food, the Ministry of Labour and the German Work Front. Discipline was a matter for the Ministry of Justice and the police. Concentration camp inmates were the responsibility of the SS. The major problem for all concerned was that air raids made it impossible to meet even the minimum standards set by various government agencies. Sauckel, for example, set exacting standards for working and living conditions, but they could seldom be met. Flächsner produced a number of documents that showed that Speer had been concerned about the wellbeing of Soviet workers. They were all to be adequately fed. Civilian workers should not be kept behind barbed wire like prisoners of war. POWs should be given allocations of tobacco and suchlike as rewards for special achievement.[30]

Working hours lasted on average between sixty and sixty-four hours per week but they were often interrupted by air raids. Workers from concentration camps were treated in the same way as all other workers. Speer insisted that inmates in special camps built near factories had been given special treatment and that when he visited various works they gave the impression of being healthy and well fed. When asked about working conditions in the underground factories Speer replied that these were state-of-the-art factories in which conditions were beyond reproach. They were free from dust, the air was fresh, and the lighting was excellent. Working underground was exactly the same as working on the night shift in a normal factory. He added that contrary to the impression hitherto created in court, most of the workers in these factories were Germans who were interested in working on the most modern of weapons. He did not choose to mention that the underground factories had been built by slave labour and that most of these German workers were concentration camp inmates, and neither did he make reference to the appallingly high mortality rate in these death-traps.[31] Speer was fortunate that the prosecution did not follow up with questions about Mittelbau-Dora. They would have shown that Speer's statements were blatantly untrue.

When asked why he had visited the concentration camp at Mauthausen he replied that he had heard that paving stones for civilian use were being produced there. He wanted to put a stop to this and to warn the SS that they were not to waste resources on civilian production. He had been most impressed by the camp. The buildings were solidly built of stone. Living conditions for the inmates were exemplary. The camp was spotlessly clean. He did, however, admit that the commandant had been warned in advance of his arrival and that he did not actually see any of the inmates at work.[32] Speer denied that he had ever used brutality or terror to force people to work harder. He insisted that it would have been impossible to get fourteen million workers to perform well using such means. On that note the court adjourned for the day.[33]

The next morning, 20 June, Flächsner asked Speer about his relationship with Sauckel.[34] He said that he was grateful for every worker he could get. In spite of certain differences with him over production and the allocation of

German workers, they had worked well together. Before Speer took over aircraft production in August 1944, Sauckel had provided between 30 and 40 per cent of the workers in the armaments industries. They came from home and abroad. Speer made the extravagant claim that weapons production had increased sevenfold, tank production five-and-a-half times, and munitions by 600 per cent, all with a workforce that was only 30 per cent larger. Thanks to improved production methods it had been possible to achieve this without making undue demands on labour.

Flächsner questioned his client about an affidavit from a US statistician stating that according to the records of the Ministry of Armaments 400,000 prisoners of war had been employed in the armaments industry during the war.[35] Speer admitted that this was true, but he insisted that none of them were involved in making weapons as defined by the Geneva Convention. Soviet and Italian prisoners were in any case not protected by the convention. In addition to the 400,000 mentioned in the affidavit there were 200,000 to 300,000 Italian internees employed in the armaments industry.

Speer repeated that he was not responsible for the supply of labour. That was Sauckel's responsibility. His ministry constantly suffered from a shortage of labour as a result of the faulty allocation of available resources. Thus 200,000 Ukrainian women were brought to Germany in the spring of 1943 to work as domestic servants.[36] They would have been far better employed in armaments factories. Similarly, Speer had been unable to lay hands on the reserves of German labour, particularly women, that would have been readily available had he had the authority to set them to work. He argued that apart from miners, he would have had no need for foreign labourers had domestic resources been mobilised as they were in the United States, Britain and the Soviet Union.

Speer stated that he preferred to use workers from western Europe in the armaments industry, but after the defeats at Stalingrad and North Africa, combined with the increasing number of air raids in industrial regions, it became difficult to get hold of workers from this region. Therefore he decided to create 'blocked firms' in the occupied countries in which workers could avoid deportation by working in local factories. As a result, the number of workers coming to Germany from France was steadily reduced.

He was able partially to overcome the problem of the shortage of German labour in the armaments industry by taking over the Ministry of Economics. This enabled him to switch the consumer goods sector in Germany over to armaments production, while using the protected firms abroad for consumer goods. He had hoped thereby to recruit a further one million German workers for armaments production, along with additional factory space, administrative personnel, power, transportation and raw materials, but it was too late for this to be effective.

The president was extremely impatient with Flächsner's line of questioning. He interrupted the proceedings to ask him exactly what he was trying to prove. As far as the court was concerned it did not matter whether workers came from the West or the East. It did not matter whether Speer's schemes were efficient or inefficient. It did not matter whether people were forced to work in Germany or forced to work at home. It did not matter whether they were making arms or consumer goods. It was solely a matter of legality. On this testy note the president called for a recess.

When the session resumed, questions were asked about Speer's negotiations in September 1943 with the French Minister of Labour, Jean Bichelonne, which resulted in the system of 'blocked firms'. As a result the number of French workers going to Germany was reduced from the 500,000 initially proposed to 33,000 in the first half of 1944.[37] Flächsner's questioning was designed to draw a sharp distinction between Sauckel and Speer, but the president intervened, saying that this point had already been made on several occasions.

Undaunted by this intervention Flächsner now drew a clear distinction between Sauckel and the Gauleiters, who wanted to continue exploiting foreign labour, and Speer, who felt that there were sufficient reserves of labour in Germany, particularly among women, to cover immediate needs. Speer was particularly worried about the increasing number of incidents of sabotage. Differences between Sauckel and Speer were aired at a meeting with Hitler on 4 January 1944. Hitler ordered Sauckel to round up 3.5 million workers in the occupied countries and OKW was instructed to direct the armed forces to give him every assistance.

Flächsner now set out to show how Speer had resisted Sauckel and Hitler's attempts to resume sending foreign workers to Germany, particularly when, in preparation for the invasion, French industry had been crippled as a result of intensive Allied bombing. It had left one million workers unemployed. Sauckel managed to get Hitler's approval of this measure during a series of meetings between 19 and 22 June 1944. OKW issued orders that workers should be rounded up and sent to Germany, but the military authorities in France had other priorities after the invasion. In July 1944 only three thousand French workers were selected.[38]

The cross-examination now turned to the question of armaments industries within the concentration camps. Soon after his appointment as Minister of Armaments, Speer had been offered the use of Himmler's concentration camps for war production. Speer knew full well that Himmler was hoping thereby to gain control over part of the armaments industry. He was therefore determined to resist him. During his lengthy illness in 1944, Himmler set about removing concentration camp inmates from the armaments factories and sending them back to the main camps. He did this at a rate of thirty to forty thousand per month. This was done on the basis of trumped-up charges of criminal activity. Once Speer was back at work he was determined to put an end to what he described as 'kidnapping'.[39]

During the afternoon session on 20 June Speer pointed out how he and Hermann Röchling, who was responsible for iron production in western Europe, had resisted Hitler's attempt to use violent methods to discipline labour in France and to abandon 'humanitarian muddle-headedness' when dealing with saboteurs. He had urged Sauckel to make sure that French workers were at least paid and that a certain number of consumer goods should be made available to them.

When asked by Flächsner what he had done with his documents, Speer testified that he had handed them over in their entirety to Allied authorities when he was still at liberty in Flensburg. This statement was an exercise in the economy of truth. He may have given up most of the documents that he had to hand, but he certainly did not part with all of them. Had he done so, his chances of escaping the death penalty would have been very slim. In answer to a direct question, he stated that there was nothing in them about Nazi ideology or anti-Semitism. Fortunately for Speer, none of the documents concerning the expulsion of the Jews from Berlin had fallen into the prosecution's hands. The details of his dealings with Himmler and the SS were also barely mentioned.

When asked about the 20 July 1944 plot, Speer answered that he had had nothing to do with it. He assumed that he had been suggested as a possible minister by the plotters because he was on very good terms with Generals Fromm and Zeitzler.[40] Speer gave a remarkable reply to Flächsner's question as to whether he felt that his responsibility was limited to his own area of competence. 'This war was an unimaginable catastrophe for the German people and caused a worldwide catastrophe. It was therefore obviously my duty to admit my responsibility to the German people. This obligation was all the greater because the head of government avoided his responsibility towards the German people and the world. As an important member of the leadership of the Reich from 1942 I therefore accept joint responsibility.'[41]

Flächsner now turned to the question of the part played by Speer in frustrating Hitler's 'Nero Order'. Speer stated that the policy was supported by Bormann, Goebbels and Ley, but that the armed forces and the various ministries were strongly opposed to it. His tactic with Hitler was to point out that since he refused to admit that the war was lost, industrial facilities would be needed to continue the fight. His policy was to put factories near the front temporarily out of action by removing and concealing pieces of essential equipment that could easily be replaced.

It was at this point that Flächsner introduced Speer's plan to assassinate Hitler. Very understandably he had had serious reservations about even mentioning this. He feared that it would stretch the credibility of his testimony well beyond reasonable limits. It was, after all, only a plan or an intention, for which there was only one somewhat suspect witness.[42] In his autobiography Speer argues that he had mentioned his intention to kill Hitler in order to show how dangerous were his 'destructive intentions'.[43] Speer told the court that he did not wish to go into details. He was therefore alarmed when the judges told him that they would like to know more.

The issue of Speer's implausible attempt to assassinate Hitler had first been raised in the afternoon session of 3 January 1946. Flächsner was away from Nuremberg during the Christmas holidays. His place had been taken by von Papen's defence counsel, Dr Egon Kubuschok, an outstanding lawyer who had courageously defended a number of people during the war, including Czech resistance fighters who had the misfortune to stand before Roland Feisler's 'People's Court'. During the cross-examination of Otto Ohlendorf, Kubuschok asked whether he had known that Speer had tried to stop the destruction of property that Hitler had ordered. He said that he had. He was then asked whether he knew that Speer had planned to kill Hitler in mid-February 1945. Ohlendorf replied with an emphatic 'no'. In answer to further questions he said that he had known that Speer was on the 20th July plotters' list of possible ministers. To the question whether Speer could be considered as a specialist rather than a politician he replied that it was impossible to remain apolitical when one was so closely involved in the decision-making process, but he added that Speer was not known for being particularly politically active.[44]

Ohlendorf's testimony had an electrifying effect. Göring was outraged. During a pause in the proceedings he accused Speer of sabotaging the united front of the accused.[45] Speer had thereby managed to distance himself from Göring and the unrepentant Nazis even before he took the stand. Later that evening, Göring told G.M. Gilbert, the American psychiatrist who had become his confidant, that Speer was a miserable wretch who was simply trying to save his filthy neck, so that 'for a while longer he could piss in front and shit behind'.[46] During the midday break the following day Göring asked Baldur von Schirach, the former Youth Leader of the NSDAP and Gauleiter of Vienna, to persuade Speer to join forces with him. Speer rejected this advance out of hand, denouncing Göring as a coward, morphine addict and art thief, who was now trying to steal the show.[47] Speer repeated this insult in court two days later. He had initially undertaken not to say anything incriminating or insulting about any of the other accused. Now he had told the tribunal that Hitler had said of the Reichsmarschall that he was a corrupt, drug-addicted failure.[48] This put an effective end to Göring's attempt to go down in glory. The Göring saga had come to an end. It was unlikely that monuments would be built in his memory. Papen, Schirach and Schacht were delighted that Speer had delivered him the death blow.

Encouraged by the startling effect of the claim that he had thought of killing Hitler, Speer contrived to bring the matter up again during his cross-examination on 20 June.[49] Flächsner asked him why it was that in mid-February 1945 he had asked Dieter Stahl, the head of the munitions department, to provide him with poison gas in order to kill Hitler, Bormann and Goebbels. Speer replied that this was an act of desperation, because he could think of no alternative. Even before Hitler issued the Nero Order, Speer knew that he had wanted to bring down the German people with him. Speer claimed to have realised that defeat was inevitable and that there was no alternative to unconditional surrender.

He was very reluctant to reply to Flächsner's question as to whether he had intended to carry out the assassination attempt himself. On the one hand he was one of the few people who still had access to Hitler, on the other there were certain technical problems that had to be overcome. In his memoirs Speer claims that he refused to give a detailed account of this putative assassination attempt because he did not want to boast.[50] Here memory conveniently fails him. After a ten-minute recess he gave a detailed account of his plan, having first protested that he did so unwillingly because 'such things are always unpleasant'.

He told the court that Hitler frequently met Ley, Goebbels and Bormann in his bunker at the chancellery. At that time these men were his closest associates. After the 20 July assassination plot it was impossible to enter the bunker without being thoroughly searched. It would have been impossible to bring weapons or explosives past the guards. Therefore the best solution was to introduce poison gas through the ventilation system. He had asked Stahl to provide him with a gas that would penetrate the gas filter. Stahl told him that he had consulted Colonel Soika, a poison gas expert, who pointed out that explosives would have to be used. This was not possible, because the air intake was made of light metal and an explosion would have been so defused as to be ineffective. Further investigation by an engineer revealed that the gas filter was not always operative, so that a normal gas could be used. Speer went with the engineer to examine the air intake, only to find that on Hitler's orders a four-metre-high chimney had been built so that the plan came to naught.[51]

Speer's tale of his planned assassination attempt is impossible to believe. In the first place, no bunker would be built with an air intake through a thin metal or brick chimney on the roof. This would be highly vulnerable to a direct hit and the blast from a near miss would probably have created a pressure wave that would have killed everyone inside. There were two towers for the ventilation system: one for intake, the other for exhaust. There was also a second emergency intake vent. They were made of massive reinforced concrete with conical roofs. Speer's claim that he had conspired with Johannes Hentschel, the chief mechanic at the chancellery, was equally preposterous. The filter was only used during air raids.[52] But even if the bunker had been so constructed, it was still an absurd plan. As Markus Misch – who acted as a telephonist and guard in the bunker – pointed out, the bunker was guarded by a large number of men from the Security Service, the Gestapo and the SS. They were unlikely to have stood idly by while Speer climbed a ladder to introduce gas into the ventilation system.[53]

The truth behind the gas plot was eventually discovered in the archives of the company that had installed the ventilation and air-conditioning system. During a conference attended by a number of generals as well as Göring and Goebbels there was a strong smell of burning. There was a state of near panic at the possibility of sabotage. The ventilation system was immediately shut off. After a lengthy investigation the root cause was found. Göring's driver had parked the car by the ventilation tower with the engine running and the exhaust three metres below the intake. The car had a wood-burning engine, hence the smell. Once the main and auxiliary ventilation systems had been cleaned out the conference was able to proceed. Henceforth no cars were allowed to park in the vicinity of the ventilation tower.[54] Speer's account of his attempt on Hitler's life was merely imaginative embroidery of this incident.

The following morning Jackson suggested to Speer that he had been involved in several plots to remove those whom he felt were responsible for the destruction of the country. Speer modestly replied that one did not need great courage to act in this manner, because there were only a few dozen people who were stupid enough to continue the fight.[55] This remark made nonsense of his testimony of the previous day. What had been an action that only someone in Hitler's inner circle could even contemplate, was now apparently openly discussed by some eighty million Germans. Speer stated: 'During that time it was extremely easy to start a plot. One could accost practically any man in the street and tell him what the situation was, and then he would say "this is insane". If he had any courage he would place himself at your disposal.' Jackson asked: 'Isn't it a fact that in the circle around Hitler there was almost no one who would stand up and tell him that the war was lost, except yourself?' His gamble had paid off. It was fortunate for Speer that he did not allude to the alternative plan to remove Hitler that he had mentioned to Dr Gilbert. It involved kidnapping ten leading figures – including Hitler, Himmler, Goebbels, Bormann, Keitel and Göring – putting them on a plane and flying them to England. Unfortunately his co-conspirators, whom he did not mention by name, got cold feet at the last moment.[56]

Speer was quick to realise that the central issue was the treatment of forced labourers and prisoners of war. It was therefore vital for him to put as much distance between himself and Sauckel as possible. He was greatly assisted in this endeavour by Sauckel's attitude during the trial. The latter was a belligerently unapologetic Nazi, whose motto was that 'we must rid ourselves of the slag of dim-witted humanitarianism'. Speer told the Americans that Sauckel was the man who most deserved to be tried as a war criminal. Sauckel returned the compliment, telling his captors that Speer was the man they should hang.[57]

Speer knew that since his ministry had benefited the most from Sauckel's activities, he could not possibly attempt to put the entire blame on his shoulders. Both had at least a theoretical interest in workers that were fit enough to do a decent day's work. In the course of the trial Speer realised that since he had worked closely with Sauckel it would not be wise to paint him in too poor a light. Anxious to attribute the appalling conditions in which forced labourers were obliged to live to the immoral and inhuman Allied bombing campaign, Speer claimed that Sauckel had done all that he could to make sure that workers were well treated and properly fed.[58]

Himmler had taken a quite different approach. Work for him was an alternative and more economical way of getting rid of undesirable elements. If prisoners were going to die anyway they might as well be worked to death. Unfortunately for Speer it was not possible to draw a sharp distinction between the humane treatment of forced labour favoured by both him and Sauckel with Himmler's murderous brutality. Speer had worked closely with Himmler, even before he was appointed Minister of Armaments. He had made extensive use of concentration camp inmates in Nuremberg and Berlin, and had turned a blind eye to their fate.

Flächsner's line of defence was to present Speer as a man who had become Minister of Armaments against his will. He had accepted the task reluctantly, for he would have much preferred to remain in what he called the 'ideal world' of architecture. Speer's attorney quoted part of a speech that he had delivered two weeks after his appointment in which he made a statement to this effect. However, he prudently omitted a sentence in which Speer expressed his determination 'recklessly to carry out the wartime mission'.[59] The reluctant architect remained, according to this version, resolutely aloof from politics. He used as evidence an extract from the memorandum he had sent to Hitler on 20 September 1944, in which he had argued that he was acting purely as a technocrat and expert. 'The duties that I have to fulfil are apolitical. I have enjoyed my work for as long as my efforts were judged according to professional standards.'[60] Flächsner returned to this theme in his summing-up, arguing that many of those involved in the 20 July assassination attempt on Hitler had considered Speer to have been a suitable person to have as a minister in a new government. This, he argued, was proof that Speer was a man who was regarded both at home and abroad as a decent, apolitical expert.

During the morning session on 21 June, Jackson asked Speer about the Nazi Party and the government's policy towards the Jews.[61] He replied that he knew that the party was anti-Semitic and that Jews were evacuated from Germany, but he denied that he was in any way involved. On the contrary, he said that on his appointment as Minister of Armaments he had objected to the removal of Jews from armaments factories and had managed to rescind the order. In September or October 1942 Hitler had ordered that all Jews should be removed from armaments factories, but Speer had managed to postpone this until March 1943 'when resistance gave way'. Speer's case was seriously weakened, however, when a memorandum from Sauckel, dated 26 March 1943, was read in evidence against him. It was entitled 'Deportation of Jews' and addressed to the Provincial Labour Offices. It showed that Jews were deported and herded into labour camps on orders from Himmler, with Speer and Sauckel in full agreement.[62]

During his interrogation on 18 October 1945 Speer had admitted that he had not objected to a hundred thousand Hungarian Jews being evacuated to work in subterranean aircraft factories. He admitted that these and other workers were brought to Germany against their will. He used the spurious argument that, since international law in this respect had been violated before he was appointed minister, he was in no way responsible. Jackson did not pursue this line of questioning. Speer was fortunate that the mass murder of European Jews was not a central issue at Nuremberg and that the prosecution had not delved into his activities in rebuilding Berlin or his operations in the Soviet Union before he was appointed Minister of Armaments.

Jackson spent far more time on the savage treatment of Soviet prisoners of war, particularly at the Krupp works in Essen. He had an impressive collection of evidence at the ready. First came photographs of iron lockers, 1.52 metres high, 40 centimetres wide and 50 centimetres deep, reputedly specially built by Krupp for punishing recalcitrant Soviet POWs and forced labourers. There was an opening on the top, covered by a grille, through which ice-cold water was poured in winter to add to the misery. They were not released when nature called.

A further set of photographs showed a room that was 2.5 metres wide, 5 metres long and 2 metres high, in which sixteen prisoners had to sleep on bunk beds. Jackson told the court that he had more than one hundred affidavits from inmates at the Krupp work camp that described in detail the appalling treatment meted out to them. He read one such affidavit from Dr Apolinary Gotowicki, a medical officer in the Polish Army, who had been captured in January 1941. He described the inhumane conditions in which Soviet prisoners of war and forced labourers were compelled to live. They slept crowded together on a concrete floor on straw mattresses full of fleas and lice. Many of the men had been brutally manhandled and were covered in serious contusions, the result of severe beatings with iron bars, rubber hoses or clubs. Whenever Gotowicki complained to the Krupp management he was told that this was all a matter for the SS and the

Gestapo. He was warned that if he did not keep his mouth shut he too would land up in a concentration camp. He was given no medical supplies, either from the Wehrmacht or from Krupp, so that by 1942 the mortality rate averaged four deaths per day. The women were treated as badly as the men. They were fed a watery soup that smelt as vile as it tasted. They were dressed in rags, shod with shreds of cloth or wooden clogs, and were frequently beaten.[63]

Speer calmly replied that such overcrowding was due to Allied bombing causing a severe shortage of accommodation. He added that it would be a mistake to generalise from this one instance. He had to repeat this answer because Jackson was unable to understand the translation. Speer used this as an opportunity to add that he did not believe that Dr Gotowicki's story was true. Furthermore, he found it absurd that Jackson should assume that he knew what was going on at the Krupp camp. It was run by the SS.

When Jackson pointed out that Speer must have had an interest in having healthy workers, he replied that very few hours were lost due to sickness and that most of those who reported sick did so in response to Allied propaganda urging them to sabotage armaments production. In such cases he felt that punishment was appropriate. In any case, punishment was not his concern. It was a matter for Sauckel and the SS. When pressed on the question of the metal cupboards, Speer told Jackson that they were perfectly normal lockers. They had not been made especially for torture. All such lockers had ventilation holes at the top and bottom. In short, the story was a fabrication. 'I mean, after the collapse in 1945 a lot of affidavits were collected that were not quite true . . . after a defeat it is quite possible that people make things up.'[64]

Speer boldly asserted that all these statements about the brutal mistreatment of foreign workers and prisoners of war were fabrications. 'I would say that German people do not do such things. If any such individual cases occurred those concerned were punished. It is not possible to drag the German people in the dirt in such a way. The heads of enterprises were decent people. They took an interest in their workers. If the head of the Krupp plant had heard about such things, he would have certainly reacted immediately.'[65]

Since neither the British nor the French judges wished to cross-examine Speer, it was now the Soviet counsellor General M.Y. Raginsky's turn to question the accused. He argued that Speer must have known about Hitler's aggressive intentions, particularly against the Soviet Union, because he had read *Mein Kampf.* Speer coolly replied that: 'I was particularly relieved in 1939 when the Non-Aggression Pact with Russia was signed. After all, your diplomats too must have read *Mein Kampf;* nevertheless they signed the Non-Aggression Pact. They were certainly more intelligent than I. In political terms I mean.'[66] Speer outwitted the clod-hopping Raginsky at every turn. He was given a helping hand from Lord Lawrence, the President of the Tribunal, who felt obliged to intervene with the acid remark: 'What is the ultimate object of the cross-examination? You say it is leading somewhere else. Where is it leading to?'[67] Raginsky repeatedly went down blind alleys, wasted the court's time by asking questions that had already been answered exhaustively, and gave Speer every opportunity to demonstrate his superior intelligence. The president felt obliged to intervene frequently in an attempt to keep the unfortunate general on track, but to little avail. There must have been many present who were amused by the humiliation of the po-faced Russian, who soon abandoned the unequal struggle. Speer's cross-examination ended with some brief questions from Flächsner and Sauckel's defence counsel, Robert Servatius, and Biddle from the tribunal.[68]

Speer's trial came to an end on 23 July. The session began with Flächsner's summary.[69] He underlined Speer's claim that as an architect he had had nothing to do with crimes against peace; on the contrary, his activities in this regard hampered war preparations in that they required large quantities of raw materials and equipment which might otherwise have been used, directly or indirectly, for armaments. Since these were long-term projects Speer had obviously assumed that Hitler was planning for a long period of peace.

Flächsner was on more slippery ground with the charges under Article 52 of the Hague Convention on Land Warfare, which states that 'services shall not be demanded from municipalities or inhabitants except for the needs of the army of occupation. They shall be in proportion to the resources of the country, and of such a nature as not to involve the inhabitants in the obligation of taking part in military operations against their own country.'[70] This was qualified in that the Soviet Union was not a signatory, so that the conditions laid down in Article 52 did not apply to Soviet citizens.

The question was therefore whether the deportation of workers from the occupied territories constituted a violation of the Hague Convention. Here, Flächsner argued, Article 46 had to be taken into consideration. It stipulated that 'family honour and rights, the lives of persons, and private property, as well as religious convictions and practice, must be respected. Private property cannot be confiscated'. Furthermore, the question had to be considered whether these deportations were carried out in accordance with agreements made with the government of the occupied country.

The prosecution argued that any such agreements were legally invalid because they were made under duress. Flächsner insisted that in any treaty one side usually has the upper hand – especially in the case of peace treaties – but that did not affect their legality. In the case of France, Vichy was the legitimate regime. Its treaties had full legal force. France benefited from these arrangements in that the economy was revived, widespread unemployment relieved and prisoners of war released.

In the case of Holland and Belgium there were no governments with which to negotiate a treaty. The rules that applied here had already been discussed during the trial of Richard Seyß-Inquart, the Reich Commissar in the Netherlands. In the case of eastern Europe the issue was whether Article 46 was universally applicable under international law, even if a country was not a signatory to the convention. Flächsner argued that international law recognised that in a state of emergency certain otherwise illegal practices could be condoned. He claimed that the Allied declaration of unconditional surrender created such an emergency. Knowing full well that this policy dated from the Casablanca Conference in January 1943, Flächsner pointed out that a state of emergency existed before that date because the conflict had already become a total war. War as defined by the Hague Convention was between the fighting forces of the belligerent nations. Now war was aimed also at the total disruption of the enemy's economy and targeted civilians. Germany's labour policy was thus a justified response to the Allied air offensive.

At this point the president intervened to ask whether there had been an agreement made after the war of 1914–18 that suggested that the Hague Rules on Land Warfare were no longer applicable.[71] Flächsner replied that there had been no changes or modifications whatsoever. He continued his plea by arguing that air raids and the blockade had created a state of emergency and that the defendant, Speer, had reason to believe in the existence of such an emergency. By September of 1942 he knew that Soviet labourers were being forced against their will to work in Germany. He countenanced this, because there was no other way that he could have met his labour requirements. The emergency overruled all legal concerns.

Flächsner argued that Speer assessed his requirements and depended on Sauckel to satisfy them. As the witnesses Walther Schieber, who was in charge of consignments in the Ministry of Armaments, Hans Kehrl, who was head of the Armaments Office in the ministry and Fritz Schmelter from the Fighter Staff had all testified, Speer made every effort to obtain German labour. Foreign labour was a last resort. According to the testimony of Karl-Otto Saur, the number of workers in the armaments industry under Speer had increased from 4 million to 4.9 million, but output had far outstripped that increase. Speer had thus kept the employment of foreign workers down to a minimum. He had fought against stiff opposition from Sauckel for protected industries in western Europe so as to avoid deportations and to increase the number of Germans employed in the armaments industry. Forced labour in France resulted from a decree by the French government.

When Speer took over the ministry from Todt, the transfer of foreign labour to Germany was already in full swing. Flächsner argued that he had assumed that all legal questions had been duly considered. Sauckel had frequently assured him that he acted within the strict limits of the law. Speer's remit was equivalent to that of a technical plant manager. It was not therefore part of his duties to examine whether employment contracts with individual workers conformed to the law. That was the responsibility of Sauckel, whose office was analogous to that of a director of personnel.[72]

Flächsner rejected the prosecution's argument that since Speer was a member of the Central Planning Board he must have played a leading role in the procurement of foreign labour. He convincingly showed that Central Planning played no active role in this regard. Sauckel alone was responsible. He further argued that since The Hague Convention on Land Warfare covered a 'different concept of warfare' than the present form of 'economic warfare', its provisions did not apply.[73] Even if it was agreed that the deportation and employment of the compulsory labour of foreign nationals was illegal, it should be remembered that Speer was not responsible for this and that he did what he could to mitigate their living conditions. As for the 'abuses of a general nature, for which the firm of Krupp might be held responsible', these were uniquely caused by Allied bombing raids.

The main point in Flächsner's plea was that the allotment of labour was in Sauckel's hands. Speer's ministry was merely concerned with allocating the labour thereby made available, as well as transferring labour from one armament plant to another. Speer was not responsible for the means whereby foreign labour was procured, or for transportation back to Germany. He was only responsible for the utilisation of part of the labour that Sauckel provided.[74]

Flächsner now turned his attention to the charge that Speer had violated two articles of the Geneva Convention of 1929. Article 31 stated that it was forbidden to employ prisoners of war for the manufacture or transport of arms or munitions of any kind, or for the transport of material destined for combatant units. Article 32 forbade the employment of prisoners of war in unhealthy or dangerous work. Conditions of work were not to be rendered more arduous by disciplinary measures.

His defence here rested on the argument that the term 'armaments industry' as used by Speer was not coterminous with the manufacture of arms and munitions. It covered a wide range of raw materials and industrial plant such as foundries, forges and rolling works, the optical and electrical industries, factories making ball-bearings and cogwheels, and so on. Only some 20 to 30 per cent of such production was used in the manufacture of armaments as defined by the Geneva Convention. The Americans had introduced an affidavit by a statistician that purported to show the number of prisoners of war employed in the armaments industry, but Flächsner argued that it did not show in which branches of the armaments industry individual prisoners of war had been forced to work.

The French prosecution had insisted that the employment in the armaments industry of prisoners of war who had been released from captivity
constituted a violation of Article 31. Flächsner argued that such people were
free agents, even when they had agreed to work as a condition of their release.
They had been free to remain prisoners of war and were thereby protected by
the Geneva Convention. The allocation of prisoners of war was the responsibility not of Speer, but of Sauckel, in conjunction with the military authorities.
Flächsner argued that the employment of concentration camp inmates was not
in itself illegal, because it had always been the practice in Germany to make
convicts work, either in prison or outside.[75] The question of whether all concentration camp inmates could be defined as convicts did not attract the court's
attention.

Quoting a letter written by Walther Schieber to Speer on 7 May 1944,
Flächsner pointed out that the employment of concentration camp inmates was
encouraged by the Armaments Ministry because it gave them improved conditions in special camps close to their place of employment. He pointed out that
there were only 36,000 such inmates working in the armaments industry and
that the number was dwindling.[76] Flächsner argued that these figures disproved
the prosecution's contention that people were deliberately sent to concentration
camps in order to maintain a steady supply of labour. When asked by his defence
lawyer why he had built special concentration camps close to major factories
Speer had the audacity to reply: 'These work camps were built so as to have
workers in the factories who were fresh and enjoyed their work.'[77]

Flächsner pointed out that Hungarian Jews had been sent to build bomb-
proof aircraft factories during Speer's lengthy illness and that he had been
utterly opposed to the suggestion. The work had been carried out by Xaver
Dorsch from Organisation Todt, who, although he was subordinate to Speer, in
this case acted under direct orders from Hitler. The question was never asked
whether Speer's objections were to the use of Hungarian Jewish labour or to
Dorsch's scheme to build massive bunkers.[78]

On the question of sending shirkers to concentration camps, Flächsner
argued that the Allies had mounted a massive propaganda campaign, dropping
leaflets that encouraged workers to report sick on every possible occasion. He
claimed that punishment of those who feigned illness was the result of a decree
issued by Sauckel. In particularly grave cases, those found guilty could be sent
to a 'workers' training camp' for fifty-six days or permanently to a concentration camp. The decree applied equally to native and foreign workers. Only a
small number of workers received such punishment. Speer also insisted that
escaped prisoners of war who had been working in the armaments industry
should be returned to their workplace rather than be sent to a concentration
camp when they were caught.[79]

Flächsner concluded his plea with a lengthy account of Speer's assessment that the war could not be won and details of his efforts to frustrate Hitler's Nero Order. As early as June 1944 Speer had warned Hitler that if production continued to decline the war would be lost. In January 1945, according to the testimony of General Guderian, who was then chief of the army's general staff, Hitler defined any talk about the possibility of a lost war as high treason and punishable as such. Nonetheless Speer continued to tell both Guderian and Hitler that Germany's prospects were grim.[80]

Theo Hupfauer, head of the Central Office of the German Work Front, Speer's secretary, Annemarie Kempf, his adjutant, Manfred von Poser, and Carl Rudolf Stahl, who had taken over responsibility for munitions in Speer's ministry in June 1944, all testified that Speer had told the Gauleiters and army commanders that the war was lost and they should stop the senseless destruction of property.[81] Even though, on 29 March 1945, Hitler had warned Speer of the consequences of his actions, he went to Seyß-Inquart two days later to explain to him that the situation was hopeless. Seyß-Inquart began negotiations with representatives of the Allied and Soviet armies and the Dutch government to provide food for the starving Dutch population and for the total capitulation of the German forces in Holland. The results were not very impressive. Tens of thousands of Dutch people starved to death. 4.5 million suffered from acute starvation in the final months of the war.[82]

Flächsner argued that the fact that there was no evidence that industries in Poland, the Balkans, Czechoslovakia, France, Belgium and Holland were destroyed during the German retreat was due to Speer's efforts. General Guderian had testified that in February 1945 Hitler had identified his fate with that of the German people. He was determined to continue the struggle to the bitter end, although he knew it was lost. He therefore ordered the destruction of everything of real value. Hitler and Bormann issued clear orders to this effect. But, as 'Panzer' Rohland had testified, Speer was determined to ensure that vital necessities were provided, so as to make a rapid changeover to a peacetime economy possible.

In early November 1944 Speer had ordered the production of poison gas to stop. By the end of January 1945 the food situation had become his particular concern. In order to guarantee that the German people could be adequately fed he made the manufacture of agricultural machinery a priority, to ensure that the land was tilled in the spring. Flächsner added that it was greatly to Speer's credit that Bormann and Goebbels had referred to him as alien and hostile to the Party and that the 20 July conspirators had considered him as a suitable candidate for a ministerial position had their plot succeeded. He ended his plea with a rousing appeal: 'Speer had to betray Hitler in order to remain loyal to his people. One cannot but respect the tragedy which lies in this fate.'[83]

On 27 July 1946, the 189th day of the trials, Sir Hartley Shawcross outlined the British case against Speer.[84] Delivered with restrained passion, it was a brilliant summary of the prosecution's case that showed a complete mastery of the material. He dismissed out of hand Speer's argument that since all the violations of international law had taken place before he took office in February 1942, he was in no sense responsible. Speer had stated that during his first months in office he had 'used all my energy to ensure that as many workers as possible should be brought to Germany'. He had acknowledged the receipt of one million Soviet labourers in August 1942. On 4 January 1944 he had demanded 1,300,000 more workers during the coming year. Shawcross regarded the retention of French workers in France as 'a mere matter of mitigation'. Speer's manner in court might appear moderate, but his policies had caused appalling misery and suffering for millions of Soviet and other families. Shawcross insisted that Speer's gradual awareness of the true interests of the German people in the final stages of the war could in no sense absolve him from having participated in these appalling activities. His argument that any incidents of the mistreatment of workers were exceptional, so that he could not accept personal responsibility, did not hold water. The evidence showed that such conditions were widespread.

Shawcross went on to say that Speer had exploited 'to the point of exhaustion and death' the manpower supplied to him by Sauckel, Kaltenbrunner, the Gauleiters and the generals.[85] Flächsner's contention that the French government had freely given consent to sending forced labour to Germany was simply not borne out by the facts. As head of Organisation Todt, Speer had exploited more than a million men. After the Dambusters raid on the Möhne and Edersee dams in May 1943 more than fifty thousand Frenchmen were deported to repair the damage. Speer was ultimately responsible for the ill treatment of workers in German factories, especially at the Krupp plants. He had obtained authorisation from OKW to select skilled labour from the concentration camps and employed thirty-two thousand inmates in the armaments industry. In addition, four hundred thousand prisoners of war were forced to work under him. A hundred thousand Hungarian Jews were made to work in his underground armaments factories. Shawcross further asserted that Speer shared responsibility 'for the deportation of Jews to special labour camps, where they were exterminated', but had failed to produce any evidence that this was the case.[86] He also claimed that mobile gas chambers were used in various factories, including Daimler, all of which were subordinate to Speer as Minister of Armaments.[87]

On the morning of 30 July 1946 General Rudenko presented the Soviet prosecution's case. Speer had been charged by Hitler to become his Minister of Armaments. He was Hitler's intimate friend, but claimed that he knew nothing of his plans. He had been a member of the Nazi Party for fourteen years, but allegedly remained aloof from politics. He had never read *Mein Kampf*. He had lied when he said that he had never belonged to the SA or the SS. He had held several important posts within the Nazi Party. He was in charge of all technical questions, headed the Main Office of Engineering, directed the German National Socialist Union of Technicians, was deputy chief of staff for Rudolf Hess and head of a major organisation within the German Work Front. He collaborated with Hitler, Hess, Ley and Göring. He was a Reich Minister, but also a fascist political leader. As minister he ruthlessly exploited the population of the occupied countries and turned prisoners of war into slave labourers.[88]

Rudenko argued that 'when the fascist fliers bombed peaceful towns and villages, thereby killing women, old men and children, when the German artillery bombarded Leningrad, when the Hitlerite pirates sank hospital ships, when English towns were bombed by the V-weapons – [this] all came about as a result of Speer's activity'. Speer had also admitted that he had been manufacturing poison gas.

The Soviet prosecutor also claimed that Speer had refused to name anyone close to Hitler whom he had criticised for the simple reason that he had never done so. The fact that he realised that Germany had lost the war hardly counted in his favour. Who in their right mind thought otherwise?[89]

Adrian S. Fisher, legal adviser to the US Attorney General Francis Biddle, had prepared two summary memoranda for the tribunal during the summer of 1946 in which he detailed the case against Speer. He argued that for all his apparent reservations he had used at least thirty thousand concentration camp inmates as workers. Although he had recommended that they be reasonably well treated, for the simple reason that sickly and undernourished workers were useless, he undoubtedly knew that they lived in unacceptably harsh conditions. Fisher argued that the system of blocked industries was a violation of The Hague Rules, even though it may have served to save some foreign workers from deportation. Fisher refused to accept the argument that since the Soviet Union had not signed the Geneva Convention the Germans were technically within their rights when they put Soviet POWs to work in the armaments industries. A counter-argument was that even though the Soviets were not signatories to the convention, the Germans were still obliged by international law to respect 'customary laws and usages of war'. Fisher claimed the prosecution had made a major mistake by using raw statistics of the POWs set to work for Speer's ministry, so that the large number of prisoners who were other than Soviet nationals and who were covered by the convention were not specifically mentioned. This gave the impression that only Soviet POWs were thus exploited.

The fundamental problem, in Fisher's view, was not one of whether Speer was guilty or innocent – he was demonstrably guilty – but whether there was any mitigating evidence. Speer was clearly not a monster, unlike some of the other accused. He had undoubtedly resisted Hitler's scorched earth policies, often at considerable personal risk, but Fisher did not take Speer's claim to have plotted to kill Hitler very seriously. The main issue was that Speer was clearly in a uniquely powerful position. He had the education, the intelligence and the social background that should have enabled him to understand the moral implications of what he was doing. Lastly, did his critical view of Hitler in the final stages of the war outweigh the many years of full complicity?[90]

On 29 August Thomas J. Dodd, Executive Trial Counsel for the United States, summed up the case against the major war criminals. Of Speer he said: 'The Gauleiter(s), functioning as Reich Defence Commissioners, at the order of Speer and Sauckel, and under the most revolting conditions of conveyance, shunted the slaves from receiving depots to armament industries where like stanchioned beasts they were submitted to sub-human indignities and worked to death. Medical care and even the simplest medical supplies were refused them. Denied even the social advantages of the barnyard, they struggled under less than good stable standards. With a crassness unknown to ordinary domestic animal care, directives providing for the abortion of female labourers were distributed to Gauleiter(s) and Kreisleiter(s) and their staffs. Their keepers were of the Security Service and Gestapo, and the cellblocks of the concentration camp awaited any who chafed under the cruelty. Urged on by Speer, the Gauleiter(s) used prisoners of war for slave labour purposes, and Rosenberg's minions in the Eastern territories under the spur of Sauckel's demands gleaned new minions for thraldom.'[91]

Following this remarkable display of rhetoric, General Rudenko presented the Soviet prosecution's brief summary. Although all the evidence indicated the opposite, he claimed that when Speer was given plenipotentiary powers by Hitler for the destruction of industrial objectives, bridges, railways and other means of communication in March 1945, he had ordered the Gauleiters to carry out these orders.[92] Furthermore Speer was guilty of having used people from the occupied countries and prisoners of war as forced labourers.[93]

Speer made his final statement during the afternoon of 31 August 1946. He distanced himself from his admission of overall responsibility by wallowing in self-pity, bemoaning the tremendous suffering that Hitler and his system had wrought upon the hapless German people. He argued that it was the application of technology that made Hitler's dictatorship unique. According to this version, the radio had deprived the people of the ability to think for themselves. The telephone, radio and Teletype made possible the rapid transmission of orders and information, thereby reinforcing authority. Technology transformed assistants and advisers into the passive recipients of orders. Speer, the prophet of doom, warned the court that the modern world was prone to be terrorised by technology, unless individual freedoms were staunchly defended.[94]

Keenly aware of the growing rift between the Soviet Union and the Western Allies, Speer drew a dramatic Wellsian scenario of a future war with intercontinental ballistic missiles, torpedoes that sought out their targets, horrific chemical weapons and the atom bomb. He gloomily prophesied that 'nothing can prevent unconfined engineering and science from completing the work of destroying human beings, which it has begun in so dreadful a way in this war'. In a direct appeal to the Western powers he insisted that 'the more the world is dominated by technology, the greater is the need for individual freedom and self-confidence as a counterweight'.[95] This was a theme upon which he was to harp at great length upon his release. It resulted in a turgid exercise in pseudo-philosophy with the portentous title *Technology and Power*.[96]

There was still a glimmer of hope. Over centuries, the German people had contributed greatly to human civilisation and had frequently done so when they were just as powerless and weak as they were today. They may well create new and lasting works of particular significance. A nation's greatness is not only decided by warfare, but also by cultural achievements. Speer concluded this astonishing performance by saying that 'a nation that believes in its future will never perish. May God protect Germany and the culture of the West'.[97] Germany, having fallen into the clutches of technology and become victimised by it, was to lead the cultural revival of the West, thereby providing a viable alternative to the technological dictatorship of the Soviet Union.

The court adjourned on 1 September 1946 to discuss the sentences. There was a tense debate as to which of the four counts – conspiring to commit crimes against peace, planning, initiating and waging a war of aggression, war crimes and crimes against humanity – Speer should be found guilty of. The Soviet judges – Major General Nikitchenko and Lieutenant General Volchov – demanded that he be convicted on all four. The French – Professor Donnedieu de Vabres and Robert Falco – and the British – Colonel Sir Geoffrey Lawrence and Sir Norman Birkett – felt that he should only be held accountable for counts three and four. The Americans – Francis Biddle and John J. Parker – reserved their opinion on counts one and two. In the second session on 10 September the Soviets repeated their call for conviction on all four counts. Sir Geoffrey Lawrence now considered Speer to be guilty on counts two, three and four, while all the other judges felt that only counts three and four should be considered. Lawrence then spoke up in favour of Speer, using the rather curious argument that he had merely taken over a system that already existed. This overlooked the obvious fact that someone who joins a criminal organisation that already exists is not thereby absolved of guilt. Parker also felt that Speer should be moderately treated on the grounds that he was a fundamentally decent and respectable person.

Differences over the appropriate sentence were also considerable. Both French judges, as well as Lawrence and Parker, called for a limited prison sentence. Lawrence suggested fifteen years. Donnedieu de Vabres concurred. Biddle called for the death sentence. He was enthusiastically seconded by Nikitchenko. Norman Birkett, although as an alternate judge without a final vote, caused a deadlock by recommending a ten-year sentence. With the French and the British judges recommending a prison sentence and the US and Soviet judges calling for the death sentence, the meeting was adjourned.

The following day the Soviets were outvoted. Speer was to be charged only on counts three and four. Lawrence and Donnedieu de Vabres compromised by agreeing to a longer prison term. Biddle, having reconsidered his position, no longer called for the death sentence. On the morning of 11 September it was agreed by a vote of three to one that Speer should be sentenced to twenty years' imprisonment. The British and French judges, by persuading Biddle to drop his demand for the death sentence, had saved Speer's life.[98]

A severe dent in Speer's testimony was made on 30 September, during Major General I.T. Nikitchenko's reading of the judgment on the plunder of public and private property. He referred to a meeting of Central Planning on 1 March 1944 at which Speer's representative, Hans Kehrl, had reported that a great number of Frenchmen went voluntarily to work in Germany. At this point he was interrupted by Sauckel, who said that some were recruited forcibly. Kehrl claimed that force was only used when voluntary recruitment no longer produced satisfactory results. Sauckel replied that of the five million workers who came to Germany, less than two hundred thousand were volunteers. Kehrl responded: 'Let us forget for the moment whether or not some slight pressure was used. Formally, at least, they were volunteers.'[99]

Nikitchenko then quoted an earlier meeting of Central Planning, on 16 February 1943, at which Speer and Sauckel were present. It was reported that thirty thousand Soviet prisoners of war were used to man anti-aircraft batteries and that it was intended to use twenty thousand more. The minutes recorded that it was considered most amusing that Russians were forced to work these guns.[100] Speer had thereby condoned a serious breach of the Geneva Convention. His attitude towards foreign workers was also called into serious question later in the day. Speer's circular directive of 10 November 1944 was quoted, in which he transmitted an order from Himmler that the Local Group Leaders, on instructions from the District Leaders, should instruct all party members to keep foreign workers under strict observation.[101]

On the afternoon of 1 October 1946 Francis Biddle read the indictment of Albert Speer.[102] He had been indicted on all four counts. The tribunal agreed that he was not involved in initiating, planning, or preparing wars of aggression, or of conspiring to that end. Nor was he guilty of waging aggressive war as charged under count two. The evidence introduced against Speer under counts three and four related entirely to his involvement in the slave labour programme. He had no direct administrative accountability for this measure, for which Sauckel was fully responsible. However, he had instructed Sauckel to provide the workers needed in industries under his control. Sauckel obtained the labour required, allocating it according to instructions given by Speer. As Adrian S. Fisher had pointed out, if Speer gave the labour quotas to Sauckel, who then rounded up the workers, was Sauckel any more guilty than Speer?[103] Sauckel was from the working class, a former longshoreman and sailor. He was crude and uneducated, lacked style and had a grating personality. He was in marked contrast to the handsome, suave, polite, cultured and solidly bourgeois Speer. The impression both men made on the court accounts in large part for the difference in their sentences.

Biddle brushed aside the question of whether or not prisoners of war had been involved in the armaments industry in contravention of the Geneva Convention. He agreed that Speer had not been directly involved in the cruel treatment of slave labour, but contended that he was aware of it. He knew that violence was used to meet his demands for labour. At a meeting of the Central Planning Board on 30 October 1943 Speer had stated that many slave labourers who claimed to be sick were malingerers and that the SS and police should take 'drastic steps' and send those found guilty to concentration camps.

In mitigation, it had to be admitted that the system of blocked industries did save some workers from deportation. At the end of the war Speer was one of the few men who had the courage to tell Hitler that the war was lost and he had taken steps to prevent the senseless destruction of essential facilities, both in the occupied territories and in Germany. In doing so he had placed himself at considerable risk. Biddle concluded by stating that the tribunal found Speer not guilty on counts one and two, but guilty under counts three and four.

The indictments of all the defendants having been read, the court immediately proceeded to deliver the sentences, between 30 September and 1 October 1946. Speer as seventeenth anxiously awaited his fate. Göring, Ribbentrop, Keitel, Kaltenbrunner, Rosenberg, Frank, Frick, Streicher, Sauckel, Jodl and Seyß-Inquart were condemned to death by hanging. Hess, Funk and Raeder were given life sentences. Baldur von Schirach was sentenced to twenty years' and Dönitz to ten years' imprisonment. Flächsner had assured Speer that he could expect between four to five years' imprisonment. As the sentences were read out this must have seemed to Speer to be absurdly optimistic. A death sentence seemed a terrifying possibility. At last it was his turn. In accordance with Article 27 of the charter, Sir Geoffrey Lawrence pronounced Speer's sentence on the indictment. 'Defendant Albert Speer, on the Counts of the Indictment for which you have been convicted, the Tribunal sentences you to twenty years' imprisonment.' Neurath was then sentenced to fifteen years' imprisonment and the absent Bormann to death by hanging. Fritzsche, von Papen and Schacht were acquitted.

Speer later claimed that he saw no point in appealing his sentence. In his memoirs he sanctimoniously stated that this was because 'any punishment would have been mild given the misfortune that we brought upon the world'.[104] In fact he knew full well that the defendants were denied the right of appeal.

Speer gave a remarkable performance at Nuremberg that impressed most of those present. It helped to save his neck, but the real reason was that no mention was made of his treatment of the Jews in Berlin and that his close cooperation with Himmler, the SS and the concentration camps was overlooked. There were some who were unconvinced. Major Airey Neave, a British officer who, at the suggestion of Lord Justice Lawrence, was given the task of reading the initial indictments to the Nazi leadership, also on behalf of the organisations and groups to which they belonged, was one of the few participants at the trials who saw through Speer's carefully constructed façade. He admired the skill with which he presented his case, his courage under stress and his obvious intelligence; but what he first thought to be urbanity he grew to see as 'smooth hypocrisy'. For him, Speer was 'more beguiling and dangerous than Hitler'. There were a few moments when he dropped his guard. When the prosecution spoke of the transportation of workers to Auschwitz and Mauthausen he momentarily lost his self-satisfied look, revealing himself as 'urbane, talented and dangerous'. In the final count 'his smoothness repelled me'.[105]

Neave's assessment of Speer is remarkably similar to that of Sebastian Haffner, who wrote in the *Observer* on 9 April 1944:

To a far lesser extent than any other German leader does he resemble anything typically German or typically National Socialist. He symbolises indeed a type, which among all the belligerents has become increasingly important: the pure technician, the classless, brilliant man without a background, who knows no other goal than to make his way in the world, purely on the basis of his technical and organisational capabilities ... This is his age. We can get rid of the Hitlers and the Himmlers, but not the Speers. Whatever may be the fate of each individual man, they will be with us for a long time.[106]

Curiously, Speer took Haffner's comments as a compliment. He had read the article at the time and passed on a translation to Hitler. Milch warned him not to do so, saying that Bormann was likely to use it against him. Hitler read it, made no comment and handed it back to him. Speer felt that he could use Haffner's argument as the basis for his defence. To Haffner, Speer was a case of someone 'exemplifying perfectly the revolution of the managers'. He was neither a conman nor loud-mouthed, as were most Nazis, but appeared to be courteous and honest. He symbolised the type of individual that rose to the top during the war. He was the pure technician, the brilliant person who did not belong to a given class or was bound by any tradition, who knew no other objective than to make his way in the world. His 'absence of either psychological or moral preoccupations' enabled him to serve 'the frightening machinery . . . of our times'.[107] All this serves to underline Speer's son Albert's remark that most people began by liking his father, but then soon changed their minds about him.[108] Speer assiduously cultivated this image of himself as the apolitical technocrat, but there were moments when he admitted this to be untrue. In describing his intrigues against Bormann and Lammers he wrote: 'In an authoritarian system one necessarily becomes engaged in the political battlefield if one wishes to remain among the leadership.'[109] He was to spend the rest of his life bolstering this image of himself as the apolitical artist entrapped by technology. In this endeavour he was remarkably successful.

CHAPTER THIRTEEN

SPANDAU

HAVING SPENT THE first nine months of his sentence in his cell at Nuremberg, Speer served the remainder of his twenty-year sentence in Spandau gaol. It was a military prison built in Berlin shortly after the Franco-Prussian war. After the First World War it was used as a civilian gaol. Among the prisoners at that time were the prominent left-wing journalists Carl von Ossietzky and Egon Erwin Kisch. It was then a Gestapo prison where, among others, members of the Communist Red Orchestra awaited their execution in cells similar to that occupied by Speer.[1] After Speer and Baldur von Schirach's release in 1966, Rudolf Hess remained as the sole prisoner in this vast building. When he died in 1987 it was torn down, lest it become a place a pilgrimage for those who saw Hess as a martyr to the cause and a sacrificial victim of Allied and Soviet injustice. A shopping centre now marks the site.

Initially Speer's fellow inmates were Dönitz; Konstantin von Neurath, Ribbentrop's predecessor as Foreign Minister, then Reich Protector of Bohemia and Moravia; Baldur von Schirach, the Reich Youth Leader and Gauleiter of Vienna; Walther Funk, the Minister of Economics; Erich Raeder, the navy's commander-in-chief; and Rudolf Hess, Hitler's deputy until 1941. Speer claimed that Dönitz and Raeder detested him because of his confession of 'overall responsibility' during the trial. In the case of Dönitz this was a radical change in attitude. At Nuremberg he had told the psychiatrist Leon Goldensohn that Speer was his only friend among the prisoners. He spoke warmly of the musical evenings they had spent together along with their wives.[2] Baldur von Schirach, who had supported Speer at Nuremberg, now sided with the admirals. Neurath and Funk nodded in approval when Schirach attacked Speer. Hess remained apart in his private delusional world.[3] There were times when Speer was on reasonable terms with Schirach, but with frequent clashes. Neurath was distantly courteous. Speer therefore tended to be left with Hess, who lived in a troubled world of his own, occasionally firing salvos of malicious wit. Four hundred soldiers and fifty gaolers guarded this odd group of former grandees. Four doctors were at their disposal. Commandants from the four powers served monthly tours of duty.

Speer's initial reaction to his sentence was one of self-pitying resentment. He began to imagine that he had been scrupulously honest and open in his confession of guilt and that he had been unjustly punished for his truthfulness. Rather than thanking his lucky stars that none of the evidence had been produced that would inevitably have cost him his life, he begrudged Schacht and Papen's acquittals, which he attributed to their 'lies, deceptions and dishonest testimony'.[4]

Speer, who now was known simply as Prisoner Number Five, was given a cell that was 3 metres long and 2.7 metres wide. It measured 4 metres from floor to ceiling, which somewhat relieved the cramped feeling. There was a window that could be reached when he stood on a small wooden chair. Grey cellophane had replaced the window-panes for fear that prisoners would use a glass splinter to slash their wrists. Through this window he could vaguely see the top of an acacia tree and at night a few stars. There was a small shelf measuring 43 by 54 centimetres where he could place a few oddments, underneath which were a few hooks from which he could hang some items of clothing. A table measuring 48 by 81 centimetres was in a poor state of repair. In place of a plank-bed with a straw mattress, he now had an iron bedstead 1.9 metres long, but only 79 centimetres wide, with a cotton-filled mattress from San Antonio, Texas. Unlike his cell in Nuremberg he had sheets and a pillow. Ironically his five blankets were stamped GBI: Inspector General of Buildings. They had been provided for the foreign workers and concentration camp inmates who were forced to work for the Germania project. There was a flush toilet in a recess in the corner and a tin washbasin. The plasterwork was peeling, the paint faded, but the cell was clean. There was a penetrating smell of disinfectant in the toilet, in the clothing that was returned from the laundry, and in the water with which he washed the floor every day. Speer comforted himself with the thought that his 8.1 square metres provided a slightly more practical space than the 650 square metres of the study he had planned for Hitler.[5]

The prisoners were allowed precious little contact with their families. Every four weeks they were permitted to write a letter with a strictly limited number of words. Family members were allowed to visit for fifteen minutes every eight weeks. It was possible to save up the visiting times. Margarete Speer thus first visited her husband in 1949. They spent an uncomfortable hour together, closely watched by six guards. His son Albert and daughter Hilde paid their respects in 1953 to a patriarch whom they hardly knew. Speer was to tell Eugene Bird, an American guard who was to become the prison governor, that the hardest part of his imprisonment was the visits from his children. Once he had asked the standard questions 'How is Mother?' and 'How is school?' he found that he had nothing left to say.[6] Visits from his wife were equally awkward and frustrating.

By nature a depressive, Speer found prison life particularly hard to bear. He quickly realised that he needed to work out a survival plan, the carefully edited details of which he was to publish nine years after his release in his best-selling *Spandau: The Secret Diaries*.[7] He was determined to keep physically and mentally fit so as to be able put all his energy into recreating his image as a technocrat of outstanding talent, whose decency set him apart from all the other leading figures in the Third Reich. Although there were many obstacles to overcome and he frequently stumbled, he was in the end remarkably successful in this effort to refashion his image.

To keep fit he became a passionate gardener. The gaol had a large walled garden that had been left unattended for years. The prisoners were given individual plots to cultivate as they wished. Funk specialised in tomatoes, Dönitz favoured beans, while Speer grew a variety of flowers. Gradually the other inmates lost interest or became too ill to keep their plots in working order. At the British prison director's suggestion, Speer, who was the youngest and fittest of the prisoners, turned this space into an intricate garden with pathways, lawns, flowerbeds, shrubberies, a rock garden and fruit trees.

In the summer months he spent hours every second day watering it by refilling a watering can fifty times. He sowed four thousand square metres of lawn, which then had to be regularly mowed by hand. The garden was Speer's private world where he could do whatever he wanted. Here he was free to use his imagination, to create and to dream. But this was only part of his fitness programme. He regularly made long walks around the garden, keeping an exact record of the distance covered each day. His record was 24.7 kilometres. His fastest pace was 5.8 kilometres in one hour. To make walking in a confined space more interesting he set out on an imaginary walk around the globe.

To keep intellectually alive Speer decided to turn his cell into a monkish study. He regularly studied professional architectural journals to keep himself up to date in his field. He made a systematic study of history from the earliest times, but the prison authorities did not allow the Spandau Seven to read anything about recent events. He dabbled in philosophy and theology. To escape the drab, tedious and routine life in prison he turned to great works of fiction. He worked hard to build on the remnants of his schoolboy knowledge of English and French. With his obsession for figures he kept a tally of everything that he had read. On his release from Spandau he announced that during his captivity he had read five thousand books.[8] Like many of Speer's statistics, this figure is grossly exaggerated. He spent roughly 7,300 days in prison after his trial. Therefore we are asked to believe that he read each book in an average of one-and-a-half days. Given that he spent up to six hours a day gardening and a couple of hours for the daily average of 7.3 kilometres of his 'walk around the world', plus the time spent writing thousands of pages of material, this seems exceedingly far fetched. Even the speediest and most expert of readers could not wade through the daunting volumes of Houston Stewart Chamberlain, Karl Jaspers or Karl Barth in a matter of hours.[9]

Speer's life changed dramatically on 14 October 1947 when Toni Proost ('Anton Vlaer' in the diaries), a young Dutchman working in the Spandau sick bay, offered to smuggle his messages out of the prison.[10] Proost had been deported during the war and had been forced to work in an armaments factory in Berlin. He had fallen ill and had been very well treated in one of the special hospitals that Speer had established for forced labourers in the armaments industry. After his recovery he worked as an assistant in the operating theatre. He became a close friend of the chief physician, who treated him as if he were a family member. Speer wrote that the possibility of writing secret messages on toilet paper, thereby making contact with the outside world, gave his life 'a new dimension'.[11]

At first the messages were sent either to his secretary, Annemarie Kempf, or to his family in Heidelberg. From 1951 the post was directed to the architectural office of his close friend and associate Rudolf Wolters in Coesfeld. Wolters immediately set about trying to make Speer's life in prison as comfortable as possible, for which he earned no thanks. Speer was so intent on presenting a grim picture of the 'endless monotony' of prison life in the published version of his prison diaries that there was no room for the gratitude he owed to Wolters. Speer wrote that he had kept the names of those who had helped him anonymous for 'obvious reasons', although he did mention 'Anton Vlaer', the man who had made it all possible. The main reason for this singular ingratitude was to mislead future historians. To this end he moved the anonymous Wolters' office from Coesfeld to Coburg.[12]

Wolters had been looking after Speer's interests long before 1951. All Speer's substantial assets had been seized, leaving his wife and six children in a desperate situation. Wolters therefore set about contacting all of Speer's co-workers and the wealthy industrialists who had profited from the industries that he had controlled in order to establish an emergency fund. Money soon began to flow into a 'Tuition Account'. Wolters kept a meticulous record of all payments in and out of this account between 1948 and Speer's release in 1966. The three volumes of account books show that the considerable sum of 154,183.34 Deutschmarks was paid into the account.[13]

Speer's financial worries were over at the end of 1953 when the German Federal Government released all his assets. In the final stages of the war he had deposited considerable sums of money with friends as an insurance policy for his family and for himself, were he to survive. He was now a wealthy man and was able to control how his money was spent through the secret messages that Proost took to the outside world. Speer told Wolters that his personal fortune should not be touched and that the family should be maintained exclusively from the charitable donations in the Tuition Account.[14] Although a man of considerable wealth, who was later to become a best-selling author, he had a neurotic attitude towards money. Margarete complained bitterly to Wolters that with six children it was impossible for her to live without support from her husband. She had been obliged to take paying guests into her home in Heidelberg so as to make both ends meet. Speer ignored these entreaties. He issued orders from Spandau prison that the Tuition Account was to pay the handsome sum of 1,200 Deutschmarks for the children's birthday and Christmas presents. It was also to provide Toni Proost with a two-week skiing holiday in the Tyrol at a cost of 400–500 Deutschmarks.[15] Money from the Tuition Account was used to buy thirty red roses for his daughter Hilde on the occasion of her marriage and a bouquet of roses for the bride's mother.[16]

Speer placed a virtually intolerable burden on Wolters. He was flooded with messages from Spandau, to the point that two of his assistants were fully occupied with Speer's affairs. Over the years many thousands of messages arrived in Coesfeld, prompting Wolters to remark to the historian Matthias Schmidt that in an emergency the 'Black Post' worked as quickly and as efficiently as the 'Red Telephone' in Washington and Moscow.[17] A major problem was that Speer had to write in minuscule handwriting in order to save scarce paper. At the best of times his handwriting was sloppy and difficult to read. The miniaturised version was virtually illegible. Marion Reisser, Wolters' eagle-eyed mistress, managed to decipher the scribble and for fifteen years transcribed it into a readable form.

Marion Reisser was the daughter of a distinguished Jewish professor of pharmacology from Breslau who managed to escape to Holland, where he remained in hiding throughout the war. He died in 1949. Marion's grandmother had been evicted from her apartment in the Lichtensteinallee in Berlin on Speer's orders. It was adjacent to the site of Speer's new studio.[18] In Wolters' heartless words, she was then 'given a free ticket to Theresienstadt', where she died in 1945.[19] Marion was a draughtswoman who joined Speer's Berlin staff in 1944. Immediately after the war she worked for Wolters in Coesfeld. As a man who enjoyed his hock, he referred to his beautiful and charming mistress, whom he ruthlessly dominated, as 'Riesling-Spätlese'.

Wolters was not only burdened with collecting funds to support the family and where possible to meet Speer's immediate needs. Between January 1953 and January 1954 he was also charged with providing Speer with material to help him write his memoirs. He had begun work on this project while at Nuremberg, where he gave a visiting clergyman one hundred pages of manuscript to pass to Wolters.[20] His messages were smuggled out of Spandau on a regular basis and were typed up in Coesfeld by Marion Reisser. Speer initially appears to have been genuinely grateful to Wolters for all that he had done to help. He promised to dedicate the published work to 'My and my family's trusted friend'.[21]

The assistance that Wolters provided for Speer was not restricted to the financial and the literary. It also included a generous effort to make the prisoner's life as pleasant as possible. He augmented the rations provided by the four powers with deliveries of champagne, foie gras and caviar. Speer, who took great pains to present himself as a man of frugal habits and modest demands, proved a difficult man to please. When Wolters sent him some cheap pressed caviar he received a sharp rebuke. Even the Beluga was criticised. Thanking Wolters for the caviar he had sent for his birthday in 1959 – along with some foie gras with truffles, venison and a Winkler Massenpflug 1957 [sic] – he could not resist remarking that: 'even though for us experts Beluga comes second to that other outrageously expensive one we tasted together at the Kuban bridgehead: remember?'[22] Wolters was obliged to pay 145 Deutschmarks for a Group 1 Dunhill pipe. He thought this to be an unnecessary extravagance. Without the little white spot it looked like a pipe costing 3.50 Deutschmarks.[23]

Anxious to make prison life seem as grim and austere as possible, Speer makes no mention of Wolters' generosity in the Spandau Diaries. There are, however, certain hints that life was not quite so hard. In 1950 he claimed that an American doctor had prescribed half a bottle of champagne per day as a remedy for his irregular heartbeat.[24] Given that alcohol can cause cardiac arrhythmia this would seem a most dubious prescription and is almost certainly untrue. Speer admits that the faithful Proost smuggled a quarter of a litre of cognac into his cell, which he drank at one go and then put coffee in the glass to fool the Russian guards.[25] A couple of months later Schirach celebrated his birthday with half a bottle of cognac.[26] Funk is then described as smoking a cigar and sipping at a bottle of cognac.[27] Speer reported being given a bottle of cognac and some Swiss chocolate, but did not say from whence they came. That day Speer pointed out that the *Empire News* had reported that prisoners were smuggling letters out of Spandau, but no stricter controls were applied.[28] In February 1954 he wrote that one of the guards was delivering Hennessy and Canadian Club 'without limit'. Again he did not say who was the benefactor.[29] He celebrated the New Year of 1961 with a bottle of Pommard.[30]

Nothing seems to have changed when, in 1957, the NKVD attempted to recruit Toni Proost as an agent in Spandau. He prudently reported this to the Allied authorities, who decided that he should leave Spandau and return to his native Holland.[31] A friendly US sergeant now acted as Speer's courier. Thanks to him, New Year's Day was celebrated with lobster mayonnaise, washed down by British beer. Again we are not told who footed the bill. In all these cases we can safely assume that it was Wolters.

Even though Speer became increasingly exigent, Wolters regarded him with genuine affection. They maintained a lively correspondence, its intimacy enhanced by a coded language. Spandau became 'Spain', the prison 'hotel', the memoirs 'aria', his diary 'wood shavings' and champagne the onomatopoeic 'Plöpp'. Wolters' messages were full of wry humour, jovial encouragement and friendly support.

Wolters' main efforts were devoted to his determined attempt to get Speer's sentence reduced. To this end he contacted Dönitz's defence attorney, Dr Otto Kranzbühler, a former naval officer who had served in the Spanish Civil War and who had acted as a naval judge in France and Wilhelmshaven during the war. He proved to be the outstanding defence lawyer at Nuremberg, quickly adapting his tactics to Anglo-Saxon court procedure. He saved Dönitz from a death sentence for ordering the sinking of merchant ships without due warning by his brilliant questioning of Admiral Nimitz, in which he forced the admiral to admit that the US Navy had done exactly the same. Kranzbühler also defended Alfried Krupp von Bohlen und Halbach, Friedrich Flick and Hermann Schmitz – the latter in the IG Farben trial. After the war he enjoyed a spectacular legal career defending German industrial concerns against claims from former slave labourers. He was appointed to the board of directors of a number of major companies and was known as 'Krupp's Grey Eminence'. He also had close contacts with a number of leading politicians, including the chancellor, Konrad Adenauer.[32]

Thanks to Kranzbühler's skilful handling of his case, Dönitz had only received a ten-year prison sentence and was due for release in 1956. Kranzbühler and Wolters therefore hoped to draw parallels between the cases of Dönitz and Speer so as to secure Speer's release at the same time. Prisoner Number Three, Konstantin von Neurath, who had been given a fifteen-year sentence, was released in November 1954 at the age of eighty-one for reasons of health. He received congratulatory telegrams from Chancellor Adenauer and President Theodor Heuss, which provoked considerable criticism in some circles. As a psychosomatic reaction to Neurath's release and a painful reminder that he still had several years of his sentence left to serve, Speer's right leg once again flared up. It swelled to twice its normal size and he developed bronchitis. Prisoner Number Four, the 79-year-old Erich Raeder, was released in September 1955, also for health reasons. On 1 October 1956 Dönitz was released, having served his full term. In May 1957 prisoner Number Six, Walther Funk, who had received a life sentence and was in poor health, was released at the age of sixty-seven. He died three years later.

Speer's efforts to gain an early release were doomed to failure. Kranzbühler had met Speer in Nuremberg shortly after Christmas 1946.[33] The relationship between them was uncomfortable from the outset. The lawyer thought it wise for Speer not to mention that he had planned to assassinate Hitler. Flächsner and Wolters agreed.[34] No appeal was permitted against judgments at Nuremberg. Speer was thirty-two years younger than von Neurath and in reasonable health. The Soviet Union had no intention of showing any clemency to Speer – a man for whom they had demanded the death sentence.

Speer was somewhat encouraged when he heard that there were a number of people outside the prison who had some consideration for his plight. The Catholic author Anne Freemantle wrote to Wolters saying that the widows of the prominent resisters Adam von Trott zu Solz and Wessel Freytag von Loringhoven showed respect and 'a certain sympathy' for him. She also said that their friends Bertrand Russell and Jacques Maritain agreed, but cautioned that Speer was not noted for his loyalty. Speer tried to turn this charge to his own advantage by arguing that loyalty was a form of 'ethical blindness', thereby hoping to conceal his allegiance to Hitler and his total lack of moral insight. Speer's meditations on the meaning of the word 'loyalty' make astonishing reading. He claimed to have been loyal to Stauffenberg by not denouncing him for describing Hitler, Goring, Himmler and Keitel as 'idiots'. He was equally 'loyal' to General Friedrich Fromm, the commander of the reserve army, and Stauffenberg's co-conspirator General Helmuth Stieff, who frequently criticised the leadership.

Indeed Speer regarded himself as having been loyal to everyone – even to the slave labourers, whom he 'treated well' – and also to Sauckel, who rounded them up on his behalf. Above all Speer was loyal to Germany, claiming to have been the only one among the prisoners in Spandau who had made a clear distinction between the Third Reich and Germany. Unlike them he had boldly confronted Hitler, Göring and Bormann on numerous occasions.[35] His loyalty to Sauckel did not amount to much. He conveniently put all the blame for the use of forced labour upon him, but he felt obliged to argue that Sauckel had been concerned for his workers' welfare so as to buttress his claim that working for the Ministry of Armaments was hardly a dismal fate.[36]

Speer's aim in the published version of the Spandau Diaries was to present himself as having lost twenty years of his life, from the ages of forty to sixty, enduring a harsh prison sentence, in return for which he was absolved of all wrongdoing. The entire book was in a sense an amplification of his answer to a letter that his daughter Hilde had written to him on her birthday on 17 April 1953, asking how he could possibly have served a regime that was so transparently evil.[37] Speer did not reply until 14 May. He makes no mention of this painful exchange in the diaries. He began by saying that: 'There are things, you see, for which one has to carry the blame, even if purely factually one might find excuses. The immensity of the crime precludes any attempt at self-justification.'

He spoke here of blame. At Nuremberg he spoke of 'joint responsibility'. He purposefully avoided any mention of the word 'guilt', for fear of then having to justify himself. He then repeated the familiar line that although he knew nothing of the 'dreadful things' that had happened, he blamed himself for not finding out about them. He went on to compare himself with Oedipus, who was horribly punished by providence for transgressions for which he bore no responsibility. He claimed to have been overwhelmed by Hitler's friendship, by the power that he thereby gained, and by the limitless opportunities he was given to pursue his career as an architect. He was blinded by a Faustian pact, a tragic hero enmeshed in inextricable fate. He only began to question the regime when Hitler threatened to destroy what was left of Germany. His opposition, such as it was, was not to the persecution of the Jews or to an aggressive war. In conventionally anti-Semitic terms he wrote: 'I really did not have any feelings of aversion towards them [the Jews], in other words no more than the uncomfortable feeling that all of us sometimes have when in contact with them.'[38]

This makes for painful reading now that we know that not only was Speer fully aware of what had happened to the Jews, but also played an active part in their persecution. Even in the carefully edited Spandau Diaries there are moments when he lets down his guard. He tells us that 'between the soup and the vegetable course' Hitler would announce: 'I intend to destroy the European Jews! This war is a decisive contest between National Socialism and world Jewry. One will fall by the wayside, but it certainly will not be us. It is fortunate that I as an Austrian know the Jews so well. They will destroy us if we lose. Why should I show them any pity?' Speer commented that those present did not react, not because of fear but rather out of shame that they 'almost' knew, but did nothing.[39] If such were indeed the case, their shame emanated from their cowardly silence, their moral torpor, and the continued suppression of troublesome knowledge. Speer reminded himself that Hitler was constantly talking of the elimination and extermination of the Jews, but then he tried to turn the tables by asking himself whether 'Bomber' Harris used the same language when talking of the Germans.[40]

In the same manner Speer argued that the Allies had also used POWs as forced labour in armaments factories.[41] Although this was a widespread practice in Germany, particularly at Krupp and BMW, there is no evidence that German POWs were used in armaments factories in either the United States or Britain. In Britain, working outside the camp was considered a privilege from which known Nazis were excluded. They worked on a volunteer basis, mainly in agriculture and the building trades, and were paid minimum union wages. Twenty-four thousand of them chose to stay in Britain after the war. Among these was Manchester City's popular goalkeeper, Bert Trautman. Those captured by the Red Army were considerably less fortunate.

Speer agreed with his fellow prisoner Dönitz that the Nuremberg trials were a flagrant example of victor's justice.[42] He refused to accept that he was guilty in a judicial sense, on the highly dubious grounds that he had done nothing that leaders on the other side had not also done. He comforted himself with the argument that 'terror raids' by Allied aircraft were morally equivalent to the worst of the Nazis' crimes. As for the charge that he had employed slave labour, he managed to convince himself that that was Sauckel's sole responsibility, thereby conveniently forgetting that Sauckel had rounded up workers at his request.[43] Speer's concept of guilt was a curious construct. For him it was a kind of therapy helping him to overcome the ordeal of a twenty-year prison sentence. Although he thought himself to be guiltless, he realised that in the interest of mental self-survival he could not indulge in prolonged self-pity and indignation at the injustice of the Nuremberg judges. A sense of guilt, abstracted almost to vanishing point, provided some justification for his imprisonment. Wrestling with it at the intellectual level helped pass the time, as he dabbled in Karl Barth's analysis of the Epistle to the Romans and engaged in conversation with the prison chaplain, the admirable French Protestant theologian Georges Casalis. The end result was that Speer counted himself as the outstanding example of the 'denazification victim' or 'casualty of denazification'.[44]

Speer quickly developed a strategy for survival in Spandau. His conscience was relieved by accepting a conveniently vague concept of guilt. He claimed that in spite of his consultations with Kranzbühler he was resolved to remain emotionally detached by calmly accepting a lengthy imprisonment with no hope of an early release. He also managed to convince himself that by serving his sentence he would be absolved of all residual guilt, to emerge from Spandau with all wrongdoing remitted. On a practical level he was determined to organise his daily routine so as best to meet the challenges resulting from such a lengthy confinement.[45]

There are moments in the diaries when Speer drops his guard and reveals his former self. Thus he admits that he saw the campaign against the Soviet Union as a 'European Crusade' that was supported by volunteers from Belgium, Holland, France, Spain and a number of other countries. Traditional fear of the East was compounded by the horrors resulting from the Bolshevik Revolution, giving rise to an idealistic movement analogous to Eisenhower's 'Crusade in Europe'. The problem was that it was derailed by the regrettable activities of the murderous *Einsatzgruppen*.[46] He thereby failed to realise that mass murder was an essential component of Nazi Germany's civilising mission.

In a dramatic gesture of loyalty, Speer congratulated himself on the 'romantic' action of visiting Hitler shortly before his suicide. He contrasted this selfless act with the brutal anarchy as the Third Reich fell apart. As an example of the widespread depravity of those horrific final days he cites the case of the

Gauleiter of Saxony, Martin Mutschmann, who in the freezing cold was led through the streets of Dresden in an open cart and beaten to death.[47] None of this is true. Mutschmann was a ludicrously incompetent person who failed to provide adequate air raid protection for the citizens of Dresden. He fled the city, having ordered the people to fight to the last amid the ruins. He was captured by the Red Army and executed in Moscow's Lubyanka prison in 1947.

Speer frequently presents himself as sitting beside Hitler listening with awestruck attention as he launched into yet another interminable monologue. Although the National Socialists destroyed the federal system and with it the last vestiges of provincial autonomy, Speer is full of praise for Hitler's deep respect for regional differences, which was reflected in each Party District. He gave silent agreement to Hitler's definition of centralised government as 'Jewish egalitarianism.'[48] He comforted himself with the thought that other great men also fell under Hitler's 'magic spell', among them Hindenburg, Lloyd George, Sir John Simon and Mussolini.[49]

During his time in Spandau Speer came to believe that had Todt not been killed, and had he not been appointed Minister of Armaments, he would have become a truly great architect and would never have been condemned at Nuremberg. Fate, he felt, had struck him a harsh blow. He even managed to entertain the idea that he might have been able to produce a work that would have matched the Parthenon, St Peter's or a Palladian villa.[50] He also felt resentful that he was unlikely to be able to pursue a successful career as an architect upon his release. He had tried to keep up to date with modern styles and techniques, but he was totally out of sympathy with modernists like Mies van der Rohe, Walter Gropius and Le Corbusier who were now setting the tone. To make matters worse, Germany was being rebuilt by 'subaltern confectioners', whose work was greatly inferior. He made exceptions for Egon Eiermann, Hans Sharoun and Hans Schwippert.[51] Unable to adapt, he returned to Tessenow for inspiration. All the villas he sketched while in Spandau and the more modest houses he designed for some of the warders were very much in his teacher's style.[52]

Speer deeply regretted that nothing was left of his architectural work, apart from a modest house he had built for his parents-in-law, some street lighting in Berlin and a chair that he had designed for the new chancellery, which had been provided for the frail Neurath in his Spandau cell.[53] Regarding himself as the 'last classicist', he saw no future for himself as an architect in a world of 'glass, concrete and steel' in which there was no place for skilled masons and craftsmen.[54] Speer decided that upon his release he would begin a new career as a writer. He would then become a second Cellini, although without anything to match the *Salt Cellar* or *Perseus* – an artist best known for his colourful memoirs.[55]

In November 1953, after eight months' work, Speer completed his memoirs, comprising 350 typewritten pages.[56] The final draft was finished in December the following year.[57] With his somewhat indelicate interest in the pecuniary he calculated that rich pickings could be made from a carefully packaged account of his remarkable life. As early as December 1948 the American publisher Knopf offered to publish his memoirs.[58] In June 1951 the Heliopolis-Verlag in Tübingen, Ernst Jünger's publisher, expressed an interest in an autobiography.[59] Speer decided to bide his time. In October 1963 his daughter Inge brought him an attractive offer from the Berlin publisher Propyläen, part of the Ullstein publishing house that had been 'Aryanised' in 1934, restored to the Ullstein family and then, in 1960, taken over by the highly controversial newspaper mogul Axel Springer.[60] Speer had some rather coquettish doubts about taking up this offer. Did he really want to put himself in the spotlight? He still had lingering thoughts of going back to architecture or perhaps pursuing a career in the business world, where his excellent connections and organisational talents were likely to be appreciated and adequately remunerated. He decided to keep Propyläen on tenterhooks. The tactic paid off. The offer was renewed in 1965.[61] Speer said that he was 'not uninterested'. The publishers would hear from him soon after he was released from prison in six months' time. Offers were also made for him to be interviewed on television, but he was horrified when one station suggested that he should appear alongside Hermann Esser, the author of *The Universal Jewish Pestilence*, whom he aptly described as a 'petit-bourgeois Bavarian Hitlerite'.[62]

For years Speer continued his lonely walk around the world until, having walked 31,816 kilometres, he sent a message to Rudolf Wolters: 'please pick up 35 kilometres south of Guadal[a]jara Mexico'.[63] The prison director told Speer that he was to leave Spandau before Schirach. His bitter reflection was that he had hoped to leave years, not seconds, before the former Reich Youth Leader and Gauleiter of Vienna. He left his collection of gramophone records to Rudolf Hess, who was now the sole prisoner. These had mostly been given to him by his friend the pianist Wilhelm Kempff. He had already issued orders to the family to prepare certain essential items in preparation for his release. These included an inconspicuous tweed suit, a briefcase in dark brown leather and a dark brown wallet containing a couple of hundred marks. The money was naturally to come from Wolters' Tuition Account, not from his own personal account. He ordered an electric razor, shaving lotion and toothpicks, along with a series of medications, including anti-depressants, adrenalin, sleeping pills, multi-vitamins and Bellergal to relieve nervousness and tension. His daughter Hilde complained that she was driven crazy by this flood of orders that included a detailed list of menus and drinks.[64] There was enough money in the Tuition Account for Wolters to buy him the Jaeger-LeCoultre wristwatch he had ordered to celebrate his release from prison.[65]

SPEER

On the evening of 30 September 1966, after an awkward and distant farewell to Hess, Speer waited in his cell pondering the concluding passages of Tessenow's *Handwerk und Kleinstadt – Handicraft and Small Towns*. Shortly before midnight he was brought an old ski jacket, a shirt and tie and a pair of old corduroy trousers. He was then taken to see the friendly British prison director, who handed over the 2,778 obsolete Reichsmarks that he had had in his possession in May 1945. He was also given a temporary identity card that was only valid for five days.

CHAPTER FOURTEEN

THE GOOD NAZI

H IS WIFE AND Dr Flächsner were waiting for him at the prison gates. Having peremptorily shaken Gretel's hand, he made as if to take the seat beside the driver of a large black Mercedes that had been provided by the industrialist Ernst Wolf Mommsen. Flächsner pulled him back, insisting that he sit beside his wife.[1] Speer reluctantly complied. The gates swung open. They were blinded by the floodlights of numerous TV cameras and exploding flash bulbs. Having run the gauntlet of journalists they drove to the Schlosshotel Gehrhus in the Grünewald where they spent the night.

This uncomfortable scene was symptomatic of the relationship between Speer and Margarete. They did not embrace. He did not wish to sit beside her. Hans Flächsner, although by no means a demonstrative person, found the scene so bizarre that cold shivers went down his spine.[2] The couple had always found it difficult to express their emotions and there was little affection between them. Although they dutifully presented the Führer with six children, theirs was a singularly distant relationship. Georges Casalis's wife Dorothée, who was also a Protestant theologian, said of the Speers: 'I honestly don't think that either of them knew the meaning of sexuality. She was above all a mother; perhaps her attitude even to Speer was that of a mother – or a sister?'[3]

From the time he had met Hitler Speer had virtually no time for family life. He dreaded the awkwardness of the infrequent visits by his wife and children to Spandau. In an inexplicable entry in the Spandau Diaries, Speer mentions that he had a 'semi-erotic' relationship with Spandau, and that perhaps he never wanted to leave. He admitted that there had always been a screen between himself and others. He had been a stranger amid Hitler's inner circle, a stranger among his fellow prisoners in Spandau, and now he was a stranger within his own family. Insurmountable differences remained that could not be pushed aside. The situation was made all the more painful because everyone tried so hard to make it work.[4]

SPEER

The Schlosshotel Gehrhus was a small luxury hotel where Speer had often stayed. A magnificent room filled with flowers was prepared for the reunited couple. Having sampled a fine bottle of wine with Flächsner, Speer made some telephone calls, among others to Wolters. He then calmly called for a press conference to quieten the crowd of journalists that was swarming all over the hotel. When asked what he intended to do now, he replied that he was an architect and that he hoped to practise his profession.[5] This was not to be. His one attempt ended in disaster. In 1967/8 he collaborated with Ernst Neufert, a modernist from the Bauhaus and an associate of Walter Gropius, in a project to build a brewery for Dortmunder Union. Speer's attempt to learn the modernist idiom was doomed to failure.[6]

The next day the couple moved to a rented house on the Kellersee in Schleswig-Holstein. There followed weeks of awkwardness and frustration. Speer's remoteness and self-absorption had become acute after twenty cloistered years in Spandau. He missed the prison routine, his meditations and his imaginary walk around the world. He appeared to be totally uninterested in what his children thought, had done or what they aspired to do. The family never recovered from the shock of this cold aloofness and self-absorption. He made no mention of his wrestling with the question of guilt, nor of his agnostic dabbling in theology. In large part this was because he always drew a sharp distinction between guilt and responsibility. The concept of responsibility is conveniently vague. In as much as he felt any guilt it was strictly limited. As he wrote to a distinguished lawyer, Dr Werner Schütz, who had offered to help him: 'My guilt, as I voluntarily stated even before the trial, is, in my opinion, limited to the fact that I demanded that workers be brought to Germany who came against their will, and that I did not stop asking for them even when I knew that they were brought by force.'[7] This is blatantly untrue. On 24 April 1952 he wrote to Hilde saying that at Nuremberg he never spoke of guilt, but only of 'joint responsibility'. Guilt was simply not part of his vocabulary.[8]

Speer's task now was to continue reinventing his past so as to be in harmony with this new-found self-righteousness. He was not only guiltless because he had obtained absolution; he had never been guilty in the first place. Wrong had been done not by him, but by others, by an evil system or by the phantom of technology that had enslaved him. It was an extraordinary achievement for a man who was responsible for so many deaths to present himself to the world as a guiltless innocent – a *Parsifal*, as Funk had said of him – and to have been so astonishingly successful in getting away with it.

Speer was to claim that Spandau was more of a refuge for him than a prison, a place where he could study and meditate. Here, he would claim, he lived an authentic existence and discovered his real self. His daughter Hilde, however, knew that this was all a sham. He was determined to be conspicuously in the limelight and make a fortune out of his writing. The Hermit of Spandau was every bit as hungry for fame, power, status and money as he had ever been. He had every reason to believe that he would succeed. While in Spandau he had received offers from various magazines. He decided to accept the astronomical sum of DM50,000 from *Der Spiegel* for an interview. Although this was less than he had been offered by other publications, he felt that the magazine was of a suitable quality and had a wide enough circulation for his debut literary effort.[9]

The success of Speer's endeavour depended on the careful concealment of all evidence that could be used against him. He subscribed wholeheartedly to the principle in Roman law, *'quod non est in actis non est in mundo'* (what is not kept in the records does not exist). Careful weeding out of the records would thus cause any unpleasantness to disappear. It was here that his friend and close associate Dr Rudolf Wolters played a key role.[10] They had been students together in Munich and Berlin. From the outset Wolters was involved in most of Speer's important projects. He helped to plan the north–south axis. He engaged a number of architects, painters and sculptors for the new Berlin. He planned a major architectural exhibition. He was responsible for 'culture, press and propaganda' in Organisation Todt. He was also in charge of planning the rebuilding of the bomb-damaged towns. During all this time he kept a detailed diary of all Speer's activities in what was named the 'Speer Chronicle'. Wolters also kept a personal diary that included excerpts from letters, memoranda and official documents.

While in Nuremberg, Speer felt that Wolters was the ideal man to write his biography. He had already written a brief adulatory book on Speer in a series 'Contemporary German Artists', published in 1943.[11] Speer's plan was for his life's work to be examined in four parts. The first would deal with his work as an architect. It was to be lavishly illustrated. The second part would be an 'objective account of the organisation and achievements' of the Ministry of Armaments. Thirdly there would be a study of the life of the man whom Speer described as 'Number Two' in Hitler's Germany. This was to include a positive portrait of his relationship with Hitler 'in an idealistic manner as it once was'. Lastly would come his own memoirs that were to be 'open and honest'. They were to be published many years later. Speer began work on this last section while at Nuremberg and completed a rough draft of his memoirs between 1953 and 1954. While in Spandau he thought of publishing the 'Speer Chronicle', to include a detailed commentary, an architectural study entitled 'The Window' on which he had begun work, along with a selection of essays and book reviews. He told Wolters that he would give all the money that he earned from it to charity. Wolters listened in silent disbelief.[12]

While Speer was in Spandau, Wolters organised a number of meetings between the well-known conservative historian Walther Hubatsch and the

Athenäum publishing house, but Speer, who had already had offers from several publishers, told him to hold his horses. In 1964 a young historian, Gregor Janssen, wrote the equivalent of a master's thesis on the Ministry of Armaments. He showed the work to Walther Hubatsch in the hope that it could be turned into a doctoral dissertation under his supervision. Hubatsch gave it to Wolters, who arranged for it to be smuggled into Spandau. Speer was far from pleased with the work. Claiming that it was riddled with errors, he sent it back with his marginal comments. He was relieved to hear that a shortage of funds made it unlikely that Janssen would be able to finish his thesis. These difficulties were surmounted, Hubatsch agreed to supervise him, and the resulting thesis was published in 1968, the year before Speer's memoirs. It was an excellent pioneering institutional study that was well received. It did nothing to harm Speer's reputation, even though it emphasised the close cooperation between Himmler and Speer.[13]

On his way from his retreat in Schleswig-Holstein to the family home in Heidelberg, Speer paid a visit to Rudolf Wolters in Coesfeld. Wolters, furious with Speer for ordering him around and his ingratitude for all he had done for him, had not wished to see his old friend, but Annemarie Kempf had mollified him, thereby enabling what turned out to be a courteous encounter. The atmosphere was eased with a bottle of Johannesberger 1937 from Prince Metternich's estate. Wolters handed over his retyped version of the Chronicle, masses of photographs of Speer' buildings, the plans for rebuilding Berlin, all the material he had sent from Spandau, press clippings collected over the last twenty years, and the balance of DM25,000 in the Tuition Account, which Speer promptly spent on a luxurious car. It would seem that his recent enthusiasm for austerity and the simple life was soon forgotten amid the tempting materialism of the west German 'economic miracle'. Wolters also presented him with a fine Westphalian ham from a pig that had been born on the day that Stalin died.[14]

The meeting was superficially convivial, but it was clear to Wolters that their friendship was severely strained. Speer had a good reason for distancing himself from his old friend. He did not want to draw attention to a man who knew his secrets and could at any time destroy his carefully constructed self-image of 'the angel who came from hell', the guiltless scapegoat for a nation bewitched by a charismatic leader and in thrall to the tyranny of modern technology.

Wolters was contemptuous of Speer's hand-wringing and confessions of guilt, which he found self-serving, duplicitous and implausible. His precise political position is difficult to pinpoint. Although never a party member and often critical of certain aspects of the regime, as a fervent nationalist Wolters was proud of many of the achievements of National Socialist Germany. To many who knew him well he was at heart a Nazi who posed as an old-fashioned nationalist. A photograph of Speer with Hitler hung in his bedroom, even after his break with Speer. He was later to admit that his relationship with Speer was very similar to that between Speer and Hitler.[15] He gave his son Friedrich – to his acute embarrassment – a Volkswagen with the number plate COE AH 88: COE for Coesfeld, AH for Adolf Hitler and 88 for HH (*Heil Hitler*), H being the eighth letter in the alphabet. ('88' was a widely used code among Nazi sympathisers after the war.)[16]

On his return to the family home in Heidelberg, Speer set to work sifting through the vast mounds of material that Wolters had assembled over the past twenty years. He immediately contacted Wolf Jobst Siedler, the head of the Propyläen division at the Ullstein publishing house, suggesting that he should come to Berlin to discuss a contract for his memoirs. Siedler replied that he would prefer to come to Heidelberg, but Speer insisted on going to Berlin. The contract was signed over lunch. Speer claimed he had not even bothered to read it.

Speer immediately set to work preparing for the interview in *Der Spiegel*.[17] He later claimed to have done it not for the money but to enlighten young people. If that was indeed his intent, he failed miserably. Wolters was outraged at the interview, accusing Speer of being irresponsible and deliberately misleading, thereby seriously damaging his reputation. He had merely voiced the conventional wisdom handed out by German schools and universities during the previous twenty years. In answer to the question whether Germany was responsible for the war, Speer replied that Hitler, not Germany, bore the blame. Wolters pointed out that in 1939 they all believed that Hitler *was* Germany and that Poland, encouraged by support from Britain, had provoked the war. For Wolters, the attempt to demonise Hitler was a cheap way to absolve Germany of all guilt.[18] He instinctively felt that Speer's intent was to provide the Germans with an alibi, free them from guilt, and make a great deal of money in the process. He therefore refused to help Speer write his memoirs, which he knew would give a far from accurate picture of the twelve years of Nazi Germany. His daughter Hilde took over as Speer's literary executor.

In addition to the vast amount of material he had received from Wolters he made extensive use of material from the Federal Archives in Coblenz. One archivist was struck by the fact that he never asked for material relating to Jews or the treatment of foreign workers.[19] Given this mass of data, Siedler decided that Speer should write two substantial books: first the memoirs and then bits and pieces selected from his papers that were to comprise the Spandau Diaries. To help him write the memoirs Siedler hired the gifted conservative journalist Joachim Fest to act as consultant.

Fest's role is a matter of some dispute. Speer and Siedler both agree that he was in no sense a ghost-writer, but this is hard to believe. Whatever his precise role, it is quite clear that Fest played a major part in the end product. He was a past master of German prose. The fluid style of the memoirs is far removed from the awkwardness of Speer's prose in his speeches and other published works. Fest had already published an immensely influential essay on Speer. In this he painted a portrait of an upper-middle-class technocrat who fell prey to Hitler's magic charm.[20] It was a version of Speer's life that was to be elaborated in great detail in his autobiography. Towards the end of 1966, Fest was approached by the American publishers Harcourt Brace Jovanovich with the proposal that he give up his job on North German Radio to concentrate on writing a biography of Hitler. The prospect of working with Speer, Hitler's intimate associate, was therefore extremely attractive. Fest began working with Speer in 1967. In the following year he took leave of absence from North German Radio and devoted himself full time to working on the autobiography. It took almost three years to get Speer's two-thousand-page manuscript into readable form.[21]

Speer very soon realised how difficult it was for him to come to terms with his past and to give it adequate literary expression. His perceptions had radically altered after twenty years of study and reflection. He was a quite different person from the young prisoner at Nuremberg, who had expressed his determination to give a brutally honest account of the corruption, hypocrisy and brutality at the heart of National Socialism.[22] Speer had wrestled for years with the true nature of his curious relationship with Hitler. He had yet to find an answer.

The writer and resistance fighter Günther Weisenborn gave a vivid picture of Hitler and Speer in the artistic milieu of Munich in the mid-1930s. Hitler and Speer sat side by side on a sofa. The others, including Himmler, Goebbels and Franz Ritter von Epp, the Governor of Bavaria, sat around a table. Uniformed officers occupied a number of smaller tables. They represented to him 'the Aryan machinery of Germania, scampering Nazi automata, clean-shaven barbarity stemming from frozen humanity'. The relationship between Hitler and Speer was on display.

> It was a remarkable performance. Whenever the fellow that they call the Leader (*Führer*), who this evening plays the role of the simple fellow with his good-natured eyes agape, says a few words, all the paladins who surround him lean forward devotedly. They all concentrate on the same point: the mouth with the snot mop. It was as if a warm wind of devotion had silently bent these proud stems, so that all I could see was the rolls of fat on the necks of the leaders of our Reich. And that was not all. Fat-faced Hitler accepted this wave of submissiveness then nodded discreetly to Speer, who sat to his right and occasionally spoke a few well-mannered and

wearied words. The homage that Hitler received was thereby passed on to Speer, in a sort of relay race of submissiveness. Speer seemed to be an object of admiration, a lover who accepted these acts of homage as if they were loose change.[23]

Karl Maria Hettlage insisted that Speer was Hitler's 'unhappy love'.[24] Speer was troubled by, but never came to terms with, the homoerotic aspects of his relationship with Hitler. As early as 1954 he had hoped that writing his memoirs would help him answer the question 'Who am I?' Karl Jaspers' remark that objective reality did not exist was both comforting and troubling to him. It provided a means to avoid the unpleasant and disquieting, but it also stood in the way of self-discovery.[25]

It was therefore hardly surprising that Siedler and Fest had considerable difficulty editing the manuscript. Siedler often acted like a stern thesis supervisor, frequently sending Speer back to Heidelberg to rewrite passages like a recalcitrant student.[26] It is impossible to tell to what extent the memoirs differ in substance from the sketches of 1946 and 1953–4. Speer refused to bequeath this material to the archives. Fest and Siedler took a journalistic approach to the project. They relied entirely on Speer's own testimony and on picking the brains of such dubious witnesses as Field Marshal Milch, Nicolaus von Below, Hitler's Luftwaffe adjutant, and the controversial British writer, David Irving. Fest had utter contempt for academic historians, feeling that their work was little more than a mass of details on insignificant topics, tediously heaped together and written in opaque academic jargon.[27] It is therefore hardly surprising that they did not hire any historians as research assistants to comb through the archives. Since they did not visit the Federal Archives in Coblenz, where the remaining papers of Speer's ministry were lodged, they had to rely on his highly selective account of his knowledge of the treatment of forced labourers and Jews. Fest and Siedler had to force Speer to add one brief paragraph on the pogrom of 9 November 1938.[28] He was extremely reluctant to mention this, even though – or perhaps because – he was in Berlin at the time. During his cross-examination by the Allies in Kransberg he had spoken of this well-organised display of widespread thuggery that resulted in four hundred deaths, the arrest of thirty thousand Jews, plus the destruction of 1,406 synagogues and 7,500 Jewish stores, as 'a spontaneous demonstration'. At about the same time, Rudolf Wolters recalled that in November 1938 he was working with Speer on the 'Germania' project. Speer confessed to having been shocked that almost all the shops in Unter den Linden, Berlin's most elegant street, were in Jewish hands. 'We therefore considered the "Night of Broken Glass" [Kristallnacht] to have been an unavoidable side-issue of the National Socialist seizure of power that we all supported and which showed its revolutionary character.'[29]

It is impossible to know whether Siedler and Fest naively accepted Speer's account, thereby sparing themselves the arduous task of ploughing through piles of archival material, or whether they were set on producing what the historian Wolfgang Benz was to call a 'patriotic project': the reconstruction of a major Nazi war criminal, cleansed of all guilt, truly penitent and reborn. This was to be called the 'living lie' of an entire generation, for whom Speer's memoirs were a confirmation of their convenient belief that the entire burden of guilt was borne by the members of a small clique of criminals, psychopaths and sadists.[30]

Fest and Siedler never pressed Speer on the question of how much he really knew. Years later when questioned on this point Fest replied that he saw no point in doing so.[31] Was this because they did not want to face this uncomfortable question themselves? Or perhaps it would compromise their carefully constructed portrait based on Speer's self-image? Whatever the answer, Speer's memoirs were swallowed hook, line and sinker by hundreds of thousands of readers, even though it is utterly inconceivable that a man in Speer's position knew nothing of the persecution of the Jews or the ill-treatment of the slave labourers that had the misfortune to work under him. Speer admitted to Fest and Siedler that he was aware of the appalling conditions in which the forced labourers and concentration camp inmates had to live, but he laid the blame for this on Sauckel, Himmler and, ultimately, Hitler. He claimed that at Nuremberg these living conditions had been grossly misrepresented. Later he pointed to the case of Toni Proost, who had helped him in Spandau, in gratitude for the excellent treatment he had been afforded under Speer's aegis. In any case, Speer argued, war is a nasty business in which unpleasant things happen to all concerned. He claimed that conditions on the other side were not much different, 'obviously among the Russians, but also to a considerable extent among the French, Americans and others'. Neither side respected the Geneva or Hague Conventions.[32]

A major problem with the memoirs was that Speer wrote in general terms without giving concrete examples. He did not seriously question the entire regime and the role he had played in it. He could describe the general atmosphere, but was reluctant to fill it in with facts. He felt it prudent not to mention any similarities between the Dresden raid and Theresienstadt. When pressed, he had to admit that there was a certain distinction to be made between the Allied bombing and the German determination to exterminate all those they considered to be socially, biologically and racially undesirable.[33]

Siedler was disappointed with the final version of the memoirs. He felt that Speer should have analysed the structure of the regime, shown how the entire system had broken down and examined his own shortcomings, thereby revealing how he had become morally unresponsive, pliant and submissive. Instead he had constantly repeated how sorry he was for what had happened.

Fest heartily agreed, so that, much to his annoyance, Speer had to delete a number of his empty apologies.[34] When Siedler and Fest asked him whether he had left out anything that might later cause him some embarrassment, he replied emphatically that he had no secrets.

Siedler later claimed that he never expected Speer's memoirs to be a great success. He had given Speer a very modest advance and precious little time to complete the manuscript, and had planned a relatively modest first printing.[35] This is difficult to believe. Admittedly Baldur von Schirach's memoirs, published in 1968, excited little interest, but they had not yet been published when Speer signed the contract. No one had been closer to Hitler than Speer throughout the twelve years of the Third Reich. He was a highly intelligent man with a carefully considered view of the past that would ease the burden of conscience of an entire nation. Siedler had taken great pains to offer Speer optimum working conditions and had provided him with an outstanding journalist as his assistant. Major publishing houses had made handsome offers, while magazines had paid breathtaking fees for interviews. Equally strange is Siedler's claim that for an international bestseller the profits were relatively slim.

In fact, the memoirs were a phenomenal success. Speer, the major war criminal, became almost overnight a popular figure – something that he had never been at the height of his power in Nazi Germany. The general reading public was fascinated and titillated by this unique account of the inner workings of the Third Reich. Descriptions of Hitler's private life at the Berghof, the power struggles among the high and the mighty, the unreal atmosphere of overwhelming hubris and looming collapse, all made for compelling reading. Historians, however, were disappointed that Speer had revealed little that was new and had kept his cards close to his chest.

For the older generation of Germans the memoirs provided a comforting alibi for all that had happened in the twelve years of the Third Reich. Here was a man at the very top, closer than anyone to Hitler, and yet he knew nothing of the Shoah. He appeared not to have been a National Socialist in any meaningful sense of the term. His guilt – like a figure in a Greek tragedy – was guiltless. Speer the good Nazi gave comfort and reassurance to all the little Nazis, who resented the humiliation of de-nazification and re-education. They had shut their eyes, avoided any troubling moral qualms, and simply followed orders. It is for this reason that Matthias Schmidt's revelation of Speer's active part in the persecution of the Jews, published shortly after Speer's death, and Susanne Willems's detailed account of Speer's monstrous treatment of the Jews in Berlin did nothing to alter the public perception of the man. It was not until the journalist Heinrich Breloer presented his biographical film on TV in 2004 that the process of public demystification began. But even that was only a timid step forward. The very title, *Speer and Him*, is testament to the fact that the cult of the Führer has still to be exorcised. Speer had fallen under Hitler's spell, just as the German people had been bewitched. Hitler was still a fascinating subject, surrounded by an aura of mystery, against whom there was no defence. As is so often the case, a journalist – in this case an exceptionally gifted one – had a far greater influence on the public perception of the past than professional historians could ever hope to have. But it is a pity that even Breloer pulled his punches.[36]

Many of those who had been close to Speer were horrified when they read the memoirs. A senior member of his staff remarked that the new Speer was someone he had never met before. Rudolf Wolters, his friend for forty years, who had done so much to help him and to make the writing of his memoirs possible, found reading the published version exceedingly painful. He said that he was 'torn between old friendly feelings and instinctive repulsion'. He ended his letter to his former boss and oldest friend on a note of bitter irony: 'a detective story could not have been written with more spellbinding invention'.[37] He described Speer as 'a wandering preacher in a hair-shirt, handing over his fortune to the victims of National Socialism, renouncing all the vanities and pleasures of life and living on locusts and wild honey'. Speer visited Coesfeld shortly after receiving this letter. Sales were staggering, the money rolling in. 'Where,' he asked his host with a laugh, 'are the locusts?'[38] Many of his friends were equally shocked at Speer's albeit guarded and ambiguous admission of a modest share of responsibility for the regime's crimes. Speer boasted that the huge sales had silenced all criticism. Arno Breker remarked: 'I am astonished about Albert Sp. I have to radically change my view of him.'[39] On another occasion Wolters said that Speer was an acrobat, who 'could do a double somersault from a standing position'.[40]

The memoirs further bolstered the self-image that Speer had effectively presented at Nuremberg of an idealistic architect who, by force of circumstances, had been obliged to turn himself into a mover and shaker and who, when he came to realise the horrific reality behind the regime he had so loyally served, had become genuinely remorseful.[41] The carping remarks of a few historians were largely ignored. On the occasion of his seventy-fifth birthday in 1980, the *Frankfurter Allgemeine Zeitung*, with Joachim C. Fest on the editorial board, published an astonishingly servile and cliché-ridden eulogy of Hitler's favourite. Speer was presented as someone who had steered clear of politics, but who as a very young man had made a Faustian compact that brought him to the pinnacle of fame and power. He was a technocrat who disregarded the regime's crimes. He had distanced himself from the regime in 1944 and plotted to assassinate Hitler. Unfortunately the plot turned out to be 'technically impossible'. Speer was a man of unimpeachable honesty who had the courage at Nuremberg to accept responsibility for the appalling crimes committed in Nazi Germany. This outraged the unrepentant Hitlerites, who were now his implacable enemies. They scoffed at the notion that Speer was almost a tragic figure in that, although he had been given such amazing opportunities to realise his architectural fantasies, he had left virtually nothing behind. Even Fest offered some cautious criticism. He found Speer's loudly trumpeted acts of penance singularly tasteless. They merely served to give the Nazi regime a mask of respectability.[42]

The initial response to the memoirs by experts in Germany was largely negative, although this had no effect on sales. The general reading public did not pay heed to reviews in the quality press and specialist journals. The review that affected Speer the most was that by Golo Mann.[43] He pointed out that although the book was full of self-criticism, it was totally lacking in a Christian sense of contrition. He clearly saw the contradictions within Speer's character. Here was a man who had lived at the very centre of a system that he described as a 'band of murderers' and yet who professed at Nuremberg to be shocked at the revelation of their crimes. He claimed to be a technocrat, yet he was in many ways as much of an amateur and dilettante as many of the others in the inner circle. He was the favourite, an outsider who was despised by the 'old warriors' and party paladins, whose intrigues he describes so well, but who was nevertheless deeply involved in their unsavoury plots and alliances. He was a reader of Stefan George's poetry, a man who loved to be alone in the wilderness, yet who had spent days on end amid the insufferable courtiers on the Obersalzberg. Here was a man who deluded himself that his actions were apolitical. He was fascinated by Hitler, admired and worshipped him, and yet he found all the lesser Hitlers repulsive. He claimed to have wanted to assassinate Hitler, but six weeks later told him that he had his unconditional support. Then there was the unbelievable farewell scene, with Hitler weeping when Speer told him that he had disobeyed the Nero Order, followed by Speer's tears of sympathy at the trembling ruin of a dictator. Then, when all was over, Speer devoted the same amazing energy that he had expended on the monstrous building projects and his armaments empire to creating an image of himself as a guilt-ridden prophet, warning of the demonic threat from technology. For Golo Mann, there is an uncomfortable emptiness and alienation at the core of the book. The murder of six million Jews is dismissed with a hollow 'I have no defence.' Monstrous crimes committed by the Germans in the Soviet Union are dismissed in a single sentence. The appalling brutality of the occupation forces in Poland and elsewhere is not even mentioned. In the end, even though the idol had fallen, he was never able to free himself entirely from Hitler's spell. Golo Mann concluded his review with a quote from Adelbert von Chamisso's poem 'The Men in the Zobtenberg', which greatly impressed Speer. Three knights who were guilty of dreadful crimes were banished to this mountain. There they met the holy man Johannes Beer. He asked them if they admitted their deeds. Yes they replied. Were they good or bad? They were bad. Were they ashamed of them? They sank their heads, were frightened and remained silent. They did not know.

Among the strongest critics of the memoirs were Lucy Dawidowicz, Geoffrey Barraclough, Rebecca West, Elias Canetti and Heinz Höhne, but their comments had no effect on sales. There was good reason for Speer to hope that historians would have a difficult time following his traces. The Ministry of Armaments had been badly hit by Allied bombers, resulting in a large number of documents being destroyed. Towards the end of the war Speer sifted through reams of papers to see if there was anything that could be used against him. He claimed that he destroyed nothing, apart from a memorandum by an unnamed industrialist on the possible use of poison gas against the Soviets. He said that he did this in a very perfunctory manner, because he could not conceive that he would ever be held to account by the victorious powers.[44]

When combing through his papers Speer overlooked the 'Speer Chronicle'. Towards the end of 1940, Wolters, who at that time was head of the Main Office of the General Inspectorate for the Reich Capital, as well as being Speer's press secretary, suggested that he should keep a diary of Speer's increasingly varied activities. Speer agreed and Wolters began work on 1 January 1941. Speer issued instructions that all his fellow workers should cooperate fully with Wolters. He made no editorial changes. The diary was comprehensive up until September 1944, after which, as the situation rapidly deteriorated, it became increasingly sketchy. By the end of the war there were several copies, but only one complete example survived.

In March 1945 one of Wolters' colleagues deposited the Chronicle in a special depot for the safekeeping of important documents established by Wolters and the future Federal German President, Heinrich Lübke, in Höxter, a small town between Detmold and Göttingen. Shortly afterwards, it was moved to the library of the nearby castle of the Duke of Ratibor and Corvey. Wolters still did not consider this to be a safe hiding place. In 1946 he ordered the Chronicle to be sealed in lead containers and buried in his parents' garden in Coesfeld. Once he felt that the going was safe, the Chronicle was dug up and kept in his office. One version, covering the years 1942 and 1943, had been burnt in Berlin just before the war's end. A complete version was said to have been buried in the Harz Mountains, along with a number of other important documents, including some of Milch's papers, but none of these have ever been found in spite of an intensive search.

In 1964, in preparation for Speer's release from Spandau, Wolters decided to have the entire Chronicle retyped to remove stylistic and grammatical errors, omit any irrelevant or trivial passages and, above all, to suppress anything that could be used against Speer or any of his co-workers. By this time Wolters had begun to look over his shoulder at the Ludwigsburg Central Office for National Socialist Crimes, which had been founded in 1957–8 and which rapidly revealed an alarming number of Nazi crimes, committed both at home and abroad, that had been overlooked by the victors. The Auschwitz Trial in Frankfurt that began in 1963, following closely upon the Eichmann Trial in Jerusalem in 1961, for the first time brought the appalling reality of the Shoah into public awareness. The effect was shattering. Speer had every cause to be alarmed.

Wolters gave the edited version of the Chronicle to Speer upon his release from Spandau to help him write his autobiography. He gave him a rough indication of the changes he had made in the original. In 1969, having finished his memoirs, Speer presented the edited version of the Chronicle to the Federal Archives in Coblenz, without telling Wolters. The Federal Archives then sent a photocopy of the Chronicle to the Institute for Contemporary History in Munich. Both knew that the Chronicle had been retyped. Neither knew that important omissions had been made.

In the same year David Irving, who was working on a biography of Erhard Milch, discovered a section of the Chronicle in the Imperial War Museum in London that varied somewhat from the versions in Coblenz and Munich. Irving sent photocopies showing the differences between the two versions to Speer for comment. This provoked a tense exchange between Speer and Wolters. Speer accused Wolters of having put him in a very awkward position by handing over an obviously doctored version of the Chronicle when at least part of the original was extant. Since there were no substantial differences between the Imperial War Museum's extract and the edited original, Speer suggested that Wolters should send the full text of the original to the archives.

Wolters' reply was carefully worded. He pointed out that he had given Speer a full account of the kind of editing he had done, adding that since he was the author of the Chronicle he felt entitled to make certain changes. But then came the bombshell. He told Speer that he had cut out a few passages that were 'unfortunately not implicitly unimportant from the point of view of contemporary history'. Wolters bluntly stated that one of the excised passages revealed that Speer, in his capacity as Inspector General for the Reich Capital, had seized 23,765 Jewish apartments in Berlin and had forced 75,000 Jewish people to be 'resettled'. 'That,' Wolters ironically commented, 'was quite an achievement.' Wolters insisted that the original had to be made public, at least by the time that no one concerned would be caused to suffer from any of its revelations. He left Speer to determine what to do next: 'Now you decide – Oh mighty Minister of Armaments!'

Speer was horrified. His memoirs had just been published to general acclaim, he had become a media star and his rehabilitation was virtually complete, thanks in large part to the successful deception that he knew nothing of the persecution of the Jews. Were the full text of the Chronicle to become public, it would then be widely known that not only had he been fully informed of this monstrous crime but that he had also played an active role in it. Speer had to admit to Wolters that he had acted quite correctly in suppressing this incriminating evidence, thereby saving his carefully constructed public image.

Speer was determined to ensure that the original version of the Chronicle should remain hidden from view. Wolters remained loyal, although sorely tried. He wrote a letter to Speer, which he suggested should be forwarded to the Federal Archives, saying that he had been unable to discover the original of the Chronicle among his personal papers. He then told Speer that the original would be lodged in the archives upon his own death. Speer forwarded the letter to the Federal Archives, adding that he deeply regretted his failure to discover the whereabouts of the original. He comforted the director, Dr Wolfgang A. Mommsen, with the thought that the edited version of the diaries held in the archives would still be of immeasurable benefit to future historians.[45] Speer then told Wolters that the full version of the Chronicle should be retyped and made public when Speer's great-grandchildren reached their majority.[46] He disingenuously claimed that it was highly doubtful that it would reveal anything significant that was not already known from other sources.

Wolters' final break with Speer resulted not from the memoirs but as a result of an interview published in *Playboy* magazine in June 1971, extracts from which were printed in the German illustrated weekly *Quick*.[47] Speer was later to claim that the interviewer, Eric Norden, spoke no German and had taken several liberties with the text. But Norden had studied the memoirs attentively and his questions were carefully prepared.[48] Wolters found the contrast between Speer's repeated mea culpa in the article absurdly at odds with his comfortable lifestyle, cheerfulness and his boasting about his literary and financial successes. His claims for the probity of the Nuremberg trials seemed excessive, even to the Allied prosecutors. Wolters was the most outspoken of those who accused Speer of soiling his own nest. Others felt that his constantly reiterated confession of non-specific culpability, coupled with his continued insistence that he knew nothing of the mass murder of the European Jews, was nothing more than a convenient way of shifting all the blame on to Hitler and his insalubrious entourage that included the likes of Himmler, Göring, Goebbels and Ribbentrop, as well as his own personal scape-goat – Sauckel. Wolters claimed that Speer had told him that his confession of guilt, his acts of penance, the hair shirt, the public display of sackcloth and ashes and the professed yearning for atonement were nothing but 'tricks'.[49] Was this merely an angry outburst of an old friend who had been betrayed, or was there more than a grain of truth in these harsh words?

The interview – a condensation of ten days of intensive talks – reveals the extraordinary contradictions within Speer's personality. He was, as Hugh Trevor-Roper remarked in his introduction to the interview, an amazing mixture of perception and blindness, sensitivity and insensitivity, moral standards and moral neutrality. His confession of guilt was greatly weakened by his efforts to shift the blame on to others and on to historical circumstances. Speer claimed that Hitler 'not only enabled me to destroy my conscience, he also drained and perverted the creative energies of my youth'. Speer, once described by Wolters as 'Hitler's unrequited love', placed the main responsibility for the crimes of National Socialism on the modern world that is 'terrorised by technology' to the point that we are '*all* in Auschwitz'. The crimes of the Third Reich were 'essentially modern crimes made possible by twentieth-century technology, which holds within it both great promise and great danger for human values'. Speer's half-baked musings on the demonic force of technology were in a sense an attempt to stand Heidegger on his head. Whereas the philosopher, attributing the 'oblivion of being' to industrialisation and capitalism, had imagined that National Socialism would provide a means of escape, Speer – in his own words 'the technician of death' – saw it as a product of the age.

Speer was always concerned to distance himself from some of the more grotesque rogues among Hitler's myrmidons. Göring is described as a heroin addict who lived in a 'near comatose state of narcotic stupor'. Bormann was a chronic alcoholic, who was 'coarse, brutal and ruthless'. Himmler, with whom he worked closely, is described as 'my enemy at court' who was as corrupt as Göring. He did, however, show some respect for Goebbels' malignant intelligence. He was, after all, the only person among the Nazi elite who had seen a university from the inside.

In some respects the interview is more honest than the memoirs. Speer admitted that he had walked past the ruins of the synagogue on the Fasanenstraße the day after the pogrom of 9 November 1938. He confessed to sharing Sauckel's guilt in that he was just as enthusiastically in favour of the use of slave labour and treated forced workers, prisoners of war and concentration camp inmates as 'servomechanisms for our machines of war'. He said that he felt like vomiting after his visit to the Mittelbau-Dora factory. His account of his actions on 20 July 1944 at the time of the attempt on Hitler's life is somewhat more accurate than the melodramatic version in the memoirs. But there are a number of highly questionable remarks buried in the text. He has the audacity to claim that he had refused to mention his plan to assassinate Hitler during his defence at Nuremberg. He grossly overestimates his role in frustrating Hitler's Nero Order and endorses the convenient myth that the German Army would never have countenanced the 'wholesale massacre of unarmed men'.[50] His most convincing untruth was the claim, which he frequently repeated, that the Allied bombing offensive did nothing to shorten the war. This was a convenient way to shift at least part of the blame on to the other side. In this he was singularly successful.[51]

Wolters was intensely irritated by Speer's affectation of a casual attitude towards money and his claim that he lived a simple life. This too was part of the carefully constructed façade behind which Speer concealed his true self. By any normal standards he was a rich man. Born to wealth, he had no need to ape the grotesquely lavish parvenu way of life favoured by other Nazi grandees, but he lived in great comfort and had accumulated a substantial fortune. During the Spandau years, Wolters' Tuition Fund had relieved him of financial responsibility for his wife and six children. As one of his daughters remarked, he lived 'modestly in luxury'.[52] An embittered Wolters was even closer to the truth when he wrote to Speer's rival, Hermann Giesler, that Speer was motivated by two things: money and prestige.[53]

Speer was desperately lonely despite his success and wealth. At the initiative of the former head of the Central Office, Theo Hupfauer, a meeting of some of his former friends and associates was organised in Munich. This was followed by a number of similar gatherings. They were not a success. These men were prominent industrialists and businessmen who had made fortunes during West Germany's 'Economic Miracle'. They lived in the present. They were not interested in Speer's obsession with Adolf Hitler and his reminiscences of a past that now seemed so conveniently distant. The meetings became increasingly painful. Attendance dwindled until they were finally dropped.[54]

Nor did Speer find any consolation in family life. His marriage was a convenient arrangement that was not untypical of the times. As in his parents' case, love and affection seems to have been conspicuously absent.[55] Hitler was surprised to learn that Speer was married when he was introduced to Gretel in 1934. He pointed out that as a good National Socialist it was about time to have a child after six years of marriage. Speer did not feel that it was appropriate to mention that his wife was pregnant. As their firstborn, Albert, said of his mother, Gretel, thereafter she was either in 'official dirndl' or with a swollen belly.[56] Six children were born in rapid succession, for which their mother was to be awarded the Mother's Cross in silver.[57] As further evidence of their loyalty to the regime, the fifth child was named Adolf, which was later prudently changed to Arnold. As a mother Gretel was distant and cool. As Speer's career gathered momentum he was seldom at home. When the family moved to Berchtesgaden during the war their socially ambitious mother made frequent trips to Berlin so that their upbringing was left largely to the housekeeper, Wilhelmine Leidheuser, and a ferociously strict nanny, Paula Züfle, frostily known as 'Sister Paula'.[58]

The children looked forward to their father's infrequent visits. He was relaxed and easy-going, suspended Sister Paula's stern regime and allowed the dachshund Ruppi free run of the house. They had mixed feelings about his fondness for driving the entire brood at high speed in an open BMW up precipitous mountain roads. Arnold's only abiding memory of Berchtesgaden was being petrified during these excursions, while Albert junior had frequent nightmares of careering off the road into the void.[59] Theirs was not a happy childhood. Albert and Arnold developed severe stutters. Albert frequently vomited. Hilde was often in tears.

Propaganda photographs and home movies at the Berghof presented the illusion of a happy brood of healthy Aryan stock, but this was a seriously dysfunctional family. Twenty years of imprisonment with infrequent, short and awkward family visits did nothing to repair the damage. After Speer's release from prison there was no possibility of starting afresh. The knowledge that their father had been condemned as a major war criminal was hard for the children to bear in a society that was trying as best it could to free itself from its criminal past. All the children were gifted and two of them had remarkable careers. Albert became an internationally renowned architect and town planner. Hilde was to have a distinguished career as a Green politician and Professor of Education. She devoted much of her energy to the reconciliation between Germans and Jews, for which she has been widely recognised. Margret, a professional photographer, published her memoirs in 2005, in which she complained that her father had no time for his children before 1945, and after his release in 1966 devoted all his energy to the construction of his own myth.[60]

Although an extremely successful author and a prominent public figure, Speer sorely missed the immense power he had once held. Living on memories and reconstructing the past only increased this sense of loneliness and vulnerability. There were just a few people whose company he enjoyed. These included the psychologist Erich Fromm, Carl Zuckmayer – author of The Devil's General – and Eugene Davidson, author of The Trial of the Germans (1966) and The Nuremberg Fallacy (1973). There were only four people with whom he might have had a close relationship, but whose offer of friendship he was incapable of accepting: his secretary Annemarie Kempf, the Spandau chaplain Georges Casalis, the Benedictine monk from Maria Laach, Father Athanasius, with whom he spent a series of retreats over ten years, and the maverick rabbi Robert Raphael Geis.

'Abba' Geis had been interned in Buchenwald in November 1938, but was permitted to go to Palestine in February 1939. He returned to Germany in 1952 bent on working for the reconciliation of Germans and Jews.[61] Having seen Speer interviewed on television Geis wrote to him saying that although he did not understand him, possibly because he had not yet read his memoirs, 'as a devout Jew I feel that there has to be forgiveness, for today you are an honest man'. Geis was a truly remarkable personality, a man of deep spirituality, warmth and goodness. He felt a curious affinity with Speer. On his return to Germany he found that among the precious few Jews that remained, almost none had any desire for reconciliation with their tormentors. In a second letter to Speer, Geis said that it was a mistake to categorise people. He had known high-ranking Nazis who had been helpful and generous and Jews who had denounced him to the Gestapo. He blamed the great powers for their 'cowardly silence' in the face of the Nazi threat. He mentioned the war in Vietnam, the treatment of black people in South Africa and the United States, the dictatorships in Greece, Spain and Latin America, and widespread torture and starvation as examples of a universal evil. After a cordial exchange of letters they finally met in March 1970. Geis's wife Susanne later confessed that she did not share her husband's belief in Speer. She remained deeply sceptical about him. Geis's children heartily disliked Speer, and the Jewish community was appalled at his friendship with this major war criminal.[62] Speer's image was burnished by his friendship with Geis, but he was impervious to his spiritual warmth and integrity.

Speer went regularly to the Benedictine monastery of Maria Laach. Unlike most other visitors he did not stay in the guesthouse, but shared the cloistered life of the monks. Although never a Catholic and having opportunistically abandoned the Protestant Church during the Third Reich, he attend the five daily services, beginning at 5.30 a.m. He shared their silent meals while one of the monks read aloud. He told Father Athanasius that monastic life reminded him of his time in Spandau. Unlike most laymen on a retreat he did not find it at all strenuous. The monk was a far better judge of Speer than was the rabbi. He realised that Speer was totally lacking in imagination, an administrator rather than a creator, a hollow being driven by strict discipline, essentially a man without qualities. Speer to him was 'a brilliant man, incapable of abstract thinking and I think incapable of sensual love and thus, finally, an incomplete man'.[63] Pity, compassion, sympathy and empathy were not part of Speer's nature. It would seem that he could only be touched emotionally through music and art, but to a very limited extent.[64]

Speer's relationship with Georges Casalis after his release from Spandau was very tense. He made no effort to contact him and it was not until 1970, thanks to Geis and the Protestant theologian Lili Simon, that they were brought together at a meeting at the evangelical Youth Academy Radevormwald. Although they met later on three occasions they were never again as close as they had once been. Speer no longer had any need for Casalis, who in return felt that his former confidant had regressed spiritually. He appeared to have found fulfilment in his role as a public personality. The positive outcome of these encounters was that a close relationship developed between Geis and Casalis, with both men devoted to the reconciliation between Christians and Jews.[65] Speer gained precious little, other than acceptance by three outstanding men of deep spirituality and insight: a Benedictine monk, a rabbi and a Protestant minister. It was a precious gift that he truly failed to appreciate.

Speer found it increasingly difficult to face being interviewed as he found himself giving pat answers to familiar questions. Most difficult of all to answer was the persistent questioning about his knowledge of the fate of the Jews. To this his response was always that he could have known, should have known, but had not known. He must have been plagued by the fear that sooner or later he would be exposed, either by one of his associates or by the discovery of some incriminating documents. Or had he managed to convince himself during the long years of imprisonment that he was indeed ignorant? This seems improbable. When Gitta Sereny told him that she would like to talk to his wife, he begged her not to ask any questions about the Jews, as this would be too painful for her. Although she agreed to this condition, the interview never took place.[66]

Speer's carefully constructed image of himself as a man who deeply regretted having failed to discover the monstrous crimes committed by a regime in which he had played a major role threatened to implode towards the end of 1971. The Canadian historian Erich Goldhagen published an article in *Midstream*, the journal of the Theodor Herzl Foundation, in which he pointed out that Himmler had addressed Speer personally during his speech in Posen on 6 October 1943 in which he gave details of the mass murder of the Jews, saying:

> It is very easy, gentlemen, to utter the simple sentence that the Jews must be exterminated. It is exceedingly difficult and hard for those who have to carry it out. . . . We were faced with the question of what to do with the women and children. In this instance I decided to find a simple solution. I did not consider it justifiable to exterminate – in other words kill, or order to be killed – the men and to permit the children to grow up who will seek revenge on our sons and grandchildren. We had to take the difficult decision to make this race disappear from the face of the earth.[67]

Speer, who in spite of a number of hostile reviews, seemed to have been almost totally vindicated by the worldwide success of his memoirs, was suddenly confronted with a devastating disclosure. He immediately called Joachim Fest in a state of panic, insisting that Goldhagen had preconceived ideas and had got it all wrong. He said that he was determined to prove that he was not at Posen that afternoon, but let slip that he had heard about Himmler's speech 'a considerable time later'. In other words he knew all about the mass murder of the European Jews. Wolf Jobst Siedler was also bombarded with telephone messages from a distraught Speer. He concluded that Speer was worried that he had been caught out telling a lie. Fest replied that when you live among the Camorra you are unlikely to worry about telling a lie. For Fest it really did not matter whether Speer had been at Posen or not; he already knew more than enough about the regime's crimes. Fest further said that Speer's real problem was that he was beginning to doubt his own memory.[68] The journalist Gitta Sereny offered Speer some relief when she pointed out that Goldhagen had manipulated the evidence. In a footnote in the article he quoted Himmler as having said: 'Speer is not one of the pro-Jewish obstructionists of the Final Solution. He and I together will tear the last Jew alive on Polish ground out of the hands of the army generals, send them to their death and thereby close the chapter of Polish Jewry.' Himmler had said no such thing. Goldhagen's lame excuse for this shameful deceit was that it was merely the gist of what Himmler had intended to say, and that the editor of *Midstream* had mistakenly printed it as a quotation.[69]

Casalis had always advised Speer to confront the truth head on. Geis argued that if he could not confront the truth he would have to come to terms with its suppression. Ignoring this advice, Speer embarked on the virtually impossible endeavour of proving that he was not in Posen on the afternoon of 6 October 1943. Faced with Goldhagen's accusation, Speer began to shift his position somewhat. He conceded that he 'sensed' that dreadful things were happening to the Jews and that he admitted to his *Billigung* – a word meaning endorsement, agreement or approval – of the persecution and murder of millions of Jews.[70] Speer did not pause to question how one could endorse something of which one knew nothing. Had he admitted as much at Nuremberg, he would have been hanged, but he now insisted that he had served his full sentence, thereby paying his debt to society. He was now a free man, having expiated his guilt. It was an argument that did not accord with his frantic efforts to defend himself from Goldhagen's charges.

In his response Speer repeated the definition of guilt he had given at Nuremberg and in his memoirs. For him, the question of what he knew or did not know was quite irrelevant when compared with what he should have known and the consequences he should have drawn from what little he did know. When Hanke had made a veiled reference to Auschwitz, Speer was frightened of something being discovered that would have dire consequences for him. His personal responsibility for Auschwitz therefore lay in the fact that he had closed his eyes to what had happened there. As far as the Posen meeting was concerned, Speer argued that he, like Dönitz and Milch, was a guest speaker at a meeting of Gauleiters, so that there was no pressing reason why he should have stayed for the afternoon session. Furthermore, the references to Speer in the speech were all in indirect speech: 'and worked for Party Comrade Speer'; 'naturally that had nothing to do with Party Comrade Speer'; 'then I would ask Party

Comrade Speer'. Speer then argued that even if Himmler had addressed him personally this did not prove that he was there. There were, after all, some seventy people assembled in a large room so that Himmler could not have known who was present. It is difficult, however, to believe that a figure as prominent as Speer would, on this auspicious occasion, have been hiding away somewhere at the back of the room, or that he would have missed the opportunity to hear a key speech from a person of Himmler's stature.

Speer counter-attacked by saying that he, Sauckel and the military commander in the General Government, General Curt Freiherr von Gienanth, had opposed Himmler and Keitel's orders that skilled Jewish workers should be expelled from the General Government and replaced by non-Jewish Poles. He quoted Himmler's log of a message from SS-Obergruppenführer Wolff from Hitler's headquarters, dated 22 September 1942: 'Speer's (Saur) wish, Jews in armaments factories.' Both the Governor General, Hans Frank, and General Schindler, the armaments inspector in the General Government, insisted that Jewish workers should remain, on the grounds that many of them were highly skilled and irreplaceable. As a result, the number of Jewish workers in the General Government increased from 15,091 in January 1943 to 21,600 in July, in spite of all of Himmler's efforts. By April 1944 the number had reached 28,537. Hence Himmler's insistence in his Posen speech that the argument that murdering Jews was harmful to the armaments industry overlooked the deadly threat that the Jews presented to the German people. Speer was thereby able to counter Goldhagen's contention that he had assisted Himmler in his effort to send all the Jews in the General Government to their deaths, but his attempt to present himself as a saviour of the Jews is considerably less convincing. Furthermore, it is highly unlikely that Speer never asked himself why Himmler was so eager to round up all these people when they were so usefully employed.[71]

In a second note Speer presented a letter from 'Panzer' Rohland, dated 6 July 1973, almost two years after the publication of the Goldhagen article, in which he stated that on 6 October 1943 he and Speer gave presentations during the morning session at Posen. They were both worried that the Gauleiters, who were due to meet Hitler the following day, would complain bitterly about their speeches. They therefore decided to drive to Rastenburg to pre-empt the Gauleiters and persuade Hitler that their demands were fully justified. A further affidavit was written in October 1975 – four years after the Goldhagen article. It was signed by Harry Siegmund, formerly personal assistant to the Gauleiter and Reich Governor of Wartheland, Arthur Greiser. In his capacity as liaison officer with the local army command Greiser had organised the Posen meeting. It stated that Speer had left Posen that afternoon. Furthermore, Siegmund wrote that Prince Heinrich Reuss, the commander of 18 Flak Division, had told him that Speer had not been present during 'Himmler's ominous speech'.

Prince Reuss, as a military man, was not present during Himmler's speech on 6 October, at which he addressed the Gauleiters; but he could well have heard the similar speech Himmler had given in Posen two days earlier.[72] While driving in the same car as Himmler the following day, Siegmund had noticed that he wore very thick spectacles. He estimated that he would not have been able to see clearly who was present, especially as the Romanesque castle in Posen was exceptionally gloomy. But both these affidavits are worthless. They were made at Speer's request. He had carefully vetted their texts.[73]

Speer also noted that Milch had told Hitler's biographer, John Toland, that he had not been present that afternoon. Speer's pilot, Hermann Nein, further testified that it would not have been possible to fly to Rastenburg after Himmler's speech because night-time landings were not possible there. Hitler's personal pilot, Hans Baur, later dismissed this as nonsense. Landing at night at Rastenburg was not easy, but he had done so on numerous occasions.[74] Speer added that on 6 October 'Hitler's diary' showed that he had had no appointments between 5 and 9 p.m., so that there was plenty of time for discussions and dinner.[75] Speer was never confronted with the awkward fact that Hitler's manservant, Heinz Linge, made no note of a visit by Speer that evening in his immaculately kept 'Appointments Book'. It is clearly marked that he came the following day. Among the guests at supper that evening were Rosenberg, Bormann, Himmler's chief of staff Karl Wolff, and Gauleiters Hanke (Lower Silesia), Sauckel (Thuringia), Hofer (Innsbruck) and Rainer (Carinthia), all of whom had been present when Himmler had delivered his speech.[76] It is inconceivable that no mention was made of its horrifically dramatic content.

In March 2007 a series of almost one hundred letters written by Speer to Hélène Jeanty Raven, the widow of a member of the Belgian Resistance who had been shot by the Germans, and wife of the Regius Professor of Divinity at Cambridge, was sold at Bonhams in London for £18,000. In one of these letters, written soon after the publication of the Goldhagen article on 23 December 1971, Speer stated categorically that he had been present during Himmler's speech. In a curious passage he wrote that the truth of his memoirs was 'written between the lines' and that it would have been simpler to tell the truth as Schirach had done in his memoirs. The truth for Speer lay in his subconscious. In 1974 Speer returned Jeanty Raven's letters, possibly in the hope of retrieving the letter in which he had made this confession.[77]

The fuss over the Goldhagen article soon blew over. After all, the question as to whether Speer knew of the Shoah did not depend on whether or not he had stayed in Posen that afternoon. He would almost certainly have heard about Himmler's speech even if he had not been present. For the moment, clear evidence that he had lied had not yet been produced. His attention was now focused on preparing his Spandau Diaries for publication. Ullstein was determined not only that this should be at least as successful as his memoirs, but that it should also silence those who had expressed their reservations over the earlier book. Confident that it would be another international best-seller, they printed a first run in hardback of 200,000 copies. Axel Springer's *Die Welt* paid the princely sum of DM 600,000 for serialisation rights. Macmillan paid $350,000 for the American rights – according to Siedler the largest sum ever paid for a German book.

Siedler told Gitta Sereny that Ullstein, to whom Speer had given the world rights for his memoirs, had sold 500,000 hardback copies of the German edition of the memoirs and millions in both hard and paperback editions throughout the world. Speer claimed that this had brought him $577,000 in royalties. He had given $102,000 to various charities, had paid $263,000 in income tax, $96,000 for secretarial help, transport and the 'support of relatives' and $93,000 on 'family expenses'. On the basis of these dubious figures he claimed that he had been left out of pocket. Simple arithmetic shows that he would still have been left with $23,000.[78] Even on the basis of these suspect figures, Speer was making a lot of money. The average income of a German in 1970 was $3,706 per annum. If the amount spent on 'family expenses' were added to the residue, the total would have been $116,000. The average German would have had to work for thirty-one years to earn such a sum. At this rate his secretarial staff must have been treated with exceptional generosity. None of this includes the colossal sums of money he made from interviews, articles and television appearances. Once again Speer made cavalier use of the figures.

The German edition of the Spandau Diaries, with a Foreword by Joachim Fest, was published in 1975. The English edition, published the following year, was also a tremendous success. The Spandau Diaries are a highly ingenious reconstruction of the prison years. Speer had never systematically kept a diary while in prison. Only a few rough notes survived from the early years. Later entries were copied from letters he sent to Wolters. Events are rearranged and the years altered in a reconstruction of the past designed to bolster Speer's image as presented in the memoirs.[79]

The main themes are Speer's remarkable efforts to come to terms with the monotony of what, thanks to the intransigence of the Soviet authorities, amounted to life imprisonment. There was also his gradual coming to terms with the fact that his architectural work had been a disastrous mixture of neo-classicist eclecticism and historicist kitsch that was nothing but a deplorable expression of National Socialist gigantomania. For Speer, this was all part of the increasing disparity between means and ends that had led to the downfall of the Third Reich. This in turn was due to the autonomous power of technology that had destroyed the last vestiges of an ordered and predictable society. It had ended with Hitler's scorched earth policy. Speer's principled stand against the Nero Order was, for him, his finest hour. The other major

issue addressed in the diaries was to reveal the true nature of his close relationship with Hitler.

Speer spends a great deal of time brooding on his guilt in having served in
a leading position in what he admitted was a criminal regime; but at the same
time he continues adamantly to deny any knowledge of the mass murder of the
European Jews. Speer's musings on these points never go beyond the anecdotal
and personal. He never dares to look deeper into the structure of the regime.
He does not ask whose interests it served, or questions its political motivations.
The Nuremberg Tribunal had provided him with absolution from personal
guilt. Twenty years of confinement had wiped the slate clean. Public confessions of guilt by association now simply served to enhance his image as a
fundamentally decent human being, who had been punished for a past that
was not of his own choosing. His achievements outweighed his faults and
shortcomings. The Spandau Diaries are thus a further example of the reduction of the history of the Third Reich to the personalities involved, rather than
an examination of its structure and dynamics.

In early 1977 Speer received a letter from the Chairman of the South African
Board of Jews asking him to support his efforts to counter a pamphlet entitled
Did Six Million Really Die?, written on behalf of the British National Front by
'Richard E. Harwood', the pseudonym of Richard Verrall, the National Front's
Deputy Chairman. It was published by the German-born neo-Nazi holocaust
denier Ernst Zündel, whose Toronto-based Samisdat Publishers cranked out a
series of abhorrent leaflets with titles such as *The Hitler We Loved and Why* and
Auschwitz, Dachau, Buchenwald: The Greatest Fraud in History.[80] Speer was
asked to sign an affidavit to the effect that there was a plan to exterminate the
Jews, that he knew of it and that the plan was indeed put into effect. He was also
asked about the means by which it was executed. Speer's reply was based on
statements made during the Nuremberg Trials. He wrote that he had been
present in the Reichstag on 30 January 1939 when Hitler had said that in the
event of a war the Jews and not the Germans would be destroyed, and that
Hitler had repeated this threat in a speech on 30 January 1942. When Hitler
heard of the Hamburg raid in July 1943 he had repeatedly said that he would
get his revenge by killing Jews. Speer ended by saying that the Nuremberg
Trials, as well as his own sentence, were 'on the whole' fair and that: 'I still
consider it appropriate for me to accept responsibility and therefore the blame
in a general sense for all the crimes committed after I joined Hitler's government on 8 February 1942 . . . During the Nuremberg trial I therefore accepted
overall responsibility, as I do today.' Once again he used the word *Billigung* for
his acceptance of the persecution and murder of millions of Jews. Therein lay
his guilt. Speer soon realised that he had made a serious mistake by using this
equivocal word. When Gitta Sereny wrote an article on him for the weekly

newspaper *Die Zeit*, she quoted this passage. Speer insisted that she add a foot-note that read: '*Billigung* by looking away, not by knowledge of an order or its execution. The first is as serious as the second.'[81]

Another aspect of Speer's past was soon to come to light, although it did not cause many ripples. In the record of his possessions that he made while at Kransberg he mentioned a collection of paintings worth 120,000 Reichsmarks. It would seem that towards the end of the war he had handed over the bulk of his valuable collection to his friend Dr Robert Frank for safekeeping. Speer had renovated Frank's country house in Perleberg in north-western Brandenburg in 1933. Frank had been head of the Prussian Electricity Works, but was dismissed by the Nazis and had retired to private life. He remained on friendly terms with Speer, who introduced him to the leading Nazi artists, architects, and figures such as Karl Brandt and Magda Goebbels, with whom he travelled to Sicily and southern Italy in 1939. In return he offered to help Speer in 1945, looking after his family and valuables while he played a part in the Dönitz government in Schleswig. Frank not only stored Speer's art collection, but also a considerable amount of jewellery, silver and furs.[82] While in Spandau, Speer requested that investigations be made into the whereabouts of his paintings. Frank and his wife, who had moved to Mexico, gave evasive answers. At first they said that these had either been stolen or burnt. Later they claimed that all the paintings in their possession were gifts from Speer. Then, in 1955, the Franks sent three crates of paintings to the Speer family with the assurance that these was all that remained. When Speer was released from gaol, fearing that some uncomfortable legal questions might be raised, he chose not to pursue the matter any further.[83]

In 1979 or 1980, the executor of the will of a person who had died in Mexico approached the art auctioneers Lempertz in Cologne with a list of paintings for sale. They were not very impressive works and the names of various artists had been misspelt, but the experts decided that it might be worthwhile having a closer look. They were pleasantly surprised by what they saw. There was a fine Schinkel painting and a charming landscape of the Pontine Marshes by Böcklin, painted in 1852. Dr Paul Wallraf, one of Lempertz' most experienced appraisers, had an uncomfortable feeling about the painting's neo-classical frame. This was a style much beloved by the Nazi elite. It was therefore decided to ask Rolf Andree, an acknowledged expert on Böcklin, if he knew of the provenance of the painting.[84] Andree promptly replied that it had belonged to Albert Speer, who claimed that it had been burnt. He came to Cologne to examine the painting, recognised it as authentic, and asked himself why it was that Speer had told him that it had been burnt in 1945.

Lempertz contacted Speer to tell him that the Böcklin had been recovered. The auctioneers received the angry response that he did not wish to be troubled with 'such rubbish' and he slammed down the phone. Lempertz then phoned Speer's wife, asking her to calm her husband down and assure him that they were not investigative journalists, but an auction house with a long and distinguished tradition. Speer apologised for his intemperate behaviour, but remained curt and abrupt. When he was told that the paintings came from Mexico he then admitted that he had given them to his best friend, Dr Frank. When he heard the list of artists – all of them German painters of the early nineteenth century – he was speechless.[85] He asked Lempertz to call again the next day because he was convalescing after a heart attack and was in a state of shock.

Speer put the matter into the hands of Walter Oppenhoff, a highly respected commercial lawyer who had looked after the interests of Coca-Cola and other major companies during the war, and who therefore had excellent relations with the former Allies. Oppenhoff had got into difficulties during the war and had been given a position in Speer's ministry to keep him out of harm's way. He went with Henrik Hanstein, Lempertz's owner, to visit Speer in Heidelberg. On the way they were joined by Karl Maria Hettlage, Speer's former right-hand man, who had had a distinguished post-war career in the Federal Republic. They met Frank's executor, Günter Hank, at the hospital where Speer was then recuperating. Speer made it quite clear that he did not want any publicity about the matter and called for an out-of-court settlement.

On the journey back to Cologne, Oppenhoff said that if Speer was not prepared to go to court the only solution was to split the collection fifty-fifty. The matter was settled in this manner. Hanstein, who was fascinated by Speer, continued to visit him in his gloomy and foreboding house in Heidelberg. On one occasion Speer's pertness made him feel most uncomfortable. Speer noticed this and asked him what was the matter. Hanstein replied that he could not get over the fact that he was sitting in the presence of a man 'who was a member of the cabinet of one of the most criminal regimes in history', whereupon Speer invited him to pose any questions that he liked. Hanstein, who was in no position to ask any pertinent questions, realised that Speer was playing with him. He remained resistant to all Speer's attempts to charm him and treated him with considerable scepticism. On the other hand he was very impressed by Speer's knowledge of early nineteenth-century German romantic art, a genre that particularly interested him. He was also delighted with a very fine painting of this type that Speer gave him.

To avoid any untoward publicity Speer did not sell the Böcklin, but lent it to the museum in Düsseldorf. It was then given to the museum as part of a foundation and hangs there today. Speer was careful to cover his tracks. Whereas the Franks' half was sold en bloc, Speer's paintings were sold one or two at a time to avoid publicity and prying eyes. According to Hanstein he received a total of one million marks in cash.[86] He never asked for receipts, so Lempertz always had four or five witnesses when the money was handed over. It is unclear what Speer did with the money. His widow enquired after it, but received no answer. There was ample speculation among Lempertz's staff. Most agreed with Paul Wallraf's plausible answer: 'cherchez la femme'.

Another valuable source of income came from the sale of a number of architectural sketches made by Hitler. This was a substantial collection, the first dating from 1934. Speer had given Otto Apel, a former Tessenow pupil with his own architectural firm, the task of ordering and cataloguing these drawings. Apel died before Speer was released from prison, but Speer made sure that the sketches remained in safekeeping. He was quick to realise the potential value of these works. Only a small fraction of them were put on sale so as not to flood the market. They commanded the extraordinarily high prices of DM3,000 to 5,000, but Speer was angered when he discovered that many of them had been quickly resold in the United States for the identical sum in dollars.

In the final years of his life Speer became increasingly bitter as persistent questions were asked as to how a man in his position could possibly not have known of the fate of the European Jews. The publication of the Spandau Diaries served only to increase the suspicion that he had a great deal to hide. He truculently adopted the attitude that he had served his sentence, had paid his debt to society and should be left in peace. In an attempt to silence his critics he published – without Joachim Fest's guiding hand – an embarrassingly dreadful and fortunately for him largely overlooked book, Technology and Power, in 1979. The book excited little interest and was not translated into English. It is a set of recorded answers to some rather anodyne questions set by Adelbert Reif, a man who specialised in interviewing such figures as Hannah Arendt, Ernst Bloch, Martin Walser and Werner Heisenberg. The result is a muddleheaded hodge-podge of semi-digested ideas from radical ecologists and peace activists such as Herbert Gruhl, Robert Junck, Klaus Traube and Carl Friedrich von Weizsäcker. He adds some comments by John Kenneth Galbraith on increasing inequality and relies heavily on Hermann Rauschning's apocryphal volume Hitler Speaks. Speer once again harps on the familiar theme that we are ruled by a technology that has got out of control. Technology now trumps all rational concerns.[87]

The book is not without its tell-tale passages. Outrage at the Treaty of Versailles, particularly Article 231 on war guilt, coupled with Hitler's determination to make Germany once again count in the world, were the main reasons why Speer found National Socialism so appealing.[88] Hitler's great successes in foreign policy, such as the Anschluss of Austria and the destruction of Czechoslovakia 'justified the scale' of his plans for rebuilding Berlin. He then mused that perhaps Hitler indeed had a chance to dominate the world.[89] Only a few pages later he admits that the buildings he designed for Hitler were 'megalomaniac', 'out of proportion', impersonal and designed to overwhelm. Their sole purpose was to serve as monuments to Hitler's greatness. These projected buildings were an anticipation of his desire to dominate Europe and then the world. They celebrated victories that had yet to be won.[90]

Speer claims that the proclamation of the doctrine of unconditional surrender at Casablanca in January 1943 and Churchill's agreement to the Morgenthau Plan at the Second Quebec Conference in September 1944 were the main reasons why Germany continued to fight until the bitter end.[91] He again presents himself as the apolitical technocrat, a term which he defines as a blinkered specialist, using the splendid German word *Fachidiot*.[92] Adelbert Reif swallows all this without protest, making for a singularly dull read. The book is thus little more than a testament to the shallowness of Speer's thinking after almost thirty-five years contemplating the Third Reich and his place within it. It never rises above the level of platitudes, such as the belief that mankind is driven by a need for property, family life, relative freedom and religion, or that thanks to modern technology the distance between the killer and the killed grows ever wider.[93] The general impression is one of a grossly oversimplified and watered-down version of Heidegger's essays on technology as conveyed by lesser minds. Serious doubts about the historical accuracy of Speer's reflections are raised when he claims that the German aristocracy was solidly on the side of the 20 July conspirators.[94]

Late in life Speer tried to salvage that which he felt was positive about the National Socialist project. His efforts found little resonance. The neo-traditionalist architect and town planner Léon Krier, who is one of the very few admirers of Speer's plans for Germania, enthusiastically endorsed Speer's sombre reflections on the evils of technology.[95]

Speer first visited the Federal Archives in Coblenz in July 1969 shortly after the publication of the German edition of his memoirs. The purpose of the visit was to present the edited version of the Chronicle. Six months later, when David Irving discovered part of the uncut version, he went back to the archives in an attempt to repair the damage. He spent long hours in the archives, never appearing in the reading room, but hidden away in one of the archivists' rooms in a vain attempt to build a case for the defence. His efforts intensified with the publication of Goldhagen's damaging article. The end result of his research was *Infiltration: How Heinrich Himmler Schemed to Build an SS Industrial Empire*, which appeared shortly before his death in 1981.

In late 1979, while Speer was working on this new project, he was approached by Matthias Schmidt, a graduate student at the Friedrich Meinecke Institute in Berlin. Speer assured him that he would give him all the help he could with his dissertation. Assuming that his closest colleague would remain discreet, he suggested that he should get in contact with Wolters. This was a serious error of judgment. Wolters was seriously ill and still harboured resentment against his former friend.[96] He seized the opportunity to provide Schmidt with ample material to demolish Speer's carefully constructed image.[97] Schmidt visited Wolters at his home in Coesfeld in early 1980. Wolters showed him the incriminating passages that he had removed from the Chronicle that referred to the expulsion of the Berlin Jews and to the appalling conditions in the Mittelbau-Dora concentration camp. Schmidt, realising that he was in possession of sensational new material, decided to return to Heidelberg and confront Speer with the evidence. Speer was so shocked that he first denied any knowledge of the Chronicle. He also claimed never to have had any correspondence with Wolters about doctoring the Chronicle before presenting it to the Federal Archives in Coblenz. Caught completely off guard, he agreed to Schmidt's request for his permission to use this new material in his dissertation, and promised that he would not take legal action against him were it to be published.

No sooner had Schmidt left, Speer suddenly realised that he had in his hands material that might even lead to criminal action against him by the Central Office of the State Justice Administration for the Investigation of National Socialist Crimes in Ludwigsburg. After an agonising month in which he examined all possible courses of action, he decided to place the matter in the hands of his lawyers. Wolters also felt it prudent to take legal advice. There followed a heated correspondence between the two men, as a result of which Speer formally nullified the power of attorney he had given to Wolters over his private and official papers.[98] The last year of Speer's life was thus overshadowed by the nagging fear that Wolters' revenge would destroy his reputation. But it was largely unfounded. Schmidt completed his dissertation in 1982 and published it three years later. The work remained virtually unknown outside a small group within the historical profession, and Schmidt did not pursue a career as an historian. Similar works by other historians remained largely in the shadows.[99]

Speer considered it an act of treachery that Wolters had given a young scholar access to the unedited version of the Chronicle that included sections on the expulsion of the Jews from Berlin.[100] This was something that Matthias Schmidt found hard to fathom. He attributed it to a suicide wish, given the ill feeling between the two men. It is hard to believe that Speer imagined that Wolters would remain silent about his tampering with the records. Speer had earlier claimed that Wolters had insisted that he had edited the Chronicle on his orders to save others from embarrassment. When Fest asked what cuts had been made in the version lodged in the archives Speer had said that they were 'insignificant'. When asked repeatedly for details, he murmured something about seeking legal advice and then said, 'Let's drop it!'[101] Later, on reading Schmidt's book, Joachim Fest told Wolf Jobst Siedler that Speer had 'led them around by the nose', and that destiny had once again smiled on Albert Speer by his 'departing the scene' before the book was published. Siedler thought that Fest's condemnation of Speer was altogether too harsh and pitiless, and that a future judgment should be based on a careful examination of both sides. Fest conceded this point, but was outraged to have learnt that Speer had lied about the 'insignificant' cuts made in the edited version of the Chronicle. He found this 'inexcusable'. He now began to worry that there might well be further embarrassing examples of Speer's duplicity.[102]

Gitta Sereny later made light of Schmidt's charges against Speer. She admitted that by 1941 Speer certainly knew that the Berlin Jews were being deported, but argued that he did not know of their subsequent fate. She wrote that Schmidt's doctoral dissertation 'makes no claim to historical objectivity'.[103] In his biography of Speer, Fest overlooked Schmidt's revelations. To have done otherwise would have involved completely reworking the text and acting as a historian. Fest the journalist with a distinct political agenda did not wish to stoop so low.

Some time in 1980 Speer went to Berlin to discuss the publication of *Infiltration*. Over lunch Siedler discreetly told him that it would take so much time to get it into a publishable state that he regretted that he would have to turn it down. Speer took this news calmly, and then confided in him that something important had happened. He took a photograph out of his wallet that showed him with an attractive young woman on a hotel balcony in Provence. She was tall, slim and had long blonde hair. They both looked relaxed and contented. Speer was smiling and casually dressed. Siedler hardly recognised him. With all the 'embarrassment of a schoolboy' he spoke of his 'great love', saying with great regret that it was not until he was in his seventies that he first had had an intense erotic relationship.[104] He added, suggestively, 'with a woman'.[105]

In late 1979 or early 1980 Speer had received a letter from a woman with an English surname and a German first name. She had been bowled over by *Spandau: The Secret Diaries*. She described it as the most wonderful book she had ever read. She told Speer that she was married to an Englishman whose job had taken them overseas, but that they were now back in England. She found life as a German woman in England very difficult and that it was very hard for her children to have a German mother. She ended the letter saying that his book had made her cry, but it had also made her very happy. Speer promptly replied, inviting her to visit him the next time she visited Germany.[106]

The effect of this torrid affair on his long-suffering wife was devastating. Gretel was sixty-one years old when Speer was released from Spandau. He had been an absentee husband and then spent twenty years in prison. She had hoped that now at last they might have a life together, but as Speer told Joachim Fest, the family was hardly mentioned in his memoirs because 'they played no part in my life'.[107] His emotional Indian summer was a shattering blow to

Gretel's fading hopes for the future. Her daughter Margret said that throughout all the ordeals, hardships and emotional deprivation she had suffered, until now she had never seen her cry. Now she wept. Margret was convinced that this was the root cause of her mother's Parkinson's disease.[108]

The main purpose of *Infiltration* was to distance Speer from Himmler. It is a hodgepodge of material left over from his memoirs and the Spandau Diaries. Lacking the meticulous stylistic guidance of Joachim Fest and the skilful management of a publisher like Siedler, it is repetitive, often contradictory and contains chunks of material from his other books.[109] It contains such a mass of falsifications, deliberate misinterpretations and distortions that a number of complaints were made to the publishers. They in turn said that Speer would make some changes, but none appeared in print. Speer's carefully constructed image, which had proven to be so profitable, remained intact.[110]

The case of the industrialist Rudolf Egger, managing director of Büssing-NAG in Braunschweig, is an excellent example of Speer's manipulation of the evidence. Egger was one of Speer's closest associates. His firm specialised in building trucks and buses. Half the workforce in the company had been forced labour. More than a thousand prisoners from Auschwitz worked in the firm. Workers were housed in two nearby concentration camps. Executions took place at the factory on several occasions, when workers were forced to witness group hangings. In spite of these displays of National Socialist ardour, Egger was arrested by the Gestapo in June 1944 and sentenced to a symbolic three-day imprisonment for making personal use of some of the firm's building materials.[111] Speer claimed that he wrote to 'Dear Party Comrade Dr Kaltenbrunner', complaining that Egger had been arrested without his being informed. Egger was immediately released from what the Nazis euphemistically called 'protective custody'.[112] In fact Speer had written to Kaltenbrunner saying that if Egger were indeed guilty, then three days' imprisonment was far too lenient a sentence. He insisted that sentences had to be severe in order to act as a deterrent. Egger was released, not because of Speer's intervention, but because the charges against him were found to be false.[113]

Hitler's plans for a future Germany were so grotesque that there is no need for exaggeration, but Speer claims it was to include all of Poland, Bohemia and Moravia, Scandinavia and the Netherlands. Also to be included were Burgundy, Alsace-Lorraine, Belgium and the coal-mining area in north-eastern France around Lille. Speer prudently does not add a map or supporting evidence for this assertion.[114]

Speer always played fast and loose with statistics, but here his errors are mostly a matter of poor mathematics. He claims that if 100,000 hectares of land planted with the Russian dandelion Taraxacum kok-saghyz or TKS produced 8,000 metric tons of rubber, this amounted to 800 kilos per hectare (actually 80).[115] Speer failed to mention that Himmler's plans for cultivating dandelions in the Soviet Union served a double purpose. They were sown in areas where the partisans were particularly active. Dandelions were intended to replace food crops so that the population would starve. Rubber production and the Hunger Plan made a perfect match.

Speer claimed that Himmler was a mediocre businessman. He would have made far more money had he hired out concentration camp workers at rates of between 4.70 and 6 Reichsmarks per day – as he had done with Russian prisoners of war from the camps at Kaulsdorf and Falkensee in Berlin – instead of building factories in the camps to be run by the SS. This would have brought in 506,000 Reichsmarks per day or 184 million Reichsmarks per year.[116] At Nuremberg Karl Sommer, the head of Department DII-1 of the SS Economics and Administrative Main Office, who was directly responsible for putting prisoners to work, reported that by the end of 1944 an average of 50 million Reichsmarks per month were made from workers, with payments of 4.70 Reichsmarks per day for unskilled and 6 Reichsmarks per day for skilled labour. This did not include those who worked in the concentration camps.[117] Speer had the audacity to accuse Himmler of cooking the books, even though he was far worse a culprit. It is small wonder that Goebbels wrote of him: 'I don't believe Speer any more . . . he makes us all drunk with his figures. . . . For some time now he makes up for the missing airplanes and tanks with phoney statistical fairy tales.'[118]

Speer tried to enhance his own image by being unsparingly critical of his former colleagues. Bormann was 'an engine fuelled by hate'.[119] Göring was 'corrupt, lazy and addicted to morphine'.[120] SS-Obergruppenführer Oswald Pohl, the head of SS Economics and Administrative Main Office, was 'spewed up from among a mass of old party members. He was in no sense suited to the job'. He was a man of very little intellect, whose industrial empire was a 'chimera'.[121] Himmler 'gave the impression of being a jumped-up petty-bourgeois, who for no apparent reason had reached a lofty position'. He had a 'corrupt and perverted morality', 'liked to use overblown expressions' and was 'outrageous in the way he got involved in matters about which he understood nothing'.[122] Of Walther Schieber, one of his closest associates who had served him loyally until he was pushed aside, Speer wrote that 'he tended towards corpulence' and 'in spite of undeniable successes, he was far too weak a personality to be a department head. He often tended to take a euphoric view of the situation and was very careful not to disappoint Himmler.'[123] Speer also managed to convince himself, against all the evidence, that Schieber was Himmler's mole within the Armaments Ministry. This hardly squares with Himmler, Bormann, Ohlendorf, Hanke and Kaltenbrunner's massive attacks on Schieber, whom they accused of treason in his dealings with Sweden. These attacks forced Speer to drop him on 31 October 1944.[124]

The most interesting of these character portraits is that of Hans Kammler. In his memoirs Speer described him as 'cool and down-to-earth, my partner, in many ways my rival, but he was my mirror image as far as his background and working methods were concerned'.[125] Elsewhere he describes him as 'a ruthless but capable despot'. He even managed to think of him as a kind of Schindler, who like himself had given concentration camp prisoners a chance to survive by slaving away building underground factories.[126] That Speer could imagine that it was in any way merciful to work in Dora-Mittelbau is a clear indication that he knew perfectly well what would happen to those who remained in the concentration camps. Elsewhere he described his 'mirror image' as the most brutal and unscrupulous of Himmler's associates.[127] All this was designed to show that Speer was quite different from all the other brutes, incompetents and madmen in the Nazi hierarchy. In this context it is perhaps apposite to be reminded of Field Marshal Milch's assessment of Speer: 'ambitious to the point of being power-hungry, knows what he wants and what he is worth . . . moody . . . likes to be the centre of attraction, suffers from a certain degree of vanity'.[128]

Yet in spite of all these efforts at reinventing himself there are times when Speer lets down his guard. This is particularly evident in his use of language. Thus he speaks of human beings in terms of 'the great human reservoir in the General Government', 'net gain discounting deaths' and 'capital goods'.[129] Elsewhere he remarks that it made no sense to kill Jews because they made such good (slave) workers.[130] He writes that 'Himmler promised the Gauleiters that he would "liquidate" all the Jews by 1943, but he still used them for industrial purposes.' To which is added: 'The Jewish reservoir in the General Government has dried up.'[131] But Speer did not see Jews merely as victims. He argued that they were very 'powerful' in Germany prior to 1933 and asked why they had not used this power to stop the Nazis. He then undermines this argument by the all-too-familiar statement that Nazi anti-Semitism was fuelled by Jewish opposition to National Socialism.[132] On both counts it would seem that Jews were somehow responsible for the Third Reich and its crimes.

Speer worked in close cooperation with Himmler, who at his request provided him with quarries and brickyards for his mammoth building projects. It was only when Himmler tried to expand his industrial empire and have greater influence over the armaments industry that conflict arose. Speer was opposed to Himmler's idea of bringing factories into the concentration camps because he wanted to bring the concentration camp inmates into the armaments factories.

The most shameless deception in *Infiltration* is the citation of the letter – already quoted – from Speer to Himmler written on 30 May 1943. His co-workers Desch and Sander had recently visited Auschwitz and as a result of their very positive report he had allocated substantial amounts of building material 'for the extension of concentration camps, particularly Auschwitz'. He regretted that he was unable to release the additional building material requested by the Waffen-SS. In a handwritten postscript he added that 'I am delighted that the visit to other concentration camps made such a favourable impression'. Speer claims that this letter was written not by him, but by Oswald Pohl, even though it is signed by him and the postscript is clearly in his own handwriting.[133]

Matthias Schmidt gives an example of how Speer doctored documents to avoid any unpleasantness before handing them over to the Allies. During his long illness he wrote an acceptance speech on receiving the Dr Fritz Todt Prize on 8 February 1944. Willy Liebel, the mayor of Nuremberg and the head of his Central Office, read the speech on Speer's behalf. It contains a denunciation of 'Jewish wire-pullers and warmongers'. Rather than destroy the document, Speer pencilled in the margin: 'Liebel's draft, during [my] sickness. Read by Liebel.'[134]

At the end of August 1981 Speer travelled to London to be interviewed on the BBC by the Oxford historian Norman Stone. He left his holiday home in the Allgäu at seven in the morning and at six that evening Stone picked him up at the Park Court Hotel in Bayswater. They dined at Brown's Hotel and chatted easily until two in the morning. He was taken to the studio early the next day. They spent several hours taping the interview. Speer was scheduled to fly back home that afternoon, so Stone suggested that they have lunch before he left for the airport. Speer cheerily replied that he was having lunch with a lady. He returned to his hotel where he suffered a massive stroke. He died that afternoon at St Mary's Hospital in Paddington. It was not until later that the consultant who attended him admitted to finding it strange that a man should spend his last hours in a hospital in a city that he had sought to destroy. At the time it merely seemed remarkable that an old man should have been in the company of such a strikingly attractive young woman.[135]

The *Frankfurter Allgemeine Zeitung* gave Speer a generous obituary, presumably written by Joachim Fest. He is described as 'a man of ideals and integrity . . . characterised by education, broad horizons and an upper-middle-class background'. Gradually this image of Speer began to crumble. The first major breach in the protective wall he had built around himself was the publication of Mathias Schmidt's doctoral thesis shortly after Speer's death. Damage was limited because the book received limited attention. Although Fest failed to mention Schmidt's startling revelations in his biography of Speer published in 1999, in his notebook he wrote that while Schmidt's book was 'prejudiced', the evidence he produced was 'considerable'. It showed that Speer had kept secrets from him and Siedler. In presenting himself as the ingenuous 'everybody's darling' – to Tessenow, Hitler, the Nuremberg Tribunal and post-war

Germany – he had managed to deceive everyone. Siedler felt that Fest had gone too far in damning Speer for his deceit and deception, feeling that it was too early to pass final judgment on him. He pointed out that Wolters had merely told Schmidt of the doctoring of the Chronicle, but had not said anything about the ejection of Jews from their apartments. Siedler reminded Fest of Speer's statement that one had to come to terms with the contradictions one faces in daily life. This suggests that Siedler had not read Schmidt's book with close attention. Fest warily noted that this might well not be the last of such revelations.[136] He obviously felt it best not to mention these reservations about Speer in the biography. It might have damaged his carefully constructed portrait, thereby bringing the entire Speer enterprise into question. In the English version of the biography, subtitled *The Final Verdict*, Fest mentions Schmidt's book as making an admittedly significant contribution, but then minimises its significance by saying that it covered only a brief phase in his life.[137]

In 1993 an article appeared in the Austrian bi-monthly journal *Zeitgeschichte* that showed how Speer had played an important role in the expansion of Auschwitz-Birkenau by providing capital, labour and building materials. The purpose of this operation was to provide facilities for 'special treatment'.[138] Fest, with his contempt for professional historians, overlooked this important study and remained incredulous.

By the time that Sereny and Fest had published their biographies of Speer, in 1995 and 1999 respectively, historians had provided ample evidence that Speer had lied through his teeth. Reviewers were quick to point this out. The British historian Richard Evans wrote perceptively of Sereny's psychological study that Speer had lied to himself in order to live with himself.[139] And yet the Speer myth persisted, traces of which even appeared in Breloer's otherwise critical TV docudrama of 2004.[140] The truly astonishing part of this story is that in spite of the fact that a vast mass of evidence had been uncovered about Speer, including the editing of the Chronicle, the expulsion of the Berlin Jews, the ways in which Speer had amassed vast wealth from his building projects, his role in building Auschwitz, his use of forced labour including concentration camp inmates in underground factories and his close association with major criminals, Fest and Siedler stuck to their now threadbare version of Speer as the innocent technocrat. Admittedly Fest had confessed to having had some doubts about Speer, but in his interview with Breloer he stuck fast to the notion that Speer was a mere functionary who was totally unaware of the criminal nature of the regime he served. In denial of all the evidence that historians had collected over the years, Fest insisted that there was no evidence to show that Speer was aware of what was going on when he was on his watch.[141]

Fest's total inability to face the facts and his arrogant contempt for mere historians was dictated by his refusal – a stubbornness that he shared with

Siedler – to accept what had been proven beyond all doubt, that well-educated men from respectable middle-class backgrounds, often with doctorates, could act as mass murderers and were as morally reprehensible as the gangsters, psychopaths and bully-boys that were the popular image of the typical Nazi. He simply could not face the fact that 'one of us', that is a man such as Albert Speer, not only could have been complicit with Nazi crimes, but also could have been one of the regime's leading criminals.

CONCLUSION

Ａ**FTER HIS RELEASE** from Spandau prison, Speer professed to have been plagued by an oppressive feeling of guilt. In his *Playboy* interview he made the dramatic claim to have made a one-way trip to hell from which he had not yet returned. One cannot help feeling a certain sympathy for Speer's erstwhile friend Rudolf Wolters's outrage at his loudly broadcasted expressions of remorse and his public appearances in the penitent's hair-shirt. It was never at all clear what Speer meant by guilt. His expression of general or overall guilt at Nuremberg was an empty formula, although it turned out – much to the surprise of his defence attorney – to have been a masterly tactic that helped save his skin. Guilt in this context seems to have meant little more than overall responsibility for things that had happened while he was in office, but with which he was not directly concerned. In the judicial sense of the term his guilt was palpable, but this form of guilt had been exculpated by twenty years in prison. Or was this feeling of guilt merely remorse? After all, things had not turned out for him quite as he had hoped. By late 1944 Speer began to think about his place in post-war Germany. With his close connections with the captains of industry, his proven managerial skills and his untarnished popular image he imagined that he was certain of a stellar career in the business world. With so many architects indebted to him, he could also head a major architectural practice. There would certainly be a lot of work to do.

Gitta Sereny spent twelve years of research and took 747 pages to come to the conclusion that Speer had rediscovered the 'intrinsic morality' he had in his youth. This was a singularly modest return for all her efforts. Those best placed to judge were not easily impressed. Georges Casalis, the Protestant pastor in Spandau, had felt that Speer's wrestling with problems of guilt while in prison were genuine. Upon his release he rapidly became so absorbed in his wealth and fame that he was no longer troubled by conscience and abandoned his spiritual quest. Father Athanasius, in whom he confided while attending frequent retreats at Maria Laach, realised that although Speer was well aware of his mistakes, failures and shortcomings, he lacked the spiritual insight that might have enabled him to overcome any deep-rooted sense of guilt. Without any genuine expression of repentance springing from his inner being, his attempts to grapple with the past were unlikely to amount to much more than window-dressing.

It was difficult to believe that Speer's concept of guilt had much to do with what either Georges Casalis or Father Athanasius understood by the term. Speer was a typical example, as Sebastian Haffner had noted, of the new managerial type. He believed in action, without considering the consequences of his deeds. He operated in the world of the practical and the horizontal and had little patience with the moral, spiritual and vertical. Speer lived in the modern world where God is dead. He would have agreed with Mephistopheles when he said: 'The world does not remain silent to the proficient. He does not need to wander in eternity.'[1] Mephistopheles is a remarkable precursor to the Speer type. In *Faust* Part I, Goethe presents him as an old-fashioned medieval German devil, but in Part II he is a man of the world, a cynic, a technocrat and a management consultant. Unlike Speer, he then relapses into the total debauchery to which some of his epigones are prone. Speer sometimes fashioned himself as Faust, but he more closely resembles the Demon.

Joachim Fest and Wolf Jobst Siedler were both struck by the pride that Speer showed in having enabled the German armed forces to continue the struggle for as long as they did.[2] There can be no doubt that Speer did indeed help to prolong the war longer than many thought possible, as a result of which millions were killed and Germany reduced to a pile of rubble. To take pride in such an achievement did not quite fit with his public image as a public penitent, handing over a fortune to the victims of National Socialism, renouncing the material pleasures of life and living on locusts and wild honey. Speer, rejoicing in his successful and lucrative rehabilitation, was at times prepared to acknowledge that his appearance as a conscience-stricken prophet in a technological wilderness was a sham.[3]

He argued that his guilt was based on omission rather than commission. He clearly implied that guilt by omission was necessarily the less reprehensible. His self-serving public display of scrupulosity sidestepped a confrontation with the true nature of what he had done. He had not merely looked away. This was not an argument over the validity of his ignorance, nor was it a question of due moral diligence. He had been an active participant in Nazi crimes. This was something that he refused to admit, even to himself. There was no sorrow at the wrong he had caused, no hint of remorse, no genuine apology. Refusing to admit the full extent of his wrongdoing, even to those in whom he could count on absolute discretion, he could never free himself from the anxiety that he might eventually be unmasked. He lied in order to be able to live with himself. He confessed to a lesser evil so as to conceal a far greater iniquity. He saw himself as having been seduced by Hitler, a victim of the age of technology and blinded by success. Unable to confront the past honestly he could never find true peace of mind. As Goethe remarked: 'An active person is without a conscience. Only an observer has a conscience.'[4] Speer the observer was in no position to judge the active Speer. Although his sense of guilt was usually little more than a nagging unease and a lingering fear that his past might once again come under judicial scrutiny, there were moments when it seemed as if he wanted to confess so as to free himself from the burden of his Nazi past. How else to explain why he suggested that Schmidt approach Wolters or his admission to Hélène Jeanty Raven that he had indeed heard Himmler's speech in Posen.

Taking Speer's memoirs and his Spandau Diaries at face value, Mother Miriam Pollard of the Order of Cistercians of the Strict Observance saw Speer's twenty years in quasi-monastic isolation in Spandau prison, during which he trudged along the road to Emmaus, as resulting in his receiving God's redemptive embrace, having embarked on the long journey from remorse to restitution and expiation.[5] 'Hitler,' she writes, 'had taken him a fair way to hell, but when Speer finally stopped and turned, he could still find the road back to reason, humanity and grace.'[6] This is something Speer flatly denied when he told the *Playboy* interviewer that the descent into hell was an exhilarating ride, but a one-way trip. Mother Miriam has an answer to why Speer was tormented by Heidegger's 'oblivion of being'. Although to her mind Speer had been honest about the past, had accepted responsibility for wrongdoing and the punishment he had been given, had made due reparation and offered up a vicarious expiation for others, there was one critical piece missing. That was his inability, due to inadequate spiritual instruction, to accept forgiveness.[7] Nevertheless, the penitent Speer is elevated to almost saintly status. 'In his redeemed and redeeming self he was delivering the guilt of the world into the re-creative embrace of God.'[8] Speer's daughter Hilde is taken to task for her scepticism about her father's 'converted heart'.

This image of a soul-searching Speer, wrestling with the past and through years of deprivation and incarceration, living a life immersed in the redemptive death of Christ, making an act of public expiation for an entire nation, finds artistic expression in a remarkable sculpture by Yrsa von Leistner. This portrait, finished shortly before his death, shows Speer's agonised and tortured face emerging from a block of marble. A red streak in the marble runs diagonally across his face, which Mother Miriam saw as a harbinger of his imminent death, but also as 'a sublime meditation on the mystery of the redemption.'[9] Given what we now know about Speer it is difficult not to feel that Mother Miriam, out of the generosity of her soul, is reading something into the material that is simply not there. Similarly, Yrsa von Leistner's portrait suffers from a severe dose of the kitsch that mars much of her work. Speer abandoned his Protestant faith as a young man and was constitutionally incapable of finding his way back to it. Rudolf Wolters' mockery of the repentant Speer with a hair-shirt and a diet of locusts, coupled with Hilde's adamant disbelief, are far more convincing than the image of Speer the redeemer.

Speer played a dual role in post-war Germany. Here was one of the most powerful men in the Third Reich, who condemned Hitler as a criminal and who made a public, if circumscribed, confession of his own guilt at having been complicit in an immoral regime. But more importantly, he provided a thick coating of whitewash to millions of old Nazis. This was a man who was closer to Hitler than any other, yet who maintained his personal integrity as an apolitical technocrat, who told the Nuremberg Tribunal that he had only had a 'vague sentiment' of what went on in the concentration camps. Here was the man who provided exculpation for an entire generation. If a man so close to Hitler, with such immense power and with close connections to all the leading figures in the Third Reich, was unaware of the mass murder of the European Jews, how could the myriad of lesser figures possibly have known? Speer was Hitler's closest associate – so close indeed that Joachim Fest was convinced that there were distinct homoerotic overtones in the relationship – yet who kept his integrity, innocent of all the evil done by the regime.[10] For Wolters, he was Hitler's 'unrequited love'. Reinhard Spitzy, a hard-nosed diplomat seconded to military security in the Reich Security Main Office, said that whenever Speer visited the Obersalzberg he and Hitler would disappear to pore over architectural drawings like a couple of lovers. His publisher, Siedler, got so carried away by this extravagant talk that he described him as an 'angel who came from hell'. The psychologist Alexander Mitscherlich said of him that he was a 'sensitive guilty-innocent'.[11] For others, less given to such convoluted and largely meaningless utterances, he was simply the perfect example of the idealistic, hardworking German, who fell under Hitler's spell. He was stylised as a Parsifal who lacked the simple-mindedness and incorruptibility with which to resist Klingsor's magic. He was by nature detached and standoffish, awkward in society, haughty and arrogant, without any real friends and anxious to avoid the company of others. He thus appeared to be a man apart. This helped to save him from the gallows and made the successful reconstruction of his public image possible.

So great was the need to believe the Speer myth that Siedler and Fest were able to strengthen it, even in the face of mounting evidence against him by professional historians. Fest held fast to his vision of the Third Reich as a regime, like any other, held together by blinkered specialists, of whom Speer was the perfect example. He was the gentleman among the gangsters. He was not someone who ranted and raved about the world Jewish conspiracy, but a conventionally civilised anti-Semite who confessed to having had an 'unpleasant feeling' when in the presence of Jews. He did not worry his head about Jewish slave labourers in his brickyards. He did not spare a thought about his Transport Corps in the Soviet Union as it moved stolen works of art back to Germany, or when it resettled German Mennonites in Himmler's eastern outposts. Part of the Corps' remit was, after all, to help implement the resolutions of the Wannsee Conference. Speer was no more lacking in empathy than Wernher von Braun, who was unconcerned about the slave labourers worked to death in underground factories building his beloved rockets; or Ferdinand Porsche, in whose works thousands of prisoners of war and forced labourers died; or Alfried Krupp, for whom Speer built special concentration camps for a hundred thousand ruthlessly exploited slaves.

Speer made staggering profits from the 'Aryanisation' of property in Berlin. He assembled a fine collection of early nineteenth-century romantic art, much of which was purchased at bargain basement prices from legitimate dealers, many of the previous owners having been forced to sell. Göring's generous gift of a hundred hectares of woodland, adjacent to his magnificent estate at Oderbruch, was prudently overlooked. Fest took Speer's preposterous claim to have always preferred the simple life, and to have easily adjusted to the austerity of his Spandau cell, at face value. He remained silent about Speer's inhuman treatment of the Berlin Jews who stood in the way of his grotesque plans to rebuild the city. Had Fest bothered to have done his homework, he would have known that Speer was involved in the building of the prisoners' barracks at Mauthausen, later to complain, much to Oswald Pohl's irritation, that he found them far too luxurious. He was however well satisfied with the facilities at Auschwitz, on which he had commissioned a special report. Himmler, Heydrich, Oswald Pohl, Hans Kammler and Dr Karl Brandt, to name but a few, were among Speer's closest associates. All were complicit in mass murder on an unimaginable scale. It is inconceivable that Speer knew absolutely nothing of this aspect of their efforts to build a new Germany.

He ordered every effort to be made to support Hitler's last desperate gamble in the Ardennes offensive in late 1944. When it failed, it is to his credit that he did what he could to counter Hitler's Nero Order and to save whatever could be saved, at least in the Ruhr. It is all too easy to overestimate Speer's role in the final stages of the Third Reich. A scorched earth policy was impossible to implement. The vast majority of Germans had had more than enough. They wanted an end to the horror, not a horror without end. They were prepared to wave the white flag, even at the risk of the death penalty. Dying a hero's death in a war that was already lost seemed utterly pointless.

Speer the miracle worker is every bit as mythical as Speer the innocent, apolitical artist. This reputation rests on the calculations made by the Ministry of Armaments' chief statistician, Rolf Wagenführ.[12] The figures are indeed remarkable. Armaments production rose threefold from February 1942, when Speer took office, to July 1944.[13] This is all the more astonishing given that this dramatic increase happened despite the Allied bombing offensive, dwindling supplies of raw materials and labour shortages. Wagenführ attributes this to a significant increase in the productivity of labour from a baseline of 100 in January 1942 to 234 by July 1944.[14] Rationalisation also made it possible to produce more weapons using fewer raw materials. Productivity was further enhanced by drastically reducing the number of different weapons produced. The Speer ministry also put an end to the constant modification of individual weapons. Further savings were made by concentrating orders for weapons in the ministry, rather than leaving them in the hands of diverse institutions within the armed services. The self-determination of industry meant that firms were obliged to share their know-how, thereby making substantial savings. The system of committees and rings put small and inefficient enterprises out of business. The armaments industry suffered initially from start-up problems resulting from the rapid growth of capital stock and the labour force, but Speer benefited as industry rapidly learnt from experience.

Some argue that a significant improvement was made with the fixed price system that did not become the norm until 1942. Hitherto profits had been mainly calculated on the percentage of capital employed.[15] The problem here was that this did not force less resourceful producers to meet standard pricing. It also necessitated complex bureaucratic controls to make sure that all was on the level. Now fixed prices were negotiated on the basis of good to average producers. Profits were made by producing at a lower cost. No awkward questions were asked as to how costs were reduced. That this was largely due to the ruthless exploitation of all forms of labour was conveniently overlooked.

There is no evidence to show that the change from cost prices to fixed prices made a significant difference. Fixed prices were already in effect in significant sectors of the armaments industry. Furthermore, fixed prices were based on previous cost prices. Generally speaking cost prices were used to cover risks when launching a new product. Fixed prices were often adjusted – particularly in the aircraft industry – when excess profits were made. The tax authorities, however, were careful to ensure that incentives to innovation and efficiency were not removed by excessive taxation. As a result, substantial profits were made throughout the war.[16]

Wagenführ's macro-economic data, the report of the US Strategic Bombing Survey and Speer's compelling memoirs created the impression that there had indeed been an armaments miracle and that Albert Speer was the brightest star in the National Socialist firmament. It only needed a cursory examination of the evidence to show that there had already been a substantial increase in armaments production long before Speer began to work his miracles. This was deliberately disguised by choosing the exceptionally low production figures in January and February 1942 as the baseline. The relatively low production figures in 1940 and 1941 had little to do with inefficiency and low productivity. They were the result of deliberate military-political decisions. Speer's much vaunted changes in the pricing system in May 1942 did not make a significant impact. Before that date there had been price reductions that suggest there were already sufficient incentives to increase efficiency.[17]

Problems about the ways in which the armaments index was weighted are compounded by Speer's deliberate manipulation of the figures in order to appease Hitler. This left the Wehrmacht wondering where on earth these weapons were that were listed in Speer's public recitations of staggering production figures. The productivity figures are equally suspect. They were only based on productivity in firms that were under the aegis of the Armaments Inspectors. They do not include statistics from the armaments industry in the occupied countries.[18]

Further doubts about the armaments industry stem from the fact the branches that showed outstanding rates of growth were initially not under Speer's ministry. He did not take over control of naval armaments until October 1943, and Luftwaffe armaments remained independent until June 1944. Productivity in the aircraft industry was marginally higher than the overall armaments index. Naval productivity was fractionally less. This raises the question whether there was anything exceptional about Speer's much-vaunted rationalisation programme. There are serious doubts whether the dramatic increase in the number of committees and rings resulted in any significant exchange of information between firms.[19] Nor was this such a great innovation. They had been created by Todt. There had been effective exchanges of information between firms that were directly controlled by the army. Similar arrangements existed in parts of the aircraft industry.

Systematic rationalisation came relatively late and not infrequently proved to be a mixed blessing. Shipbuilding was rationalised in the summer of 1943. Production figures were impressive, but U-boats that were not seaworthy did not improve the navy's fighting power. In the aircraft industry there was a steady increase in the number of different types and their variants. It was not until the summer of 1944 that a serious effort was made to address this problem.

A report commissioned by Hans Kehrl as head of the Planning Office in early 1944 suggests that Speer's rationalisation efforts did not amount to much.[20] Shortage of labour was a constant and increasing problem. It was compounded by the waste caused by the frequent introduction of new programmes combined with ongoing technical modifications. The Krupp Grusonwerk AG in Magdeburg was obliged to make eight significant changes in its tank-building programme in the course of 1943. The Eisenwerk Oberdonau GmbH in Linz had to make 1,474 modifications to the spare parts they provided for the Panther tank between July 1942 and March 1944. The Henschel aircraft company, that had built the Ju 88 bomber for years, was ordered to cease production in 1943 and make the Me 410 'Hornet' fighter bomber. The Hornet proved ineffective in its role as a bomber destroyer, so that in 1944 the company was obliged once again to make the Ju 88. The end result was a disastrous drop in productivity. Hans Kehrl frequently complained that Speer did not address these problems with due concern.

Although many of the measures ascribed to Speer had been implemented before his appointment as Minister of Armaments, the question remains how it was that armaments production increased significantly during his time in office. In part this was due to the learning process in the first two-and-a-half years of the war. In the two years before he became minister, the amount of capital invested in enterprises controlled by the army for weapons production increased threefold. Much the same was true of the aircraft industry. In the first year of the war the workforce in the armaments industry doubled. Unskilled labourers had time to learn their trades, so that Speer inherited a highly skilled workforce. In his address to the Gauleiters in Munich on 24 February 1942, just a few days after his appointment, Speer paid ample tribute to Fritz Todt. He listed the enormous increases in efficiency, output and productivity that had been achieved by the ministry under his leadership.[21] By February 1942 there had been a fourfold increase in the value of machine tools delivered to the armaments industry. This was a rate of increase that Speer was unable to match and it provided him with the solid foundations for further growth.

One factor that inhibited growth during Todt's time in office was a widespread belief that this would be a short war. After the spectacular victories over Poland and France it seemed that the Wehrmacht would make short work of the Soviet Union. Firms such as Daimler-Benz were therefore loath to invest heavily in armaments production because they wanted to be well prepared for the post-war market.[22] With Operation Barbarossa in ruins it was obvious to most that this was going to be a long hard slog and that industry would be wise to become fully involved in war production. Ample rewards were there for those who could produce the goods.

Until 1943 wage-adjusted labour productivity remained below the 1939 level. Thereafter it made a spectacular increase, until it began to tail off by the end of 1944. Rationalisation, centralisation, standardisation, the closing down of redundant firms and pricing had little to do with this achievement. Since the overwhelming majority of the eight-million-strong workforce in the armaments industry were forced labourers, prisoners of war or slaves, and German workers were ruthlessly exploited, the unit cost of labour was necessarily extremely low. The achievement of the armaments industry under Speer was no armaments miracle. There was no discontinuity between him and his predecessor. The economy was not transformed from a 'peacetime economy in wartime' into a full-scale wartime economy. A number of rationalisation measures had taken place under Todt. Others came into force relatively late, at a time when production figures had already peaked. Fixed prices were already in place, offering ample incentives to cut costs. Many of the achievements of the armaments industry were thus due to continuity and the long-term effects of measures that had been taken before Speer took office.

Speer may not have been a miracle worker and he had no particular gift as an architect, but, recognising his own shortcomings, he readily delegated to men of exceptional talent and energy. This made him an outstanding organiser and manager. At times he claimed to be an artist who had been forced into an alien world. Alternatively he described himself as an apolitical technocrat enthralled by a world of scientific know-how and applied science. In fact he was neither. As an architect, with grim confidence he followed the example set by others: first Tessenow, then Troost, and lastly Hitler. Even his finest achievement, the Cathedral of Light at Nuremberg, was probably suggested to him by the filmmaker Leni Riefenstahl and her cameraman Walter Frentz, whom Speer had met while canoeing.[23] Having no technical expertise whatsoever, he relied on others. This left him vulnerable to attack from ambitious underlings. Being neither artist nor technocrat his unique position was solely due to his close relationship with Hitler. Once that was compromised he was left virtually powerless. All that remained was a set of mutually beneficial relationships that could only be sustained because the Third Reich was falling apart, the dictatorship crumbling.

What makes Speer so particularly frightening was that this hollow man, resolutely bourgeois, highly intelligent, totally lacking in moral vision, unable to question the consequences of his actions, and without scruples, was far from being an outsider. He was of the type that made National Socialism possible. The Third Reich would never have been so deadly effective had it relied on the adventurers, thugs, half-crazed ideologues, racist fanatics and worshippers of Germanic deities that people the public image of the regime. Speer is the outstanding representative of a widespread type that made the regime possible. That so many found his carefully staged post-war image so thoroughly convincing points to an insidious danger. As Sebastian Haffner so shrewdly remarked, we can get rid of the Hitlers and the Himmlers, but not the Speers. They are still with us. They are immediately recognisable and every bit as dangerous.

NOTES

Introduction

1. Hugh Trevor-Roper, *The Last Days of Hitler*, London, 1947.
2. H.R. Trevor-Roper, 'Porträt des wirklichen Nazi-Verbrechers' (1949) in Adelbert Reif, *Albert Speer: Kontroversen um ein deutsches Phänomen*, Munich, 1978, pp. 233–9.
3. Joachim Fest, *Die unbeantwortbaren Fragen: Notizen über Gespräche mit Albert Speer zwischen Ende 1966 und 1981*, Reinbek bei Hamburg, 2006, p. 232.
4. Ibid., p. 221.
5. Speer, *Spandauer Tagebücher*, Berlin, 1975, p. 20.
6. Margret Nissen (with Margrit Knapp and Sabine Seifert), *Sind Sie die Tochter Speer?*, Munich, 2005.
7. Dietrich Eichholtz, *Geschichte der deutschen Kriegswirtschaft 1939–1945*, 5 vols, Munich, 2002; Adam Tooze, *The Wages of Destruction: The Making and Breaking of the Nazi Economy*, London, 2006; and Rolf-Dieter Müller's contributions to *Das Deutsche Reich und der Zweite Weltkrieg*, vols 4, 5/1, 5/2, 10/1 and 10/2. Valuable additional material can be found in Heinrich Breloer, *Unterwegs zur Familie Speer: Begegnungen, Gespräche, Interviews*, Berlin, 2005, and Heinrich Breloer and Rainer Zimmer, *Die Akte Speer: Spuren eines Kriegsverbrechers*, Berlin, 2006.
8. Joachim Fest, *Speer: Eine Biographie*, Berlin, 1999, and Gitta Sereny, *Albert Speer: His Battle with Truth*, London, 1995.
9. Fest, *Die unbeantwortbaren Fragen*.

Chapter 1: The Young Architect

1. On the other hand, being a Sunday it is possible that church bells were ringing somewhere in the town. Christian Schrade, *Christuskirche Mannheim*, Mannheim, 1911, reprinted 1986; Herbert Wäldin, *50 Jahre Christuskirche Mannheim 1911–1961*, Mannheim, 1961. The bells were confiscated in 1942, thereby entering Speer's domain. Matthias Schmidt, *Albert Speer – Das Ende eines Mythos: Speers wahre Rolle im Dritten Reich*, Munich, 1982, p. 33, consulted the meteorological office for weather conditions on that day.
2. Albert Speer, *Erinnerungen*, Berlin, 1969, p. 22; H.J. Reichhardt and Wolfgang Schäche, *Ludwig Hoffmann in Berlin*, Berlin, 1987.
3. Speer, *Erinnerungen*, p. 20; Schmidt, *Albert Speer*, p. 34.
4. Gitta Sereny, *Albert Speer: His Battle With Truth*, London, 1995, p. 41.
5. Schmidt, *Albert Speer*, p. 34, quoting Rudolf Wolters.
6. William Hamsher, *Albert Speer: Victim of Nuremberg?*, London, 1970.
7. Hermann was born in 1902, Ernst in 1906. Ernst went missing, presumably killed, in Stalingrad in 1942. Hermann was unsuccessful as a photographer. After the Second World War he was financially dependent on his younger brother.
8. Gitta Sereny, 'Hat Speer alles gesagt?', *Die Zeit, Zeitmagazin*, no. 43 (20 October 1978).
9. Sereny, *Albert Speer*, p. 42. The fact that she was Jewish may perhaps explain why Speer was never given to crude anti-Semitism and harboured a number of 'half-Jews' in his office, including his invaluable secretary Annemarie Kempf.
10. Speer, *Erinnerungen*, p. 21.

11. This was an *Oberrealschule*, a nine-year school specialising in modern languages, science and mathematics.
12. Joachim Fest, *Die unbeantwortbaren Fragen: Notizen über Gespräche mit Albert Speer zwischen Ende 1966 und 1981*, Reinbek bei Hamburg, 2006, p. 27.
13. Speer, *Erinnerungen*, p. 25.
14. At the height of the inflation 1 dollar equalled 4.2 trillion marks.
15. Speer, *Erinnerungen*, p. 27.
16. Nitzan Lebovic, *The Philosophy of Life and Death: Ludwig Klages and the Rise of a Nazi Biopolitics*, London, 2013.
17. Heinrich Breloer, *Unterwegs zur Familie Speer: Begegnungen, Gespräche, Interviews*, Berlin, 2005, p. 30; Fest, *Die unbeantwortbaren Fragen*, p. 52.
18. The speech 'Mensch und Erde' is reprinted in Ludwig Klages, *Mensch und Erde*, Berlin, 2013.
19. Reinhardt's flamboyant style led to the *Großes Schauspielhaus* being renamed Reinhardt's Circus.
20. Julius Posener, 'Zwei Lehrer: Heinrich Tessenow und Hans Poelzig', in Reinhard Rürup (ed.), *Wissenschaft und Gesellschaft: Beiträge zur Geschichte der Technischen Universität Berlin 1879–1979*, vol. 1, Berlin, 1979.
21. Poelzig, a Berliner, was known as '*der Meester*'.
22. Heinrich Tessenow, *Handwerk und Kleinstadt*, Berlin, 1919.
23. Hamsher, *Albert Speer: Victim of Nuremberg?*, p. 27.
24. Schmidt, *Albert Speer*, p. 37.
25. Ibid., p. 39.
26. Sereny, *Albert Speer*, p. 49.
27. Speer, *Erinnerungen*, p. 28. This remark is quoted in the closing section of Tessenow's *Handwerk und Kleinstadt*.
28. Albert Speer, *Spandauer Tagebücher*, Berlin, 1975, p. 128, mistakenly dates the speech to November.
29. Schmidt, *Albert Speer*, p. 40. Wolfsburg was then known as the Town of the Strength Through Joy Motor Car (*Stadt des KdF-Wagens*).
30. In 1945 he was to talk at some length about racial superiority of Siberians and White Russians over the Germans – at least in terms of fortitude and resolution – and of Europeans over Arabs. Ulrich Schlie (ed.), *Albert Speer: Die Kransberg-Protokolle 1945. Seine ersten Aussagen und Aufzeichnungen (Juni–September)*, Munich, 2003, p. 447.
31. Michael H. Kater, 'Der NS-Studentenbund von 1926 bis 1928: Randgruppe zwischen Hitler und Strasser', *Vierteljahrshefte für Zeitgeschichte*, 22, 1974, pp. 148–90.
32. Jeffrey Herf, 'The Engineer as Ideologue: Reactionary Modernists in Weimar and Nazi Germany', *Journal of Contemporary History*, vol. 19, no. 4 (October 1984), pp. 631–48.
33. Ebbo Demant, *Von Schleicher zu Springer*, Frankfurt, 1971, p. 77.
34. Kurt Sondheimer, 'Der Tatkreis', *Vierteljahrshefte für Zeitgeschichte*, vol. 7, no. 3 (1959), pp. 229–60. Sefton Delmer was the bilingual correspondent of the *Daily Express* in Germany until 1933.
35. Jeffrey Herf, *Reactionary Modernism: Technology, Culture and Politics in Weimar and the Third Reich*, Cambridge, 1984, pp. 152–88.
36. Barbara Orland, 'Der Zwiespalt zwischen Politik und Technik: Ein kulturelles Phänomen in der Vergangenheitsbewältigung Albert Speers und seiner Rezipienten' in Burkhard Dietz, Michael Fessner and Helmut Maier (eds), *Technische Intelligenz und 'Kulturfaktor Technik': Kulturvorstellungen von Technikern und Ingenieuren zwischen Kaiserreich und früher Bundesrepublik Deutschland*, Münster, 1996, pp. 269–95.
37. This building was much favoured by the Nazis. After the war it was used as a concert hall where artists such as Jimi Hendrix, Patti Smith, Elvis Costello and Dire Straits performed.
38. The speech was reprinted in full in Goebbels' newspaper *Der Angriff* on the following day. Full text in Constantin Goschler and Christian Hartmann (eds), *Hitler: Reden, Schriften, Anordnungen, Februar 1925–Januar 1933: Von der Reichstagswahl bis zur Reichspräsidentenwahl. Oktober 1930–März 1932*, vol. 4/1 (*Oktober 1930–Juni 1931*), Munich, 1997. It seems that only one SA man, Theodor Sanders, died on 4 December 1930, according to the neo-Nazi site 'Blood Witnesses to the Movement' (*Blutzeuge der Bewegung*).
39. Speer, *Erinnerungen*, p. 33.
40. Schmidt, *Albert Speer*, p. 45.
41. Speer, *Erinnerungen*, p. 34.
42. Speer, *Erinnerungen*, p. 34; Albert Speer, *Inside the Third Reich*, London, 1970, p. 51.
43. Speer, *Erinnerungen*, p. 33.
44. Hamsher, *Albert Speer: Victim of Nuremberg?*, p. 52.
45. Schmidt, *Albert Speer*, p. 45.
46. Speer, *Erinnerungen*, p. 35.

47. Speer, *Erinnerungen*, p. 38. For Nagel's later career under Speer, see Franz W. Seidler, 'Das Nationalsozialistische Kraftfahrkorps und die Organisation Todt im Weltkrieg', *Vierteljahrshefte für Zeitgeschichte*, vol. 32, no. 4 (1984), pp. 625–36.
48. André François-Poncet, *Souvenirs d'une ambassade à Berlin, septembre 1931–octobre 1938*, Paris, 1947.
49. Speer, *Erinnerungen*, p. 38.
50. The building was torn down in 1938 to make way for Speer's new chancellery.
51. Speer, *Erinnerungen*, p. 40. The *Vereinigte Werkstätten für Kunst im Handwerk* in Munich and Bremen were famous for furnishing luxury liners following Troost's designs. They made the furniture for Hitler's Berghof, his Munich apartment, the new Reichskanzlei and other official buildings, following designs by Paul and Gerdy Troost, Albert Speer, Leonhard Gall and Hans Russwurm. Sonja Günther, *Design der Macht: Möbel für Repräsentanten des 'Dritten Reiches'*, Stuttgart, 1992.
52. Speer, *Erinnerungen*, p. 40; Peter Longerich, *Goebbels: Biographie*, Munich, 2010, p. 235.
53. Longerich, *Goebbels*, p. 291.
54. Anna Teut, *Architektur im Dritten Reich 1933–1945*, Berlin, 1967, p. 187.
55. Longerich, *Goebbels*, p. 226.
56. Speer, *Erinnerungen*, p. 40.

Chapter 2: Nuremberg and Berlin

1. Günter Neliba, *Wilhelm Frick: Der Legalist des Unrechtsstaates*, Paderborn, 1992; Norbert Bormann, *Paul Schultze-Naumburg: Maler, Publizist, Architekt, 1869–1949*, Essen, 1989; Paul Schultze-Naumburg, *Kunst und Rasse*, Munich, 1928. This heady mixture of eugenics, social Darwinism and cultural racism concluded that modern art was a form of 'cretinism' and 'degeneration'. Twenty-nine of the teaching staff of thirty-two were fired. Schultze-Naumburg's views on 'degenerate' art were based on the ideas of Julius Langbehn and Max Nordau, a social critic and co-founder of the World Zionist Organisation.
2. It was here that the Potsdam Conference was held. It is now a hotel. It was made a UNESCO World Heritage Site in 1990.
3. Karl Willy Straub, *Die Architektur im Dritten Reich*, Stuttgart, 1932.
4. Walther Darré, *Neuadel aus Blut und Boden*, Munich, 1930.
5. Ploetz was somewhat heterodox in his views on Jews. He felt that they had many excellent qualities, resulting from the admixture of Aryan blood. Günther remained unrepentant after 1945 and was highly regarded by American segregationists, but was also well regarded in more respectable circles. He was elected corresponding member of the American Society of Human Genetics in 1953.
6. Anon., *Bauten der Bewegung*, Berlin, 1938; Barbara Miller Lane, *Architecture and Politics in Germany, 1918–1945*, Cambridge, MA, 1968, p. 269.
7. Frederic Spotts, *Hitler and the Power of Aesthetics*, London, 2002, p. 265.
8. Wolfgang Hardtwig (ed.), *Utopie und politische Herrschaft im Europa der Zwischenkriegszeit*, Munich, 2003; Franz Lawaczeck, *Technik und Wirtschaft im Dritten Reich*, Munich, 1932.
9. Ernst Neufert, *Bauordnungslehre*, Berlin, 1943.
10. Raphael Rosenberg, 'Architekturen des "Dritten Reiches": Völkische Heimatideologie versus internationale Monumentalität' (2011), p. 9, online at ART-Dok <http://archiv.ub.uniheidelberg.de/artdok/volltexte/2011/1501>.
11. Troost's building was 175 metres wide, Schinkel's only 87. This was the beginning of National Socialist 'gigantomania' that was to reach its apogee in Speer's buildings.
12. Dan Hill, 'Senate House, University of London', *City of Sound*, 21 November 2003, at <http://www.cityofsound.com/blog/2003/11/senate_house_un.html>; Simon Jenkins, 'It's time to knock down Hitler's headquarters and start again', *The Guardian*, 2 December 2005. George Orwell thought it a suitable housing for the Ministry of Truth in *1984*. It has also been effectively used as a movie set, particularly in a distinctly fascist reading of *Richard III*. Charles Holden is best known for his superb work designing for the London Underground.
13. Albert Speer, *Spandauer Tagebücher*, Berlin, 1975, p. 202.
14. Arthur Moeller van den Bruck, *Der preußische Stil*, 1914. Although he coined the phrase 'the Third Reich' he thought Hitler to be a 'proletarian primitive'.
15. Hans J. Reichhardt and Wolfgang Schäche, *Von Berlin nach Germania: Über die Zerstörung der 'Reichshauptstadt' durch Albert Speers Neugestaltungsplanungen*, Berlin, 2008.
16. Elke Dittrich, *Ernst Sagebiel: Leben und Werk (1892–1970)*, Berlin, 2005.
17. Joachim Petsch, *Baukunst und Stadtplanung im Dritten Reich: Herleitung/Bestandsaufnahme/Entwicklung/Nachfolge*, Munich, 1976, p. 183.

18. Speer, *Spandauer Tagebücher*, p. 261.
19. Heinrich Breloer, *Unterwegs zur Familie Speer: Begegnungen, Gespräche, Interviews*, Berlin, 2005, p. 271. Some psychologists, such as Erich Fromm, try to convince us that Hitler's enthusiasm for ruins is clear evidence of a death wish.
20. David Skilton, 'Contemplating the Ruins of London: Macaulay's New Zealander and Others', *The Literary London Journal*, vol. 2, no. 1 (March 2004). Werner Hofmann, *Das Irdische Paradies: Motive und Ideen des 19. Jahrhunderts*, Munich, 1974, pp. 176ff.
21. His son Albert, who did not have a high opinion of his work, felt that much of it was done by his subordinates. Breloer, *Unterwegs zur Familie Speer*, p. 150.
22. Neville Henderson, *Failure of a Mission, Berlin, 1937–39*, Toronto, 1940, pp. 66–7.
23. Albert Speer, *Erinnerungen*, Berlin, 1969, p. 42.
24. Maybe it was not quite such an original idea. Both Leni Riefenstahl and one of her cameramen, Walter Frentz, claimed that they had suggested the idea to Speer. Frentz also claimed that Speer's work on the Tempelhof Field was the work of Tessenow's pupil Hans Peter Klinke. Gitta Sereny, *Albert Speer: His Battle With Truth*, London, 1995, p. 128f.
25. Bernhard Gelderblom, *Die Reichsverteidigungsfeste auf dem Bückeberg 1933–37*, Hameln, 1998. Excellent material is also available at <http://www.gelderblom-hameln.de>. A 'Thing' (Anglo-Saxon Folkmoot or Manx Tyn) was a governing assembly. For the Nazis it was a theatrical representation with appropriate racial, national and ideological content.
26. Paul B. Jaskot, *The Architecture of Oppression: The SS, Forced Labor and the Nazi Monumental Building Economy*, London, 1999, p. 52.
27. The House of German Art is 175 metres wide.
28. Siegfried Zelnhefer, *Die Reichsparteitage der NSDAP in Nürnberg*, Nuremberg, 2002.
29. Barbara Miller Lane, 'Architects in Power: Politics and Ideology in the Work of Ernst May and Albert Speer', *Journal of Interdisciplinary History*, vol. 17, no. 1 (Summer, 1986), pp. 283–310.
30. Albert Speer, 'Die Bauten des Führers', in *Bilder aus dem Leben des Führers*, Hamburg, 1936, pp. 72–7. The book contains articles by Speer, Ley, Schirach and other prominent Nazis.
31. Thomas Mann, 'Deutschland und die Deutschen', in *Thomas Mann: Essays*, vol. 2, *Politik*, ed. Herman Kunzke, Frankfurt, 1977, p. 294.
32. Jaskot, *The Architecture of Oppression*, p. 59.
33. Speer, *Erinnerungen*, p. 82. The *Bismarck* cost 196.8 million Reichsmarks. As Minister of Armaments Speer was to spend as much in four days.
34. Speer, *Erinnerungen*, p. 75.
35. Jaskot, *The Architecture of Oppression*, p. 59.
36. Ibid., p. 22.
37. Speer, *Erinnerungen*, p. 158, says that it was Himmler. Karl Mummenthey, DEST's business manager, said at Nuremberg that it was Speer. *Trials of War Criminals before the Nuernberg Military Tribunals Under Control Council Law No. 10*, 'Green Series', 15 vols, http://www.loc.gov/rr/frd/Military_Law/NTs_war-criminals.html, vol. 5 (1950), p. 567. Hermann Kaienburg, 'Vernichtung durch Arbeit': *Der Fall Neuengamme*, Bonn, 1990, p. 74, says the order came from Hitler.
38. SS-Obersturmbannführer Karl Mummenthey, DEST's manager, received a life sentence on this count, but it was reduced to twenty years. He was released in 1953. Pohl was hanged in 1951 after several appeals for clemency including a delegation from the Bundestag that included a prominent Social Democrat, Carlo Schmid.
39. Susanne Willems, *Der entsiedelte Jude: Albert Speers Wohnungsmarktpolitik für den Berliner Hauptstadtbau*, Berlin, 2002, pp. 22f.
40. Speer, *Erinnerungen*, p. 177. In an interview ('Die Bürde werde ich nicht mehr los', *Der Spiegel*, 7 November 1966) Speer claimed that only Hitler wanted war. He said that he regarded it as an unnecessary war of aggression.
41. Jaskot, *The Architecture of Oppression*, p. 61.
42. Speer, *Spandauer Tagebücher*, p. 173.
43. This meant that this became the responsibility of Fritz Todt as Generalbevollmächtigter für die Regelung der Bauwirtschaft or Plenipotentiary for Building within the Four-Year Plan, but in effect his deputy, Günther Schulze-Fielitz, was in charge. Rüdiger Hachtmann and Winfried Süß (eds), *Hitlers Kommissare: Sondergewalten in der nationalsozialistischen Diktatur*, Göttingen, 2006, p.119; Jaskot, *The Architecture of Oppression*, p. 63.
44. Speer, *Erinnerungen*, p. 47. Siedler, a distinguished architect, was the uncle of Wolf Jobst Siedler, the publisher of Speer's memoirs.
45. Adolf Hitler in Albert Speer, *Die Neue Reichskanzlei*, Munich, n.d. (1940?), p. 7.
46. Speer, *Erinnerungen*, p. 43.
47. Sereny, *Albert Speer*, p. 103.

48. Speer, *Erinnerungen*, p. 48. To Werlin's credit he helped save Wilhelm Haspel's Jewish wife, who had the improbable name of Bimbo. Haspel was the head of Mercedes-Benz from 1942 until his death in 1952.
49. Hermann Giesler, *Ein anderer Hitler: Bericht seines Architekten Hermann Giesler – Erlebnisse, Gespräche, Reflexionen*, Leoni am Starnberger See, 1978. Giesler remained an impassioned National Socialist and played a prominent role in right-wing extremist circles after the war. Speer deliberately misspelt his name throughout his memoirs.
50. Debussy said of the Palais Garnier that it looked like a railway station outside and a Turkish bath inside.
51. Speer, *Spandauer Tagebücher*, p. 166.
52. Ibid., p. 260. Among Bruno Schmitz's other monstrosities are the monument to the Battle of the Nations in Leipzig and the Kyffhäuser Monument in Thuringia.
53. William Hamsher, *Albert Speer: Victim of Nuremberg?*, London, 1970, p. 26. In fact Hitler frequently interfered with musicians. He told Tietjen (correctly) that the oboe had played out of tune during a performance at Bayreuth. He imposed Furtwängler on Winifred Wagner at the Bayreuth Festival in 1936. He alone appointed conductors and Kappelmeister as well as appointing all professors of music. He censored music and did much temporarily to destroy Germany's rich musical culture.
54. Speer, *Spandauer Tagebücher*, pp. 45ff.; Joachim Fest, *Speer: Eine Biographie*, Berlin, 1999, p. 65.
55. Speer, *Spandauer Tagebücher*, p. 536.
56. Ibid., p. 538. Ziegler, who was described by Goebbels as 'the dumbest of the dumb', landed up in a concentration camp for 'defeatism'. After 1945 Padua painted portraits of Richard Strauss, Friedrich Flick and Herbert von Karajan. Peiner's historicist horrors, styled at the time as 'announcements of the racial myth', have been recast as ironic examples of 'inner immigration' and still command a good price.
57. Ibid., pp. 538 and 402.
58. Ibid., p. 538.
59. Speer, *Erinnerungen*, p. 62. Although Speer expressed great admiration for Troost, describing him as one of his teachers, and although he worked under him, the two never met – in spite of Speer's insistence in his memoirs that they did. This information comes from Gerdy Troost. Schmidt, *Albert Speer*, p. 55.
60. The quote comes from Hitler's adjutant Fritz Wiedemann, whose private papers are in the archives of the Institut für Zeitgeschichte in Munich.
61. Speer, *Erinnerungen*, p. 66.
62. Hitler's drawing can be seen in Angela Schönberger, *Die Neue Reichskanzlei von Albert Speer: Zum Zusammenhang von nationalsozialistischer Ideologie und Architektur*, Berlin, 1981, p. 35.
63. Ibid., pp. 177–82.
64. Speer, *Erinnerungen*, p. 116.
65. Werner Rittich, *New German Architecture*, Berlin, 1941, p. 46, makes the preposterous claim that Speer built the new chancellery in nine months.
66. Heinrich Breloer and Rainer Zimmer, *Die Akte Speer: Spuren eines Kriegsverbrechers*, Berlin, 2006, p. 40.
67. Schönberger, *Die Neue Reichskanzlei*, pp. 38ff.
68. Since Germany had ceased to be a federal state, ousting the legations presented no great difficulty. The Gau offices were the property of the Jewish Wertheim Group that was officially designated as Jewish in 1935, even though Georg Wertheim had signed over his entire wealth to his 'Aryan' wife Ursula. In 1937 the company was 'Aryanised'.
69. Schönberger, *Die Neue Reichskanzlei*, p. 40.
70. Wilhelm Treue, 'Hitlers Denkschrift zum Vierjahresplan 1936', *Vierteljahrshefte für Zeitgeschichte*, vol. 3, no. 2 (April 1955), pp. 184–210.
71. Schönberger, *Die Neue Reichskanzlei*, p. 43. Piepenburg is best known as the architect of Hitler's bunker in the Reich Chancellery, which was built in 1943–4 by the construction company Hochtief.
72. Ibid., p. 45.
73. Friedrich Hossbach, *Zwischen Wehrmacht und Hitler 1934–1938*, Göttingen, 1965, pp. 219ff.
74. Dietmar Petzina, *Autarkiepolitik im Dritten Reich: Der nationalsozialistische Vierjahresplan*, Stuttgart, 1968, pp. 73ff.
75. Schönberger, *Die Neue Reichskanzlei*, p. 51.
76. Hitler's speech is printed in full in ibid., pp.177ff. I have tried to give an impression of the awkwardness of the original. Hitler used the common Austrian adverb *heuer*, meaning 'this year'.
77. Pinnau had a successful post-war career. Among his commissions were the interior design of Aristotle Onassis' luxury yacht *Christina O.* and a number of office buildings for Olympic Maritime.

78. A quote from Wagner's *Siegfried*: '*Das Fürchten lernen*'. Karl Arndt, 'Architektur und Politik', in Albert Speer, *Architektur: Arbeiten 1933–1942*, Berlin, 1995, pp. 113–35, esp. p. 128.
79. Speer, *Erinnerungen*, p. 128.
80. Ibid., p. 129.
81. Schönberger, *Die Neue Reichskanzlei*, p. 132.
82. The *Vereinigte Werkstätten für Kunst im Handwerk*. The company, founded in 1898, had factories in Munich and Bremen.
83. Sereny, *Albert Speer*, p. 108.
84. Fest, *Speer*, p. 69.
85. Schönberger, *Die Neue Reichskanzlei*, p. 144.
86. Ibid., p. 69.
87. Speer, *Erinnerungen*, p. 129.
88. Fest, *Speer*, p. 153.
89. Dietmar Arnold, *Neue Reichskanzlei und 'Führerbunker': Legenden und Wirklichkeit*, Berlin, 2005, p. 106. The cost of the elaborate wooden ceiling was estimated at 900,000 Reichsmarks.
90. Speer, *Erinnerungen*, p. 65.
91. Schönberger, *Die Neue Reichskanzlei*, p. 155.
92. *Völkischer Beobachter*, 3 August 1938.
93. Schönberger, *Die Neue Reichskanzlei*, p. 63.
94. Berliners with their typical humour took to saying: '*Wir haben keine Wurst, kein Brot und kein Ei, / aber eine Neue Reichskanzlei!* (We have no sausages, bread or eggs / but we do have a New Reich Chancellery!).

Chapter 3: Germania

1. Goebbels, *Tagebücher*, 3/2/1932.
2. Jost Dülffer, Jochen Thies and Josef Henke, *Hitlers Städte: Baupolitik im Dritten Reich. Eine Dokumentation*, Cologne, 1978, p. 85.
3. This came as no surprise since the Academy sponsored such Jewish and or degenerate artists as Max Liebermann, Arnold Schönberg, Thomas Mann, Ernst Barlach and Käthe Kollwitz. The building on the same site is once again the Academy of Arts.
4. Hans J. Reichhardt and Wolfgang Schäche, *Von Berlin nach Germania: Über die Zerstörung der 'Reichshauptstadt' durch Albert Speers Neugestaltungsplanungen*, Berlin, 2008, p. 61.
5. See, for example, Werner Lindner and Erich Böckler, *Die Stadt: Ihre Pflege und Gestaltung*, Munich, 1939.
6. Hitler, Adolf, *Mein Kampf*, 85th–94th edn, Munich, 1934, pp. 290ff.
7. John Toland, *Adolf Hitler*, New York, 1976, pp. 414ff. Gerdy Troost did however build a number of 'Führer Buildings' and designed jewellery, among others for Göring, using diamonds stolen from Dutch Jews. See Adolf Galland, *Die Ersten und die Letzten*, Munich, 1993.
8. For the 'Ästhetisierung des politischen Lebens' see Walter Benjamin, *Das Kunstwerk im Zeitalter seiner technischen Reproduzierbarkeit*, Frankfurt, 1963, p. 48.
9. Gerdy Troost, *Das Bauen im Neuen Reich*, vol. 1, Bayreuth, 1938, p. 10.
10. For an insightful discussion of Nazi art and culture see Peter Reichel, *Der schöne Schein des Dritten Reiches: Gewalt und Faszination des deutschen Faschismus*, Hamburg, 2006.
11. Frank Lloyd Wright, 'Architecture and Life in the USSR', *Architectural Record* (October 1937). The brilliant caricaturist Osbert Lancaster in *Pillar to Post*, London, 1938, echoed the current opinion that the German and Soviet Pavilions were virtually identical expressions of totalitarian architecture.
12. Danilo Udovički-Selb, 'Facing Hitler's Pavilion: The Uses of Modernity in the Soviet Pavilion at the 1937 Paris International Exhibition', *Journal of Contemporary History*, vol. 47, no. 1 (January 2012), pp. 13–47.
13. Schmidt-Ehmen, who was on friendly terms with Hitler and Troost, specialised in making statues of eagles. They adorned many public buildings.
14. Karen Fiss, *Grand Illusion: The Third Reich, the Paris Exposition, and the Cultural Seduction of France*, Chicago, 2009, p. 70.
15. Dieter Bartetzko, 'Die Architekten', in Hans Sarkowicz (ed.), *Hitlers Künstler: Die Kultur im Dienst des Nationalsozialismus*, Frankfurt, 2004, pp. 110–34, esp. pp. 110ff.
16. Joachim Fest, *Speer: Eine Biographie*, Berlin, 1999, p. 110.
17. Ella Fitzgerald and David Bowie performed in the Deutschlandhalle. It was demolished in 2011. The Rolling Stones, Jimi Hendrix, and the Berlin Philharmonic were later to perform in the open-air theatre. It was originally known as the Dietrich Eckart Theatre, named after one of the

founder members of the Nazi Party, to whom Hitler had dedicated volume 2 of *Mein Kampf*. It is now the popular *Waldbühne*.

18. Albert Speer, *Erinnerungen*, Berlin, 1969, p. 94.
19. Alexander Kropp, *Die politische Bedeutung der NS-Repräsentationsarchitektur: Die Neugestaltungspläne Albert Speers für den Umbau Berlins zur 'Welthauptstadt Germania' 1936–1942/43*, Neuried, 2005, pp. 77ff; Reichhardt and Schäche, *Von Berlin nach Germania*, pp. 78ff.
20. Chipperfield's Museum of Modern Literature in Marbach strongly echoes Troost's House of German Art.
21. There is some unintentional humour in that *Führerbau* is the word for the cab of a truck or a locomotive.
22. Speer estimated the total cost at six billion Reichsmarks, equivalent to five per cent of GDP in 1939. This was almost certainly an underestimation, although the use of slave labour and the seizure of Jewish property greatly reduced costs.
23. Speer, *Erinnerungen*, p. 89.
24. Karl-Dietrich Bracher, 'Die Speer-Legende', in Adelbert Reif, *Albert Speer: Kontroversen um ein deutsches Phänomen*, Munich, 1978, pp. 408–10.
25. Dieter Rebentisch, *Führerstaat und Verwaltung im Zweiten Weltkrieg: Verfassungsentwicklung und Verwaltungspolitik 1939–1945*, Stuttgart, 1989, pp. 337ff. The quote is from Edmund Glaise von Horstenau, the German Commissioner General in Croatia, at a meeting of the OKW on 25 January 1940.
26. Ibid., p. 341.
27. Behrens died in February 1940, aged 71. Stanford Anderson, *Peter Behrens and a New Architecture for the Twentieth Century*, Boston, 2002.
28. It is noticeable that Speer was not included in this list, which was compiled in 1944.
29. Wolfgang Voigt and Roland May (eds), *Paul Bonatz (1877–1956)*, Tübingen, 2010.
30. A point underlined by Frederic Spotts, *Hitler and the Power of Aesthetics*, London, 2002, p. 357.
31. Reichhardt and Schäche, *Von Berlin nach Germania*, pp. 78ff.
32. Albert Speer (ed. Adelbert Reif), *Technik und Macht*, Esslingen, 1979, p. 33.
33. Klaus Herding and Hans-Ernst Mittig, *Kunst und Alltag im NS-System: Albert Speers Berliner Straßenlaternen*, Gießen, 1975, pp. 9ff.
34. Reichhardt and Schäche, *Von Berlin nach Germania*, p. 90.
35. Dustmann was to return to a modified Bauhaus style after the war when, like many of the Nazi architects, he pursued a successful career.
36. Rosenberg objected strongly to the choice of Behrens, who was effectively AEG's house architect, but Hitler admired Behrens' design for the German Embassy in Saint Petersburg, built in 1913, so that the ideologue was overruled. It was never built.
37. Speer, *Erinnerungen*, p. 196.
38. Such as *The Enigma of the Hour* (1911) or *The Enigma of a Day* (1914).
39. Gerald D. Feldman, *Die Allianz und die deutsche Versicherungswirtschaft 1933–1945*, Munich, 2001.
40. Joachim Petsch, *Baukunst und Stadtplanung im Dritten Reich: Herleitung/Bestandsaufnahme/Entwicklung/Nachfolge*, Munich, 1976, p. 111.
41. The Battle of the Skagerrak is known in English as the Battle of Jutland. Both sides claimed it to be a victory, however qualified.
42. Friedrich Tamm, 'Die Kriegerdenkmäler Wilhelm Kreis', *Die Kunst im Deutschen Reich*, no. 3, 1943, p. 57.
43. Petsch, *Baukunst und Stadtplanung im Dritten Reich*, pp. 112ff.
44. Speer, *Erinnerungen*, p. 151.
45. Fest, *Speer*, p. 129. Speer's father agreed with Nervi. When he saw the model of Germania he said: 'You've all gone completely mad!' (Speer, *Erinnerungen*, p. 148).
46. Reichhardt and Schäche, *Von Berlin nach Germania*, pp. 127ff.
47. Speer, *Erinnerungen*, pp. 170ff.
48. The influence of the Palazzo Pitti can also be seen in the Marriner S. Eccles Federal Reserve Board Building in Washington, D.C. The Oval Office is a mere 76 square metres.
49. Speer, *Erinnerungen*, pp. 170ff.
50. Roger Fornoff, *Die Sehnsucht nach dem Gesamtkunstwerk: Studien zu einer ästhetischen Konzeption der Moderne*, Hildesheim, 2004; Hilton Kramer, 'At the Bauhaus: the fate of art in "the Cathedral of Socialism"', *The New Criterion*, vol. 12, no. 7 (March 1994), pp. 4–10; Michael Chapman and Michael Ostwald, 'Laying Siege to the Stadtkrone: Nietzsche, Taut and the vision of a Cultural Aristocracy', in John Macarthur and Antony Moulis (eds), *Additions to architectural history: XIXth annual conference of the Society of Architectural Historians, Australia and New Zealand*, Brisbane, 2002, available at <http://hdl.handle.net/1959.13/37963>.

51. Speer, *Erinnerungen*, p. 167.
52. Speer, *Erinnerungen*, p. 175.
53. Letter from Speer to Lammers, 1 December 1937, in Dülffer, Thies and Henke, *Hitlers Städte*.
54. Joseph Goebbels, *Die Tagebücher von Joseph Goebbels*, ed. Elke Fröhlich, Part 1, *Aufzeichnungen 1923–1941*, vol. 9, *Dezember 1940–Juli 1941*, Munich, 1998, entry for 8 May 1941.
55. Speer, *Erinnerungen*, p. 170.
56. Léon Krier, 'An Architecture of Desire', in *Albert Speer: Architecture 1932–1942*, ed. Leon Krier, Brussels, 1985, p. 225.
57. Reichhardt and Schäche, *Von Berlin nach Germania*, pp.142ff.
58. For a brilliant study of these statues see R.E. Hardt, *Die Beine der Hohenzollern*, East Berlin, 1960.
59. Peter Longerich, *Heinrich Himmler: Biographie*, Berlin, 2008, p. 254.
60. Hermann Kaienburg, *Die Wirtschaft der SS*, Berlin, 2003, pp. 696 and 715; Paul B. Jaskot, *The Architecture of Oppression: The SS, Forced Labor and the Nazi Monumental Building Economy*, London, 1999, p. 70. Natzweiler eventually produced 25,000 cubic metres of granite for the Nuremberg project.
61. Heinrich Breloer, *Unterwegs zur Familie Speer: Begegnungen, Gespräche, Interviews*, Berlin, 2005, p. 558.
62. Ibid., p. 245. When Speer's older brother Hermann heard of this remark he denounced him for being utterly cold-hearted and for 'accepting all this stupid hatred of the Jews without the slightest resistance'.
63. Jan Erik Schulte, 'Das SS-Wirtschafts-Verwaltungshauptamt und die Expansion des KZ-Systems', in Wolfgang Benz and Barbara Distel, *Ort des Terrors: Geschichte der nationalsozialistischen Konzentrationslager*, vol. 1 (*Die Organisation des Terrors*), Munich, 2005, pp. 141–55; Jaskot, *The Architecture of Oppression*. Speer's financial officer, Karl Maria Hettlage, allocated 5.3 million Reichsmarks to build Oranienburg II. Among the items required were 810 metres of electric fencing, with reinforced concrete pillars, that was 2.5 metres high and covered in barbed wire, costing 8,100 Reichsmarks with 36,000 Reichsmarks for lighting.
64. Susanne Willems, *Der entsiedelte Jude: Albert Speers Wohnungsmarktpolitik für den Berliner Hauptstadtbau*, Berlin, 2002, p. 25.
65. Susanna Schrafstetter, 'Verfolgung und Wiedergutmachung – Karl M. Hettlage: Mitarbeiter von Albert Speer und Staatssekretär im Bundesfinanzministerium', *Vierteljahrshefte für Zeitgeschichte*, vol. 56, no. 3 (2008), pp. 431–66.
66. *Drei von der Planung*. Hans Stephan was also a talented caricaturist. His witty comments on the plans for Germania can be found in Lars Olof Larsson, Sabine Larsson and Ingolf Lamprecht, 'Fröhliche Neugestaltung' oder: *Die Gigantoplanie von Berlin 1937–1943: Albert Speers Generalbebauungsplan im Spiegel satirischer Zeichnungen von Hans Stephan*, Kiel, 2008.
67. Speer, *Erinnerungen*, p. 90.
68. Willems, *Der entsiedelte Jude*, p. 31. By comparison in 1936 (a good year) the average male blue-collar worker earned 1,761 Reichsmarks per year, female workers 952 Reichsmarks. The average white-collar worker earned 3,000 Reichsmarks per year, roughly twice the income of his female counterpart. Only 17 per cent of the population earned more than 2,400 Reichsmarks per year. Adam Tooze, *The Wages of Destruction: The Making and Breaking of the Nazi Economy*, London, 2006, p. 142.
69. Gitta Sereny, *Albert Speer: His Battle With Truth*, London, 1995, p. 145.
70. Speer, *Erinnerungen*, p. 231.
71. Ibid., p. 76.
72. Frank Bajohr, *Parvenus und Profiteure: Korruption in der NS-Zeit*, Frankfurt, 2001, p. 63. These figures are admittedly to be taken with caution because they are based on somewhat dubious tax returns. Although such equivalents are impossible to calculate accurately, 1 Reichsmark is equivalent to about 16 dollars today.
73. Heinrich Breloer and Rainer Zimmer, *Die Akte Speer: Spuren eines Kriegsverbrechers*, Berlin, 2006, p. 80.
74. Ibid.
75. Speer, *Erinnerungen*, p. 81.
76. Facsimile in Breloer and Zimmer, *Die Akte Speer*, p. 100.
77. Ludolf Herbst and Thomas Weihe (eds), *Die Commerzbank und die Juden*, Munich, 2004.
78. Speer, *Erinnerungen*, p. 87.
79. Breloer and Zimmer, *Die Akte Speer*, pp. 69ff.
80. Goebbels, *Die Tagebücher*, Part I, vol. 6, *August 1938–Juni 1939*, ed. Jana Richter, Munich, 1998, entry of 1 January 1939.
81. Jaskot, *The Architecture of Oppression*, pp. 91ff.

82. Ulrich Herbert, 'Labour and Extermination: Economic Interests and the Primacy of *Weltanschauung* in National Socialism', *Past and Present*, vol. 138, no. 1 (1993), pp. 144–95, esp. pp. 148–9.
83. Jaskot, *The Architecture of Oppression*, p. 99.
84. Ibid., p. 100.
85. Willems, *Der entsiedelte Jude*, p. 30.
86. 'Baugruppe Giesler' in the northern sector and OT-Einsatzgruppe VI in Bavaria and the Danube.
87. Breloer, *Unterwegs zur Familie Speer*, p. 243.
88. Willems, *Der entsiedelte Jude*, p. 434.
89. http://www.ghwk.de/fileadmin/user_upload/pdf-wannsee/dokumente/protokoll-januar1942_barrierefrei.pdf.
90. Schrafstetter, 'Verfolgung und Wiedergutmachung', p. 441.
91. Petsch, *Baukunst und Stadtplanung im Dritten Reich*, p. 107.
92. Werner Durth and Niels Gutschow, *Träume in Trümmern: Stadtplanung 1940–1950*, Munich, 1993.
93. Raul Hilberg, *The Destruction of the European Jews*, New Haven, 1961, p. 116.
94. Letter from Ministry of Economics to Lammers, 12 November 1937; letter from Speer to Lammers, 24 November 1937, in Dülffer, Thies and Henke, *Hitlers Städte*.
95. Willems, *Der entsiedelte Jude*, p. 48.
96. Ibid., pp. 48ff (the meeting is misdated 1938 in the footnote).
97. Heinz Boberach (ed.), *Meldungen aus dem Reich: Die geheimen Lageberichte des Sicherheitsdienstes des SS 1938–1945*, vol. 2, Herrsching, 1984, p. 210.
98. Fest, *Speer*, pp. 122ff.
99. Wolf Gruner, *Judenverfolgung in Berlin 1933–1945: Eine Chronologie der Behördenmaßnahmen in der Reichshauptstadt*, Berlin, 1996, pp. 10f.
100. Willems, *Der entsiedelte Jude*, pp. 73ff.
101. Ibid., p. 77.
102. Ibid., p. 80.
103. Willems, *Der entsiedelte Jude*, p. 78.
104. Susanne Heim and Götz Aly, 'Staatliche Ordnung und "organische Lösung": Die Rede Hermann Görings "Über die Judenfrage" vom 6. Dezember 1938', *Jahrbuch für Antisemitismusforschung*, vol. 2 (1993), pp. 378–405. Schmeer was described in an internal report as 'a sinister character who does not come up to snuff'. Speer chose him to play a key organisational role in the Ministry of Armaments.
105. Speer, *Erinnerungen*, p. 125.
106. Sereny, *Albert Speer*, p. 165. Simon later wrote *Das Herz unserer Städte*, Essen, 1963, a sensitive work on urban morphology.
107. Albert Speer, *Spandauer Tagebücher*, Berlin, 1975, p. 20.
108. Paul B. Jaskot, 'Anti-Semitic Policy in Albert Speer's Plans for the Rebuilding of Berlin', *The Art Bulletin*, vol. 78, no. 4 (December 1996), pp. 622–32.
109. A friend of Hans Frank, he was appointed governor of the Lublin district, where he crossed swords with the sadistic mass-murderer SS and Police Chief Odilo Globocnik. He was dismissed on Himmler's orders. He then worked for Organisation Todt in Bohemia and Moravia.
110. Willems, *Der entsiedelte Jude*, p. 86.
111. Ibid., p. 98.
112. Ibid., p. 117.
113. Ibid., p. 124.
114. Ibid., p. 133.
115. Ibid., pp. 140ff.
116. Breloer and Zimmer, *Die Akte Speer*, pp. 97ff.
117. Willems, *Der entsiedelte Jude*, p. 144.
118. It was published in the *Berliner Lokal-Anzeiger* on 25 June 1939.
119. Willems, *Der entsiedelte Jude*, p. 145.
120. Archives of the Ministry of Armaments, Bundesarchiv Berlin, R3/1737, p. 6.
121. Ibid., p. 22.
122. Willems, *Der entsiedelte Jude*, p. 161. For more details see Götz Aly, 'Endlösung': Völkerverschiebung und der Mord an den europäischen Juden, Frankfurt, 1995.
123. Willems, *Der entsiedelte Jude*, p. 162.
124. Susanne Willems, *Netzeitung*, 31 January 2005.
125. Speer, *Erinnerungen*, p. 187.

126. Willems, *Der entsiedelte Jude*, p. 170. She argues that this was at Speer's urging. Although this is likely, she produces no evidence in support of this contention. The protocol does not show who was present. Willi A. Boelcke, *Kriegspropaganda 1939–1941: Geheime Ministerkonferenzen im Reichspropagandaministerium*, Stuttgart, 1966, p. 82; Peter Longerich, *Goebbels: Biographie*, Munich, 2010, p. 459.
127. Breloer, *Die Akte Speer*, p. 101.
128. Willems, *Der entsiedelte Jude*, p. 173.
129. Ibid., p. 174.
130. Willems, *Der entsiedelte Jude*, p. 183. It is unclear who represented Speer at the meeting. Matthias Schmidt, *Albert Speer – Das Ende eines Mythos: Speers wahre Rolle im Dritten Reich*, Munich, 1982, pp. 218ff, suggests that it was Clahes. Goebbels was represented by Leopold Gutterer, who was later to attend the Wannsee Conference and who was responsible for forcing German Jews to wear the badge of the Star of David. He was given a moderate sentence after the war on account of his 'mild attitude towards the Jewish question'.
131. Gruner, *Judenverfolgung*, p. 12.
132. Willems, *Der entsiedelte Jude*, p. 187.
133. Jaskot, 'Anti-Semitic Policy', p. 630.
134. Willems, *Der entsiedelte Jude*, p. 180.
135. Jaskot, 'Anti-Semitic Policy', p. 630.
136. Fest, *Speer*, p. 164.
137. Willems, *Der entsiedelte Jude*, pp.199ff.
138. Ibid., p. 225.
139. Klaus Hildebrandt, *Vom Reich zum Weltreich: Hitler, NSDAP und koloniale Frage 1919–1945*, Munich, 1969.
140. In Mohr's defence it should be mentioned that he fell foul of the Gestapo for deceiving them and the GBI by trying to help Jews avoid deportation. How far this was a selfless act is unclear. Willems, *Der entsiedelte Jude*, pp. 331ff.
141. Their objection to the fine was that it would force Jews to sell their bonds, thereby weakening a severely strained economy.
142. Willems, *Der entsiedelte Jude*, pp. 241ff. Konti Öl was created by the Deutsche Bank and IG Farben. Blessing was the president of the Bundesbank from 1958 to 1969.
143. Ibid., pp. 253ff.
144. Breloer, *Unterwegs zur Familie Speer*, p. 333. Schlippenbach acted as a witness for the prosecution at Nuremberg against the SS Race and Settlement Main Office. In a chequered post-war career he was among other things the promoter of the British vocal harmony group Wall Street Crash.
145. Jaskot, *The Architecture of Oppression*, p. 101.
146. Willems, *Der entsiedelte Jude*, p. 257.
147. The other two apartments were put at the disposal of the army's social services and were rented by two women. The owner, Bronislaw Schütze, managed to emigrate to the USA in March 1941. Ibid., p. 258.
148. Konrad Kwiet, 'Nach dem Pogrom: Stufen der Ausgrenzung', in Wolfgang Benz (ed.), *Die Juden in Deutschland 1933–1945: Leben unter nationalsozialistischer Herrschaft*, Munich, 1988, pp. 545–659.
149. Gruner, *Judenverfolgung*, p. 94.
150. The most impressive of these was in Berlin by a group of mostly women demonstrating against the proposed deportation of Jews living in mixed marriages: see Antonia Leugers (ed.), *Berlin, Rosenstraße 2–4: Protest in der NS-Diktatur – Neue Forschungen zum Frauenprotest in der Rosenstraße 1943*, Annweiler, 2005.
151. Willems, *Der entsiedelte Jude*, p. 323.
152. Facsimile of the 'Speer Chronicle' in Breloer and Zimmer, *Die Akte Speer*, p. 116.
153. Kwiet, 'Nach dem Pogrom', p. 638.
154. Goebbels, *Die Tagebücher*, Part II, *Diktate 1941–1945*, vol. 7, *Januar–März 1943*, Munich, 1993. There were, however, a number of snitches, even among the Jews. The most notorious of these was Stella Goldschlag. See Claudia Schoppmann, ' "Fabrikaktion" in Berlin: Hilfe für untergetauchte Juden als Form des humanitären Widerstandes', *Zeitschrift für Geschichtswissenschaft*, vol. 53, no. 2 (2005), pp. 138–48.
155. Speer, *Erinnerungen*, p. 98. Helene Bechstein, part owner of the famous piano company, was one of Hitler's earliest supporters. She introduced him into Munich society. The company was in serious difficulties. Helene's grotesque anti-Semitism alienated many distinguished customers and the consequences of the Great Depression were dire. During the war the company produced propellers.

156. Fröhlich starred in Fritz Lang's *Metropolis*. He was Goebbels' predecessor as Lída Baarová's lover, which did not improve his prospects as a movie star.
157. Dietmar Arnold, *Neue Reichskanzlei und 'Führerbunker': Legenden und Wirklichkeit*, Berlin, 2005, p. 149.
158. Breloer, *Unterwegs zur Familie Speer*, p. 123.
159. Bajohr, *Parvenus und Profiteure*, p. 64.
160. Jonathan Petropoulos, *Kunstraub und Sammelwahn: Kunst und Politik im Dritten Reich*, Berlin, 1999, p. 445.
161. Barbara Schröter, *Stoff für Tausend und Ein Jahr: Die Textilsammlung des Generalbauinspektors für die Reichshauptstadt (GBI) – Albert Speer*, Berlin, 2013, p. 143.
162. Breloer, *Unterwegs zur Familie Speer*, p. 95; Rainer Maria Rilke and Marianne Gilbert, *Le tiroir entr'ouvert*, Paris, 1956. 'Marianne Gilbert' was Marie-Anne von Goldschmidt-Rothschild's pseudonym. Gilbert was her son's name.
163. Willems, *Der entsiedelte Jude*, p. 423.
164. The Automobil-Verkehrs- und Übungsstrecke (Automobile, Traffic and Test Track) was a 9.8 km circular track where Speer liked to test his skills as a driver.
165. Albert Speer, *Der Sklavenstaat: meine Auseinandersetzung mit der SS*, Berlin, 1981, p. 355.
166. Speer, *Sklavenstaat*, p. 347. Sereny, *Albert Speer*, p. 228, believes that although Speer certainly knew that the Jews were being expelled from Berlin, he knew nothing of their subsequent fate.
167. Breloer and Zimmer, *Die Akte Speer*, pp. 146f.
168. Isabel Heinemann, *Rasse, Siedlung, deutsches Blut: Das Rasse- und Siedlungshauptamt der SS und die rassenpolitische Neuordnung Europas*, Göttingen, 2003.
169. Michael Hepp, 'Fälschung und Wahrheit: Albert Speer und "Der Sklavenstaat"', *Mitteilungen der Dokumentationsstelle zur NS-Sozialpolitik*, vol. 1, no. 3 (1985), pp. 1–37, esp. p. 22.
170. Willi A. Boelcke (ed.), *Deutschlands Rüstung im Zweiten Weltkrieg: Hitlers Konferenzen mit Albert Speer 1942–1945*, Frankfurt, 1969, p. 183.
171. The future Federal German President, Heinrich Lübke, worked for the Baugruppe Schlempp, which gave rise to some awkward questions.
172. Dirk Zabel, 'Das Projekt der "Stadt X für 20,000 Einwohner" bei Trassenheide oder die Militarisierung des Urbanen im Nationalsozialismus', in Bernfried Lichtnau, *Architektur in Mecklenburg und Vorpommern 1800–1950*, Greifswald, 1996, pp. 340–50.
173. *Bauhandbuch für den Aufbau im Osten*.
174. Breloer and Zimmer, *Die Akte Speer*, p. 156.
175. Ibid., pp. 158ff. The town was renamed Litzmannstadt in April 1940 in honour of General Karl Litzmann, an NSDAP member whose Guards Infantry Division had defeated the Russians there in the First World War. The word for 'removed' was *herausbekommen*.
176. Klaus-Peter Friedrich (ed.), *Die Verfolgung und Ermordung der europäischen Juden durch das nationalsozialistische Deutschland 1933–1945*, vol. 4, Munich, 2011, p. 174.

Chapter 4: The State of German Armaments In 1942

1. John Kenneth Galbraith, 'Germany Was Badly Run', *Fortune*, vol. 22 (December 1945), pp. 173–8 and 196–200. For criticism see Peter Hayes, 'Polycracy and Policy in the Third Reich: The Case of the Economy', in Thomas Childers and Jane Caplan (eds), *Reevaluating the Third Reich*, New York, 1993, pp. 190–230.
2. Notably: Albert Speer, *Inside the Third Reich*, London, 1970; Rolf Wagenführ, *Die deutsche Industrie im Kriege 1939–1945*, Berlin, 1954; Hans Kehrl, *Krisenmanager im Dritten Reich*, 2nd edn, Frankfurt, 2007; Hans Kehrl, 'Kriegswirtschaft und Rüstungsindustrie', in *Bilanz des Zweiten Weltkrieges: Erkenntnisse und Verpflichtungen für die Zukunft*, Oldenburg, 1953, pp. 267–85; Hans Kehrl, 'Zum Untergang des Dritten Reiches', *Historische Tatsachen*, vol. 8, Vlotho, 1981 (a journal specialising in Holocaust denial).
3. Albert Speer, *Erinnerungen*, Berlin, 1969, pp. 229ff.
4. Wagenführ, *Die deutsche Industrie*; for criticism see Matthias Schmidt, *Albert Speer – Das Ende eines Mythos: Speers wahre Rolle im Dritten Reich*, Munich, 1982, pp. 135ff., and Karl-Heinz Ludwig, *Technik und Ingenieure im Dritten Reich*, Dusseldorf, 1974.
5. Christoph Buchheim, 'Die Wirtschaftsentwicklung im Dritten Reich – mehr Desaster als Wunder: Eine Erwiderung auf Werner Abelshauser', *Vierteljahrshefte für Zeitgeschichte*, vol. 49 (2001), pp. 653–64.
6. Thomas Speckmann, 'Erst Kanonen, dann Butter', *Frankfurter Allgemeine Zeitung*, 9 February 2000.
7. Dan P. Silverman, *Hitler's Economy: Nazi Work Creation Programs, 1933–1936*, Cambridge, MA, 1998, pp. 219ff; Hans-Joachim Braun, *The German Economy in the Twentieth Century*, London, 1990, p. 83.

8. Harold James, 'Innovation and Conservatism in Economic Recovery: The Alleged "Nazi Recovery" in the 1930s', in W.R. Garside (ed.), *Capitalism in Crisis. International Responses to the Great Depression*, London, 1993, pp. 70–96.

9. Adam Tooze, *The Wages of Destruction: The Making and Breaking of the Nazi Economy*, London, 2006, p. 53.

10. Contemporaries were well aware of the unsound foundations of the Germany economy. See Hans Erich Priester, *Das deutsche Wirtschaftswunder*, Amsterdam, 1936.

11. Particularly by Tooze, who contends that consumption stagnated in the 1930s, but his statistics on this topic are patchy. Werner Abelshauser, 'Germany: guns, butter and economic miracles', in Mark Harrison (ed.), *The Economics of World War II: Six Great Powers in International Comparison*, Cambridge, 1998, p. 169. For criticism of Tooze see Robert J. Gordon's review in *The Journal of Economic History*, vol. 69, no. 1 (March 2009), pp. 312–16.

12. Avraham Barkai, *Nazi Economics: Ideology, Theory, and Policy*, New Haven, 1990, p. 232.

13. Abelshauser, 'Germany: guns, butter and economic miracles', p. 148 and table 4.2.

14. Wilhelm Deist, *The Wehrmacht and German Rearmament*, London, 1981.

15. Wilhelm Treue, 'Hitlers Denkschrift zum Vierjahresplan 1936', *Vierteljahrshefte für Zeitgeschichte*, vol. 3, no. 2 (April 1955), pp. 184–210.

16. Tooze, *The Wages of Destruction*, p. 234.

17. For the full text see <http://www.worldfuturefund.org/wffmaster/Reading/Hitler%20Speeches/Hitler%20rede%201939.01.30.htm>.

18. Hans-Erich Volkmann, in *Das Deutsche Reich und der Zweite Weltkrieg*, vol. 1, Stuttgart, 1979, pp. 349ff; Rolf-Dieter Müller, *Das Deutsche Reich und der Zweite Weltkrieg*, vol. 5/1, Stuttgart, 1988, p. 361.

19. Georg Thomas, *Geschichte der deutschen Wehr- und Rüstungswirtschaft 1918–1943/45*, Boppard, 1966, pp. 11ff. and 173. Wolfgang Birkenfeld, who edited Thomas' papers, takes this as evidence that he should be counted among the resisters. This is rubbish. Thomas was in favour of war, but felt that Germany was not yet ready.

20. Boelcke, Willi A., *Die deutsche Wirtschaft 1939–1945: Interna des Reichswirtschaftsministeriums*, Düsseldorf, 1983.

21. The best-known expressions of these ideas are Alan S. Milward, *The German Economy at War*, London, 1965, and Timothy W. Mason, *Sozialpolitik im Dritten Reich: Arbeiterklasse und Volksgemeinschaft*, Opladen, 1977.

22. Richard Overy, 'Hitler's War and the German Economy: A Reinterpretation', *The Economic History Review*, vol. 35, no. 2 (May 1982), pp. 287–313, and his *War and Economy in the Third Reich*, Oxford, 1994.

23. For example, Christoph Buchheim, 'Der Blitzkrieg, der keiner war' ('The Blitzkrieg that never was'), *Die Zeit*, 10 July 2007.

24. For some interesting reflections on these problems see Ludolf Herbst, *Der Totale Krieg und die Ordnung der Wirtschaft: Die Kriegswirtschaft im Spannungsfeld von Politik, Ideologie und Propaganda 1939–1945*, Stuttgart, 1982.

25. These decisions were made in November and December 1939. See Rolf-Dieter Müller, *Das Deutsche Reich und der Zweite Weltkrieg*, vol. 5/1, Stuttgart, 1988, p. 410.

26. *Wirtschaftliche Volksgemeinschaft*. *Volk* means 'people' as well as 'race'. In Nazi terminology the racial implication is strongest.

27. Rolf-Dieter Müller, DRZW 5/1, p. 417.

28. Ibid., p. 446.

29. Speer, *Erinnerungen*, p. 223; Shulamit Volkov, *Walther Rathenau: The Life of Weimar's Fallen Statesman*, New Haven and London, 2012; trans. by Ulla Höber as *Walther Rathenau: Ein jüdisches Leben in Deutschland 1867 bis 1922*, Munich, 2012.

30. An *alter Kämpfer* was one who had joined the NSDAP before the Reichstag election in 1930.

31. Ronald Smelser, *Robert Ley: Hitler's Labour Front Leader*, Oxford, 1988.

32. Rüdiger Hachtmann and Winfried Süß (eds), *Hitlers Kommissare: Sondergewalten in der national-sozialistischen Diktatur*, Göttingen, 2006, p. 19.

33. Rolf-Dieter Müller, DRZW 5/1, p. 461.

34. Ibid., p. 467.

35. Hans-Ulrich Wehler, *Deutsche Gesellschaftsgeschichte*, vol. 4 (*Vom Beginn des Ersten Weltkriegs bis zur Gründung der beiden deustchen Staaten 1914–1949*) Munich, 2003, pp. 631ff.

36. Rolf-Dieter Müller in DRZW 5/1, p. 463, takes Dietrich Eichholtz to task for claiming that this 'new stage in the organisation and structure of the wartime economy marks the beginning of a new phase in the development of state monopoly capitalism': Dietrich Eichholtz, *Geschichte der Deutschen Kriegswirtschaft*, 5 vols, Munich, 2002, vol. 1 (first published in Berlin, 1968), p. 121. He thereby overlooks the fact that Eichholtz was obliged to use Marxist-Leninist terminology in his

fine study of the German war economy and was thereby saying that heavy industry had won considerable freedom of action and enjoyed a very cosy relationship with the ministry. For a nuanced assessment see Tooze, *The Wages of Destruction*, pp. 350ff.

37. Rolf-Dieter Müller, DRZW 5/1, p. 472.
38. It is unclear quite what these 'family problems' were and to what degree Becker was 'defamed'. There is a suggestion that two Gestapo officers were present when he took his life.
39. Eichholtz, *Geschichte der Deutschen Kriegswirtschaft*, vol. 1, p. 131.
40. Rolf-Dieter Müller, DRZW 5/1, p. 476.
41. Sandkastenspiel: literally, playing in a sandpit. Speer, *Erinnerungen*, p. 188.
42. Marie-Louise Recker, *Nationalsozialistische Sozialpolitik im Zweiten Weltkrieg*, Munich, 1985, p. 82.
43. He made this remark at a meeting at Plassenburg in July 1940 between representatives of the military and civilian armaments committees. Rolf-Dieter Müller, DRZW 5/1, p. 507.
44. Ulrich Schlie (ed.), *Albert Speer: Die Kransberg-Protokolle 1945: Seine ersten Aussagen und Aufzeichnungen (Juni–September)*, Munich, 2003, p. 275.
45. Tooze, *The Wages of Destruction*, p. 347.
46. The Ju 88 turned out to be an ineffective weapon. It was slow, reaching a maximum of 500 kilometres per hour without bombs, lacked effective armament and its bomb-load of up to 2,400kg was insufficient for strategic bombing. Crews remarked that they were more scared of the machine than they were of the enemy. The Lancaster had a bomb load of 3,600 kg, increasing to 5,400kg.
47. Rolf-Dieter Müller, DRZW 5/1 p. 513.
48. 'Nebeneinanderarbeit, viel Übereinander- Untereinander- und Gegeneinanderarbeit': ibid., p. 518.
49. Kehrl, *Krisenmanager*, p. 194.
50. Rolf-Dieter Müller, DRZW 5/1, p. 518; Kehrl, *Krisenmanager*, p. 202.
51. For civilian morale see Heinz Boberach (ed.), *Meldungen aus dem Reich: Die geheimen Lageberichte des Sicherheitsdienstes des SS 1938–1945*, vol. 7, Herrsching, 1984.
52. Joseph Goebbels, *Die Tagebücher von Joseph Goebbels*, ed. Elke Fröhlich, Part 1, *Aufzeichnungen 1923–1941*, vol. 9, *Dezember 1940–Juli 1941*, Munich, 1998, entry for 16 June 1941.
53. Rolf-Dieter Müller, DRZW 5/1, p. 553.
54. Ibid., p. 564. Thomas' memorandum was dated 'end of June 1941'. It was thus presumably written after the invasion of the Soviet Union on 22 June.
55. Quoted in ibid., p. 574. In fact German estimates of US aircraft production were as much as three times less than the actual figures.
56. Memorandum from Thomas, 22 October 1941, quoted ibid., p. 601.
57. Ibid., p. 626.
58. Goebbels, *Die Tagebücher*, Part II (*Diktate 1941–1945*), vol. 2 (*Oktober–Dezember 1941*), entry of 30 November 1941.
59. Thomas, *Geschichte der deutschen Wehr- und Rüstungswirtschaft*, pp. 307ff.
60. Rolf-Dieter Müller, DRZW 5/1, p. 655.
61. Ibid., p. 667.
62. Ibid., p. 668.
63. Ibid., p. 673.
64. The theory that Fritz Todt was murdered is revived in Robert Wilson's novel *The Company of Strangers*, 2001.
65. See Gitta Sereny, *Albert Speer: His Battle With Truth*, London, 1995, pp. 277–83, for the following.

Chapter 5: Minister of Armaments

1. Max Müller, 'Der plötzliche und mysteriöse Tod Dr. Fritz Todts', *Geschichte in Wissenschaft und Unterricht*, vol. 18 (1967), pp. 602–4; Reimer Hansen, 'Der ungeklärte Fall Todt', *Geschichte in Wissenschaft und Unterricht*, vol. 18 (1967), pp. 604–5; Richard Reinhardt, 'Heute vor 25 Jahren starb Fritz Todt als unbequemer Warner', *Pforzheimer Zeitung*, vol. 32, 8 February 1967. Udet, with 62 'kills', was second only in the number of victories to Richthofen with 80. He was heavily addicted to alcohol and crystal meth. He shot himself after the failure of the Battle of Britain.
2. Karl-Heinz Ludwig, *Technik und Ingenieure im Dritten Reich*, Düsseldorf, 1974, pp. 388ff; Walter Rohland, *Bewegte Zeiten: Erinnerungen eines Eisenhüttenmannes*, Stuttgart, 1978, p. 75; Hans Kehrl, *Krisenmanager im Dritten Reich*, 2nd edn, Frankfurt, 2007, pp. 217ff; Gregor Janssen, *Das Ministerium Speer: Deutschlands Rüstung im Krieg*, Berlin, 1968, p. 33ff; Gert Buchheit, *Hitler der Feldherr: Die Zerstörung einer Legende*, Rastatt, 1958, p. 283; Gerald Reitlinger, *Die Endlösung: Hitlers Versuch der Ausrottung der Juden Europas 1939–1945*, Berlin, 1956, p. 397; Lutz Graf Schwerin von Krosigk, *Die große Zeit des Feuers: Der Weg der deutsche Industrie*, vol. 2, Tübingen, 1957, pp. 299ff.

3. Dietrich Eichholtz, *Geschichte der deutschen Kriegswirtschaft 1939–1945*, 5 vols, Munich, 2002, vol. 1, pp. 55ff; Matthias Schmidt, *Albert Speer – Das Ende eines Mythos: Speers wahre Rolle im Dritten Reich*, Munich, 1982, pp. 71ff; Franz W. Seidler, *Fritz Todt: Baumeister des Dritten Reiches*, Munich, 1986.

4. Franz W. Seidler, 'Das Nationalsozialistische Kraftfahrkorps und die Organisation Todt im Weltkrieg', *Vierteljahrshefte für Zeitgeschichte*, vol. 32, no. 4 (1984), pp. 625–36.

5. Heinrich Breloer and Rainer Zimmer, *Die Akte Speer: Spuren eines Kriegsverbrechers*, Berlin, 2006, p.127. Organisational details of the *NSKK-Transportstandarte Speer* can be found in the archives of the Ministry of Armaments, Bundesarchiv Berlin, R50-II.

6. Breloer and Zimmer, *Die Akte Speer*, pp. 135ff.

7. Ulrich Schlie (ed.), *Albert Speer: Die Kransberg-Protokolle 1945: Seine ersten Aussagen und Aufzeichnungen (Juni–September)*, Munich, 2003, p. 274. On 2 December 1942 Oswald Pohl wrote to Himmler: 'Reich Minister Speer has given industrial organisation clear and simplified direction by the *reintroduction* of self-determination.' Albert Speer, *Der Sklavenstaat. Meine Aufeinandersetzungen mit der SS*, Berlin, 1981, p. 251.

8. Alan S. Milward, 'Fritz Todt als Minister für Bewaffnung und Munition', *Vierteljahrshefte für Zeitgeschichte*, vol. 14, no. 1 (1966), pp. 40–58; Rolf-Dieter Müller, DRZW, 5/1 p. 678.

9. Rolf-Dieter Müller, DRZW 5/2, p. 301.

10. Gitta Sereny, *Albert Speer: His Battle With Truth*, London, 1995, p. 366.

11. Seidler, *Fritz Todt*, pp. 215ff; Ludwig, *Technik und Ingenieure*, p. 400.

12. Rolf-Dieter Müller, DRZW 5/1, p. 680.

13. Albert Speer, *Erinnerungen*, Berlin, 1969, p. 217.

14. Joseph Goebbels, *Die Tagebücher von Joseph Goebbels*, ed. Elke Fröhlich, Part II, *Diktate 1941–1945*, vol. 3, *Januar–März 1942*, Munich, 1995, entries for 14 and 15 February 1942.

15. Marie-Luise Recker, 'Der Reichskommissar für den sozialen Wohnungsbau: Zu Aufbau, Stellung und Arbeitsweise einer führerunmittelbaren Sonderbehörde', in Dieter Rebentisch and Karl Teppe (eds), *Verwaltung contra Menschenführung im Staat Hitlers*, Göttingen, 1986, pp. 333 50.

16. Speer, *Erinnerungen*, p. 220.

17. The major sections of this speech are in Breloer and Zimmer, *Die Akte Speer*, pp. 243ff.

18. Janssen, *Das Ministerium Speer*, p. 65.

19. Ibid., pp. 65ff.

20. Schmidt, *Albert Speer*, p. 144.

21. Speer, *Erinnerungen*, p. 227.

22. Ulrich Herbert, *Fremdarbeiter: Politik und Praxis des 'Ausländer-Einsatzes' in der Kriegswirtschaft des Dritten Reiches*, Bonn, 1985, p. 176.

23. There are good examples of these struggles in the Ministry of Armaments archives, Bundesarchiv Berlin, R3/1739.

24. These conferences can be found in Willi A. Boelcke (ed.), *Deutschlands Rüstung im Zweiten Weltkrieg: Hitlers Konferenzen mit Albert Speer 1942–1945*, Frankfurt, 1969.

25. Speer, *Erinnerungen*, pp. 245f.

26. Boelcke (ed.), *Deutschlands Rüstung im Zweiten Weltkrieg*, p. 5.

27. Kehrl, *Krisenmanager*, p. 284.

28. Eichholtz, *Geschichte der deutschen Kriegswirtschaft*, vol. 2/1, p. 49, describes this as a 'centralised state-monopolistic regulatory system', but qualifies this by saying that it was not always unreservedly in the interest of the monopolies. Translated into more conventional language this is an excellent analysis.

29. Industrialists often referred to Todt as 'Totila' after the King of the Ostrogoths: Seidler, *Fritz Todt*, p. 392.

30. Rolf-Dieter Müller, DRZW 5/1, p. 688.

31. Adam Tooze, *The Wages of Destruction: The Making and Breaking of the Nazi Economy*, London, 2006, p. 559.

32. Janssen, *Das Ministerium Speer*, p. 40.

33. Joachim Fest, *Die unbeantwortbaren Fragen: Notizen über Gespräche mit Albert Speer zwischen Ende 1966 und 1981*, Reinbek bei Hamburg, 2006, p. 29.

34. Karl-Otto Saur, *Er stand in Hitlers Testament*, Berlin, 2007

35. Kehrl, *Krisenmanager*, p. 244.

36. Susanna Schrafstetter, 'Verfolgung und Wiedergutmachung – Karl M. Hettlage: Mitarbeiter von Albert Speer und Staatssekretär im Bundesfinanzministerium', *Vierteljahrshefte für Zeitgeschichte*, vol. 56, no. 3 (2008), pp. 431ff.

37. Kehrl, *Krisenmanager*, p. 245.

38. Bundesarchiv Berlin, R3/1737, p. 22.

39. Ibid., R3/1739, p. 10.
40. Bundesarchiv Berlin, R3/1742, pp. 2ff.
41. Eichholtz, *Geschichte der deutschen Kriegswirtschaft*, vol. 2/1, pp. 65ff.
42. Eichholtz, 2/I, pp. 65f.
43. Eichholtz, 2/1, p. 69.
44. Ibid., 2/1, p. 67. Otto Fitzner was a fanatical National Socialist and close friend of Karl Hanke, the 'Hangman of Breslau'. He told his superior at Georg von Giesches Erben, Eduard Schulte, of a meeting between Hanke and Himmler in which full details of the 'Final Solution' were revealed. Schulte passed this information on to the Allies via Jewish contacts in Switzerland. See Walter Laqueur and Richard Breitman, *Breaking the Silence*, New York, 1986. Röchling was a rapacious exploiter of the occupied territories and a ruthless employer of forced labour, for which he received a ten-year prison sentence.
45. Tooze, *The Wages of Destruction*, p. 563. The telephone book can be found in the Foreign Office files: FO 935/137.
46. Rolf-Dieter Müller argues in DRZW, V.2, p. 313, that the activity of these engineers is further evidence that the influence of 'big business' (*Großkapital*) and the 'bosses' over the armaments industry is often exaggerated. The personnel at the head of these circles belie this point.
47. Janssen, *Das Ministerium Speer*, p. 46.
48. The Army Armaments Office or Heereswaffenamt was a prime example of bureaucratic hypertrophy. Its personnel rose from 7,000 in 1939 to 195,000 in 1944.
49. Götz Aly, *Hitlers Volksstaat: Raub, Rassenkrieg und nationaler Sozialismus*, Frankfurt, 2005, pp. 61 and 168.
50. Eichholtz, *Geschichte der deutschen Kriegswirtschaft*, vol. 3, p. 700; Tooze, *The Wages of Destruction*, p. 566.
51. Eichholtz, *Geschichte der deutschen Kriegswirtschaft*, vol. 2/1, p. 71.
52. Georg Thomas, *Geschichte der deutschen Wehr- und Rüstungswirtschaft 1918–1943/45*, Boppard, 1966, p. 309.
53. Ibid., p. 308.
54. *Kriegstagebücher des Oberkommandos*, vol. 2/1, *1. Januar bis 31. Dezember 1942*, ed. Andreas Hillgruber, Frankfurt, 1963, p. 349.
55. Tooze, *The Wages of Destruction*, p. 587.
56. For Leyers' relationship with Karajan, see Reinhard J. Brembeck, 'Nazi-Dirigent oder Deserteur?', *Süddeutsche Zeitung*, 19 May 2010.
57. Eichholtz, 2/1, pp. 157ff.
58. SS-Oberführer Schlotterer, a vigorous proponent of Nazi occupation policy, was also head of the Eastern Section of the Ministry of Economics: see Ludolf Herbst and Thomas Weihe (eds), *Die Commerzbank und die Juden*, Munich, 2004, p. 18; Götz Aly and Susanne Heim, 'Die Ökonomie der "Endlösung": Menschenvernichtung und wirtschaftliche Neuordnung', in Götz Aly (ed.), *Sozialpolitik und Judenvernichtung: gibt es eine Ökonomie der Endlösung?*, Berlin, 1987, pp. 11–90, esp. p. 36.
59. Janssen, *Das Ministerium Speer*, pp. 53ff.
60. Eichholtz, *Geschichte der deutschen Kriegswirtschaft*, vol. 2/1, p. 94.
61. Ibid., p. 73.
62. Kehrl, *Krisenmanager*, p. 273.
63. Alfred Gottwaldt and Diana Schulle, *'Juden ist die Benutzung von Speisewagen untersagt': Die antijüdische Politik des Reichsverkehrsministeriums zwischen 1933 und 1945*, Teetz, 2007. After the war Ganzenmüller worked for Hoechst AG. In 1973 he was charged with complicity in the deaths of millions of Jews, but the trial was abandoned because he had a heart attack. He died in 1996 aged ninety-one.
64. Janssen, *Das Ministerium Speer*, p. 253; Schlie (ed.), *Albert Speer: Die Kransberg-Protokolle 1945*, p.195; Kehrl, *Krisenmanager*, pp. 272ff.
65. Kehrl, *Krisenmanager*, p. 276.
66. Janssen, *Das Ministerium Speer*, p. 259.
67. Koll was given command of the 1st Panzer Division in January 1944, but having failed to relieve the Cherkassy pocket he was posted back to his desk job at the end of February.
68. Körner played a leading role in formulating the 'Hunger Plan' designed to starve tens of millions to death after Operation Barbarossa. He held many important positions in industry, including a seat on the board of Lufthansa. Göring preferred to call him 'Billy'. Joachim Fest, in *Speer: Eine Biographie*, Berlin, 1999, p. 196, mistakenly assumes that Körner's first name was Wilhelm.
69. Rolf-Dieter Müller, DRZW, V/2, p. 305.
70. Janssen, *Das Ministerium Speer*, p. 57; Kehrl, *Krisenmanager*, p. 254.

71. Kehrl, *Krisenmanager*, p. 298.
72. Ibid., p. 297.
73. Eichholtz, 2/1, pp. 80ff.
74. Kehrl, *Krisenmanager*, pp. 288f.
75. Ibid., p. 262.
76. Tooze, *The Wages of Destruction*, p. 559.
77. Janssen, *Das Ministerium Speer*, p. 59.
78. The result of discussions between Speer and Hitler held on 5 and 6 March: ibid., p. 67, note 22.
79. Eichholtz, *Geschichte der deutschen Kriegswirtschaft*, vol. 2/1, p. 84; Kehrl, *Krisenmanager* p. 254.
80. Kehrl, *Krisenmanager*, p. 257.
81. Bundesarchiv, R3/1737, p. 36.
82. Eichholtz, *Geschichte der deutschen Kriegswirtschaft*, vol. 2/1, p. 86.
83. Poensgen's foster-son was the Marxist economist and philosopher Alfred Sohn-Rethel. At the age of 16 he had asked Poensgen for the three volumes of *Das Kapital* as a Christmas present.
84. Ibid., p. 88.
85. Keitel, Lammers and Bormann also formed another set of 'Three Kings'.
86. Tooze, *The Wages of Destruction*, p. 571.
87. Eichholtz, 2/1, pp. 89f.
88. Boelcke (ed.), *Deutschlands Rüstung im Zweiten Weltkrieg*, pp. 170f.
89. Kehrl, *Krisenmanager*, p. 278.
90. Janssen, *Das Ministerium Speer*, p. 74.
91. Tooze, *The Wages of Destruction*, p. 575.
92. Janssen, *Das Ministerium Speer*, pp. 74ff.
93. Boelcke (ed.), *Deutschlands Rüstung im Zweiten Weltkrieg*, p. 171.
94. Eichholtz, *Geschichte der deutschen Kriegswirtschaft*, 2/1 p. 12. The full designation was *Industrierat des Reichsmarschalls für die Fertigung von Luftwaffengerät*.
95. Peter Kohl and Peter Bessel, *Auto Union und Junkers: Geschichte der Mitteldeutschen Motorenwerke GmbH Taucha 1935–1948*, Stuttgart, 2003, p. 110.
96. Janssen, *Das Ministerium Speer*, p. 89.
97. Ibid., p. 90.
98. Ferdinand von Senger und Etterlin, *Die deutschen Panzer 1926–1945*, Bonn, 1998.
99. Janssen, *Das Ministerium Speer*, p. 91.
100. Walter J. Spielberger and Hilary Louid Doyle, *Panzer VI Tiger und seine Abarten*, Stuttgart, 2010.
101. Janssen, *Das Ministerium Speer*, p. 93. Speer made this remark in June 1942.
102. Ferdinand von Senger und Etterlin, *Die deutschen Panzer 1926–1945*, Bonn, 1998.
103. *Kriegstagebücher des Oberkommandos*, vol. 2/2, *1. Januar bis 31. Dezember 1942*, ed. Andreas Hillgruber, Frankfurt, 1963, pp. 1310ff.
104. Eichholtz, *Geschichte der deutschen Kriegswirtschaft*, vol. 2/1, p. 121.
105. Hitler's decree, dated 22 January 1943: Janssen, *Das Ministerium Speer*, p. 96.
106. Tooze, *The Wages of Destruction*, p. 595.
107. Erich von Manstein, *Verlorene Siege*, Bonn, 1955, p. 490. The official designation of the Ferdinand was Panzerjäger Tiger (P).
108. Tooze, *The Wages of Destruction*, p. 595. Aircraft construction is a far more complex undertaking than the manufacture of tanks, but it also uses considerably fewer resources.
109. Lutz Budraß, *Flugzeugindustrie und Luftrüstung in Deutschland 1918–1945*, Düsseldorf, 1998, p. 893.

Chapter 6: Labour: Free, Forced and Slave

1. Dietrich Eichholtz, *Geschichte der deutschen Kriegswirtschaft 1939–1945*, 5 vols, Munich, 2002, vol. 2/1, p. 75; Kees Gispen, *Poems in Steel: National Socialism and the Politics of Inventing from Weimar to Bonn*, New York, 2002, pp. 241ff; Hein A.M. Klemann and Sergei Kudryashov, *Occupied Economies: An Economic History of Nazi-Occupied Europe, 1939–1945*, London, 2011, p. 127.
2. Jürgen Nürnberger and Dieter G. Maier, *Präsident, Reichsarbeitsminister, Staatssekretär: Dr. Friedrich Syrup; Präsident der Reichsanstalt für Arbeitsvermittlung und Arbeitslosenversicherung; Leben, Werk, Personalbibliographie*, Ludwigshafen, 2nd edn, 2007. A document used in evidence against Mansfeld in a British Military Court on 15 May 1946 contains a marginal note written by him on 20 February 1942: 'The present difficulties with labour would not have arisen had we decided early enough to make extensive use of Russian prisoners of war. 3.9 million Russians were available. Now there are only 1.1 million.' *Braunbuch – Kriegs- und Naziverbrecher in der Bundesrepublik und in West Berlin: Staat; Wirtschaft; Verwaltung; Armee; Justiz; Wissenschaft*, East Berlin, 1968 p. 20.

3. Ulrich Schlie (ed.), *Albert Speer: Die Kransberg-Protokolle 1945: Seine ersten Aussagen und Aufzeichnungen (Juni–September)*, Munich, 2003, pp. 173f.

4. Gregor Janssen, *Das Ministerium Speer: Deutschlands Rüstung im Krieg*, Berlin, 1968, p. 61.

5. Eichholtz, *Geschichte der deutschen Kriegswirtschaft*, vol. 2/1, p. 77.

6. Hans Kehrl, *Krisenmanager im Dritten Reich*, 2nd edn, Frankfurt, 2007, p. 342.

7. Janssen, *Das Ministerium Speer*, p. 61.

8. Eichholtz, *Geschichte der deutschen Kriegswirtschaft*, vol. 2/1, p. 78.

9. Janssen, *Das Ministerium Speer*, pp. 62ff; Berenice A. Carroll, *Design for Total War: Arms and Economics in the Third Reich*, The Hague, 1968, p. 241; David Irving, *Die Tragödie der deutschen Luftwaffe: Aus den Akten und Erinnerungen von Feldmarschall Milch*, Berlin, 1970, p. 224 and passim.

10. At the beginning of the war the number of women employed dropped from 14.39 million in 1940 to 14.19 million in 1941. It did not reach the pre-war rate of 14.6 million until 1943 and even in September 1944 it was only 14.9 million. Hans-Ulrich Wehler, *Deutsche Gesellschaftsgeschichte*, vol. 4 (*Vom Beginn des Ersten Weltkriegs bis zur Gründung der beiden deutschen Staaten 1914–1949*), Munich, 2003, pp. 755f.

11. Hitler signed a decree to this effect on 23 June 1942: Janssen, *Das Ministerium Speer*, p. 78.

12. Wigbert Benz, *Der Hungerplan im 'Unternehmen Barbarossa' 1941*, Berlin, 2011.

13. Ulrich Herbert, *Fremdarbeiter: Politik und Praxis des 'Ausländer-Einsatzes' in der Kriegswirtschaft des Dritten Reiches*, Bonn, 1985, p. 194.

14. The ELFI or Elektro- und Feinmechanische Industriegesellschaft was a subsidiary of Bosch. See Manfred Overesch, *Bosch in Hildesheim 1937–1945: Freies Unternehmertum und nationalsozialistische Rüstungspolitik*, Göttingen, 2008.

15. Eichholtz, *Geschichte der deutschen Kriegswirtschaft*, vol. 2/1, pp. 215ff.

16. Janssen, *Das Ministerium Speer*, p. 97.

17. Lutz Budraß, *Flugzeugindustrie und Luftrüstung in Deutschland 1918–1945*, Düsseldorf, 1998, p. 775.

18. Leon Goldensohn, *The Nuremberg Interviews*, ed. Robert Gellately, New York, 2004, p. 411.

19. Schieber was an SS-Brigadeführer, the equivalent of a brigadier in the British Army or a US one-star general.

20. For Speer's tendentious account see Speer, *Der SklavenStaat*, pp. 31ff.

21. Longerich, *Himmler*, pp. 652ff. Eichholtz, 3/1, pp. 301ff, for an account of conditions in Ravensbrück.

22. Peter Longerich, *Heinrich Himmler: Biographie*, Berlin, 2008, pp. 653f.

23. Ibid.

24. Herbert, *Fremdarbeiter*, p. 425.

25. See the testimony of Rudolf Höss, the commandant of Auschwitz, in Dietrich Eichholtz and Wolfgang Schumann (eds), *Anatomie des Krieges: Neue Dokumente über die Rolle des deutschen Monopolkapitals bei der Vorbereitung und Durchführung des Zweiten Weltkrieges*, Berlin, 1969, p. 478.

26. Herbert, *Fremdarbeiter*, p. 425.

27. Kammler has been described as an 'extermination technocrat': Rainer Fröbe, 'Hans Kammler, Technokrat der Vernichtung', in Ronald Smelser and Enrico Syring (eds), *Die SS: Elite unterm Totenkopf – 30 Lebensläufe*, Paderborn, 2000, pp. 305–19.

28. Breloer, *Die Akte Speer*, pp. 187ff.

29. Ibid., pp. 202ff. Kammler had since been promoted to SS-Brigadeführer.

30. Matthias Schmidt, *Albert Speer – Das Ende eines Mythos: Speers wahre Rolle im Dritten Reich*, Munich, 1982, pp. 226f.

31. The original of this letter is in the archives of the Ministry of Armaments, Bundesarchiv, R3/1542. Schmidt, *Albert Speer*, pp. 226–7, reproduces this letter in full. See also Michael Hepp, 'Fälschung und Wahrheit: Albert Speer und "Der Sklavenstaat"', *Mitteilungen der Dokumentationsstelle zur NS-Sozialpolitik*, vol. 1, no. 3 (1985), p. 16.

32. Heinrich Breloer and Rainer Zimmer, *Die Akte Speer: Spuren eines Kriegsverbrechers*, Berlin, 2006, pp. 198f.

33. Breloer, *Die Akte Speer*, pp. 200f.

34. Schmidt, *Albert Speer*, p. 208.

35. Gitta Sereny, *Albert Speer: His Battle With Truth*, London, 1995, p. 378.

36. Florian Freund, Bertrand Perz and Karl Stuhlpfarrer, 'Der Bau des Vernichtungslagers Auschwitz-Birkenau: Die Aktenmappe der Zentralbauleitung Auschwitz "Vorhaben: Kriegsgefangenenlager Auschwitz (Durchführung der Sonderbehandlungen)" im Militärhistorischen Archiv Prag', *Zeitgeschichte*, vol. 20 (1993), pp. 187–214.

37. Longerich, *Heinrich Himmler*, p. 586.

38. Albert Speer, *Der Sklavenstaat: meine Auseinandersetzungen mit der SS*, Berlin, 1981, p. 350.

39. Peter Longerich, *Goebbels: Biographie*, Munich, 2010, p. 508.
40. Herbert, *Fremdarbeiter*, pp. 349ff; Walter Naasner, *Neue Machtzentren in der deutschen Kriegswirtschaft 1942–1945: Die Wirtschaftsorganisation der SS, das Amt des Generalbevollmächtigten für den Arbeitseinsatz und das Reichsministerium für Bewaffnung und Munition, Reichsministerium für Rüstung und Kriegsproduktion im nationalsozialistischen Herrschaftssystem*, Boppard, 1994, pp. 176 and 349; Bernhard R. Kroener, "'Menschenbewirtschaftung", Bevölkerungsverteilung und personelle Rüstung in der zweiten Kriegshälfte (1942–1944)', *Das Deutsche Reich und der Zweite Weltkrieg*, vol. 5/2, Stuttgart, 1999, pp. 777–1001, esp. 928ff.
41. *Kriegstagebuch des Oberkommandos*, vol. 2/2, *1. Januar bis 31. Dezember 1942*, ed. Andreas Hillgruber, Frankfurt, 1963, p. 1152. 'Hero Snatcher' (*Heldenklau*) was based on the propaganda figure 'Coal Snatcher' (*Kohlenklau*), urging people not to waste energy.
42. Ibid., pp. 111f.
43. Dieter Rebentisch, *Führerstaat und Verwaltung im Zweiten Weltkrieg: Verfassungsentwicklung und Verwaltungspolitik 1939–1945*, Stuttgart, 1989, pp. 471f.
44. These were the figures given by Sauckel at Nuremberg. Janssen, *Das Ministerium Speer*, p. 80, note 130.
45. For an overview see Edward L. Homze, *Foreign Labor in Nazi Germany*, Princeton, 1967 and Herbert, *Fremdarbeiter*.
46. Janssen, *Das Ministerium Speer*, p. 83.
47. Ibid., p. 84.
48. Eichholtz, *Geschichte der deutschen Kriegswirtschaft*, vol. 2/1, p. 206.
49. Eichholtz, 2/1, pp. 207ff.
50. Ministry of Armaments archives, Bundesarchiv, R3/1737, p. 3.
51. Wolfgang Bleyer, *Staat und Monopole im totalen Krieg: Der Staatsmonopolistische Machtapparat und die 'totale Mobilisierung' im ersten Halbjahr 1943*, Berlin, 1970, p. 96.
52. Bleyer, *Staat und Monopole im totalen Krieg*, pp. 62 and 91. Speer used the word *Lebenshaltung*.
53. Willi A. Boelcke, (ed.), *Deutschlands Rüstung im Zweiten Weltkrieg: Hitlers Konferenzen mit Albert Speer 1942–1945*, Frankfurt, 1969, p. 252.
54. Eichholtz, 2/1, pp. 203f.
55. Janssen, *Das Ministerium Speer*, p. 125.
56. Fred Kupferman, *Le Procès de Vichy: Pucheu, Pétain, Laval*, Paris, 2006, pp. 383ff.
57. Jean-Pierre Azéma, *De Munich à la Libération, 1938–1944*, Paris, 1979, pp. 210ff.
58. Archives of the Ministry of Armaments, Bundesarchiv R3/1737, p. 107.
59. Ibid., p. 120.
60. Guy Sabin, *Jean Bichelonne: Ministre sous l'occupation 1942–1944*, Paris, 1991; Albert Speer, *Erinnerungen*, Berlin, 1969, p. 323.
61. Kehrl, *Krisenmanager*, p. 317.
62. Ibid., p. 344.
63. Bundesarchiv R3/1742, p. 16.
64. See the protocol of these conferences on 16 and 17 December in Boelcke (ed.), *Deutschlands Rüstung im Zweiten Weltkrieg*, p. 323.
65. Dieter Rebentisch, *Führerstaat und Verwaltung*, pp. 356–62.
66. Janssen, *Das Ministerium Speer*, p. 128. Minutes in Breloer and Zimmer, *Die Akte Speer*, pp. 261f.
67. Kehrl, *Krisenmanager*, pp. 347f.
68. Bleyer, *Staat und Monopole im totalen Krieg*, pp. 177f.
69. Bundesarchiv, R3/1737, p. 83.
70. Bleyer, *Staat und Monopole im totalen Krieg*, p. 147.

Chapter 7: The Consolidation of Power

1. Adam Tooze, *The Wages of Destruction: The Making and Breaking of the Nazi Economy*, London, 2006, p. 634.
2. Frank Bajohr, 'Gauleiter in Hamburg. Zur Person und Tätigkeit Karl Kaufmanns (1900–1969)', *Vierteljahrshefte für Zeitgeschichte*, 43, 1995.
3. Bundesarchiv R3/1739, p. 134.
4. Eberhard Rössler, *U-Boottyp XXI*, Bonn, 2000.
5. Erich Raeder, *Mein Leben*, 2 vols, Tübingen, 1956–7, vol. 2, p. 277.
6. Gregor Janssen, *Das Ministerium Speer: Deutschlands Rüstung im Krieg*, Berlin, 1968, p. 111.
7. Bundesarchiv R3/1737, p. 107.
8. Janssen, *Das Ministerium Speer*, p. 112.

9. Tooze, *The Wages of Destruction*, p. 616.
10. Rössler, *U-Boottyp XXI*.
11. Susanne Wiborg, *Walther Blohm: Schiffe und Flugzeuge aus Hamburg*, Hamburg 1993, pp. 104ff.
12. Tooze, *The Wages of Destruction*, p. 618.
13. Albert Speer, *Erinnerungen*, Berlin, 1969, p. 284.
14. Gitta Sereny, *Albert Speer: His Battle With Truth*, London, 1995, p. 372.
15. Ian Kershaw, *Hitler 1936–1945: Nemesis*, London, 2000, pp. 569–77. Goebbels often complained in his diary of Hitler's shortcomings as a leader, citing his indecision, his reluctance to settle disagreements and his procrastination: Speer, *Erinnerungen*, p. 271.
16. Duquesne University, Gumberg Library Digital Collections, Mussmano Collection: Interview of Speer at 'Dustbin' by Mr O. Hoeffding, Economic and Financial Branch FIAT (US), 1 August 1945.
17. Speer, *Erinnerungen*, p. 277.
18. Wolfgang Bleyer, *Staat und Monopole im totalen Krieg: Der Staatsmonopolistische Machtapparat und die 'totale Mobilisierung' im ersten Halbjahr 1943*, Berlin, 1970, p. 63.
19. Peter Longerich, *Goebbels: Biographie*, Munich, 2010, p. 550.
20. Albert, Speer, *Spandauer Tagebücher*, Berlin, 1975, p. 354. Funk was quick to realise that Speer had skilfully used Goebbels as a front man.
21. Körner was a particular favourite of the Nazis. The text comes from his poem *Men and Lads* (*Männer und Buben*): 'Das Volk steht auf, der Sturm bricht los.'
22. Longerich, *Goebbels*, p. 554.
23. Janssen, *Das Ministerium Speer*, p. 121.
24. Longerich, *Goebbels*, p. 577.
25. These included Pleiger, Krauch, Röchling, Rohland, William Werner, Frydag, Heyne, Geilenberg, Tix, Degenkolb, Porsche, Erich Müller, Albert Wolff, Saur and Schieber. He prudently made no mention of the staggering amounts of money showered upon these magnates. Degenkolb, for example, was given 250,000 marks for his efforts. For excerpts from Speer's speech see Dietrich Eichholtz and Wolfgang Schumann (eds), *Anatomie des Krieges: Neue Dokumente über die Rolle des deutschen Monopolkapitals bei der Vorbereitung und Durchführung des Zweiten Weltkrieges*, Berlin, 1969, pp. 424f. The full text is in Bundesarchiv R3/1547.
26. Hans Kehrl, *Krisenmanager im Dritten Reich*, 2nd edn, Frankfurt, 2007, p. 298.
27. Heinz Boberach (ed.), *Meldungen aus dem Reich: Die geheimen Lageberichte des Sicherheitsdienstes des SS 1938–1945*, vol. 14, Herrsching, 1984, pp. 5341f and 5596.
28. Longerich, *Goebbels*, p. 577.
29. Speer, *Erinnerungen*, p. 281.
30. Bleyer, *Staat und Monopole im totalen Krieg*, p. 159.
31. By 4,938 to 2,465.
32. Tooze, *The Wages of Destruction*, p. 605.
33. Bundesarchiv R3/1737, p. 89.
34. Kehrl, *Krisenmanager*, p. 300.
35. Ibid., p. 311.
36. Ibid., pp. 310ff.
37. Ulrich Schlie (ed.), *Albert Speer: Die Kransberg-Protokolle 1945: Seine ersten Aussagen und Aufzeichnungen (Juni–September)*, Munich, 2003, pp. 155 and 196.
38. Bundesarchiv R3/1737, pp. 123f.
39. Dietrich Eichholtz, *Geschichte der deutschen Kriegswirtschaft 1939–1945*, 5 vols, Munich, 2002, vol. 2/1, pp. 147f. See also Alan S. Milward, *War, Economy and Society 1939–1945*, London, 1977, and Friedrich Forstmeier and Hans-Erich Volkmann (eds), *Kriegswirtschaft und Rüstung 1939–1945*, Düsseldorf, 1977.
40. Kehrl, *Krisenmanager*, p. 312.
41. Ibid., p. 310.
42. Ibid., p. 313.
43. Ibid., p. 321.
44. Kehrl, *Krisenmanager*, p. 176.
45. Figures from Enzo Angelucci, *The Rand McNally Encyclopedia of Military Aircraft, 1914–1980*, New Delhi, 1988.
46. Schlie (ed.), *Albert Speer: Die Kransberg-Protokolle*, p. 336.
47. Reichsleiter was a state appointment, Gauleiter was a party official. Some held both offices. Goebbels was Gauleiter of Berlin and Reichsleiter as Minister of Propaganda.
48. Longerich, *Goebbels*, p. 600. A German infantry division had about 18,000 men at full strength, but most were seriously undermanned. By 1945 a full-strength division had 12,000 men, but none had that many.

49. *Bummelanten und Simulanten.*
50. For an excellent account of the Posen conference, see Tooze, *The Wages of Destruction*, p. 605. See also Eichholtz, *Geschichte der deutschen Kriegswirtschaft*, vol. 2/1, p. 175f. Janssen, *Das Ministerium Speer*, p. 124, claims that Speer's three-point definition is clear indication that he realised that the war could not be won.
51. Breloer, *Die Akte Speer*, pp. 210ff.
52. Breloer, *Die Akte Speer*, pp. 217ff.
53. Eichholtz, *Geschichte der deutschen Kriegswirtschaft*, vol. 2/1, p. 174. Speer makes no mention of the pact in his memoirs.
54. Speer, *Erinnerungen*, p. 326f.
55. Joachim Fest, *Die unbeantwortbaren Fragen: Notizen über Gespräche mit Albert Speer zwischen Ende 1966 und 1981*, Reinbek bei Hamburg, 2006, p. 47.
56. Ibid., p. 48.
57. Kehrl, *Krisenmanager*, p. 335.
58. Noble Franklin and Charles Webster, *The Strategic Air Offensive against Germany, 1939–1945*, vol. II, London, 1961, pp. 141ff.
59. Franklin and Webster, op. cit., pp. 64–70
60. Janssen, *Das Ministerium Speer*, p. 145.
61. John Sweetman, *The Dambusters Raid*, London, 1999.
62. Bundesarchiv R3/1737, p. 107.
63. Noble Franklin and Charles Webster, *The Strategic Air Offensive against Germany, 1939–1945*, 4 vols, London, 1961, vol. 2 (*Endeavour*); Ralf Blank, *Ruhrschlacht: Das Ruhrgebiet im Kriegsjahr 1943*, Essen, 2013; Richard Overy, *Bomber Command 1939–45: Reaping the Whirlwind*, London, 1997.
64. Bundesarchiv R3/1737, p. 116. Krupp's 'little villa' – the Villa Hügel – has 269 rooms with 8,100 square metres of living space set in 28 hectares of parkland.
65. Eichholtz, *Geschichte der deutschen Kriegswirtschaft*, vol. 2/1, p. 143. In May 1942 Speer had described Erdmann as 'energetic and active', but too much of an officer. He felt that he should be 'brought in line' (ibid., p. 94).
66. Ibid., p. 142.
67. For a graphic account of the raid see Hans Erich Nossack, *Der Untergang*, Frankfurt, 1976.
68. The local units were known as Damage Removal Squads (*Aufräumtrupps* or *A-Trupps*) and Auxiliary Building Squads (*Bauhilfstrupps* or *B-Trupps*).
69. Kehrl, *Krisenmanager*, pp. 299f.
70. Speer, *Erinnerungen*, p. 297.
71. Janssen, *Das Ministerium Speer*, p. 48, note 95.
72. Kehrl, *Krisenmanager*, p. 329.
73. Ibid., p. 330.
74. Ibid., p. 336.
75. Speer, *Erinnerungen*, p. 291. The famous '88' was used both as an anti-tank and anti-aircraft gun.

Chapter 8: The Challenge to Power

1. Dietrich Eichholtz, *Geschichte der deutschen Kriegswirtschaft 1939–1945*, 5 vols, Munich, 2002, vol. 3/1, p. 13.
2. Ibid., p. 31.
3. Gregor Janssen, *Das Ministerium Speer: Deutschlands Rüstung im Krieg*, Berlin, 1968, p. 157.
4. Gitta Sereny, *Albert Speer: His Battle With Truth*, London, 1995, p. 406.
5. Bundesarchiv R3/1739, p. 4. For details of the simplification of payments and the reduction of paperwork see R3/1744.
6. Ibid., R3/1739, p. 7.
7. Sereny, *Albert Speer*, p. 409, comes up with the fanciful idea that Speer's sickness was exacerbated by an 'inkling' (*Ahnung*) of Hitler's 'crimes'.
8. Hugh Trevor-Roper, *The Last Days of Hitler*, London, 1947, p. 74.
9. Bundesarchiv, R3/1739, p. 15.
10. Ernst Klee, *Dokumente zur 'Euthanasie' im NS-Staat*, Frankfurt, 1985; Ernst Klee, *'Euthanasie' im NS-Staat: Die 'Vernichtung lebensunwerten Lebens'*, Frankfurt, 1983; Götz Aly (ed.), *Aktion T4 1939–1945: Die 'Euthanasie'-Zentrale in der Tiergartenstraße 4*, Berlin, 1989; Michael H. Kater, *Doctors Under Hitler*, Chapel Hill, 1989; Ulf Schmidt, *Karl Brandt: The Nazi Doctor – Medicine and Power in the Third Reich*, London, 2007.
11. Albert Speer, *Der Sklavenstaat. Meine Auseinandersetzung mit der SS*, Berlin, 1981, p. 323.

12. Bundesarchiv, R3/1739, p. 24.
13. Ibid., R3/1739, p. 32; Hans Kehrl, *Krisenmanager im Dritten Reich*, 2nd edn, Frankfurt, 2007, p. 354.
14. Eichholtz, *Geschichte der deutschen Kriegswirtschaft*, vol. 3/1, p. 16; Lutz Budraß, *Flugzeugindustrie und Luftrüstung in Deutschland 1918–1945*, Düsseldorf, 1998, p. 867.
15. Janssen, *Das Ministerium Speer*, p. 158.
16. Albert Speer, *Sklavenstaat*, p. 317.
17. Sereny, *Albert Speer*, p. 424.
18. Ibid., p. 425. Bichelonne and Hohenlychen feature in Céline's remarkable novel '*D'un château l'autre*' (1957).
19. Speer to Himmler, 23 February 1944, in Heinrich Breloer and Rainer Zimmer, *Die Akte Speer: Spuren eines Kriegsverbrechers*, Berlin, 2006, pp. 178f.
20. Albert Speer, *Erinnerungen*, Berlin, 1969, pp. 339ff.
21. Janssen, *Das Ministerium Speer*, p. 162.
22. Carl Birkenholz, *Die Betreuung der Bauarbeiter: Sozialpolitisches Handbuch für die Bauwirtschaft*, Berlin, 1940; Carl Birkenholz and Wolfgang Siebert, *Der ausländische Arbeiter in Deutschland: Sammlung und Erläuterungen der arbeits- und sozialrechtlichen Vorschriften über die Arbeitsverhältnisse nicht volksdeutscher Beschäftigter*, Mainz, 1942.
23. Birkenholz and Siebert, *Der ausländische Arbeiter*, p. 23. 'POWs, Eastern workers, Poles etc' were exempt from these perks. Concentration camp inmates working in the armaments industry were allowed between 1,300 and 1,700 calories per day.
24. Rolf-Dieter Müller, DRZW, 5/2, pp. 383ff.
25. Bundesarchiv, R3/1629, pp. 3–25.
26. Speer, *Erinnerungen*, p. 349.
27. Sereny, *Albert Speer*, p. 427.
28. Bundesarchiv, R3/1739, p. 98.
29. Janssen, *Das Ministerium Speer*, pp. 164ff.
30. Eichholtz, *Geschichte der deutschen Kriegswirtschaft*, vol. 3/1, pp. 12ff.
31. Speer, *Erinnerungen*, p. 353.
32. Martin Moll, *'Führer'-Erlasse 1939–1945*, Stuttgart, 1997, p. 404.
33. Speer, *Erinnerungen*, p. 345; Sereny, *Albert Speer*, p. 422.
34. Sereny, *Albert Speer*, p. 192.
35. Bundesarchiv, R3/1739, p. 36.
36. Ibid., R3/1739, 17 April 1944.
37. Janssen, *Das Ministerium Speer*, pp. 116f.
38. Joachim Fest, *Speer: Eine Biographie*, Berlin, 1999, p. 286.
39. Kehrl, *Krisenmanager*, p. 364.
40. Walter Rohland, *Bewegte Zeiten: Erinnerungen eines Eisenhüttenmannes*, Stuttgart, 1978, p. 99; Speer, *Erinnerungen*, p. 350. Speer claims that this meeting with Rohland was at Klessheim, Rohland that it was in Meran.
41. Olaf Groehler, *Bombenkrieg gegen Deutschland*, Berlin, 1991, p. 291.
42. Speer, *Erinnerungen*, pp. 349ff. Andreas Heusler, Mark Spoerer and Helmuth Trischler (eds), *Rüstung, Kriegswirtschaft und Zwangsarbeit im 'Dritten Reich'*, Munich, 2010, pp. 202ff. The factories were to be 600–800,000 square metres.
43. Bundesarchiv, R3/1739, p. 57.
44. Speer gives a sketchy account of this meeting in *Erinnerungen*, pp. 351ff.
45. Sereny, *Albert Speer*, pp. 478–81; Dan van der Vat, *Der gute Nazi: Leben und Lügen des Albert Speer*, Berlin, 1997, p. 300. He takes Dorsch's promise for fact and wrongly states that the first bunker was operational in November 1944.
46. Bundesarchiv, R3/1739, p. 38f.
47. Ibid., R3/1739, pp.17ff.
48. Ibid.
49. Eichholtz, *Geschichte der deutschen Kriegswirtschaft*, vol. 3/1, p. 32.
50. Speer, *Sklavenstaat*, p. 330.
51. Kehrl, *Krisenmanager*, p. 365.
52. Willi A. Boelcke (ed.), *Deutschlands Rüstung im Zweiten Weltkrieg: Hitlers Konferenzen mit Albert Speer 1942–1945*, Frankfurt, 1969, p. 363.
53. Janssen, *Das Ministerium Speer*, p. 164.
54. Kehrl, *Krisenmanager*, p. 378.
55. Bundesarchiv, R3/1739, pp. 138 and 144.
56. Ibid., R3/1739, part II, p. 65.

57. Ibid., R3/1739, p. 97. Sauckel visited Speer at the Pariser Platz on 31 May 1944. A fierce argument ensued over this issue.
58. Boelcke (ed.), *Deutschlands Rüstung im Zweiten Weltkrieg*, p. 367.
59. Eichholtz, *Geschichte der deutschen Kriegswirtschaft*, vol. 3/1, pp. 43ff.
60. Ludolf Herbst, *Der Totale Krieg und die Ordnung der Wirtschaft: Die Kriegswirtschaft im Spannungsfeld von Politik, Ideologie und Propaganda 1939–1945*, Stuttgart, 1982, pp. 318f., 327ff., 333f.
61. Rolf-Dieter Müller, DRZW, 5/2, p. 722.
62. Ibid. Speer later made the lame excuse that he was carried away by the optimistic atmosphere in Hitler's headquarters: Speer, *Erinnerungen*, p. 368.
63. Rolf-Dieter Müller, DRZW, 5/2, p. 745.
64. Eichholtz, *Geschichte der deutschen Kriegswirtschaft*, vol. 3/1, p. 45.
65. Riecke escaped prosecution after the war and enjoyed a successful career in the Federal Republic. Eigruber was hanged.
66. Eichholtz, *Geschichte der deutschen Kriegswirtschaft*, vol. 3/1, p. 46.
67. Speer, *Erinnerungen*, p. 368, claims that this concluding remark was an expression of his belief that for him the needs of the German people came first.
68. Bundesarchiv, R3/1739, p. 132.
69. Herbst, *Der Totale Krieg*, pp. 333ff.
70. The Morgenthau Plan to destroy German industry and convert Germany into a mainly agricultural country did not become public until the Quebec Conference in September 1944.
71. Hildegard von Kotze and Herbert Krausnick, *Es spricht der Führer. 7 exemplarische Hitler-Reden*, Gütersloh, 1966, pp. 351ff.
72. Kehrl, *Krisenmanager*, p. 397; Speer, *Erinnerungen*, p. 369.
73. Rolf-Dieter Müller, DRZW, 5/2, p. 550.
74. Boelcke, *Deutschlands Rüstung im Zweiten Weltkrieg*, p. 417.
75. Janssen, *Das Ministerium Speer*, p. 269. Here Kennes is demoted to the rank of Colonel. Speer, *Erinnerungen*, p. 390, wrongly states that Stauffenberg issued the invitation.
76. Rolf-Dieter Müller, DRZW, 5/2, p. 752.
77. Budraß, *Flugzeugindustrie*, p. 872.
78. Sereny, *Albert Speer*, pp. 443ff.
79. Janssen, *Das Ministerium Speer*, p. 268, argues that Speer no longer believed that victory was possible but is unable to back it up with any concrete evidence.
80. Speer, *Erinnerungen*, p. 401.
81. Wilfred von Oven, *Finale Furioso: Mit Goebbels bis zum Ende*, Tübingen, 1974, p. 416.
82. Claudius returned to Romania and was captured by the Red Army a few weeks later. He died in a Soviet POW camp in 1952. Eckart Conze, Norbert Frei, Peter Hayes and Moshe Zimmermann, *Das Amt und die Vergangenheit: Deutsche Diplomaten im Dritten Reich und in der Bundesrepublik*, Munich, 2010, pp. 323f.
83. Bundesarchiv, R3/1739, Part II, p. 52.
84. Speer, *Erinnerungen*, pp. 398f.
85. Duquesne University, Gumberg Library Digital Collections, Mussmano Collection: Interview of Speer at 'Dustbin' by Mr O. Hoeffding, Economic and Financial Branch FIAT (US), 1 August 1945.
86. BA R3/1552.
87. Eichholtz, *Geschichte der deutschen Kriegswirtschaft*, vol. 3/1, pp. 49f; Breloer and Zimmer, *Die Akte Speer*, pp. 281f.
88. Bundesarchiv, R3/1739, Part II, p. 21.
89. Ibid., p. 19.
90. Janssen, *Das Ministerium Speer*, pp. 268f.
91. The full text of Speer's memorandum to Hitler is in Janssen, *Das Ministerium Speer*, pp.172f.
92. Speer, *Erinnerungen*, p. 406.
93. The SS Main Leadership Office or SS-Führungshauptamt (SS-FHA) was responsible for logistics, wages, training and medical services.
94. Speer, *Sklavenstaat*, p. 442. Buhle was also Stauffenberg's commanding officer and wondered why he had suddenly left the conference room. Jüttner played a leading role in the Mutual Help Association of Former Waffen-SS Members (HIAG) after the war.
95. Hartmut Knittel, 'Deutsche Kampfpanzerproduktion und Fertigungstechnik 1939–1945' in Roland G. Förster and Heinrich Walle (eds), *Militär und Technik: Wechselbeziehung zu Staat, Gesellschaft und Industrie im 19. und 20. Jahrhundert*, Herford and Bonn, 1992; Emil Leeb, 'Aus der Rüstung des Dritten Reiches (Das Heereswaffenamt 1938–1945): Ein amtlicher Bericht des letzten Chefs des

Heereswaffenamtes', *Wehrtechnische Monatshefte*, vol. 55, no. 4 (1958). The Bundeswehr also adopted this new institution.

96. Eichholtz, *Geschichte der deutschen Kriegswirtschaft*, vol. 3/1, p. 50.
97. The man concerned was Alfred-Ingemar Berndt, responsible for branding Rommel 'The Desert Fox'. He had been attached to the Afrika Korps as Rommel's propaganda manager. He was killed in March 1945 in Hungary while serving in the SS-Panzer Regiment 'Viking'.
98. Eichholtz, *Geschichte der deutschen Kriegswirtschaft*, vol. 3/1, p. 50.
99. Janssen, *Das Ministerium Speer*, p. 272.
100. Barth was head of a department concerned with increasing the output of energy: Boelcke, *Deutschlands Rüstung*, p. 477. He had a distinguished career in post-war Germany.
101. Janssen, *Das Ministerium Speer*, p. 270.
102. Ian Kershaw, *The End: The Defiance and Destruction of Hitler's Germany, 1944–1945*, London, 2011, p. 30, gives a characteristically sure-footed account of the consequences of the plot's failure.
103. Speer, *Erinnerungen*, p. 407.
104. Rolf-Dieter Müller, DRZW, 5/2, p. 551. It is noticeable that this embarrassing memorandum is not mentioned in Speer's memoirs and was edited out of the 'Speer Chronik' now in the Federal Archives. Speer had added the production figures for the first week of August to those of July and had ordered the Weapons Office to cook the books in the same manner so that the figures balanced.
105. Speer, *Erinnerungen*, p. 370.
106. Janssen, *Das Ministerium Speer*, p. 167.
107. Ibid., p. 169.
108. Ibid., p. 170.
109. Bundesarchiv, R3/1739, p. 82.
110. Eichholtz, *Geschichte der deutschen Kriegswirtschaft*, vol. 3/1, p. 279.
111. Duquesne University, Gumberg Library Digital Collections, Mussmano Collection: Interview of Speer at 'Dustbin' by Mr O. Hoeffding, Economic and Financial Branch FIAT (US), 1 August 1945.

Chapter 9: Miracle Weapons

1. Horst Boog, Gerhard Krebs and Detlef Vogel, *Das Deutsche Reich und der Zweite Weltkrieg*, vol. 7 (*Das Deutsche Reich in der Defensive: Strategischer Luftkrieg in Europa, Krieg im Westen und in Ostasien, 1943 bis 1944/45*), Stuttgart, 2001.
2. Gregor Janssen, *Das Ministerium Speer: Deutschlands Rüstung im Krieg*, Berlin, 1968, p. 186.
3. Eichholtz, 3/1, pp.14ff.
4. Willi A. Boelcke (ed.), *Deutschlands Rüstung im Zweiten Weltkrieg: Hitlers Konferenzen mit Albert Speer 1942–1945*, Frankfurt, 1969, pp. 375f: minutes of Hitler's conference 3–5 June 1944.
5. Lutz Budraß, *Flugzeugindustrie und Luftrüstung in Deutschland 1918–1945*, Düsseldorf, 1998, p. 871.
6. In July 1944 Speer personally fired the head of the Heinkel works in Vienna: Dietrich Eichholtz, *Geschichte der deutschen Kriegswirtschaft 1939–1945*, 5 vols, Munich, 2002, vol. 2/1, p. 19.
7. Janssen, *Das Ministerium Speer*, p. 188.
8. Ulrich Herbert, *Fremdarbeiter: Politik und Praxis des 'Ausländer-Einsatzes' in der Kriegswirtschaft des Dritten Reiches*, Bonn, 1985, p. 310.
9. Ibid., p. 364.
10. Bundesarchiv, R3/1739, p. 33.
11. Eichholtz, *Geschichte der deutschen Kriegswirtschaft*, vol. 3/1, p. 19.
12. Boelcke (ed.), *Deutschlands Rüstung im Zweiten Weltkrieg*, pp. 424f.
13. Janssen, *Das Ministerium Speer*, p. 189.
14. For the dismal tale of the He 177 see Joachim Dressel and Manfred Griehl, *Heinkel He 177–277–274: Eine luftfahrtgeschichtliche Dokumentation*, Stuttgart, 1989.
15. Eichholtz, 3/1, pp. 199ff.
16. Boelcke, *Deutschlands Rüstung*, p. 214.
17. The nickname 'Cherrystone' came from the so-named directional device in the rocket that 'spat' the device from one antenna to another, analogous to spitting a cherrystone. Goebbels suggested that it should be called the 'Hell Hound'. The British cheerily dismissed it as the 'buzz bomb' or 'doodlebug'.
18. Benjamin King and Timothy Kutta, *Impact: The History of Germany's V-Weapons in World War II*, New York, 2003; Michael J. Neufeld, *The Rocket and the Reich: Peenemünde and the coming of the Ballistic Missile Era*, New York, 1995; Frederick Ordway and Mitchell R. Sharpe, *The Rocket Team*, Cambridge, MA, 1982; David Irving, *The Mare's Nest*, New York, 1965.

19. Stahlknecht was responsible for developing A4 factories at the Zeppelin Works and Wiener Neustadt.
20. A total of 5,200 were built by the end of the war.
21. The Lancasters took off in England, bombed Friedrichshafen and landed in Algeria. They then bombed targets in Italy.
22. Hans Kehrl, *Krisenmanager im Dritten Reich*, 2nd edn, Frankfurt, 2007, pp. 336f. Speer deliberately obfuscates his relationship with Himmler with regard to Peenemünde in Albert Speer, *Erinnerungen*, Berlin, 1969, p. 379.
23. *Wasserfall* was one of a number of other surface-to-air missiles developed at Peenemünde. They included the Henschel Hs 117 *Schmetterling*, *Enzian* and *Rheintochter*.
24. It was intended to produce 10,000 Waterfall rockets per month.
25. Speer, *Erinnerungen*, pp. 374f., for Speer's self-criticism.
26. Ibid., p. 377.
27. Ernst Klee, *Das Personenlexikon des Dritten Reich: Wer war was vor und nach 1945*, Frankfurt, 2003, p. 521.
28. Janssen, *Das Ministerium Speer*, p. 196.
29. Ulrich Schlie (ed.), *Albert Speer: Die Kransberg-Protokolle 1945: Seine ersten Aussagen und Aufzeichnungen (Juni–September)*, Munich, 2003, p. 289.
30. Speer, *Erinnerungen*, p. 385.
31. Rickhey was the only V2 engineer tried for war crimes. He attributed the charges against him to the 'vilification and perjury of Communists and Russian agents'. Charged with murdering concentration camp inmates in March 1945, he was acquitted and worked for the Americans at Wright Field. Ernst Klee, *Das Personenlexikon zum Dritten Reich: Wer war was vor und nach 1945*, Frankfurt 2007, p. 496.
32. 'Dora' was the letter 'D' in the German phonetic alphabet.
33. Karin Orth, *Das System der nationalsozialistischen Konzentrationslager: Eine politische Organisationsgeschichte*, Hamburg, 1999, p. 247.
34. Albert Speer, *Der Sklavenstaat. Meine Aufeinandersetzungen mit der SS*, Berlin, 1981, p. 332.
35. Speer, *Erinnerungen*, p. 385.
36. Heinrich Breloer, *Unterwegs zur Familie Speer: Begegnungen, Gespräche, Interviews*, Berlin, 2005, p. 290, based on the testimony of two inmates, Carl Schwerdtfeger and Albert van Dijk.
37. Jens-Christian Wagner, *Produktion des Todes: Das KZ Mittelbau-Dora*, Göttingen, 2001; Adam Tooze, *The Wages of Destruction: The Making and Breaking of the Nazi Economy*, London, 2006, p. 623.
38. Joachim Neander, *'Hat in Europa kein annäherndes Beispiel': Mittelbau-Dora, ein KZ für Hitlers Krieg*, Berlin, 2000, p. 69.
39. Speer, *Erinnerungen*, p. 384.
40. Breloer, *Unterwegs zur Familie Speer*, p. 18, quoting from the 'Speer Chronicle'.
41. Bundesarchiv, R3/1739, p. 9. Dr Poschmann testified to this effect at Nuremberg. See Dennis Piszkiewicz, *The Nazi Rocketeers: Dreams of Space and Crimes of War*, Mechanicsburg, PA, 1995, p. 122.
42. Bundesarchiv, R3/1739, p. 12. Berlitz was Wolters' associate after the war.
43. Speer, *Sklavenstaat*, p. 299.
44. The von Brauns worked for the Americans after the war, Göttrup for the Soviets. Riedel was killed in a car crash in 1944.
45. Peter Longerich, *Heinrich Himmler: Biographie*, Berlin, 2008, pp. 708f.
46. David Irving, 'Unternehmen Armbrust. Der Kampf des britischen Geheimdienstes gegen Deutschlands Wunderwaffen,' *Der Spiegel*, 17 November 1965.
47. Sönke Neitzel and Harald Welzer, in *Soldaten: Protokolle vom Kämpfen, Töten und Sterben*, Frankfurt, 2012, provide ample evidence that many soldiers still believed that new 'miracle weapons' were imminent. The authors felt that were this not the case the war would have been ended.
48. *Das Reich*, 30 July 1944.
49. See Neitzel and Welzer, *Soldaten*, for numerous examples.
50. Ralf Schabel, *Die Illusionen der Wunderwaffen. Die Rolle der Düsenflugzeuge und Flugabwehrraketen in der Rüstungspolitik des Dritten Reiches*, Munich, 1994, p. 268.
51. Rolf-Dieter Müller, DRZW, 5/2, p. 696.
52. Janssen, *Das Ministerium Speer*, p. 205.
53. Rolf-Dieter Müller, DRZW, 5/2, p. 696. Waterfall was never developed beyond the prototype. Work stopped on the project at the end of February 1945. Other surface-to-air missiles such as the *Feuerlilie* and the *Taifun* were also abandoned before deployment.

54. Janssen, *Das Ministerium Speer*, p. 207.
55. Edgar Jones, Robin Woolven, Bill Durodie and Simon Wessely, 'Public Panic and Morale: Second World War Civilian Responses Re-examined in the Light of the Current Anti-terrorist Campaign', *Journal of Risk Research*, vol. 9, no. 1 (January 2006), 57–73. The bomb payload of a Lancaster was twice that of a V1 or V2. A Flying Fortress carried three times the amount.
56. Mark Walker, *Nazi Science: Myth, Truth, and the German Atomic Bomb*, New York, 2001; Irving, *The Mare's Nest*; Arnold Kramish, *The Griffin: The Greatest Untold Espionage Story of World War II*, New York, 1986; Thomas Powers, *Heisenberg's War: The Secret History of the German Bomb*, New York, 1994.
57. Speer, *Erinnerungen*, pp. 239ff.

Chapter 10: The End in Sight

1. Hans Kehrl, *Krisenmanager im Dritten Reich*, 2nd edn, Frankfurt, 2007, p. 356.
2. Albert Speer, *Erinnerungen*, Berlin, 1969, p. 357, argues that these attacks marked 'the end of German armaments'.
3. Bütefisch had a distinguished career in industry after the war for which he was awarded the Grand Cross of the Order of Merit. This distinction was annulled when he was unmasked as a war criminal. See Ernst Klee, *Das Personenlexikon des Dritten Reich: Wer war was vor und nach 1945*, Frankfurt, 2003.
4. Kehrl, *Krisenmanager*, p. 368.
5. Gregor Janssen, *Das Ministerium Speer: Deutschlands Rüstung im Krieg*, Berlin, 1968, pp. 236f.
6. Dietrich Eichholtz, *Geschichte der deutschen Kriegswirtschaft 1939-1945*, 5 vols, Munich, 2002, vol. 3/1, p. 375. Speer gives a more positive gloss on this meeting in *Erinnerungen*, pp. 357ff.
7. Bundesarchiv, R3/1739, Part II, p. 128.
8. *Trial of the Major War Criminals before the International Military Tribunal*, 'Blue Series', 42 vols, Nuremberg, 1947–9, vol. 16, p. 533.
9. Heinrich Breloer and Rainer Zimmer, *Die Akte Speer: Spuren eines Kriegsverbrechers*, Berlin, 2006, p. 369.
10. Speer, *Erinnerungen*, p. 361.
11. Eichholtz, *Geschichte der deutschen Kriegswirtschaft*, vol. 3/1, pp. 34f.
12. Kehrl, *Krisenmanager*, p. 382.
13. Tobias Bütow and Franka Bindernagel, *Ein KZ in der Nachbarschaft: Das Magdeburger Außenlager der Brabag und der 'Freundeskreis Himmler'*, Cologne, 2004, pp. 77–111.
14. Bundesarchiv R3/1739, Part II, p. 13.
15. Seuss was condemned to death at the US Military Court's Dachau Trial and executed on 5 April 1946.
16. Michael Grandt, *Unternehmen 'Wüste' – Hitlers letzte Hoffnung: Das NS-Ölschieferprogramm auf der Schwäbischen Alb*, Tübingen, 2002.
17. Wolfgang Birkenfeld, *Der synthetische Treibstoff 1933-1945: Ein Beitrag zur nationalsozialistischen Wirtschafts- und Rüstungspolitik*, Göttingen, 1964, pp. 238ff.
18. Bundesarchiv R3/1739, p. 13.
19. Janssen, *Das Ministerium Speer*, pp. 241f.
20. Bundesarchiv BA R3/1739, Part II, p. 13.
21. Ibid., R3/1739, Part II, p. 39.
22. Kehrl, *Krisenmanager*, p. 389.
23. Ibid., p. 390.
24. Speer, *Erinnerungen*, p. 417.
25. Eichholtz, *Geschichte der deutschen Kriegswirtschaft*, vol. 2/1, p. 150.
26. Janssen, *Das Ministerium Speer*, p. 242.
27. Bundesarchiv R3/1739, Part II, p. 109.
28. Kehrl, *Krisenmanager*, pp. 403f.
29. Bundesarchiv R3/1739, Part II, p. 19.
30. Ibid., p. 68.
31. Pölitz is now Police in north-western Poland on the German border. It was then on the border between Western and Eastern Pomerania.
32. Janssen, *Das Ministerium Speer*, p. 244.
33. *Kriegstagebücher des Oberkommandos*, vol. 4/1, *1. Januar 1944 bis 22. Mai 1945*, ed. Percy Ernst Schramm, Frankfurt, 1961, p. 945.
34. Joseph Goebbels, *Die Tagebücher von Joseph Goebbels*, ed. Elke Fröhlich, Part II, *Diktate 1941-1945*, vol. 15, *Januar-April 1945*, ed. Maximillan Gschaid, Munich, 1995, entry of 28 March 1945.

35. Kehrl, *Krisenmanager*, p. 414.
36. Willi A. Boelcke (ed.), *Deutschlands Rüstung im Zweiten Weltkrieg: Hitlers Konferenzen mit Albert Speer 1942–1945*, Frankfurt, 1969, p. 361.
37. Ulrich Schlie (ed.), *Albert Speer: Die Kransberg-Protokolle 1945: Seine ersten Aussagen und Aufzeichnungen (Juni–September)*, Munich, 2003, p. 392.
38. Birkenfeld, *Der synthetische Treibstoff*, pp. 198ff.
39. Janssen, *Das Ministerium Speer*, pp. 246f.
40. Ibid., p. 249.
41. Götz Aly, *Hitlers Volksstaat: Raub, Rassenkrieg und nationaler Sozialismus*, Frankfurt, 2005, p. 73.
42. *Kriegstagebücher des Oberkommandos*, vol. 4/1, p. 381, 18 September 1944.
43. Janssen, *Das Ministerium Speer*, p. 295.
44. Ibid., p. 260.
45. Bundesarchiv, R3/1743, p. 14.
46. Ibid., R3/1528, pp. 5f.
47. *Kriegstagebücher des Oberkommandos*, vol. 4/2, p. 987. These staggering figures show the vital importance of coal during the war. Germany with 2,420.3 million metric tons out-produced the US with 2,149.7 million metric tons, the Soviet Union with 590.8 million metric tons and the UK with 1,1441.2 million metric tons.
48. Bundesarchiv, R3/1739, Part II, p. 144.
49. *Kriegstagebücher des Oberkommandos*, vol. 4/2, p. 1323.
50. Some bombs landed inadvertently on Basle, Zurich and Schaffhausen.
51. Janssen, *Das Ministerium Speer*, p. 274.
52. It was designed by Speer's arch-rival Hermann Giesler. It is richly ironical that the slave-driver's palace is now a training school for the Federal Ministry of Labour.
53. Janssen, *Das Ministerium Speer*, p. 278.
54. See Boelcke (ed.), *Deutschlands Rüstung im Zweiten Weltkrieg*, pp. 293f. for examples.
55. Willi A. Boelcke, *Kriegspropaganda 1939–1941: Geheime Ministerkonferenzen im Reichspropaganda-ministerium*, Stuttgart, 1966, pp. 55f. Naumann played an ugly role in post-war Germany in a neo-Nazi group within the Free Democratic Party (FDP).
56. Bundesarchiv, R3/1739, Part II, p. 79.
57. Eichholtz, *Geschichte der deutschen Kriegswirtschaft*, vol. 3/1, pp. 51f.
58. Bundesarchiv, R3/1739, Part II, pp. 35f.
59. Ibid., p. 44.
60. Eichholtz, *Geschichte der deutschen Kriegswirtschaft*, vol. 3/1, p. 56; Janssen, *Das Ministerium Speer*, p. 290.
61. Boelcke, *Deutschlands Rüstung im Zweiten Weltkrieg*, pp. 424f.
62. Bundesarchiv, R3/1739, Part II, p. 129.
63. Adolf Galland, *Die Ersten und die Letzten*, Munich, 1993. Most of Galland's planes were destroyed on the ground. He never had more than twelve Me 262s operational.
64. Bundesarchiv, R3/1739, Part II, p. 44.
65. Ibid., R3/1739, report of 9 July 1944; F.H. Hinsley, E.E. Thomas, C.A.G. Simkins and C.F.G. Ransom, *British Intelligence in the Second World War: Its Influence on Strategy and Operations*, vol. 3, part 2, London, 1998, p. 459ff.
66. Speer, *Erinnerungen*, p. 403. General Schneider had reputedly said that Hitler knew nothing of technical matters. Speer demotes Generalleutnant Fichtner to the rank of colonel. He had supposedly shown such a lack of initiative in developing new tanks as to amount to sabotage.
67. Eichholtz, *Geschichte der deutschen Kriegswirtschaft*, vol. 3/1, pp. 68f; Roman Sandgruber, 'Dr. Walter Schieber: Eine nationalsozialistische Karriere zwischen Wirtschaft, Bürokratie und SS', in Reinhard Krammer, Christoph Kühberger and Franz Schausberger (eds), *Der forschende Blick: Beiträge zur Geschichte Österreichs im 20. Jahrhundert*, Vienna, 2010.
68. Gitta Sereny, *Albert Speer: His Battle With Truth*, London, 1995, p. 470.
69. Peter Longerich, *Der ungeschriebene Befehl*, Munich, 2001, p. 188.
70. He was shot in the left temple. As a right-hander it was unlikely to have been suicide.
71. Brandt's wife had moved to the West to avoid capture by the Soviets. This was construed as desertion at Brandt's behest. Hitler condemned him to death, but Himmler and Speer managed to save him. He was hanged by the US Military in June 1948.
72. Eichholtz, *Geschichte der deutschen Kriegswirtschaft*, vol. 3/2, p. 599.
73. Partly due to the deployment of the Flak 40 gun from June to August 1944. One third of bombers were destroyed due to Flak. Previously the figure had been a fifth: Bundesarchiv, R/3 1739, Part II, p. 53.
74. Janssen, *Das Ministerium Speer*, p. 280.

75. Ibid., p. 281.
76. David K. Yelton, *Hitler's Volkssturm: The Nazi Militia and the Fall of Germany 1944–1945*, Lawrence, KS, 2002.
77. Boelcke, *Deutschlands Rüstung im Zweiten Weltkrieg*, p. 452.
78. Joachim Fest, *Speer: Eine Biographie*, Berlin, 1999, p. 317.
79. Breloer and Zimmer, *Die Akte Speer*, pp. 289f.
80. Ibid., pp. 287f.
81. Schlie (ed.), *Albert Speer: Die Kransberg-Protokolle*, p. 402.
82. Richard J. Overy, Gerhard Otto and Johannes Houwink ten Cate (eds), *Die Neuordnung Europas: NS-Wirtschaftspolitik in den besetzten Gebieten*, Berlin, 1997; Aly, *Hitlers Volksstaat*.
83. Adam Tooze, *The Wages of Destruction: The Making and Breaking of the Nazi Economy*, London, 2006, p. 642.
84. Ibid., p. 648. For an overview see Alfred C. Mierzejewski, *The Collapse of the German War Economy, 1944–1945*, Chapel Hill, NC, 1988.
85. Bundesarchiv, R3/1739, p. 151.
86. Ilka Richter, *SS-Elite vor Gericht: Die Todesurteile gegen Oswald Pohl und Otto Ohlendorf*, Marburg, 2011; Ronald Smelser and Rainer Zitelmann (eds), *Die braune Elite I: 22 biographische Skizzen*, Darmstadt, 1999. See also the chapter 'SS Wirtschaftsideologie' in Albert Speer, *Der Sklavenstaat. Meine Aufeinandersetzungen mit der SS*, Berlin, 1981, pp.122–33.
87. Speer, *Sklavenstaat*, pp. 107 and 440.
88. Bundesarchiv, R3/1739, p. 21.
89. Schlie (ed.), *Albert Speer: Die Kransberg-Protokolle*, pp. 197 and 287.
90. Bundesarchiv, R3/1739, Part II, p. 109; Rolf-Dieter Müller, DRZW, 5/2, p. 762.
91. Bundesarchiv, R3/1739, Part II, p. 127.
92. Haspel had been demoted at Daimler-Benz in 1935 because of complaints from the NSDAP about his 'half-Jewish' wife. He gradually worked his way back to the top.
93. Schlie (ed.), *Albert Speer: Die Kransberg-Protokolle*, p. 403.
94. Bundesarchiv, R3/1739, Part II, p. 130.
95. Janssen, *Das Ministerium Speer*, p. 286.
96. See Eichholtz, *Geschichte der deutschen Kriegswirtschaft*, vol. 3/2, p. 631, for a detailed list.

Chapter 11: Defeat

1. Bundesarchiv, R3/1739, Part II, pp. 112ff.
2. The Me 163 was a revolutionary design capable of flying at up to 698mph. 300 were built but they only had 9 'kills'. The cockpit was unpressurised, limiting the ceiling to the pilots' ability to remain conscious and obliging them to have low-fibre diets to avoid the expansion of gastrointestinal gas upon descent.
3. Willi A. Boelcke (ed.), *Deutschlands Rüstung im Zweiten Weltkrieg: Hitlers Konferenzen mit Albert Speer 1942–1945*, Frankfurt, 1969, p. 444.
4. Gregor Janssen, *Das Ministerium Speer: Deutschlands Rüstung im Krieg*, Berlin, 1968, p. 297.
5. *Kriegstagebuch des Oberkommandos*, vol. 3/2, *1. Januar bis 31. Dezember 1943*, ed. Walther Hubatsch, Frankfurt, 1963, p. 1159.
6. Michael Hepp, 'Fälschung und Wahrheit: Albert Speer und "Der Sklavenstaat" ', *Mitteilungen der Dokumentationsstelle zur NS-Sozialpolitik*, vol. 1, no. 3 (1985), p. 26.
7. Rolf-Dieter Müller, 'Endkampf im Reichsgebiet? Die Bedeutung der Oderlinie im Frühjahr 1945', in Werner Künzel and Richard Lakowski (eds), *Niederlage – Sieg – Neubeginn: Frühjahr 1945*, Potsdam, 2005.
8. Albert Speer, *Erinnerungen*, Berlin, 1969, p. 430.
9. Rolf-Dieter Müller, DRZW, 10/2, p. 111.
10. Heinz J. Nowarra, *Die Deutsche Luftrüstung 1933–1945*, Coblenz, 1993. Michel Ellenbogen, *Gigantische Visionen. Architektur und Hochtechnologie im Nationalsozialismus*, Graz, 2006, pp. 147–92. Among such projects were the Heinkel He 274 heavy bomber and the jet-propelled bomber He 343.
11. Boelcke (ed.), *Deutschlands Rüstung im Zweiten Weltkrieg*, p. 468.
12. Rolf Wagenführ, *Die deutsche Industrie im Kriege 1939–1945*, Berlin, 1954, pp. 116f.
13. Ibid.
14. Dietrich Eichholtz, *Geschichte der deutschen Kriegswirtschaft 1939–1945*, 5 vols, Munich, 2003, vol. 3/2, p. 616.
15. Wolfgang Bleyer, *Staat und Monopole im totalen Krieg: Staatsmonopolistische Machtapparat und die 'totale Mobilisierung' im ersten Halbjahr 1943*, Berlin, 1970, p. 17.

16. Janssen, *Das Ministerium Speer*, p. 291.
17. Ulrich Schlie (ed.), *Albert Speer: Die Kransberg-Protokolle 1945: Seine ersten Aussagen und Aufzeichnungen (Juni–September)*, Munich, 2003, p. 407.
18. Eichholtz, *Geschichte der deutschen Kriegswirtschaft*, vol. 3/2, p. 624.
19. Janssen, *Das Ministerium Speer*, p. 296.
20. Bundesarchiv, R3/1743, p. 69.
21. Willi A. Boelcke, 'Hitlers Befehle zur Zestörung oder Lähmung des deutschen Industriepotentials 1944/45', *Tradition: Zeitschrift für Firmengeschichte und Unternehmerbiographie*, vol. 13, no. 6 (1968), pp. 301–16.
22. Boelcke (ed.), *Deutschlands Rüstung im Zweiten Weltkrieg*, p. 402.
23. Janssen, *Das Ministerium Speer*, p. 304.
24. Ibid., pp. 305ff.
25. Rüdiger Overmans, 'Die Kriegsgefangenenpolitik des Deutschen Reiches' in Jörg Echternkamp (ed.), *Das Deutsche Reich und der Zweite Weltkrieg*, vol. 9/2, Stuttgart, 2005, pp. 825–34; Gerhard Schreiber, *Die italienischen Militärinternierten im deutschen Machtbereich 1943–1945: verraten – verachtet – vergessen*, Munich, 1990. Their fate is the subject of Lina Wertmüller's black comedy 'Seven Beauties' (1975).
26. Janssen, *Das Ministerium Speer*, p. 253.
27. *Kriegstagebuch des Oberkommandos*, vol. 3/2, p. 1386.
28. Six Armaments Plenipotentiaries with responsibility for between five and eight Party Districts (*Gaue*) had only recently been created. The system worked very well. Speer deeply regretted that he had not thought of the idea earlier (Bundesarchiv, R3/1623a, p. 18).
29. Speer, *Erinnerungen*, p. 426. This headquarters was known as the Eagle's Nest or *Adlerhorst*.
30. Ibid., pp. 426f.
31. Duquesne University, Gumberg Library Digital Collections, Mussmano Collection: Interview of Speer at 'Dustbin' by Mr O. Hoeffding, Economic and Financial Branch FIAT (US), 1 August 1945.
32. Speer, *Erinnerungen*, p. 427.
33. Albert Speer, *Der Sklavenstaat. Meine Aufeinandersetzungen mit der SS*, Berlin, 1981, p. 188.
34. Boelcke (ed.), *Deutschlands Rüstung im Zweiten Weltkrieg*, p. 466.
35. Ibid., p. 460. The rocket launchers were known as *Nebelwerfer* (fog launchers) to fool enemy intelligence into thinking this was a device to create smokescreens.
36. A fierce debate followed between Marshal Chuikov, who argued that Berlin could have been taken and Marshal Zhukov, who insisted that his decision to halt the offensive on 31 January was correct. See Antony Beevor, *Berlin: The Downfall 1945*, London, 2002, and Christopher Duffy, *Red Storm on the Reich: The Soviet March on Germany, 1945*, London, 1993.
37. Peter Longerich, *Goebbels: Biographie*, Munich, 2010, p. 657.
38. Speer ignored the January 1944 imports, so that he claimed that in January 1945 coal supplies were 51.7 per cent of the previous year's amount.
39. Janssen, *Das Ministerium Speer*, pp. 301f.
40. Bundesarchiv, R3/1535, pp. 4f.
41. Ibid., R3/1623a, p. 2.
42. OKW issued detailed instructions for dispersal, removal, deactivation and destruction (*ARLZ-Maßnahmen: Auflockerung, Räumung, Lähmung und Zerstörung*): ibid.
43. Speer, order drafted by Hupfauer, 25 January 1945, ibid., R3/1623a, pp. 10f.
44. Rolf-Dieter Müller, DRZW, 10/2, p. 82.
45. According to Speer's testimony at Nuremberg, Hitler threatened to charge him with treason. This is unlikely. *Trial of the Major War Criminals before the International Military Tribunal, 'Blue Series'*, 42 vols, Nuremberg, 1947–9, vol. 16, p. 541.
46. Speer, *Erinnerungen*, p. 432.
47. Bundesarchiv, R3/1623a, p. 18.
48. Boelcke (ed.), *Deutschlands Rüstung im Zweiten Weltkrieg*, pp. 468ff.
49. Rolf-Dieter Müller, DRZW, 10/2, p. 82.
50. Ibid., p. 6.
51. *Kriegstagebuch des Oberkommandos*, vol. 3/2, p. 1323.
52. Ibid., p. 1116; Bundesarchiv, R3/1623a, p. 28.
53. Bundesarchiv, R3/1623a, p. 41.
54. Speer, *Erinnerungen*, pp. 442f.
55. Eichholtz, *Geschichte der deutschen Kriegswirtschaft*, vol. 3/2, pp. 660f.
56. Heinrich Schwendemann, '"Drastic Measures to Defend the Reich at the Oder and the Rhine . . .": A Forgotten Memorandum of Albert Speer of 18 March 1945', *Journal of Contemporary History*, vol. 38, no. 4 (October 2003), pp. 597–614. It is not quite forgotten. See Janssen, *Das Ministerium Speer*,

400 NOTES to pp. 263–275

p. 311, and Eichholtz, *Geschichte der deutschen Kriegswirtschaft*, vol. 3/2, p. 662, note 212, also Bundesarchiv, R3/1537, memorandum 18 March 1945.

57. This point of view is well described by Dönitz's adjutant: Walter Lüdde-Neurath, *Regierung Dönitz: Die letzten Tage des Dritten Reiches*, Göttingen, 1964, p. 24. Also in Joseph Goebbels, *Die Tagebücher von Joseph Goebbels*, ed. Elke Fröhlich, Part II, *Diktate 1941–1945*, vol. 15, *Januar–April 1945*, ed. Maximillan Gschaid, Munich, 1995, p. 572.

58. *Trial of the Major War Criminals before the International Military Tribunal*, 'Blue Series', 42 vols, Nuremberg, 1947–9, vol. 41, p. 520.

59. Longerich, *Goebbels*, p. 666.

60. Rolf-Dieter Müller, XRZW, 10/2, p. 80.

61. Speer, *Erinnerungen*, pp. 431f.

62. Goebbels, *Die Tagebücher*, Part II, vol. 15, entry of 15 March 1945.

63. Rolf-Dieter Müller, XRZW, 10/2, p. 118.

64. Speer, *Erinnerungen*, pp. 442ff.

65. Bundesarchiv, R3/1623a, p. 46; Eichholtz, *Geschichte der deutschen Kriegswirtschaft*, vol. 3/2, p. 663.

66. Bundesarchiv, R3/1623a, p. 50.

67. Eichholtz, *Geschichte der deutschen Kriegswirtschaft*, vol. 3/2, p. 664; Speer, *Erinnerungen*, p. 448.

68. Longerich, *Goebbels*, pp. 666f.

69. Wagner, a bestial anti-Semite who terrorised Alsace during the occupation, was executed in August 1946. His wife was sent to a brothel in Paris where, having been repeatedly raped, she committed suicide: Jean-Laurent Vonau, *Le Gauleiter Robert Wagner: Le Bourreau de l'Alsace*, Strasbourg, 2011.

70. Bundesarchiv, R3/1623a, pp. 52ff.

71. Speer, *Erinnerungen*, p. 454.

72. Eichholtz, *Geschichte der deutschen Kriegswirtschaft*, vol. 3/2, p. 665; Speer, *Sklavenstaat*, p. 298.

73. Goebbels, *Die Tagebücher*, Part II, vol. 15, entry of 28 March 1945.

74. *Kriegstagebuch des Oberkommandos*, vol. 3/2, pp. 1581ff. The original is in the Bundesarchiv, R3/1538.

75. Eichholtz, *Geschichte der deutschen Kriegswirtschaft*, vol. 3/2, p. 666.

76. Speer, *Erinnerungen*, pp. 457ff.

77. Speer, *Erinnerungen*, p. 462.

78. Bundesarchiv, R3/1623a.

79. Ibid., pp. 75f.

80. *Kriegstagebuch des Oberkommandos*, vol. 4/2, *1. Januar 1944 bis 22. Mai 1945*, ed. Percy Ernst Schramm, Frankfurt, 1961, p. 1212.

81. Bundesarchiv, R3/1623a, pp. 108ff. Uiberreither survived under an assumed name, contracted Alzheimer's, and died in 1984, aged seventy-six.

82. Ibid., p. 144.

83. Ibid., p. 165.

84. Ibid., p. 183.

85. Ibid., p. 189.

86. Ibid., p. 123.

87. Heinrich Breloer, *Unterwegs zur Familie Speer: Begegnungen, Gespräche, Interviews*, Berlin, 2005, p. 63. While in Spandau Speer wrote a long letter to his daughter Hilde claiming to have saved western Germany from Soviet domination.

88. IMG vols 16 and 41 as well as in Speer's *Erinnerungen*.

89. Heinrich Breloer and Rainer Zimmer, *Die Akte Speer: Spuren eines Kriegsverbrechers*, Berlin, 2006, p. 316.

90. Michael Hepp, 'Fälschung und Wahrheit: Albert Speer und "Der Sklavenstaat"', *Mitteilungen der Dokumentationsstelle zur NS-Sozialpolitik*, vol. 1, no. 3 (1985), p. 29.

91. Speer, *Erinnerungen*, p. 356.

92. Manfred Messerschmidt, 'Generalfeldmarschall Models letztes Gefecht', *Die Zeit*, vol. 14, 31 March 2005.

93. Breloer and Zimmer, *Die Akte Speer*, p. 308.

94. Gitta Sereny, *Albert Speer: His Battle With Truth*, London, 1995, p. 507.

95. Heinrich Schwendemann, 'Strategie der Selbstvernichtung: Die Wehrmachtführung im "Endkampf" um das "Dritte Reich"', in Rolf-Dieter Müller and Hans-Erich Volkmann (eds), *Die Wehrmacht: Mythos und Realität*, Munich, 1999, pp. 232ff.

96. Speer, *Sklavenstaat*, p. 316f.

97. Ian Kershaw, *The End: The Defiance and Destruction of Hitler's Germany, 1944–1945*, London, 2011, p. 311.

98. Dietmar Arnold, *Neue Reichskanzlei und 'Führerbunker': Legenden und Wirklichkeit*, Berlin, 2005, p. 150. This sum would be roughly 480,000 dollars today. The GBI had 9 million Reichsmarks on hand on 19 April 1944. This vanished in the last stages of the war.

99. Kershaw, *The End*, pp. 204 and 311. For Karl Dönitz's version see his *10 Jahre und 20 Tage*, Bonn, 1958, and *Mein wechselvolles Leben*, Göttingen, 1968.

100. Marlis G. Steinert, *Die 23 Tage der Regierung Dönitz: Die Agonie des Dritten Reiches*, Munich, 1982, p. 140. Hugh Trevor-Roper, in *The Last Days of Hitler*, London, 1947, p. 106, describes Krosigk as a 'ninny'; but this is an example of Lord Dacre in his less than charitable mode.

101. Joachim Fest, *Die unbeantwortbaren Fragen: Notizen über Gespräche mit Albert Speer zwischen Ende 1966 und 1981*, Reinbek bei Hamburg, 2006, p. 10.

102. Speer, *Erinnerungen*, p. 289.

103. Fest, *Die unbeantwortbaren Fragen*, p. 44.

104. See ibid., pp. 106ff., for Speer's musings to this effect.

105. In his memoirs Speer says the opposite. He claims to have said to his adjutant, Manfred von Poser: 'Thank God, I won't have to play the role of Prince Max von Baden.' This, as so much else in the memoirs, can be taken with more than a grain of salt. *Erinnerungen*, p. 488.

106. Jürgen Thorwald, *Das Ende an der Elbe*, Stuttgart, 1952, pp. 330f.

107. Fest, *Die unbeantwortbaren Fragen*, p. 183.

108. See Heike B. Görtemaker, *Eva Braun: Leben mit Hitler*, Munich, 2010, for a reassessment of Eva Braun's influence as a key to access to Hitler.

109. Speer, *Erinnerungen*, p. 482ff.

110. Speer asks us to believe that this meeting with Himmler was 'on impulse'. Sereny, *Albert Speer*, pp. 534f.

111. Speer, *Erinnerungen*, p. 489.

112. Steinert, *Die 23 Tage der Regierung Dönitz*, p. 141.

113. Janssen, *Das Ministerium Speer*, p. 320.

114. Steinert, *Die 23 Tage der Regierung Dönitz*, p. 87.

115. Ibid., p. 165.

116. Ibid., p. 166.

117. Ibid., p. 179.

118. Kershaw, *The End*, p. 377.

119. *Kriegstagebuch des Oberkommandos*, vol. 3/2, p. 1475.

120. Bundesarchiv, R3/1624.

121. John Kenneth Galbraith, *A Life in our Times*, Boston, 1981, p. 207.

122. Paul H. Nitze, *From Hiroshima to Glasnost: At the Centre of Decision – a Memoir*, London, 1990, p. 33.

123. Margret Nissen (with Margrit Knapp and Sabine Seifert), *Sind Sie die Tochter Speer?*, Munich, 2005. Susanne von Beyer, Vater und Verbrecher', *Der Spiegel*, 31.01.2005.

124. Most of the other major war criminals were held at 'Camp Ashcan': John Kenneth Galbraith, 'The "Cure" at Mondorf Spa', *Life*, 22 October 1945.

Chapter 12: Nuremberg

1. Joachim Fest, *Speer: Eine Biographie*, Berlin, 1999, p. 383.

2. Ulrich Schlie (ed.), *Albert Speer: Die Kransberg-Protokolle 1945: Seine ersten Aussagen und Aufzeichnungen (Juni–September)*, Munich, 2003.

3. Ibid., p. 135.

4. Fest, *Speer*, p. 384.

5. Schlie, *Albert Speer: Die Kransberg-Protokolle*, p. 206.

6. Matthias Schmidt, *Albert Speer – Das Ende eines Mythos: Speers wahre Rolle im Dritten Reich*, Munich, 1982, p. 174.

7. Hans Kehrl, *Krisenmanager im Dritten Reich*, 2nd edn, Frankfurt, 2007, p. 435.

8. Albert Speer, *Erinnerungen*, Berlin, 1969, p. 507. Twenty-four were indicted; but Bormann was tried in absentia, Ley committed suicide before the trial began and Gustav Krupp von Bohlen und Halbach was too sick to stand trial.

9. Speer, *Erinnerungen*, p. 508.

10. Kehrl, *Krisenmanager*, p. 435.

11. Ball was fond of quoting Ian Fleming's adage 'nothing propinks like propinquity'. Nowhere was this truer than in the Third Reich.

12. J.K. Galbraith, *A Contemporary Guide to Economics, Peace and Laughter*, Boston, 1972; Gitta Sereny, *Albert Speer: His Battle With Truth*, London, 1995, p. 559.

13. Sereny, *Albert Speer,* p. 561.
14. Duquesne University, Gumberg Library Digital Collections, Mussmano Collection: Interview of Speer at 'Dustbin' by Mr O. Hoeffding, Economic and Financial Branch FIAT (US), 1 August 1945, p. 49.
15. Heinrich Breloer, *Unterwegs zur Familie Speer: Begegnungen, Gespräche, Interviews,* Berlin, 2005, p. 354; Richard W. Sonnenfeldt, *Mehr als ein Leben,* Bern, 2003, and *Witness to Nuremberg,* New York, 2006.
16. Speer, *Erinnerungen,* p. 514.
17. Ibid., p. 278. During the Weimar Republic he had defended Göring against a charge of possessing illegal drugs.
18. Schmidt, *Albert Speer,* p.176.
19. *Trial of the Major War Criminals before the International Military Tribunal, 'Blue Series',* 42 vols, Nuremberg, 1947–9 [IMT] vol. 16, p. 616.
20. Jack El-Hai, 'The Nazi and the Psychiatrist', *Scientific American Mind,* January/February 2011.
21. Werner Maser, *Nürnberg: Tribunal der Sieger,* Düsseldorf, 1977, p. 386.
22. Sereny, *Albert Speer,* pp. 584f.; Adelbert Reif, *Albert Speer: Kontroversen um ein deutsches Phänomen,* Munich, 1978, pp. 224f. Maser, *Nürnberg,* claims that Speer wrote directly to Jackson. There is no evidence that this was the case.
23. David Irving, *Der Nürnberger Prozess: Die letzte Schlacht,* Munich, 1979, p. 92.
24. Reif, *Albert Speer,* pp. 223–30.
25. Albert Speer, *Welt am Sonntag,* 31 October 1976.
26. Fisher was assistant to the U.S. Attorney General Francis Biddle.
27. The charges are reprinted in Reif, *Albert Speer,* pp. 22ff.
28. International Military Tribunal (IMT), vol. 16, p. 430.
29. Ibid., p. 433.
30. Ibid., p. 440.
31. Ibid., p. 444.
32. Mauthausen was the only camp in Greater Germany that had its own gas chambers. 119,000 men, women and children were murdered there between 1938 and 1945. See Gordon J. Horwitz, *In the Shadow of Death: Living Outside the Gates of Mauthausen,* New York, 1990.
33. IMT, vol. 16, p. 446.
34. For the the the day's proceedings see ibid., pp. 447ff.
35. Ibid., p. 452.
36. Ibid., p. 456.
37. Ibid., p. 463.
38. Ibid., p. 470.
39. Ibid., p. 474.
40. Ibid., p. 482.
41. Ibid., p. 483. The English translation of *Gesamtverantwortung,* 'total responsibility', is too strong.
42. Ibid., p. 493. Schmidt, *Albert Speer,* p. 190.
43. Speer, *Erinnerungen,* p. 519.
44. IMT, vol. 4, p. 343.
45. G.M. Gilbert, *Nuremberg Diary,* New York, 1947, p. 102.
46. Ibid., p. 103.
47. Ibid., p. 105.
48. IMT, vol. 16, p. 531.
49. IMT, vol. 16, p. 543.
50. Speer, *Erinnerungen,* p. 519.
51. This prompted Giesler to write to the publisher of Speer's memoirs on 22 November 1970 pointing out that it was difficult to believe that 'the second most important man in the country could not get a ladder': Fest, *Speer,* p. 334.
52. Breloer, *Unterwegs zur Familie Speer,* pp. 141ff., based on the testimony of Dietmar Arnold, an engineer and expert on Hitler's bunker. See Dietmar Arnold, *Neue Reichskanzlei und 'Führerbunker': Legenden und Wirklichkeit,* Berlin, 2005.
53. Breloer, *Unterwegs zur Familie Speer,* p. 328.
54. Arnold, *Neue Reichskanzlei und Führerbunker,* p. 128. The company Drägerwerk AG of Lübeck, founded in 1889, still exists. It specialises in medical ventilators, gas detection and diving equipment.
55. IMT, vol. 16, p. 583.
56. Gilbert, *Nuremberg Diary,* p. 103.
57. John Kenneth Galbraith, *A Life in our Times,* Boston, 1981, p. 212.

58. Statement made during cross-examination by US authorities on 4 July 1945, in Schmidt, *Albert Speer*, p. 187.
59. This speech was given in Munich on 24 February 1942 at a meeting of Gauleiters and Reichsleiters: ibid., p. 189.
60. IMT, vol. 16, p. 479.
61. Ibid., p. 518.
62. IMT, vol. 15, p. 139.
63. IMT, vol. 16, p. 558.
64. IMT, vol. 16, p. 543.
65. Ibid.
66. Ibid., p. 566.
67. Ibid., p. 573.
68. Servatius, who served as a frontline officer throughout the entire war, also defended Dr Karl Brandt, Paul Pleiger and Adolf Eichmann.
69. IMT, vol. 19, p. 177.
70. Ibid., p. 180.
71. Ibid., p. 183.
72. Ibid., p. 188.
73. Ibid., p. 191.
74. Ibid., p. 197.
75. Ibid., p. 206.
76. Ibid., p. 207.
77. IMT, vol. 16, p. 487.
78. IMT, vol. 19, p. 208.
79. Ibid., p. 210.
80. Ibid., p. 211.
81. Ibid., p. 213.
82. C. Banning, 'Food Shortage and Public Health, First Half of 1945', *Annals of the American Academy of Political and Social Science*, vol. 245, *The Netherlands during German Occupation* (May 1946), pp. 93–110.
83. IMT, vol. 19, p. 216.
84. Ibid., p. 524.
85. Ibid., p. 543.
86. Ibid., p. 557.
87. Ibid., p. 573.
88. IMT, vol. 20, pp. 6ff.
89. Ibid., p. 7.
90. Bradley F. Smith, *Reaching Judgment at Nuremberg*, New York, 1977, pp. 218ff.
91. IMT, vol. 22, p. 253.
92. Ibid., p. 317.
93. Ibid., p. 362.
94. Speer, *Erinnerungen*, p. 522.
95. IMT, vol. 22, p. 407.
96. Albert Speer (ed. Adelbert Reif), *Technik und Macht*, Esslingen, 1979. It was never translated into English.
97. IMT, vol. 22, p. 407.
98. Smith, *Reaching Judgment at Nuremberg*, pp. 222f.
99. IMT, vol. 22, p. 487.
100. Ibid., p. 490.
101. Ibid., p. 504.
102. Ibid., pp. 576ff.
103. Smith, *Reaching Judgment at Nuremberg*, p. 209.
104. Speer, *Erinnerungen*, p. 524.
105. Airey Neave, *Nuremberg: A Personal Record of the Trial of the Major Nazi War Criminals in 1945–6*, London, 1978, pp. 133, 138, 144, 244 and 329.
106. Quoted in Speer, *Erinnerungen*, p. 356.
107. For a brilliant analysis of this type see Michael Wildt, *Generation des Unbedingten: Das Führungskorps des Reichssicherheitshauptamtes*, Hamburg, 2003. Speer's friend Dr Karl Brandt was also a typical example. See Ulf Schmidt, *Karl Brandt: The Nazi Doctor – Medicine and Power in the Third Reich*, London, 2007.
108. Breloer, *Unterwegs zur Familie Speer*, p. 7.
109. Speer, *Erinnerungen*, p. 272.

Chapter 13: Spandau

1. See the harrowing description of the life of a Spandau inmate who was a member of the Red Orchestra: Günther Weisenborn, *Memorial*, Berlin, 1962.
2. Leon Goldensohn, *The Nuremberg Interviews*, ed. Robert Gellately, New York, 2004, p. 17.
3. Albert Speer, *Spandauer Tagebücher*, Berlin, 1975, p. 42.
4. Ibid., p. 17.
5. Ibid., p.116. Actually Hitler's study would have measured 900 square metres.
6. Heinrich Breloer, *Unterwegs zur Familie Speer: Begegnungen, Gespräche, Interviews*, Berlin, 2005, p. 373
7. Albert Speer, *Spandauer Tagebücher*, Berlin, 1975.
8. Albert Speer, 'Die Bürde werde ich nicht mehr los' (interview), *Der Spiegel*, 7 November 1966.
9. Matthias Schmidt, *Albert Speer – Das Ende eines Mythos: Speers wahre Rolle im Dritten Reich*, Munich, 1982, p. 203.
10. Speer, *Spandauer Tagebücher*, p. 119.
11. Ibid., p. 120.
12. Ibid., p. 14. Schmidt, *Albert Speer*, p. 203.
13. Schmidt, *Albert Speer*, p. 205.
14. Ibid.
15. Gitta Sereny, *Albert Speer: His Battle With Truth*, London, 1995, pp. 641ff. In 1955, the year of this request, the average working-class family with two children had a gross income of 470 Deutschmarks per month.
16. Speer, *Spandauer Tagebücher*, p. 542.
17. Schmidt, *Albert Speer*, p. 206.
18. Breloer, *Unterwegs zur Familie Speer*, p. 411.
19. Ibid., p. 423.
20. Speer, *Spandauer Tagebücher*, p. 20.
21. Schmidt, *Albert Speer*, p. 206.
22. Sereny, *Albert Speer*, p. 649. There is no such wine. It must have been a Winkler Hasensprung. Probably the error springs from the difficulty of transcribing his minute handwriting. The Kuban caviar was undoubtedly Beluga.
23. Schmidt, *Albert Speer*, p. 209.
24. Speer, *Spandauer Tagebücher*, p. 229.
25. Ibid., p. 344.
26. Ibid., p. 346.
27. Ibid., p. 352.
28. Ibid., p. 356.
29. Ibid., p. 360.
30. Ibid., p. 535.
31. Ibid., p. 474.
32. Otto Kranzbühler, *Rückblick auf Nürnberg*, Hamburg, 1949; Norbert Frei, *Vergangenheitspolitik: Die Anfänge der Bundesrepublik und die NS-Vergangenheit*, Munich, 1996, pp. 163–7 and 248.
33. Speer, *Spandauer Tagebücher*, p. 53.
34. Schmidt, *Albert Speer*, p. 211.
35. Speer, *Spandauer Tagebücher*, pp. 282–4.
36. Ibid., p. 81.
37. Sereny, *Albert Speer*, pp. 634ff.
38. The letter is printed in full in Heinrich Breloer and Rainer Zimmer, *Die Akte Speer: Spuren eines Kriegsverbrechers*, Berlin, 2006, p. 378.
39. Speer wrote 'so gut wie gewusst'.
40. Speer, *Spandauer Tagebücher*, pp. 46f.
41. Ibid., p. 55.
42. Ibid., p. 83.
43. Ibid., pp. 81ff.
44. *Entnazifizierungsopfer* and *Entnazifizierungsgeschädigte* were popular words in post-war western Germany.
45. Ibid., p. 108.
46. Ibid., p. 98.
47. Ibid., p. 323.
48. *Jüdische Gleichmacherei*: ibid., p. 142.
49. Michael Foot wrote in 'Cato', *Guilty Men*, London, 1940, that to describe Sir John as 'the worst Foreign Minister since Ethelred the Unready' was unfair to the latter.

50. Speer, *Spandauer Tagebücher*, p. 610.
51. Ibid., p. 617.
52. Ibid., p.113. These designs closely resemble Osbert Lancaster's 'Stockbroker's Tudor': see his *Pillar to Post*, London, 1938.
53. Speer, *Spandauer Tagebücher*, p. 339.
54. Ibid. Speer overlooked the superb craftsmanship involved in the reconstruction and repair of many of Germany's historic buildings.
55. Ibid., p. 341.
56. Ibid., p. 353.
57. Ibid., p. 406.
58. Ibid., p. 169. *Inside the Third Reich* was published in the United States by Simon and Schuster, in Britain by Weidenfeld and Nicolson, both in 1970.
59. Ibid., p. 233.
60. Ibid., p. 582; Hans-Peter Schwarz, *Axel Springer: die Biographie*, Berlin, 2008.
61. Ibid., p. 654.
62. Ibid., p. 653; Hermann Esser, *Die jüdische Weltpest: Judendämmerung auf dem Erdball*, Munich, 1939. The book is basically a rehash of 'The Protocols of the Elders of Zion'.
63. Speer, *Spandauer Tagebücher*, p. 653.
64. Sereny, *Albert Speer*, p. 660. Bellergal was a curious choice. It is normally used to treat menopause symptoms.
65. Speer, *Spandauer Tagebücher*, p. 650.

Chapter 14: The Good Nazi

1. Albert Speer, *Spandauer Tagebücher*, Berlin, 1975, pp. 660ff.
2. Gitta Sereny, *Albert Speer: His Battle With Truth*, London, 1995, p. 665.
3. Ibid., p. 640.
4. Speer, *Spandauer Tagebücher*, p. 663.
5. Sereny, *Albert Speer*, p. 663.
6. Heinrich Breloer, *Unterwegs zur Familie Speer: Begegnungen, Gespräche, Interviews*, Berlin, 2005, p. 150.
7. Sereny, *Albert Speer*, p. 627.
8. Ibid., p. 635.
9. Ibid., p. 666.
10. Matthias Schmidt, *Albert Speer – Das Ende eines Mythos: Speers wahre Rolle im Dritten Reich*, Munich, 1982, pp. 16ff.
11. Rudolf Wolters, *Albert Speer*, Oldenburg, 1943.
12. Schmidt, *Albert Speer*, p. 19.
13. Gregor Janssen, *Das Ministerium Speer: Deutschlands Rüstung im Krieg*, Berlin, 1968; Schmidt, *Albert Speer*, p. 20.
14. Sereny, *Albert Speer*, p. 668.
15. Breloer, *Unterwegs zur Familie Speer*, p. 432.
16. Ibid., p. 401. Friedrich did not know the significance of '88' until Breloer explained it to him many years later.
17. Albert Speer, 'Die Bürde werde ich nicht mehr los' (interview), *Der Spiegel*, 7 November 1966.
18. Sereny, *Albert Speer*, p. 671.
19. Ibid., p. 679.
20. Joachim C. Fest, 'Albert Speer und die technizistische Unmoral' in *Das Gesicht des dritten Reiches: Profile einer totalitären Herrschaft*, Munich, 1963, pp. 271–85. This was published in English as 'Albert Speer and the Immorality of the Technicians', *The Face of the Third Reich: Portraits of the Nazi Leadership*, trans. Michael Bullock, London, 1970, pp. 299–314.
21. Joachim Fest, *Speer: Eine Biographie*, Berlin, 1999, p. 441.
22. G.M. Gilbert, *Nuremberg Diary*, New York, 1947, p. 122.
23. Günther Weisenborn, *Memorial*, Berlin, 1962, pp. 189f.
24. Speer, *Spandauer Tagebücher*, p. 216.
25. Ibid., p. 359.
26. Schmidt, *Albert Speer*, p. 21
27. Joachim C. Fest, 'Noch einmal: Abschied von der Geschichte – Polemische Überlegungen zur Entfremdung von Geschichtswissenschaft und Öffentlichkeit', in Joachim Fest, *Aufgehobene Vergangenheit: Portraits und Betrachtungen*, Munich, 1983. This diatribe was delivered to an appreciative audience of German industrialists in November 1977. Martin Broszat gave a reasoned

response in the *Frankfurter Allgemeine Zeitung*, 30 October 1978. Fest's contempt for the profession was such that in 2005 he described Heinrich Schwendemann, born in 1956, as an 'elderly historian'. Joachim Fest, *Die unbeantwortbaren Fragen: Notizen über Gespräche mit Albert Speer zwischen Ende 1966 und 1981*, Reinbek bei Hamburg, 2006, p. 12.

28. Fest, *Die unbeantwortbaren Fragen*, pp. 112ff.
29. Ulrich Schlie (ed.), *Albert Speer: Die Kransberg-Protokolle 1945: Seine ersten Aussagen und Aufzeichnungen (Juni–September)*, Munich, 2003, pp. 36ff.
30. Wolfgang Benz, 'Idealtypus Speer: Das patriotische Projekt des Duos Speer und Siedler', *Netzzeitung*, 27 May 2005. Siedler, Fest and Johannes Gross tweeked the evidence in a similar fashion with the memoirs of the political scientist Theodor Eschenburg, thereby disguising the murky past of a prominent public figure: Udo Wengst, *Theodor Eschenburg: Biographie einer politischen Leitfigur 1904–1999*, Berlin, 2005.
31. Markus Brechtken, 'Persuasive illusions of the Self: Albert Speer's Life Writing and Public Discourse about Germany's Nazi Past' in Birgit Dahlke, Dennis Tate and Roger Woods (eds), *German Life Writing in the Twentieth Century*, Rochester, NY, 2010, p. 75.
32. Fest, *Die unbeantwortbaren Fragen*, pp. 108f.
33. Ibid., pp. 128f.
34. Ibid., pp. 149f.
35. Sereny, *Albert Speer*, p. 680.
36. Matthias Schmidt, *Das Ende eines Mythos, Aufdeckung einer Geschichtsverfälschung*, Munich, 1985; Susanne Willems, *Der entsiedelte Jude: Albert Speers Wohnungsmarktpolitik für den Berliner Hauptstadtbau*, Berlin, 2002; Heinrich Breloer, *Speer und Er*, TV series, 3 parts, 270 minutes, 2004; Brechtken, 'Persuasive illusions of the Self', pp. 73ff.
37. Schmidt, *Albert Speer*, p. 23.
38. Fest, *Speer*, p. 444. An additional irony was that the meeting was on 19 November, *Buß- und Bettag*, the Protestant day of repentance.
39. Sereny, *Albert Speer*, pp. 683 and 685.
40. Fest, *Speer*, p. 444.
41. This was a version accepted by Erich Fromm in *The Anatomy of Human Destructiveness*, New York, 1973.
42. *Frankfurter Allgemeine Zeitung*, 19 March 1980.
43. Golo Mann, 'Des Teufels Architekt: Albert Speers Erinnerungen', *Süddeutsche Zeitung*, 20 and 21 September 1969.
44. Speer, *Spandauer Tagebücher*, p. 55.
45. Schmidt, *Albert Speer*, p. 25ff.
46. Sereny, *Albert Speer*, p. 12. Wolters died in January 1983, shortly after Schmidt published his book. Presumably he had made testamentary disposition of the typescript some time beforehand.
47. *Playboy*, June 1971, 69–96, 168–71,192–203.
48. Sereny, *Albert Speer*, p. 684.
49. Wolters to Giesler, 21 May 1971, quoted in Dan van der Vat, *Der gute Nazi: Leben und Lügen des Albert Speer*, Berlin, 1997, p. 552.
50. See Hannes Heer and Klaus Neumann (eds), *Vernichtungskrieg: Verbrechen der Wehrmacht 1941–1944*, Hamburg, 1995, for a contrary view.
51. See, for example, Jörg Friedrich, *Der Brand: Deutschland im Bombenkrieg 1940–1945*, Berlin, 2002, and A.C. Grayling, *Among the Dead Cities: The History and Moral Legacy of the WWII Bombing of Civilians in Germany and Japan*, London, 2007.
52. Sereny, *Albert Speer*, p. 678.
53. Wolters to Giesler, 21 May 1971, quoted in van der Vat, *Der gute Nazi*, p. 552.
54. Fest, *Speer*, p. 447.
55. Breloer, *Unterwegs zur Familie Speer*, p. 432.
56. Ibid., p. 109.
57. Albert (1934), Hilde (1936), Fritz (1937), Margret (1938), Adolf/Arnold (1940) and Ernst (1943).
58. Breloer, *Unterwegs zur Familie Speer*, p. 432.
59. Ibid., pp. 221f.
60. Margret Nissen (with Margrit Knapp and Sabine Seifert), *Sind Sie die Tochter Speer?*, Munich, 2005. Speer was highly successful in this endeavour. Karl-Günter Zelle, *Hitlers zweifelnde Elite: Goebbels – Göring – Himmler – Speer*, Paderborn, 2010, says that Speer was an 'enigma' and a 'doubter'. This was precisely the effect that Speer wanted to achieve in his memoirs.
61. Andrea Sinn, 'The Return of Rabbi Robert Raphael Geis to Germany: One of the Last Witnesses of Germany Jewry?', *European Judaism*, vol. 45, no. 2 (Autumn 2012), pp. 123–38.
62. Sereny, *Albert Speer*, p. 694.

63. Ibid., p. 697.
64. Father Athanasius OSB (Hermann Wolff, born 1931) as a Protestant convert and philosopher was an exceptionally open-minded and controversial figure. During a fatal illness he went through a severe crisis of faith, but died peacefully in 2013.
65. Sereny, *Albert Speer*, p. 701.
66. Ibid., p. 690.
67. Erich Goldhagen, 'Albert Speer, Himmler, and the Secrecy of the Final Solution', *Midstream* (October 1971), pp. 43–50. Erich Goldhagen is the father of Daniel Goldhagen, the author of *Hitler's Willing Executioners*.
68. Fest, *Die unbeantwortbaren Fragen*, pp. 160–4.
69. Sereny, *Albert Speer*, p. 393.
70. Ibid., pp. 706f.
71. Albert Speer, 'Antwort an Erich Goldhagen', in Adelbert Reif (ed.), *Albert Speer: Kontroversen um ein deutsches Phänomen*, Munich, 1978, pp. 395–403.
72. Himmler gave a speech at Posen on 4 October to ninety-two SS officers that lasted for three hours, in which he made brief mention of the 'eradication of the Jewish race'. Prince Reuss might well have been present at this speech at which Speer was definitely absent.
73. Heinrich Breloer and Rainer Zimmer, *Die Akte Speer: Spuren eines Kriegsverbrechers*, Berlin, 2006, pp. 397–404.
74. Sereny, *Albert Speer*, p. 398.
75. Albert Speer, 'Ein Nachtrag', in Adelbert Reif, *Albert Speer. Kontroversen um ein deutsches Phänomen*, Munich, 1978, pp. 404–7.
76. Michael Hepp, 'Fälschung und Wahrheit: Albert Speer und "Der Sklavenstaat"', *Mitteilungen der Dokumentationsstelle zur NS-Sozialpolitik*, vol. 1, no. 3 (1985), p. 9. Linge made a record of the day's visitors. It was not an appointments book in the normal sense of the term.
77. 'Zeitgeschichte: Brisanter Brieffund: Log Albert Speer?', *Die Presse*, 14 March 2007; Sven Felix Kellerhoff, 'Neuer Beleg für Speers Lügengebäude', *Die Welt*, 11 March 2007; Brechtken, 'Persuasive illusions of the Self', p. 76. The letter is partly reproduced and translated in <https://www.bonhams.com/auctions/15230/lot/621>
78. Sereny, *Albert Speer*, p. 678.
79. Breloer, *Unterwegs zur Familie Speer*, p. 574. See also Hans Mommsen, 'Spandauer Tagebücher: Bemerkungen zu den Aufzeichnungen Albert Speers im internationalen Militärgefängnis 1946–1966', *Politische Vierteljahresschrift*, vol. 17 (1976), pp. 8–14, and Karl-Heinz Ludwig, 'Die wohlreflektierten Erinnerungen des Albert Speer – einige kritische Bemerkungen zur Funktion des Architekten, des Ingenieurs und der Technik im Dritten Reich', *Geschichte in Wissenschaft und Unterricht*, vol. 21 (1970), pp. 695–708.
80. *Did Six Million Really Die* was eventually banned in Germany and South Africa. Zündel was eventually deported from Canada, where he had lived since 1958. In 2007 a German court sentenced him to five years' imprisonment for inciting hatred.
81. Fest, *Speer*, p. 450; Sereny, *Albert Speer*, p. 708. Sereny translates *Billigung* as 'tacit acceptance'. Were this the case Speer would have written *stillschweigende Billigung*. 'Acceptance' would also have been an accurate translation. This footnote is repeated in Albert Speer (ed. Adelbert Reif), *Technik und Macht*, Esslingen, 1979, p. 135.
82. Speer, *Erinnerungen*, pp. 160f.
83. See Breloer, *Die Akte Speer*, pp. 415–23 for the below.
84. In his study of Böcklin, Andree claims that the painting vanished in 1945. It had belonged to the great Anglo-Austrian collector and art historian Count Antoine Seilern, who sold it when he left Austria in 1939. Rolf Andree, *Arnold Böcklin: die Gemälde*, Basel and Munich, 1977, catalogue number 70.
85. They included Franz Karl Leo von Klenze, Eduard Schleich, Johann Jakob Frey, Gerhard Fries, Johann Wilhelm Schirmer and Rudolf Kuntz.
86. Stefan Koldehoff, 'Nazi-Gemälderaub: Kunst und Kriegsverbrecher', *Der Spiegel*, 3 September 2007.
87. Speer, *Technik und Macht*, pp. 66 and 70.
88. Ibid., pp. 25f.
89. Ibid., p. 20.
90. Ibid., pp. 29f.
91. Ibid., p. 157.
92. Ibid., p. 74. The term originates from Karl Marx, *Das Elend der Philosophie*, Stuttgart, 1885. He derived it from *idiotisme du métier* and *idiot savant*.
93. Ibid., pp. 77 and 105.
94. Ibid., p. 213.

95. Léon Krier, 'An Architecture of Desire' in *Albert Speer: Architecture 1932–1942*, ed. Léon Krier, Brussels, 1985. Krier helped form Prince Charles' views on architecture and disaffection with the modern.
96. Fest, *Speer*, pp. 452ff
97. Sereny, *Albert Speer*, p. 675.
98. He did this by placing an advertisement in the *Börsenblatt für den deutschen Buchhandel*, a weekly trade paper for publishers, booksellers and the interested public. It has a very modest circulation.
99. For example the work of Susanne Willems, Eckart Dietzfelbinger and Jens-Christian Wagner.
100. Breloer, *Unterwegs zur Familie Speer*, p. 432.
101. Fest, *Die unbeantwortbaren Fragen*, p. 253.
102. Ibid., pp. 257f.
103. Sereny, *Albert Speer*, p. 228.
104. Fest, *Die unbeantwortbaren Fragen*, p. 256.
105. Ibid., p. 712.
106. Sereny, *Albert Speer*, pp. 711ff.
107. Ibid., p.144.
108. For a full account see Nissen, *Sind Sie die Tochter Speer?*
109. Albert Speer, *Der Sklavenstaat. Meine Auseinandersetzungen mit der SS*, Berlin, 1981; translated as *Infiltration: How Heinrich Himmler Schemed to Build an SS Industrial Empire*, London, 1981.
110. Hepp, 'Fälschung und Wahrheit', pp. 1–69.
111. Rolf-Dieter Müller, *Das Deutsche Reich und der Zweite Weltkrieg*, vol. 5/2, Stuttgart, 1999, p. 408, note 335. For Egger see Karl Liedke, 'Hinzert, Auschwitz, Neuengamme', in Wolfgang Benz and Barbara Distel, *Der Ort des Terrors. Geschichte der nationalsozialistischen Konzentrationslager*, vol. 5 (*Hinzert, Auschwitz, Neuengamme*), Munich, 2007, p.357ff.
112. Speer, *Sklavenstaat*, pp. 163f.
113. Hepp, 'Fälschung und Wahrheit', p. 5.
114. Speer, *Sklavenstaat*, p. 407.
115. Ibid., pp. 272f. The Russian dandelion is also known as the Rubber Dandelion. It produces latex comparable to that of the rubber tree. Rubber from dandelions was not quite such a crackpot scheme as Speer and other writers claim. It was widely used in the Soviet Union from 1931 to 1950, with yields of up to 200 kilos of rubber per hectare, also in wartime Britain and the USA. See Susanne Donner, 'Gummi aus Löwenzahn: Von der Kriegsforschung zur neuen Biotechnologie', *Frankfurter Allgemeine Zeitung*, 5 May 2008.
116. Speer, *Sklavenstaat*, p. 62.
117. Hepp, 'Fälschung und Wahrheit', p. 25. Sommer received a death sentence in 1947. This was reduced to life imprisonment, then to twenty years. He was released from Landsberg in 1953.
118. Wilfred von Oven, *Finale Furioso: Mit Goebbels bis zum Ende*, Tübingen, 1974, pp. 490–5.
119. Speer, *Sklavenstaat*, p. 21.
120. Ibid., p. 66.
121. Ibid., pp. 19, 33 and 196.
122. Ibid., pp. 47, 29, 37 and 14.
123. Ibid., p. 37.
124. Ibid., pp. 81ff.
125. Speer, *Erinnerungen*, p. 383.
126. Speer, *Sklavenstaat*, p. 332.
127. Hepp, 'Fälschung und Wahrheit', p. 28.
128. David Irving, *Die Tragödie der deutschen Luftwaffe: Aus den Akten und Erinnerungen von Feldmarschall Milch*, Berlin, 1970, p. 389.
129. Speer, *Sklavenstaat*, pp. 92–4.
130. Ibid., p. 96.
131. Ibid., p. 11.
132. Ibid., p. 346.
133. Quoted above, pp. 373–4. The original of this letter is in Bundesarchiv, R3/1542. Schmidt, *Albert Speer*, pp. 226–7 reproduces this letter in full.
134. Schmidt, *Albert Speer*, p. 24.
135. Ibid., pp. 716f.
136. Fest, *Die unbeantwortbaren Fragen*, pp. 257f. 'Everybody's darling' is in English in the original.
137. Joachim Fest, *Speer: The Final Verdict*, New York, 1999, p. 2.
138. Florian Freund, Bertrand Perz and Karl Stuhlpfarrer, 'Der Bau des Vernichtungslagers Auschwitz-Birkenau: Die Aktenmappe der Zentralbauleitung Auschwitz "Vorhaben: Kriegsgefangenenlager Auschwitz (Durchführung der Sonderbehandlungen)" im Militärhistorischen Archiv Prag', *Zeitgeschichte*, vol. 20 (1993), pp. 187–213.

139. Richard Evans, 'The Deception of Albert Speer', *Times Literary Supplement*, 20 September 1995.
140. Breloer, *Speer und Er*, TV series.
141. Sven Felix Kellerhoff, 'Speer war kein unwissender Technokrat: Der Stand der Forschung', *Die Welt*, 10 May 2005; Susanne Willems, 'Er betrieb aktiv die Zerstörung jüdischer Existenzen', *Die Welt*, 12 April 2005; Brechtken, 'Persuasive illusions of the Self', pp. 82f.

Conclusion

1. Goethe, *Faust* Part II: 'Dem Tüchtigen ist diese Welt nicht stumm/Was braucht er in die Ewigkeit zu schweifen.'
2. Joachim Fest, Wolf Jobst Siedler and Frank A. Meyer, *Der lange Abschied vom Bürgertum*, Berlin, 2005, p. 100.
3. Joachim Fest, *Speer: Eine Biographie*, Berlin, 1999, p. 444.
4. Goethe, 'Maximen und Reflexionen', *Sämtliche Werke*, vol. 17, Munich, 1991, p. 758.
5. Miriam Pollard, *The Other Face of Love. Dialogues with the Prison Experience of Albert Speer*, New York, 1996.
6. Ibid., p. 54.
7. Ibid., p. 73.
8. Ibid., p. 77.
9. Yrsa von Leistner, *Große Begegnungen: Aus der Sicht einer Künstlerin*, Tübingen, 1986; Pollard, *The Other Face of Love*, p. 175.
10. Joachim Fest, *Die unbeantwortbaren Fragen: Notizen über Gespräche mit Albert Speer zwischen Ende 1966 und 1981*, Reinbek bei Hamburg, 2006, p. 9.
11. Klaus Wiegrefe, 'Der charmante Verbrecher', *Der Spiegel*, 2 May 2005.
12. Rolf Wagenführ, *Die deutsche Industrie im Kriege 1939-1945*, Berlin, 1954.
13. Ibid., p. 178.
14. Ibid., p. 125.
15. Jochen and Sabine Streb, 'Optimale Beschaffungsverträge bei asymmetrischer Informationsverteilung: Zur Erklärung des nationalsozialistischen "Rüstungswunders" während des Zweiten Weltkriegs', *Zeitschrift für Wirtschafts- und Sozialwissenschaften*, vol. 118 (1998), pp. 275-94. Adam Tooze, *The Wages of Destruction: The Making and Breaking of the Nazi Economy*, London, 2006, p. 565.
16. See Dietrich Eichholtz, *Geschichte der deutschen Kriegswirtschaft 1939-1945*, 5 vols, Munich, 2003, vol. 2/2, p. 564 for some examples.
17. Jonas Scherner and Jochen Streb, 'Das Ende eines Mythos? Albert Speer und das so genannte Rüstungswunder', *Vierteljahreshefte für Sozial- und Wirtschaftsgeschichte*, vol. 93 (2006), p. 190.
18. Jochen Streb and Sabine Streb, 'Optimale Beschaffungsverträge bei asymmetrischer Informationsverteilung: zur Erklärung des nationalsozialistischen "Rüstungswunders" während des Zweiten Weltkriegs', *Zeitschrift für Wirtschafts- und Sozialwissenschaften*, vol.118, 2, 1998, pp. 275-94.
19. Michael C. Schneider, *Unternehmerstrategien zwischen Weltwirtschaftskrise und Kriegswirtschaft: Chemnitzer Maschinenbauindustrie in der NS-Zeit 1933-1945*, Essen, 2005, pp. 473ff.
20. Streb, op. cit.
21. The speech is in the archives of the Ministry for Armaments, Bundesarchiv, R3/1547, pp. 42-5.
22. Neil Gregor, *Stern und Hakenkreuz: Daimler-Benz im Dritten Reich*, Berlin, 1997.
23. Gitta Sereny, *Albert Speer: His Battle With Truth*, London, 1995, p. 129.

BIBLIOGRAPHY

Bundesarchiv Berlin

Archives of the Ministry of Armaments

R3/1522
R3/1528
R3/1535
R3/1538
R3/1539
R3/1540
R3/1542
R3/1543
R3/1544
R3/1547
R3/1618
R3/1623a
R3/1624
R3/1629
R3/1694
R3/1699
R3/1737
R3/1739
R3/1740
R3/1742
R3/1744

Works by Albert Speer

Speer, Albert, 'Die Bauten des Führers', in *Bilder aus dem Leben des Führers*, Altona, 1936
Speer, Albert, *Die Neue Reichskanzlei*, Munich, n.d. (1940?)
Speer, Albert, 'Die Bürde werde ich nicht mehr los' (interview), *Der Spiegel*, 7 November 1966
Speer, Albert, *Erinnerungen*, Berlin, 1969
Speer, Albert, *Inside the Third Reich*, London, 1970
Speer, Albert, *Spandauer Tagebücher*, Berlin, 1975
Speer, Albert, *Spandau: The Secret Diaries*, New York, 1976
Speer, Albert, *Der Sklavenstaat. Meine Austeinandersetzungen mit der SS*, Berlin, 1981
Speer, Albert, *Infiltration: How Heinrich Himmler Schemed to Build an SS Industrial Empire*, London, 1981
Speer, Albert (ed. Adelbert Reif), *Technik und Macht*, Esslingen, 1979

Printed Sources

Abelshauser, Werner, 'Germany: guns, butter and economic miracles' in Mark Harrison (ed.), *The Economics of World War II: Six Great Powers in International Comparison*, Cambridge, 1998

Abelshauser, Werner, 'Kriegswirtschaft und Wirtschaftswunder: Deutschlands wirtschaftliche Mobilisierung für den Zweiten Weltkrieg und die Folgen für die Nachkriegszeit', *Vierteljahrshefte für Zeitgeschichte*, vol. 47 (1999), pp. 503–38

Abetz, Otto, *Das offene Problem: Ein Rückblick auf zwei Jahrzehnte deutscher Frankreichpolitik*, Cologne, 1951

Aly, Götz and Susanne Heim, 'Die Ökonomie der "Endlösung": Menschenvernichtung und wirtschaftliche Neuordnung, in Götz Aly (ed.), *Sozialpolitik und Judenvernichtung. Gibt es eine Ökonomie der Endlösung?* Berlin 1987, pp. 11–90

Aly, Götz (ed.), *Aktion T4 1939–1945: Die 'Euthanasie'-Zentrale in der Tiergartenstraße 4*, Berlin, 1989

Aly, Götz, *'Endlösung': Völkerverschiebung und der Mord an den europäischen Juden*, Frankfurt, 1995

Aly, Götz and Christian Gerlach, *Das letzte Kapitel, Der Mord an den ungarischen Juden*, Stuttgart, 2002

Aly, Götz, *Hitlers Volksstaat: Raub, Rassenkrieg und nationaler Sozialismus*, Frankfurt, 2005

Améry, Jean, 'Offener Brief an Herrn Ex-Minister Albert Speer', *Frankfurter Rundschau*, 14 October 1975

Anderson, Stanford, *Peter Behrens and a New Architecture for the Twentieth Century*, Boston, 2002

Andree, Rolf, *Arnold Böcklin: die Gemälde*, Basel and Munich, 1977

Anon., *Bauten der Bewegung*, Berlin, 1938

Arad, Yitzhak, *Belzec, Sobibor, Treblinka: The Operation Reinhard Death Camps*, Bloomington, 1986

Arndt, Karl, 'Architektur und Politik', in Albert Speer, *Architektur: Arbeiten 1933–1942*, Berlin, 1995, pp. 113–35

Arnold, Dietmar, *Neue Reichskanzlei und 'Führerbunker': Legenden und Wirklichkeit*, Berlin, 2005

Azéma, Jean-Pierre, *De Munich à la Libération, 1938–1944*, Paris, 1979

Bajohr, Frank, *Parvenus und Profiteure: Korruption in der NS-Zeit*, Frankfurt, 2001

Banning, C., 'Food Shortage and Public Health, First Half of 1945', *Annals of the American Academy of Political and Social Science*, vol. 245, *The Netherlands during German Occupation* (May 1946), pp. 93–110

Barkai, Avraham, *Nazi Economics: Ideology, Theory, and Policy*, New Haven, 1990

Barker, Nicolson, *Human Smoke: The Beginnings of World War II, the End of Civilization*, New York, 2008

Bartetzko, Dieter, 'Die Architekten', in Hans Sarkowicz (ed.), *Hitlers Künstler: Die Kultur im Dienst des Nationalsozialismus*, Frankfurt, 2004, pp. 110–34

Bartov, Omer, *Hitler's Army: Soldiers, Nazis and War in the Third Reich*, Oxford, 1991

Beevor, Antony, *Berlin: The Downfall 1945*, London, 2002

Benjamin, Walter, *Das Kunstwerk im Zeitalter seiner technischen Reproduzierbarkeit*, Frankfurt, 1963

Benz, Wolfgang, 'Idealtypus Speer: Das patriotische Projekt des Duos Speer und Siedler', *Netzeitung*, 27 May 2005

Benz, Wolfgang and Barbara Distel, *Der Ort des Terrors. Geschichte der nationalsozialistischen Konzentrationslager*, vol. 5 (*Hinzert, Auschwitz, Neuengamme*), Munich, 2007

Benz, Wigbert, *Der Hungerplan im 'Unternehmen Barbarossa' 1941*, Berlin, 2011

Besson, Waldemar, 'Wem diente Albert Speer?', *Die Zeit*, 10 October 1969

Birkenfeld, Wolfgang, *Der synthetische Treibstoff 1933–1945: Ein Beitrag zur nationalsozialistischen Wirtschafts- und Rüstungspolitik*, Göttingen, 1964

Birkenholz, Carl, *Die Betreuung der Bauarbeiter: Sozialpolitische Handbuch für die Bauwirtschaft*, Berlin, 1940

Birkenholz, Carl and Wolfgang Siebert, *Der ausländische Arbeiter in Deutschland: Sammlung und Erläuterungen der arbeits- und sozialrechtlichen Vorschriften über die Arbeitsverhältnisse nicht volksdeutschen Beschäftigter*, Mainz 1942

Blank, Ralf, *Ruhrschlacht: Das Ruhrgebiet im Kriegsjahr 1943*, Essen 2013

Bleyer, Wolfgang, *Staat und Monopole im totalen Krieg. Der staatsmonopolistische Machtapparat und die 'totale Mobilisierung' im ersten Halbjahr 1943*, Berlin, 1970

Boberach, Heinz (ed.), *Meldungen aus dem Reich: Die geheimen Lageberichte des Sicherheitsdienstes des SS 1938–1945*, 17 vols, Herrsching, 1984

Boelcke, W.A., 'Hitlers Befehle zur Zerstörung oder Lähmung des deutschen Industriepotentials 1944/45', *Tradition*, vol. 13, no. 6 (1968), pp. 301–16

Boelcke, Willi A. (ed.), *Deutschlands Rüstung im Zweiten Weltkrieg: Hitlers Konferenzen mit Albert Speer 1942–1945*, Frankfurt, 1969

Boelcke, Willi A., *Die deutsche Wirtschaft 1939–1945: Interna des Reichswirtschaftsministeriums*, Düsseldorf, 1983

Boelcke, Willi A., *Kriegspropaganda 1939–1941: Geheime Ministerkonferenzen im Reichspropagandaministerium*, Stuttgart, 1966

Boog, Horst, Gerhard Krebs and Detlef Vogel, *Das Deutsche Reich und der Zweite Weltkrieg*, vol. 7 (*Das Deutsche Reich in der Defensive: Strategischer Luftkrieg in Europa, Krieg im Westen und in Ostasien, 1943 bis 1944/45*), Stuttgart, 2001

Bormann, Norbert, *Paul Schultze-Naumburg: Maler, Publizist, Architekt, 1869–1949*, Essen, 1989

Bracher, Karl-Dietrich, 'Die Speer-Legende', in Adelbert Reif, *Albert Speer: Kontroversen um ein deutsches Phänomen*, Munich, 1978, pp. 408–10

Braun, Hans-Joachim, *The German Economy in the Twentieth Century*, London, 1990

Braunbuch – Kriegs- und Naziverbrecher in der Bundesrepublik und in West Berlin: Staat; Wirtschaft; Verwaltung; Armee; Justiz; Wissenschaft, East Berlin, 1968

Brechtken, Markus, 'Persuasive illusions of the Self: Albert Speer's Life Writing and Public Discourse about Germany's Nazi Past' in Birgit Dahlke, Dennis Tate and Roger Woods (eds), *German Life Writing in the Twentieth Century*, Rochester, NY, 2010, pp. 71–91

Breloer, Heinrich, and Rainer Zimmer, *Die Akte Speer: Spuren eines Kriegsverbrechers*, Berlin, 2006

Breloer, Heinrich, *Unterwegs zur Familie Speer: Begegnungen, Gespräche, Interviews*, Berlin, 2005

Brembeck, Reinhard J., 'Nazi-Dirigent oder Deserteur?', *Süddeutsche Zeitung*, 19 May 2010

Brenner, Hildegard, 'Die Kunst im politischen Machtkampf der Jahre 1933/34', *Vierteljahrshefte für Zeitgeschichte*, vol. 10, no. 1 (January 1962), pp. 17–42

Broszat, Martin, 'Abschied von der Geschichte', *Frankfurter Allgemeine Zeitung*, 30 October 1978

Brown, Eric Melrose, *Berühmte Flugzeuge der Luftwaffe 1939–1945*, Stuttgart, 1999

Buchheim, Christoph, 'Die Wirtschaftsentwicklung im Dritten Reich – mehr Desaster als Wunder: Eine Erwiderung auf Werner Abelshauser', *Vierteljahrshefte für Zeitgeschichte*, vol. 49 (2001), pp. 653–64

Buchheim, Christoph, 'Der Blitzkrieg, der keiner war', *Die Zeit*, 10 July 2007

Buchheit, Gert, *Hitler der Feldherr: Die Zerstörung einer Legende*, Rastatt, 1958

Budraß, Lutz, *Flugzeugindustrie und Luftrüstung in Deutschland 1918–1945*, Düsseldorf, 1998

Burrin, Philippe, *France under the Germans, Collaboration and Compromise*, New York, 1996

Bütow, Tobias and Franka Bindernagel, *Ein KZ in der Nachbarschaft: Das Magdeburger Außenlager der Brabag und der 'Freundeskreis Himmler'*, Cologne, 2004, pp. 77–111

Carroll, Berenice A., *Design for Total War: Arms and Economics in the Third Reich*, The Hague, 1968

'Cato' (Michael Foot, Peter Howard and Frank Owen), *Guilty Men*, London, 1940

Chapman, Michael and Michael Ostwald, 'Laying Siege to the Stadtkrone: Nietzsche, Taut and the vision of a Cultural Aristocracy', in John Macarthur and Antony Moulis (eds), *Additions to architectural history: XIXth annual conference of the Society of Architectural Historians, Australia and New Zealand*, Brisbane, 2002, available at <http://hdl.handle.net/1959.13/37963>

Conze, Eckart, Norbert Frei, Peter Hayes and Moshe Zimmermann, *Das Amt und die Vergangenheit: Deutsche Diplomaten im Dritten Reich und in der Bundesrepublik*, Munich, 2010

Darré, Walther, *Neuadel aus Blut und Boden*, Munich, 1930

Darré, Walther, *Das Schwein als Kriterium für nordische Völker und Semiten*, Munich, 1933

Diest, Wilhelm, Manfred Messerschmidt, Hans-Erich Volkman, Wolfram Welte, *Das Deutsche Reich und der Zweite Weltkrieg*, vol. 1, Stuttgart, 1979

Deist, Wilhelm, *The Wehrmacht and German Rearmament*, London, 1981

Dettmar, Werner, *Die Zerstörung Kassels im Oktober 1943*, Fuldabrück, 1983

Dittrich, Elke, *Ernst Sagebiel: Leben und Werk (1892–1970)*, Berlin, 2005

Donner, Susanne, 'Gummi aus Löwenzahn: Von der Kriegsforschung zur neuen Biotechnologie', *Frankfurter Allgemeine Zeitung*, 5 May 2008

Dönitz, Karl, *10 Jahre und 20 Tage*, Bonn, 1958

Dönitz, Karl, *Mein wechselvolles Leben*, Göttingen, 1968

Dressel, Joachim and Manfred Griehl, *Heinkel He 177-277-274: Eine luftfahrtgeschichtliche Dokumentation*, Stuttgart, 1989

Duffy, Christopher, *Red Storm on the Reich: The Soviet March on Germany, 1945*, London, 1993

Dülffer, Jost, *Hitler, Weimar und die Marine. Reichspolitik und Flottenbau 1920–1939*, Düsseldorf, 1973

Dülffer, Jost, Jochen Thies and Josef Henke, *Hitlers Städte: Baupolitik im Dritten Reich. Eine Dokumentation*, Cologne, 1978

Duquesne University, Gumberg Library Digital Collections, Mussmano Collection: Interview of Speer at 'Dustbin' by Mr O. Hoeffding, Economic and Financial Branch FIAT (US), 1 August 1945

Durth, Werner, *Deutsche Architekten: Biographische Verflechtungen 1900–1970*, Brauschweig and Wiesbaden, 1986

Durth, Werner, and Niels Gutschow, *Träume in Trümmern: Stadtplanung 1940–1950*, Munich, 1993

Eichholtz, Dietrich and Wolfgang Schumann (eds), *Anatomie des Krieges: Neue Dokumente über die Rolle des deutschen Monopolkapitals bei der Vorbereitung und Durchführung des Zweiten Weltkrieges*, Berlin, 1969

Eichholtz, Dietrich, 'Die Vorgeschichte des "Generalbevollmächtigten für den Arbeitseinsatz"', *Jahrbuch für Geschichte*, vol. 9 (1973), 339–83

Eichholtz, Dietrich, *Geschichte der deutschen Kriegswirtschaft 1939–1945*, 5 vols, Munich, 2003

El-Hai, Jack, 'The Nazi and the Psychiatrist', *Scientific American Mind*, January/February 2011

Ellenbogen, Michael, *Gigantische Visionen: Architektur und Hochtechnologie im Nationalsozialismus*, Graz, 2006

Evans, Richard, 'The Deception of Albert Speer', *Times Literary Supplement*, 20 September 1995

Feldman, Gerald D., *Army, Industry and Labour in Germany 1914–1918*, Princeton, 1966

Feldman, Gerald D., *Die Allianz und die deutsche Versicherungswirtschaft 1933–1945*, Munich, 2001

Fest, Joachim C., 'Albert Speer und die technizistische Unmoral' in *Das Gesicht des dritten Reiches: Profile einer totalitären Herrschaft*, Munich, 1963, pp. 271–85; translated by Michael Bullock as 'Albert Speer and the Immorality of the Technicians', *The Face of the Third Reich: Portraits of the Nazi Leadership*, London, 1970, pp. 299–314

Fest, Joachim C., 'Noch einmal: Abschied von der Geschichte – Polemische Überlegungen zur Entfremdung von Geschichtswissenschaft und Öffentlichkeit', in Joachim Fest, *Aufgehobene Vergangenheit: Portraits und Betrachtungen*, Munich, 1983

Fest, Joachim, *Speer: Eine Biographie*, Berlin, 1999

Fest, Joachim, *Speer: The Final Verdict*, New York, 1999

Fest, Joachim, *Die unbeantwortbaren Fragen: Gespräche mit Albert Speer*, Reinbek bei Hamburg, 2006

Fest, Joachim, Wolf Jobst Siedler and Frank A. Meyer, *Der lange Abschied vom Bürgertum*, Berlin, 2005

Fiss, Karen, *Grand Illusion: The Third Reich, the Paris Exposition, and the Cultural Seduction of France*, Chicago, 2009

Fornoff, Roger, *Die Sehnsucht nach dem Gesamtkunstwerk: Studien zu einer ästhetischen Konzeption der Moderne*, Hildesheim, 2004

Forstmeier, Friedrich and Hans-Erich Volkmann (eds), *Kriegswirtschaft und Rüstung 1939–1945*, Düsseldorf, 1977

François-Poncet, André, *Souvenirs d'une ambassade à Berlin, septembre 1931–octobre 1938*, Paris, 1947

Franklin, Noble, and Charles Webster, *The Strategic Air Offensive against Germany, 1939–1945*, 4 vols, London, 1961, vol. 2 (*Endeavour*)

Frei, Norbert, *Vergangenheitspolitik: Die Anfänge der Bundesrepublik und die NS-Vergangenheit*, Munich, 1996

Freund, Florian, Bertrand Perz and Karl Stuhlpfarrer, 'Der Bau des Vernichtungslagers Auschwitz-Birkenau: Die Aktenmappe der Zentralbauleitung Auschwitz "Vorhaben: Kriegsgefangenenlager Auschwitz (Durchführung der Sonderbehandlungen)" im Militärhistorischen Archiv Prag', *Zeitgeschichte*, vol. 20 (1993), pp. 187–214

Fried, Erich, 'Offener Brief an Jean Améry', *Frankfurter Rundschau*, 16 October 1975

Friedrich, Jörg, *Der Brand: Deutschland im Bombenkrieg 1940–1945*, Berlin, 2002

Fröbe, Rainer, 'Hans Kammler, Technokrat der Vernichtung', in Robert Smelser and Enrico Syring (eds), *Die SS: Elite unterm Totenkopf – 30 Lebensläufe*, Paderborn, 2000, pp. 305–19

Fromm, Erich, *The Anatomy of Human Destructiveness*, New York, 1973

Galbraith, John Kenneth, 'The "Cure" at Mondorf Spa', *Life*, 22 October 1945

Galbraith, John Kenneth, 'Germany Was Badly Run', *Fortune*, vol. 22 (December 1945), pp. 173–8 and 196–200

Galbraith, J.K., *A Contemporary Guide to Economics, Peace and Laughter*, Boston, 1972

Galbraith, John Kenneth, *A Life in our Times*, Boston, 1981

Galland, Adolf, *Die Ersten und die Letzten*, Munich, 1993

Gelderblom, Bernhard, *Die Reichserntedankfeste auf dem Bückeberg 1933–37*, Hameln, 1998

Gellately, Robert, *The Gestapo and German Society: Enforcing Racial Policy 1933–1945*, Oxford, 1991

George, Enno, *Die wirtschaftlichen Unternehmungen der SS*, Stuttgart, 1963

Gerlach, Christian, *Krieg, Ernährung, Völkermord: Forschungen zur Deutschen Vernichtungspolitik im Zweiten Weltkrieg*, Hamburg, 1998

Gerlach, Christian, *Kalkulierte Morde: die Deutsche Wirtschafts- und Vernichtungspolitik in Weißrussland 1941 bis 1944*, Hamburg, 1999

Giesler, Hermann, *Ein anderer Hitler: Bericht seines Architekten Hermann Giesler – Erlebnisse, Gespräche, Reflexionen*, Leoni am Starnberger See, 1978

Gilbert, G.M., *Nuremberg Diary*, New York, 1947

Gispen, Kees, *Poems in Steel: National Socialism and the Politics of Inventing from Weimar to Bonn*, New York, 2002

Goebbels, Joseph, *Die Tagebücher von Joseph Goebbels*, ed. Elke Fröhlich,
Part 1, *Aufzeichnungen 1923–1941*:
vol. 6, *August 1938–Juni 1939*, ed. Jana Richter, Munich, 1998

vol. 9, *Dezember 1940–Juli 1941*, ed. Elke Fröhlich, Munich, 1998
Part II, *Diktate 1941–1945*:
vol. 7, *Januar–März 1943*, ed Elke Fröhlich, Munich, 1993
vol. 15, *Januar–April 1945*, ed. Maximillan Gschaid, Munich, 1995
Goldensohn, Leon, *The Nuremberg Interviews*, ed. Robert Gellately, New York, 2004
Goldhagen, Erich, 'Albert Speer, Himmler, and the Secrecy of the Final Solution', *Midstream* (October 1971), pp. 43–50
Gordon, Robert J., Review of 'The Wages of Destruction: The Making and Breaking of the Nazi War Economy', *The Journal of Economic History*, vol. 69, no. 1 (March 2009), pp. 312–16
Görtemaker, Heike B., *Eva Braun: Leben mit Hitler*, Munich, 2010
Goschler, Constantin and Christian Hartmann (eds), *Hitler: Reden, Schriften, Anordnungen, Februar 1925–Januar 1933: Von der Reichstagswahl bis zur Reichstagspräsidentenwahl. Oktober 1930–März 1932*, vol. 4/1 (*Oktober 1930–Juni 1931*), Munich, 1997
Gottwaldt, Alfred and Diana Schulle, *'Juden ist die Benutzung von Speisewagen untersagt': Die antijüdische Politik des Reichsverkehrsministeriums zwischen 1933 und 1945*, Teetz, 2007
Grandt, Michael, *Unternehmen 'Wüste' – Hitlers letzte Hoffnung: Das NS-Ölschieferprogramm auf der Schwäbischen Alb*, Tübingen, 2002
Grayling, A.C., *Among the Dead Cities: The History and Moral Legacy of the WWII Bombing of Civilians in Germany and Japan*, London, 2007
Gregor, Neil, *Stern und Hakenkreuz: Daimler-Benz im Dritten Reich*, Berlin, 1997
Groehler, Olaf, *Bombenkrieg gegen Deutschland*, Berlin, 1991
Gruner, Wolf, *Judenverfolgung in Berlin 1933–1945: Eine Chronologie der Behördenmaßnahmen in der Reichshauptstadt*, Berlin, 1996
Günther, Sonja, *Design der Macht: Möbel für Repräsentanten des 'Dritten Reiches'*, Stuttgart, 1992
Hachtmann, Rüdiger, and Winfried Süß (eds), *Hitlers Kommissare: Sondergewalten in der nationalsozialistischen Diktatur*, Göttingen, 2006
Hamsher, William, *Albert Speer: Victim of Nuremberg?*, London, 1970
Hansen, Reimer, 'Der ungeklärte Fall Todt', *Geschichte in Wissenschaft und Unterricht*, vol. 18 (1967), pp. 604–5
Hardt, R.E., *Die Beine der Hohenzollern*, East Berlin, 1960
Hardtwig, Wolfgang, (ed.), *Utopie und politische Herrschaft im Europa der Zwischenkriegszeit*, Munich, 2003
Hayes, Peter, 'Polycracy and Policy in the Third Reich: The Case of the Economy', in Thomas Childers and Jane Caplan (eds), *Reevaluating the Third Reich*, New York, 1993, pp. 190–230
Heer, Hannes and Klaus Neumann (eds), *Vernichtungskrieg: Verbrechen der Wehrmacht 1941–1944*, Hamburg, 1995
Heiber, Helmut, 'Der Generalplan Ost', *Vierteljahrshefte für Zeitgeschichte*, vol. 6, no. 3 (1958), 281–325
Heim, Susanne and Götz Aly, 'Staatliche Ordnung und "organische Lösung": Die Rede Hermann Görings "Über die Judenfrage" vom 6. Dezember 1938', *Jahrbuch für Antisemitismusforschung*, vol. 2 (1993), pp. 378–405
Heinemann, Isabel, *Rasse, Siedlung, deutsches Blut: Das Rasse- und Siedlungshauptamt der SS und die rassenpolitische Neuordnung Europas*, Göttingen, 2003
Hellack, Georg, 'Architektur und Bildende Kunst als Mittel nationalsozialistischer Propaganda', *Publizistik*, vol. 5 (1960), pp. 77–95
Henderson, Neville, *Failure of a Mission, Berlin, 1937–39*, Toronto, 1940
Hepp, Michael, 'Fälschung und Wahrheit: Albert Speer und "Der Sklavenstaat"', *Mitteilungen der Dokumentationsstelle zur NS-Sozialpolitik*, vol. 1, no. 3 (1985), pp. 1–69
Herbert, Ulrich, *Fremdarbeiter: Politik und Praxis des 'Ausländer-Einsatzes' in der Kriegswirtschaft des Dritten Reiches*, Bonn, 1985
Herbert, Ulrich, 'Labour and Extermination: Economic Interests and the Primacy of *Weltanschauung* in National Socialism', *Past and Present*, vol. 138, no. 1 (1993), pp. 144–95
Herbert, Ulrich, Karin Orth and Christoph Dieckmann (eds), *Die Nationalsozialistischen Konzentrationslager: Entwicklung und Struktur*, 2 vols, vol. 1, Göttingen, 1998
Herbst, Ludolf, *Der Totale Krieg und die Ordnung der Wirtschaft: Die Kriegswirtschaft im Spannungsfeld von Politik, Ideologie und Propaganda 1939–1945*, Stuttgart, 1982
Herbst, Ludolf and Thomas Weihe (eds), *Die Commerzbank und die Juden*, Munich, 2004
Herding, Klaus and Hans-Ernst Mittig, *Kunst und Alltag in NS-System: Albert Speers Berliner Straßenlaternen*, Gießen, 1975
Herf, Jeffrey, 'The Engineer as Ideologue: Reactionary Modernists in Weimar and Nazi Germany', *Journal of Contemporary History*, vol. 19, no. 4 (October 1984), pp. 631–48

Herf, Jeffrey, *Reactionary Modernism: Technology, Culture and Politics in Weimar and the Third Reich*, Cambridge, 1984

Heusler, Andreas, Mark Spoerer and Helmuth Trischler (eds), *Rüstung, Kriegswirtschaft und Zwangsarbeit im 'Dritten Reich'*, Munich, 2010

Hilberg, Raul, *The Destruction of the European Jews*, New Haven, 1961

Hildebrandt, Klaus, *Vom Reich zum Weltreich: Hitler, NSDAP und koloniale Frage 1919–1945*, Munich, 1969

Hill, Dan, 'Senate House, University of London', *City of Sound*, 21 November 2003, at http://www.cityofsound.com/blog/2003/11/senate_house_un.html

Hinsley, F.H., E.E. Thomas, C.A.G. Simkins and C.F.G. Ransom, *British Intelligence in the Second World War: Its Influence on Strategy and Operations*, vol. 3, part 2, London, 1998

Hitler, Adolf, *Mein Kampf*, 123rd–124th edn, Munich, 1934

Hofmann, Werner, *Das Irdische Paradies: Motive und Ideen des 19. Jahrhunderts*, Munich, 1974

Homze, Edward L., *Foreign Labor in Nazi Germany*, Princeton, 1967

Horwitz, Gordon J., *In the Shadow of Death: Living Outside the Gates of Mauthausen*, New York, 1990.

Höschle, Gerd, *Die deutsche Textilindustrie zwischen 1933 und 1939: Staatsinterventionalismus und ökonomische Rationalität*, Stuttgart, 2004

Hossbach, Friedrich, *Zwischen Wehrmacht und Hitler 1934–1938*, Göttingen, 1965

Hüttenberger, Peter, *Die Gauleiter: Studie zum Wandel des Machtgefüges in der NSDAP*, Stuttgart, 1969

Irving, David, 'Unternehmen Armbrust: Der Kampf des britischen Geheimdienstes gegen Deutschlands Wunderwaffen', *Der Spiegel*, 17 November 1965

Irving, David, *The Mare's Nest*, New York, 1965

Irving, David, *Der Traum von der deutschen Atombombe*, Gütersloh, 1967

Irving, David, *Die Tragödie der deutschen Luftwaffe: Aus den Akten und Erinnerungen von Feldmarschall Milch*, Berlin, 1970

Irving, David, *Der Nürnberger Prozess: Die letzte Schlacht*, Munich, 1979

James, Harold, 'Innovation and Conservatism in Economic Recovery: The Alleged "Nazi Recovery" in the 1930s', in W.R. Garside (ed.), *Capitalism in Crisis. International Responses to the Great Depression*, London, 1993, pp. 70–96

Janssen, Gregor, *Das Ministerium Speer: Deutschlands Rüstung im Krieg*, Berlin, 1968

Jaskot, Paul B., 'Anti-Semitic Policy in Albert Speer's Plans for the Rebuilding of Berlin', *The Art Bulletin*, vol. 78, no. 4 (December 1996), pp. 622–32

Jaskot, Paul B., *The Architecture of Oppression: The SS, Forced Labor and the Nazi Monumental Building Economy*, London, 1999

Jenkins, Simon, 'It's time to knock down Hitler's headquarters and start again', *The Guardian*, 2 December 2005

Jones, Edgar, Robin Woolven, Bill Durodie and Simon Wessely, 'Public Panic and Morale: Second World War Civilian Responses Re-examined in the Light of the Current Anti-terrorist Campaign', *Journal of Risk Research*, vol. 9, no. 1 (January 2006), pp. 57–73

Kahn, Daniela, *Das Europa der Diktatur: Die Steuerung der Wirtschaft durch Recht im nationalsozialistischen Deutschland*, Frankfurt, 2006

Kaienburg, Hermann, *'Vernichtung durch Arbeit': Der Fall Neuengamme*, Bonn, 1990

Kaienburg, Hermann, *Die Wirtschaft der SS*, Berlin, 2003

Kater, Michael H., *Doctors Under Hitler*, Chapel Hill, 1989

Kedward, H. Roderick, *STO et Maquis dans La France des années noires*, vol. 2, Paris, 1993

Kehrl, Hans, 'Kriegswirtschaft und Rüstungsindustrie', in *Bilanz des Zweiten Weltkrieges: Erkenntnisse und Verpflichtungen für die Zukunft*, Oldenburg, 1953, pp. 267–85

Kehrl, Hans, 'Zum Untergang des Dritten Reiches', *Historische Tatsachen*, vol. 8, Vlotho, 1981

Kehrl, Hans, *Krisenmanager im Dritten Reich*, 2nd edn, Frankfurt, 2007

Kellerhoff, Sven Felix, 'Speer war kein unwissender Technokrat: Der Stand der Forschung', *Die Welt*, 10 May 2005

Kellerhoff, Sven Felix, 'Neuer Beleg für Speers Lügengebäude', *Die Welt*, 11 March 2007

Kempner, Robert M.W., 'In Spandau gab es keine Märtyrer', *Vorwärts*, 18 September 1975

Kershaw, Ian, *Hitler 1936–1945: Nemesis*, London, 2000

Kershaw, Ian, *The End: The Defiance and Destruction of Hitler's Germany, 1944–1945*, London, 2011

King, Benjamin and Timothy Kutta, *Impact: The History of Germany's V-Weapons in World War II*, New York, 2003

Klages, Ludwig, *Mensch und Erde*, Berlin, 1913

Klee, Ernst, *'Euthanasie' im NS-Staat: Die 'Vernichtung lebensunwerten Lebens'*, Frankfurt, 1983

Klee, Ernst, *Dokumente zur 'Euthanasie' im NS-Staat*, Frankfurt, 1985

Klee, Ernst, *Das Personenlexikon des Dritten Reich: Wer war was vor und nach 1945*, Frankfurt, 2003

Klee, Ernst *Das Kulturlexikon zum Dritten Reich: Wer war was vor und nach 1945*, Frankfurt, 2007
Klein, Burton H., *Germany's Economic Preparations for War*, Cambridge, MA, 1959
Klemann, Hein A.M., and Sergei Kudryashov, *Occupied Economies: An Economic History of Nazi-Occupied Europe, 1939–1945*, London, 2011
Knittel, Hartmut, 'Deutsche Kampfpanzerproduktion und Fertigungstechnik 1939–1945' in Roland G. Förster and Heinrich Walle (eds), *Militär und Technik: Wechselbeziehung zu Staat, Gesellschaft und Industrie im 19. und 20. Jahrhundert*, Herford and Bonn, 1992
Kogon, Eugen, 'Albert Speer und die politische Moral', *Frankfurter Hefte*, vol. 1, January 1976
Kohl, Peter and Peter Bessel, *Auto Union und Junkers: Geschichte der Mitteldeutschen Motorenwerke GmbH Taucha 1935–1948*, Stuttgart, 2003
Koldehoff, Stefan, 'Nazi-Gemälderaub: Kunst und Kriegsverbrecher', *Der Spiegel*, 3 September 2007
Kramer, Hilton, 'At the Bauhaus: the fate of art in "the Cathedral of Socialism"', *The New Criterion*, vol. 12, no. 7 (March 1994), pp. 4–10
Kramish, Arnold, *The Griffin: The Greatest Untold Espionage Story of World War II*, New York, 1986
Kranzbühler, Otto, *Rückblick auf Nürnberg*, Hamburg, 1949
Kriegstagebuch des Oberkommandos des OKW:
  vol. 1/1 and 1/2, *1. August 1940 bis 31. Dezember 1941*, ed. Hans-Adolf Jacobsen, Frankfurt, 1965
  vol. 2/1 and 2/2, *1. Januar bis 31. Dezember 1942*, ed. Andreas Hillgruber, Frankfurt, 1963
  vol. 3/1 and 3/2, *1. Januar bis 31. Dezember 1943*, ed. Walther Hubatsch, Frankfurt, 1963
  vol. 4/1 and 4/2, *1. Januar 1944 bis 22. Mai 1945*, ed. Percy Ernst Schramm, Frankfurt, 1961
Krier, Léon, 'An Architecture of Desire', *Albert Speer: Architecture 1932–1942*, ed. Léon Krier, Brussels, 1985
Kroener, Bernhard R., Rolf-Dieter Müller, Hans Umbreit, *Das Deutsche Reich und der Zweite Weltkrieg*, vol. 5/1, Stuttgart, 1988
Kroener, Bernhard R., Rolf-Dieter Müller, Hans Umbreit, *Das Deutsche Reich und der Zweite Weltkrieg*, vol. 5/2, Stuttgart, 1999
Kroener, Bernhard R., '"Menschenbewirtschaftung", Bevölkerungsverteilung und personelle Rüstung in der zweiten Kriegshälfte (1942–1944)', *Das Deutsche Reich und der Zweite Weltkrieg*, vol. 5/2, Stuttgart, 1999, pp. 777–1001
Kropp, Alexander, *Die politische Bedeutung der NS-Repräsentationsarchitektur: Die Neugestaltungspläne Albert Speers für den Umbau Berlins zur 'Welthauptstadt Germania' 1936–1942/43*, Neuried, 2005
Kupferman, Fred, *Le Procès de Vichy: Pucheu, Pétain, Laval*, Paris, 2006
Kwiet, Konrad, 'Nach dem Pogrom: Stufen der Ausgrenzung', in Wolfgang Benz (ed.), *Die Juden in Deutschland 1933–1945: Leben unter nationalsozialistischer Herrschaft*, Munich, 1988
Lancaster, Osbert, *Pillar to Post*, London, 1938
Lane, Barbara Miller, *Architecture and Politics in Germany, 1918–1945*, Cambridge, MA, 1968
Lane, Barbara Miller, 'Architects in Power: Politics and Ideology in the Work of Ernst May and Albert Speer', *Journal of Interdisciplinary History*, vol. 17, no. 1 (Summer 1986), pp. 283–310
Laqueur, Walter and Richard Breitman, *Breaking the Silence*, New York, 1986
Larsson, Lars Olof, Sabine Larsson and Ingolf Lamprecht, *'Fröhliche Neugestaltung' oder: Die Gigantoplanie von Berlin 1937–1943: Albert Speers Generalbebauungsplan im Spiegel satirischer Zeichnungen von Hans Stephan*, Kiel, 2008
Lawaczeck, Franz, *Technik und Wirtschaft im Dritten Reich*, Munich, 1932
Lebovic, Nitzan, *The Philosophy of Life and Death: Ludwig Klages and the Rise of a Nazi Biopolitics*, London, 2013
Leeb, Emil, 'Aus der Rüstung des Dritten Reiches (Das Heereswaffenamt 1938–1945): Ein amtlicher Bericht des letzten Chefs des Heereswaffenamtes', *Wehrtechnische Monatshefte*, vol. 55, no. 4 (1958)
Leistner, Yrsa von, *Große Begegnungen: Aus der Sicht einer Künstlerin*, Tübingen, 1986
Leugers, Antonia (ed.), *Berlin, Rosenstraße 2–4: Protest in der NS-Diktatur – Neue Forschungen zum Frauenprotest in der Rosenstraße 1943*, Annweiler, 2005
Lindner, Werner and Erich Böckler, *Die Stadt: Ihre Pflege und Gestaltung*, Munich, 1939
Longerich, Peter, *Politik der Vernichtung. Eine Gesamtdarstellung des nationalsozialistischen Judenverfolgung*, Munich, 1998
Longerich Peter, *Der ungeschriebene Befehl*, Munich, 2001
Longerich, Peter, *Heinrich Himmler: Biographie*, Berlin, 2008
Longerich, Peter, *Goebbels: Biographie*, Munich, 2010
Loubet, Jean-Louis, *La Maison Peugeot*, Paris, 2009
Lüdde-Neurath, Walter, *Regierung Dönitz. Die letzten Tage des Dritten Reiches*, Göttingen, 1964
Ludwig, Karl-Heinz, 'Die wohlreflektierten Erinnerungen des Albert Speer: Einige kritische Bemerkungen zur Funktion des Architekten, des Ingenieurs und der Technik im Dritten Reich', *Geschichte in Wissenschaft und Unterricht*, vol. 21 (1970), pp. 695–708

Ludwig, Karl-Heinz, *Technik und Ingenieure im Dritten Reich*, Düsseldorf, 1974

Maier, Dieter, *Arbeitseinsatz und Deportation: Die Mitwirkung der Arbeitsverwaltung bei der national-sozialistischen Judenverfolgung in den Jahren 1938–1945*, Berlin, 1994

Mann, Golo, 'Des Teufels Architekt: Albert Speers Erinnerungen', *Süddeutsche Zeitung*, 20 and 21 September 1969

Mann, Thomas, 'Deutschland und die Deutschen', in *Thomas Mann: Essays*, vol. 2, *Politik*, ed. Herman Kunzke, Frankfurt, 1977

Manstein, Erich von, *Verlorene Siege*, Bonn, 1955

Martin, Bernd (ed.), *Martin Heidegger und das Dritte Reich. Ein Kompendium*, Darmstadt, 1989

Maser, Werner, *Nürnberg: Tribunal der Sieger*, Düsseldorf, 1977

Mason, Timothy W., *Arbeiterklasse und Volksgemeinschaft: Dokumente und Materialien zur deutschen Arbeiterpolitik 1936–1939*, Opladen, 1975

Mason, Timothy W., *Sozialpolitik im Dritten Reich: Arbeiterklasse und Volksgemeinschaft*, Opladen, 1977

Messerschmidt, Manfred, 'Generalfeldmarschall Models letztes Gefecht', *Die Zeit*, vol. 14, 31 March 2005

Mierzejewski, Alfred C., *The Collapse of the German War Economy, 1944–1945*, Chapel Hill, NC, 1988

Milward, Alan S., *The German Economy at War*, London, 1965

Milward, Alan S., 'Fritz Todt als Minister für Bewaffnung und Munition', *Vierteljahrshefte für Zeitgeschichte*, vol. 14, no. 1 (1966), pp. 40–58

Milward, Alan S., *War, Economy and Society 1939–1945*, London, 1977

Mitscherlich, Alexander and Fred Mielke (eds), *Medizin ohne Menschlichkeit: Dokumente des Nürnberger Ärzteprozesses*, Frankfurt, 1960

Moll, Martin (ed.), *'Führer-Erlasse' 1939–1945*, Stuttgart, 1997

Mommsen, Hans, 'Spandauer Tagebücher: Bemerkungen zu den Aufzeichnungen Albert Speers im internationalen Militärgefängnis 1946–1966', *Politische Vierteljahresschrift*, vol. 17 (1976), pp. 8–14

Mouret, Jean-Noël, *Louis Renault*, Paris, 2009

Mühlen, Norbert, *Der Zauberer: Leben und Anleihen des Dr Hjalmar Horace Greeley Schacht*, Zurich, 1938

Müller Max, 'Der plötzliche und mysteriöse Tod Dr. Fritz Todts', *Geschichte in Wissenschaft und Unterricht*, vol. 18 (1967), pp. 602–4

Müller, Rolf-Dieter, 'Die Mobilisierung der deutschen Wirtschaft für Hitlers Kriegführung' in *Das Deutsche Reich und der Zweite Weltkrieg*, vol. 5/1, Stuttgart, 1988

Müller, Rolf-Dieter, *Der Manager der Kriegswirtschaft: Hans Kehrl – Ein Unternehmer in der Politik des Dritten Reiches*, Essen, 1999

Müller, Rolf-Dieter (ed.), *Das Deutsche Reich und der Zweite Weltkrieg*, vol. 10/1, Stuttgart, 2008

Müller, Rolf-Dieter, 'Endkampf im Reichsgebiet? Die Bedeutung der Oderlinie im Frühjahr 1945', in Werner Künzel and Richard Lakowski (eds), *Niederlage – Sieg – Neubeginn: Frühjahr 1945*, Potsdam, 2005

Müller, Rolf-Dieter *Das Deutsche Reich und der Zweite Weltkrieg*, vol. 10/2, Stuttgart, 2008

Naasner, Walter, *Neue Machtzentren in der deutschen Kriegswirtschaft 1942–1945: Die Wirtschaftsorganisation der SS, das Amt des Generalbevollmächtigten für den Arbeitseinsatz und das Reichsministerium für Bewaffnung und Munition, Reichsministerium für Rüstung und Kriegsproduktion im nationalsozialistischen Herrschaftssystem*, Boppard, 1994

Neander, Joachim, *'Hat in Europa kein annäherndes Beispiel': Mittelbau-Dora, ein KZ für Hitlers Krieg*, Berlin, 2000

Neave, Airey, *Nuremberg: A Personal Record of the Trial of the Major Nazi War Criminals in 1945–6*, London, 1978

Neitzel, Sönke and Harald Welzer, in *Soldaten: Protokolle vom Kämpfen, Töten und Sterben*, Frankfurt, 2012

Neliba, Günter, *Wilhelm Frick: Der Legalist des Unrechtsstaates*, Paderborn, 1992

Neufeld, Michael J., *The Rocket and the Reich: Peenemünde and the coming of the Ballistic Missile Era*, New York, 1995

Neufert, Ernst, *Bauordnungslehre*, Berlin, 1936.

Nissen, Margret (with Margrit Knapp and Sabine Seifert), *Sind Sie die Tochter Speer?*, Munich, 2005

Nitze, Paul H., *From Hiroshima to Glasnost: At the Centre of Decision – A Memoir*, London, 1990

Nossack, Hans Erich, *Der Untergang*, Frankfurt, 1976

Nowarra, Heinz J., *Die deutsche Luftrüstung 1933–1945*, 4 vols, Coblenz, 1993

Nürnberger, Jürgen and Dieter G. Maier, *Präsident, Reichsarbeitsminister, Staatssekretär: Dr. Friedrich Syrup; Präsident der Reichsanstalt für Arbeitsvermittlung und Arbeitslosenversicherung; Leben, Werk, Personalbibliographie*, Ludwigshafen, 2nd edn, 2007

Ordway, Frederick and Mitchell R. Sharpe, *The Rocket Team*, Cambridge, MA, 1982

Orland, Barbara, 'Der Zwiespalt zwischen Politik und Technik: Ein kulturelles Phänomen in der Vergangenheitsbewältigung Albert Speers und seiner Rezipienten', in Burkhard Dietz, Michael Fessner and Helmut Maier (eds), *Technische Intelligenz und 'Kulturfaktor Technik': Kulturvorstellungen von Technikern und Ingenieuren zwischen Kaiserreich und früher Bundesrepublik Deutschland*, Münster, 1996, pp. 269–95

Orth, Karin, *Das System der nationalsozialistischen Konzentrationslager: Eine politische Organisationsgeschichte*, Hamburg, 1999

Oven, Wilfred von, *Finale Furioso: Mit Goebbels bis zum Ende*, Tübingen, 1974

Overesch, Manfred, *Bosch in Hildesheim 1937–1945: Freies Unternehmertum und nationalsozialistische Rüstungspolitik*, Göttingen, 2008

Overmans, Rüdiger, 'Die Kriegsgefangenenpolitik des Deutschen Reiches', in Jörg Echternkamp (ed.), *Das Deutsche Reich und der Zweite Weltkrieg*, vol. 9/2, Stuttgart, 2005, pp. 825–34

Overmans, Rüdiger, *Deutsche militärische Verluste im Zweiten Weltkrieg*, Munich, 2004

Overy, Richard, *The Air War: 1939–1945*, London, 1980

Overy, Richard, 'Hitler's War and the German Economy: A Reinterpretation', *The Economic History Review*, vol. 35, no. 2 (May 1982), pp. 287–313

Overy, Richard, *War and Economy in the Third Reich*, Oxford, 1994

Overy, Richard J., Gerhard Otto and Johannes Houwink ten Cate, *Die Neuordnung Europas: NS-Wirtschaftspolitik in den besetzten Gebieten*, Berlin, 1997

Overy, Richard, *Bomber Command 1939–45: Reaping the Whirlwind*, London, 1997

Overy, Richard J., *The Bombing War: Europe 1939–1945*, London, 2013

Ozsváth, Zsuzsanna, *In the Footsteps of Orpheus: The Life and Times of Miklós Radnóti*, Bloomington, 2000

Pehle, Walter H. (ed.), *Der Judenpogrom 1938: Von der 'Reichskristallnacht' zum Völkermord*, Frankfurt, 1988

Petropoulos, Jonathan, *Kunstraub und Sammelwahn: Kunst und Politik im Dritten Reich*, Berlin, 1999

Petsch, Joachim, *Baukunst und Stadtplanung im Dritten Reich: Herleitung, Bestandsaufnahme, Entwicklung, Nachfolge*, Munich, 1976

Petzina, Dietmar, *Autarkiepolitik im Dritten Reich: Der nationalsozialistische Vierjahresplan*, Stuttgart, 1968

Pingel, Falk, *Häftlinge unter SS-Herrschaft: Widerstand, Selbstbehauptung und Vernichtung im Konzentrationslager*, Hamburg, 1978

Piszkiewicz, Dennis, *The Nazi Rocketeers: Dreams of Space and Crimes of War*, Mechanicsburg, PA, 1995

Ploetz, Karl (eds Percy Ernst Schramm and Hans O.H. Stange), *Geschichte des Zweiten Weltkrieges*, vol. 2, *Die Kriegsmittel*, Würzburg, 1960

Pollard, Miriam, *The Other Face of Love. Dialogues with the Prison Experience of Albert Speer*, New York, 1996

Posener, Julius (ed.), *Hans Poelzig: Gesammelte Schriften und Werke*, Berlin, 1970

Posener, Julius, 'Zwei Lehrer: Heinrich Tessenow und Hans Poelzig', in Reinhard Rürup (ed.), *Wissenschaft und Gesellschaft: Beiträge zur Geschichte der Technischen Universität Berlin 1879–1979*, vol. 1, Berlin, 1979

Powers, Thomas, *Heisenberg's War: The Secret History of the German Bomb*, New York, 1994

Priester, Hans Erich, *Das deutsche Wirtschaftswunder*, Amsterdam, 1936

Raeder, Erich, *Mein Leben*, 2 vols, Tübingen 1956–7

Rebentisch, Dieter, *Führerstaat und Verwaltung im Zweiten Weltkrieg: Verfassungsentwicklung und Verwaltungspolitik 1939–1945*, Stuttgart, 1989

Rebentisch, Dieter and Karl Teppe (eds), *Verwaltung contra Menschenführung im Staat Hitlers*, Göttingen, 1986

Recker, Marie-Luise, 'Der Reichskommissar für den sozialen Wohnungsbau: Zu Aufbau, Stellung und Arbeitsweise einer führerunmittelbaren Sonderbehörde', in Dieter Rebentisch and Karl Teppe (eds), *Verwaltung contra Menschenführung im Staat Hitlers*, Göttingen, 1986, pp. 333–50

Reichel, Peter *Der schöne Schein des Dritten Reiches: Gewalt und Faszination des deutschen Faschismus*, Hamburg, 2006

Reichhardt, H.J. and Wolfgang Schäche, *Ludwig Hoffmann in Berlin*, Berlin, 1987

Reichhardt, Hans J. and Wolfgang Schäche, *Von Berlin nach Germania: Über die Zerstörungen der 'Reichshauptstadt' durch Albert Speers Neugestaltungsplanungen*, Berlin, 2008

Reif, Adelbert, *Albert Speer: Kontroversen um ein deutsches Phänomen*, Munich, 1978

Reinhardt, Richard, 'Heute vor 25 Jahren starb Fritz Todt als unbequemer Warner', *Pforzheimer Zeitung*, vol. 32, 8 February 1967

Reitlinger, Gerald, *Die Endlösung: Hitlers Versuch der Ausrottung der Juden Europas 1939–1945*, Berlin, 1956

Richter, Ilka, *SS-Elite vor Gericht: Die Todesurteile gegen Oswald Pohl und Otto Ohlendorf*, Marburg, 2011

Riecke, Hans-Joachim, 'Ernährung und Landwirtschaft im Kriege', in *Bilanz des Zweiten Weltkrieges: Erkenntnisse und Verpflichtungen für die Zukunft*, Oldenburg, 1953, pp. 329–46

Riedel, Matthias, *Eisen und Kohle für das Dritte Reich: Paul Pleigers Stellung in der NS-Wirtschaft*, Göttingen, 1973

Rilke, Rainer Maria and Marianne Gilbert, *Le tiroir entr'ouvert*, Paris, 1956

Rittich, Werner, *New German Architecture*, Berlin, 1941

Rohland, Walter, *Bewegte Zeiten: Erinnerungen eines Eisenhüttenmannes*, Stuttgart, 1978

Rohwer, Jürgen, *Der Krieg zur See, 1939–1945*, Munich, 1992, translated as *War at Sea 1939–1945*, Annapolis, 1996

Rosenberg, Raphael, 'Architekturen des "Dritten Reiches": Völkische Heimatideologie versus internationale Monumentalität' (2011), p. 9, online at ART-Dok <http://archiv.ub.uniheidelberg.de/artdok/volltexte/2011/1501>

Rössler, Eberhard, *U-Boottyp XXI*, Bonn, 2000

Sabin, Guy, *Jean Bichelonne: Ministre sous l'occupation 1942–1944*, Paris, 1991

Salewski, Michael, *Die deutsche Seekriegsleitung 1935–1945*, 3 vols, Frankfurt, 1970–5

Sandgruber, Roman, 'Dr. Walter Schieber: Eine nationalsozialistische Karriere zwischen Wirtschaft, Bürokratie und SS', in Reinhard Krammer, Christoph Kühberger and Franz Schausberger (eds), *Der forschende Blick: Beiträge zur Geschichte Österreichs im 20. Jahrhundert*, Vienna, 2010

Saur, Karl-Otto, *Er stand in Hitlers Testament*, Berlin, 2007

Schabel, Ralf, *Die Illusionen der Wunderwaffen: Die Rolle der Düsenflugzeuge und Flugabwehrraketen in der Rüstungspolitik des Dritten Reiches*, Munich, 1994

Schäche, Wolfgang and Norbert Szymanski, *Das Reichssportfeld: Architektur im Spannungsfeld von Sport und Macht*, Berlin, 2001

Scherner, Jonas and Jochen Streb, 'Das Ende eines Mythos? Albert Speer und das so genannte Rüstungswunder', *Vierteljahreshefte für Sozial- und Wirtschaftsgeschichte*, vol. 93 (2006), pp. 172–96

Schlie, Ulrich (ed.), *Albert Speer: Die Kransberg Protokolle 1945: Seine ersten Aussagen und Aufzeichnungen (Juni–September)*, Munich, 2003

Schmidt, Matthias, *Albert Speer – Das Ende eines Mythos: Speers wahre Rolle im Dritten Reich*, Munich, 1982

Schmidt, Ulf, *Karl Brandt: The Nazi Doctor – Medicine and Power in the Third Reich*, London, 2007

Schneider, Michael C., *Unternehmerstrategien zwischen Weltwirtschaftskrise und Kriegswirtschaft: Chemnitzer Maschinenbauindustrie in der NS-Zeit 1933–1945*, Essen, 2005

Schönberger, Angela, *Die Neue Reichskanzlei von Albert Speer: Zum Zusammenhang von nationalsozialistischer Ideologie und Architektur*, Berlin, 1981

Schoppmann, Claudia, ' "Fabrikaktion" in Berlin: Hilfe für untergetauchte Juden als Form des humanitären Widerstandes', *Zeitschrift für Geschichtswissenschaft*, vol. 53, no. 2 (2005), pp. 138–48

Schrade, Christian, *Christuskirche Mannheim*, Mannheim, 1911, reprinted 1986

Schrafstetter, Susanna, 'Verfolgung und Wiedergutmachung – Karl M. Hettlage: Mitarbeiter von Albert Speer und Staatssekretär im Bundesfinanzministerium', *Vierteljahrshefte für Zeitgeschichte*, vol. 56, no. 3 (2008), pp. 431–66

Schreiber, Gerhard, *Die italienischen Militärinternierten im deutschen Machtbereich 1943–1945: verraten – Verachtet – vergessen*, Munich, 1990

Schröter, Barbara, *Stoff für Tausend und Ein Jahr: Die Textilsammlung des Generalbauinspektors für die Reichshauptstadt (GBI) – Albert Speer*, Berlin, 2013

Schulte, Jan Erik, 'Das SS-Wirtschafts-Verwaltungshauptamt und die Expansion des KZ-Systems', in Wolfgang Benz and Barbara Distel, *Ort des Terrors: Geschichte der nationalsozialistischen Konzentrationslager*, vol. 1 (*Die Organisation des Terrors*), Munich, 2005, pp. 141–55

Schultze-Naumburg, Paul, *Kunst und Rasse*, Munich, 1928

Schwarz, Hans-Peter, *Axel Springer: Die Biographie*, Berlin, 2008

Schwendemann, Heinrich, 'Strategie der Selbstvernichtung: Die Wehrmachtführung im "Endkampf" um das "Dritte Reich" ', in Rolf-Dieter Müller and Hans-Erich Volkmann (eds), *Die Wehrmacht: Mythos und Realität*, Munich, 1999, pp. 224–44

Schwendemann, Heinrich, ' "Drastic Measures to Defend the Reich at the Oder and the Rhine . . .": A Forgotten Memorandum of Albert Speer of 18 March 1945', *Journal of Contemporary History*, vol. 38, no. 4 (October 2003), pp. 597–614

Schwerin von Krosigk, Lutz Graf, *Die große Zeit des Feuers: Der Weg der deutschen Industrie*, vol. 2, Tübingen, 1957

Seidel, Robert, *Deutsche Besatzungspolitik in Polen: Der Distrikt Radom 1939–1945*, Berlin, 2006

Seidler, Franz W., 'Das Nationalsozialistische Kraftfahrkorps und die Organisation Todt im Weltkrieg', *Vierteljahrshefte für Zeitgeschichte*, vol. 32, no. 4 (1984), pp. 625–36

Seidler, Franz W., *Fritz Todt: Baumeister des Dritten Reiches*, Munich, 1986
Sereny, Gitta, 'Hat Speer alles gesagt?' *Die Zeit, Zeitmagazin*, no. 43, 20 October 1978
Sereny, Gitta, *Albert Speer: His Battle With Truth*, London, 1995
Silvermann, Dan P., *Hitler's Economy: Nazi Work Creation Programs, 1933–1936*, Cambridge, MA, 1998
Simon, Hans, *Das Herz unsere Städte*, Essen, 1963
Sinn, Andrea, 'The Return of Rabbi Robert Raphael Geis to Germany: One of the Last Witnesses of Germany Jewry?', *European Judaism*, vol. 45, no. 2 (Autumn 2012), pp. 123–38
Skilton, David, 'Contemplating the Ruins of London: Macaulay's New Zealander and Others', *The Literary London Journal*, vol. 2, no. 1 (March 2004)
Smelser, Ronald, *Robert Ley: Hitler's Labour Front Leader*, Oxford, 1988
Smelser, Ronald, and Rainer Zitelmann (eds), *Die braune Elite I: 22 biographische Skizzen*, Darmstadt, 1999
Smith, Bradley F., *Reaching Judgment at Nuremberg*, New York, 1977
Smith, Bradley F., 'Die Überlieferung der Hossbach–Niederschrift im Lichte neuer Quellen', *Vierteljahrshefte für Zeitgeschichte*, vol. 38 (1990), pp. 329–36
Sondheimer, Kurt, 'Der Tatkreis', *Vierteljahrshefte für Zeitgeschichte*, vol. 7, no. 3 (1959), pp. 229–60
Sonnenfeldt, Richard W., *Mehr als ein Leben*, Bern, 2003
Sonnenfeldt, Richard W., *Witness to Nuremberg*, New York, 2006
Speckmann, Thomas, 'Erst Kanonen, dann Butter', *Frankfurter Allgemeine Zeitung*, 9 February 2000
Spotts, Frederic, *Hitler and the Power of Aesthetics*, London, 2002
Steinert, Marlis G., *Die 23 Tage der Regierung Dönitz: Die Agonie des Dritten Reiches*, Munich, 1982
Straub, Karl Willy, *Die Architektur im Dritten Reich*, Stuttgart, 1932
Streb, Jochen and Sabine Streb, 'Optimale Beschaffungsverträge bei asymmetrischer Informationsverteilung: Zur Erklärung des nationalsozialistischen "Rüstungswunders" während des Zweiten Weltkriegs', *Zeitschrift für Wirtschafts- und Sozialwissenschaften*, vol. 118 (1998), pp. 275–94
Sweetman, John, *The Dambusters Raid*, London, 1999
Tamm, Friedrich, 'Die Kriegerdenkmäler Wilhelm Kreis', *Die Kunst im Deutschen Reich*, no. 3, 1943
Taylor, Robert R., *The Word in Stone. The Role of Architecture in the National Socialist Ideology*, Berkeley, 1974
Tessenow, Heinrich, *Handwerk und Kleinstadt*, Berlin, 1919
Teut, Anna, *Architektur im Dritten Reich 1933–1945*, Berlin, 1967
Thomas, Georg, *Geschichte der deutschen Wehr- und Rüstungswirtschaft 1918–1943/45*, Boppard, 1966
Thorwald, Jürgen, *Das Ende an der Elbe*, Stuttgart, 1952
Toland, John, *Adolf Hitler*, New York, 1976
Tooze, Adam, *The Wages of Destruction: The Making and Breaking of the Nazi Economy*, London, 2006
Treue, Wilhelm, 'Hitlers Denkschrift zum Vierjahresplan 1936', *Vierteljahrshefte für Zeitgeschichte*, vol. 3, no. 2 (April 1955), pp. 184–210
Trevor-Roper, Hugh, *The Last Days of Hitler*, London, 1947
Trial of the Major War Criminals before the International Military Tribunal, 'Blue Series', 42 vols, Nuremberg, 1947–9
Trials of War Criminals before the Nuernberg Military Tribunals Under Control Council Law No. 10, 'Green Series', 15 vols, http://www.loc.gov/rr/frd/Military_Law/NTs_war-criminals.html
Troost, Gerdy, *Das Bauen im Neuen Reich*, vol. 1, Bayreuth, 1938
Udovički-Selb, Danilo, 'Facing Hitler's Pavilion: The Uses of Modernity in the Soviet Pavilion at the 1937 Paris International Exhibition', *Journal of Contemporary History*, vol. 47, no. 1 (January 2012), pp. 13–47
Vat, Dan van der, *Der gute Nazi: Leben und Lügen des Albert Speer*, Berlin, 1997
Voigt, Wolfgang and Roland May (eds), *Paul Bonatz (1877–1956)*, Tübingen, 2010.
Volkov, Shulamit, *Walther Rathenau: The Life of Weimar's Fallen Statesman*, New Haven and London, 2012; trans. by Ulla Höber as *Walther Rathenau: Ein jüdisches Leben in Deutschland 1867 bis 1922*, Munich, 2012
Vonau, Jean-Laurent, *Le Gauleiter Robert Wagner: Le Bourreau de l'Alsace*, Strasbourg, 2011
Wagenführ, Rolf, *Die deutsche Industrie im Kriege 1939–1945*, Berlin, 1954
Wagner, Jens-Christian, *Produktion des Todes: Das KZ Mittelbau-Dora*, Göttingen, 2001
Wäldin, Herbert, *50 Jahre Christuskirche Mannheim 1911–1961*, Mannheim, 1961
Walker, Mark, *Nazi Science: Myth, Truth, and the German Atomic Bomb*, New York, 2001
Weber, J.B., 'Aspects of National Socialist Architecture', *Architectural Association Quarterly*, vol. 1 (1969)
Wedekind, Michael, *Nationalsozialistische Besatzungs- und Annexionspolitik in Norditalien 1943 bis 1945: Die Operationszonen 'Alpenvorland' und 'Adriatisches Küstenland'*, Munich, 2003
Wehler, Hans-Ulrich, *Deutsche Gesellschaftsgeschichte*, vol. 4 (*Vom Beginn des Ersten Weltkriegs bis zur Gründung der beiden deutschen Staaten 1914–1949*), Munich, 2003

Weidenbach, Uli, *Geheimnisse des Dritten Reichs 6/6: Speers Täuschung*, Phoenix TV programme, broadcast 15 February 2012

Weisenborn, Günther, *Memorial*, Berlin, 1962.

Wengst, Udo, *Theodor Eschenburg: Biographie einer politischen Leitfigur 1904–1999*, Berlin, 2005

Wiegrefe, Klaus, 'Der charmante Verbrecher', *Der Spiegel*, 2 May 2005

Wildt, Michael, *Generation des Unbedingten: Das Führungskorps des Reichssicherheitshauptamtes*, Hamburg, 2003

Willems, Susanne, *Der entsiedelte Jude: Albert Speers Wohnungsmarktpolitik für den Berliner Hauptstadtbau*, Berlin, 2002

Willems, Susanne, 'Er betrieb aktiv die Zerstörung jüdischer Existenzen', *Die Welt*, 12 April 2005

Wolters, Rudolf, *Albert Speer*, Oldenburg, 1943.

Wright, Frank Lloyd, 'Architecture and Life in the USSR', *Architectural Record* (October 1937)

Wysocki, Gerd, *Arbeit für den Krieg: Herrschaftsmechanismen in der Rüstungsindustrie des 'Dritten Reiches'; Arbeitseinsatz, Sozialpolitik und staatspolizeiliche Repression bei den Reichswerken 'Hermann Göring' im Salzgitter-Gebiet 1937/38 bis 1945*, Brunswick, 1992

Yelton, David K., *Hitler's Volkssturm: The Nazi Militia and the Fall of Germany 1944–1945*, Lawrence, KS, 2002

Zabel, Dirk, 'Das Projekt der "Stadt X für 20,000 Einwohner" bei Trassenheide oder die Militarisierung des Urbanen im Nationalsozialismus', in Bernfried Lichtnau, *Architektur in Mecklenburg und Vorpommern 1800–1950*, Greifswald, 1996, pp. 340–50

Zelnhefer, Siegfried, *Die Reichsparteitage der NSDAP in Nürnberg*, Nuremberg, 2002

Zelle, Karl-Günter, *Hitlers zweifelnde Elite: Goebbels – Göring – Himmler – Speer*, Paderborn, 2010

Zuckmayer, Carl, 'Albert Speer hat überwunden', *Die Welt*, 31 July 1975

INDEX